ONLY THE GOOD NEWS
On the Law of the Press in India

Other books by the author

The Supreme Court and Parliamentary Sovereignty (1976)
Black People in Britain: The Way Forward (1976)
The Supreme Court of India: A Socio-legal Analysis of its Juristic Techniques (1977)
The Amendment: Conspiracy or Revolution (1978)
Censorship and Obscenity (1978 co-edited)
The Indian Constitution: Trends and Issues (1978 co-edited)
Selection and Appointment of Supreme CourtJudges: A Case Study (1978, Co-authored with Alice Jacob)
President's Rule in the States (1979)
The Supreme Court under Strain: The Challenge of Arrears (1979)
Justice on Trial: The Supreme Court Today (1980)
Contempt of Court and the Press (1981)
Judges and the Judicial Power (1985 co-edited)
Litigation Explosion in India (1986)
Public Interest Law (1987 edited)
Marc Galanter's *Law and Society in India* (edited, with a critical introduction, 1988, forthcoming)

ONLY THE GOOD NEWS

On the Law of the Press in India

RAJEEV DHAVAN

MANOHAR
1987

ISBN 81—85054—38—X

First Published 1987

Published by
Ramesh Jain
For Manohar Publications
1 Ansari Road, Daryaganj
New Delhi-110002

Printed at
Bharat Enterprises
Delhi-110053

for
Bhagwan Sahay

CONTENTS

A PREFATORY INTRODUCTION

This book caused the accidental death of an article. Commissioned to write an article on the law of the press in India, I was surprised to discover how little material there was on the subject; and that most of it was concerned with questions of 'hard' black letter law and decided cases. Useful for lawyers to track down statutory provisions and judicial precedents, such material did not even explain legal doctrine. It told us next to nothing about where the laws came from, why they were introduced and how they became absorbed in social and political reality. So, willy nilly, the article acquired elasticity and grew, and grew and grew.

The press, like the law, is a lively political arena. While the pundits of the Indian press display a profound confusion about their predicament and role, other conceptive ideologists have slowly, but surely, sought to contain the press within a political and moral disciplinary framework. Obsessed with issues of law and order and anxious to subjugate the press by re-structuring the market economy within which the press operates, successive governments have tried to control the press. The Imperial government of the British Raj successfully argued the case for law and order, and depicted the press as divisive and unprincipled. British laws and policy settled a law and order paradigm which was gratefully adopted by the Constituent Assembly drafting India's Constitution. The First Press Commission (1952-4) endorsed the concern about law and order and the extent to which government servants were being criticised. Unable to set both these concerns in the wider context of social change, the First Press Commission passed the blame on to the so-called press barons. The Second Press Commission (1982) decided that the press was a nuisance and monopolistic. As it happens, there was no real proof. The *Report of the Fact Finding Committee into Newspaper Economics* (1977) could not establish monopolistic practices in the newspaper industry except to the extent of asserting that not everyone could start a newspaper. The research commissioned by the Second Press Commission establishes the existence of healthy competition rather than monopolism. The reports of both Press Commissions often reproduce part of the government's repertoire against its political enemies. In order to lend credibility to its stand, the government has tried to put forward the view that it is acting for the small newspapers (as evident from the stance of the Diwakar Committee Report on Small Newspapers (1966)) or in the interests of promoting a development oriented journalism, a view that was somewhat indelicately handled during the Emergency (1975-77).

But government politics apart, all this settled three paradigms within which much of the debate about the press is imprisoned. The *first* paradigm concerns 'law and order'. Established by the British, the ideology of 'law and order' has unassailably dwarfed all other considerations important to the growth of a real democracy and distributive justice in India. The *second* paradigm concerns the monopolism of the Indian press. Designed to break the capability of the larger papers without empowering strength to the smaller newspaper, it has provided an excuse to use the regulatory State to contain the press. Faced with this paradigmatic assumption even the Supreme Court, which stepped in to question an irresponsible use of regulatory powers in the *Bennett Coleman* case (1973), has not been able to reexamine the institutional needs of the press. The *third* paradigm argues that journalism must be 'committed' to developmental aims. It is never clear whether 'developmental' progress means the same thing as regime interests. Together, these paradigms describe and prescribe what the 'good news' is and how it must be produced. Put together they determine—for the government, for the press and for the public at large—the disciplinary framework within which the press must act. Within the contours of this disciplinary framework, the press must publish 'only the good news.'

Indian law captures and reinforces many of these insights. But a deeper analysis of the nature of Indian law is necessary. Indian law represents striking contrasts. In terms of formal description, it looks like modern Western law. Institutionally and socially it is operated through courts and professional lawyers interpreting norms articulated by designated government authorities. But this is where the similarity ends. The most important feature of Indian law is its privatisation. Social forces have assured the privatisation of the Indian State. The Indian State is not an effective third party intermediary between diverse interests. It is increasingly being owned by some at the expense of others. This process is stronger at local levels where privatisation takes a direct and crude form. At higher levels of government, it is more sophisticated. What is true of the legislature and the administration is also true of the judiciary. At certain levels, the judiciary and legal processes (including the police and the administration) have become the private property of certain interests. At other levels, the judiciary and legal processes have been manipulated so that—to borrow a phrase—the 'haves come out ahead.' At yet other levels, the judiciary acts as an independent third party making hegemonic gains which favour certain interests and parties. Indian legal institutions are unable to find a moderating corrective to this process of privatisation. The higher judiciary has been paralysed by, and drawn into dispensing, an increasingly irrelevant interim justice. At all levels, the litigation game transforms legal processes into reflecting social wrangles with an indignity that does not help to legitimise the system as a whole. The effect is to totally transform the meaning of the laws that are promulgated. These matters are dealt with at length in my *Litigation Explosion in India* (1986).

The laws of the press present two distinct pictures. One picture features tough law against the press. Another picture displays the pathology of litigation and administrative practice which makes a nonsense of these laws. Laws relating to religious strife have been used to exacerbate religious strife and those relating to public order have sown the seeds of further disorder. The laws of defamation have become meaningless because the damages threatened are too low. The government which set up the Press Council for the public and to protect the Press is the biggest user of the Council which explicates government ideology as a seemingly neutral body. Examples can be multiplied to show that the law is both a declaratory ideology as well as an institutional trap which draws consensus and enables control as it articulates and renegotiates social and political reality.

The significance of the press lies in its fast becoming a prime political arena in Indian politics. The privatisation of the constitutionally designated political arenas and the destruction of the ground rules under which they should operate has given greater importance to the press. Along with, but less credible than, grass root activism, it represents the only other political arena not wholly controlled by the government. Parts of the political arena are controlled by vested interests. Who can doubt that? But the struggle over the press is part of a wider struggle for *political arenas* in a society where more and more such arenas are being savagely restricted by an emergent capitalism. Forces across the political spectrum—no less the government as its political opponents—realise the importance of the press as a *political arena.* The present battle is not just over who should control this *arena* but whether there should be such an arena at all. Once the latter battle is won, and a secure victory seems probable, the fight for supremacy of this arena will continue. The law and legal institutions are wound up in this political debate. The disadvantaged may lose in all these arenas but they rely on a strategic activism and tend to use these arenas selectively. So, these may be controversies between competing middle class elites but they are of consequence to the political economy of the system as a whole.

Since these essays were first conceived, written and revised, the material on the law of the press has been enriched in more ways than one. P.M. Bakshi's *Press Law: An Introduction* (1986), accompanied by his more detailed *Law of Defamation, Some*

Aspects (1986) are valuable additions to the slender material on the subject. Justice E.S. Venkataramiah's admirable *Freedom of the Press: Some Recent Trends* (1986) helps to explain his courageous declarations in the *Newsprint* case (pp. 97-9 *infra*). The lacunae in information about the Press Council has been neatly filled by Usha Loghani's painstaking summary and analysis of the Council's determinations in her *Violations of Journlistic Ethics and Public Taste* (1984), followed closely on its heels by *Violation of Freedom of the Press* (1986). These are joined by N.K. Trikha's *The Press Council: A Self Regulatory Mechanism for the Press*, which contains inside knowledge of the working of the Council with an informed critical analysis, and the Press Council's *Annual Report 1986*. Continuing interest in the historical origins of regulatory control of the press is evident from B.M. Sankdher's *Press, Politics and Public Opinion in India* (1984).

The *Newsprint* case (1986), read with an obscure judgment of the Delhi High Court in the *Jansatta/Punjab Kesari* case (*Times of India*, 22 May 1986) which gives partial immunity for journalists regards the disclosure of the sources of information, suggests the development of a jurisprudence on the press as distinct from theoretical formulations on free speech. But the Delhi view has to be contrasted with Justice Sujata Manohar's order in the *Stardust* case (*Statesman*, 22 July 1987) and the Supreme Court's laconic and cryptic judgment in the *Malayalam Manorma* case (*M.K. Sasidharan* v. *Malayalam Manorma* (1987) 1 *Scale* 1231). However, the cause of an unregulated press freedom has received great impetus from Justice Pendse's judgment in *Bennett Coleman* v. *Union of India* (A.I.R. 1986 Bombay 321) which declares freedom of the press as part of the inviolable basic structure of the Constitution and asserts the controversial proposition that the provisions of the Monopolies and Restrictive Practices Act, 1969 requiring prior approval of the government to expand its undertakings do not apply to newspaper concerns. Despite this bold precedent—and, it is almost certainly much more than that—one has to be hesitant—notwithstanding Justice Venkataramiah's partial espousal, on and off the Bench, of freedom of the press—about the establishment of a secure new trend in the constitutional law of the press.

Any optimism, inevitably, sinks into disquiet on a closer examination of Tamil Nadu's Cinemas (Regulation) Amendment Bill 1987, giving the government vast powers to censor films contemptuos of the legislature or its members, and the Tamil Nadu Compulsory Censorship of Publicity Material Bill 1987 which allows powers to ban and precensor virtually anything and everything. All this suggests that the *Bihar Bill* controversy of 1982 (pp. 318-322, 336-339 *infra*) was not the idiosyncratic excesses of just one Chief Minister but part of a standard response of government to stifle criticism from the press on the unconvincing ground that the latter must, perforce, be not just mischevious but dangerous. The Union Government's Indecent Represenation of Women (Prohibition) Act 1986 is a recent example of a clumsy compromise between the competing demands of feminists and advertizers in ways that will adversely affect the press. The disquiet about recent events deepens further into apprehension in the light of the Tamil Nadu Assembly's order—later withdrawn—of three month's rigorous imprisonment of the editor of *Ananda Vikatan* (*Indian Express*, 4 April 1987). No sooner was the ink dry on this story, the Priveleges Committee chose to ignore an order of the Supreme Court to temporarily desist from proceeding with an alleged breach of privelege by the Tamil daily *Dinakaran* (*Times of India*, 4 June 1987). Undoubtedly, the priveleges of parliament in relation to the press merit close scrutiny but not in a manner which declares war between two organs of government. This must be contrasted with the other extreme situation of alleged collusive control of the judiciary so that the *Illustrated Weekly* has to petition the Supreme Court to have a defamation case by a powerful Chief Minister transfered from the latter's state (*Times of India*, 18 September 1987). Meanwhile, the press continues to be seduced or intimidated by the government. Even if the press being offered gift coupons to attend government press conferences is a peccadillo (*Indian Express*, 4 August 1987), the actual beating up of journalists by the police and hired ruffians on wild allegations of trumped up charges needs severe condemnation (*e.g. Hindustan Times*, 13 June 1987) and highlights the sinister preoccupations of some sections of government on the need to discipline the press. The recent raid on the *Indian Express*—in the aftermath of *Bofors*—raises an important issue which has not received adequate juridical treatment when considering the institutional needs of the press. And, the issue is really quite crucial. There is a case for discussing *whether certain operational needs of the press media* (including newsprint, machinery etc.,) *should be wholly free from regulatory* (*including fiscal*) *control*? The Supreme Court's refusal in the *Newsprint* case (1986) to exempt non-onerous taxes and duties on newsprint weakly flirts with an affirmative answer whilst Justice Pendse in *Bennett Coleman* (1986) states the case for the press much more strongly. But until his issue is debated at length unease over governmental regulation of the basic requirements of the running of newspapers will continue (see further p. 42 *infra*). The press is not *sui generis* and in this book I argue that no stronger a case can be made out for the press than accepting it as a private fiduciary of the public interest. Yet its private status does not obviate the need for a sensitive weighing up what it needs to discharge its public function.

Despite these scattered onslaughts, the causes of the press does not go unchampioned. Soli Sorabjee, P.M. Bakshi and A.G. Noorani maintain a steady stream of vigilant newspaper comment and protest (see also *Seminar* 292; *A Messy Media* (1983) and No. 327 *Web of Censorship* (1986). This has been accompanied by litigation in court as evidenced by the *Newsprint* (1986), *Bennett Coleman* (1986) and other cases. The late Romesh Thapar's notice to the Union Government questioning the monopolistic autonomy of All India Radio and Doordarshan (television) will help to review some of the Delhi High Court's more dogmatic assertions about the technological limitations on developing a democratic audio-visual set up in the 'air'. (pp. 112-113 *infra*).

All these events fortify the comments in this book exposing the unprincipled basis on which the government obtains moral consensus for a law and order society. But our circumnavigation of the world of this year's events affecting media freedom is not intended to obscure the anxiety in the last chapter of this book which shows how much of our faith hangs precariously and indelicately on the notion of 'professionalism' and 'professional' ethics which is supposed to circumscribe the behaviour of the press. Both a general analysis of 'professionalism' and its unchecked pathological practice in India—no less in its handling of the recent *Bofors* crisis concerning corruption in government defence deals as in the various varieties of responsible and irresponsible journalism that exist in India—do not instill the confidence they are supposed to inspire. Arbitrary and biased control, selection and presentation of what is alleged to constitute the 'good news' remains a worry as long as 'professionalism' remains—as it must inevitably be—an insecure form of press accountability.

I have relied almost exclusively on Indian materials; and—except where absolutely necessary—resisted the alluring temptation of drawing cosmopolitan analogues to interpret and assess the material. Implicit in this choice of method, is a diffident assertion about the uniqueness of the Indian example. Even though primarily concerned with India, I have not attempted a political assessment of the Indian press; but only of the law relating to it inasmuch as the latter provides an institutional framework, articulates and generates a disciplining ideology and creates its own patterns of pathological use which may defeat the intention of the lawmakers. If I have sided with the press against the government, this should not incite the assumption that I think the Indian press has a radical pedigree and future. Even after two Press Commissions, several seminars, articles and books, the social and political potential of the Indian press needs to be more elaborately and firmly assessed. It is only when that is done that we can assess whether the press as a public political arena will service a wider distributive justice.

I would like to take this opportunity to thank those who have assisted me. Discussions with Upendra Baxi helped greatly to develop some of the wider political concerns in which some of the discussion is set. Marc Galanter's work on how various groups used law courts as a socio-political forum in the nineteenth century provided a framework for exploration. The Late S.N. Jain, (of the Indian Law Institute) and Justice Grover (former Chairman, Press Council) permitted me to draw from my earlier book on *Contempt of Court and the Press* (Tripathi, 1982) which was written for their respective institutions. Monisha Kapur was an exacting editor and critic. Usha Vaidyanathan edited the manuscript into its final shape and Pramodh Singh displayed his usual indifatigible skills in collecting research material. I benefited greatly from discussions with Marc Galanter, Girilal Jain, Soli Sorabjee, Pramodh Singh, Alice Jacob, Chhatrapati Singh, Thomas Paul, Justice Mathew, Imtiaz Ahmad, Mark Yudott, Ravi Jain, R. Sudarshan, Monisha Kapur and Pnina Lahav. Pnina Lahav commissioned the essay from which this book grew and provided much encouragement. It was a pleasure to work with Ramesh Jain of Manohar who provided energy, encouragement and much valued advice.

Those that typed this book—P.L. Batra, Margaret Cook and Angela Duncan—are not an 'also ran' in the list of acknowledgements. They know—and I know—that, but for them, the editors and an energetic publisher, this book would not have surfaced.

Then there is Bhagwan Sahay to whom this book is dedicated. Much of this book was written in his house, and discussed with him. He is no longer with us. He passed away a few months ago, and as memory intermingles with emotion, I feel a certain emptyness in thinking of a Delhi without him. Artist, sculptor, civil servant, diplomat, the erstwhile gubernatorial head of five political units, polymath and more, this wonderful old man stood, and will always stand, in a class of his own. He was of a kind the likes of which we will never see again. This small dedication is my way of publicly thanking him for good times spent with him and recalling something of his humour, something of his insight and something of his wisdom. Those who knew him, know exactly what I am talking about.

RAJEEV DHAVAN
SEPTEMBER 1987

PART ONE

Confusions and Controversies

1

A PROFOUND CONFUSION

In a country like India where competition for status finds expression in modern and traditional forms, the press operates at different levels in differing ways. At some levels, it is the direct expression of social and economic power. At others, it is left to its own devices—sometimes operating as professionals; sometimes forced to operate as an industry. The rural press has produced its own distinctive pattern of operation. The metropolitan press constantly takes refuge in cosmopolitan ideals as a justification for its existence. India's press, like its legal and political system, is 'palpably foreign'.[1] But these foreign transplants have, inevitably, become a property of the social system and not an independent variable outside it. Indeed, the working of the press in India—and of the internal and external rules which seek to circumscribe its behaviour—have to be understood in the context of its multi-dimensional presence in the social system rather than on the basis of certain universalistic functions attributed to the press generally.[2]

Throughout its history India's press has had an inchoate idea about its function and role. This is adequately demonstrated by the literature on the press. Some of the early histories of the press in India convey exaggerated contemporary notions of the dangers and contributions of the press.[3] Later accounts tend to assimilate information about the press,[4] correlate it to broad political trends,[5] or consist of research commissioned by the government.[6] Some of the material is openly partisan attacking the Indian press for not playing the game and seeking to persuade them to fall into line.[7] While a lot of attention has been paid to the political framework within which the press operated, little attention has been given to social factors which have influenced the work of the press. There is some work on the regional press[8] but certainly not enough to show that the "throbbing of the country... was best reflected in the vernacular press".[9]

Since independence, much of the literature on the press proceeds on the assumption that something "ails" the Indian press[10] which is caught in a "creeping paralysis" or "stagnation".[11] The press is described as being "under pressure" which is attributed partly to the government's "ideological distrust of a capitalist owned press".[12] Opinions have been expressed that the "emerging estate" would be benefited by fresh expertise, better technology and economic management, better correspondent links in Asia (and, presumably elsewhere) and better training.[13] Some of the depression may have been caused by the fact that it is made to perceive itself as being over-concentrated and as contributing little to the development of India[14]—a point often emphasized by the government.[15] The press is given all kinds of political roles ranging from promoting unity[16] to emphasizing its socialistic nature in a planned economy.[17] All this has introduced a lot of confusion into what the press ought to do. At least one famous editor has declared that the Indian press is quite good[18] and attacked the monopolism of the government's hold on the radio and other agencies.[19] The 'right' have held on to a view of the press which traces its intellectual pedigree to Milton's *Aeropagation* and Tom Paine's *Rights of Man*,[20] supports the need for private enterprise, paints a foreboding future for the development of a liberal press[22] and blames the government for its stranglehold on the press through advertising control and the active sponsorship of some sections of the press.[23] Compromise solutions have suggested the "prospects of internal freedom" by interposing a trusteeship system between the editors and the owners.[24] Perceptions of how the press operates also vary. On the one hand, the press is described as routine, dull and without accountability or money.[25] It has been said that the Indian press lacks a "well founded public or collegiate critique . . . (or) the art of relevant or objective criticism" and has an ambivalent attitude towards government.[26] On the other hand, a prominent member of the ill-fated Janata government attributes the fall of that government to the severe exposure it had from the press.[27] Successive governments in the sixties and seventies have entered into controversies and controversial legislation about the press.[28] The control of the press during the Emergency (1975-77) represents the high tide of governmental reaction.

Most of the literature revolves around doctrinaire and well thrashed out but indecisive claims about the role of the press. This is as true of individually published works as it is of anthologies of papers delivered at conferences about the press.[29] Such declarations serve many useful purposes. Like similar declarations made by lawyers,[30] the making of the declaration is the message.[31] Journalists find that establishing a connection with foreign cosmopolitan ideals enables them to strike a social pose which gives them all the advantages of status mobility that such a course of action affords them.[32] Sometimes such declarations represent a serious, even if immature, attempt to look at present problems and for future solutions—even if these solutions consist of an adaption or transplant of imported solutions.[33] Sometimes a conference is called not to discuss the issues but to demonstrate a show of strength by politically like-minded editors.[34] Various forms of political lobbying on a broad liberal platform were also campaigned for by the Press Institute of India.[35]

The social context within which the press operates is often ignored even though it is developed more fully in the literature on the vernacular press.[36] The Indian Institute of Mass Communications—initially set up by the Ministry of Information and Broadcasting in 1965—has, apart from setting up training courses and the like, adopted what appears to be an 'instrumental' approach by asking how the press can be harnessed to developmental perspectives.[37] It has looked at the impact of various kinds of governmental programmes (*e.g.* agrarian information[38] or family planning[39]) and various policies and events[40]—including the impact of the government's famous 20 point programme during the Emergency.[41] It has cast its net wide looking at the impact of the media on elections or reactions to film censorship.[42] But its skeletal reports do not wander too greatly from its developmental perspectives: how can the press aid development? The Press Council's latest research into how selected papers report on various social problems also fall within an impact analysis, instrumental framework.[43] This is not wholly surprising. All this fits in with other more general approaches to development in the third world.

Discussion and debate on the press has got locked into a prototype. The parameters of this prototype have been clearly set by the government. Even the most ingenious and formidable pressmen have not really been able to critically assail this prototype in any meaningful way. The British government's prototype was built upon the importance of law and order. The Indian press' response to this prototype lay largely in emphasising that 'law and order' was really a cloak to prevent nationalistic agitation from taking root.[44] Significantly, the press continued the debate and discussion on the 'order/disorder/national freedom' frame of reference without giving adequate attention to its own structure, its campaigns, it social and class loyalties and its perception of its own roles And all this while there were a lot of exciting matters to. report and comment on. Each and every peasant uprising yielded tensions which offered innumerable possibilities for the discerning journalist or commentator.[45] There was no doubt that the press was doing interesting things. Gandhi's contempt case[46] and various sedition cases are excellent examples of using oppressive laws to revitalize press campaigns.[47]

But whilst all this was happening the press was also permitting the self-perpetuation of two important tendencies. The first was to make the activities and discussions of the nationalist leaders central to the concerns of the press. This is not to suggest that the elite activity of nationalistic leaders was not important. What the press did was to create a new kind of hegemonic relation in respect of the national leaders based on traditional—and somewhat uncritical—notions of patrimony. This hegemonic relationship became quite central to the kinds of expectations that the government of independent India had from the press.

This hegemonic relationship had a second effect. It ascribed a central line teleological dimension to all participants in public activity. While the Nationalist movement chose 'free-dom'—and that, too, a particular form of it—as the 'to-be-achieved' central consensus value, Nehru's regime chose socialism and national progress as its focal projection. Woven together with overtly over-emphasized British notions of public order Nehru's socialism stalked through the corridors of journalism like a colossus. Dissenting members of the Second Press Commission (1982) describe the mood well:

> For many of the distinguished members of the First Press Commission refashioning the Press was part of the larger enterprize of refashioning society. When the Press Commission came to the end of its labours, the Avadhi Session of the Indian National Congress, which adopted, too hesitantly for some, a 'socialist pattern of society' as the nation's goal (not realizing it—*sic*!) was still some months away. The middle class intelligentsia were waiting to watch and to participate in, the working of an alchemy which would fuse together the concepts of democracy and socialism in a gigantic crucible. And the Press was to be one component of the alchemy.[48]

Indian journalism was, therefore, to be tested on the basis of the extent to which they could contribute to the self-perpetuation of this socialism. Not that the press did not listen to its patrons or give up reflecting factional rivalries. Trapped in this rhetoric and being unable to articulate any-thing more than stereotyped arguments drawn from pundits of the Western press, Indian journalism was not able to develop an informed critique of its own function and role.[49] A somewhat artificial debate seems to have persisted between the 'liberalists' (who wanted the press to have as full a freedom to operate as possible and who ascribed eclectic roles to the press in a plural democracy) and the 'teleologists' who pointed out to India's developmental goals and claimed to examine the structural foundations on which these goals could be realised. The line of division is as nebulous as the constantly shifting supports of the press. Many of the 'liberalists' are themselves willing to countenance the importance of developmental goals just as many teleologists join hands with the liberals in fighting for a common pool of resources, respectability and status.[50] The aridity of the debate is highlighted by the fact that both sides are quite firmly entrenched in the existing social, economic and political status quo. The teleologists in this debate do not really wish to make structural changes in society and are justly rebuked for pretending "that the grand experiment envisioned in 1954 is still on and that the restructuring of the ownership of the Press is still a part of the grand design of restructuring the society and its property relationships".

In truth, the teleologists do not wish the government criticised. And the liberalists are really staking a claim for preferring the interests and ideologies of those in partial, and apparent, polarity with the government. The advent of Mrs. Gandhi strengthened the hands of the teleologists. After her initial term in the Ministry of Information and Broadcasting she sought to intensify her control of the Press by an ardent appeal to her own socialism. The same plea had been made to expel dissidents from her party, control bureaucrats, supersede judges in the Supreme Court of India, declare an Emergency and return to power. Never was a plea of 'you-can't-criticise-me' more artfully argued. Never, too, was it so transparently estranged from reality. This broad appeal to teleology was strengthened greatly as a result of the war with China (1962) and two wars with Pakistan (1965 and 1971).[51] On all these occasions Mrs. Gandhi claimed greater control over the press. While the press was willing to support the government at a time of war, respectability for the teleological hegemony that was sought to be perpetuated eluded the government. This is partly because exhaustion, cynicism and increasing differentials between various classes of people had made the nation as a whole suspicious about this election-post hustings socialism. More especially, there is a transparency about the structural argument that supports this quest for hegemonic coercion.

This argument which owes its origins to the Report of the Press Commission (1952-4)[52] was recharged when the Diwakar Committee[53] espoused the cause of the small newspapers. What started as a small investigative campaign, matured as a policy of newsprint control. The Supreme Court anxious to lend support to the broad hegemony of socialism was less keen to support the newsprint control.[54] The fact remained that none of the investigations appointed was really able to establish the kind of monopolistic tendencies that existed or that the small newspapers which were sought to be protected really needed protection.[55] What was emerging was a different pattern. Having demanded a 'committed' administration and a committed judiciary[56] it was unnatural for that demand to be extended to a 'committed' press. The real question was: committed to whom? To the highly suspect teleological projections of the government or the people who ran it? The answer to this question became clearer during the Emergency (1975-77) which not only re-projected the teleology argument in the form of the 20 point programme but also imposed a rigorous censorship which denied legitimacy to any form of journalism—teleological, liberal or otherwise.[57] But the teleological approach—like John Brown's soul—lived on even though the Emergency lay a-smouldering in its grave. The Kuldip Nayar Committee established after the Emergency was trapped in the debate. Minutes of Dissent accused the majority of paying lip service to the same apparatus of values that formed the basis of legitimation during the Emergency.[58] The press under the Janata regime was not really successful in providing a critique of or an alternative to the teleological approach. Advani's protest about the press being the reason for the downfall of the government does not really establish either the integrity or the wisdom of the Janata press.[59]

Much rather it reflects on its mindlessness. No press in the world operates in such a total vacuum as not to be able to voice some kind of value structure that the press would try and sustain. The post-Emergency press was wholly eclectic. In an effort to claim their own power and find social and political status for a core of journalists, the press entered into a mindless exposure. In a sense it did everything and nothing.[60] With no understanding of the institutional structure needed to sustain the kind of democracy that the press wished to protect, no appreciation of the factors that give (or deny legitimacy) to a cause, no clear feel for any sense of direction, the press pushed and was manipulated in all directions. Pretending to act as a "part of (some) . . . rich plurality",[61] the press found itself dominated by a philos ophy of mindless eclectism,[62] the press was never really able to evolve any kind of distinct theory to legitimate its role, understanding and function in the India of the late seventies. Reporting for its sake, and being susceptible to manipulation in any direction, became part of the operating principles of the Indian press. Its own stance could never be identified amongst its shifting loyalties; nor could the potential vulnerability of its opponents. It was surprising that this open-ended pluralism was never able to effectively dislodge the teleological theory. The latter surfaced in full force in the report of the Second Press Commission (1982). Chaired by Justice Mathew, the Press resurrected the old debates all over again. Trying to ward off the argument that the debate about the press has nothing to do with the debate about whether the government ought to be criticised, the Commission felt that the press should not be either "a mindless adversary or an unquestioning ally" but a "constructive critic".[63] Paradoxically, this seemingly objective role led back to all the demands made by the teleologists.

The next step lay in defining what a "constructive critic" was. The answer to that question seemed to take us back to the earlier notion of a committed press.

The formal expectation of the Commission had to ascribe an independence to the press—

> The role of the Press in a developing and democratic society should neither be that of an adversary nor an ally of the

> government. . . . A free Press should be, in our view, a constructive critic.[64]

And though the press was counselled to do more than report on official programmes through "official handouts",[65] the Commission had a clear idea of the value structure that they wished to depict. Dedicated to a particular form of secularism and the development of a scientific temper[66] newspapers were asked to "discontinue the publication of astrological predictions".[67] In an effort to redefine religions within a new hegemony it was decreed that "(s)uperstitious beliefs which are unrelated to the essence of religions and are inimical to physical and social health must be relentlessly exposed and fought".[68] The press was to "strengthe(n) . . . the moral fabric of society", fight excessive consumption[69] and "give news values a different orientation in the interest of social health and national development".[70] Many of the epithets of the Emergency about controlling 'anti-national activities' were expressly denied.[71] Instead the press was being asked to maintain a 'due sense of responsibility'[72] commence sustained campaigns to promote the concept of human brotherhood[73] and to commence a new kind of 'development reporting'.[74] Of course, an 'objective presentation of news'[75] was called for in all cases and the press should tell the 'story of what is going well as well as what is going wrong'.[76] But all this has to take place within a preordained value structure of 'socialism' and 'secularism' about which it is assumed there can be little discussion.[77] This was accompanied by a further plea that a 'law and order' society must be maintained at all costs. Journalists were warned "against attempts by the authorities or by landlords to pass off agrarian revolts against exploitation as Naxalite or other politically motivated violence"[78] and asked not to report on communal tensions.[79] The British policy of a "stricter enforcement of the provisions in the Indian Penal Code with regard to communal incitement"[80] was endorsed. The role of the press in all this was to ensure the continued maintenance of a 'law and order' society, to advocate adherence to lawful methods of ventilating grievances",[81] and "take a forthright stand against unconstitutional methods of agitation".[82]

If we read between the lines, this whole set of projected values, the underlying instrumental purpose of the Commission and the broad consensus values that are being projected become clear. Firstly, it cannot be overlooked that 'secularism' and 'socialism' were the major ideological weapons of the Emergency.[83] It is quite clear that the pathological practice of the Emergency lay in using these values in order to silence criticism and control the opposition. For, who is to be the judge of what constitutes the 'essence of a religion', a scientific temper or a superstitious belief?[84] Would not such a judgment be a covert public mal-identification of opponents?[85] Secondly—and this is important—the Report gave a national role to the press but no political role. Thus the press was supposed to do wonderful things for the nation but could not be part of the political process. This whole approach is as fallacious as it is suspect. Most things have to be fought for by political campaigns. To say that the press should not be party to politics and political campaigning in the present constitutional and political set-up seems absurd. It also reposes a spurious faith in existing governmental and institutional political processes. It would be an irresponsible pressman truly committed to distributive justice who would pledge a 'trust-the-government-at-all-times' stand and counsel the abdication of agitational acts of political necessity.[86] Trying to strait-jacket the press into this kind of thinking can only be explained in two ways. The more generous interpretation is that offered by the dissenting members of the Commission:

> Pressmen cannot be turned into charming goldfish as swimming effortlessly in an artificially lit aquarium, protected from the eddies and whirls of their natural habitat. Is it feasible or desirable to put the Press under a glass domed oxygen tent of its own, so that pure minds may breathe pure oxygen and survive under a round-the-clock vigil.[87]

The more insidious—but more insightful—interpretation is to reiterate that the teleologists are really trying to create an atmosphere, an ideology and fidelity to law and order which seeks to control the press rather than to make it a public forum which can be used to fight exploitation, disadvantage and socio-economic differentials.

Quite apart from the problem of suspect ideologies, the Report also projects an image of the kind of the press that it envisages and would like to create. Starting with the idea that there is too much monopolism in the Indian press, it seeks to remedy that situation. The charge of monopolism is not really borne out. *The fatal flaw in the analysis lies in the fact that it is not necessary to prove the existence of monopolism in order to substantiate patterns of class domination.* But to that we shall return later.

For the present let us see the kind of structure that is being presented. There are less difficulties with the analysis to the extent to which a more equitable sharing of basic resources, research and development and financial facilities is sought to be rationalized,[88] as long as the institutional structure by which this process of rationalization is to be achieved is itself not riddled with all the contrivances of manipulative control. The real problem lies in the 'de-linking' from business policy voiced in the Report so as to give currency to the original proposal of interposing a trustee between the owners of newspapers and journalists.[89] The central purpose of the 'de-linking' policy is to prevent a person involved in the newspaper business from being directly or indirectly involved in other business except to the extent of a maximum prescribed limit.[90] This crude adaptation of an even cruder Marxism not only fails to appreciate the methods of emerging capitalism but begins to seem to be both an empty, as well as a political, exercise when we come across the Commission confessing that it is 'conscious that the newspapers which will come within the ambit of the proposed legislation are all quality papers rendering good service to the community'.[91] If we take this concession to represent the state of facts perceived by the Commission we are forced to ask why these measures are necessary. The answer that the "public have a vital interest in their water supply"[92] seems to have its match only in a kind of brahmanical Hindu orthodoxy whereby the Commission seems to be more interested in purity than in cleanliness.

Yet, let us imagine what the logical consequences of any legislation about monopolism would be? Firstly, in a country like India where we have seen the market subvert the putative import of agrarian reform legislation, it is hardly likely that such a legislation will escape the contrivances of manipulation. The Commission is forced to establish its own case by pointing out to such facts as the marriage relationship between Bennett Coleman Ltd. and the House of Sahu Jain.[93] All this would lead us to the rather confusing area of what the minority called "nebulous (concepts) of doubtful utility".[94] Secondly, let us work on the assumption that such a de-linking process is possible. One possible result would be a complete denial of investment resources for the newspaper world. These resources would then come from the public sector which in turn would secure them from government.[95] The other logical possibility goes to the other extreme of creating press barons who can claim that their prime business interests are newspapers. Given a combination of both possibilities, we are left with a strange mix of press barons, small low financed private groups and a large sector dependent greatly on government dominated public sector funds.

Faced with this self-defeating set of alternatives, the Commission then proposes that a new kind of editorial management will be created. The minority wanted to include in the Board of Directors men drawn from journalism, literature, social science or law.[96] The majority, similarly, wanted to create such "public men of unquestionable integrity and eminence" and constitute them into a board of trustees appointed by management with the approval of the Chairman of the Press Council and the Chief Justice—with the latter to have the final say.[97] Such a proposal can only increase the power of patronage of the Press Council which, as a statutory body, works much too closely with the government.[98] Even though the proposals of the minority are really no different from those of the majority, the minority do forcefully remind us of the harsh reality that the socio-economic forces of society cannot be dissolved in such a superficial way:

> (N)ewspapers . . . shall still be run by owners whoever they may be. Their ideological alignments will not necessarily be

> different from those of today's owners. The production relations of our society shall not leave them untouched. Even monastic Buddhism, let it be remembered, could not be delinked from the prosperity of trading Vaishya castes whose emergence made it possible for this non-conformist religion to prosper.[99]

The whole approach of the Commission appears to rest on a mistaken left-wing analysis that certain formal changes in the super-structure will create turn around solutions in the deeper socio-economic structure which feeds the press and creates the ideological consciousness that dominates it. Its solutions rest on a superficial analysis of the power structure in society as well as an unconvincing understanding of how the ideological domination of class interests takes place in a plural society. But the views of the Commission represent the prototype around which much of the discussion about the press revolves.

Why has there been this 'intellectual paralysis'[100] on the nature of the discussion of the press? At one level, there is an intellectual tradition associated with Hinduism which lays great emphasis on arguing within an established consensus rather than on the basis of an independent critique. For centuries, resilient Hinduism has set up an art form whereby dominant ideologies absorb discussion on the basis of parameters set by them. Hinduism was assisted greatly by an all-encompassing ideology which sought to explain the nature of life and society as part of one non-dualistic understanding.[101] Supported by a State whose raison d'etre rested on the basis of such an understanding, an uncritical relationship was developed between the ruler and the ruled.[102] The attempt of Modern India's rulers to replicate a new ideological construct on the basis of a suspect socialism and establish a 'you-must-believe-in-us' relationship between the ruler and the ruled has done much to paralyse intellectual growth and re-assessment without adding a layer of conviction to the entire process. The dominance of the government eclipses not just the quest for alternative solutions but also alternative analysis. So, we are faced with an intellectual paralysis accompanied by a frustration for ideas which is quite apparent in the debates about the press.

The paralysis is part of the predicament of socio-economic forces of which the press is a part. The Indian press is a part of emergent capitalism. Supported and supportive of the government in their business dealings, modern Indian business-houses use the strength of the press as a social and political weapon to create a bargaining arena in which they have exclusive control. It is not unnatural for political elites which are often at the receiving end of this bargaining arena to try and 'discipline' and control it. It is also not unnatural for the business-houses to try and resist this attack on their relatively autonomous hold on this arena. While there is a great unity between political and economic elites, there are contradictions in the political economy. Both the political and business elites have not only to maintain power but legitimize it on a basis that espouses the public interest. The tussle for the press as an arena of power and sphere of influence has also been camouflaged as a genuine argument of principle. One group has unconvincingly talked of monopolistic dominance over the press whilst others have loosely linked the issue of press freedom to freedom generally. In one sense, the argument is merely a visible storm in an invisible tea cup. In another sense, like other aspects of political life, the fight over the press is part of a power struggle between competing elites.[103] Controversies at local and regional levels often take on a different complexion. But the same tensions continue even though they are tackled more on the basis of direct negotiations and threats. The central government's championship of a 'responsible' local press at the expense of an 'irresponsible' metropolitan press is more often than not not the whole story; and very often not even a part of it.

But, to return to the press as a bargaining arena of power. The nature and complexion of this arena is altering greatly. This must, perforce, affect the manner in which those in power will seek to use it. In an expanding consumer economy, the press is increasingly serviced by an increased labour force of journalists and has to be responsive to a more discerning public.[104] We have already witnessed in India an explosion of magazines and newspapers. The new corps of journalists is beginning to realise its own importance; and, to some extent, its bargaining strengths. Taking on board the rhetoric of both kinds of elites they have indulged in both developmental journalism (to expose the government) and the liberal freedom of the press to discover truths about management. Professionalism—defined as we shall see later as a new set of bargaining strengths—is creating a new force in the political economy of India.

Hitherto profoundly confused about its own role and the multiple pressures that seek to contain it, the press is slowly coming into its own. *This is not because of its performance but because of its increasing importance as the more credible power filter in India's political economy.* Heavily biased, greatly pressurized and manipulated, subject to enormous strains, starved of resources and riddled with varying degrees of competence and incompetence in management techniques and journalism, the press remains a formidable weapon. With radio and television as part of the monopoly of the State, the press commands more response than the promises of politicians. The emergence of a group of journalists who wish to increase the arena of bargaining to include themselves and various sections of the public, the nature of this arena itself is changing. Even the left—when they are not making their usual allegations about press monopolism and governmental control—have come to realize that it is important to join the fight not just for the control of information in society but also because the press is an important theatre of politics.

The press is a political instrument. Controversies about the press are part of the struggle for its political mastery. It is one of the few political instruments not wholly insensitive to multiple use. If it becomes too crude a political instrument, it will lose legitimacy. It operates through various levels of direct and indirect expression and through various techniques designed both to maintain its viability and legitimacy and have an affective influence on power. There are enormous problems with its structure. It is subject to great pressures. But it is not wholly surprising that the freedom of the press is defended by a diverse range of unholy alliances from both the left and the right.

Given India's existing polity, the press will increasingly become the arena for political exchange, the release of information and the creation of conceptive ideology. The struggle for the mastery of the press is an important item on the legal, political and social agenda. In that sense we need to begin a new debate about the nature of the press as a political institution and the ground rules and conditions under which this institution will be run. And, by whom. And for what.

NOTES

1. A phrase used by Marc Galanter: "The displacement of traditional law in Modern India", (1968) 24 *Journal of Social Issues* 65.
2. Cf. T.I. Emerson: *Towards a General Theory of the First Amendment* (1961) 1-15; C.E. Baker: "The Scope of the First Amendment Freedom of Speech", (1978) 28 *U.C.L.A.L.R.* 964. Much of the analytical literature on the press in India falls in this mould e.g. C. Sarkar (ed.): *The Press and the Law* (1968).
3. e.g. Leicester Stanhope: *History and Influence of the Press in British India* (1823); Stanford Arnof: *History of the Indian Press* (1829).
4. Note the significant articles by S.C. Sanial on the "History of the Indian Press" in the (1907, 1908) *Calcutta Review*; Sir Roper Lethbridge: *The Press in India* (1914); H. Barnes: *The Indian Press* (1940).
5. e.g. S. Natrajan: *A History of the Press in India* (1962) which looks at broad trends. A less analytical account is that of S. Agarwala: *Press, Public Opinion and Government* (1970); P.S. Khare: *The Growth of the Press and Public Opinion in India 1857-1918* (1964); M. Moitra: *History of Indian Journalism* (1969). To be preferred are more incisive undertakings which look at specific periods and contributions within more closely defined parameters (e.g. P. Narain: *Press and Politics in India 1885-1905*, (1963).
6. e.g. J. Natrajan: *History of Indian Journalism* (1954) which formed Part II of the Report of the Press Commission (1954).
7. See Valentine Chirol: *Indian Unrest* (1910). Cf. Pat Lovett: *Journalism in India* (1928) on some of the aspects of the inevitable influence of the national movement on the Press.
8. T.J.S. George: *Provincial Press in India* (1839-41); T.V. Parvate: *Marathi Journalism* (1969); G. Singh (ed.): *Panjab Akhbars 1839-41* (National Archives) (1932); N. Kumar: *Journalism in Bihar* (1971—supplement to Bihar State Gazetteer); R.B. Bhatnagar: *Rise and Growth of Hindi Journalism* (1970). See also F.E. Keay: *Hindi Literature* (1933); P.N. Basu and H.W.B. Moreno: *Hundred Years*

of Bengali Press (1920); D.V. Gundappa: *The Press in Mysore* (1940); K. Tripathi and P.D. Tandon: *Patra aur Patrakar* (1950); R.G. Ranade: *History of Marathi Periodicals 1832-1937*; V.R. Joshi and K.L. Ramachandra: *History of Newspapers* (1951—in Marathi); A.A. Nair: *Peeps at the Press in South India: A short survey of the achievements of editors and publishers* (1966); K.R. Seshagiri Rao (ed.): *Studies in the History of Indian Journalism* (1968).

9. P. Narain (*supra* note 5) 287.
10. As in the title of D.R. Manekar (ed.): *What ails the Indian Press: Diagnosis and Remedies* (1970—Proceedings of a Seminar sponsored by the All India Newspaper Conference), *ibid.* (Chanchal Sarkar) 26-32.
11. Chanchal Sarkar: *Challenge and Stagnation: The Indian Mass Media* (1969) attributing such stagnation *inter alia* to a lack in technological development (1-2, 78-79) and what he had termed earlier in his *Changing Press* (1967) as the lack of "adequate recognition of the right to know" (15).
12. D.R. Manekar: *The Press under Pressure* (1973) 58.
13. Chanchal Sarkar (ed.): *Emerging Estate* (1966). Note the suggestions of U.K. Narasimhan on technology (97-123), D.K. Rangnekar on expertise (124-38), Sarkar on correspondent exchanges in Asia (155-61)—on the latter note also the comments of L. Hoffman (147-54) and Susman Ejiro (161 ff.).
14. R. Ayyangar (a retired Supreme Court judge) in D.R. Manekar (*supra* note 10) 2-6.
15. e.g. I.K. Gujral in A.G. Noorani: *Freedom of the Press in India* (1971) 56-68.
16. V.K. Narasimhan: *Press, the Public and the Administration* (1961) refers casually to this. Miss Shireen Mehdi of the Press Council has done some interesting research on how the press reports on communal incidents (1979-80—not published as yet).
17. S.C. Jha: *The Concept of a Planned Free Press* (1958) setting up a Soviet style press divided into a planned press run by a branch of the planning board (72) and a party press (77) run by the public within planning allocations and with censorial functions.
18. F. Moraes in D.R. Manekar (ed.) (*supra* note 10) 413.
19. F. Moraes in A.G. Noorani (ed.): *Freedom of the Press in India* (1971) 82-5.
20. S. Sorabjee: *The Law of Press Censorship in India* (1976).
21. M.R. Masani in A.G. Noorani (*supra* note 19) 69-88.
22. S. Mulgaonkar in A.G. Noorani (*supra* note 19) 13-23.
23. C.R. Irani in A.G. Noorani (ed.) (*supra* note 19) 100-115.
24. e.g. M. Chalapati Rau in C. Sarkar (ed.): *Emerging Estate* (1966) 67-84.

25. D.R. Manekar in D.R. Manekar (ed.) (*supra* note 10) 8-17, and asking for editorial autonomy and better training—on the latter see also C. Sarkar in Noorani (ed.) (*supra* note 19) 116-33.
26. Manfred Lokmann in Noorani (ed.) (*supra* note 19) 96.
27. L.K. Advani: *The People Betrayed* (1980). "Perhaps the most devastating pieces about the Janata Government's failings came from the pen of supposedly pro-Janata journalists . . . than from pro-Indira scribes. . . ."
28. Discussed *infra*.
29. Examples of anthologies include A.G. Noorani (*supra* note 19); D.R. Manekar (*supra* note 10); Sarkar (ed.) (*supra* note 13). These are matched by general discussions on democracy in which many defenders of the press participate, e.g. N.C. Joshi (ed.): *Democracy and Human Values* (Essays in honour of V.M. Tarkunde (1979)). There are occasionally interesting and illuminating views in all these. For an exceptional account, collection of information and ideas see R.E. Wolseley (ed.): *Journalism in Modern India* (1964). Of individual works consider, for example, K. Ghosh: *Freedom on Fraud of the Press* (1973) which written in the form of a platonic dialogue is generally ambivalent in obtaining a solution between "control" and "abuse". More incisive views include those of journalists Sachin Sen: *The Press and Democracy* (1957); V.K. Narasimhan: *Press, the Public and the Administration* (1961) and S. Natrajan: *Democracy and the Press* (1965) despite the latter's unfortunate predictions that the government would not and could not interfere. (*supra* notes 10, 13 and 15).
30. See R. Dhavan: *The Supreme Court of India: A Socio-legal Analysis of its Juristic Techniques* (1977) Chapter 1.
31. What Austin called performative acts in J.L. Austin: *How to do things with words* (1954).
32. Implicit, for example, in some of the publications of Chanchal Sarkar: *The Changing Press* (1967); *Challenge and Stagnation* (1969); *Press Councils and their Role* (Press Institute of India).
33. e.g. Noorani (*supra* note 19).
34. e.g. *supra* note 7. Consider also R.D. Parikh: *The Press and Society: A Sociological Study* (1965) which after analysing the new educated readers concludes with the much overworked observation: "It has now become neither a campaigner for the needs and grievances of the people nor a crusader for social reforms. It has now struck a convenient balance in these respects because its survival no longer depends upon the readers alone; may be because being an industry it is run more for profits than for anything else."
35. See C. Sarkar (ed.) *The Press and the Law* (1968); C. Sarkar: *Press Councils and their Role* (1966); C. Sarkar (ed.): *Emerging Estate* (1967); C. Sarkar (ed.): *The Changing Press* (1967); T.J.S. George:

The Provincial Press in India (1967); R. Jansen (ed.): *The Newspaper and the Community* (1968); S. Banerjee: *Advertizing and small Newspapers* (1967); T. Lingam: *Circulation Problems in Indian Newspapers* (1968).

36. See references cited in note 5 *supra*.
37. It juxtaposes its work against "traditional media" and examines "developmental communication", "communications research" and "campaign planning". It is interesting to see the general affirmation of this approach in its *Evaluation: Sixth Anniversary* (Mimeo, 1980)—notably G.S.N. Murthy (3-5A) and Smt. Taruna Tanwar (11-15). See also M.U. Desai: "Communicating with Rural India—A two-fold task" (1973-4); *Approaches to Research on use of more communication for development in Africa and Asia*, (1944-5); D.A. Wora: *Communication for Rural Development* (1975-6); *Development Journalism* (1976).
38. e.g., "Agro-information flow at village level" (1967-68).
39. e.g., *Communication and Family Planning* (1967-8); I.P. Tewari: *Family Planning Problems and Perception*" (1972-3); *Impact of Mass Media on Family Planning Programme in India* (1972-3); "Administration and Organisational Communication Behavior in family Planning Programme" (1973-6); "Communication and Message" Reception in Family Planning" (1973-6); "Motivational training for rural leaders in family planning" (1973-6); "Sociological Characteristics of Family Planning Opinion Leaders" (1973-6).
40. e.g., "Perception of Indo-Pakistan War: Study at Village Level" (1971-2); "Impact of Field Publicity Activities in Four Rajasthan Districts" (1973-6).
41. e.g., "Awareness about the knowledge on 20 points programme and implementation" (1976-77).
42. e.g., "A Study on Election Campaign Broadcasts" (1978-9); "Film Censorship and Censorship Policy (Western Zone & Hindi Zone)" (1979-80—still in progress).
43. Note the research of Shireen Mehdi for the Press Council of India on the amount of coverage of various newspapers of various socio-economic items (see Press Council *Annual Report* (1981) A.R. 220-28. I am grateful to Justice Grover, Chairman of the Press Council, for a full text of the Report.
44. See P. Narain (*supra* note 5); and generally S. Natrajan (*supra* note 5). This is explored in Chapter VII later.
45. Indian historiography has neglected peasants by either representing them as an 'also ran' or as meddlesome interlopers who aberrated their assigned role in the scheme of things. They need to be rescued—in E.P. Thompson's memorable phrase—*The Making of the English Working Classes* (1968) 13—from "the enormous condescension of posterity". Yet it is not enough to examine the relationship between the peasant and the Raj in the context of the 1857 revolt

(see E. Stokes: *The Peasant and the Raj*: *Studies in Agrarian Society and Peasant Rebellion in Colonial India* (1978) and the review article of T. Metcalf (1979) XXXIX *Journal of Asian Studies* 111-9 or to show peasants as part of social movements; (see M.S.A. Rao (ed.): *Social Movements in the Nineteenth and Twentieth Centuries* Volumes I and II (1978). There is a need to study history as it affects the large bulk of people—of whom, in the Indian context, the peasant is a significant part. For a provocative beginning see R. Guha (ed.): *Subaltern Studies* Volume I (1982); Volume II (1983). For a general survey and a good bibliography see S. Sen: *Peasant Movements in India*: (*Mid*) *Nineteenth and Twentieth Centuries* (1982).

46. The *Young India* case (*In re Mohandass Karamchand Gandhi*) A.I.R. 1920 Bom. 175; for an analysis of which see R. Dhavan: *Contempt of Court and the Press* (1981) 45-6.
47. The leading cases on sedition are discussed in W.R. Donough: *History of the Law of Sedition* (1914 edn.); see also the discussion *infra* Chapter 7.
48. *Report of the Second Press Commission* (1982) pr. 2, p. 224.
49. See anthologies edited by A.G. Noorani (*supra* note 19); C. Sarkar (*supra* notes 11, 13, 35).
50. Note the diversity of participants and the extent of common ground amongst them in A.G. Noorani (*supra* note 19). We can see a considerable amount of common ground between the majority and the minority in the *Kuldip Nayar Report on News Agencies* (1978) during the Janata regime and in the *Report of the Second Press Commission* (1982) during Mrs. Gandhi's second regime.
51. For patterns of controls during the Emergency see the *White Paper on the Misuse of the Media during the Emergency* (1978) and S.J. Sorabjee: *The Emergency, Censorship and the Press in India (1975-77)*.

    This is discussed later in Chapter 2 *infra*.
52. *Report of the Press Commission* (1952-4).
53. *Diwakar Committee Report on Small Newspapers* (1966).
54. The culmination of this was the Supreme Court's ruling in *Bennett Coleman* v. *Union of India* A.I.R. 1973 S.C. 106.
55. On this see futher Chapter 2 *infra*.
56. On the campaign for a 'committed judiciary' see the different viewpoints expressed by N. Palkhivala (ed): *A Judiciary made to Measure* (1973) and M. Kumaramanglam: *Judicial Appointments* (1973).
57. S. Sorabjee: *The Emergency, Censorship and the Press in India, 1975-77* (1977).
58. See Kuldip Nayar: *Committee Report on the Committee on News Agencies* (1977) 94-5 (dissent of C.R. Irani and A.K. Sarkar).
59. L.K. Advani: *The People Betrayed* (1980).

60. Some of this eclectism can be seen in Arun Shourie's reports, many of which have been collected in his *The Second Reign of Mrs. Gandhi* (1983). It is not clear as to whether Shourie is trying to protect the institutions of democracy or simply asserting his animosity for Mrs. Gandhi.
61. Note the pluralist framework within which the Minority (*viz.* Justice Sisir Kumar Mukherjee, Rajendra Mathur, Girilal Jain and H.P. Paranjpe) locate their analysis in their dissent to the *Report of the Second Press Commission* (1982) pr. 15 p. 225.
62. Anne Lapping (ed.): *Media, Government and the Law* (1978—report of the proceedings of a seminar on the media held in Delhi in 1978).
63. *Report of the Second Press Commission* (1982) p. 20. This is apart from its "primary function to provide comprehensive and objective information on all aspects of the country's social, economic, political and cultural life . . . ." However, this 'objectivity' seems compromised in respect of all its detailed recommendations on a larger number of specific aspects of social and political life (pp. 186 8).
64. *Ibid.*, pr. 7 p. 20. But note the emphasis on development (prs. 9-11 p. 20) which really defines the parameters of constructive discussion.
65. *Ibid.*, pr. 81 p. 29. Note, however, the limited definition given to 'investigative reporting' (prs. 83-5 p. 30). The plea for investigative reporting becomes less convincing when the Press Commission while criticising private agencies simply asks the official handout agencies (*i.e.* radio and television) to be more objective (pr. 95 p. 31).
66. *Ibid*, prs. 8-11 p. 20; prs. 71-90, pp. 23-31. Note that the Constitution (Forty-second Amendment) Act, 1976 (s. 2) introduced "secularism" and "socialism" as part of the Preamble to the Constitution; see further R. Dhavan: *The Amendment: Conspiracy of Revolution* (1978), 64-72.
67. *Report of the Second Press Commission* (1982), prs. 28-9 pp. 22-3. Astrology should accordingly be the subject of special publications.
68. *Ibid.*, pr. 55 p. 26 and generally prs. 53-5 pp. 25-6 ("Promoting the concept of brotherhood"). Note the reliance on teleological approaches by the reference to Nehru and the Institute of Mass Communication (pr. 54 pp. 25-6).
69. *Ibid*, prs. 56-7 p. 26 with particular emphasis on social health. The irony is that it is accepted that "(w)hether the source is religion or the humanism of a non-theological ideology like socialism it is clear that every society needs a value system which will include self-restraint in the larger social interest". We are thus thrown back to arguments about the nature of the value system. Indeed, that is where the arguments begin; not, as the Commission pre-supposes, ends.
70. *Ibid.*, pr. 75 p. 28. This is after contrasting the relative space given on the front page and in editorials to 'development,' 'conflict and

tensions' and 'politics'. To attempt to tell the press about the areas they should cover is the beginning of censorship.

71. *Ibid.*, pr. 32 p. 23. Though this comment is made in the context of 'foreign relations' it has more general undertones. During the Emergency, Article 31C was introduced to deny civil liberty protections to those indulging in 'anti-national' activities.
72. *Ibid.*, pr. 44 p. 24. This is said in the context of communal reporting. The argument and solution is disingenuous. It is assumed that no voluntary method of restraint has, or could, work. So, there should be a strict enforcement of law (pr. 45 p. 24).
73. *Ibid.*, pr. 53 pp. 25-6 in the name of all religions.
74. *Ibid.*, prs. 78-82 p. 29 on 'development reporting'. Note the innumerable caveats on 'investigative reporting' (prs. 83-90, pp. 30-1). In his minute of dissent K.R. Ganesh seems to express the fear that liberal reporting usually results in vilifying national leaders like Nehru and others. The overall impression left by the Commission is to urge—and where necessary pressurize—the press into a particular kind of reporting in the name of the social and public interest.
75. *Ibid.*, pr. 95 p. 31.
76. *Ibid.*, prs. 81-2 p. 29. Clearly the object of all this is "to meet the extension workers who are the agents of change or the beneficiaries of change". However, there is some doubt as to whether reporting can countenance a critique of change from a totally different standpoint ? Would such a critique be regarded as anti-social or against the public interest?
77. *Ibid.*, prs. 56-95 pp. 27-31 on secularism and socialism generally.
78. *Ibid.*, pr. 51 p. 25. Note the interesting example of newspaper distortion of 'naxalite' activity by a Patna daily.
79. *Ibid.*, prs. 34-63 pp. 23-7. This taken to its logical limit leads N.P. Nande (Congress I)'s attempt to introduce a Banning of Communal Parties in India Bill, 1983 where "communal party means a party based on religious community and sectional appeal to serve its communal interests and whose activities are against the interest of the nation". Times of India, August 7, 1983. In all this there is a tendency to try and reduce all forms of tension, publicity, protest and discussion within the framework of control of a 'law and order' society (of pr. 51 p. 25; but note the treatment of the Press (Objectionable Matter) Act, 1951 at pr. 60 p. 56).
80. *Ibid.*, pr. 45 p. 24.
81. *Ibid.*, pr. 58 p. 26.
82. *Ibid.*, pr. 61 p. 26.
83. See generally the discussion of how the major controversies were tackled during the Emergency in R. Dhavan: *The Amendment: Conspiracy or Revolution* (1978) and "Amending the Amendment" (1978) 20 *J.I.L.I.* 249-72.

84. For an interesting Supreme Court attempt to re-define a 'Hindu' in the light of modern Indian secularism see Gajendragadkar J.'s judgment in *Yagnapurushdasji* v. *Muldas*, A.I.R. 1966 S.C. 111; see further J.D.M. Derrett: "The definition of a Hindu" (1966) 2 *S.C.J.Jnl.* 67; *ibid.* "Hindu—want of a definition for the purpose of applying a personal law" (1968) 70 Z.U.R. 110; M. Galanter: "Hinduism, secularism and the Indian judiciary" (1971) 21 *Philosophy East and West* 467.
85. One way in which this is done is demonstrated by how Government (and others) have used the Press Council's jurisdiction to harass various papers about communal tensions. These cases have all been collected in an unpublished research by A. Jacob and U. Loghani of the Indian Law Institute for the Press Council of India (1983). I am grateful to these researchers and the Director of the Institute for having made this research available to me. This is explored further in Part V (*infra*).
86. *Ibid.*, prs. 58-61 p. 26. Thus there is a complementary duality in the Press maintaining a reliance in reporting many social questions and preserving a 'law and order' society for government.
87. *Ibid.*, pr. 15 p. 225.
88. On finance (92-3) a development council (94-5) and generally on the problems of the press as an industry. But there are limits on the kinds of controls that are introduced and the purpose they serve especially in respect of price and page control (239) and advertisements (239-43) and newsprint control (246-7).
89. *Ibid.*, prs. 52-62 pp. 150-153; cf. Minority, pr. 19 p. 230; prs. 45-57 pp. 234-36.
90. *Ibid.*, pr. 52 p. 150.
91. *Ibid.*, pr. 61 p. 153. This point is forced home by the Minority both in its final peroration (pr. 34, p. 254) and more specifically in respect of the newspapers fairness (pr. 150, p. 249) advertisements (pr. 85 p. 240) editorial independence (pr. 67 p. 237) property control (pr. 424 p. 234; prs. 13-14 p. 230).
92. *Ibid.*, pr. 61 p. 153.
93. *Ibid.*, pr. 58 p. 152; cf. Minority pr. 53 p. 235.
94. *Ibid.*, pr. 19 p. 230.
95. *Ibid.*, prs. 75-86 pp. 94-96 shows how the National Development Commission could well be the instrument of such a control.
96. pr. 68 p. 237.
97. pr. 113 p. 162.
98. On the Press Council see below Chapter 4 for a preliminary assessment about the working of the Press Council. *Report of the Second Press Commission* (1982), pr. 11-53 pp. 79-85 and some of the controversies referred to there.
99. *Report of the Second Press Commission* (1982), pr. 36 p. 227.

100. Mckim Marriot: "Hindu Transactions—Diversity without Dualism" in Kapferer (ed.): *Transaction and Meaning* (1976).
101. Note the emphasis on breaking this intellectual paralysis in a democracy by Justice Beg in *Bennett Coleman* v. *Union of India*, A.I.R. 1973 S.C. 106 at pr. 157 p. 449.
102. For a good account of the relationship between the ruler and the ruled see J.D.M. Derrett: "Rulers and Ruled in Ancient India" (1969) *Recueils de Societies Jean Bodin XXII Gouvernes et Gouvernants* 417. R. Dhavan (*supra* note 30). *The Supreme Court of India: A Socio-legal Analysis of its Juristic Techniques* (1977) 216-8 reviews the literature.
103. J. Schumpeter: *Capitalism, Socialism and Democracy* (1941 edn.).
104. This does not necessarily attribute an elite "educating the masses" function to the press (see *Report of the Second Press Commission* (1982), pr. 48 p. 149). Cf. Minority, prs. 16-20 pp. 225-6. The Minorities are right to explain (pr. 20 p. 226) that "a newspaper is a newspaper, and not a newspaper journal or a sociological tract." However, the view presented here suggests that newspapers—amongst other things—are, and ore increasingly becoming, more of a political forum. The public is happy to be entertained, but also resistant to both trivia as well as indoctrination.
105. This is explored more extensively in Chapter 2 *infra*.

2

CONTROLS AND INFLUENCES

I

The controls and influences on the press are too complex to admit to simple explanation, too varied to admit to a simple descriptive summary and too important to be allowed to suffer eclectic analysis. Yet the question seems simple enough. A lawyer might proceed to answer queries about controls and influences on the press by examining the relevant rules and regulations, examining their severity and pronouncing judgment on the basis of this examination.[1] A slightly more discerning lawyer might turn to the loopholes in the law and examine the depth of legal manoeuvre.[2] Further analysis may take us away from the lawyer's library—and the cases that bear testimony to his art—to the actual social and litigational use of the law.[3] And, indeed, much can be learnt from that. But, whilst all this would suggest one framework within which the press operates, it does not exactly tell us of the kinds of controls and pressures exerted on the press. For this it is necessary to sustain some kind of insight into one's understanding of power, how it is exercised, whom it controls and in what way it replicates the conditions for its future use. So, leaving our lawyer behind, let us proceed to our student of government who would look at the government and the extent to which the government directly dominates the press.[4] But the government does not just control the press directly. Given the nature of India's political economy, it is also an important intermediary in controlling the market conditions under which the press exists. Quite apart from general systemic control of the economy as a whole, a change in government advertisement policy, control of newsprint, the interposition of a statutory wage structure and a thousand other things affect the viability of the press.[5] Nor does this influence stop with the government. The economic structure of the press, the manner in which it is financed, the impediments on its future growth and the possibility of concerted practices all exert their influence.[6] Many of the debates in India concentrate either on the severity of the law, the extent of direct government control or the accusatory insight that big business dominates the press. These three issues have attracted the attention of the two Press Commissions which have been appointed by the Government of India.[7] In a sense that is inevitable. These commissions were appointed to advise the government and naturally looked at the laws, government policy and direct economic pressures. Their strategy seems to have been to suggest marginal changes in the law, confess governmental pressures but continue to protect the government and to pass the major blame on to business houses. This strategy has gathered momentum and is taken as settled.[8] Here, we are concerned, in part, with considering whether this strategy is correct.

There is yet another level at which the discussion about controls and influences must be discussed. We cannot assume that questions of control and influence are be concerned only with crude issues of direct control—whether economic or political. At another level systemic control over a society manifests itself. The point is particularly relevant for a discussion on India. Hinduism has dominated Indian society for thousands of years on the basis of a subtle combination of coercive power and ideological domination. Dealing with both a particular notion of the predicament of man and of his place in society, Hinduism provided legitimacy to the extensive domination of various groups passing through various stages of economic growth. It has offered power to rulers, servitude to untouchables and various other groups and control to various dominant interests.[9] Such a set of values needs consideration, transformation and adaptation when faced with a new emergent economy, a varied range of occupational relationships and different methods of control.[10]

New ideologies were created by a combination of British nineteenth century utilitarianism, and imperial need.[11] The freedom movement resting on new ideological principles of democracy and liberalism sought to translate these into the Constitution and the post-constitutional framework along with a heavy incorporation of the ideology of the British Raj and the mechanisms through which the Raj had functioned.[12]

It is a fallacy to assume that the Constitution represents a clear break from the Raj. This is particularly important as far as the press is concerned. The British first assumed the policy of treating the press as mischief makers. This was easier to sustain in the late eighteenth and early nineteenth centuries. The Calcutta press fought out all the battles of the Governor General's council and played the politics of press embarrassment to the full.[13] Much later, this policy came to be modified so as to reduce press questions to law and order questions. The Indian Penal Code was amended to make this possible.[14] This policy of treating press issues as law and order issues forms an important part of the strategy of British laws and of the struggle to legitimate harsh laws as being consistent with a progressive patrimony. The makers of India's Constitution relied greatly on this tactic of creating a consensus in favour of law and order so that it would be regarded as a reasonable and legitimate intrusion on civil liberties.[15] This policy was then adopted by the Supreme Court and proved so convincing that even civil libertarians consider law and order issues to be an overall legitimate intrusion on civil liberties under virtually all circumstances. In this sense, the Emergency (1974-77) was also for the defence of law and order as, indeed, was the famous Bihar Press Bill, 1982. What is at issue here is the process of ideological reductivism which simultaneously gives the State both arbitrary power as well as a liberal identity and legitimacy.

In addition, Independent India has also to accommodate the claims of liberal socialism. The government has tried to trade off the classic conflicts between pure liberalism and the State's formally declared duty to re-distribute ownership, wealth and power in society.[16] This results in the contradictory position of it having to package and present an ideology which will be credible to the vast bulk of people, not affect the power of emergent interests and yet give the government the capability to ward off public exposure and criticism. However, this is where difficulties arise. The Indian State is being privatized. But its privatization is at present taking place at the hands of an emerging class of power brokers. These power brokers are linked to emergent interests, who manipulate them and are, in turn, manipulated by them. They are still able to hold their own because the apparatus of State control has given them an array of regulatory powers in a political economy which cannot dispense with such controls.[17] Since emergent interests do not want to be totally defenceless against these power brokers, several discrete political arenas have been created to maintain a polarity of tension and influence. Sometimes the government and emergent interests use these powers jointly; sometimes they use them in opposition. The press has become a strange arena for conflict.[18] The government faced with the power of the media recognizes that the press does much to give support to the values which the government wishes to sustain. *At the same time, the government cannot be sure of two things. It cannot be sure that the media will do exactly what the government wishes it to do.* Further, since the media operates under conditions of open liberalism, there is no effective guarantee that it will not be used either by elite political opponents or even the exploitative disadvantaged. This has made the government in India feel that it must not only seek a broad alliance with the press to establish—amongst disagreements—certain hegemonic values, but also that the press must be controlled directly. This feeling was even more pronounced in the case of Mrs. Gandhi who found it impossible to brook any kind of opposition. To this end, she has collapsed Indian federalism by imposing State emergencies on various States,[19] attacked the Supreme Court and tried to humble it into submission[20] and suspend Parliament by declaring a national Emergency.[21]

Anyhow, Mrs. Gandhi discovered that as long as she swore some kind of allegiance to liberal democracy she could not deal with the press as she liked. Appeals to law and order could be used in only a limited way and to a limited extent. They could not be used to give credence to a policy of the total annihilation of the press. So, some other explanation and some subtler method of control had to be found.[22] Several attempts have been made to try and control the press in the name of socialism by attacking the monopolism of the big newspapers in the name of the smaller papers in order to control the lot.[22] In the end what emerged was a somewhat complex ideology in which intra-elite class tensions found expression, whilst power brokers negotiated with emergent interests to produce a favourable status quo. A facade of appealing to universal principles was designed to legitimate and sustain the whole apparatus of control.

When all this is fought through in the bargaining arena of law courts, the pattern becomes even more awkward. Here is another arena which is theoretically a free-for-all. It is not surprising that those with litigational skills are able to trivialize much of law through the pathology of litigation.

So, law comes to be associated with many functions. It is a means to declare a set of values not just through its rules but also through its institutions which are represented as just. It is itself a process where the institutions and processes are such that it has been said of law that often 'the process is the punishment'.[24] Litigation can transform rules so as to alter their social meaning, import and reality. So, the legal system far from bringing a universality to society, replicates many power struggles in society—whether ideological or otherwise. This is not to deny that 'law' like the 'press' constitutes an area which contains some potential benefits for the disadvantaged—even if it is also the primary means to control and secure the latter's domination. These arenas can bring commutative rather than distributive benefits.[25] But, since they are couched in terms of universal access they also contain the possibilities of providing marginal arenas affording turn around capabilities for the disadvantaged.[26] So both the 'press' and 'law' beeome instruments of domination, and theatres for playing games and finding possibilities for reverse turn around action.

So, when we concern ourselves with looking at the nature of controls and influences on the press we are concerned with many things. But after we have got past our initial catalogue of strict laws, tough government policy and crude administrative and economic control, we find ourselves thrown into a much more sophisticated area where power is legitimated and where people are taught to delegate others to oppress them with their own consent. Since this exercise cannot be considered in a vacuum, it must be drawn out historically. There is a cumulative paradigm of control over the press which draws links with the past with the same alacrity with which it makes concessions to the present.

II

Direct Governmental Control

Direct governmental control has been a constant and indelible part of the law relating to the press. The pattern for such an extensive control was set in the early days of the British Raj.

The Indian press, which began its life in the late eighteenth century, invoked the immediate displeasure of the government.[27] The first editor was deported. J.A. Hicky's *Gazette* (1780), which produced invectives about Calcutta's social and political pressure, denial of postal facilities and litigation was jointly sponsored by the Governor-General and Chief Justice. This pattern of control was also exercised elsewhere. Boyd was deprived of the editorship of *Hurkaru* in Madras and William Duane and, later, Maclean were deported from India. By 1799, Wellesley's government had introduced Regulations which, *inter alia*, required pre-inspection of all papers by the government and prescribed deportation as a punishment for violation. Lord Hastings' attempts in 1818 to create a pattern of responsibility with the editor were opposed in his own Council and in London. Instead the censor, John Adam, created considerable support for a pattern of censorship and in 1823—during his temporary tenure as Governor-General—a full and comprehensive censorship was established. The press was to be licensed with powers of search of unlicensed premises. Certain papers or publications could be prohibited.[28] "Regulations", which were registered by Chief Justice Macnaghten over a petition by Raja Ram Mohun Roy's lawyer, were a direct consequence of disagreements between Adams and the English press; men like James Buckingham were deported just before the Regulations were issued. The impact of some of these Regulations was redressed in 1835.[29] Substituted for a system of direct control was the requirement of supplying information about the publisher and printer. This concession was made as a result of a change in administration and as a result of strenuous lobbying by the vernacular and English press.

After the Mutiny, the Press Act, 1857 imposed a rigorous control on the possession of printing material, granting printing licences and gave the government the power to "prohibit the publication or circulation . . . of any particular newspaper, book, or other printed paper or any newspaper of any particular description, whether printed in the said territories or not. . . ."[30] This Act lasted only one year.

So far vernacular and English presses were similarly treated. The Press and Registration of Books Act, 1867 regulated (rather than restrained) English and vernacular presses by introducing a system of registration. In 1878, "an Act for the better control of publications in Oriental Languages" was passed. The vernacular press was placed under an extensive control, forced to make deposits vulnerable to forfeit and subjected to arbitrary powers of licensing and search and seizure. Meanwhile, the Indian Penal Code, 1860 introduced the offence of criminal defamation, and was amended to include offences against obscenity, defamation, sedition, the promotion of enmity between groups and outraging religious feelings.[31] Official Secrets Act patterned on British legislation was introduced as were other statutes dealing with law and order, contempt and the like.[32] As the movement for Indian Independence gathered momentum, further restraints were imposed to control the incitement of offences, provide for the forfeiture of deposits and to empower the seizing of presses.[33]

The deposit forfeiture system crippled the smaller, and frightened the larger, newspapers. In its crucial initial years the effect of the system was as tabled below:

TABLE I: Showing the use of the 'forfeiture deposit' system between 1910-1914

Year	*No. of newspapers affected*	*Range of Security deposited (in Rs.)*	*No. unable to make deposit and, therefore, closed*	*Language of newspapers*	
				English	*Indian*
1910	10	1000-5000	9	2*	10
1911	5	500-5000	3		5
1912	2	2000-5000	1		2
1913	3	500-2500	2		3

*These papers were published in Anglo-Gujerati and Anglo-Marathi respectively. They were essentially Indian language papers.

The symbolic effect of this control was even greater. It posed a non-negotiable threat. This whole system was heavily criticised in the Press Law Committee after the First World War, and after a relaxation of control in 1922 a more stringent control was again introduced in 1931.[34] It was extensively used although exact figures are not available.

The fact that some of this legislation was *ultra vires* the freedom of speech provisions guaranteed by the Constitution of India, 1950 led to the formal repeal of these provisions.[35] However, since the freedom of speech provisions are suspended during an Emergency, a limited pattern of pre- and post-censorship exists as part of the Defence of India Regulations and operates during national emergencies. This system was fully reintroduced in a modified form during the famous internal Emergency (1975-7).[36]

The pattern of control intensifies greatly when an Emergency is declared under the Constitution. The government is empowered to prohibit the publication of any items prejudicial to the public safety, the defence of India, the maintenance of public order and so on.[38] Any papers can be closed down or be required to make a forfeitable deposit of money. The flow of information through postal and other services can also be controlled. A much more elaborate version of such provisions was used in the famous Emergency of 1975-77. All this is in addition to the normal powers to control the publication and circulation of such information which would incite people to offences or threaten the public safety. The low key 'registration' and 'information gathering' control on the press can be gradually increased during an Emergency to impose a more or less total and complete censorship on the press.

The first major Emergency (1962-8) promulgated during the Chinese invasion (1962) and continued during and after the Indo-Pakistan War (1965) resulted in a relatively mild control. Apart from scrutiny by the Press Advisory Unit, a warning system was introduced through a Central Emergency Press Advisory Committee. A formal warning also resulted in the cessation of government advertising. Later, a procedure of show cause notices was also introduced. Since the press were generally co-operative, a committee of newspapers was also created to advise the government. Between 1962-65 (the operative years) the Central Government considered infractions by 54 newspapers and magazines (4 in 1962, 38 in 1963, and 12 in 1965) involving 100 items. Action was proposed in 33 cases involving 77 items. A formal warning was given in 11 cases, informal advice in 11, one case was treated as a security issue, one case invited pre-censorship and one a ban. The figures for the State governments were as follows: 93 cases were considered resulting in formal warnings in 12 cases, pre-censorship in 10 cases, a security issue in 2 cases, proscription in 25 cases, arrests in 9 cases, prosecution in 23 cases, a press closure in one case and a ban on publication in another case.[37]

The Emergency (1975-77) saw a much more stringent revival of the forfeiture deposit system. But rather than use that system extensively—though it stood out as a threat—a more direct censorship programme was introduced. Fifty-one pressmen were discredited including 43 correspondents, 2 cartoonists and 6 cameramen. Seven correspondents were expelled and 29 correspondents were banned from India. Censorship was imposed on 161 items and it has been estimated that 99 fell outside the scope of the censorship guidelines. Censorship by telephone was rampant.[39] A private account[40] of censorship estimates 158 attempts to muzzle the press including 41 attempts at pre-censorship, 67 banned items and the rest a mixture of what was called 'newspaper management, including management, banning and pre-censorship'. Ninety-seven newspapers and periodicals (not including action against multiple editions of the same newspaper or periodical) were denied advertisements and 12 requests for government advertisements were not acceded to. Two hundred and fifty-three journalists were preventively detained during the Emergency—110 under the Maintenance of Internal Security Act, 1971 as amended, 60 under Defence of India Regulations and 83 under other provisions. The press, radio and television were extensively used to highlight news items and programmes at the request of the government. An Enquiry Committee[41]—formed after the Emergency—received 1037 complaints, 820 of which were outside the scope of the terms of reference, 103 involved harassment of journalists, 45 misuse of censorship provisions, 8 allegations of certifications in films, 23 the manipulation of the mass media and 38 'incidental matters'. These statistics do not do justice to the 'total censorship' which had been imposed and which was openly proclaimed by the government as being essential to the future and progress of the Indian nation.

Even in 'ordinary' as opposed to 'emergency' times, various provisions were enacted to prevent the publication of certain kinds of information. This was continued till 1957.[42] At the same time, the Indian Penal Code 1860 (as amended) contains a large number of provisions which declare offences committed on the publication of certain kinds of material which constitutes an impressive array of controls discussed in full later.[43]

Various State governments were not happy with either the range of these offences or the manner in which they were enforceable. Legislation was enacted by the Tamil Nadu and Orissa Governments against "grossly indecent or scurrilous matters or matter intended for blackmail". Such offences carried severe penalties for the original (imprisonment of up to two years or fine or both) and subsequent offences (imprisonment for up to five years or fine or both). They were also made non-bailable and cognizable.[44] In 1982, the Government of Bihar—much plagued by political opposition from the press—enacted a similar Bill. Here the government was given political control of the decision to proceed with the trial, the police were given the discretion to arrest and the executive magistrate the power to determine questions of bail.[45] On the one hand, this Bill followed the logic of the Indian Penal Code and the theory of the British Raj towards the press. On the other hand, it also created fresh moves to empower State governments to harass their media opponents with, at least, arrest and denial of bail—if not trial, conviction, imprisonment and fine. A massive lobby was organised against the Bill which having passed the Bihar legislatures was reserved for the assent of the President.[46] The lobby—accompanied by large scale agitation—succeeded and the Bill was formally withdrawn a year later.[47] During this period of time, the government was obviously waiting to slip the Bill through as a statute as soon as the temperature of the agitation died down and while the controversy faded from memory into obsolescence.

The Bihar Bill controversy brings to the surface the persistence of—what can be called—local emergencies. Local emergencies exist where a combination of police, executive and lower judicial officers can harass their opponents through the exercise of legal emergency action. The most gruesome illegal example of this is the murder of a journalist by a policeman when the former was investigating corrupt police practices.[48] The most potent political legalization of this process is the Bihar Bill. The cohesive—even if differential—use of the Indian Penal Code provisions along party political lines follow both the privatization and partisan politicization of the Indian State.

In a sense the national Emergency (1975-77) is a demonstration of this process of privatization and partisan politicizationship. This process results in alliances between socio-economic class interests and emergent political power brokers. Police harassment constitutes continuous minor examples of this process just as the Bihar Bill and the declaration of an Emergency represent its high points.

The existing pattern of control is contained in the Press and Registration of Books Act, 1867. A person in possession of a press has to register a declaration to that effect.[49] Changes of residence to a new local jurisdiction for a period longer than sixty days should be notified to the magistrate of the latter jurisdiction. If the press remains within the same jurisdiction, a notification should be made within 24 hours if the keeper of the press is the same, otherwise a fresh registration is necessary.[50] Every newspaper shall contain the names of the owner and editor and the date of publication.[51] Changes for more than thirty days have to be notified in the same way as for the owner of the press.[52] Since the British—and now the Indian—government did not trust their subjects, there are extensive provisions for the proof and verification of the information that is made available.[53] The registration of presses and papers can be cancelled if there is a newspaper with a similar name, a change of printer or publisher, a contravention of the rules, a false representation or a concealment of any material fact.[54] Penalties for contravention of the rules are a fine not exceeding two thousand rupees or imprisonment for a term of six months or more.[55] There is also a small fine for failing to supply the government with a copy of the newspaper or for an improper disclosure of certain relevant information.[56] The office of the Press Registrar was introduced following a recommendation of the Press Commission in 1954.[57] He compiles information on all the newspapers including information on editors, publishers' ownership and control, circulation, price and such matters. Newspapers have to file Annual Statements before the Registrar who shall have:—

> access to any relevant record or document and may enter at any reasonable time any premises where he believes some

> record or document to be had and may inspect or take copies of the relevant record or ask any question necessary for obtaining any information required to be furnished under . . . (the) . . . Act.[58]

These powers have not really been used. So far, the purpose of all the above provisions is to identify those responsible for a paper and provide for the cumulation of information about newspapers. Such information would be useful to the public and the government and could be used for future analysis. Under another statute, copies of newspapers have also to be supplied to the government—presumably so that they can be preserved in the government's archives.

The Second Press Commission (1982)[59] has advanced a series of proposals which may well have the effect of politicizing the routine, administrative, registration role of the Press Registrar. Following the government's so-called lead in attacking the so-called monopolism of the metropolitan press, the Press Commission has commissioned the services of the Press Registrar to assist in this process.[60] To be given the grand title of 'Registrar of Newspapers in India',[61] he will if these recommendations are implemented, not just classify papers on the basis of circulation but also by ownership,[62] separately classify 'daily newspapers', 'news magazines' and 'periodicals',[63] collect a vast array of statistical information including the number of persons employed,[64] the capital invested and the capacity of machinery in use,[65] require newspapers to supply "techno-economic data (including edition-wise and publication-wise financial data)[66] not only in respect of individual publications" but also separate editions of the same newspaper brought out from different centres whether by conventional methods of printing or by facsimile reproduction and ensure the supply of regular information on the volume of advertizing revenue from advertizing agencies in the country.[67] All this information will be made public and available to competitors. The Press Registrar will have the power to impose a fine—hitherto exercised by a magistrate.[68] All this is despite a tremendous backlog of cases with the Registrar.[69] He would be invested with the pre-censorship power to determine whether a magazine is a sex or cinema magazine or not so that newsprint may or may not be allocated to it.[70] He will verify the regularity in publication of the newspapers and declare non-regular publications as non-genuine,[71] keep control over inflated circulation figures and liaise with the Institute of Chartered Accountants to take disciplinary action against such chartered accountants who may have falsified such figures.[72] Apart from all this, the Press Registrar is to have an advisory team of experts to discharge his non-statutory functions[73] (whatever they might be!), regional officers,[74] and a statistical and economic cell to collect

> data on some important aspect of the press, for example, the average page level of individual publications . . . keep himself informed of all significant developments in the field of newspaper publications including developments in printing technology . . . and have information on the profile of readership of newspapers.[75]

While recommendations that a refusal by a magistrate to authenticate or cancel a declaration should call for an appeal to a central board[76] are welcome, *there is no doubt that the Press Registrar contemplated in the Report is like a Press Commission in continuous session with powers to investigate, subpoena, threaten, intimidate and harass.* Theoretically such information is useful to the researcher, government and politicians. But whom is it intended for? The implementation of such proposals can only transform the office of the Press Registrar into a powerful bureaucratic—and political—office. Without specifying details the Report naturally goes on to recommend that the Registrar should be a professional, capable of autonomous functioning, be appointed for five years and be someone with "suitable background and experience".[77] The utility of the information that is collected should not blind us to the manner in which it is collected or the power that would be given to those who shall collect it.

Apart from direct censorship, there are also a range of controls on the press because it operates as a business or an industry. To the extent to which the press is organised as a business, it is subject to all the laws that apply to any other business ventures—*e.g.*, the law relating to partnerships, companies and monopoly control. The press as a business has the right to some protection under the Constitution even though the Constitution does permit anti-monopoly restrictions on the right to business.[78]

The Monopolies Commission did not look at the nature of press monopolies.[79] The government and others have made much of the monopoly structure of the press. But, despite the fact that provisions exist to control the monopoly structure of the press, the government has not really used these provisions. In the sixties and seventies, the government did try to control the price, page and advertisement structure and the supply of newsprint to newspapers. All these attempts were struck down by the Supreme Court on the grounds that they violated the freedom of the press.[80] But a price control statute nevertheless continues unscathed on the statute book.[81]

At a policy level, the Report of the Second Press Commission (1982) represents the revival of an attack on the allegedly monopolistic press. The Report refuses to accept the constitutional doctrine set out in *Sakal Newspapers*:[82]

> It may well be within the power of the State to place, in the interest of the general public, restrictions on the right of a citizen to carry on business but it is not open to the State to achieve this object by directly and immediately curtailing any other freedom of that citizen guaranteed by the Constitution and which is not susceptible of abridgement on the same grounds . . . Freedom of speech cannot be taken away with the object of placing restrictions on the business activities of a citizen.[83]

The Report simply moves on the assumption that the Supreme Court is wrong,[84] that the decision should be looked at afresh[85] and proceeds on the basis that reforms can be made even though the decision poses a constitutional restraint on such reforming impulses.[86] The Minority not only asserts the correctness of the *Sakal* doctrine[87] and the inappropriateness of the

Press Commission to "pronounce upon the correctness or otherwise of Supreme Court judgments"[88] but also on the fact that Justice Mathew (the Chairman of the Press Commission) had himself affirmed the correctness of *Sakal*[89] even if he was now using the Press Commission to re-assert his theories on the economic control of the press which had not been accepted by the rest of the Supreme Court in 1972.[90] The Report recommends extensive changes. The Monopolies and Restrictive Trade Practices Commission (MRTP) should apply to the Press.[91] The effective market for determining monopolistic or restrictive practices should be the State or even the region.[92] This could mean that a district where there is a single newspaper could be deemed to be called a monopoly! While the MRTP would give a public hearing,[93] it could also act *suo motu* where allegations of monopolistic practices come to its notice.[94] We know that the government is a major complainant against the press in the Press Council:[95] could—indeed, would—not a similar result occur with the MRTP? The Minority in the Press Commission were convinced that this proposal is to single out the larger newspapers without assisting the smaller ones.[96] They recall, with some irony, that official policy had precluded the MRTP from being used to prevent the decentralisation of economic power[97] and suggest that it would be invidious to single out the newspaper industry to be presented as a sacrificial ideological example in persuasion.[98] While they are right to smell a political rat and to point out to the hypocrisy of a government that allows the practice of monopolism and preaches socialist ownership at the same time, they are aware that the use of the MRTP is both necessary and desirable.[99] We shall see later[100] that although the incidence of monopolism in the press is not significant, there is room for concerted practices. The Supreme Court's pronouncements in *Sakal*[101] are not an absolute bar on anti-monopoly control but were definitely intended to limit ingenious attempts to impose either price and page or newsprint control.[102]

Newsprint control has always posed a problem in that it is an essential commodity that has import control connotations and must be distributed equitably. The present policy—objected to by at least one member—allows an initial quota for new publications for four months for eight pages (16 for periodicals) and a circulation can be shown.[103] The Report recommends an increase in import quotas of up to 12 pages for newspapers,[104] suggests direct handling by newspapers of this quota through a proposed Newspapers Development Corporation[105] rather than through the much complained about State Trading Corporation,[106] suggests stopping the quota where the newspaper ceases to be regular,[107] increasing the expected regularity rate to 90 per cent (for the present 50 per cent) after allowing for "failure to publish on account of strikes, lockouts, power cuts and other circumstances beyond the control of newspapers".[108] A progressive rate of import duty—designed to hit bigger newspapers—would be imposed ostensibly to reduce "the tendency to increase the number of pages to accommodate more and more advertisements with a view to earning higher profits (and make it) uneconomical".[109] One can understand the problems of equitable distribution, but the imposition of a tax to prevent growth in size has precisely the kind of implications which were declared unconstitutional in the *Bennett Coleman* case.[110] This is even more important if we remember that there is no real indication that import quotas were, in fact, being misused.[111] Moral considerations are also suggested for this form of pre-censorship in that it is declared that sex and cinema magazines should not be allocated newsprint irrespective of whether the material they contain is obscene, immoral or indecent.[112] The Minority rightly use the Majority's argument that the import bill for newsprint is no drain on resources (1.3 per cent in 1981).[113] Stressing what we have earlier identified as the political role of the press they point out to the State monopoly on broadcasting (which competes with the newspapers),[114] forecast an increase in literacy[115] and argue that it is consistent with democracy to allow an Open General (Import) Licence for newsprint.[116] More recently, the Supreme Court has insisted that the government do a periodic review of its newsprint import policy; and put it on a rational basis.[117] While in the long run better technology may result in indigenous newsprint,[118] the real achievement would be the elimination of the possibility of government harassment of the press:

> (This approach) will eliminate the continuous wrangling between the Press and the Government. It will also discourage fake claims in respect of circulation figures. To the best of my knowledge the Government has not used newsprint allocations to put pressure on newspapers. But a government, in future, may, if it is so disposed. The possibility will be greatly reduced if newsprint is put on (an Open General Licence .) . . . It would also eliminate the difficulties that many smaller papers experience in ensuring that their quotas are met.[119]

Some of these arguments have also been made about the import of technology and machinery.

The Report also suggests price:page and news:advertisement ratio controls. It recommends the imposition of a minimum price for a particular size of newspaper in order to create effective competition[120] and a 60:40, 50:50, 40:60 news: advertisement ratio for large, medium and small newspapers respectively.[121] We have already noted that these provisions may be unconstitutional in the light of the decisions of the Supreme Court in the *Sakal* and *Bennett Coleman* cases.[122] While the mechanics of advertizing policy (including government advertizing) are looked at later,[123] some of the implications of these proposals need to be examined. The Minority point out that small is not always beautiful[124] and that price and page control may be an issue for consideration by the Monopolies and Restrictive Trade Practices Commission.[125] They draw attention to the simple economic fact that advertisements subsidize newspaper finance to keep prices low:

> We are surprized that our colleagues should have proposed news:advertisement ratios without any reference to the present day economics of newspaper publishing. We have little doubt that its implementation will make it extremely difficult for larger newspapers to survive. A price and page schedule . . . will have a similar effect on their fortunes . . . (A)s the economy is organised at present, advertisement revenue cannot be treated as an evil form of finance. So long as we have a largely free enterprize and market oriented

economy, advertisement will remain an integral part of the system.[126]

There is much substance in the argument that the problem must be studied at the deeper level of the structure of the economy and newspaper finance. While there is a need to control the news:advertisement ratio, the ultimate control on this must be a bored readership that finds excessive advertising boring or a prudent readership that would cause high prices to reduce circulation.[127] Where the situation gets serious in any one sector of the economy, the application of anti-monopoly and restrictive trade practices legislation can be applied—both as an act of necessity and as an act of a faith.

The major proposal for governmental control is the plan to de-link ownership patterns.[128] This involves proposals for legislation to "make it mandatory for persons carrying on the business of publishing newspapers to sever their connections with other business".[129] Thus, other businesses cannot have more than a ten per cent interest in a newspaper business and a newspaper cannot have more than a ten per cent interest in other businesses.[130] We have already argued that this will have the ridiculous effect of either creating more newspaper magnates, or a heavy dependence on State finance. Since the Report also suggests that a Newspaper Development Commission should enter this field,[131] the argument about creating the conditions for dependency on State finance becomes more and more cogent. In any event, the real problem does not concern formal ownership but effective control. And since, to prevent such effective control involves lifting the veil on *benami* transactions and—the Commission seems to think—marriage alliances,[132] the control mechanisms threaten to be quite extensive. All this is coupled with recommendations for a Board of Trustees interposed between editors and proprietors.[133]

So, it would appear that a new round of State control mechanisms are being discussed and proposed through the aegis of the Press Commission. Whether they find their place in policy or legislation, they hang threateningly like a Damocles' sword. But is it really necessary to achieve a greater freedom of the press? No one can doubt that business houses and newspaper magnates have influence. Newspapers cost money![134] It is hardly surprising that newspaper finance depends greatly on a mixture of private investment, advertisement revenue and public finance. The government can arbitrate on questions of the equitable distribution of resources and raw material. It can also redress market situations and prevent concerned practices. But is it really necessary—in the name of a free press and to help small newspapers—to control everything? The press in India is created by a series of hybrid forces. To superimpose governmental control on these forces does not necessarily improve the situation. The press needs to be controlled by a range of contradictions within the industry itself. The press has to deal with a range of pressures from the public, from proprietors, government and its own journalists. This results in equations which even though not wholly satisfactory do not create a situation wholly insensitive to differential use and application! Perhaps, this is the reason why a government that is created by certain forces is scared of the forces that created it; and these, in their turn, are scared of the institutions and mechanisms they generate and sustain for their own protection and advantage.

As an industry, the press is also subject to labour and factory legislation dealing with the conditions of work and service. More importantly, any dispute amongst labour and management is subject to a compulsory adjudication machinery under the Industrial Disputes Act. This enactment has been interpreted to cover a wide field and almost certainly the whole press.[135] Since article 19 of the Constitution guarantees to each citizen, the right to form associations (subject to reasonable restrictions in the public interest), journalists and other workmen of the press can form unions and use these unions to mobilize themselves against management. An analysis of these aspects of the press indicates that such unionization has affected the press.[136] The post-independent press in India has seen an increase in illegal and other strikes and a much more extended use of industrial dispute settlement machinery. In addition, the government has enacted legislation to deal with the conditions of service of working journalists.[137] The Supreme Court pronounced on the validity of this legislation by upholding the broad purpose of the legislation and refusing to interpret the legislation as being concerned only with the issue of minimum wages.[138] It validated mechanisms whereby the wage structure of the industry could be determined by a Wage Board and invalidated particular sections of the legislation which gave a gratuity to journalists who retired after only three years of service.[139] But having strait-jacketed the press within an industrial dispute machinery and agreed to increased economic security for journalists, it assumed a supervisory control of the kind of economic factors the Wage Board could take into account. The actual determination of the Wage Board was struck down because, *inter alia*, it had not looked at the circumstances relating to the newspaper industry in different regions of the country.[140] The Wage Board whose inquiries had met with little co-operation had decided on whatever information was placed before it after an extended consultative programme. In one of its quixotic moments of Olympian detachment (or, perhaps, legal guile) the Court both approved the legislation and also made it impossible for a Wage Board to operate unless it possessed a degree of omniscience their lordships themselves were not able to muster. The Court emphasized the need for social control but virtually promised to make it impossible to effectuate this social control in providing security for journalists. But the Court has not been able to protect the press from the general use by labour of organised rights.

Journalists have pressed hard for better working conditions. The Report of the Press Commission (1952-4)[141] was responsible for creating legislation[142] and a political climate which was dampened by the Supreme Court's impossible ruling in the *Express Newspaper* case.[143] Since then, several bodies have examined the conditions of service of journalists. The Palekar award called for better pay and security of tenure.[144] Since the award has been made for working journalists, the smaller newspapers—indeed, the industry as a whole—have resisted the award.[145] It is neither possible nor right that the conditions of service of journalists should vary according to the financial viability of newspapers. The Indian Federation of Journalists have rightly pointed out that the prediction that newspapers will close down as a result of these has happily proved to be false.[146] For that has simply not happened. Even so, the newspaper industry as a whole is fighting back to resist these awards.

In 1982, the Railway Ministry has followed the recommendation of the Rail Tariff Inquiry Committee to abolish the travel concessions of journalists (of 15 per cent in the first class and 50 per cent in the second class) on the grounds that "expenditure on travel is essentially a business expense which should legitimately be borne by their employers".[147] Since it would be tax deductible—even for freelance journalists—an existing governmental subsidy already exists. Slightly more problematic is the problem of house allocations. The Report of the Second Press Commission (1982) has argued that the governmental allocation of houses (110 houses for 615 journalists accredited to the government) in Delhi and the allocation of plots of land (for construction of houses) in various towns should be abolished.[148] This is not only because of the marginal incidence of abuse[149] but because the Commission—whose own Report is riddled with the politics of the patrimonial control of the press—feels that such allocations smack of patronage[150] and because the Commission was unable to persuade itself that "... accredited correspondents as a class are more useful to society than teachers or public health staff".[151] This argument was resisted by some of the Minority who felt that such facilities ought to continue.[152] The problem is an intractable one. There is no doubt that the problem of housing is crucial to ill-paid journalists living in expensive metropolitan towns. Equally, this has obviously not been adequately built into the wage structure! The government's intervention in this area is unsavoury, though it may have proved to be important for the journalists themselves. Even if public sector housing is made available it should be on the basis of short leases rather than allowing journalists to buy land cheap and construct houses which are passed on to their progeny, rather than remain as permanent assets for journalists as a corps—except to the extent to which children of journalists replicate the profession of their parents and themselves become journalists.

In controlling labour-management relations and improving the working conditions of journalists the government has tried to have it both ways. It has made awards which seek to please the journalists. It has also created a negotiating machinery which makes it impossible for journalists to get what they need and what is promised to them. Journalists are forced to think of themselves as underpaid employees, with insufficient security of tenure, bad working conditions and dependent on editors and proprietors without adequate machinery to resolve disputes and better their own lot.

Inevitably, the effect of direct governmental action and legislation must be read along with the informal controls which the government exercised.

The pattern for the government controlling the press by informal methods was developed no sooner had the press emerged as a viable nuisance in the late eighteenth century. Apart from stringent controls imposed on the private press and its editors, who were threatened and deported, the government also entered into a '*if-you-cannot-beat-'em-join-'em*' policy of starting or funding newspapers. The India Gazette was started in 1730 with Governor-General Hastings' blessings. The Calcutta Gazette (1784), the Madras Courier (1785) and the Bombay Gazette (1791) were all government publications. This policy continued and a century later the Pioneer (Allahabad, 1869) and the Civil and Military Gazette (Lahore, 1874) were important sources of governmental information. This was the logical result of the government's refusal to trust the private press. In 1877, Lethbridge, the Press Commissioner, admitted that the Pioneer was close to governmental sources but hastened to add that "however loyally the Pioneer endeavoured to reflect the views of the Viceroy, the latter had no power to enforce his wishes being set forth and followed".[153]

The government linked papers were gradually eclipsed by the private press in terms of their respective expertise, efficacy, credibility or popularity. It was not until the Emergency (1975-77) when the government virtually took control of the National

Herald. But political parties have constantly used various newspapers as propaganda devices. Reformers like Raja Ram Mohun Roy, leaders like Gokhale, Tilak and Gandhi used the press as a powerful political instrument. This has meant that the Congress, as the party in power, has been able to use its newspapers to propagate and support its government. In answer to a parliamentary question, the government revealed that maximum use of newspapers was made by the Congress which had 5 dailies, 16 weeklies, 3 fortnightlies and 6 monthlies. The newspapers were not very prominent. Indeed, the dailies serviced Hyderabad, Srinagar, Manipur and parts of Calcutta.[154] But they were, nevertheless, instruments through which the government could speak. Some of the private press have also been close to the government (*e.g.*, the *National Herald* was begun by Nehru and, less convincingly, Maneka Gandhi's *Surya*). On the whole the private press has evolved a public viability of its own even though it responds to governmental moods in and out of crisis situations.

The pressures provided by a mischievous and unwanted press did pressurize the British Government into thinking about a public relations policy. It has been rightly observed: "To give information to the press was regarded as derogatory to the prestige of the government . . . Government publicity in India was, therefore, a sickly infant".[155] But good public relations was necessary for a foreign government. Since relations with the press had always been "somewhat strained and often really embittered",[156] C.E. Buckland and, later, Robert Lethbridge were appointed the first Press Commissioners from 1877-81. Special publicity arrangements lapsed until the First World War when publicity boards were set up and continued under Dr. Rushbrook Williams. Even though the object of this was to provide propaganda, it was declared that the "most important" aspect of the work of this office (the Department of the Central Bureau of Information—a sub-section of the Home Department) was to find "topics in which the public is interested and on which it requires information and of finding out matters in connection with which the action of the government is criticised".[157] This Department was re-organised in 1935 recruiting native Indian journalists as well to become a formidable publicity and propaganda department during the War. Directed both against the 'enemy' and the national independence movement, the Bureau of Press Information remained an important governmental machine.

Since Independence, apart from the Bureau, governmental publicity has been in the hands of the Ministry of Information and Broadcasting which controls governmental propaganda, a films division including the certification and pre-censorship of private films and controls over the exclusively government owned radio and television. The Press Commission (1952-54) noted with concern—

> the continued expansion of the scope and activities of Press Information and Public Relations Organisations in the State Governments and the comparative neglect of machinery by which representatives of the Press could observe themselves and report in their own way.[158]

It seemed to deplore "an excessive tendency to consider the press as a means of publicity for certain selected activities of the State or for certain individuals" and felt that "insufficient importance is attached to the functioning of the press as reporter and interpreter acting for the people".[159] The government was criticised for favouring certain accredited correspondents, placing insufficient facilities at the disposal of the press, providing insufficient access to information, pre-scrutinizing foreign despatches, putting pressure on foreign correspondents, using publicity stunts and 'puffs', using a proliferation of its own periodicals to provide unfair competition and using the Press Advisory Committee set up by the government to control the incidence of suggested reform.[160]

But a discerning public finds crude government propaganda boring. The private press—never very exciting since Independence at a national level and unscrupulously mischievous at a local level—is still a force to be reckoned with. A Press Consultative Committee was set up by the Ministry of Information and Broadcasting between 1962-64. The Chanda Committee

Report (1964-66), looked more closely at the role of the Ministry, recommended that All India Radio should be made autonomous and generally expressed dismay that the government had failed to inform, educate and enthuse support for its Five Year Plans and what it was doing.[161] The idea of autonomy for the government owned radio was recommended again in 1978 by a Committee under the brief Janata Government.[162] No action has been taken or is proposed on this.

The government has extended its publications considerably. In 1956, Central and State governments had 213 periodicals (91 in English and 54 in Hindi). This increased to 284 in 1960 (English 128, Hindi 55), 396 in 1965 (189 English, 89 Hindi), 396 in 1970 (182 English, 81 Hindi), 470 in 1975 (197 English, 97 Hindi) and 559 in 1979 (209 English, 120 Hindi).[163] The maximum number are in news and current affairs (112), with the rest in social welfare (68), agriculture (52), commerce and industry (42), education (37), transport and communication (34), culture (34), science and technology (64), radio (21), law and public administration (21), medicine and health (15), labour (13) and so on. Of these in 1979, 44 were weeklies, 61 fortnightlies, 243 monthlies, 161 quarterlies, 12 annuals and 37 others.[164] This is quite an impressive list of publications. In 1976 two weeklies [Employment News in English (circulation 1,75,668, in 1979 and Rozgar Samachar (circulation 47,350)] were added.[165] There are three State owned dailies. Plans have been suggested to add more government owned dailies to the list.[166]

There are two important points to be noted about the government propaganda machine. The point of principle was stated by the First Press Commission:

> (There is) no objection to their (*i.e.* government's) publication so long as they confine themselves to publicising the activities and achievements of Government and are not utilized for political propaganda! In their case, too, as in the case of press releases, we would repeat the advice that the aim should be to provide factual information regarding achievements and objectives and to eschew personal publicity for individuals.[167]

On the other hand lies the reality:

> Many government periodicals have very limited circulation and incur losses. Even where the circulation is large, it is, to some extent, a captive audience since State governments provide grants for the purchase of books and periodicals to institutions and Panchayats, and also draw up a list of approved periodicals for subscription.[168]

The Report of the Second Press Commission (1982) has passed a number of strictures on governmental publicity. Although not wholly able to make up its mind as to whether the government should indulge in general publications,[169] it has suggested that the government should not establish competitive daily papers—except perhaps in the Andaman and Nicobar Islands where there are none.[170] Nor should it take over papers even if they are faced with financial or other difficulties.[171] It has stressed that government press releases are biased and one-sided and give the impression of "being the mouthpieces of the party and of persons for the time being in power".[172] The Press Information Bureau and the Principal Information Officers are not well organized, efficient,[173] credible or balanced.[174] The Report calls for more autonomy,[175] professional appointments[176] and better conditions of service for government journalists.[177] However, we should return to the point of principles that are involved. Firstly, it is the government's duty to keep the people informed and persuade them. To that extent any advice on making governmental agencies more balanced is more an exercise in strategy rather than truth! This applies equally to comment about the dull and routine nature of government propaganda. Secondly, having allowed a powerful propaganda function to the government, there is little reason for putting forward the pretence that propaganda is not really propaganda but also the truth. And the propaganda—at present clumsy—has all the potential of being effective. What is important is to allow public participation in the work of such newspapers by allowing them to become forums of public discussion. The Gujarat High Court has stressed this in its judgment in the

Life Insurance Corporation case[178] by insisting that all government journals should allow a right to reply to their readers. Thirdly, there is something unsatisfactory in the government controlling such a large share of the media. The Central Government—already in control of radio and television[179]—controlled 303 periodicals in 1979 (268 in 1975, 225 in 1970, 227 in 1965, 164 in 1960 and 93 in 1956).[180] Considerable increases have taken place since 1970 when Mrs. Gandhi began to consolidate her power against her party political opposition. Such a share of the media is wholly disproportionate to its educative and developmental needs. There is no doubt that information and planning has to be sent to rural areas. But it is precisely because this is so that the government needs to explore alternative and more effective communication techniques. Instead it has chosen to follow the policy chosen by the British in India to create newspapers. Such papers neither allay fears and suspicions nor contribute to spreading functional education. An extensive review of the kind that the Press Commission has not conducted of government monopolism is long overdue.

Anxious to affect the influence of the national private press and set up a firm control of small newspapers, the government sought to embarrass the larger newspapers by making allegations about the irresponsible nature of the monopolistic national press. While the press in India does have oligopolistic tendencies, the Monopolies Commission in 1965 did not really have anything to say on the subject.[181] The government decided to pose as the champion of the small newspaper and took the *pro bono publico* position that it was only just and right that small newspapers should be developed. Attempts to impose a Price and Page Schedule on the larger papers was struck down by the Supreme Court in 1962.[182] The Diwakar Committee on Small Newspapers suggested a re-introduction of the Price and Page Schedule and a 50 per cent allocation of governmental advertisement to small papers and also recommended the institution of annual awards to encourage the quality and production standards of such papers. But the government was a bit hesitant.[183] However, scarcity conditions gave the government the policy leverages and options it was looking for.

The major controversial issue became the control of the supply of newsprint. From 1964—following a suggestion of the Estimates Committee of Parliament—a Newsprint Advisory Committee was set up with a large membership of government nominees. This was reconstituted in 1971 and again after the Emergency. The fight for newsprint was on. It resulted in a planned governmental campaign in the early seventies to ration the newsprint quota. The policy promulgated was a very tight one. It even made internal transfers of unused quota within firms illegal. The larger newspapers fought back to win a major Supreme Court victory in which the government's newspaper policy was declared unconstitutional.[184] Keen to pursue the campaign against the larger newspapers—allegedly on behalf of the small newspapers—the government established an expanded fact-finding committee on the economics of newspapers and news agencies.[185] This was unsuccessfully resisted by the Statesman.[186] The report favoured better foreign exchange and governmental advertisement facilities for smaller newspapers, asked for a thorough examination on monopolistic practices and price fixing and recommended the setting up of a Newspaper Finance Corporation. The basic strategy involved a much more extensive use of governmental control to rationalize the distribution of resources within the system.[187]

Inspired more by a desire to establish effective control over the press—and especially the larger papers—the Report of the Second Press Commission (1982) espouses the cause of the small papers further. Apart from the indirect methods of controlling monopolism,[188] interposing trustees, establishing newsprint quotas and price and page control and de-linking ownership patterns, direct methods of helping the small papers were also envisaged. The major proposal is to promote a Newspaper Development Corporation (NDC)[189] which would play a crucial role in direct and indirect financial assistance, bring and subsidize technology for such papers, create newspapers in remote areas, promote technical research, training programmes and survey research on the press and, generally, oversee the industry as a whole.[190] To be funded by a cess on newspapers and a tax on advertisement revenue[191] (for which the Constitution would have to be amended), the NDC would set up Advisory Councils which would, *inter alia*, maintain an advisory financial control.[192] It is difficult to react to what seems like a sensible proposal except to the extent that it will increase government patronage and control. The mechanics of how it is set up, who will run it and what degree of independence it will have, are crucial. Its members will be drawn from industry (Chairman and one managing director), three representatives each from newspaper management and working journalists respectively, representatives from the government sponsored Press Council of India and Institute of Mass Communications and with three government appointed nominees.[193] Its independence will depend upon the selection of members, its operational freedom and the extent to which it will support rather than interfere with the removal of operational differentials amongst classes of newspapers. But quite apart from the NDC, the biggest problems of newspapers is the non-availability of flexible credit facilities. On this the Press Commission offers sympathy rather than support.[194] So, at the end, we are left with a private funding system, insensitive to the special funding needs of the press and a public financial support system which cannot be wholly divorced from governmental control.

All these measures have caused a certain amount of suspicion. The suspicion relates less to the merits of the proposals and more to the real reason for controlling the private press. All these measures are not seen as part of an agreed consultative consensus but an imposed solution as a result of which the larger ones will lose their independence and the smaller ones will become increasingly dependent on the government. Since the mid-sixties, there has been real tension between the government and the press. The 'rational' statement and discussion of alternative policy perspectives obscures the raw distrust that separates them. The charge of anti-monopolism and press irresponsibility in a developing nation have become key issues in which rhetoric plays a greater role than constructive policy-making.

The government has also sought to control the news agencies which relay information to the press. Between 1978-81 a Press Commissioner was appointed to give information to the English and, later, the vernacular press. Meanwhile, pressmen in India combined their resources to create the Associated Press in India (A.P.I.) followed by a breakaway Press Bureau. Financial and other problems led to the abandonment of the latter and its replacement by a telegraphic based Indian News Agency, the main customers of which were the government. This eventually phased itself out. Associated Press in India itself was taken over by the international news agency, Reuters, which came to be virtually owned by 190 England based newspapers. A historian on the press in India has observed:

> By the early twenties, Reuters and Associated Press were well under official control. News of the non-cooperation and civil disobedience movement was kept down to the barest minimum and Indian leaders in politics and business felt that on controversial matters (such as the rupee ratio, for example) their views were not adequately carried to England.[195]

An independent experiment to set up an alternative Free Press of India and its connected venture (1927-35) failed because the government forfeited its security deposit and Reuters and Associated Press in India refused to supply information to those who did not respect their monopoly. Later, two other agencies—United Press of India (U.P.I.) and the Press Trust of India (P.T.I.)—were set up in 1933 and 1942 respectively. The latter took over A.P.I. and formed a co-operative system with Reuters. The former continued and was finally replaced by the United News of India (U.N.I.). A few years later, vernacular agencies (like Hindustan Samachar) were also set up. But the State played an important role in the functioning of these agencies. The Press Commission (1952-4) thought it appropriate to emphasize—

> . . . the fundamental point . . . that news agencies should not be state owned or state controlled. . . The fact that the government is ours does not make the slightest difference to the basic objection to any sort of governmental control or influence. Witnesses who appeared before us also stressed this point and urged that government should not participate in the ownership and control of any news agency.[196]

The government's 'direct influence' became greater because it was a subscriber to these services. But the Commission went on to suggest that the leading Indian news agency (the Press Trust of India) should not only be given government loans but also be reconstituted as a public corporation with its chairman appointed by the Chief Justice of India and half the Committee would be composed of lay non-newspaper people.[197] The other agency (U.N.I.) which produced one-third of the wordage was supposed to provide viable competition. The government was expected to make concessions to the then called U.P.I. to help to rationalize its working.[198] It was noted that many newspapers relied on the radio, which was and remains a government corporation.[199] The Commission naively believed that the public corporation status for a major news agency and incidental government support for the competitive unit would protect these agencies from governmental influence and control.[200] These plans were not implemented. Meanwhile, the agencies depend greatly on governmental subscription. The government has exploited the magic word 'autonomy' to present the agencies as invulnerable units. The 'autonomizing' of an Indian language agency (Samachar Bharati) was also suggested in 1969. Governmental influence continues to affect Board and correspondent appointments. Government news is prioritized and an informal system is used to place an embargo on such information which the government feels ought not to be fed through the news agency system. The government has been wary of using the 'autonomy' technique suggested by the Press Commission because it may, in part, lose some of the informal control it possesses.

During the Emergency (1975), all these ideas about legitimizing control by formally autonomizing news agencies gave way to a more stringent and direct control. The idea that all the news agencies should be placed under one umbrella organization—Samachar—was mooted almost within a month of the promulgation of the Emergency. An inter-departmental Working Group in the Ministry of Information and Broadcasting wanted to nationalize the news agencies. The news agencies owed money to the government which used its services greatly. A 'voluntary' merger was effected. But the government virtually controlled appointments to Samachar—both in respect of internal appointments and management.[201] A *putsch* of communal elements took place in the monsoon of 1976 and new plans were laid to purge disloyal and unreliable employees in January 1977. News items were censored and a system was set out to ensure that news agencies would "evolve positive action" in their reporting and transmission of news.

The Kuldip Nayar Committee—appointed after the Emergency—reported fresh proposals on the future of news agencies which had reverted to their original pre-Emergency structure. The Committee had overtly political motives. Its chairman was a newspaperman who had been preventively locked up during the Emergency and many of its members were still smarting from the treatment they had received during the Emergency. The Committee was anxious to order an inquiry into the Emergency, urge the government to "follow a self-denying policy of not interfering in any way in the work of news agencies", accept that such agencies would file reports which would be critical of the government and request that the selection and promotion of personnel should be on merit and not governmental influence. Its solution lay in the creation of two news agencies (Sandesh and Varta—catering to English and vernacular needs respectively) which would, in turn, set up an international agency: News India. All these were to be established by an Act of Parliament which would be reviewed after 10 years. Sandesh and Varta would be run by managing boards including 9 subscriber representatives, one employee representative and two co-opted members. Indian television (doordarshan) and radio (akashvani) would be allowed participating representatives if they became autonomous. News India would have six representatives from Sandesh and Varta not including their two Chief Editors and two co-opted members. This 'subscriber' dominated system was to ensure the freedom of the press. The government was kept away from management appointments but was intended to provide financial help to Varta in respect of teleprinter facilities, be an important subscriber to News India, appoint a small body to effect the transition from the present system, provide additional revenue for the agencies and ensure that radio and television would underwrite the funds needed by these agencies. The news agencies were also charged with the function of reporting on the cultural variety of India, and on rural and socio-economic development.[202] In brief, they were asked to report on the very matters which the government wanted reports on during the Emergency and which were used to control and dominate the press.

The Notes of dissent in the report were very distrustful of the teleological and developmental aims which were saddled on the news agencies. They attacked the financial dependence of the agencies on the government and suggested a competitive system.[203] Some notes were also concerned with the big newspaper domination of news agencies and thought that the social aims set out for these agencies were essentially rhetorical in nature.[204]

There is no doubt that newspaper agencies are in bad shape. Samachar Bharati (SB) has shown a consistent loss (from Rs. 3 lakhs in 1970 to Rs. 70,000 in 1976). Hindustan Samachar (HS) has shown a loss from 1957-8 to 1975-6—showing profits in 1960-1 and from 1966-8. For the years 1961-76 UNI has shown profits for only 1962, 1970-1 and 1975. Press Trust of India (PTI)—the most viable of all the news agencies—showed losses from 1965-70 and in 1974 and 1976. In 1976, its loss was over Rs. 8 lakhs.[205] Sponsored and owned by newspapers,[206] these agencies are ailing financially. They have wide networks including 585 correspondents (193 PTI, 164 UNI, 134 HS and 94 SB), at 152 centres (44 PTI, 43 UNI, 37 HS and 28 SB)—with mutual competition at only 19 centres[207] and a total of 1800 customers

(839 PTI, 747 UNI, 178 HS and 136 SB) 555 of which are government bodies including government media (299 PTI, 156 UNI, 50 HS and 249 SB).[208] Only 39 per cent of daily newspapers in 1980 subscribed to these 'wire agencies'[209] with subscriptions by the newspapers being made on the basis of need and the quality of the service provided.[210] In addition to these wire agencies, there are other agencies and syndicated services.[211] These have increased from 9 in 1952 to 108 reported to be in existence in 1981.[212] Of the 48 agencies analysed by the Second Press Commission, 24 were owned by individuals, 6 by companies or co-operatives and one by the Communist Party.[213] They are usually small and specialised, have varying rates, operate in different languages and vary in the services they provide from comic strips, charts and diagrams to feature articles and routine news.[214] It is quite clear that the total back up support of news agencies in India is under great financial pressure and differs in quality and consistency. This does not mean they should be pressurized to pool together.[215] That will make their news/reports worse. The Report of the Second Press Commission (1982) speaks of an over-reporting of politicians,[216] an emphasis on 'spot' as opposed to 'in-depth' reporting,[217] imbalances in socio-economic reporting[218] and a lack of rural coverage.[219] This may—as the Palekar Report (1980) points out—be due to the financial structure of these agencies:

> (They) . . . are according to their constitutions, similar to non-profit making consumer societies. Their membership is restricted to proprietors of newspapers to the services provided by the Agencies and are run by them on a no-profit basis. No dividends are declared. As in consumer co-operatives their natural anxiety is to keep down expenditure on the one hand, and provide services to the members as cheaply as possible, on the other. This distorts their economies.[220]

There is certainly a case for an increase in subscription which even if increased by 50 per cent will "hardly have an impact on the production cost of a newspaper".[221] The kind of coverage that these agencies provide may also be due to political pressures which reached their high point during the Emergency.[222] Suspecting continuing political affiliations with both the Indian language agencies,[223] the Report of the Second Press Commission (1982) holds faith in the co-operative *modus operandi* of PTI and UNI.[224] However, it offers its favourite remedy of appointing one or two directors appointed by the Chairman of the Press Council and jointly by the Speakers of the two houses of Parliament respectively and one director each from the small and medium newspapers and from the proposed National Development Commission.[225] If all this fails, the old Emergency proposal of setting up a unified statutory corporation is suggested.[226] This follows a predictable pattern based on the belief that some kind of governmental hold on the press can alone provide a free and impartial press.

We can see that the government looms large in its control of the information and agencies that feed the press. It knows that a wide ranging competitive system is beyond the growth and capacity of even many of the larger papers. At the same time, it uses its position as a government to control the press and the manner in which it operates. That the press has survived all this can be traced back to the tenacity of the private press and those who own it not to give in too easily.

III

Proprietor Control

The influence of the proprietor owner is very significant. In the nineteenth century such control was self-evident. Despite the growth and maturity of Indian journalism, seasoned editors continued to be influenced by proprietors. An interesting exchange with an Indian editor before the Press Laws Committee, 1921 confirmed a leading Indian politician—Sir Tej Bahadur Sapru's—worst fears about such control:

> *Question*: Don't you think that the editior is responsible there and not the Directors?

Answer: Not always the editor; poor man, he has many gods to propitiate. Take the case of Horniman; first under the Board which was composed of Moderates, then under Home Rulers.

Question: Do you mean to say that a powerful personality like Mr. Horniman would be influenced by a Board of Directors?

Answer: What was he when he was on the staff of the Statesman?[227]

The story may, to some extent, be apochryphal, but the Press Commission (1952-4) found that proprietors continued to maintain control.[228] This extended to pleasing advertizers and others and appointing non-press managing editors as well as general editors for chains of newspapers.[229] Proprietors have dictated policy changes for political reasons and forced editors who disagree to resign from their posts. Job insecurity amongst editors continues to reinforce these pressures. The Press Commission observed:

> There are some papers which have managed to retain their traditions irrespective of changes in the form of ownership. Unfortunately, these are not numerous enough to provide a solid base for the future expansion of the press in this country. There have been instances where traditions of general objectivity and of a high standard of journalism (whatever the political policy might have been) were, after a change of ownership, no longer maintained at the same level.[230]

The pressure is intensified with the growth of newspaper oligopolies. *Prima facie*, the overall picture painted by the Press Commission (1952-4) was not so startling.[231] Thus, the leading Goenka chain had only 9.2 per cent of the total circulation, followed by 6.6 per cent, 5.7 per cent, 5.6 per cent, and 4.1 per cent of the Amrita Bazar, Dalmia, Ananda Bazar and Birla chains respectively. But this is too gross a statistic. The Commission itself was able to show that language, region and city breakdown revealed a much greater influence for the big chain.[232] This picture has been confirmed by the Registrar of Newspapers Annual Reports which have been filed since 1947.[233] Inevitably, it is not easy to measure the extent of monopoly in the newspaper industry but there is no doubt that the newspaper industry has become much too expensive for new ventures to be started from scratch. The Fact Finding Committee (1977), having assessed the situation, made the following observation:

> The extent of monopoly in the newspaper industry is not easily measurable, but one can start with the proposition that the existence of big groups and the heavy initial capital outlay needed to start a newspaper make effective new competition practically impossible.[234]

Monopolism of the press in India is more of a bogey than a fact. But, then, this begs the question as to what a monopoly is. The Second Press Commission (1982) has struggled to establish a belief in the existence of monopolism in the press in India. It began by commissioning a study from the Indian Institution of Public Administration (IIPA).[235] The IIPA study starts off with certain preconceived notions and is said to have "failed to have arrived at clear and indisputable conclusions.[236] Its premises are:

> The changing character in ownership and control structures of the Indian press has far-reaching socio-economic implications. It is of common knowledge that press reporters and senior staff of many a newspaper are also employed to promote non-newspaper interests of their managements. Inspired news stories are timed and planted to influence decision making in government. While use of press for promotion of House interests is known, it is not very often realised that newspaper managements exercise their choice to ignore or build up public images of chosen public personalities.[237]

The Indian press is 'fiddled' to the same—though perhaps to a lesser—extent as the Indian government. Whether this can be traced back to monopolism and remedied on the basis of the prescriptions offered by the Second Press Commission is another matter. Anyway, the IIPA study sought to reveal the existence of large "national monopoly houses".[238] This concept itself—as the Minority in the Second Press Commission point out—was ambiguous and soon abandoned by the Commission.[239] Before we abandon it, let us be clear as to whether there is a monopolistic situation here at all. Monopoly is used here in the sense in which it is used as part of the legislation on anti-monopolism. The statistics collected are grouped to show the preponderance of eight business houses.[240] But a closer look at the statistics would show that these houses own 1.42 per cent of the newspaper establishments, 7.23 per cent of the newspapers and 30.22 per cent of the circulation.[241] Noting that there are eight houses operating in widely different markets, the average per monopoly house is 0.17 per cent of the establishments, 0.9 per cent of the newspapers and 3.78 per cent of the circulation.[242] The actual circulation share of the eight business houses in the total market varies from 0.14 per cent to 10.45 per cent;[243] and this includes circulation sharing in the markets of all the newspapers in all languages owned by them. All this does not, by itself, show any kind of monopolistic presence in the newspaper market. Nor is there any reason to suppose that business enterprises are subsidizing newspapers. Of 50 newspaper undertakings listed by the Second Press Commission, newspapers recouped all their costs from circulation, advertisements and other revenue.[244] Twelve out of the 50 ran at a loss and 5 per cent ran at a profit in their own right.[245] So, the charge of monopolism does not really hold until more information showing connections between the various undertakings can be shown. Nor can it be shown that there are conspiratorial concerted practices. The only concerted practice referred to was a matrimonial alliance between the House of Goenka and the House of Sahu Jain.[246] This is hardly credible as evidence; still less as proof. On the other hand, newspapers and periodicals are increasing under conditions of relatively healthy competition. This does not mean that the disadvantaged can start newspapers.[247] But that is another matter altogether.

The Second Press Commission, therefore, hit on a second idea to establish monopolism. This was to show ownership links between business and newspaper magnates and vice versa. The approach was to create at least two broad categories including (A) Newspapers where 50 per cent or more was invested in by outside interests; and (B) where the newspaper was owned by families. The IIPA study is itself based on '*prima facie*' evidence[248] and the real conclusions in the case of at least three major groups of papers is to show the absence of private business house control.[249] The Monopolies Commission specifically cleared one major group[250] and some of the outside investments of another group were approved by the government.[251] Despite this slender evidence, the Press Commission came to the conclusion that "a very significant part of the press in the country in general and a major proportion of the all important daily press in particular is controlled by persons having strong links with other business industry".[252] This conclusion was reinforced by the following Table II.

What all this really establishes is that newspaper finance is drawn from industry and business. Acloser look would suggest the existence of competition rather than monopolism. Each category is large and looks monolithic only because a lot of investors and newspaper links have been clubbed together so as to make the category look monolithic. There are some newspapers that do have close links within dustry. The classic example is the Hindustan Times owned by Birla. But this is not the norm. The only case that is made out is one of ensuring review by the Monopolies and Restrictive Trade Practices Commission (MRTP).

But the Second Press Commission was not really interested in economic realities but its own prescriptive cures for imagined situations. So, all this was only an elaborate argument to fortify the Press Commission's position in making proposals for legislation delinking newspapers from business so that neither can have holdings of more than 10 per cent in each other.[254] It can hardly be said to overstress the point to say that the economic consequences of such a proposal can only be described as ridiculous.

Newspaper finance can only come from two sources—private finance or the public sector. De-linking can only create two immediate situations. Newspaper magnates alone will be able to run newspapers. The alternative can only be described as worse. This would entail a dependence on public sector funding—perhaps, putting the government in the position of control which the Second Press Commission wants it to be in.

TABLE II: **Categories of Newspaper[253] Ownership**

Sl. No.	*Category*	*No.*	*Circulation*	*Per cent of the total circulation*
1.	Newspapers owned or controlled by companies or undertakings or businessmen with interests in other businesses or industries.	27	54,05,711	40.87
2.	Newspapers owned or controlled by companies or families or individuals or groups of individuals with primary interest in newspaper business.	20	24,86,969	18.80
3.	Newspapers owned or controlled by individuals or groups of individuals representing a variety of interests.	1	3,08,833	2.33
4.	Newspapers owned or controlled by Trust or educational organisations with primary interest in newspaper business.	1	1,56,689	1.18
5.	Newspapers owned or controlled by Trusts or educational, cultural or religious organisations as a means to achieve their wider objectives.	5	3,33,515	2.52
	Total	54	86,91,717	65.70

But all this should not blind us to the tremendous influence of the media. The media does present a cohesive picture which must alarm even the most objective observer. It supports the institutional morality of existing power structures, legitimates the demands of business, the middle classes and the haute bourgeoisie and operates its critique in a narrow framework giving support to the sustenance of a 'law and order' society. What the newspapers protect is not just an entire system of control but create consent for the values that make the people agree to their own exploitation. This calls for a sophisticated balance rather than crude propaganda. The mistake made by those who have been arguing against the monopolistic press has been to concentrate on the pattern of ownership of certain sectors rather than to look at the manner in which hegemonic domination preserves both structure and power. The effect of such domination is infinitely more complete and pervasive. Since 'democracy' and the 'free press' are parts of eliciting consent for this domination, the press must recognise some of the demands that emanate from adherence to such ideologies. It does this by adding pragmatism to the process of accommodation by which these demands can be superimposed upon a stratified, structured and already controlled society. Many contradictions develop as a result of accommodating democratic pressures in a credible way. These contradictions are largely confined to intra-class struggles; but they have inter-class connotations that may suffer the press to become a more realistic and meaningful political playground than it was intended to be. So, whatever the strictures of the Second Press Commission on matters of ownership, the real problem lies in the kind of 'consent domination' that the press as a whole seeks to perpetuate. Common values, class identity, common affinities and a commonality of values rather than direct financial control is what makes the press establish a monopoly of values and exploitation by consent.

Apart from proprietors, advertising also plays an important role. The Press Commission (1952-4) reported that sixty per cent of advertising came from advertizing agencies—the leading 34 amongst which had a considerable influence. While the sale of goods may not have been editorially supported, news

TABLE III : **Showing the Expenditure and Revenue Data of 50 Newspaper Undertakings**

Item	*Big*	*Medium*	*Small*	*Total*
1. *Expenditure*				
(a) Material	6,279,10	268.37	30.69	6,578.16
	(56.20)	(55.45)	(41.24)	(56.08)
(b) Salaries and wages	2,041.96	72.68	17.50	2,132.14
	(18.28)	(15.02)	(23.52)	(18.18)
(c) News gathering	543.28	21.00	3.92	568.20
	(4.86)	(4.34)	(5.27)	(4.84)
(d) Others	2,307.99	121.92	22,30	2,452.21
	(20.66)	(25.19)	(29.97)	(20.90)
(e) Total	11,172.33	483·97	74.41	11,730.71
	(100.00)	(100.00)	(100.00)	(100.00)
2. *Revenue*				
(a) Circulation	6,154.03	275.41	31.36	6,460.80
	(46.80)	(59.32)	(42.15)	(47.20)
(b) Advertisement	6,195.50	179.84	33.67	6,409.01
	(47.11)	(38.74)	(45.26)	(46.82)
(c) Others	800.30	9.02	9.37	818.69
	(6.09)	(1.94)	(12.59)	(5.98)
(d) Total	13,149.83	464.27	74.40	13,688.50
	(100.00)	(100.00)	(100.00)	(100.00)
3. (+) Surplus (−) Deficit	(+)1,977.50	(−)19.70	(−)0.01	(+)1,957.79
4. (+) Surplus (−) Deficit as a percentage of total revenue.	(+)15.04	(−)4.24	–	(+)14.30

Note: The expenditure figures exclude depreciation. Figures in brackets indicate percentage.

items may well have been suppressed.[255] Government advertising has also played a considerable role.[256] No real measures have been taken to prevent this advertising control. The Fact Finding Committee on newspapers in 1977 reported on the continued dependence of newspapers on advertising and recommended an advertisement:news ratio 60:40. The government's own Directorate for Advertising and Visual Publicity (D.A.V.P.) was used by the government and various autonomous corporations.[257]

The Report of the Second Press Commission (1982) seems to take a fairly anxious view of the advertisement problem.[258] Discovering an average advertisement space allocation of 39 per cent—varying from 23 per cent in Sindhi up to 49 per cent in English newspapers[259]—it seeks to establish that the space given to advertisements has been growing, especially, in the larger papers.[260] Such anxieties are misplaced if we note that the average is not very much greater than the average that was proposed by the Fact Finding Committee on Newspaper Economics.[261] In any event, such a finding should cause further reflections about the financial insecurity of newspapers and the extent to which they are forced to look for funding through diverse sources. This can be shown by looking at the Expenditure and Revenue data on the funding of 50 newspapers.[262]

The economics of the newspaper business are such that it is virtually impossible to dispense with the dependence of advertisement revenue. The Commission has suggested 60:40; 50:50; and 40:60 news:advertisement ratio for big, medium and small papers.[263] This suggestion goes against the grain of its own finding of fact that it is the larger newspapers that are increasing advertisements and need funds.[264] That such control would probably be unconstitutional,[265] and must be left to the readership has already been suggested earlier. Here, we are concerned with the extent to which advertising constitutes a form of precensorship control.

The Second Press Commission also reported that advertising agencies during 1979-80 earned Rs. 16.48 crores with 6 earning more than one crore each.[266] One agency had a turnover of Rs. 9.24 crores including its non-newspaper advertisements.[267] But it is difficult to estimate to what extent advertising agencies influence newspaper editors and reporting. There is certainly a diversity of ownership of the wire agencies.[268] They tend to rely on the circulation figures of the Audit Bureau of Circulations and readership surveys.[269] The agencies themselves claim to consider the "readership and circulation of the newspapers", the nature of the product to be advertised and the cost-efficiency of the medium.[270] Two agencies claimed to be influenced by non-commercial considerations,[271] two claimed that it was impossible for advertisers and advertising agencies to influence the big papers,[272] one claimed political interference[273] and an economist suggested that advertisements were used by big business "to transfer resources to interconnected newspaper companies and to influence the policy of newspapers."[274] There is no doubt that the small newspapers are neglected with the same ease as are rural areas.[275] This is not surprising considering the nature of advertising and maldistributions in the consumer economy in India. Although there is some measure of crude advertising by private business and government applauding the people who run them, there is room to believe that the ethical codes of advertising carry some credibility[276] even in a political economy of country where all forms of institutional morality seem to defy consistency. This belief has earned greater credibility since the Monopolies Commission expressed satisfaction with what was going on in this area.[277]

The really big problem is government advertisement.[278] These constitute 30 per cent to one-third of the total advertising in the country increasing from Rs. 1.92 million to Rs. 6.96 million in 1980-1.[279] The share of big newspapers has remained about the same although the number of newspapers to whom advertisements have been given, has increased from 1678 in 1972-3 to 2457 in 1980-1.[280] At least two governments of two States—Bihar and Jammu & Kashmir—have made it clear that policy treatment and support for government policy are important considerations as far as giving advertisements are concerned.[281] There is considerable dissatisfaction with government policy. 332 out of 392 newspaper respondents thought it was unfair.[282] At various points in time advertisements have been withheld from at least 42 important daily papers including several chain papers,[283] rates were increased for 53 papers[284] and 33 papers were not getting advertisements because the Department of Visual Publicity rates were too low.[285] There are several examples of abuse of advertisement which show that the "aberrations were not restricted to the Internal Emergency period and (that) . . . (t)here have been fluctuations in the amount of advertisements released to various papers during the periods in office of Governments of different hues".[286] Having observed all this, the Second Press Commission blesses a ruling of the Andhra Pradesh High Court which can only be described as creating the framework for 'further and more oppression'.[287] Advertisements can be refused on a large variety of grounds including "abusive and slanderous attacks on Government and its functionaries".[288] While it is only right that government should publicly announce its policy and adhere to it,[289] there are clear links between government advertising and policy interference which make any allegations against private advertising agencies seem marginal and most insignificant. The setting up of an autonomous corporation[290] merely means the introduction of another situation to remedy rather than a cure.

The whole issue of proprietor and advertising control feeds on the financial insecurity of journalists. The government's attempts to provide some such security to working journalists have not been very effective. Nor has the government tried to control proprietor influence. The 'trusteeship' system whereby a Board of Trustees would cushion the editor from undesirable influences has not really taken root. The trustees find themselves vulnerable to removal and influence.

The trustee system seems to have become an obsession with government and governmental bodies and it is not surprising that it has been proposed by the Second Press Commission (1982).[291] What is surprising is that even the Minority—although unhappy with the trustee proposal—have suggested the presence of litterateurs and men of scholarship to constitute at least a minority on the board of control.[292] The Majority's proposal follows the usual course of suggesting that such trustees should be set up with the help of the Press Council—itself not removed from governmental control—or the Chief Justice of India who is hardly likely to wish to be drawn into controversy.[293] The appointment of these "public men of unquestionable integrity"[294] will be to arbitrate in disputes between managements and editors.[295] Since they are to be introduced by legislation they will have statutory authority and statutory powers.[296] Hardly likely to be divorced from political interference, they will form another layer of manipulation rather than the fulfilment of editorial freedom. They will generate politics, personality conflict and friction.[297] The growth of better working conditions for journalists, a better bargaining position for editors and the development of some kind of countervailing power in the hands of those who work in the industry (including using institutions like the Press Council) must form the basis of remedial action rather than nineteenth century Chancery notions of the amount of faith that can be reposed in publicly recognised "pillars of society".[298] For, these notions are concerned with the further perpetuation of the domination of an even smaller circle of elite control than that thrown up by the political economy as a whole.

The government has been happier to exercise its own pattern of control and domination even though it has taken the formal policy to defend the right of growth of the small newspapers. We have already seen that the government's war on behalf of the small newspapers has been somewhat suspect in that it would not really help the smaller newspaper and would simply have the effect of increasing the government's control over small newspapers alike.

IV

The Pathology of Press Laws

The actual pathology of the operation of laws defines their real, social and operational content. For law as a social reality is constantly transforming under the pressures of social life. Analytical perceptions of what the law is, or ought to be, obscure our understanding of law as a social reality. Certain people mobilise laws more easily than others. The laws themselves may have a range of social effects and implications restraining some, offering opportunities to others, building symbolic images for certain purposes, having instrumental effects for other purposes and serving as socially legitimating and delegitimating devices of various kinds. Studies and proposals for reform which look at laws within the context of certain discrete notions of legal reality and argument ignore fundamental aspects of law as a social phenomenon.

In a special Report to the Press Council of India on the laws relating to contempt of court, the present writer examined some of the implications of looking at the laws of the press in a wider social context.[299] Perhaps, the point is best illustrated with an example. Analytically, it seems absurd that 'truth' should not be a defence in contempt cases where the press has made allegations against a judge. But, if it were to be permitted every disgruntled litigant could be tempted to make allegations that the judge was incompetent or corrupt. Even if—at the end of the contempt case—the allegations were found to be not true, the judge would have been taken through an embarrassing public *tamasha* (spectacle) in a case started by his well-wishers or even himself. The contempt case is merely seen as a device converting the court into another public forum for the continuance of a dispute. Significantly, some people are more equipp ed to effect this transformed use than others. Indeed, certain political minded lawyers in India could well have been tempted to do just that so that the press could repeat the allegations they made as part of a campaign against certain judges. Again, civil defamation cases are few and far between in India. Amongst the reasons for this is that such cases involve considerable litigation expenses and a manipulation and control of the evidence. They also take a considerable amount of time to reach a final conclusion. Criminal defamation is more popular than civil defamation. All these factors also explain why few people in India are able to protect their rights to privacy against intrusions by the press and others. Many of the reported cases of prosecutions under the Official Secrets Act are on procedure rather than substance. The accused, in these cases, with their lawyers are able to play the system to gain various advantages by playing the procedure game rather than quickly moving to considering the case on its merits. Many constitutional cases have as much to do with the political embarrassment of the government as they have to do with the legal dispute which is at issue.

The pathology of the operation of the laws is important not just in respect of the Court system but also in other aspects of institutional and social life. Certain people are better equipped to exercise their rights than others. They may be better institutionally organized, have better links and have the capacity and preparedness to take more risks. They may be able to stifle, stall or contain the machinery of government moving against them. Equally, they may be subject to restraints which the law does not perceive or be able to do anything about. It is useful to keep this in mind even though, for obvious reasons, this paper will deal more fully with the pathology of litigation and the operation of the courts.

An interesting example of how this can take place was given by a British official, Sir William Vincent, in an important debate on the press in 1922. He explained how Indian editors by-passed the exacting demands of difficult criminal laws—

> As soon as an editor was prosecuted . . . the proceedings were protracted for an indefinite time, the paper sold like hot cakes while the case was pending—on some occasions many thousand copies being sold at a rupee a copy—the editor became a martyr, and, finally, when he was convicted, he usually got some short sentence, an appeal being made for mercy on account of his youth. On one occasion no less than five editors were put up, one after another, and convicted for disseminating seditions (*sic*) throughout the whole of Bengal. They were convicted and fresh dummy editors took their place.[300]

Other governmental procedures are vulnerable to similar controls.

But this is not just a comment on the incipient possibility of law being subject to aberrational use. It should persuade us to ask more meaningful questions about law and its relationship to society. At the level of both rhetoric and ideological projection, law is represented as attractively universal and relatively autonomized from outside pressures. An aberrational pathology is, thus, seen as an example of entropy at the edges which can be rectified if the system is more effective. But this is looking at the subject with a legal ethnocentrism. If we pause to consider how litigants, lawyers and various groups and interests look at law a different image altogether appears. It seems hardly tenable that those in power will create an autonomous area of power where they are willing to countenance compromises and the terms of their surrender.

So, the legal arena although projected for its even-handed and just application of a well-balanced equity turns out to an arena where society does much to obtain consent for the system as a whole and create opportunities for differential use by the advantaged against the disadvantaged. This is not the place to discuss "why the 'haves' come out ahead" in the precarious skillful arena of the law.[301] It is, however, important to spell out the fact that the aberrational use of law is not really an aberration at all. Those skilled at manipulating the other various political and administrative 'power filters' in society also find the skills to maximise their use of the legal system. The transformation of the legal system through its pathological use cannot be studied independent of the social structure and the latter's capacity to define the social terrain in which law finds meaning as a social reality.

NOTES

1. *e.g.* D.D. Basu: *The Law of the Press in India* (1980). P.M. Bakshi: *Press Law: An Introduction* (Delhi: TRF Institute for Social Sciences, 1986).
2. *e.g.* S.N. Jain: *Official Secrecy and the Press* (1982); M.P. Jain: *Parliamentary Privileges and the Press* (1984).
3. *e.g.* See L. Sarkar: "Criminal Law and the Press" in C. Sarkar (ed): *The Press Law in India* (1968) 31-39; J.R. Mudholkar: *Press Law* (1975—to a limited extent); R. Dhavan: *Contempt of Court and the Press* (1982) which is set in a wider perspective.

4. Oddly enough, the relationship of the press with the government has not really had attention (*e.g.* this subject being ignored in C. Sarkar (ed.) *supra* note 3; Mudholkar: *Press Law* (1975)). The only really considered attention has been in the *Report of the Second Press Commission* (1982) 86-106.
5. Matters of concern for the *Report of the Second Press Commission* (1982); see further S. Banerjee: *India's Monopoly Press: A Mirror of Distortion* (1973). That the legal framework to this is evidenced from the otherwise informative, C. Sarkar (*supra* note 3).
6. See S.K. Goyal and C. Rao: *Ownership and Control Structure of the Indian Press* (1981). As a Report to the Second Press Commission, it is reproduced in the *Second Press Commission* (1982) 227-325; note also their rejoinder to criticisms at pp. 326 ff.
7. *Report of the Press Commission of India* (1952-4) in two volumes including a volume on the history of the press. *Report of the Second Press Commission of India* (1982)—in two volumes including one volume of Appendices.
8. Not, however, a strong dissent of the Minority in *Report of the Second Press Commission* (1982) 224-268. But the Majority view was so preponderant that the Minority who should have frankly stated that they were dissenting—which is what they were doing on a large number of substantive questions—preferred to marginalise their dissent as "(a)n area of difference" (*ibid.* 224).
9. For a general look note the acerbic but incisive N. Chaudhary: *Hinduism* (1980). For a more socio-legal analysis of the relationship between social structures, property and control. J.D.M. Derrett: "The development of concept of property in India", C.A.D. 800-18 of (1962) 64 *Z.V.R.* 15-130. See also S.G. Sardesai: "Peculiarities of Hinduism" in S.G. Sardesai and D. Bose: *Marxism and the Bhagvad Gita* (1983); This kind of control effect of Hinduism is usually ignored (*e.g.* R.S. Sharma: *Material Culture and Social Formation made in Ancient India* (1983)).
10. No real extended study has been done of this specifically even in sociological literature. V.S. Naipaul: *India: A Wounded Civilization* (1977) does not do credit to the subject.
11. See generally E. Stokes: *The English Utilitarians and India* (1969 edn.) especially on the Penal Code at pp. 219-33, which unfortunately does not look at how the Code was influenced by need and policy as much as it was by Bentham's architectural designs.
12. Once again no real work has been done on this. Of interest are V. Dhagamvar: *Law, Order and Power* (1975); U. Baxi: *Crisis in the Indian Legal System* (1982) is an interesting but by no means systematic exposition of this process.
13. See S. Natrajan: *History of the Press in India* (1962).
14. See *infra* Part III.

15. See *infra* Chapter 3 especially in respect of the demands of public order. Note also how a 'due process' clause was reduced to becoming an 'any process' clause (see R. Dhavan: *Due Process in India: A Preliminary Analysis* (1981—Mimeo: Report of the Indian Law Institute)).
16. This has been part of a continuing rhetoric which culminates in the Emergency (1975-77). On the nature of ideological discourse during the Emergency see R. Dhavan: *The Amendment: Conspiracy or Revolution* (1978).
17. For a preliminary exploration of the notion of the 'intermediary' state mediating between multiple demands in a complex economy see R. Dhavan: "*For Whom? And For What?. . .*" (Paper to a Conference on Social Action Groups and the Law, Ahmedabad, 1982); for an interesting analysis see A.K. Bagchi: *The Political Economy of Underdevelopment* (1982).
18. Some of the reasons and nature of this development are evidenced in Arun Shourie: *The Symptoms of Fascism* (1978); *ibid.*: *The Institutions Under Janata Rule* (1980); *ibid. The Second Reign of Mrs. Gandhi* (1983): see also L.K. Advani: *The Betrayed* (1980).
19. See R. Dhavan: *President's Rule in the States* (1978).
20. R. Dhavan: *Justice on Trial: The Supreme Court Today* (1980) generally.
21. See R. Dhavan: *The Amendment: Conspiracy or Revolution* (1978).
22. *Supra* Chapter 1.
23. The elementary and most cogent expression of this is the *Report of the Second Press Commission* (1982).
24. The title of a book by M. Feeley: *The Process is the Punishment* (1978). This is generally true of any kind of government by institution which devises procedures. It requires a great number of skills to work these procedures without gettimg bogged down in them.
25. Much controversy surrounds E.P. Thompson: *Whigs and Hunters* (1975) and the extent to which law can be used to redress wrongs. Of course, much depends on the kind of 'power filter' law is. Eighteenth century law provided less opportunities than twentieth century law. This may be because the problems of legitimating the State in the context of today's political economy are greater requiring a greater grant of power to courts and other institutions. However, law courts do not possess re-distributive powers over the political economy. This is also true of the press. The press can bring situational redress or create a situation whereby a more effective demand for redress may be quantified.
26. For the view that the disadvantaged should acquire institutional and technical skills to obtain turn around results see M. Galanter: "Making Law Work for the Oppressed' (1983) *III The Other Side* (No. 2); Cf. R. Dhavan: *Public Interest Litigation in India: A*

Preliminary Investigation (1982—Report to the National Committee for the Implementation of Legal Aid Schemes).

27. For a good historical account see S. Natrajan: *A History of the Press in India* (1962); M. Barnes: *The Indian Press* (1940); Articles by S.C. Sanial on the "History of the Indian Press" in (1907, 1908) *Calcutta Review*. J. Natrajan: *History of the Indian Jonrnalism* (1954) which forms Part II of the *Report of the Press Commission* (1950-54).
28. Hastings Regulations issued on 19 August, 1818 which virtually abolished press censorship. The editors were expected not to publish or reprint any material which was injurious to the British authorities and caused discontent amongst the natives or scandalized individuals. On 18 December, 1823 a fresh ordinance was issued replacing this flexible system with a licensing system.
29. In 1835 what came to be called the Metcalfe Act (Act XI of 1935) was passed lifting all these restrictions—see Charles Metcalfe Minutes of 17 April 1835 (quoted in J. Natrajan, *supra* pp. 36-38).
30. The Press Act (XV of) 1857.
31. Indian Penal Code 1860, S. 268 (obscenity), Ss. 499-500 (defamation), S. 124A (added in 1870), S. 153A (promoting enmity amongst groups—added in 1898), S. 295A (outraging religious feelings). In 1972, S. 153B was added in connection with offences relating to national integration.
32. On official secrecy see the Official Secrets Act (XV of) 1889; Official Secrets Act (V of) 1904; Official Secrets Act (19 of) 1923. On contempt of court see Contempt of Courts Act, 1920 later expanded into Contempt of Courts Act, 1952 and reformed into Contempt of Courts Act, 1971. In 1922 the Police (Incitement to Disaffection) Act, 1922 was passed. There were also general public order controls in various provisions of the Criminal Procedure Code, 1898.
33. These statistics are re-tabled from *Report of the Press Commission of India* (1952-54) II, 266-8; The system operated under the Newspaper (Incitement to Offences) Act, 1908, and the Indian Press Act, 1910. For the earlier regulatory system see Press and Registration of Books Act, 1867. During the First World War, further restraints were imposed under the Criminal Law Amendment Act, 1913 and the Defence of India Regulations under the Defence of India Act, 1914.
34. Press Laws Repeal and Amendment Act, 1922 and then the Press (Objectionable Matter) Act, 1931.
35. The constitutionality of the 1931 statute was challenged, see *Srinivasa* v. *State of Madras*, A.I.R. 1951 Mad. 70; *Amarnath* v. *State*, A.I.R. 1951 Punjab 18; *Ram Shankar* v. *State* (1954) Cr. L.J. 1212. Modified legislation was then introduced (to deal with the tensions following partition) in the form of the Press (Objectionable Matter) Act, 1951. This statute was challenged (*State of Bihar* v. *Shailabala*, A.I.R. 1952 S.C. 329; see also *Tilok* v. *State* (1954) Cr. L.J. 549). It was a temporary statute which had its life extended in 1952 and repealed in 1957.

36. S. 3(2) of the Defence of India Act, 1962 and the Regulations made thereunder. This was followed by the Defence of India Act, 1971. The Emergency of 1975-77 stands in a class of its own. The controlling censorship order [S.O. 275(E) applied from 26 June, 1975 to 22 March, 1977]. Comprehensive legislation about the press was contained in the Prevention of Publication of Objectionable Matter Act, 1976 (replacing an Ordinance with the same name from 1975). During the Emergency there was control on the publication of parliamentary proceedings [Parliamentary Proceedings (Protection from Publication) Act, 1976] and the Press Council established by the Press Council Act, 1965 was abolished [Press Council (Repeal) Act, 1976]. These last three measures were themselves repealed by the Janata Government in 1977-79 (see Prevention of Publication of Objectionable Matter (Repeal) Act, 1977; Parliamentary Proceedings (Protection of Publication) Act, 1977; Press Council Act, 1978).
37. These statistics are taken from tables collated by C. Sarkar in an appendix to his article "The Emergency and the Indian Press" in C. Sarkar (ed.): *The Press and the Law* (1968) 70-1.
38. Note the effect of Articles 358 and 359 of the Constitution; see further C. Sarkar (*supra* note 37).
39. White paper on the use of Media and other Agencies (1979), 61-4.
40. S. Sorabjee: *The Emergency, Censorship and the Press 1975-77* (1977).
41. This was a Committee under K.K. Das appointed on 21 May 1977 (report not published). On the basis of this report the Government Published *White Paper on the Misuse of the Media and News Agencies* (1979) 1-2. See further Appendix 13 "News items disallowed by the Censors" 52-60), Appendix 14 "Pressman discredited" (61-2), Appendix 15 "Correspondents Expelled", Appendix 16 "Correspondents whose entry was banned", Appendix 20 "Newspapers/Periodicals which remained on the banned list during Emergency" (72).
42. See the Press (Objectionable Matter) Act, 1951 which was repealed in 1957 following an unsuccessful constitutional challenge (see *State of Bihar* v. *Shaibala*, A.I.R. 1952 S.C. of 329. For a full account of this note the observations and see *infra* Part III.
43. *Infra* Part III.
44. See Code of Criminal Procedure (Tamil Nadu Amendment) Ordinance 12 of 1980 (Tamil Nadu Ordinance 12 of 1981) replaced by Indian Penal Code and Code of Criminal Procedure (Tamil Nadu) Amendment Act (13 of) 1982; The Indian Penal Code and Code of Criminal Procedure (Orissa) Amendment Act (13 of) 1962 (16 May, 1962).
45. Bihar Bill to amend the Indian Penal Code and the Code of Criminal Procedure, 1983 in their application to the State of Bihar adding S. 292A by way of a substantive offence (clause 2 of the Bill) and adding the offence as Non-Bailable Cognizable in the First Schedule

of the Criminal Procedure Code, 1973 (clause 3 of the Bill); see S.N. Jain and J.K. Mittal: *Working Paper and Report to the Press Council of India on the Bihar Bill* (Mimeo, 1982, Indian Law Institute).

46. See *India Today*, 15 August, 1982; *Sunday* (10(2) 8-14 August, 1982).
47. See *India Today*, 15 August, 1983.
48. See *India Today*, 15 August, 1983.
49. S. 4(1) Press and Registration of Books Act, 1867 (as amended by Act 55 of 1955).
50. *Ibid.*, S. 4(2) (inserted by Act 55 of 1955). Such a person is the 'keeper' of the press not its owner. He is still liable for the contents of what is printed; see *Emp.* v. *Shankar S. Dev* (1910) 35 Bom. 55.
51. *Ibid.*, S. 5 (as amended by Act 55 of 1955 and Act 26 of 1960). This is not a system of licensing just a mandatory request for information: *Madanlal* v. *S.D.M.*, A.I.R. 1965 M.P. 128 at pr. 6, pp. 730-1; *Ganesh* v. *D.M.*, A.I.R. 1959 Mad. 519 (on an ownership dispute about a newspaper). Such a declaration also identifies the person *prima facie* liable for contents of the publication. *Man Mohan Ghosh* v. *Emp.* (1910) 35 Cal. 253; *Surendra Prashad Lahiri* v. *Emp.* (1910) 38 Cal. 227. *In Red K. Rajgopala Rao* A.I.R. 1951 Mad. 714. Under S. 8C (inserted by Act 26 of 1960) and amended by the Press Council Act, 1978 (S. 27) a person may appeal against a refusal by a magistrate to authenticate a declaration. Such an appeal shall lie to the Press Registration Appellate Board consisting of the Chairman and one other person nominated by the Press Council of India.
52. *Ibid.*, S. 5(3).
53. *Ibid.*, S. 6 provides for the authentication of the declaration. The authenticated office copy shall determine under S. 7 the designated liability of the people responsible for and other details in respect of the paper. *Koya* v. *Muthu Koya*, A.I.R, 1979 S.C. 154 at pr. 19, p. 162. This presumption is rebuttable: *H.E. Mohanty* v. *Surendra Mohanty*, A.I.R. 1974 S.C. 47. This settles editorial liability: *Mishra* v. *Sharma*, A.I.R. 1971 S.C. 856 at pr. 14, p. 860, as well as that of the printer and publisher: *In re D. Pandurangam* (1953) Cr. L.J. 763 at pr. 9, p. 764 (Mad.) but not necessarily of a nominated but not active editorial board: *State of Maharashtra* v. *R.B. Chowdhari*, A.I.R. 1968 S.C. 110 at pr. 6, p. 111.
54. *Ibid.*, S. 8B, see further *Madan Lal* v. *S.D.M.*, A.I.R. 1965 M.P. 128 and note the right to appeal to a Press and Registration Appellate Board under S. 8C.
55. *Ibid.*, Ss. 12, 13, 14, 15.
56. *Ibid.*, Ss. 16A, 16B, 15A.
57. *Report of the Press Commission* (1952-54).
58. The Press and Registration of Books Act, 1867 Part VC deals with the registration of newspapers (Ss. 19A-19C). The relevant section

giving the Registrar powers of access is S. 19F. Note that Part V (S. 18) deals with the registration of books.

59. *Report of the Second Press Commission* (1982) prs. 5-21 pp. 5-7; pr. 14 p. 6; prs. 131-157 pp. 58-62; prs. 2-10, pp. 86-7.
60. The Report nowhere attributes this new function to the Registrar. But it is clear that this is what the import of the new proposed powers will be. See classification of papers at pr. 14 p. 6 and other regulating controls discussed in this chapter.
61. *Ibid.*, pr. 138 p. 59.
62. *Ibid.*, pr. 14 p. 6.
63. *Ibid.*, pr. 147 p. 59.
64. *Ibid.*, pr. 149 pp. 60-1 calling for the additional entries in Form I of the Schedule to the Registration of Newspapers (Central) Rules, 1956.
65. *Ibid.*, pr. 149 pp. 60-1.
66. *Ibid.*, pr. 150 p. 61 calling for amendments to Section 19B(2)—if necessary.
67. *Ibid* , pr. 151 p. **61**.
68. *Ibid.*, pr. 151 p. 61.
69. *Ibid.*, pr. 162 p. 61 noting that the percentage of default before the Registrar rose from 24.44 to 45.7 per cent in 1971, came down to 37 per cent in 1972-5, went up to 53.1 per cent in 1976-9; see further Report Volume II Appendix IV p. 141. Note that some 90,000 cases are pending largely because there is a right to property in a name (see *Printers Mysore Pvt. Ltd.* v. *Union of India*, (W.P. 1054 of 1965 decided 4 December, 1965). Perhaps, the Act should be amended (pr. 153 p. 61).
70. *Ibid.*, pr. 133 p. 127 cf. Minority view at pr. 148 p. 249 referring to Report Volume II Appendix IX. 25, p. 210 showing that such magazines do not make a significant 'dent' into use. They call this view 'puritanical' and argue that it might affect the family planning programme (pr. 148 p. 249).
71. *Ibid.*, pr. 4 p. 86.
72. *Ibid.*, pr. 4 p. 86. An example is cited of the Calcutta High Court recommending that the deletion of a name of an accountant from the List of Chartered Accountants with the Institute of Chartered Accountants. But, if, as the Report argues this is a professional matter, should not the profession rather the Registrar, deal with it? The Registrar will presumably have only referred powers. cf. *ibid.* pr. 5, pp. 86-7.
73. *Ibid.*, pr. 7 p. 87.
74. *Ibid.*, pr. 9 p. 87.
75. *Ibid.*, pr. 10 p. 87. The object of all this is that "future surveys should be wide enough in their coverage so as to be useful to policy planners in Government and not only to advertisers and advertizing agencies".

76. *Ibid.*
77. *Ibid.*, pr. 157, pp. 61-2 recommending the amendment of S. 8C of the Press and Registration of Books Act, 1867 and the deletion of S. 27 of the Press Council Act, 1978 which created an Appellate Board set up by the Press Council.
78. Article 19(1)(g) read with Article 19(6) of the Constitution.
79. *The Report of the Monopolies Commission* (1965) does not look at newspaper monopolies at all. Clearly the Monopolies and Restrictive Trade Practices Act, 1969 applies to newspapers.
80. Newspaper (Price and Page) Act, 1956 read with the Daily Newspapers (Price and Page) Control Order, 1960 struck down in *Sakal Newspapers* v. *Union of India*, A.I.R. 1962 S.C. 305. The Newsprint Control Order, 1972 passed under S. 3 of the Essential Commodities Act, 1955 which was struck down in *Bennett Coleman* v. *Union of India*, A.I.R. 1973 S.C. 106.
81. The Newspaper (Price Control) Act, 1972.
82. *Sakal Newspapers* v. *Union of India*, A.I.R. 1962 S.C. 305.
83. See *Report of the Second Press Commission* (1982) pr. 93 pp. 157-8.
84. *Ibid.* pr. 94 p. 158 arguing that it is *per in curiam* in that it ignored earlier case law.
85. *Ibid.*, pr. 101 pp. 159-60.
86. *Ibid.*, prs. 99-100 p. 159.
87. *Ibid.*, prs. 112-3 pp. 243-4.
88. *Ibid.*, pr. 117 p. 245.
89. *Ibid.*, pr. 115 p. 244.
90. *Ibid.*, pr. 112 p. 243.
91. *Ibid.* pr. 31 p. 144 following the recommendations of the *Sachar Committee Report of the High Powered Committee on Companies and MRTP Acts* (1978) and once again concentrating less on concerted practices and more on the conditions under which small papers can be established.
92. *Ibid.*, pr. 32 p. 144—also suggested that the criterion for a dominant share of the market should be one-fourth rather than one-third—following the *Sachar Committee Report* (*supra* note 10).
93. *Ibid.*, pr. 32 p. 144.
94. *Ibid.*, pr. 32 p. 144.
95. We shall see later in Part V that the Press Council remains flooded by government complaints against the press; also Alice Jacob and Usha Loghani's work on classification of the complaints and jurisdiction of the Press Council shows how the latter has followed greatly the government's ideologies on 'law and order' and communal disturbances. (This research has been done by the Indian Law Institute for the Press Council of India).
96. *Ibid.*, pr. 35 pp. 232-3. " . . . (T)here is enough evidence to suggest that there has been an increasing tendency on the part of Government to create difficulties especially in the way of those newspapers

which show an independent outlook. The larger newspaper undertakings are in a better position to maintain their independence than the smaller ones, though there have been excellent examples of some small newspapers who have shown courage to brave the wrath of the authorities. It would, therefore, be risky to arm the Government with further powers in relation to newspaper undertakings." But, there remains the question of creating market conditions for the smaller papers to be viable.

97. *Ibid.*, pr. 32 p. 232 noting the non-implementation of S. 27 of the Monopolies and Restrictive Trade Practices Act, 1969 and the recommendations of the *Report of the Industrial Licensing Policy Inquiry Committee* (1969).
98. *Ibid.*, pr. 32, p. 232. This is while not denying adherence to the socialist goals in Article 39 of the Directive Principles of State Policy in the Constitution of India.
99. *Ibid.*, prs. 141-6 p. 248. Note that the Minority feel that it should be crucial to have a government official (i.e. the Press Registrar) associated with the case (*ibid.*, pr. 144 p. 248) and the forum should be a public inquiry (pr. 145, p. 248) to which the press can obviously give publicity, though the Minority have in mind specialized use of the monopolies legislation (*e.g.* in the sphere of advertizing pr. 109 p. 243).
100. *Infra* this chapter.
101. *Sakal Newspapers* v. *Union of India* A.I.R. 1962 S.C. 305. For Comments see H.M. Seervai: *Constitutional Law of India* (1975) Vol. I, 451-2; J.R. Mudholkar: *Press Law* (1975) 32-4 does not look at the deeper questions either.
102. These were the issues in *Sakal Newspapers* v. *Union of India* A.I.R. 1962 S.C. 305 (price and page); and *Bennett Coleman* v. *Union of India* A.I.R. 1962 S.C. 106 (newsprint).
103. *Ibid.*, pr. 142 p. 127. Note Dr. H.K. Paranjpe did not approve of even the existing system of control. One can understand his reasons (even though he does not specify them) if they stem from the fact that regulating newsprint supply regulates the existence, expression and growth of all or any newspapers. Note that a system of bank guarantees was introduced in pr. 143, p. 127 which has since been increased from 10 per cent to 20 per cent of the value of the order involved. On making the indigenous supply of newsprint better (see prs. 123-32 pp. 125-6); also suggestions for eliminating wastage (prs. 169-73 pp. 130-1).
104. *Ibid.*, pr. 156 pp. 128-9, Cf. Minority prs. 124-30 p. 246.
105. *Ibid.*, pr. 167 p. 130.
106. *Ibid.*, prs. 160-66 pp. 129-30 (for a review of the system established).
107. *Ibid.*, pr. 143 p. 127.
108. *Ibid.*, pr. 143 p. 127.
109. *Ibid.*, pr. 156 pp. 128-9. Cf. Minority prs. 131-2 pp. 246-7.

110. *Bennett Coleman* v *Union of India* A.I.R. 1973 S.C. 106.
111. *Report of the Second Press Commission* (1982) pr. 154 p. 128 cf. pr. 150 p. 128; also Minority prs. 131-2 pp. 246-7 drawing support from the policy of the Ministry of Information and Broadcasting on the discriminatory effects of such a policy.
112. *Ibid.*, pr. 139 p. 127; cf. Minority pr. 148 p. 249. Note in Report Volume II Appendices, Appendix IX. 25, p. 210 that the demands for such magazines is really quite low.
113. *Ibid.*, pr. 124 p. 246 referring to Majority pr. 154 p. 128, see further Report Volume II Appendix IX. 26, p. 210.
114. *Ibid.*, pr. 125 p. 246.
115. *Ibid.*, pr. 125 p. 246.
116. *Ibid.*, prs. 127-30 p. 246.
117. *I.E. Newspapers (Bombay) P. Ltd.* v. *Union of India* A.I.R. 1986 S.C. 515. at pr. 109 p. 554-5.
118. *Ibid.*, prs. 123-32 pp. 125-6 e.g. the NEPA newsprint factory in Madhya Pradesh which started in 1956-7, produced 30,000 tons in 1963-6 and 40,000 tons in 1971 and may have produced 60,000 tons in 1981-2 (pr. 123 p. 124); the Mysore Mills due to start in 1982-3 with a capacity of 75,000 and in Kerala with a capacity of 80,000 tons (pr. 128 p. 126). The expected capacity is to rise to 2,20,000 tons and it is possible India has good raw materials in *bagase* and *kenaf* to improve quality.
119. *Ibid.*, pr. 129 p. 246.
120. *Ibid.*, pr. 65 p. 153.
121. *Ibid.*, pr. 156 p. 256.
122. Cf. *ibid.*, pr. 120 p. 160 making the additional point that this would not emasculate the basic structure of the Constitution (under *Kesavananda* v. *State of Kerala* (1973) 4 S.C.C. 225) which gives special place to freedom of speech.
123. *Infra*.
124. *Ibid.*, pr. 81 p. 239. The argument is nonsensical in the context of monopolism in that it small is not beautiful then, given the economics, large may be impossible.
125. *Ibid.*, pr. 109 p. 243. Note that the Majority claim (at pr. 81 p. 156) that the *Enquiry Committee on Small Newspapers* (1965) opted for 5:4 for price and page control. For a different interpretation of that Enquiry Report see Minority "Appendix A to Minute of Dissent" pp. 262-3 esp. M.Y. Dehlvi that there was no evidence during the period of control that all this helped the small newspapers.
126. *Ibid.*, pr. 95 p. 241.
127. Prs. 90-1 pp. 240-1 referring also to *Business World* (1981) June 8-21 pp. 26-39.
128. *Ibid.*, pr. 152 p. 50 proposing legislation on the same lines as the French Ordinance of 26 August, 1944 of which all the Commission knows was a letter (dated 19 February, 1982) from the Press Attache

of the French Embassy saying the provisions have never been implemented (*ibid.*, pr. 51 p. 150 footnote); see also Minority pr. 45 p. 234.

129. *Ibid.*, pr. 52 p. 150.
130. *Ibid.*, pr. 56 p. 151. Note also the concept of 'control' explored at pr. 57 pp. 151-2.
131. *Ibid.*, prs. 75-9 pp. 94-5.
132. *Ibid.*, prs. 57-8 pp. 151-2. Cf. Minority prs. 49-53 p. 235.
133. *Ibid.*, pr. 113 p. 162. Cf. Minority prs. 62-6, pp. 236-7.
134. *Ibid.*, prs. 7-41 pp. 108-17 for examples of budgets of some newspapers.
135. See generally D.D. Basu: *Law of the Press in India* (1980).

The Factories Act, 1948 applies to a press if more than twenty persons are employed there. The Industrial Disputes Act, 1947 covers the press; see *Bombay Union of Journalists* v. *The Hindu* A.I.R. 1963 S.C. 318; *Bombay Union of Journalists* v. *State of Bombay* A.I.R. 1964 S.C. 1617; *Bennett Coleman* v. *Punya* (1971) 3 S.C.C. 96; *Anand Bazar Patrika* v. *Workmen* (1970) 3 S.C.C. 248; *Workmen* v. *Statesman* A.I.R. 1976 S.C. 758.

Press establishments fall within Employees State Insurance Act, 1948 (see further *Hindustan Times* v. *Workmen* A.I.R. 1963 S.C. 1332; *E.S.I. Corporation* v. *Central Press* A.I.R. 1977 S.C. 1351). The Payment of Wages Act, 1936 also applies to the press (see *Searchlight Press* v. *Factories Inspector* A.I.R. 1960 Pat. 33) as do the provisions of the Payment of Bonus Act, 1965, the Employees' Provident Fund and Miscellaneous Provisions Act, 1952, the Workmen's Compensation Act, 1923. The leading statute is the Working Journalists (Conditions of Service) and Miscellaneous Provisions Act, 1975. All these statutes make the press like any other business and subject to the dispute settlement machinery set up under these statutes. Needless to say, journalists and management are very conscious of their statutory rights and their relative bargaining strength.

136. The *Palekar Report* (1980) has made extensive proposals in respect of the press and journalists and has received considerable attention.
137. Working Journalists (Conditions of Service and Miscellaneous Provisions) Act, 1955.
138. *Express Newspapers Ltd.* v. *Union of India* A.I.R. 1958 S.C. 579 at prs. 50-61, pp. 600-03.
139. *Ibid.*, pr. 205 p. 629.
140. *Ibid.*, pr. 251 p. 639.
141. *Report of the Press Commission* (1952-4).
142. Working Journalists and Other Newspaper Employees (Conditions of Service) and Miscellaneous Provisions Act, 1955.
143. *Express Newspapers Private Ltd.* v. *Union of India* A.I.R. 1958 S.C. 578.

144. *Palekar Report*: "Recommendations of the Tribunals for Working Journalists and Non-Journalist Newspaper Employees" (12 August, 1980).
145. *Report of the Second Press Commission* (1982) pr. 12 p. 88. However note at pr. 14 p. 88: "It came to the Commission's notice that many small papers have not been able to implement the Palekar Awards. Some big newspaper undertakings have also not fully implemented the Awards. Some newspaper undertakings have challenged the Awards in courts of law." All this also suggests a refusal to reduce profit.
146. *Ibid.*, pr. 13 p. 88. Also no doubt that the profits in the newspaper industry are quite handsome, see Volume II, Appendix IX., 4, pp. 164-9.
147. *Ibid.*, pr. 52 p. 92. This should not foreclose discussion about priority in meeting genuine urgent demands for travel by journalists.
148. *Ibid.*, pr. 42 pp. 90-1 that housing facilities were created in Haryana, Himachal Pradesh, Jammu & Kashmir, Madhya Pradesh, Manipur, Orissa, Punjab, Tamil Nadu, Uttar Pradesh. Delhi decided to refuse accommodation to those who had enough money, but subsidies and land grant allocations (*ibid.*, pr. 43 p. 91). The provision itself was abolished during the Emergency. Special rents and land allotments were also part of the scheme in Delni (*ibid.*, prs. 44-50 p. 91).
149. *Ibid.*, pr. 48 p. 91.
150. *Ibid.*, pr. 49 p. 91.
151. *Ibid.*, pr. 49 p. 91.
152. *Ibid.*, pr. 50 p. 91 (Girilal Jain and K.R. Ganeshi).
153. S. Natrajan: *A History of the Press in India* (1962) 94.
154. Information supplied to Parliament, by the Minister of Information, 1969.
155. *Report of the Press Commission* (1952-4) II, 256.
156. S. Natrajan (*supra*).
157. *Ibid.*, 201.
158. *Report of the Press Commission* (1952-4) I, pr. 452 p. 161.
159. *Ibid.*, pr. 452 p. 161.
160. *Ibid.*, prs. 451-485 pp. 161-9 (Chapter X: Liaison with governments generally).
161. *Committee on Broadcasting and Informatian Media—on Coordination of Media and Mass Communication* (1966). A small document with 41 pages of substantive text.
162. This report is known as the *Verghese Committee Report* (1978).
163. *Report of the Second Press Commission* (1982) Vol. II, Appendix VIII. 13, pp. 157-8 (also VII.14).
164. *Ibid.*, Appendix VIII. 15, pp. 158-9.
165. *Report of the Second Press Commission* (1982), pr. 150, pp. 101-2.
166. *Ibid.*, prs. 157-160 pp. 102-3. *The Daily Telegrams* (circulation 1208) was set up in Andaman and Nicobar (*Ibid.*, pr. 157 p. 102); *Basumali*

was taken over by the West Bengal Basumali Private Ltd. (Acquisition of Undertakings) Act, 1974 (*ibid.*, prs.150-9); *Samukta Karnataka* taken over by the Karnataka Government, the Lok Shikshana Trust (Taking over of Management) Ordinance, 1981 (*ibid.*, pr. 160 pp. 102-3). Note also the proposed action of the Government of Maharashtra (pr. 164 p. 103). The Second Press Commission has opposed this trend (*ibid.*, pr. 168 p. 103). This accords with the view of the Central Government (*ibid.*, pr. 163 p. 103) who may be worried about Opposition State Governments—more the left wing ones than any other—acquiring their own proposal and a machine. K. Ganesh (*ibid.*, pr. 169 pp. 103-4) clearly sees the wisdom of such a course of action (pr. 169 pp. 103-4).

167. *Ibid.*, pr. 148 p. 101 quoting from the Report of the Press Commission (1952-4) pr. 477.
168. *Ibid.*, pr. 153 p. 102.
169. *Ibid.*, prs. 165-7 p. 103.
170. *Ibid*, pr. 168 p. 103.
171. *Ibid.*, prs. 160-2 p. 103.
172. *Ibid.*, pr. 155 p. 102.
173. *Ibid.*, prs. 176-8 pp. 104-5.
174. *Ibid.*, pr. 179 p. 105.
175. *Ibid.*, prs. 190-1, p. 106.
176. *Ibid.*, prs. 195-8 p. 106 (for earlier recruitment policy see *ibid*, prs. 181-197 p. 105).
177. *Ibid.*, pr. 198 p. 106.
178. *Manubhai Shah* v. *Life Insurance Corpn. of India*, A.I.R. 1981 Guj. 15.
179. The controversy of delinking broadcasting from government is as old as the *Chanda Committee Report on All India Radio* (1965). The government's monopoly is legally secure as a result of *P.L. Lakhanpal* v. *Union of India* A.I.R. 1982 Delhi 167.
180. *Report of the Second Press Commission* (1982) Vol. II, Appendix VII, 13, pp. 157-8.
181. See *Report of Monopolies Inquiry Commission* (1964).
182. *Sakal Newspapers* v. *Union of India* A.I.R. 1962 S.C. 305.
183. *Enquiry Committee into Small Newspapers* (1966). An extended report, 300 pages long.
184. *Bennett Coleman* v. *Union of India* A.I R. 1973 S.C. 106.
185. *Report of the Fact-Finding Committee on Newspaper Economics* (1975). For a private account of patterns of concentration see A. Bhattacharjee: *The Indian Press: Profession to Industry* (1972). More importantly see Sumanta Banerjee: *India's Monopoly Press: A Mirror Distortion* (1973).
186. *Statesman Ltd.* v. *Fact Finding Committee* A.I.R. 1975 Cal. 14. See further V.V. Johan and A.B. Shah (eds.): *What Price A Free Press*: The Statesman *Case* (Calcutta, 1974).

187. *Report of the Fact-Finding Committee on Newspaper Economics* (1975)—see generally: "Summary of Recommendations" (pp. 219-37). On the Newsprint Finance Corporation see pp. 209-12.
188. *Report of the Second Press Commission* (1982) Chapter X pp. 139-64.
189. *Ibid.*, prs. 73-9.
190. *Ibid.*, pr. 75 pp. 91-5. Note Dr. H.K. Paranjpe wanted to eliminate a general "any other item" power clause (pr. 75 p. 95).
191. *Ibid.*, pr. 77 p. 95. Note Article 269(1)(f) of the Constitution of India would—as the Second Press Commission recognizes—have to be amended.
192. *Ibid.*, pr. 79 p. 95. Note *ibid.* pr. 73 p. 94 arguing that the NDC will promote regional growth but "in the prevailing atmosphere of animosity between political parties and the tendency to exercise executive discretion for the advantage of those for the time being in power" not provide a direct financial subsidy. *Quaere*: Does a denial of credit (or some credit resource) not amount to the same thing?
193. *Ibid.*, pr. 76 p. 95.
194. *Ibid.*, pr. 64 p. 93 reacting to the Memorandum of the Indian and Eastern Newspaper Society (IENS) that about the peculiar long (75 days) credits needed by newspapers. Some mention has been made of prioritizing newspaper loans with banks by the Ministry of Industries on 4 February, 1982 (also pr. 60 pp. 92-3). Loans have also been given by the Industrial Development Bank of India to big newspapers (*ibid.*, pr. 57 p. 92) as also by the Industrial Credit and Investment Corporation of India (ICICI). In 1970, there was a Bill to set up a Newspaper Finance Corporation (*i.e.*, Bill 12 of 1970). The Bill lapsed (1971) was reintroduced and lapsed again (pr. 69 p. 93). This then is the pedigree of NDC. The problem here is a difficult one of raising money for new emerging papers; for this is an expensive business.
195. J. Natrajan in *Report of the Press Commission* (1952-54) II, 245.
196. *Ibid.*, I, pr. 452 p. 161.
197. *Ibid.*, I, prs. 417-21 pp. 149-50.
198. *Ibid.*, I, prs. 425-32 pp. 151-3.
199. *Ibid.*, I, prs. 441-50 pp. 157-60.
200. *Ibid.*, I, prs. 407-32 pp. 146-53. This is the thrust of the recommendations discussed above.
201. See *Report of the Committee on News Agencies* (1977), prs. 58-79 pp. 28-38; *White Papers on Misuse of Mass Media during the National Emergency* (1977), 43-50.
202. *Report of the Committee on News Agencies* (1977) 55-69 (on structure), 73-81 (on finances) 82-93.
203. *Report of Committee on News Agencies* (1975), pp. 94-113. A.K. Sarkar and C.R. Irani cf. the reply by K. Nayar, Chairman at pp. 119-23.

204. *Ibid.*, pp. 94-96 (per C.R. Irani and A.K. Sarkar); 115 (per Ishraf Ali Siddiqui on big newspaper domination); 117-8 (K. Chathunni Master).
205. *Report of the Second Press Commission* (1982), Vol. II, Appendix XI. 4 p. 387.
206. *Ibid.* Appendix XI. 5, pp. 388-390 on the "Shareholding and management of wire agencies". The *Palekar Report on the Working Conditions of Journalists* (1980)—quoted in *Report of the Second Press Commission* (1982), prs. 24-5 pp. 166-7, suggests that the ownership structure "distorts their economies and lends an aspect of unreality".
207. *Report of the Second Press Commission* (1982), Volume II, Appendix XI.2: "History Organization and Operations of Wire Agencies" at p. 381.
208. *Ibid.*, p. 382 (Extracted from the Table on that page).
209. *Ibid.*, p. 382.
210. *Ibid.*, Main Report pr. 51 p. 170.
211. *Ibid.*, Volume II, Appendix XI. 3 pp. 384-6.
212. *Ibid.*, p. 384.
213. *Ibid.*, Main Report pr. 7 p. 164.
214. *Ibid.*, Volume II, Appendix XI. 3 p. 385.
215. *Ibid.*, Main Report pr. 11 p. 165 propagating such pooling subject to professional competence and organizational ability.
216. *Ibid.*, pr. 14 p. 165.
217. *Ibid.*, pr. 15 p. 165.
218. *Ibid.*, prs. 15-16 p. 165.
219. *Ibid.*, pr. 11 p. 165; pr. 15 p. 165.
220. *Ibid.*, pr. 15 p. 166.
221. *Ibid.*, pr. 25 pp. 166-7.
222. Pr. 5 p. 164; see further the *Report of the Committee on News Agencies* (1977) and *White Paper on Misuse of Mass Media during the National Emergency* (1977).
223. *Ibid.*, pr. 46 pp. 169-70.
224. *Ibid.*, pr. 47 p. 170.
225. *Ibid.*, prs. 59-60 p. 171.
226. *Ibid.*, pr. 50 p. 170. Note reference dissent of Minority on this point.
227. Quoted S. Natrajan: *History of the Press in India* (1962).
228. *Report of the Press Commission* (1952-4), pp. 265-312 (Chapter XV Ownership and Control; XVI Competition and Monopolies).
229. *Ibid.*, pp. 313-38 (Chapters XVII Bias and External Pressure; Chapter XVIII Editorial Control); on managing editors see specifically pr. 897 pp. 334-5.
230. *Ibid* , pr. 679 p. 267.
231. *Ibid.*, pp. 280-312 (Chapter XVI Competition and Monopolies).
232. *Ibid.*, pp. 306-7 (where a comprehensive table is set out).

233. *Ibid.*, pp. 281-303 (details of local monopolies) and pr. 806 p. 303 for an overall conclusion note pr. 807 p. 161: "On the whole our inquiry establishes that there is freedom of choice for the reader".
234. *Report of the Fact-Finding Committee on Newspaper Economics* (1977) pr. 13. 1.6 p. 198.
235. S.K. Goyal and Challapathi Rao: *Ownership and Control Structure of the Indian Press* (1981) reprinted *Report of the Second Press Commission* (1982) Volume II, Appendix X. 2, pp. 227-317.
236. *Report of the Second Press Commission* (1982) pr. 1, p. 228.
237. S.K. Goyal and Challapathi Rao (*supra* note 234) pr. 5 p. 233.
238. *Ibid.*, Chapter III 241 ff. esp. 247; further *Report of the Second Press Commission* (1982) prs. 1-26 pp. 139-42 carefully avoiding references to 'National Monopoly Houses'; cf. Minority at prs. 1-9 pp. 228-9.
239. *Report of the Second Press Commission* (1982) pr. 2 p. 228.
240. S.K. Goyal and Challapathi Rao (*supra* note 234) Table IV, p. 242.
241. *Ibid.*, calculated from Table IV, p. 242.
242. *Ibid.*, calculated from Table IV, p. 242.
243. *Ibid.*, see Table V, p. 242.
244. *Report of the Second Press Commission* (1982) Volume II, Appendix IX. 3, pp. 164-9.
245. *Ibid.* The papers running at a loss are *Amrita Bazar Patrika* (0.83 per cent loss against total revenue), Janana Mandal (0.40 per cent); R.G. Baruah (5.61 per cent); Ushodaya Publicat ons (2.13 per cent); Traders (P) Ltd. (2.63 per cent); Express Trichur (14.90 per cent); Deshabmani (5.12 per cent); Weekshanam (24.90 per cent); Basumali (56.05 per cent); Swatantra Journals (1.12 per cent); Vishwakeralam (2.77 per cent); Newspaper Ltd. (6.5 per cent).
246. *Ibid.*, Main Report pr. 58 p. 152; cf. Minority pr. 53 p. 235.
247. This is a telling point made by the *Report of the Fact-Finding Committee on Newspaper Economics* (1977), pr. 13. 1.6 p. 198.
248. *Report of the Second Press Commission* (1982) pr. 3 p. 228 (Minority); see also IIPA Study Appendix II, p. 241.
249. *Ibid.*, prs. 5-9 p. 229 (Minority).
250. *Ibid.*, prs. 5-6 p. 229. Minority referring to Goenka's *Indian Express* which had since the investigation in 1965 owned 'steel' shares subsequently nationalized.
251. *Ibid.*, prs. 37-8 p. 233. Minority referring to letter from the Company Affairs Department of the Ministry of Law (dated 16 Febuary, 1982).
252. *Ibid.*, pr. 16 p. 141.
253. *Ibid.*, pr. 12 p. 141.
254. *Ibid.*, pr. 56 p. 151.
255. *Report of the Press Commission* (1952-4), prs. 836-55 pp. 314-20.
256. *Ibid.*, prs. 855-7 pp. 320-4.
257. *Report of the Fact-Finding Committee on Newspaper Economics* (1975), pp. 119-39.

258. *Report of the Second Press Commission* (1982), prs. 30-104, pp. 112-24 (private advertizing) and prs. 87-131 pp. 96-100 (government advertizing).
259. *Ibid.*, pr. 65 p. 13.
260. *Ibid.*, pr. 65 p. 13. See also Volume II, Appendix II. 22, p. 101 giving gross figures. Clearly 60 per cent advertisement component barrier was broken only in 1970. Equally the reliance on advertisement has increased for all papers since 1965. This follows a general increase in newspapers anyway see Volume II Appendix, pp. 77-84.
261. *Report of the Fact-Finding Committee on Newspaper Economics* (1977).
262. *Ibid.*, pr. 15 p. 109 from where the Table is derived.
263. *Ibid.*, pr. 78 p. 156.
264. *Ibid.*, prs. 7-51 pp. 108-18 esp. prs. 30-51 pp. 112-3 (on advertizing revenue).
265. *Ibid.*, cf. prs. 93-4 pp. 157-8 and Minority 112-7, 243-5.
266. *Ibid.*, pr. 76 p. 121.
267. *Ibid.*, pr. 76 p. 121 (the agency in question is not specified; on Advertizing Agencies see also Volume II, Appendix XI. 3, pp. 384-7).
268. *Ibid.*, Volume II, Appendix IX. 17, 191-3 for details.
269. *Ibid.*, pr. 79 p. 121.
270. *Ibid.*, pr. 78 p. 121.
271. *Ibid.*, pr. 78 p. 121.
272. *Ibid.*, pr. 82 p. 121.
273. *Ibid.*, pr. 83 p. 122.
274. *Ibid.*, pr. 82 p. 121.
275. *Ibid.*, pr. 86 p. 122.
276. *Ibid.*, prs. 92-3 pp. 122-3. The following Codes are in operation:
    (i) Codes of Standards of Practices of the Advertizing Agencies (AAA Code).
    (ii) Code of Advertisements in India (AI Code).
    (iii) Codes of the Indian Eastern Newspapers Society (IENS Code).
277. Pr. 295 p. 122. The Monopolies Commission thought the Code was apposite unless there was legislation for future consumer protection. Note also the recommendations of the (Sachar) *Report of the High Powered Expert Committee on Companies and MRTP Acts* (1978) prs. 21.12-9 pp. 259-60. On the need for looking at unfair practices and consumer protection.
278. *Ibid.*, prs. 87-131 pp. 96-100.
279. *Ibid.*, Volume II, Appendix VIII.7 pp. 145-6.
280. *Ibid.*, Volume II, Appendix VIII.7, pp. 145-6. Cf. the impression in the Main Report pr. 90 p. 96.
281. Main Report pr. 94 p. 97—for other instances of political interference or forbearance see Volume II, Appendix VIII. 9 at p. 152 and some of the deliberations of the Press Council.
282. *Ibid.*, pr. 106 p. 96.
283. *Ibid.*, Volume II, Appendix VIII.10, Enclosure I, p. 153.

284. *Ibid.*, Volume II, Appendix VIII·10, Enclosure II, pp. 153-4.
285. *Ibid.*, Volume II, Appendix VIII. 10, Enclosure III, p. 154.
286. *Ibid.*, Main Report pr. 105, p. 97.
287. *Ibid.*, prs. 123-4 p. 99. (This decision is discussed in Chapter 3, *infra*).
288. *Ibid.*, pr. 123 p. 99. This follows from the Andhra Pradesh High Court judgment in W.P. No. 7763 of 1979 decided, 10 October on 1980.
289. *Ibid.*, pr. 113 p. 98.
290. *Ibid.*, pr. 112 p. 98.
291. *Report of the Second Press Commission* (1982) pr. 113 p. 162.
292. *Ibid.*, pr. 68 p. 237. They feel that "it would be wrong to impose external control on newspaper undertakings because their owners and managers must remain responsible for their financial soundness and viability". The Chairman of the Press Council, it is felt, would not know enough to exercise the right kind of judgment (pr. 70 p. 237).
293. *Ibid.*, pr. 113 p. 162 cf. Minority pr. 70 p. 237.
294. *Ibid.*, pr. 113 p. 162 cf. Minority pr. 68 p. 237.
295. *Ibid.*, pr. 113 p. 162. This function is not clearly spelled out, but in addition to an ombudsman on coverage and comments (prs. 116-117 p. 162).
296. Pr. 113 p. 162. Once again it is not clear that the statutory functions would be defined.
297. *e.g.*, pr. 109 p. 161. Where the editor took the matter to the Press Council whose powers to investigate were given a constitutional blessing as part of the freedom of speech provisions by the Delhi High Court in *K.K. Birla* v. *Press Council of India* (1976) ILR 1 Delhi 753.
298. This is really a victorian method of putting private and public power in the hands of a pre-defined elite who were given a fairly free hand in respect of its exercise.
299. See R. Dhavan: *Contempt of Court and the Press* (1981).
300. Sir William Vincent, Speech reported in *I.L.A.D.* 340 (22 February, 1921).
301. See M. Galanter: "Why the 'Haves' come out ahead: Speculations on the Limits of Legal Change" (1974) 9 *Law and Society Review* 95. As to alternative methods of achieving legal change in India note the views put forward in R. Dhavan: *Public Interest Litigation in India: Some Introductory Readings* (1982), Mimeo, Committee for the Implementation of Legal Aid Schemes.

3

CONSTITUTIONAL CONTROVERSIES

I

No discussion about the granting of constitutional rights is meaningful without asking a range of questions about the social and ideological terrain in which constitutional rights are set. What are constitutionally guaranteed rights? What do they signify? Are they real or illusory? What needs to be done in order to make them effective? Who uses them? For what purpose? And why?

These questions are even more important in the context of the Indian Constitution which was passed under a considerable euphoria[1] and which has, since, been assessed with a misleading optimism.[2] While the Constitution was being made, this optimism was apparent on the face of the record even if a deeper examination revealed uneasy tensions.[3] After the Constitution, lawyers complimented its makers (in effect, but never explicitly) for the enlarged professional possibilities that the Constitution created.[4] All this generated both an ideological projection about the Constitution as well as a framework for future analysis.

A much exaggerated paradigm for assessing the Constitution was set by a foreign observer who examined the process of Constitution-making and came to the conclusion that it well and truly constituted "a rationalised basis for political behaviour".[5] He was promptly reminded by an acute Indian scholar of the "little done (and) the vast undone".[6] This exaggerated paradigm runs through the literature like a locust.

Succeeding assessments of the Constitution have pointed out to specific problems without really assessing the social reality perpetrated by the Constitution or the true social nature of constitutional rights.[7] Meanwhile a national Emergency has come and gone. A group of academics meeting soon after the Emergency were unable to shake out of this optimism to force a re-assessment of the Constitution.[8] Meanwhile, a leading commentator on the Constitution has been content to make a plea for more sophisticated—even if a more contextual—doctrine[9] whilst a well known academic seems rest content to argue for a more overtly ruthless political and populist use of the Supreme Court.[10] Meanwhile, the euphoria continues.

To argue—as our foreign observer did—that the Constitution provides a 'durable framework for government in the midst of social and economic change'[11–12] seems to fly in the face of facts. This book is not really concerned with broad questions about the failure of institutional morality,[13] the nature of constitutional discourse during and after the Emergency (1975-77),[14] alternative methods of constitutional interpretation[15] or the successive transformations that the Indian Constitution has gone through to service existing socio-economic demands[16] or the spurious ideological accompaniments that form part of a distrusted rhetoric about the link between constitutional possibilities and distributive justice.[17] We are, however, concerned with the nature of constitutional rights—and, in particular, the constitutional rights of the press.

This optimistic analysis of the Constitution as a whole also visits analysis of the 'Fundamental Rights' and 'Directive Principles' chapters of the Constitution.[18] However, even optimistic accounts of the process of Constitution-making cannot disguise the fact that decisions on this chapter of the Constitution were riddled with compromises.[19] This is not just true of broader issues like the substitution of an 'any process', for a 'due process', clause.[20] There were compromises on every fundamental right. Patient research has shown the various positions that contended for recognition as far as property rights and agrarian reform legislation were concerned.[21] The Constituent Assembly left behind an imbroglio that took many years, many judgments and many constitutional amendments to clear.[22] Meanwhile, the old zamindars were routed to be replaced by a new class of landowners.[23] Compromises—as we shall see later—were also made on the press.

These compromises reflect not so much on doctrinal disputes as arguments between vested and emergent interests about existing, incipient and foreseeable struggles for power. These arguments also concern the legitimation of power as a whole, that is between these various disputants and society as a whole (including the powerless). So, the constitutional discussion runs on with an eye on the real politic, an eye to build a flexible but secure power base and a third eye on the legitimating effects of all this. The discussion is necessarily urbane, replete with references about civil liberties and couched in the language of a universal liberalism to attract support from as large a constituency of people in the most incontrovertible way. Appeals to 'liberty', 'equality' and 'freedom' tend to carry weight with a large number of people. Even potential victims of social and economic processes are made to see themselves as potential beneficiaries. This is not to deny that the broad, universally couched, ideologies so promulgated may contain the seeds of destruction for those who use them as legitimating devices. For the present we are only concerned with placing the whys and wherefores of legal analysis within the more realistically assessable terrains of social and political analysis. Such an analysis should not imply that what is a legitimating device for some cannot be a more tangible vehicle containing 'turn around' solutions for others.

This is certainly true about arguments in respect of freedom of the press. Given—as has been indicated earlier[24]—that the press is the most viable remaining general arena for politics in India, there are a great number of people from all kinds of political and social complexions who would form unholy alliances to preserve the sensitivity of this political arena. This has added social and political complexity to constitutional discussions about the freedom of speech and expression. On its part, the government has tried to oversimplify the discussion about the freedom of the press. On the one hand the press has constantly been projected as creating disorder and disharmony. This paradigm is inherited from certain British regimes and consolidated with devastating effect so that political protest is characterized in terms of problems of "law and order".[25] On the other, it is argued that the constitutional guarantees of freedom of speech and expression can only be fulfilled if the alleged monopolism of the metropolitan press is broken. This attitude is writ large across the deliberations of the Second Press Commission:

> A realistic view of Article 19(1)(a) (of the Constitution) has to recognise that right to expression is somewhat thin if it can be exercised only at the sufferance of the managers of mass communication. While we recognise that the majority in a democracy may occasionally exercise its power to throttle opportunities for discussion, we do not seem to realise that non-governing minorities who control the machinery of communication can also throttle ideas before their birth.[26]

The real problem, however, concerns providing both the constitutional mechanisms and providing legitimacy for an operation which would preclude the press becoming a major political arena, destroying existing media-based power bases and prevent the creation of alternative power basis. This should not imply that the existing press should not be regulated but simply that this regulation should not be judged through formal legal doctrine but should be more firmly assessed on an understanding of social and political realities.

Thus, constitutional discussions about freedom of the press in India must be set against the backdrop of the government's insistence that the press not only constitute monopolistic power bases but are also creators of disorder.

The fact that the Indian Constitution guarantees freedom of speech and expression did not mean that freedom of the press was protected with any kind of sensitivity. The old equations with the government precipitated during the days of the British Raj seem to have been superimposed upon the constitutional order. This process of superimposition was greatly facilitated by the partition of India. Those were troubled times. Partition itself exploded into disorder and massacre. There was the incipient threat of communal disharmony. There was also a feeling that the state of affairs was so fragile that the press and the media could disrupt this state of affairs with an irresponsible ease. It was in this mood that the freedom of speech provisions to the Constitution came to be discussed. A mixture of anxiety, ill-feeling, concern and jingoism were responsible for an ever increasing list of permissible reasonable restrictions on the exercise of the freedom of speech and expression. Attempt to tilt the balance in favour of freedom of speech were met with an uncompromising irritation. Senior politicians at the helm of affairs were committed to resolving the problems of law and order and all too easily slipped back into legitimating the same legal mechanisms which were used during British rule. There is no doubt that the situation was serious. But it obscured some very real concerns about freedom of speech; and of the press. This was not all. A paradigm of control seemed to to have been established whereby the freedom of speech and expression has almost invariably yielded to the demand that it must be restrained and restricted. This attitude has become so firmly entrenched that even the judiciary have incorporated it as part of their jurisprudence and approach.

The Constitution did not really guarantee freedom of the press. It only guaranteed freedom of speech and expression. While this was taken to mean that freedom of the press was also constitutionally protected, the full implications of this constitutional guarantee to the press have never really been worked out either by Parliament or by the courts. The emphasis has been on the expressions of the press, not the manner in which the press is institutionally guaranteed. Although the courts have, on a couple of occasions, protected indirect threats to the press, they have not fairly and squarely asked the question: What is the social, economic and legal environment in which the press can flourish as a viable institution. No discerning examination of the needs of the press has taken place. The Court has abandoned the press to a formal jurisprudence in which too few significant questions have been asked and too few real solutions found. It is almost as if the courts have ignored the fact that the modern press exists in a network of needs and relationships—each of which is vital to its existence and fundamental to its functioning. The press is part and parcel of a system of mass communication—a system that is at once, both daunting and fragile. The courts have had enormous difficulties in recognising what the needs of this system are and how it forms part of the Indian social, political and economic order.

Recently Justice Sen has reiterated the old common law bias that journalists do not need extra special powers and immunities in order to investigate their reports other than those powers possessed by the ordinary citizen:

> (Some Courts) . . . appear to be labouring under an impression that journalists enjoy some kind of special privilege, and have greater freedom than others to make any imputation and allegations sufficient to ruin the reputation of a citizen. We hasten to add that journalists are in no better position than any other person.[27]

The severity of this comment contrasts sharply with the observations of Justice Venkataramiah in the later *Newsprint* case (1986).[28]

"In today's free world", he said, "freedom of press is the heart of social and political intercourse. The press has now assumed the role of the public educator making formal and non-formal education possible on a large scale particularly in the developing world, where television and other kinds of modern communication are not still available for all sections of society. The purpose of the press is to advance the public interest by publishing facts and opinions without which a democratic electorate cannot make-responsible judgments. Newspapers being purveyors of news and views having a bearing on public administration very often carry material which would not be palatable to governments and other authorities. The authors of the articles which are published in newspapers have to be critical of the actions of government in order to expose its weaknesses. Such articles tend to become an irritant or even a threat to power. Governments naturally take recourse to suppress newspapers publishing such articles in different ways. Over the years governments in different parts of the world have used diverse methods to keep the press under control. They have followed carrot-stick methods. Secret payments of money, open monetary grants and subventions, grants of lands, postal concessions, Government advertisements, conferment of titles on editors and proprietors of newspapers, inclusion of press barons in cabinet and inner political councils etc. constitute one method of influencing the press. The other kind of pressure is one of using force against the press. Enactment of laws providing for pre-censorship, seizures, interference with the transit of newspapers and demanding security deposit, imposition of restriction on the price of newspapers, on the number of pages of newspapers and the area that can be devoted for advertisements, withholding of Government advertisements, increase of postal rates, imposition of taxes on newsprint, canalisation of import of newsprint with the object of making it unjustly costlier etc. are some of the ways in which Governments have tried to interfere with freedom of press. It is with a view to checking such malpractices which interfere with free flow of information, democratic constitutions all over the world have made provisions guaranteeing the freedom of speech and expression laying down the limits of interference with it. It is, therefore, the primary duty of all the national Courts to uphold the said freedom and invalidate laws or administrative actions which interfere with it contrary to the constitutional mandate."[29]

But this effusive rhetoric belies a much more cautious line of decision making, within an approving affinity to the broad aims of governmental regulation.[30] While agreeing in principle to strike down onerous taxes, the *Newsprint* case (1986) refuses to grant total immunity from taxes on newsprint and does not address itself to the core issue of freedom to control those matters—like newsprint, machinery and so on—indispensable to the working of the press. Nevertheless, there is an identifiable flutter in the case law, demonstrating greater sensitivity to the investigative and institutional needs of the press. *Prabha Dutt's* case (1982),[31] and now *Sheela Barse's* case (1986) allowing a journalist to interview two persons accused of heinous murders is accompanied by an unreported judgment of the Delhi High Court in the *Jansatta* case (*Times of India*, 22 May 1986) allowing partial immunity on the confidentiality of the journalist's sources of information. Justice Pendse's unprecedented and one sided Judgment in the *Bennett Coleman* case (A.I.R. 1986 Bombay 321) throws caution to the winds in declaring freedom of the Press as part of the basic structure of the Constitution and, consequently, exempts the press from anti-monopoly statutory provisions requiring the government's permission as a pre-requisite to an expansion of undertakings.

Despite these attempts at juristic innovation, the Courts have, by and large, lapsed into an undeclared traditionalism. They have protected the press with caution rather than on the basis of well-established principles. They have underlined the need for governmental control and for restrictions. They have restrained the press from intruding on traditional preserves of state and of morality. At times, they have the spoken with a cosmopolitan rhetoric about the importance of the press. Their decision-making, however, has been very cautious and tentative. And all this pertains to their approach during times of peace, when there has been no declared constitutional or national crisis.

II

But let us start from the beginning—from the Constitution itself, how it was framed and how the judges interpreted it.

The Constitution of India includes the following provision:

Article 19: *Protection of certain rights regarding freedom of speech etc.*

(1) All citizens shall have the right—(*a*) to freedom of speech and expression. . . .

(2) Nothing in sub-clause (*a*) of clause (1) shall affect the operation of any existing law, or prevent the State from making any law, in so far as such law imposes reasonable restrictions on the exercise of the right conferred by the said sub-clause in the interests of the sovereignty and integrity of India, the security of the State, friendly relations with foreign states, public order, decency or

> morality or in relation to contempt of court, defamation or incitement to an offence.

The original Constitution did not allow reasonable restrictions in favour of "public order" which was introduced in 1951[32] following some Supreme Court judgments.[33] The restrictions in the interests of "the sovereignty and integrity of India" were introduced in 1963 following the war with China.[34]

The makers of India's Constitution did not pay much attention to freedom of the press. Earlier suggestions that[36] freedom of the *press* should be specifically guaranteed were not reflected in the text of the Constitution which guaranteed only the freedom of speech and expression.[35] Living in the shadow of tremendous upheavals in the country, the mood of the draftsmen was to retain, with some concession, the apparatus of controls weilded by the British. A.K. Ayyar expressed this mood while discussing the Report of the Sub-Committee on Fundamental Rights:

> The recent happenings in different parts of India have convinced me, more than ever, that all the fundamental rights guaranteed under the Constitution must be subject to public order, security and safety though such a provision may to some extent neutralise the effect of the fundamental rights guaranteed under the Constitution.[37]

This mood must have been accepted *sub silentio*, for the other comments on the Draft Report on Fundamental Rights of 3 April, 1947[38] do not challenge this mood.[39] Indeed, the Committee itself accepted the need to impose further "limitations on fundamental rights in cases of grave emergency and when the security of the state is endangered".[40] What followed were cosmetic changes and the emergence of a general consensus that public order, lessening tension and security of state were much too important not to be regarded as legitimate restrictions on the freedom of speech and expression.[41] One member thought that the phrase "public order and morality" was vague,[42] whilst others wanted incitement of communal and class hatred to be included in the list of restrictions[43] because "fundamental peace and orderly progress of our country depend on communal peace and harmony".[44] Others proposed the amendment that a grave danger or emergency[45] or violence[46] would justify such an intrusion. The matter was decided by vote against the amendment.[47] It is important to recognise the deep concerns (or paranoia, as the case may be) of front bench spokesmen to accord priority to public order over free speech.

On the floor of the Constituent Assembly, the official approach was questioned by some who felt that permitting restrictions was really clawing back the rights which had been granted.[48] Others found many of the restrictions vague,[49] and some complained that the existing repressive system of laws was being safeguarded.[50] Some members demanded that the public order and other restrictions should apply only where there was a danger of the overthrow of the state.[51] Memories of how the laws relating to "sedition" had been used to control and crush the Independence movement were still fresh in peoples' minds.[52] The government accepted that the laws relating to "sedition" be dropped from the list of permissible restrictions.[53] But there was considerable support for the need to control public order and prevent communal and other kinds of tension.[54] Not surprisingly, the amendment to give a citizen the right to bear arms was decisively rejected[55] as was a request for a general due process clause.[56] There was, however, a specific move to demand that freedom of the press be guaranteed as a fundamental right.[57] It was argued that this was

> one of the items around which the greatest, the bitterest of constitutional struggles have been waged in all constitutions and in all countries where liberal constitutions prevail . . . I cannot imagine why these draftsmen, so experienced and seasoned, should have felt it desirable to leave out the freedom of the press, and leave it to the charity of the administrators of the Constitution when the occasion arose to include it by convention or implication and not by express provision.[58]

Clearly the "extraordinary stress and strain . . . (and) [t]he tragic happenings of some twelve or fourteen months" were seen as the reason why personal liberty was being "soft-pedalled".[59]

"Freedom of the press" was not included as a specific guaranteed right. B.R. Ambedkar, who piloted the Constitution through the Assembly, made short work of this argument by taking the traditional Common Law line that the press should not have rights greater than those of the individual:

> The press has no special rights which are not to be given or which are not to be exercised by the citizen in his individual capacity. The editor of a press or the manager are all citizens and, therefore, when they choose to write in newspapers, they are merely exercising their right to expression, and in my judgment, therefore, no special mention is necessary of the freedom of the press at all.[60]

The core of the general argument on listing the kind of restrictions that can be imposed on the guaranteed freedoms lay in determining the extent to which the legislatures or the judiciary should be responsible for protecting fundamental rights.[61] The compromise solution was to accept an amendment which required that all such restrictions had to be "reasonable"—thus, leaving the initiative of proposing amendments with the legislature subject to the final approval of the courts on whether it was reasonable.[62] The mood of the front bench that fundamental rights must exist within a restrictive framework was readily accepted.[63] Too many people were much too concerned about the contemporary upsurge of tension to be receptive to the civil liberties emphasis, that it was the rights that were fundamental and not the restrictions.[64]

In a formal sense the fact that the freedom of the press has not been specifically mentioned in the Constitution has not made a difference. The courts have assumed that the phrase "freedom of speech and expression" include, *inter alia*, the freedom of the press.[65] But the Supreme Court has also emphasized the classic Common Law view[66] that as

> a right flowing from the freedom of speech and expression, the liberty of the press stands on no higher footing than the freedom of speech and expression of a citizen and . . . no

privilege attaches to the position of the press as such, that is to say, as distinct from the right of the citizen.[67]

The result is that the rights of the press as an institution (that is those rights which the press needs to enable it to effectively perform its functions) have never really been adequately considered by the courts.

The fact that the press performs services in a democracy is not denied by the courts. But this has not led to a comprehensive examination of the institutional needs of the press. There is a marked confusion about the criteria by which the validity of legislation affecting the press will be adjudged. Equally, there is no clear understanding about what rights of the press need to be protected. In the *Express Newspaper's* case (1958),[68] certain provisions of the Working Journalists (Conditions of Service and Miscellaneous Provisions) Act, 1956—aimed at ameliorating the conditions of the working journalists and other employees—was challenged as *ultra vires*. We have already discussed this earlier. The Supreme Court upheld the Act over the plea of the newspapers that there would be an increase in their financial burden and this, in turn, would restrict the dissemination of news and views. At the same time the court refused, in a spirit of detachment to allow a Wage Board to function so that it could protect the working conditions of journalists. It demanded impossible tasks from the Wage Board and struck down its award because it could not do these impossible things.[69] But the Court hinted that a tax on publishing advertisements would be invalidated if designed to limit the circulation of information which was seen as part of the guaranteed fundamental right.[70] What is missing from the judgment is a clear statement of what constitutes the various bundles of rights the press is constitutionally entitled to (*e.g.* advertising, circulation, business autonomy *et al*). Instead the Court concentrated on the kind of effect a legislation would have to have before it was deemed to be *ultra vires* the freedom of speech provisions. After proposing a multitude of tests,[71] the Court observed:

All the consequences which have been visualised in this

regard by the petitioners viz. the tendency to curtail circulation and thereby narrow the dissemination of information, fetters the petitioners' freedom to choose the means of exercising the right, likelihood of the independence of the press being undermined by having to seek government aid, the imposition of penalty on the petitioners' right to choose the instruments for exercising the freedom or compelling them to seek alternative media etc. would be remote and depend on various factors which may or may not come into play. Unless these were the *direct and inevitable* consequences of the measures enacted in the impugned Act it would not be possible to strike down the legislation as having that effect and operation. A possible eventuality of this type would not necessarily be the consequence which could be in the contemplation of the legislature while enacting a measure of this type for the benefit of the workmen concerned.[72] (emphasis added)

It would appear that the Court wanted the *direct and inevitable* test to be operated in such a way that where the infringement was brought about by the likely occurrence of some connected social, economic, political or other event other than the one formally stated in the statute, the effect will not be *direct and inevitable* because that event, even if likely to happen, may or may not happen. Clearly, the petitioner was arguing that, given the nature of the industry, certain things are more than likely to happen even if one had to concede the theoretical possibility that these things may not happen.[73] The 'direct and inevitable' effect test formulated in this case seems to have been carefully restricted to examine the formal effect of a legislation on the operation of a press.

In the *Sakal Newspapers* case,[74] the Newspapers (Price and Page) Act, 1956 and the Daily Newspapers (Price and Page) Order, 1960 regulated the number of pages of a newspaper according to the price charged, prescribed the number of supplements to be published and prohibited the publication and sale of newspapers in violation of this Order. The alleged subject of these regulatory measures was to combat "unfair competition" in the newspaper industry. The Act also provided for regulating the size and area of advertising matter in relation to other matters contained in the newspaper. Responding to challenges by newspaper owners, the Supreme Court held that the Act and Order directly interfered with the freedom of the press as it affected not only the right of a citizen to circulate news and views but also its volume of circulation. The Court took the view that there was a link between price, size, advertisements, price of advertisements and circulation. The upshot of all the restrictions in the Order would affect the circulation of newspapers and violate the constitutional guarantee of free speech. In order to determine which freedoms of the press were constitutionally protected, the Court talked of the "essential part" of the freedom of speech and expression (and presumably the press).[75] But how this "essential part" was determined was not disclosed. It was assumed that the circulation of newspapers was an "essential part". But, so many things affect the circulation of newspapers. Although the Court remained trapped in the language of "direct and inevitable effects", it seemed to want to prevent "excessive and prohibitive" burdens on the press:

> The correct approach in such cases should be to examine as to what, in substance, is the loss or injury caused to the citizen and not merely what manner or method has been adopted by the State in placing the restriction.[76]

This takes a broader approach of the variety: what will the effect of these burdens be on an "essential part" of this freedom? And if it does have such an effect, is the restraint imposed reasonable?

Looking at the *effect* of legislation in this wide-ranging way came to be firmly established in the *Bank Nationalisation* case:[77]

> . . . (I)t is not the object of the authority making the law impairing the right of the citizen nor the form of the action taken that determines the protection he can claim. It is the effect of the law and the action upon the right which attract the jurisdiction of the Court to grant relief. If this view be

> the true view, and we think it is, in determining the impact of State action upon constitutional guarantees which are fundamental, it follows that the extent of protection against the impairment of a Fundamental Right is determined not by the object of the legislature nor the form of the action but its direct operation upon the individual right.[78]

The analysis of the effects that the nationalisation measure would have on banking indicates a wide range of inquiry.[79]

This approach is of crucial importance to the press—partly because the legislature often seeks to do indirectly what it cannot do directly[80] and partly because the government often pretends to enact legislation for *pro bono publico* reasons when its real object is to infringe private and public rights. In *Bennett Coleman's* case,[81] it was precisely this kind of issue that was mooted before the courts. The government enacted measures to control the import and supply of newsprint on a quota system. The new import policy was contained in the Newsprint Import Control Policy (1972-3) which was effectuated by the Newsprint Control Order, 1972 passed under Section 3 of the Essential Commodities Act, 1955. The salient features of the Newsprint Control Policy were:

(a) no newspaper or a new edition could be started by a common ownership even within the authorised quota of newsprint;

(b) the maximum number of pages was limited to ten and no adjustment was permitted between circulation and the pages so as to increase the pages;

(c) no inter-changeability was permitted between different papers of common ownership units or different editions of the same paper;

(d) allowance of a twenty per cent increase in the page level up to a maximum of ten had been given to newspapers with less than ten pages.

The upshot of the new import policy was to prevent a newspaper from increasing the number of pages, page area, periodicity by reducing circulation to meet its requirements within the admissible quota. The Supreme Court (by a majority of four to one) declared the impugned measures as violative of the Constitution. Justice Ray for the majority relied on the *Sakal Newspapers* case[82] to reiterate that the Constitution in protecting freedom of the press entitled a citizen to propagate and publish his ideas, disseminate and circulate them. He stressed that any restraints on the number of pages, circulation or advertisements which would detrimentally affect the freedom of the press to control the circulation and content of newspapers was not constitutional. Justice Ray followed a broad 'effect' theory:

> The correct approach should be to inquire what in substance is the loss or injury caused to the citizen and not merely what manner and method has been adopted by the State in placing restrictions.[83]

Returning to the language of 'direct' effects, he observed:

> The various provisions of the newsprint import policy have been examined to indicate as to how the petitioner's fundamental rights have been infringed by the restrictions on page limit, prohibition against new newspapers and new editions. The effect and consequence of the impugned policy upon the newspapers is directly controlling the growth and circulation of newspapers. The direct effect is the restriction upon circulation of newspapers. The direct effect is upon the growth of newsprint through (the limitation of) pages. The direct effect is that newsprint are defined of their area of advertisement. The direct effect is that they are exposed to financial loss. The direct effect is that freedom of speech and expression is infringed.[84]

At this stage, Ray J. considered another argument pertaining to the 'effect' of the impugned legislation. The Additional Solicitor General, Mr. F.S. Nariman, made a very clever argument which seemed to suggest that one of the 'effects' of the impugned legislation would be to break the monopolistic nature of the press and to create an open society in which there will be a greater freedom of speech and expression.[85] This was, conceivably, visualised as a direct effect of the legislation. Ray J. rejected this argument without really considering it:

> It is indisputable that by freedom of the press is meant the right of all citizens to speak in public and express their views. The freedom of the press embodies the right of people to read. The freedom of the press is not antithetical to the right of the people to speak and express. . . American decisions establish that a governmental regulation is justified in America as an important or essential government interest which is unrelated to the suppression of free expression. This court has established freedom of the press to speak and express. That freedom cannot be abridged or taken away in the manner the impugned policy has done.[86]

It is not clear from Ray J.'s judgment as to what he thought a permissible restriction was. His judgment seems to suggest that there are certain parts of freedom of the press which are "essential" or important to the press and any effect likely to affect these essential or important parts is likely to invite an inquiry by the courts.

Justice Mathew, adhering to a much more formal test[87] in preference to the new 'effect' doctrine, responded to Mr. Nariman's argument in his dissenting judgment. Relying on American case law, he explained that in the United States free speech was vital to the sustenance of the democratic system of government but an extensive regulation was permitted.[88] He took the view that an attack on monopolistic tendencies and to check unfair competition was fundamental to the protection of the freedom of the press.[89] Justice Mathew's reliance on the American position was countered by Justice Ray arguing that in the absence of express constitutional limitations on the right to free speech and press, the American Supreme Court evolved a theory of regulation as an essential government interest which was un related to the suppression of free speech.[90]

The Court was not really able to clarify the permissible threshold of inquiry in the nature of the effects of the impugned governmental action. The confusion was worse confounded in an important non-press constitutional case in 1977 where the language of "remoteness" replaced the references to the effect doctrine.[91] Justice Bhagwati's return, in 1978, to the 'direct and inevitable effect' doctrine—formulated by his father twenty years earlier in the *Express Newspapers* case[92]—added to the confusion. This last case was a *cause celebre* because it involved the journalistic claims of Mrs. Gandhi's daughter-in-law (and Sanjay Gandhi's wife) Maneka's right to travel abroad.[93] Was freedom to travel abroad part of freedom of speech or the rights of the press which were considered ancillary to freedom of speech? What was the effect of the government withholding Maneka's passport?

The Court had enormous difficulty in identifying what freedom of speech and expression was.[94] Following earlier *dicta*, it took the view that the Constitution protected a Fundamental Right, not a "concomitant or peripheral" right, and stressed the need to discourage a state of affairs where all kinds of rights were given protection "by a series of ever-expanding concentric circles in the shape of rights concomitant to concomitant rights and so on, lead(ing) to grotesque results".[95] But where and how does one draw the line? In the *Maneka* case, some judges took the simple view that fundamental rights could not be exercised abroad.[96] Other judges seemed to take the view that the freedom of the press should be interpreted in the context of a global technology.[97] Having done this and declared that travelling was a good thing, they held that the right to travel abroad was not *per se* a part of the freedom of speech, but that in certain circumstances it could be.[98] One judge does not really explain this—other than by declaring that "concomitant" rights could not be expanded further.[99] Justice Bhagwati made a curious distinction that certain Fundamental Rights were guaranteed but concomitant rights facilitating their exercise were not. He argues:

> We cannot, therefore, accept the theory that a peripheral or concomitant right which facilitates the exercise of a

named fundamental right or gives it meaning and substance or makes its exercise effective is itself a guaranteed right included within the Fundamental Rights.[100]

The right to exercise one's right abroad was therefore not a fundamental right, and not necessarily a part of the freedoms of journalists and pressmen.

Prima facie, this approach seems to be quite strange. Bhagwati J. seems to be making a distinction between a 'right' and its 'exercise' and arguing that the right is guaranteed as a fundamental right but its exercise is not. If this is taken seriously—as, indeed, it must be—all the rights which are guaranteed in the Fundamental Rights chapter are really no more than declaratory in nature because their exercise is not part of the guaranteed fundamental right. Bhagwati J. seems to support his approach on the basis of the 'direct and inevitable' effect theory by showing that the 'direct and inevitable' effect is on the right to go abroad and not on 'freedom of speech and expression'. This interpretation of the 'effect' approach which was put forward in the *Bank Nationalisation* case shows the weakness of Bhagwati J.'s formulation of the 'effect' doctrine in terms of 'direct and inevitable' effect. There would be no difficulty in arguing that the inevitable effect in all cases would not be to restrict the freedom of speech and expression.

The extent of direct and indirect intervention by the government can be gauged from the *Express Newspapers* case (1986)[101] where the Lieutenant Governor of Delhi issued forfeiture and demolition notices in respect of a building being constructed by the *Indian Express*. Only one judge saw this as a clear, direct and immediate threat to freedom of speech.[102] Again in the later *Newsprint* case (1986)[103] the Court while celebrating the rights of the press[104] tends to avoid a systematic discourse on the kind of direct and indirect pressures that can be placed on the press.[105]

The great confusion surrounding the subject has arisen because three separate and distinct questions have been merged into one. *First*: what is considered to be part of a Fundamental Right including rights that enable its effective exercise? *Second*:

when does governmental action infringe or have an effect on a Fundamental Right? *Three*: even if an infringement takes place, can it be considered a reasonable restriction? Mobilising speech and expression in any society has social, economic and other implications. A part of this mobilisation process depends on the institutional capabilities of those who exercise this right. The requirements of this institutional capability (*e.g.* as in the case of the press) have to be perceptively appreciated and recognised. Protecting a right but not protecting the institutional capabilities which are needed for its effective exercise has the effect of undercutting the right itself. There is no doubt that certain people are more institutionally capable than others. What should be done to equalise these policy differentials is related to question three (*supra*), not question one. In order to define the extent of the constitutional protection given to the press, extensive inquiries have to be undertaken of what it takes to run an effective press. Critics of a liberal press in a oligopolistic market economy should not think that a wide definition of the guaranteed rights of the press means the end of permissible governmental control and regulation. There are still two other questions to be answered. We have still to determine how governmental action affects the press. The Supreme Court's profound confusion on this question can be resolved by formulating the question: What is the real and intended effect? The emphasis on the intention of the government is retained to give the government the opportunity to explain their intentions. So far we have merely looked at the facts: the extent of the right and the extent of the infringement. There is still left the policy question: What kind of infringement is permissible as a reasonable restriction? What is the theory of regulation that the Court wants to follow?

The Supreme Court's theory of social and economic regulation is not at all clear. Its general stand has been that the Court can inquire into a large number of factors when determining the reasonability of governmental action and legislation. It accepts the need to control the working conditions of journalists even though this may impose financial burden on some sections of the press, disapproves of price and page control, does not accept certain forms of newsprint control and does not regard the executive power to withhold passports as offending freedom of the press. It has not really explained the permissible areas of control, *i.e.*, given conditions of scarcity, what kind of control of raw materials, prices, market conditions can the government exercise in order to arrange the equal opportunities vis-a-vis freedom of press for all? Or, should such questions be left to market forces?

The inability—or refusal—of the courts to fully understand both the institutional needs of the press and the multiple socio-economic and technical contexts in which the press operates lies at the root of the Delhi High Court's decisions to protect the monopoly of the State over radio broadcasting[106] and postal services.[107] Undoubtedly inherited British notions—as opposed to their American counterparts—about these being the exclusive sphere of the State's domain made it impossible for the judges to give anything other than a pre-constitutional interpretation to a post-constitutional situation. No satisfactory explanation is found in the judgments as to why such a State monopoly is justified in these areas even though such an explanation could be found on the basis of both existential and long term considerations. While accepting that broadcasting is part of free speech, Justice Kapur seemed to cut short all the important questions by asserting:

> In any event, the ban is not on broadcasting as such, but on ownership of the broadcasting media which is different from freedom of speech. There is no bar on the petitioner utilising *someone else's* radio station for the purpose of broadcasting.[108]

To separate 'ownership' issues from 'expression' and 'access' issues seems strange and makes nonsense of the deliberations of at least two Press Commission Reports. Who is that someone else? Who controls that someone else? Would the Court intervene to protect free speech if that someone else refused freedom of access to a person?[109] Can arguments about expression, access and ownership be that neatly separated? This does not mean that denial of claims of ownership cannot ever constitute part of the apparatus of control. But the learned judge was only able to make out a case for a very limited partial control:

> So every citizen can claim to have a broadcasting station. If everyone has a broadcasting station and can use it in an uncontrolled manner there will be chaos in the field of broadcasting. So, public order demands that there should be a regulation of the system. One possible regulation is to give exclusive right of using standard broadcasting wavebands for government radio stations and to allow others to use other wavebands. Broadcasting is covered by international conventions which have earmarked particular wavelengths to particular countries. There is no unrestricted right to broadcast.[110]

Two logical lines of inquiry should have followed. The first was to look at how the other foreign countries manage to observe international conventions and allow broadcasting by private individuals. The Court was not prepared to look at foreign examples.[111] The second relates to predictions about chaos which is really concerned with technical questions about the prevention of a technical chaos which in this case—even in the judge's own admission—would certainly not have been perpetuated.[112] So, an over-arching logic unrelated to the issue, a blanket unspecified appeal to the restraining clause of the Constitution[113] and a feeling that there was something wrong about a citizen wishing to broadcast to the public[114] replaced the quest for appropriate constitutional problematics. What we are left with is a defense of the official government policy and the existing *status quo* by reasoning that hardly constitutes credible constitutional doctrine.

Equally difficult is the decision about the monopoly of the post office. The court ruled that the penal anti-monopoly provisions do not affect the vendee but only the vendor:

> It specifically excludes the non-commercial conveyance of letters from their operation. Commercial activity is indulged in only by the carrier of the letter or the conveyer of the

letter and not the sender. The sender only comes in as an abettor. . . . Therefore, the challenge of the petitioners has to be rejected.[115]

However accurate this may be a legal description of the liabilities of the parties involved, both *constitutionally* and otherwise it seems absurd to distinguish between the activity of one party as commercial and, therefore, penal and the other as subsidiary (and, as it happens equally, penal). We are dealing here with mutually supportive transactions which affect a whole range of activity concerning the rights of the press and the freedom of communication. The press depends greatly upon a network of efficient, freely available complaint sensitive (and where necessary specifically adapted and differentiated) services in order to function.[116] This point becomes even more important if we bear in mind that both the Indian Telegraph Act and the Post Office Act permit even press messages to be intercepted. The Post Office Act contains wider powers than the Telegraph Act which permits interception if "necessary . . . and expedient to do in the interests of the sovereignty and integrity of the State, the security of the State, friendly relations with foreign States, or public order or for preventing incitement to the commission of an offence".[117] The Press Commission's hint that a corresponding but differently drafted part of the Post Office Act[118] may be unconstitutional[119] suggests that a rigorous constitutional examination of the modes of communication is urgently needed.

The partial attention paid to the operational and institutional needs of the press in the *Bennett Coleman*[120] and *Sakal Newspapers*[121] cases seems to have died out.[122] No further innovative extensions have been made. *Sakal Newspapers* had suggested that although the anti-monopolism of business could be attacked, such an attack could not directly or indirectly curtail the freedom of the press. This entire doctrine which has caused some alarm to the Second Press Commission[123] does not seem to have perturbed the Delhi High Court in deciding on the constitutional proprieties of a monopolistic State-owned post office and radio station. More importantly, no attention has been paid to broader questions about what the rights of the press are, the extent of their operation and what constitutes an "effect" on such rights. Predictably the courts have extended the rights of all kinds of people to have freedom of expression including those incarcerated in jail.[124] They have stressed that even civil servants have the right to run a newspaper.[125] But no real attention is paid as to what it takes for a newspaper to be established and be run effectively. Typical in this regard is the decision on advertising policy of the government.[126] *Ushodaya Publications*[127] were told by the Court that the constitutional guarantee of the freedom of speech and expression included a guarantee of the freedom of press and of circulation.[128] However, the constitutional generosity of the Court did not get past this formal declaration. Trapped in the confusing jurisprudential conundrum of direct and indirect effects,[129] it was stressed that no one had a right to a contract from the State;[130] and, therefore, for government advertisements. As an analytical question about whether a tangible legal right had been pre-established, the Court may have been right. But this is not a satisfactory explanation about the *constitutional rights* involved. For, a constitutional examination must, perforce, lead to examining the funding needs of newspapers, the advertisement market, the government's share of such a market and so on.[131] But let us look a little further at the advertisement relationship that the court found to be constitutionally legitimate. The court approved the withholding of advertisements where the newspapers in question indulged in activities which were anti-national, communal, provoked tensions in society, indulged in malicious and inadvertent character assassination and made abusive and slanderous attacks on Government or its functionaries. The Court struck down guidelines whereby advertisements were withheld when newspapers were rabid and abusive, distorted news for a mischievous purpose and fomented group rivalries by mischief, gossip-mongering and sensationalism. It is not clear as to why these two classes of categories are distinguishable.[132] Was it because the latter were vague? If so, both classes of categories were couched in equally vague terms. Was it because the former class-category was concerned with graver issues? This does not seem to be the case. In any event does it seem right to institute a constitutional norm which effectively gives the government the power to shut down a newspaper (by withholding advertisements)? Such a constitutional norm is as uncomfortable in its formulation as it would be arbitrary in its application. But the logic of the court's decision becomes clearer when we come across the following observation:

> One cannot legitimately expect the government to give its advertisements to those newspapers which make abusive and slanderous attacks on the government and its functionaries, in effect, paving the way for others to make abusive and slanderous attacks.[133]

This has the effect of pre-empting a responsible authority deciding whether or not the newspaper in question has violated the law. The Press Commission which has blessed this decision[134] seems to think that it is not necessary for a responsible body to judge these issues which should go to the Courts (presumably after the decision to withdraw advertisements has been made). Not looking at such forms of pre-censorship[135] constitutes a failure to deal with crucial financial and market considerations which are fundamental to the existence of the press and a consideration of its constitutional rights. *At one level*, we can conceive of this as a failure in jurisprudence. That the Court has simply not shown the imagination or assimilated the jurisprudence to look at this matter properly.[136] There is no doubt that the constitutional rights of the press call for a very challenging examination of various issues. Indian jurisprudence looks at public law through limited British administrative law techniques concerning narrow issues about the width and procedural aspects of the exercise of governmental power. Indian judges have not been able to take issues behind the range of this jurisprudence. This has also been the approach of the courts used in preventive detention matters![137] Such an administrative law approach is writ large across the *Ushodaya advertisement* case where the Court—despite this jurisprudence—continued to place power in the hands of a single official[138] and refused to recognise the nexus between political events and the withholding of advertisement revenue.[139] *At another level,* these decisions and the assumption of these narrow juristic techniques themselves involve an intuitive political judgment about the predicament of the courts and what they can do in the given constitutional and political situation. So, it is necessary to probe—at least at the level of suspicion—beyond the argument of intellectual paralysis and intellectual domination by the preponderant influence and use of English jurisprudence.[140] It has been shown that despite much publicised areas of controversy, the Supreme Court has been a willing ally both to sustain governmental power as well as support a large number of governmental plans.[141] The constitutional decisions on the press support the broad governmental demands to regulate the press even though the Supreme Court did intervene in the newsprint case where a powerful press lobby made the discreet intentions of the government patently untenable and colourable. But apart from a few controversial instances, the judiciary supports the government's restrictive socio-economic interpretation of the constitutional rights of the press. Although the government continues to call attention to the wider monopolism of the metropolitan press the restrictive interpretation of the courts deprives the press of an important arena to fight governmental policy. In most instances, the courts—faced with difficult political cases or political situations—have simply ducked the issue. They seem happier to decide matters on narrow technical grounds connected with direct and inevitable effects or the nature of the administrative power involved. But in dabbling with technicalities it may have thrown the baby out with the bathwater in not frankly examining the kind of regulations and market conditions which should form the substratum of constitutionally permissible governmental control of the press.

Though the Supreme Court—and High Courts—have not evolved a clearly discernible theory of the economic and other effects of economic and other legislation on the press, it has been clearer in its attitude to the public order and other restrictions on the press. Its initial position—soon abandoned—was to protect the press. In *Romesh Thappar*[142] and *Brij Bhushan*, [143] the Court refused to accept that restrictions in the interests of public order were linked to the security of state. The Constitution permitted reasonable restrictions only in respect of the latter. In 1951, the Constitution was amended to include "public order" within the list of permissible restrictions.[144] The next year, in the *Bihar* case,[145] the Court held that the amendment was not necessary and that the earlier cases had been misunderstood:

> It is plain that speeches and expression on the part of an individual which invite or encourage commission of violent crimes such as murder cannot but be matters which would undermine the security of the State and come within the ambit of law sanctioned by Article 19.[146]

The majority in the Press Commission (1954), supporting the government line and criticising the Court, took the view that the amendment was necessary; and further that it was not an infringement of the freedom of the press ". . . insofar as it relates to public order and incitement to an offence".[147] This provoked a spirited response from the minority who pointed out that the spirit of the *Bihar* case was to limit the restrictions on free speech in "aggravated forms of prejudicial activity".[148] A general public order restraint was seen as being very wide and opening new and previously forbidden channels.

Subsequent cases have affirmed that the minority were justified in their predictions. Expanding on the literal interpretation of the Constitution, the Court has validated several general public order statutory controls on the press. The width of the restrictions was emphasised in *Ramji Lal Modi's* case[149] where the Court validated a section of the Indian Penal Code which forbade insults to the religions or religious beliefs of a class of citizens, even where this may not have led to a disturbance of public order. Taking a wide view of the government's brief to maintain public order at the expense of the rights of the press, the Court took refuge in the fact that—

> reasonable restrictions on the exercise of freedom of speech and expression 'in the interests of public order' which is

> much wider than 'for the maintenance of' public order. If, therefore, certain activities have a *tendency* to cause public disorder, a law penalizing such activities cannot but be held to be a law imposing reasonable restrictions 'in the interests of public order' although in some cases those activities may not actually lead to a breach of public order.[150]

Such an interpretation could give the government a vast reservoir of preventive, punitive and other powers. Virtually everything could be deemed to be "in the interests of public order".

In 1962, the Court also validated the notorious Section 124A of the Indian Penal Code which dealt with 'sedition' and which had been used to contain public protests during India's Independence movement.[151] The Court justified its decision by arguing that the law of 'sedition' had been validated only if it were interpreted on the basis of an earlier Federal Court decision[152] that the act complained of "must either incite to disorder or must be such as to satisfy reasonable men that this is their intention or tendency". Implicit in this is a rejection of the 'British' view that a suspicion that disorder may be caused was enough.[153] But it is important that, at a constitutional level, what we have called the 'British' view does lie at the root of the *Ramji Lal Modi* interpretation of the phrase 'in the interests of public order'. The *Sedition* case was not proposing a general constitutional 'reasonable man' test.

What, then, was the test to be used? In *Babu Lal's* case,[154] the Court had specifically rejected the 'clear and present danger test' (*i.e.* is there a clear and present danger to public order?) which had been used by American courts. It agreed to give extensive preventive and other powers to local officials as long as some pattern of control existed. *Lohia's* case[155] tried to tackle this question, *inter alia*, by narrowing the sweep of the 'public order' restrictions so as to exclude normal 'law and order' situations and 'security of state' situations and include only such situations where there were threats to "public peace, safety and tranquillity". Further, a new 'remoteness' test was introduced:

> The limitations introduced in the interests of public order to be a reasonable restriction should be one which has a proximate connection or nexus with public order but not one far-fetched, hypothetical or problematical or remote in the chain of its relation with public order.[156]

This seems a step in the right direction even though the decision has been criticised as "contrary to well-settled principles laid down by the Supreme Court itself, and ought to be overruled as being clearly wrong and productive of public mischief".[157] Since the law under the statute in question was activated under discretionary powers vested in the government, it has been suggested that the *bona fides* and opinion of the government should be respected:

> (I)t is an expression of the opinion of the executive Government that circumstances have arisen which require the provisions of the Act to be applied and, *prima facie*, that judgment is entitled to respect unless it is affirmatively shown that the judgment is wrong.[158]

But, this begs the question. How can one show that the government was wrong? What could be the basis of the challenge?

The constitutional position is visited with a vulnerable lack of clarity. On the one hand, cases like *Ramji Lal Modi's* case stress that the phrase "in the interests of public order" must be widely interpreted. Consistent with this approach, a challenge to a Punjab statute failed because the Court held that "anything tending to overthrow the State must necessarily be prejudicial to the security of state".[159] On the other hand, cases like *Lohia's* case suggest that some criteria (reasonable man, reasonable nexus, remoteness) are available for testing the validity of governmental action. The interposition of such a test in the *Sedition* case seemed politically necessary because sedition had an 'imperial' history and was specifically dropped from the list of reasonable restrictions. *Lohia's* case must, alas, be explained in terms of the social dynamics of the litigation before the Court.

The petitioner, Dr. Lohia, was a leading opposition politician. The statute in question originated out of the British government's move to contain the 'no tax' campaign started during the Independence movement. The case was decided in the Supreme Court by a sympathetic judge who was crusading for a pro-libertarian position and who, later, resigned from the Supreme Court bench to fight for the election of President of India. The decision in the *Sedition* and *Lohia* cases are minor deviations from a general support of controlling freedom of press in the interests of public order.

By and large, the Court has supported—often without being discerning—the plea of the government for an almost blanket power to deal with these situations. The emergence of the Constitution has not affected the basic paradigm operated during the days of British Rule in India.

Connected with general public order controls, is the issue of pre-censorship. In *Brij Bhushan's* case,[160] the printers and publishers were required to get pre-publication approval for certain items in order to prevent the further proliferation of communal tension in the aftermath of the partition of India. The Court reacted very sharply to a policy of pre-censorship and quoting Blackstone observed:

> . . . the liberty of the press consists in laying no previous restraint upon publications and not in freedom from censure for criminal matter when published. Every freeman has an undoubted right to lay what sentiments he pleases before the public. To forbid this is to destroy the freedom.[161]

This broad approach was questioned in *Virendra's* case.[162] Massive, violent and virtually unmanageable agitation had begun on the sensitive language issue of promoting Hindi. The government used their statutory powers to prohibit news on this question for two months including carrying such news in a newspaper brought from without the control area. The Court upheld the legislation and the exercise of this power after talking of the extensive influence of the press on public order. Public order was seen as being very important and it was not considered unreasonable to give it priority over the freedom of the press. The Court was happy to give the government virtually a *carte blanche* in these matters:

> Quick decision and swift and effective action must be of the essence of these powers and the exercise of it must, therefore, be kept to the subjective satisfaction of the Government charged with the duty of maintaining law and order. To make an exercise of these powers justiciable and subject to judicial scrutiny will defeat the very purpose of the enactment.[163]

One section of the statute was invalidated because it permitted, without allowing any representation, indefinite prohibition orders.[164] Despite this, it has been rightly observed: "This decision shows that restrictions, more stringent than pre-censorship, can be imposed. . . in the interest of public order and the publication of certain matters could be totally prohibited for a limited period of time."[165] In this case, there was no doubt of the existence of wide-scale agitation. But suppose the existence of such a state of affairs was not publicly known beyond a carefully guarded, but foreboding, government affidavit in Court. For a short duration, the government could exercise absolute powers akin to those it can exercise during an Emergency when civil liberties are threatened.

Earlier at least one High Court upheld the provision in the Press (Objectionable Matter) Act, 1951 that prompt action by the government to prevent disorder was valid even if this involved giving no prior notice to the newspaper concerned.[166] There were some safeguards in terms of getting approval from certain designated political law officers and a power of post-preventive decisional judicial review. However, various States set up their own legislation to deal with 'objectionable matter'.[167] Some of these went unnoticed until the famous Bihar Bill controversy of 1982.[168]

All this goes to reinforce the view that the tradition for a free press has not really taken root. At its best, the press is seen as useful, but dispensable as soon as some incipient threats to public order become visible. At its worst, the press is viewed by the judges as a disorganised, dangerous, agitational corps which was a good instrumental weapon to fight for India's Independence but dangerous to the development of a free India. This latter view is consistent with the policy of the British before Independence. In some senses, such a view is also not totally at variance with a view taken by judges in the West who see the breakdown of public order (or, even law and order) as creating a general collapse of the conditions in which liberty occurs.[169] The Indian paradigm, however, is set in a tradition of general control. Further reforms in this area may take place in the light of the new 'due process' doctrine invented by the Court whereby laws interfering with procedural liberty, and other preferred rights like freedom of speech, should not be arbitrary, conflict with the principles of natural justice or be capable of indiscriminate use.[170] But, it is impossible to predict whether the strong tradition of control would be contained or dislodged by this challenge. Meanwhile, the techniques of pre-Independence days will continue unscathed.

III

Apart from public order, security of state and cognate areas, "reasonable restrictions" can also be imposed in the interests of decency or morality, contempt of court and defamation.[171] Since the itemisation of the list of permissible restrictions is qualified by a reference to the concept of reasonableness, the latter concept merits examination. In *V.G. Row's* case,[172] a broad view was taken of this. The case involved freedom of speech and the right to association. The Court invalidated a general uncontrolled executive discretion to control the press. It took a very wide view of reasonableness:

> It is important in this context to bear in mind that the test of reasonableness, wherever prescribed, should be applied to each individual statute impugned, and no abstract standard or general pattern of reasonableness can be laid down as applicable in all cases. The nature of the right alleged to be infringed, the underlying purpose of the restrictions imposed,

> the extent and urgency of the evil sought to be remedied thereby, the disproportion of the imposition, the prevailing conditions at the time should all enter into the judicial verdict. In evaluating such elusive factors and forming their conception of what is reasonable in all the circumstances of a given case, it is inevitable that the social philosophy and the scale of values of the judges participating in the decision should play an important part, and the limit to their interference with legislative judgment in such cases can only be dictated by their sense of responsibility and self-restraint that the Constitution is meant not only for people of their way of thinking but for all, and the majority of the elected representatives have in authorising the imposition of these restrictions considered them to be reasonable.[173]

Despite this declaration, the idea of reasonableness has not been used in a wide and challenging way. Two tendencies are significant. The first—which was apparent in *V.G. Row*, *Lohia* and other cases—is to concentrate on a procedural due process technique using English administrative law techniques to quantify the content of the procedure. Provisions which give wide discretionary or potentially arbitrary power and which deny the right to make a representation against the desirability of governmental action would be considered unreasonable. Such an approach has been further reinforced by the equality provisions of the Constitution (Article 14) which enjoin "equality before law and equal protection of all laws". There is a strong, though not always firm, line of interpretation of Article 14 to prevent extensive and unchecked authority reposing in governmental authorities. This is regarded as fundamental to the maintenance of the rule of law. Recently, Justice Bhagwati in *Maneka Gandih's* case,[174] has made a brave attempt to quantify reasonableness in this way and suggested that a "procedure established by law" which invaded personal liberty and other rights would become unreasonable if it did not conform to these requirements. But the impact of this decision cannot, as yet, be gauged.

A second approach in the interpretation of reasonableness seems to accept the putative 'social' and 'public' interests underlying the permitted restrictions. This has, in fact, meant that as long as the restraint falls within one of the items listed among the restrictions in Article 19(2), it would be constitutionally valid. "Reasonableness" was not seen as an independent criteria. The more important question is the question of "nexus" (*i.e.* did the impugned provisions fall within the list of restrictions?) and not one of reasonableness. This has been followed in the public order and other areas. At one stage, the Court even hinted that the reasonableness criteria applied to pre- and not post-constitutional laws on defamation and contempt of court.[175] The crucial question is to identify the law as falling within the category without questioning the reasonableness of the category itself.

This second approach may be called the 'typological' approach. As long as the restriction falls within one of the typologies mentioned in Article 19(2) of the Constitution,[176] the Court will ask few further questions. Some of these typologies are 'iron-clad' typologies. In such cases, the Court neither asks any questions about the nature and width of the typology nor the nexus between the impugned legislation and the typology. A formal statement to the effect that the impugned legislation falls within the typology is enough. This is certainly true of contempt of court, defamation and official secrecy. Anything formally claimed to be contempt of court or defamation is accepted as falling within the ambit of these typologies.[177] There is no case on official secrecy and all the constitutional questions about it seem to have proceeded on the assumption that the Official Secrets Act, 1923 must be regarded as a constitutionally legitimate restriction within the meaning of Article 19(2) of the Constitution.[178] This is presumably true of the sovereignty and integrity of India and friendly relations with States.[179] In the areas of public order and security of State we have seen how the Supreme Court did try and ask questions about the nexus between the impugned government legislation and corresponding typology. But that was in 1950[180] and these questions are not widely asked today. 'Decency' and 'public morality' seem to have posed a slightly more complex problem. The Court—as we shall see later—have assumed the American approach[181] that immoral and indecent speech unless socially worthy is not free speech anyway.[182] They have also used the typological approach while examining to a limited extent the 'reasonableness' of the restrictions from both the narrow and broad point of view.[183] Typically, public order cases also contain some discussion on 'reasonableness' in the narrow sense of examining whether the legislation reposes arbitrary power in the hands of an official.[184] However, the typological approach has been an all-embracing approach that has done much to make the rights of the press meaningless and to make the restrictions and any formal appeal to the restrictions more fundamental than the rights. Judges will usually accept at face value governmental assertions that a particular legislation falls within a particular typology. Lawyers have not really sought to reassess the approach through constitutional litigation. Nor has the press bothered to mount constitutional or public advocacy campaigns because of the government's ability to appeal to public order considerations. However, the Bihar Bill campaign of 1982 shows that blanket appeals to public order are not always acceptable to the public which, if properly informed, may question the government's attempt to assimilate power under the guise of quelling incipient disorder or maintaining the security of state.[185] Representing as it does a total faith in the government, the typological approach is a major stumbling block in the quest for an effective constitutional jurisprudence on the permissible constitutional limitations on the rights of the press.

A third approach is to deal with some of these restrictions by raising questions of moral desert: does this right deserve to be protected? The question is then answered on the basis of a covert Indian intuition read with heavily laden cosmopolitan learning. In *Ranjit Udeshi's* case,[186] the Court was called upon to consider whether D.H. Lawrence's *Lady Chatterly's Lover* was an obscene book under provisions akin to the Common Law provisions that the offending item must not deprave or corrupt those in whose hands it might fall. The Constitution permits reasonable restrictions in favour of decency or morality. The courts have accepted that the common law test in this and other areas was connected with decency or morality. That would normally have disposed of the matter under the nexus test: but for the fact that the book before the Court was a literary classic and hailed as such by one of India's leading novelists in the trial below.[187] The presiding judge in the Supreme Court had himself been a part-time lecturer in a provincial university.[188] The Court was anxious to provide an explanation for holding the book obscene and rejecting the constitutional challenge. In doing so, it also affirmed a restrictive interpretation to the definition of "freedom of speech and expression":

> (I)t can hardly be claimed that obscenity which is offensive to modesty or decency is within the constitutional protection given to free speech and expression. That cherished right on which our democracy rests is meant for the expression of free opinions to change political and social conditions or for the advancement of human knowledge. . . .It is, however, clear that obscenity by itself has poor value in the propagation of ideas, opinions of public interest or profit. Where there is (such) . . . public interest or profit, the approach to the problem may become different because the interest of society may tilt in favour of free speech and expression.[189]

The Court seems to have made a judicial amendment of the Constitution so that "freedom of speech and expression" has been re-drafted as "freedom of socially and politically relevant public interest free speech and expression". This is a totally different approach and has little to do with the "reasonableness" doctrine. The Court did connect the two questions by asserting that India's own literature would suffer and be perverted if it emulated Lawrence's and similar works.[190] The judge re-assessed the literary merit of the book by taking on the role of a critic and ignoring the expert evidence given at the trial.[191] The Court also ignored important questions relating to intent and liability without giving them the attention they deserve under the reasonableness doctrine.[192] In one sense the judgment represents a traditional Indian public reaction to obscene literature. But the urbane judge needs to do more than accept this structure of social reality. What is significant is that in this the learned judge responded to this challenge not by just looking at the question of public interest but entrenching a new concept of free speech. That a liberal-minded judge should have done this merely testified to the prevailing trend to simply accept the provisions at face value, follow a traditional approach and make no serious attempt to revaluate the purpose and intendment of the free speech provisions.

The judge's approach to free speech can be seen as part of a broader approach to fundamental rights. The judges have been anxious to assert the constitutional position that moral questions are not just relevant to inquiries into the public interest or reasonableness but also in respect of the definition of the fundamental rights themselves. Thus, the Supreme Court has held that gambling, selling liquor and trading in rural debts are so morally unworthy that they do not fall within the constitutional definition of the freedom of trade.[193] This approach has also been applied to the interpretation of the free speech provisions in the *Hamdard Dawakhana* case[194] where the Court decided that commercial advertisements which offended against morality or decency were not protected by the free speech provisions. Out of this has grown a new set of moral and policy restrictions on the recognition of the ambit of various fundamental rights, including the freedom of speech provisions. What has emerged is a new restriction of the variety: Is the act, or class of acts, worthy of constitutional protection? This question is answered on the basis of an implied appeal to an intuitive understanding of a community consensus. The community consensus is visualised as a static entity without any dynamic components. A monolithic concept of consensus is created which requires conformity, permits little dissent and is intolerant to idiosyncracies of taste. This, in turn, represents a picture of society as perceived by a policy-maker spurred on by views of an integrated society. It does little justice to society as it really works and the many diversities that people are heir to.

There is one other set of constitutional questions posed by the press. This relates to the relationship between the press and the various institutions of State and the controversies that this may precipitate between them. While more detailed attention will be given to the manner in which the institutions of State are protected from the press,[195] it is important to note some of the constitutional issues that arise in conflict situations. Each of the institutions of government—*i.e.*, the legislature, the judiciary and the executive—are protected through the laws relating to parliamentary privilege, contempt of court and secrecy respectively. The press and politicians often play political games in one institution which affects and attracts the jurisdiction and powers of one of the others. Rules of official secrecy concerning the executive may violate the demands of the judiciary for information to determine a particular matter. Thus, in one case, the Supreme Court was called upon to adjudicate on the extent to which official secrecy can be claimed as regards the information that has to be made available to the accused under the procedure according to requirements of the Constitution.[196] The issue becomes equally charged when someone begins a litigation witha view to get information concerning an official or an official matter so that this information may be given more publicity. This lies at the root of the proceedings against Mrs. Gandhi[197] when she refused to testify and part with official information concerning her activities as Prime Minister during the Emergency. The Court had to resolve the somewhat awkward question in which politics, publicity and institutional conflict get inter-mingled. As we shall see later, the judiciary has sought to protect official secrecy except to the extent it would de-legitimate the viability of and confidence in the judicial process and judges. On this basis, there is a partial denial of even the operation of the Official Secrets Act where 'restricted information' should be released as part of constitutional guarantees concerning process rights.[198] Indian courts tend to be respectful of claims of executive privilege (other than those connected with official secrecy) as far as ordinary non-constitutional litigation is concerned.[199] But political groups have recently begun to push the Court to break this respectful forbearance with embarrassing results. Much to the delight of the press, in the *Transfer of Judges* case,[200] the Supreme Court ordered the release of all confidential documents between the Chief Justice and the Minister of Law pertaining to the non-appointment of some High Court judges. While all this has been put within certain limits, an uneasy equation exists about the extent to which political groups and pressmen will be able to agitate judicial process to procure official secrecy. Unable to assert the absolute rights of the judiciary to have the information litigants and the Courts need to adjudicate matters, the Court follows the pragmatic approach. The real difficulties begin after it has been established—as it would be in practically all cases—that the information is needed for the litigation in question. The judges are unable to examine the authenticity of the reason behind the litigation for that would involve making political imputations which would generate an even more aggravated publicity.[201] Nor have they—like English Courts[202]—solidly settled principles which might be agreeable to the executive, prevent abuse by the press and politicians and provide some consistency and principled decision-making for the future.

The position of the Court is even more embarrassing in examining the constitutionality of laws protecting the judiciary. In 1978, the press fought an extensive campaign against certain Supreme Court judges being appointed as Chief Justice of India.[203] Using what has been earlier identified as the typological approach the Court was happy to give a blanket protection to the law of contempt of court. At the same time, the Court discharged the contempt notices—presumably on the ground that contempt proceedings would only embroil the judges and the Court in further controversy. The guidelines evolved by the Court for restrained comment on the part of the press were much too ambiguous to constitute credible constitutional doctrine.[204]

Finally, there is the constitutional relationship between the press, parliament and the courts. On two occasions,[205] the press has petitioned the Court in order to protect the press from punitive visitations arising out of the parliamentary privilege jurisdiction of the legislatures. At first, the Court was firm in asserting its power to offer protection to the press. This approach was quickly abandoned when—in another context—the legislature summoned judges to answer for the protection they had offered to a litigant.[206] The Court, then, recognised the mutual autonomy of both processes without any definitive result. Meanwhile, the legislature—which also has constitutional provisions and rules about not discussing the conduct of judges—frequently encounters situations where such discussion occurs.[207] Such questions, being unresolved by courts, are left for resolution by the informal creation of patterns of institutional morality. Such patterns increasingly defy cumulative and consistent aggregation in India. All in all, the court has not brought clarity to constitutional questions concerning the press and the institutional demands of the State. The Constitution itself seems to have stated the demands of each of the institutions in absolute terms. Set against the guaranteed freedom of speech and expression in the Constitution, the Court has felt it easier to accommodate these institutional demands against the press. The press and politicians, in turn, play hop-skotch on the incipient possibilities of institutional conflict between the various organs of the State, simultaneously tempting providence and publicity.

It would appear that many of the paradigm notions underlying the press law of the British Raj have been approved by judges in post-Independent India. A clear statement that this is what the framers of the Constitution wanted is discernible in the records of the Constituent Assembly. Yielding both to the demands of the government and traditional pressures, the Court has neither wholly understood the market pressures on the press nor properly evaluated their approach to what the free speech provisions are about. In some of the cases they have controlled some of the economic constraints on the circulation, distribution and other economies of newspapers. But these have not been linked to a broader consideration of the kind of market conditions within which a free press can be deemed to exist. Beyond that, the constitutional provisions have made little difference apart from the use occasionally of the administrative law remedy of controlling the exercise of power. But such remedies would have been available even in a country like England which has a flexible Constitution and which has no entrenched Bill of Rights. Traditional perceptions of a low key press have been further strengthened by a nebulous requirement that the constitutionally protected freedoms enshrined in the Constitution must be morally worthy of protection.

At the root of all this lies a failure on the part of the Courts to make an independent assessment of the role of the press in Indian democracy. They seem to have adopted the view taken by the British in India that the press consists of private individuals who are irresponsible troublemakers, disturbers of the peace and exciters of sectarian violence. While there is a case for arguing that the press consists of private groups performing public functions in a distortionist way, this does not absolve having to decide important questions about the nature of the press, the conditions that protect its viability and its demands for protection from the State and others. Indeed, the government itself has realised the potentialities of the press to constitute an alternative political forum and, like its Press Commission, analysed the rights of the press in a broader social and economic context in order to strengthen its indirect control on the enlargement of the press as a hostile political arena inimical to the government. The courts, in turn, have preserved the formal status quo and refused to get drawn into examining even preliminary questions about the extent of press rights and what constitutes reasonable restrictions on them. This might account for the fact that apart from a handful of cases the press has ceased to use the court for the protection of press rights. Whether they will be tempted to do so as the political climate changes remains to be seen. For the press, in the present proxical situation, is increasingly becoming more important as the rest of India's political institutions are slowly sucked away from democratic viability with the increasing privatisation of the Indian state.

NOTES

1. Some of this euphoria depicted an impatience with criticism as can be seen in the discussion of the Draft Constitution (1948) VII C.A.D. 31-395 (4, 5 and 8 November 1948; and at the end of the process of Constitution making XI C.A.D. 607, 995 (17, 21, 23-26 November 1949). This is not to deny the enormous work put into its making—on which see B. Shiva Rao: *The Framing of India's Constitution* (Study Volume plus Volumes I-IV).
2. e.g. K.C. Wheare: "India's New Constitution Analysed" (1950) 48 *All. L.J. Jnl.* 21-4. On the assumption that doctrine and the development of a public morality are all that are needed to make the Constitution work see H.M. Seervai: *Constitutional Law of India* (1978) Volume III; M.C. Setalvad: *The Indian Constitution 1950-65* (1967); see also A. Jacob (ed.): *Constitutional Developments Since Independence* (1975) as example of an eclectic critique to the Constitution; R. Dhavan and Alice Jacob (eds.): *The Indian Constitution: Trends and Issues* (1978); A.G. Noorani (ed.): *Public Law in India* (1982) for essays, with some exceptions, not too removed from this eclectic mould. For formal critical estimates see I. Jennings: *Some Characteristics of the Indian Constitution* (1953); Even *V.* Baxi's critique: "The Little Done the Vast Undone." Some reflections on reading Granville Austin's: 'The Indian Constitution' (1967) 9 *J.I.L.I.* 323-430 maintains a guarded optimism on most questions.
3. This requires a look at Shiva Rao (*supra*) 1 note Volumes I-IV and the Constituent Assembly Debates (C.A.D.) Volumes I to XII. There are few accounts by the participants; see, however, B.N. Rao; *India's Constitution in the Making* (1950): G. Austin: *Indian Constitution: Cornerstone of a Nation* (1966) and Shiva Rao (*supra* note 1) Study Volume records many of these tensions. A proper critique of the process of Constitution-making which examines this process in the context of the socio-economic forces still needs to be written.
4. For a review of lawyers' reactions to the Constitution see R. Dhavan: *The Supreme Court of India: A Socio-legal Analysis of its Juristic Techniques* (1977) 2-19.
5. G. Austin (*supra* note 3) 309.
6. *V.* Baxi (*supra* note 2).
7. What we have is a lot of political rhetoric about the Constitution being for the poor e.g. V.R. Krishna Iyer: *Law and the People* (1971); *ibid*: *Some half hidden aspects of Social Justice* (1979). This gives the Constitution legitimacy and talks power into respectability; see also P. B. Gajendragadkar: *Constitution of India: Philosophy and Basic Postulates* (1970) cf. P.C. Joshi: "Indian Constitution and Social e" (1971) *Ind. Left Review* 58-64.

8. R. Dhavan and A. Jacob (*supra* note 2).
9. H.M. Seervai (*supra* note 2).
10. U. Baxi: *The Supreme Court and Politics* (1982).
11. G. Austin (*supra* note 3) Preface IX.
12. G. Austin (*supra* note 5).
13. See R. Dhavan: *President's Rule in the States* (1979).
14. See R. Dhavan: *The Amendment: Conspiracy or Revolution* (1978); *ibid*: *Amending the Amendment* (1979).
15. This controversy looms large. For the arena of conflict see R. Dhavan: ' Judicial Law Making and Committed Judges: Doctrinal differences in the Supreme Court and a recent case" (1978) 6-7 *Delhi Law Review* 24-47 and R. Dhavan: *Justice on Trial: The Supreme Court* (1980) Chapters IV-V for an assessment of the Supreme Court.
16. No real account of this has ever been written. R. Sudarshan's Ph.D. dissertation in Cambridge promises to be a seminal contribution on this subject.
17. e.g. U. Baxi: "Taking Suffering Seriously: Social Action Litigation in the Supreme Court" in R. Dhavan and S. Khurshid (eds.): *Judges and the Judicial Power*: *Essays in honour of Krishna Iyer* (Bombay, Tripathi 1985).
18. The literature follows three kinds of patterns: (a) Supreme Court cases till 1973 that Directive Principles are subordinate to Fundamental Rights (on which see R. Dhavan *supra* note 4 pp. 87-94); (b) Declarations of the primacy of Directive Principles (Dhavan, J. in *Balwant Raj* v. *Union of India* A.I.R. 1968 All. 14; P.K. Tripathi: "Directive Principles of State Policy" (1954) *S.C.J. Jul.* 50; K.S. Hegde: *Directive Principles of State Policy* (1972); Bhagwati, J. in *Minerva Mills* v. *Union of India* A.I.R. 1980 S.C. 1789); (c) Directive Principles as an independent source of responsibility (Bhagwati, J. in *Peoples Union of Democratic Rights* v. *Union of India* A.I.R. 1982 S.C. 1473). The literature on the Directive Principles is too numerous to cite here see M.S. Rana: *Writings on Indian Constitution* (1973) Entries 2814-2934.
19. This is why T.T. Krishnamachari called these principles a "veritable dustbin of sentiment" (1948) VII C.A.D. 583; For the compromises see Austin (*supra* note 3) 50-115; See generally D.G. Markandan: *Directive Principles of State Policy* (1966); N.V. Paranjpe: *The Role of Directive Principles under the Indian Constitution* (1975); see also P. Diwan and V. Kumar (eds.): *Directive Principles Jurisprudence* (1983-two volumes).
20. See R. Dhavan: *Due Process in India*: *A Preliminary Explanation*, Mimeo, study for the Indian Law Institute, 1981; also G. Austin (*supra* note 3) 84-113.

21. See H.C.L. Merrillat: "Compensation for the taking of property: A historical footnote to *Bela Banerjee's* case" (1959) 1 *J.I.L.I.* 375-401.
22. This resulted in the famous *Kesavananda* v. *Union of India* (1973) 4 S.C.C. 225 on which see R. Dhavan: *The Supreme Court and Parliamentary Sovereignty* (1976).
23. See H.C.L. Merrillat: *Land and the Constitution* (1970). Cf. more specifically consider Planning Commission assessments of agrarian reform legislation e.g., A. M. Khusro: *Economic and Social Effects of Jagirdari Abolition and Land Reforms in Hyderabad* (1957); R.R. Mishra: *Effect of Land Reforms in Saurashtra* (1961); B.D. Mishra: *Land Reforms in Orissa* (1968); G. Parathasarthi and B. Prasada Rao: *Implementation of Land Reforms in Andhra Pradesh* (1969); V.M. Dandekar and S. S. Khadanpur: *A Study of the Bombay Tenancy Act* (1948); K.R. Manekar: *Land Reforms in Vidarbha* (1968); B. Singh and S. Mishra: *A Study of Land Reforms in Uttar Pradesh* (1964); D. Singh: *Land Reforms in Rajasthan* (1964).
24. *Supra* Chapter 1.
25. *Supra* Chapter 3 for the Constitutional cases and Chapter 5 for the Press cases on the Indian Penal Code and *Report of the Second Press Commission* (1982) prs. 34-63 pp. 23-27.
26. *Report of the Second Press Commission* (*supra* note 25) pr. 30 p. 37.
27. *Sewakram* v. *R.K. Karanjia* A.I.R. 1981 S.C. 1514 at pr. 11 p. 1519. Note the reference at pr. 12 p. 1519 to *Arnold* v. *King Emperor* A.I.R. 1914 P.C. 116 at 124.
28. *I.E. Pvt. Ltd.* v. *Union of India* A.I.R. 1986 S.C. 515.
29. *Ibid* at pr. 31 p. 527.
30. *Ibid* at pr. 80-2 pp. 543-9.
31. *Prabha Dutt* v. *Union of India* (1982) 1 S.C.C. 1; See further K.K. Mathew "Right to know: A critiqne of *Prabha Dutt's* case" (1982) IX *J.B.C.I.* 116.
32. Section 3, Constitution (First Amendment) Act, 1951.
33. *Romesh Thappar* v. *State of Madras* A.I.R. 1950 S.C. 124; *Brij Bhushan* v. *State of Delhi* A.I.R. 1950 S.C. 129.
34. Inserted by the Constitution (Sixteenth Amendment) Act, 1963 with effect from 5 October 1963.
35. See B. Shiva Rao: *The Framing of India's Constitution* (1965-8) in four volumes and a 'study' volume. The 'four' volumes—all the preparatory and committee work of the Constituent Assembly which drafted India's Constitution. This series is hereafter referred to as *Shiva Rao* and by Volume number. II, 75 (K. M. Munshi's Draft Article 5 (2)), 87 (B.R. Ambedkar's Draft Article II (1)) 12.
36. It appears to have been dropped without any discussion fairly early in the deliberations: see Minutes of the Sub-Committee on

Fundamental Rights II Shiva Rao 119-121. Note Munshi's comment (Article 7) at p. 120.

37. II Shiva Rao 143—in a letter dated 4 April, 1947 in the context of the freedom to religion clause; note also his comments on the "incitement to class hatred" as a restriction to freedom of speech (II, 158) in his Note of 14 April, 1947.
38. II Shiva Rao 137-43. Article 9 being the clause that dealt with freedom of speech.
39. For comments (or, indeed, their absence) see II Shiva Rao 143-63 including Minutes of Dissent (II, 161-3). The Constitutional Adviser points to the Irish pedigree of the clause (II, 148) and then ignores it (II, 152).
40. II Shiva Rao 164: "It was decided that a separate clause should be included in the chapter on Fundamental Rights." This is clearly the origin of the idea that certain constitutional rights (including the freedom of speech and expression) should be suspended during an Emergency—an idea which was actually included in Articles 358-9 of the Constitution. The revised provisions of the Drafting Committee can be found at II, 172 (Report of the Sub-Committee on Fundamental Rights, 16 April, 1947).
41. The Minutes of Dissent to the Report (*supra* note 9) do not take up this matter (II Shiva Rao 176-98). At the Sub-Committee, suggestion was made by Mr. Brihan for more restrictions to control the tribal belts in Assam (II, 201, 208).
42. II Shiva Rao 230 (per C. Rajagopalachari—a point, it later transpired, related to what B.R. Ambedkar called a "symmetry of language").
43. II Shiva Rao 231 (per. A.K. Ayyar).
44. II Shiva Rao 232 (per C. Rajgopalachari).
45. II Shiva Rao 232 (per B.R. Ambedkar and Bakshi Tek Chand).
46. II Shiva Rao 233 (per P.K. Salve).
47. II Shiva Rao 233.
48. *e.g.* VII Constituent Assembly Debates (hereafter C.A.D.) 732-4 (Hukam Singh requesting that all the restrictions be deleted); 712 (D.S. Seth); 749-50 (B.S. Mann); 757 (Kazi S. Karimuddin); 764 (H.J. Khandekar); 774-5 (L.N. Sahu). Both K. Hanumanthiya (754) and T.T. Krishnamachari (771) accepted that the restrictions invaded the guaranteed freedoms but regarded this as inevitable. *Note*: All references are to the debates of 1 December, 1948 (711-48) and 2 December, 1948 (749-89). The pagination in various editions of the Debates varies.
49. C.A.D. 770-1 (A.K. Ghosh: ". . . I think it will take centuries for the Supreme Court to exactly say what really these words mean . . .").
50. VII C.A.D. 713 (D.S. Seth); 714 (K.T. Shah); 734 (A. Baig); 736,

739 (T.D. Bhargava); 756 (K.S. Karimuddin). Cf. 740 (B.R. Ambedkar).

51. *e.g.*, VII C.A.D. 730 (K.M. Munshi); 743-4 (S. Sahaya that restrictions should be allowed only for a limited period). Note also M.H. Mohani's brilliant intervention that such extensive power should not be used by political groups in power against their political opponents (758-9).
52. VII C.A.D. 731-2 (K.M. Munshi); 735-8 (T.D. Bhargava); 750-1 (G. Das); 762 (R.K. Chaudhri); 763 (S.L. Saxena); 771 (T.T. Krishnamachari); 777 (M.A. Ayyangar).
53. VII C.A.D. 780 (B.R. Ambedkar accepting M.A. Ayyangar's forceful retreat on this, (at 777)).
54. *e.g.* VII C.A.D. 727-8 (M.A. Baig—note his Amendment 447); 742 (M. Tahir); 718 (N. Ahmad—that all rights must be peaceably exercised).
55. VII C.A.D. 718 (supported by H.V. Kamath) arguing that this was for freedom lovers not saboteurs); 758 (M.H. Mohani); 764 (S.L. Saxena); cf. 778 (M.A. Ayyangar); 780-1 (B.R. Ambedkar).
56. VII C.A.D. 726 (K.T. Shah); 728 (M.A. Baig); 724 (M. Ismail Sahib).
57. VII C.A.D. 716 (K.T. Shah); 763 (S.L. Saxena).
58. VII C.A.D. 716 (K.T. Shah).
59. VII C.A.D. 726 (K.T. Shah).
60. VII C.A.D. 780 (B.R. Ambedkar).
61. VII C.A.D. 739 (T.D. Bhargava reposing faith in the courts). On the limits of effective court action see M.H. Mohani (759) and, perhaps, T.T. Krishnamachari (771). S.A. Rouf suggested parliament and not the State should have the right to impose these restrictions (745). Faith in the legislatures was reposed by K. Hanumanthiya (154-5) and A.R. Shastri (767).
62. VII C.A.D. 735 (T.D. Bhargava) and accepted by B.R. Ambedkar (741, 780); see also 774 (T.T. Krishnamachari); 776-7 (D. Gupta).
63. VII C.A.D. 750 (G. Das); 752 (J. Singh—only in passing); 754 (K. Hanumanthiya); 760-1 (B. Prashad on the need for a powerful State); 767 (A.R. Shastri); 771 (T.T. Krishnamachari); 776 (D. Gupta).
64. This attitude seemed to have continued in the Supreme Court where the Court appears to have interpreted the restrictions at face value without examining the reasonableness of the restrictions that were imposed.
65. *Romesh Thappar* v. *State of Madras* A.I.R. 1950 S.C. 124; *Express Newspapers* v. *Union of India*, A.I.R. 1958 S.C. 578; *Sakal Newspapers* v. *Union of India* A.I.R. 1962 S.C. 305; *Bennett Coleman & Co. Ltd.* v. *Union of India* A.I.R. 1973 S.C. 106. Note also the *Report of the Press Commission* (1952-4) 358.

66. This was forcefully stated by the P.C. in *Arnold* v. *King* (1914) 41 I.A. 149 at 167 quoted in *M.S.N. Sharma* v. *Sri Krishan Sharma* A.I.R. 1959 S.C. 395 at pr. 13 p. 402 followed in *Ramnarayan* v. *State* A.I.R. 1970 M.P. 102. See further H.M. Seervai: *Constitutional Law of India* (1975) 346.
67. *Arnold* v. *King* (1914) 41 I.A. 149 at 169; for its post-constitutional implications see Seervai: *Constitutional Law of India* (1975) 346-7.
68. *Express Newspapers Ltd.* v. *Union of India* A.I.R. 1958 S.C. 578.
69. *Ibid.* prs. 227-70 pp. 634-43.
70. *Ibid.* prs. 134-5 p. 615; pr. 144 p. 616 relying on *Grosjean* v. *American Press Co.* (1935) 297 U.S. 233.
71. *Ibid.* prs. 159-60 pp. 619-20.
72. *Ibid.* pr. 160 p. 620.
73. *Ibid.* pr. 160 p. 620. "A possible eventuality of this type would not necessarily be a consequence within the contemplation of the legislature."
74. *Sakal Newspapers (P) Ltd.* v. *Union of India* A.I.R. 1962 S.C. 305.
75. *Ibid.* pr. 39 p. 314.
76. *Ibid.* pr. 29 p. 311-2, see also pr. 32 p. 313, pr. 44 p. 315 ("direct" and "immediate"); pr. 39 p. 314 "direct". Note the emphasis on "direct" impact at pr. 39 p. 314 and the statement that the result shall "still be 'direct' notwithstanding that it does not appear so on its face"; also see pr. 40 p. 314; pr. 42 p. 315; pr. 45 p. 315 (the reference to the danger to democracy; the discussion on intent at prs. 93-6 p. 315 is also interesting).
77. *R.C. Cooper* v. *Union of India* A.I.R. 1970 S.C. 564.
78. *Ibid.* pr. 56 p. 596.
79. *Ibid.* pr. 71A-72 pp. 600-1.
80. See further D.K. Singh: "What cannot be done directly cannot be done indirectly: Its meaning and logical status in constitutionalism" (1966) 29 *Modern L.R.* 273.
81. *Bennett Coleman & Co. Ltd.* v. *Union of India* A.I.R. 1973 S.C. 106.
83. *Ibid.* pr. 42 p. 120.
84. *Ibid.* pr. 43 pp. 120-1.
85. *Ibid.* pr. 44 p. 121.
86. *Ibid.* pr. 45. p. 121, pr. 49 p. 122 (after citing at pr. 47-8 p. 122 *Citizen Publishing Co.* v. *U.S.* (1969) 394 U.S. 131; *U.S.* v. *O'Brien* (1968) 391 U.S. 367. Cf. the approach of Beg. J. on this at prs. 160-1 pp. 150-1 emphasizing the object of the legislation and the fact that real evidence to suggest that the legislation served the purpose the government claimed it did.
87. pr. 119 p. 136—adhering to what is called the "pith and substance" doctrine: What is the pith and substance of this doctrine? On this doctrine note the case of *Gallagher* v. *Lynn* (1937) A.C. 863. This

case has been heavily criticized because it does not ask the question: What is this legislation in respect of? See H. Calvert: *Constitutional Law in Northern Ireland* (1968) 188-9; *ibid*: "*Gallagher* v. *Lynn* re-examined—a legislative fraud" 2 (1972) *Public Law* II and *R.* v. *Hume* (1972) decided by the Northern Ireland Court.

88. *Ibid.* prs. 121-26 pp. 139-41; prs. 140-42 pp. 144-5.
89. *Ibid.* pr. 126 pp. 140-1.
90. *Ibid.* pr. 36 pp. 118-19; prs. 47-49 pp. 121-2.
91. *State of Rajasthan* v. *Union of India* A.I.R. 1977 S.C. 1318 prs. 114-16 p. 1397 (per Chandrachud J.) pr. 137 p. 140 (per Bhagwati J.). Here some legislators claimed that the dissolution of their legislatures by Presidential proclamation took away their right to property in their salaries. Only Fazl Ali, J.—it is submitted, correctly—decided that no right to property was involved (at pr. 192 p. 1432). The rest either did not decide the question or argued that the effect was too remote. In actual fact it was direct and inevitable within the meaning of test formulated in *Express Newspapers* (*supra*).
92. *Supra* note 68.
93. (1978) 1 S.C.C. 248.
94. Citing this idea from *All India Bank Employees* v. *National Insurance Tribunal* A.I.R. 1962 S.C. 171.
95. (1978) 1 S.C.C. 248 at pr. 33-4 pp. 310-12; (per Bhagwati J.); pr. 55 p. 327 (per Chandrachud J.).
96. *Ibid.* pr. 213 p. 399 (per Beg C.J.); pr. 128 p. 359, pr. 132 p. 369-a (per Kailasam J.).
97. *Ibid.*, pr. 27 p. 304 (per Bhagwati J.); pr. 68 p. 333, pr. 102 p. 346. and esp. pr. 104 pp. 346-7 (per Krishna Iyer J.).
98. *Ibid.* pr. 193 p. 346; cf. pr. 101 p. 345, pr. 102 p. 346.
99. *Ibid.* pr. 54 pp. 326-7.
100. *Ibid.* pr. 33 p. 310.
101. *Express Newspapers Pvt. Ltd.* v.*Union of India* A.I.R. 1986 SC 872, per Sen J. at pr. 76 p. 900 esp. pr. 77 p. 909 cf. Venkataramiah J. at pr. 200 p. 953, Misra J. pr. 206 p. 954.
102. *Ibid.*, pr. 77 p. 909 follow in *Bennett Coleman* v. *Union of India* A.I.R. 1973 S.C. 106; *R. C. Cooper* v. *Union of India* A.I.R. 1970 S. C. 564. However, this version of the direct and immediate effect is far too narrow.
103. *IE Newspapers* (*Bombay*) *P. Ltd.* v. *Union of India* A.I.R. 1986 S. C. 515.
104. *Ibid.*, prs. 31-7 pp. 527-9.
105. *Ibid.*, prs. 38-9 pp. 529-31 where it does not really look at the implications of the earlier case law or direct/indirect effects but merely quotes extracts from it after a cursory summary of the facts of earlier judgments.
106. *P. L. Lakhanpal* v. *Union of India* A. I. R. 1982 Delhi 167.

107. *M/s Inland Commercial (Tpt) Service* v. *Union of Journalists* A.I.R. 1982 Delhi 393.
108. *P. L. Lakhanpal* (*supra* note 106) pr. 17 p. 174.
109. See the Gujarat High Court decision on government publications and the right to reply: *Manubhai Shah* v. *Life Insurance Corporation of India*, A. I. R. 1981 Guj 15.
110. *P.L. Lakhanpal* (*supra* note 106) pr. 12 p. 172.
111. *Ibid.* pr. 15 p. 173.
112. *Ibid.* pr. 14 p. 173.
113. *Ibid.* pr. 17 p. 174.
114. *Ibid.* pr. 15 p.173 col. 2.
115. *M/s Inland Commercial* (*supra* note 107) pr. 32 p. 402.
116. This is exactly what the whole debate in the Kuldip Nayar *Report on News Agencies* (1978) and the *Report of the Second Press Commission* (1982) is about—see *supra* Chapter II.
117. Section 5 (2) Telegraph Act, 1885.
118. Section 20 Post Office Act, 1892.
119. *Report of the Second Press Commission* (1982) prs. 158-67 pp. 62-3.
120. *Bennett Coleman* v. *Union of India* A. I. R. 1973 S. C. 106.
121. *Sakal Newspapers* v. *Union of India* A. I. R. 1962 S. C. 305.
122. *P. L. Lakhanpal* (*supra* note 96) does not refer to these cases at all and *M/s Inland Commercial* (*supra* note 107) uses the 'direct' doctrine in *Sakal* (at pr. 24 p. 401) in a restrictive way and makes a cursory reference to both cases at pr. 26 p. 401.
123. *Report of the Second Press Commission* (1982) prs. 97-102; pp. 159-60; cf. Minority prs. 112-7 pp. 243-4.
124. *K. Narayan* v. *State* A. I. R. 1973 Kerala 97.
125. *Bank of India Affairs Association, M. P.* v. *Bank of India* (1979) M. P. L. J. 561.
126. *Report of the Second Press Commission* (1982) prs. 122-4 p. 97.
127. *Ushodaya Publications (P) Ltd.* v. *Government of A. P.* A. I. R. 1981 A. P. 109.
128. *Ibid.* pr. 11 p. 116 (relying on *Maneka Gandhi* v. *Union of India* A. I. R. 1978 S.C. 578).
129. *Ibid.* prs. 8-9 pp. 114-5 referring to *Sakal* (*supra* note 121) and *Bennett Coleman* (*supra* note 120).
130. *Ibid.* pr. 11 pp. 115-6.
131. *Report of the Second Press Commission* (1982) pr. 18 p. 35.
132. *Ushodaya Publications* (*supra* note 127) pr. 21 p. 120.
133. *Ibid.* pr. 21 p. 120.
134. *e.g., Report of the Second Press Commission* (1982), prs. 123-4 p. 99.
135. For direct forms of pre-censorship *e.g., Virendra* v. *State of Punjab* A. I. R. 1957 S. C. 896.
136. R. Dhavan: *The Supreme Court of India: A Socio-legal Analysis of its Juristic Techniques* (1977) Chapters I & II.

137. *Ibid.*, Chapter IV.
138. *Ushodaya Publications* (*supra* note 127) pr. 23 p. 120.
139. *Ibid.* prs. 27-8 pp. 121-2.
140. Cf. J. D. M. Derrett: "Lawyers as Leaders" (Paper at School of Oriental and African Studies, London).
141. R. Dhavan: *Justice on Trial: The Supreme Court Today* (1980).
142. *Romesh Thappar* v. *State of Madras* A. I. R. 1950 S. C. 124.
143. *Brij Bhushan* v. *State of Delhi* A. I. R. 1950 S. C. 127.
144. Article 19 (2) Constitution of India as unamended in 1951. The Constitution (First Amendment) Act, 1951 added public order to the list of permissible reasonable restrictions.
145. *State of Bihar* v. *Shaibala Devi* A. I. R. 1952 S. C. 329.
146. *Ibid.* at pr. 4 p. 330 col. 2.
147. *Report of the Press Commission* (1952-54) pr. 969 p. 363.
148. *Ibid.* pr. 1144 p. 443.
149. *Ramjilal Modi* v. *State of U. P.* A. I. R. 1957 S. C. 620.
150. *Ibid.* at pr. 9 p. 623.
151. *Kedar Nath* v. *State of Bihar* A. I. R. 1962 S. C. 955.
152. *Niharendu Datt Majumdar* v. *R.* A. I. R. 1942 F. C. 38.
153. *R.* v. *Sadashiv Narayan Bhalerao* (1947) 74 I. A. 89 approving the formulation in the famous *Tilak* trial, *Bal G.T.* v. *Queen Empress* (1898) 22 Bom. 528.
154. *Babulal Parate* v. *State of Maharashtra* A. I. R. 1961 S. C. 884; see further *R. M. Lohia* v. *State* A. I. R. 1968 All. 110 and *Madhu Limaye* v. *S. D. M. Monghyr* A. I. R. 1971 S. C. 2487 generally.
155. *Supdt., Central Prison* v. *Ram Manohar Lohia* A. I. R. 1960 S. C. 633.
156. *Ibid.* pr. 13 p. 640.
157. H. M. Seervai: *Constitutional Law of India* (1975) Vol. I, 369.
158. *Ibid.* I, 368.
159. *Santok Singh* v. *Delhi Administration* A. I. R. 1973 S. C. 1691 on Section 9 of the Punjab Security of the State Act, 1953.
160. *Brij Bhushan* v. *State of Delhi* A. I. R. 1950 S. C. 129.
161. *Ibid.*
162. *Virendra* v. *State of Punjab* A. I. R. 1957 S. C. 896.
163. *Ibid.* at pr. 11 p. 901.
164. *Ibid.* at pr. 12 p. 901.
165. H. M. Seervai: *Constitutional Law of India* (1975) Vol. I 365.
166. *Gopal Das* v. *State of Assam* A. I. R. 1934 Assam 193.
167. *e.g.* Code of Criminal Procedure (Tamil Nadu) Amendment Ordinance (12 of) 1981 replaced by Indian Penal Code and Code of Criminal Procedure (Tamil Nadu) Amendment Act (13 of) 1982; Indian Penal Code and Code of Criminal Procedure (Orissa Amendment) Act (13 of) 1962 (16 May, 1962).

168. Bihar Bill to amend the Indian Penal Code and the Code of Criminal Procedure in their Application to the State of Bihar, 1983.
169. *e.g.*, Lord Denning in *Hubbard* v. *Pitt* (1975) 3 All. E. R. 1; Justice Black in his dissent, in *Brown* v. *Lsuioiana* (1964) 383 U. S. 1; and his majority judgment in *Adderley* v. *Florida* (1966) 385 U. S. 39.
170. See *Maneka Gandhi* v. *Union of India* (1978) 1 S. C. C. 248; see further *Charles Sobhraj* v. *Supdt.*, *Central Jail* A.I.R. 1978 S.C. 1514; *M.H. Hoskot* v. *State of Maharashtra* A. I. R. 1978 S. C. 1548; *Sunil Batra* v. *Delhi Administration* A. I. R. 1978 S. C. 1675; *Hussainara Khatoon* v. *State of Bihar* A. I. R. 1979 S. C. 1360, 1362, 1377, 1819.
171. Article 19 (2) Constitution of India.
172. *V. G. Row* v. *State of Madras* A. I. R. 1952 S. C. 196.
173. *Ibid.* p. 200.
174. *Maneka Gandhi* v. *Union of India* (1978) 1 S. C. C. 243.
175. *e. g.* on contempt *E.M.S. Namboodripad* v. *T.N. Nambiar* A. I. R. 1970 S.C. 2015 and H.M. Seervai: *Constitutional Law of India* (1975) Vol. I, 361-3. On defamation, the constitutional question has not been fairly and squarely raised but see *State* v. *Editor*, *Matrubhumi* A.I.R. 1955 Orissa 36 at 39 and the comment of H.M. Seervai (*supra*) I, 364. The issue is generally discussed in R. Dhavan: *Contempt of Court and the Press* (1982), Indian Law Institute.
176. Note the various restrictions listed earlier.
177. *e.g.*, *E.M.S. Namboodripad* v. *T.N. Nambiar* A. I. R. 1970 S.C. 2015 see further R. Dhavan: *Contempt of Court and the Press* (1982).
178. In *Supdt. and Remembrancer, Legal Affairs, West Bengal* v. *S. Bhowmick* A. I. R. 1981 S. C. 917 the Court decided that *in camera* trials interfered with the requirements of the process clause to deprive the accused of all pre-trial process rights. Cf. *Anthony* v. *State* (1975) Cr. L. J. 304; *Naresh* v. *State of Maharashtra* A.I.R. 1967 S. C. 17. However, no broad constitutional discussion took place on any aspect of the constitutionality of Official Secrets legislation other than to refer to the process requirements (*ibid.* pr. 22 p. 923).
179. *Kedar Nath* v. *State of Bihar* A.I.R. 1962 S.C. 995.
180. *Romesh Thappar* v. *State of Madras* A.I.R. 1950 S.C. 124; *Brij Bhushan* v. *State of Delhi*, A.I.R. 1950 S.C. 129.
181. *Roth* v. *U. S.* (1957) 354 U. S. 476.
182. *Hamdard Dawakhana* v. *Union of India* A.I.R. 1960 S.C. 554; Note the Law Commission seeking a amendment to make indecent advertisements a punishable offence, *Indian Express* 22 September 1984.
183. Questions of 'broad' reasonableness have been raised in *Ranjit Udeshi* v. *State of Maharashtra* A.I.R. 1965 S.C. 1881. Most of the questions are questions relating to 'discretionary powers' (an equality Article 14 question). However, all this is in the shadow of

an understanding that having fallen within the typology the legislation is almost impregnable.

184. Questions of nexus between the power and actual or potential exercise were really asked in *Romesh Thappar* (*supra* note 180) and *Brij Bhushan* (*supra* note 180) and *Supdt., Central Prison* v. *Lohia*, A.I.R. 1960 S.C. 633. "Discretionary Power" questions were asked in *Virendra* v. *State of Punjab* A.I.R. 1957 S.C. 896 and, thereafter, less frequently. So, it is assumed that even discretionary power questions are no longer important given an understanding of the entrenched status given to the constitutional categories.

185. Discussed in Chapter 2 *supra* and Part III *infra*.

186. *Ranjit Udeshi* v. *State of Maharashtra* A.I.R. 1965 S.C. 881. For a more balanced judgment now see *Samaresh Bose* v. *Amal Mitra* A.I.R. 1986 S.C. 967 at prs. 34-5 pp. 982-3.

187. *Ibid.*, pr. 3. p. 884 col. 2. The technical argument that the final responsibility of deciding the matter belongs to the judge does not really dispose the issue for expert opinion was deemed to be admissible and later Justice Hidayatullah himself relied on English experts (at p. 890).

188. Justice Hidayatullah has himself written an eminently readable autobiography entitled *My Own Boswell* (1979).

189. *Ranjit Udeshi's* case (*supra*) at pr. 8 p. 885, pr. 9 p. 886.

190. *Ibid.*, pr. 21 p. 888.

191. *Ibid.*, pr. 3 p. 884.

192. *Ibid.*, pr. 12 p. 896 rejecting American decisions on the issue of *scienter*. The judgments may not be totally reliable but the issue needs to be explored.

193. *R.M.D.C. Chamarabaghwallah* v. *State of Bombay* A.I.R. 1957 S.C. 699 (on gambling); *Coverjee* v. *Excise Commissioner* A.I.R. 1954 S.C. 220 (on selling liquor). Cf. see *K. Krishnan* v. *State of J. & K.* A.I.R. 1967 S.C. 1368 but now see *Har Shankar* v. *Dy. Excise and Taxation Commissioner* (1975) 1 S.C.C. 737; *Fateh Chand* v. *State of Maharashtra* (1977) 2 S.C.C. 670. See further R. Dhavan: "The Morality of Trade—A Socialist Supreme Court's animadversions to rural debt collectors" (1978) 1 *S.C.C.* (*Jour*) 10.

194. *Hamdard Dawakhana* v. *Union of India* A.I.R. 1960 S.C. 554.

195. *Infra* Part II.

196. *Supt. and Remembrancer Legal Affairs, West Bengal* v. *S. Bhowmick* A.I.R. 1981 S.C. 917.

197. Justice Chawla's decision in *Indira Gandhi* v. *J.C. Shah Commission* (1980) ILR 1 Delhi 552.

198. *Supra* note 2.

199. see *Union of India* v. *S.S. Singh* A.I.R. 1961 S.C. 493 esp. the judgment of Justice J.L. Kapur and the pragmatic compromises of Justice Gajendragadkar.

200. *S.P. Gupta* v. *Union of India* A.I.R. 1982 S.C. 149.
201. Thus, this question is largely ignored in *S. P. Gupta* v. *Union of India* (*supra*). While it is true that the legal test must be relevant to the litigation, the *constitutional* test must be more widely countenanced with reference to the social and political mischief sought to be caused.
202. *e.g., S.S.R.C.* v. *Nasse* (1980) A.C. 1028; *Burmah Oil Ltd.* v. *Bank of England* (1980) A.C. 1090.
203. See *In re Mulgaonkar* A.I.R. 1978 S.C. 727; *In re Shri Sham Lal* (1978) 2 S.C.C. 479.
204. See R. Dhavan and Balbir Singh: "Publish and be damned—The Press at the bar of the Supreme Court" (1979) 21 *J.I.L.I.* 1-30
205. *Gunpati* v. *Nagisul Hasan* A.I.R. 1954 S.C. 636; *M.S.N. Sharma* v. *Sri Krishan Sharma* A.I.R. 1959 S.C. 395.
206. *In re Article 143* A.I.R. 1965 S.C. 745. Note there is a new case involving the Kerala High Court and the Kerala legislature admitted for hearing in the Supreme Court where the judges were deemed to be in contempt because they gave relief in a freedom of press case to a petitioner.
207. For recent examples see *Chief Justice of India* case (1981) XXVI PD (No. 2) 2 (discussion of Judge in Parliament—Lok Sabha); *Govind Bhatt* (1982) XXVII PD (No. 1) 18 (former Chief Justice criticizing an Act of Legislature—Karnataka); *Shraddha Devi* v. *K. C. Pant* (1982) XXVII PD (No. 2) 17 (returning officers and court control, Vidhan Sabha (U.P)); *Varsha Joshi and K.W. Desai* case (1982) XXVII PD (No. 1) 14 (proceedings against Speaker on allowing discussion on a sub judice matter-Gujarat).

For recent head-on controversies between the legislatures and the Courts see *State of Kerala* v. *R. Sudarshan* A.I.R. 1984 Kerala 1 (F. B.) and the *Eenadu* case in Karnataka (see M.P. Jain: *Parliamentary Privileges and the Press* (1984 epilogue). In both these cases the legislature defied court orders giving relief to journalists found in contempt of the legislatures.

PART TWO

Protecting the Institutions of State

4

COURTS AND THEIR CONTEMPT

I

Courts are the legitimating arm of the semi-autocratic State and the pride of 'liberal' democracy. Classical political theory grounded in overworked principles of separation of powers awards greater credibility to regimes which allow a judiciary to 'independently' adjudicate on the affairs of State. Not to have a judiciary which goes some way towards this overworked image characterizes the State in question as a non-democratic authoritarian regime.[1] In itself, this must indubitably pose a paradox. The defence of democracy is left in the hands of an elite; and, any attempt to relieve this elite of its custodial role is considered to offend 'liberal' democracy. This faith in the judiciary is justified either on the weak principle that any re-assessment of the exercise of power by State authorities by an independent institution must, perforce, be good. It is also justified on the strong principle that judges are concerned with providing an interpretative rectification which is, at least, concerned with commutative—if not distributive—justice. That Marxists[2] have concerned themselves with a defense of the 'rule of (bourgeois) law' on the basis of moderating commutative role of judges against the tyrannies—both actual and potential—of the State, lends credibility to this justification!

Making 'law' or some version of 'justice' central to our understanding of the judiciary, over-proposes the case for the judiciary without enriching our understanding of the judiciary in the context of a theory of power and State. It is impossible to understand the law of contempt without understanding the position of the judiciary in the overall context of the State and without some kind of understanding of the kind of 'power filter' and judiciary has become for emergent groups in a transforming political economy.

By itself very little of the law of contempt is really concerned with the 'efficient' execution of the court's powers. The law of civil contempt is concerned with obeying the orders of the Court. While the difference between civil and criminal contempt is conceptually thin, only a marginal part of the latter law of contempt is concerned with the court's powers to enforce law and order during the sessions of the court. The bulk of the law of contempt is not directly concerned with the efficiency of the law. Known as constructive contempt, this whole area of the law of contempt is concerned with notions of 'status', 'reputation', the institutional exclusivity of the judicial process and creating an aura around the judicial process. This whole development took place largely as a result of the development of modern journalism and the advent of political attacks on the judiciary.[3]

But protecting the judiciary was by no means easy. It could not be protected on the principles of democracy because it was not by itself a democratic institution. It could not be protected for reasons of State because it was claimed that it occupied a semi-autonomous existence independent of the State. It could not be cloaked in official secrecy because its quest for legitimacy depended very greatly on the openness of its proceedings and the fact that it gave detailed and written reasons in support of its decisions. Its strength lay in the fact that it floated an ideology which obtained consent for what it was doing from the populace at large and from those who were the beneficiaries of the judicial process. But this consent was not bought and sold in the marketplace of democracy. It lay beyond and above. Democracy operates concepts like 'demand', 'expectations', 'want' and 'need' at one level and concepts like 'power', 'control' and 'authority' at another. To accommodate democracy judges invented techniques of constitutional consecration whereby certain 'wants', 'powers' etc. were consecrated as law. The modern judiciary had little choice but to accept as an objective fact the 'laws' which were consecrated by the political process. The whole jumble of constitutional law is devoted to disguising this simple fact. Critics of the Supreme Court of India during the Emergency (1975-77) attack the judiciary for its lack of subtlety in consecrating the detention laws of the Emergency.[4] Hedged in from all sides the modern judiciary is a very limited creature. It does not create much of the law it deliberates on. Nor does it have an extensive freedom to manufacture the equity with which the applicative use of law is moderated. Its quest for self-definition rests on exaggerated claims of what it is able to do. Unlike the other organs of the State it cannot legitimate itself on the basis of democracy. Nor can it wholly create an illusion of affairs by appealing to 'justice'. It remains, however, a powerful arena in which many things can be re-negotiated, and its litigative and lawyering processes lend themselves to much manipulation.

The law of contempt remains a weak attempt to retain a composition of illusions about the judiciary both as a corrective of the exercise of political power as well as an instrument of justice. Yet this attempt runs foul of other illusions which are a part of democratic expectations. The 'law of contempt' rests uncomfortably on the fact that its social and political objectives are to provide 'status' for an institution which is otherwise *sui generis*; it usually provides this status within the constraints of a democratic system which theoretically does not suffer such claims gladly. In order to achieve its objective the law of contempt has to be quick, decisive and to ensure that its exercise is not itself an occasion for controversy. For the law of contempt would be self-defeating if its use excited the very controversies it was designed to exclude. If the law of contempt suffers criticism in its efforts to stifle criticism it suffers even more in its attempts to prevent an abuse of the contempt process. It uses a 'summary procedure'.[5] It does not allow truth as a defence. It does not readily admit the plea of public interest. Such a 'law' is difficult to defend in a modern society in which ascribed status is not accorded to any process other than democracy. The American law of contempt has to be purged of many of the absolutist techniques which mar the English law.[6] The English law of contempt was itself radically altered by the Contempt of Courts Act 1981 so that it could be justified more easily on the basis of the ideologies of liberal democracy.

The Indian law of contempt rests on very insecure foundations. It grew as an analogue to 'sedition' laws and was in its present statutory form in 1926 when its applicability to the Indian judicial system was in question. The 'British Indian' State was determined to provide protection to the judiciary even if this meant courting unpopularity. At least what was protected was not disclosed. The post-Independence State is marginally ambivalent about the judiciary. The judiciary is simultaneously a legitimating device for the political and constitutional system as a whole as well as a bloody nuisance in which embarrassing decisions can be made against the other institutions of the State as well as the political masters of these institutions. While the British had limited the potential uses of the judiciary, the Constitution has structured a judiciary which is susceptible to indiscriminate use.[7] Support for the imperial British judiciary came from the rest of the State, lawyers and the projected ideology of the law. An ambivalence marks the nature of the support of the judiciary in post-independence India. Its indiscriminate users are more concerned with the immediate advantages that they are able to wreak from the litigative uses it has to offer rather than creating a systematic framework which can be justified to a wider constituency of people. Forced to protect their own status through the law of contempt, discerning Indian judges are painfully aware that this law cannot be easily defended on the basis of contemporary political ideology. Yet it may be risky to relax the rigours of this law. Disrespect of the judiciary is on the increase.[8] The incidence of contempt petitions against those who criticise the judiciary has increased.

Such petitions linger on to benefit the prestige of the contemnors. This reflects on the vulnerability of the judiciary, its own capacity for over-sensitivity as well as the manner in which the judiciary can be trapped by its own processes in an unequal battle with an unscrupulous adversary, on the latter's terms.

The press in India reflects local power and influence with a tenacity that delights as it intimidates. To the press the judiciary is not a dispenser of justice but just an arena in which social and political conflicts get trapped in the eye of public attention. And, if the press is to reflect local power, it can hardly resist superimposing the 'press' game on the litigation game. Since both games in their Indian idiom are essentially vexatious and frivolous, what emerges is a nonsense which seeks to question the legitimating function of the law of contempt. The development of the law of contempt in India is wound up with the development of the press. Both developments are characterised by ruthless use. What emerges is a jumble in which 'law' and 'social politics' are not dignified by even a notional separation.

II

The courts emerged as the second arm of the British administration in India. Though the courts sought to legitimate British rule in India, they were under constant attack. The newspapers in the late eighteenth century were open in their assaults on the judiciary and the executive alike and newsmen like Hicky were certainly crippled by a combination of collusive executive and judicial action.[9] It was not until the middle of the nineteenth century that the courts began to feel the pressure of indigenous insult. The first few cases did not involve the press but did entail the courts protecting the dignity of its processes from irreverent outrage[10]—even though the courts were in some doubt as to the range of its summary contempt jurisdiction.[11] The first broadside from the press came from an English owned paper, the *Englishman*,[12] which had questioned the integrity of a distinguished Indian High Court judge and refused to retract this allegation in a later review petition. The courts used this opportunity to establish its contempt powers in respect of the press and left the issue with the plea that the press which "is one of the main bulwarks of the rights of the people" should make sure "that there should be no misrepresentation and no wilful or unfair concealment of the facts; and that those who deny infallibility to the Judges shall not claim infallibility for themselves."[13] A warning was given. A totally different picture of the potential use of the contempt jurisdiction emerged when it was against the *Bengalee*—the newspaper of a distinguished Indian leader, Surendranath Banerjee, who had criticised the obstinacy of an English judge in asking that a Hindu idol be presented in court.[14] Over the dissent of an Indian judge, Surendranath Banerjee was punished for contempt, not just let off with a warning and acceptance of apology. Meanwhile, the Indian press began to attack the administration of justice often making important public interest points. A historian looking at the press between 1885-1905 has observed:

> Complaints regarding the expensiveness of getting justice, of the delay in deciding cases, the corruption that existed in courts, occupied the press at length because the editors were in many cases themselves lawyers.[15]

Though in 1913 the courts promised to be sparing in their use of the contempt jurisdiction,[16] it continued to pose a threat. As the National movement for independence caught up with the courts, the latter were criticised. Criticism of the trial of the Indian leader, Lokmanya Tilak, led to a severe contempt action.[17] Gandhi himself was cited for contempt in 1920 but let off (presumably, by way of strategy) on the grounds that the "principles of contempt which are quite familiar in England are imperfectly known or understood in India".[18] Gandhi expressed definite views about the press and the public interest which were reiterated years later by the Sunday Times in the *Thalidomide* case in England in 1973.[19]

Meanwhile, some doubt was expressed as to the extent to which the summary process of contempt could be used.[20] Even greater doubt was expressed as to whether the contempt jurisdiction could be used to protect the lower judiciary (other than the

High Courts) from attacks on its judges or interference with its processes.[21] The British government was anxious to provide the same protection to the judiciary which the wide ranging laws of sedition and incitement to offence provided for the executive. Earlier proposals to enable this were not taken further because of World War I.[22] Anxious not to be seen to be making a significant change, the British presented the proposed legislation as technical, necessary and humane. Sir Alexander Muddiman, who piloted the Bill, observed:

> Although in one direction we are enlarging the jurisdiction in a contempt, we are fettering the power of the courts in regard to punishment. As the courts stand at present they are unlimited. We seek in the Bill to fetter those powers. . . . We reduce the punishments to six months whereas I am informed the power now vested in the courts in India is as unlimited as it is in England. These are the main points of the Bill and I do not think that at this stage I need detain the House much longer. The Bill affirms and confirms the jurisdiction of the courts; it confers the jurisdiction of chartered High Courts on certain other High Courts. It further limits and controls the powers of the High Courts as provided in the Bill in respect of punishment.[23]

The imprisonment and fine thresholds (of six months and Rs. 2,000 respectively) was high enough both as a deterrent and a symbolic act. Sir Alexander's explanation was broadly speaking accepted by a lawyer dominated Assembly some of whom nurtured the thought that future court action could be used to whittle down the power.[24] In fact, the Bill had given the Courts a total power to deal with attacks on them and its processes by a summary procedure. Kelkar, an editor who had himself been the victim of a High Court contempt case was one of the few persons who was alert enough to see the sequel between the law of sedition and the contempt jurisdiction. He went on to say: "Government is giving individually to each judicial officer the whole of the artificial protection which they claim for themselves as a corporate body."[25] Sir Alexander was not able, however, to persuade the Assembly to extend the Chief Commissioner's contempt power to deal with contempt of its subordinate courts or increase the fine tariff so that it was unlimited.[26] He treated these concessions as representing his flexibility in accepting half a loaf of bread instead of the whole.[27] In actual fact, he had been able to obtain what he wanted.

The 1926 statute was amended because of an inconvenient Lahore High Court decision claiming an unlimited power to punish outside the prescribed tariff.[28] Attempts to discuss the problems of the press were muzzled both on this occasion and in 1939 when Mr. Datta raised the question of the general amendment of the 1926 statute.[29] Even after independence, a general discussion was not allowed when a 1950 statute gave Chief Commissioners' courts the power to deal with the contempt of courts subordinate to them—an issue on which Sir Alexander Muddiman had been defeated in 1926.[30] Again, when the 1926 statute was consolidated in 1952, no general discussion on the problems of the law of contempt in relation to the press or otherwise was created.[31]

Let us examine the effect of the legislation. The 1926 and later the consolidated 1952 statute formalised the general power possessed by the English High Court. Basically, this meant the power to enforce its processes (civil contempt), and the power to punish contempt in the face of the court, the scandalizing of judges and the interference with the due administration of justice (criminal contempt). Rigorously interpreted this could have the effect of stifling criticism of judges and judicial decisions by lowering its dignity as well as muzzling the press as soon as it becomes clear that the hearing of a criminal or civil case is 'imminent'. The offence was one of strict liability and the person's intentions or motives were treated as irrelevant. Justification (truth) and 'fair comment' in the public interest were not defences. An accused could only plead that the words or action did not interfere with the due administration of justice or affect the dignity of the court. He was virtually at the mercy of the Court and could negotiate the leniency of the court on the basis of a retraction or an apology.

Bearing this in mind, let us consider how the Contempt of Courts Act, 1926 affected the press. The contempt jurisdiction was used quite ruthlessly—often with severe sentences.[32] This may have something to do with the extreme comments that were made of the courts. While the jurisdiction to punish the press was being phased out in other parts of the Common Law world, it was being more and more firmly established in India.[33] It was used to punish attacks and criticism of the judges and to ensure that the judiciary did not lose its social legitimacy.[34]

It is by no means being suggested that the large bulk of the cases did not deservedly attract the attention of the contempt jurisdiction or were border-line cases. On the contrary, a large number of the cases constituted clear contempt and fell fairly and squarely within the contempt jurisdiction. But dealing as they did with a vast *tour de force* of attacks on the judiciary, the High Courts of India often lost sight of the difference between a fair and justified criticism of the judiciary and an unfair and unwarranted attack or interference with the due administration of justice. As the volume of the contempt cases increased in the docket of the courts, the courts' sensitivity to such distinctions also diminished.[35]

The courts also used this jurisdiction to silence press comment when a cause of action was pending or 'imminent'. But as the nature of the contempt jurisdiction came to be better understood, the contempt power was also used as part of the litigation strategies of private litigants. Disgruntled litigants having lost their case—or uneasy about its outcome—would take the issue to the local press only to be invited back to the legal forum to answer charges for contempt.[36] Such contempt cases were also welcomed as an opportunity to further air the grievances of litigants. The pathology of Indian litigation has thus transformed the contempt jurisdiction into a strategic weapon.

Let us now consider the impact of the promulgation of India's Constitution which guaranteed freedom of speech but permitted 'reasonable restrictions' in the interests, *inter alia*, of contempt of court.[37] The issue of contempt of court did not receive critical attention by the Constituent Assembly. There is no discussion on it in the Interim Report on Fundamental Rights, the discussion on the Interim Report, the Draft Constitution or the discussion of the latter.[38] Although J.P. Narayan wanted a forum for complaints against all officials, including judges, the issue of contempt of court was not raised.[39] 'Contempt of court' was suggested as a restraint by Krishnamachari on October 17, 1949 just a few months before the Constitution was adopted.[40] After a discussion on whether the restrictions had to be qualified by the concept of reasonableness,[41] R.K. Sidhwa and B. Das attacked the contempt provisions on the grounds that the judges were being converted into a kind of 'super god' and that contempt of court was really an instrument to keep the people down.[42] This caused Naziruddin Ahmad to emphasize the need to conduct "a trial in an atmosphere of calm".[43] The President, sensing a general attack on the judiciary as a whole, administered the rebuke: "[The] individual judge. . . may have erred, but we should not cast aspersions on the judiciary as a whole."[44] The argument went no further.

The courts did not create any deep constitutional wrangles. They accepted that if there was a law of contempt of court it was a reasonable restriction within the meaning of the restrictions permitted by the Constitution.[45] This was treated as axiomatic, something that did not require an extended discussion. The reasonableness of the law of contempt as a restriction on the exercise of the freedom of speech was for the most part assumed; and, indeed, continues to be assumed.[46] The constitutional guarantee has not made any fundamental difference to the approach that the courts had to the contempt jurisdiction. The American approach that the courts must use the contempt jurisdiction only when there is a clear and present danger was not accepted.[47] Nor was some alternative balancing mechanism accepted. In later years, Justice Krishna Iyer echoed the sentiment that the courts should be a little more tolerant in contempt cases because the jurisdiction was a "vague and wandering jurisdiction with uncertain frontiers". He added:

> [A] sensitive and suspect power to punish . . . vested in the

> prosecutor, a law which makes it a crime to publish regardless of truth and public good and permits a process of *brevi manu* conviction may unwittingly (en)trench upon civil liberties and so the special jurisdiction and jurisprudence bearing on [the] contempt jurisdiction must be delineated and operated with serious circumspection by the higher judicial echelons. So it is that as the palladium of our freedoms, the Supreme Court and the High Courts, must vigilantly protect free speech even against judicial umbrage—a delicate but sacred duty whose discharge demands tolerance and detachment of a high order.[48]

But this analysis which may have led to a partial policy of restraint has not resulted in the creation of a new constitutional doctrine to balance the contempt power and the free speech requirements.[49]

The bulk of the cases before the Supreme Court after 1950 and before the new legislation of 1971 took effect have been concerned with the contempt of scandalizing the judges.[50] The Supreme Court's expectation that such cases would be rare has been belied by its docket. While constantly taking the view that the Court should not be strict, it has evolved a strict law. Thus, in a 1984 case, the court let off a Chief Minister of Kashmir, who allegedly said that people should not follow the orders of the Court on the grounds that he may not have made the statement but at the same time affirmed the strict liability of the law.[51] The *cause celebre* before the Court arose when the Court punished a Marxist politician because he had said that the judges suffered from class bias.[52] The Court, through the Chief Justice, took pains not to use the 'scandalizing' jurisdiction to cover cases other than serious allegations of corruption but went out of its way to prove to the erring Chief Minister that he had also misunderstood his Marxism and was, therefore, entitled to a reduction in fine.[53] This made a leading Communist weekly react by quipping that if people were going to have their sentences reduced for misunderstood Marxism, the queue of offenders demanding clemency before the Supreme Court was likely to be very long.[54]

Apart from the contempt cases, the Supreme Court has not really taken the law any further even where the press (or politicians) have commented on a pending case—perhaps in the public interest. Justice Kapur delivered a significant unreported judgment that the mere filing of a First Information Report before the police did not mean that the press was silenced.[55] But this point was not picked up until it was clarified by the Contempt of Courts Act, 1971.[56] The limits of permissible comment were not explored by the court even though the court got an excellent opportunity to do so in two significant cases where the newspapers had reported speeches by politicians who could have claimed that they were simply commenting on contemporary events in the public interest.[57] Justice Bhagwati in a later case, tried to show that comments during the pendency of cases were justified even if they were misleading.[58] The implications of this were, however, incompletely worked out.

The cases before the High Courts represent a much more authentic and representative sample of press reporting about the judiciary. To begin with the bulk of the cases are not concerned with the scandalizing jurisdiction. They are concerned with interference with the due administration of justice. The scandalizing cases are either examples of the allegation of corruption or badly articulated criticism.[59] The cases dealing with comments on a pending or 'imminent' case often had a political flavour whether local or national. Press comments include allegations that the criminals were Communists[60] or that Communists were not getting a fair deal.[61] Politicians often made comments on criminal incidents—as for example, a rape case[62] or a riot.[63] A notice to answer charges for contempt was also issued to Jawaharlal Nehru because he made comments about the criminal nature of the activities of a political party when, unknown to him, some members of that party were being tried.[64] The courts discharged many of the notices against politicians[65] and, indeed, again judges where lawyers complained that judges were in contempt of their own court.[66] Sometimes—as in Nehru's case—on a basis which was then not open to the judges *i.e.* that Nehru had no reason to believe that proceedings were pending or imminent.[67] The Court overlooked the fact that contempt being an offence of strict liability such a defence before the 1971 statute was not available to the then Prime Minister of India. Some of the contempt cases were discharged as being only local in nature. Local situations excited local controversies. Thus, there were comments that the Raja of Kapurthala's treatment of his tenants,[68] or the pressures put on peasants who took advantage of the zamindari abolition reform,[69] or on the High Court interfering in University matters,[70] or the allegation that Congressmen were responsible for having the braids of women pulled,[71] or passing judgment on whether liquor was diluted,[72] or who sabotaged a mine,[73] or caused a flood.[74] Newspapers commented on the corruption and bias of politicians,[75] the police[76] and prosecutors[77] and the innocence or guilt of those taken into custody.[78] They also talked about private disputes and local controversies, labour matters or criminal cases.[79] All these were comments in pending or imminent cases. The Indian press is such that it does not always restrain itself to separate mere allegations from public interest issues. But there is no doubt that in a large number of these cases, the courts had ample opportunities to reconsider, re-interpret and re-value the law of contempt and the press's public and private interest in discussing matters which came before the court. The courts did not make many innovative changes. They punished severely in some cases; and in some cases simply let the newspaper off with a warning, a costs order and accepting an apology.[80] In some cases, like the *Statesman* case (1958),[81] the court suggested that reports which were mildly inaccurate but otherwise not very misleading would be treated as technical contempts and discharged with an apology.

By and large, the contempt jurisdiction was used to try and restrain clumsy reporting or prevent local politics from having a field day in reporting on pending and imminent cases. Occasionally, the cases involved the right to criticise the administration of justice or to campaign for an inquiry into the administration of justice. Such comments were accommodated by the courts to a limited extent. Again, in an occasional case like the *Blitz* case (1963)[82] the accused editor consciously claimed to comment on a pending case in the public interest. But the courts made little attempt to look into these matters in any depth. No clear statement about the limits of permissible discussion emerged even though the judgments of the Delhi High Court in the *Congress Party Split* case (1971)[83] and *Supersession of Judges* case[84] (1974) did insist on the right of the public to discuss matters of public importance even if such matters were pending determination before the courts.

But a movement for reform was afoot which began with a private Member's Bill on April Fools' day 1960[85] and—after consideration by two Committees[86] and considerable debate in Parliament—culminated in the Contempt of Courts Act, 1971. This movement for reform had a tortured development. To begin with the Sanyal Committee (1963) which first considered the matter put a brake on the reforming genius of any of its members by insisting that the contempt jurisdiction was given to the courts by the Constitution and it was outside the competence of the legislature to make any reformist proposals without a constitutional amendment.[87] The Committee then made some proposals—broadly speaking on the same lines as proposals and legislation in England[88]—making provision for appeals,[89] permitting a defence to innocent distributors who did not know a case was imminent or pending,[90] allowing fair and accurate reporting of judicial procedure[91] and permitting fair comments on a case after it had been disposed of.[92] It was essentially a lawyer's report which took into account contemporary changes in the jurisprudence of contempt case law in England. Five years elapsed before the matter was taken up by Parliament. The Bhargava Committee—a joint committee of both Houses of Parliament—retained a wide law of contempt, tied up loose ends in the law and suggested some changes. It laid down the exact time when proceedings would be deemed to be pending before which free comment was allowed.[93] It facilitated the making of complaints against the lower judiciary[94] and, while allowing for the fair and accurate reporting of judicial proceedings,[95] did not define with exactness the limits to which such comment could go. The court's power to exact unconditional apologies was limited[96] and a rule was incorporated that for a case to constitute contempt it must substantially interfere with the due administration of justice.[97] A new clause was to be added which would make it possible to punish judicial officers who committed contempt of their own courts.[98] Time limits were imposed within which contempt actions would be commenced[99] and village courts were to be exempted from the contempt jurisdiction.[100] The Minority Report—after much rhetoric about the British Raj[101]—raised the fundamental question of the press espousing the public interest[102] and tried to introduce a *mens rea* element by making contempt punishable only where there was a wilful or malicious intent.[103]

When all these matters went back to Parliament, the Law Minister made the unexpected manoeuvre of reverting back to the Sanyal Committee's argument that far-reaching changes in the law of contempt could not be made.[104] This led to a furious debate.[105] Although the Law Minister had to accept some changes which he did not want,[106] his manoeuvre succeeded in containing the reforming impulse of Parliament.

The Contempt of Courts Act, 1971 introduced the following new features in the law of contempt. Firstly, the Act carried a definition of contempt of court. 'Civil contempts' would henceforth involve only 'wilful default'. Criminal contempt could be committed only by "publication (whether by words, spoken or written, or by signs or by visible representations or otherwise) of any matter or the doing of any act whatsoever which—

(i) scandalizes or tends to scandalize, or lowers or tends to lower the authority of, any court; or

(ii) prejudices, or interferes, or tends to interfere with, the due course of a judicial proceeding; or

(iii) interferes or tends to interfere with, or obstructs, or tends to obstruct, the administration of justice in any other manner."[107]

The definition of criminal contempt was kept very wide. Secondly, the Act gave protection to innocent publishers and distributors from criminal contempts (other than scandalizing the judges) if they had reason to believe that court proceedings were pending at the time.[108] Thirdly, guidelines were laid down so that civil proceedings were deemed to commence with a plaint and criminal proceedings where a challan, charge-sheet or plaint is filed or where a court takes cognizance of proceedings.[109] Fourthly, the Act permitted fair and accurate accounts of proceedings in courts (except where such publication was prohibited)[110] and allowed "any fair comment on the merits of any case which has been heard or finally decided".[111] Whether this meant that a plea of justification (truth) could be offered as a defence is not clear. An *Explanation* to Section 12 suggested that a qualified apology could be made".[112] Fifthly, an important limitation was imposed that a sentence of imprisonment would not be imposed unless "the contempt is of such a nature that it substantially interferes, or tends to interfere with the administration of justice".[113] Sixthly—and this is related to the fifth point—the Act continued the policy of contempt legislation since 1926 to keep punishments within a limited threshold—in this case two thousand rupees or imprisonment for six months[114] subject to a premium on accepting an apology[115] and not sentencing where there is no substantial interference with the due course of justice.[116] Seventhly, the Act tried to reduce the extended use of contempt by limiting the right to initiate contempt proceedings in the hands of the higher judiciary, *viz.*, by the Courts *suo motu* through Advocates and Attorney Generals and designated law officers and on reference by subordinate courts to the High Court.[117] By a curious oversight, there is some question as to whether the High Court's power to *suo motu* issue notices for contempt in respect of contempts of subordinate courts was not specifically dealt with, and has given rise to controversy.[118] In addition, a limitation period of one year was also imposed.[119] Eighthly, an elaborate procedure was laid down for hearing contempt cases by certain kinds of benches in certain cases.[120] Provision was also made for appeals.[121] Ninthly, it was made clear that judges, magistrates and other persons acting judicially could also be found guilty of contempt of their own courts.[122] Finally, the Act seemed to preserve the law of contempt prevailing before the passing of the Act including the defence.[123] It was declared that new contempts had not been created.[124] This implied that, in spite of the new definition and other changes, nothing had really changed.

Let us now consider the impact of the Contempt of Courts Act, 1971. The passing of the Act coincided with a time when the courts were constantly under pressure because their orders were being flouted—no less by the government than by others.[125] The courts were constantly harassed with allegations of corruption and contempt cases were themselves used to give further and better circulation to the things that were being said.[126] The contempt jurisdiction was also used to further local controversies and settle personal scores. The *cause celebre* of the day was the *Baradakant Mishra* cases where a subordinate judicial officer carried a campaign against his own High Court and used the contempt jurisdiction to get more publicity.[127]

Under these circumstances the courts felt that they needed a strong and undiluted law of contempt. Confronted with the limiting effect of the Contempt of Courts Act, 1971, some of the High Courts made the gesture of approving the Sanyal Committee and Law Minister Gokhale's line of argument that such provisions of the new statute which conflicted with the inherent contempt powers of the High Courts as Courts of Record were unconstitutional and outside the competence of the legislature.[128] Equally, there was a tendency to ignore the provisions of the statute. The Supreme Court openly allowed a violation of the statute in allowing the plea of fair comment when a case was still pending.[129] Even the Bombay High Court accepted the statutory bar that an individual could not move a petition for contempt; the Delhi High Court—and to a lesser extent the Allahabad High Court—seemed to bypass this statutory restriction.[130] Again, the Allahabad High Court seems to have paid insufficient attention to the fact that the statute made the innovative change that a *bona fide* qualified apology was not to be rejected simply because it was qualified.[131] In many cases the Act was simply not referred to.[132] There was a tendency to assume that the old law was still in force and could be used as effectively as before.

Before we turn to the press cases in particular, it might be useful to look at some cases where allegations of corruption were made against the lower judiciary not in newspapers but in letters to the High Courts or other courts. The Contempt of Courts Act, 1971 permitted such complaints which would provide a more discreet forum than the press for the investigation of the judiciary. But such complaints had to be made in 'good faith'.[133] The Punjab and Haryana High Court took the view that 'good faith' meant honestly even if negligently.[134] The Allahabad High Court and Orissa High Court took the view that this phrase required that the allegations should be made with 'due care and attention'.[135] There were also other decisions—from Rajasthan and Allahabad—requiring an examination of the overall circumstances and the motive of the alleged contemnor.[136] The proportion of mischievous to careful allegations is quite high. Nor had the press stopped being used as a vehicle for such allegations.

The press cases involving allegations of corruption include allegations that a Magistrate was under the influence of a woman politico and was supplied women by a particular litigant,[137] a campaign that the Magistrate was taking bribes and a drunk,[138] a declaration that the Magistrate was bribed with wine, women and money,[139] a repetition of the allegation that the Chief Reader of the Delhi Magistrates was corrupt,[140] an accusation that the Chief Justice of Uttar Pradesh had been unfair in his administrative distribution of jurisdiction to regional benches of his High Court,[141] a statement that the Chief Justice had influenced the local press in his favour,[142] the reporting of a personal campaign of a litigant against a judge,[143] an insinuation that wealth and power had influenced an election petition,[144] the reporting of Prime Minister Indira Gandhi's statement that the adverse result in her election case was known to various politicians before it was declared,[145] a campaign against two judges of the Supreme Court alleging that such pusillanimous judges should not be appointed Chief Justice of India[146] and a pamphlet alleging that a Magistrate was wayward.[147] Each of these cases is firmly set in its own background and does not form part of a linear progression of precedents whereby the new Act is reinterpreted. In an Allahabad 'alleged-corrupt-magistrate' case, the High Court virtually permitted the making of a plea of justification by examining both the truth content and effect of an allegation.[148] Yet, on another occasion it seemed to have overlooked the statutory provisions permitting a qualified apology.[149]

The Supreme Court has not provided a lead in considering the permissible limits of criticism. It got an excellent opportunity to do so in the case where the Chief Justice of U.P. was accused of partiality in respect of his administrative distribution of work.[150] In a cryptic judgment, the Supreme Court was not really clear whether the High Court had discharged the notice after, or irrespective of, making a finding of contempt. The Court could have, but did not, clarify the kinds of official duties for which the judge could be more openly criticized and the extent to which such criticism can be made. The Supreme Court did, however, get an opportunity to discuss the limits of criticism and the nature of fair comment in the *Chief Justice Appointment* case (1978)[151] where certain judges were alleged to be unsuitable for appointment to that office because they made a pro-government decision in certain preventive detention cases during the Emergency. The sitting Chief Justice was also criticised for bowing to executive pressure in framing a code of ethics for High Court judges. To have continued with these cases would have itself generated more controversy. The cases were dropped but Krishna Iyer J. launched into a long inconclusive essay and then laid down certain guidelines asking (i) for a policy of restraint; (ii) for a balance between free criticism and protecting the supremacy of the law; (iii) for an avoidance of the use of the jurisdiction for the personal protection of a judge; (iv) for giving the press free play to make criticisms within responsible limits; (v) to avoid judicial hypersensitivity even where the limits are crossed; (vi) to use the jurisdiction only in extreme cases where the public interest requires it.[152] These principles merely reiterate a policy of restraint without conceptualizing the apparatus by which the lines of permissible speech are drawn. The Supreme Court itself did not clarify matters in the *Umaria Pamphlet* case[153] in which a Magistrate was, amongst other things, described as wayward. The Court was anxious to maintain the legitimacy of the court system in rural and other areas[154] and after allowing the contemnor to make a plea of fair comment (which he had no right to make)[155] refused to take into account the effect of Section 13 of the 1971 statute whereby it was enjoined to consider whether there had been a substantial interference with the administration of justice before sentence was passed.[156] The fact that the fine in this case was reduced from Rs. 1,000 to Re. 1 simply complicates the *ratio decidendi* of the decision and makes it all the more difficult to explain.[157] The Court seems keen to rely on intuition rather than on principle of statute in its consideration of cases involving the contempt of scandalizing the judges.

Let us turn to the post 1971 *press* cases where comments were made on pending matters.[158] In one of these cases a politician had made a comment about certain pending cases. The High Court was able to avoid deciding the issue by relying on a statutory restriction that the Attorney General's consent was needed before such a case could be brought.[159] The Supreme Court dealt with this kind of contempt in the *Test Book Release* case[160] where a press release had virtually pre-judged the issue as to which set of rival text books would be used by schools while the issue was pending before the courts. Justice Bhagwati observed:

> It is quite possible that some of the statements in the Press Note, if incorrect, might prejudicially affect the business of the appellant by bringing down sales of the text books printed and published by him, but that is very much different from saying that he would be prejudiced in the appeal or the writ petition.[161]

But the whole purpose of the appeal or the writ petition was to safeguard his business interests which had, by the Supreme Court's own admission, been affected. It is possible that Justice Bhagwati was trying to make a distinction between affecting or pre-judging the outcome of the case and prejudicing the minds of the judges. Clearly, if he limited contempt to the latter issue (*i.e.*, would a judge's mind be prejudiced?) he was enunciating a new doctrine which not only re-defined the definition of contempt in the statute (*i.e.*, as being concerned with the due administration of justice) but also gave the press a considerable leeway in making comments. This precedent was not followed.

The courts have been anxious to allow discussion on matters of public importance. In the *Supersession of Judges* case[162] the Delhi High Court ruled that matters of public importance (such as the appointment of the Chief Justice of India) must be fully canvassed publicly even if the issue was being considered by the courts at the time. Unfortunately, their lordships provide little guidelines about the parameters within which this discussion must be contained. In the *Daily Deccan Chronicle* case,[163] the Andhra Pradesh High Court permitted a discussion of the law of curfew while it was an issue before the courts and relied on the *English Sunday Times* case[164] to ask for a greater accommodation of the freedom of the press. But the *Sunday Times* case in England followed a stringent pre-judgment test which was disapproved by the European Court of Justice.[165] The recent judgment of the Madras High Court in the *Video Recordings*, case reverts back to impose severe limitations suggesting that virtually no discussion can take place while litigation is pending if the parties knew of the case, referred to it and evaluated its merits.[166]

While accepting the statutory change that a case is deemed to be pending only when a charge or challan or plaint is filed (as in the *Vikholi riot* case)[167] the courts in India, including the Supreme Court, have produced a confused response to the permissible areas of comment even though they have been anxious to state that genuine and *bona fide* discussion on matters of public importance should not be stifled.

Some judges have been tolerant even about irresponsible statements made about the judiciary because the judges understand the social context in which the statements are made. But the contempt jurisdiction has not served as a means to enforce a code of ethics and careful expression on journalists. The contempt jurisdiction has been used to judge a social event and evolve an accommodation between the relative frustrations of all the parties involved. It does not set standards. It evolves compromises, asserts the symbolic authority of the courts and ritualises the respect that is due to them. Whereas in England, this jurisdiction has been used to educate the press through the most severe methods which the courts could muster, the Indian cases on the press try and achieve only episodic results.

There remains the question of future reform. To begin with, the Contempt of Courts Act, 1971 was seen as a major reform achieved after 11 years of considered thought and discussion. At the same time, a shadow has been cast on future reform because of the assertion—supported by the courts in part—that the inherent contempt jurisdiction of the High Courts and the Supreme Court cannot be altered by the legislature without the amendment of the Constitution. The amendment of the Constitution may be considered too important to hazard for such a relatively unimportant public issue. At the same time, even those who propagate reform are aware that the pathology of contempt litigation is such that the jurisdiction provides more possibilities than restrictions to a mischievous press which seeks to court publicity. Analytically, it seems only right that the press should be able to plead that what they have said is true (*i.e.*, the plea of justification). Pathologically, it will have the effect of converting an already over-exploited jurisdiction into a spectacle in which allegations will be 'justified' in open courts to the disadvantage of the judiciary even if they are found to be untrue. The courts themselves have to deal with the issue of the extent of permissible comment and criticism. Judges are aware that they are themselves vulnerable and are not keen to give up their contempt jurisdiction or diminish the potential power and the use that it can be put to.[169] There remains the issue of judicial corruption—particularly amongst the lower judiciary. It is an important question whether this should be exposed by the press, or first considered by a more discreet process. The present writer, in a report to the Press Council, suggested *in camera* preliminary examination by the High Courts before such allegations are aired in the press. The contempt cases offer sufficient proof that the press has not shown itself capable of being trusted with such an exposure without affecting the viability of the judiciary as an institution.

A study of the contempt cases in India offers an important lesson for comparative theorists of public law. Law, as a social reality, exists at various constantly transforming levels. As such, solving problems created by the law is not just an analytical juristic challenge but requires an examination of how and why various laws are used, abused and manipulated.

III

The law of contempt explicates many of the contradictions of the Indian legal system. Hitherto, the Indian legal system was manned by a cohesive and identifiable elite that controlled and manipulated the use of the judiciary. The impact of economic growth and the ideology of democracy have jointly precipitated a much more extensive use of the political and legal system as a whole. But a political and legal system must command prestige coterminously with increased use. The Indian political and legal system revels in increased use but falters awkwardly in its efforts to legitimate itself. When the English political and legal system was faced with this challenge in England, a desperate effort was made both to control indiscriminate use as well as separately legitimate each of the institutions which formed identifiable parts of the State. Such a method of government may be called government by institution. It operates at two levels. At the first level, increased use is promised as part of the rhetoric of participation, democracy and justice. At the second level lie a plethora of institutions which are charged to control this use and seek legitimation for their activities.

Such a system promises extensive potential use. At the same time political providence and the need for systematic control dictates a biased rationalization of use consistent with the rhetoric of egalitarian democracy. The needs and circumstances of the institutions of democracy are defended in their own right. Institutional government controls democracy. Emerging from feudalism, institutional government was first justified on the basis of 'status' and, then, on the need for rational control. The British concentrated greatly on establishing relatively autonomous and seemingly self-regulating key institutions. The courts were among the key institutions which formed part of a framework of systemic control. The English system in England was assisted greatly in all this by a controlled exposure to democratic demands in the nineteenth century. They were also assisted by the cohesiveness of the elites that contended for recognition and power. Government by institution emphasized a high consensus about ground rules and a ruthless enforcement against any violation of these rules. The law of contempt fitted in very nicely into this framework of elite cohesiveness, ground rule consensus and controlled use.

Given the altered conditions of India, the law of contempt has suffered untimely strains and critiques. Neither the Raj nor its successor was able to justify the law of contempt. As the economy expanded, emerging classes were less able to convince themselves and their established and emerging adversaries about the need for elite cohesiveness, consensus ground rules and controlled use. What emerged was a reliance around dependence on power acculturations that arose out of society rather than those that grew around the institutions of State. This made it very difficult to legitimate the institutions of State. The gradual erosion of government by institution created a free-for-all which made it difficult to obtain credence for the apparatus of government. This, in turn, unleashed a government by coercion accompanied by the rhetoric of promising. The Indian law of contempt is symptomatic both of coercion and of some future promise of justice. Through this law, judges punish contemnors but at the same time offer themselves for critique and criticism. They are aware that this offer cannot really border on generosity. They are caught up in an impossibility theorem in which the demands of democracy, justice and effective decision-making cannot be reconciled. The law of contempt was originally a fall-back reserved for marginal use. Its eclipse denotes either the fulfilment of institutional morality or its abandonment. Its heightened use plays out the contradictions generated within the judicial system and the judges' helplessness in having to exact what they cannot expect. The Indian State wants to relax the laws of contempt gradually. Yet it may have played out the ground conditions under which such a gradual relaxation can be efficient.

Since the Emergency, the judiciary has tried to come into its own by claiming that it can offer more people more and simultaneously allow more outspoken criticism. If this is risky, then the law of contempt offers insurance. But the more it is used, the more it exposes and publicises disrespect for the judiciary. In India, the law of contempt is an expression of crude power. It stands defeated on ideological grounds in that it is difficult to justify; it is defeated as a result of the vagaries of litigation which trivialize its aims and objects into mischievous entropy.

NOTES

1. On the importance of judicial review to the rule of law, one can do no better than refer to A.V. Dicey: *Introduction to the Law of the Constitution* (1885). For Lord Heward's classic restatement of this see *The New Despotism* (1929). The cause of judicial review is championed by H.W.R. Wade: *Constitutional Fundamentals* (1982).
2. *e.g.*, E.P. Thompson: *Whigs and Hunters* (1975); D. Hay, P. Linebaugh and E.P. Thompson (eds.): *Albion's Fatal Tree: Crime and Society in Eighteenth Century England* (1975). For critical accounts see A. Merritt: "The nature and function of law: A criticism of E.P. Thompson's *Whigs and Hunters*" (1980); *P. Brit J. of Law and Soc.* 194-214; D. Phillips: "A just measure of crime, authority, hunters and blue locusts": The 'Revisionist' social history of crime and the law in Britain" in S. Cohen and A. Scull: *Social Control and the States* (1983). For the view that Thompson has blurred the economic and the socio-political see E. Johnson: "Thompson Genovese and Socialist-Humanist History" (1978) 6 *History Workshop* 79. Cf. R. McClelland: "Some Comments on Richard Johnson (1979) 7 *History Workshop* 101; for an illuminating account about studying law through history see D. Sugarman: "Theory and Practice in law and history: A prologue to the study of the relationship between law and economy from a socio-historical perspective" in Poob Fryer, A. Hunt, D. McBarnet and B. Moorhouse (eds.): *Law, State and Society*

(1981). For an appreciative account of E.P. Thompson's contribution see P. Anderson: *Arguments within English Marxism.*

3. For an account of the development of the modern law of contempt from the days of the Wilkes controversy see R. Dhavan: "The Phillimore Committee Report and Contempt of Court" (1976) 5 *Anglo American Law Review* 186.
4. *e.g.*, H.M. Seervai: *The Emergency, Future Safeguards and the Habeas Corpus Case* (1978) on the denial of judicial review in detention cases by the Supreme Court during the National Emergency (1975-77).
5. On the development of the summary procedure see J. Fox: "The summary process to punish for contempt" (1909) 25 L.R. 185; *ibid*: *Contempt of Courts* (1927).
6. see Donnelly and Goldfarb: "Contempt of Court by Publication in the United States" (1961) 26 *M.L.R.* 239; Donnelly: *The Contempt Power* (1963).
7. By giving wide judicial review of State action to the High Courts and the Supreme Court, the Constitution of India altered the basic political relationship between the judiciary and the executive. For some of the implications of this see R. Dhavan: "On the future of Western law in India: Reflections on the predicament of the Post-Emergency Supreme Court" (1981) VIII *Journal of the Bar Council of India* 61.
8. Note the case of *Hasmukhlal C. Shah* v. *State of Gujarat* (1978) 19 Guj. L.R. 378 at pr. 12 pp. 383-4 where the court talks of the government and others flouting the orders of the court; also *Amrit Nahata* v. *Union* A.I.R. 1986 S.C. 791; *Principal R.P. Arts K.B.C.* v *M.A. Shah* A.I.R. 1986 S.C. 1074; *Alpana* v. *Mehta* A.I.R. 1984 S.C. 1826; and note the new idea of exemplary costs by D.A. Desai, J. in *Sebastian M. Hongray* v. *Union of India* A.I.R. 1984 S.C. 1026. For further examples see R. Dhavan: *Contempt of Court and the Press* (1981) 93-99.
9. S. Natarajan: *A History of the Press in India* (1962) 14-20.
10. *Chattoo Singh* v. *Raj Kissen Singh* (1842) Fulton, 29 at 30; I Ind. Dec. (Bengal) 660; *Sreemutty Ranee Hurrossondry Dossee* v. *Cower Kistonath Roy* (1842) Fulton 85; I Ind. Dec. (Bengal) 693: *Rammohun Mullick* v. *Nubkissore Sen* (1839) Morton 297; I Ind. Dec. 1068.
11. *The Queen* v. *Hume* (1848—27 April) G. Taylor 368; 2 Ind. Dec. (Bengal) 220; *Bose Maria de Lime* v. *Fernandez* (1841—June 11) Perry O.C. 331; IV Ind. Dec. 302; *In re Abdool and Mehtab* (1867) 8 W.R. (Cr.) 32; *In the matter of Pifferd* 1 Hyde. 79; *Hedger* v. *Maha Ranee Kummul Koomaree* (1841—22 April) 7 Select Rep. 33; 8 Ind. Dec. 25.
12. *In the matter of William Taylor* (1869) but reported years later in A.I.R. 1918 Cal. 713

13. *Ibid.* p. 735. These sentiments were repeated in a later case: *In the matter of Banks and Fenwick* (1868) reported years later in A.I.R. 1918 Cal. 752.
14. *Surendra Nath Banerjee* v. *The Chief Justice and Judges of the High Court at Fort William in Bengal* (1883) 10 Cal. 109 relying on *Rainy* v. *Justices of Sieera Leone* 8 Moo. P.C. 47; *McDermott* v. *The Justices of British Guiana* 5 Moore's P.C. (N.S.) 466.
15. P. Narain: *Press and Politics in India: (1885-1905)* (1970) 154.
16. *Legal Remembrancer* v. *Motilal Ghose* (1913) 41 Cal. 173 at 231.
17. *In re Narasinha Chintaman Kelkar* (1908) 33 Bom. 240.
18. *In re Mohandas Karamchand Gandhi*, A.I.R. 1920 Bom. 175.
19. *Att. Gen.* v. *Times Newspapers Ltd.* (1972) 3 All. E.R. 1136; (1973) 1 All. E.R. 855; (1973) 3 All. E.R. 54.
20. *In re Motilal Ghose* (1918) 45 Cal. 169; *E.* v. *Balkrishna Govinda Kulkarni* A.I.R. 1922 Bom. 52.
21. The Madras, Bombay and Allahabad High Courts took the view that High Courts in India have such power but Calcutta High Court dissented from it. See *In the matter of K. Venkata Row* 12 Cri. L.J. 525; *In re Mohandas Karamchand Gandhi* (1920) 22 Bom. L.R. 368; *In re Hadi Husain* v. *Nasir Uddin* A.I.R. 1926 All. 617; *Government of Bengal* v. *Moti Lal Ghosh* (1914) 41 Cal. 177.
22. Lord Minto's Government, after consulting all the Provincial Governments in 1901-09 prepared a Bill in 1911, penalising contempt of authority of courts of justice. This Bill, as revised in the light of comments received, was introduced in the Legislative Council on 18 March, 1914. But the consideration of the Bill was postponed on account of the outbreak of the First World War. After further consideration, Government finally abandoned the 1914 Bill and decided in favour of introducing legislation on the line of Sir Tej Bahadur Sapru's suggestions: see *Sangal Committee Report* (1963) prs. 4 and 5 p. 5-6.
23. (1925) V *L.A.D.* at 991 (11 Feb. 1925). Note the discussion at 990 on the conflict of opinion amongst the courts.
24. (1925) VII L.A.D. 758.
25. (1952) VI L.A.D. 361.
26. (1926) VII L.A.D. 749-56.
27. *Ibid.* 884.
28. *Hari Krishan Lal* v. *The Crown*, A.I.R. 1937 Lah. 497.
29. (1939) II L.A.D. 1122-3 and (1939) V L.A.D. 596-600.
30. (1950) P. D. Part II Vol. II 930, 1297-1304.
31. (1952) P. D. Part II Vol. I col. 1504-10 (28 February, 1952).
32. *In the Matter of Habib son of Sadullah* A.I.R. 1927 Lah. 1; *In the Matter of the Muslim Outlook, Lahore* A.I.R. 1927 Lah. 601; cf. *In the Matter of Contempt of Court* A.I.R. 1935 Lah. 212; *E.* v. *Murli Manohar* A.I.R. 1929 Pat. 72; *In the Matter of an Advocate of*

Allahabad, A.I.R. 1935 All. 1; *Debi Prasad Sharma* v. *E.* A.I.R. 1943 P.C. 202.

33. For the decline of this jurisdiction outside India see *McCleod* v. *St. Aubyn* (1899) A.C. 549; *Ambard* v. *Attorney General of Trinidad and Tobaggo* (1936) 1 All. E.R. 704; *R.* v. *Metropolitan Police Commissioner* (1968) 2 All. E.R. 318.
34. See the case cited *infra* note 50 and R. Dhavan: *The Supreme Court of India: A Socio-legal Analysis of its Juristic Techniques* (1977) 390-99.
35. *e.g.*, *E.* v. *Marmaduke Pickthall*, A.I.R. 1923 Bom. 8; *E.* v. *Marmaduke Pickthall*, AIR. 1923 Bom. 242; *In the Matter of Habib, son of Sadullah*, A.I.R. 1926 Lah. 1: *In the Matter of Muslim Outlook* A.I.R., 1928 Lah. 610; *E.* v. *Jaganath Prasadh*, A.I.R. 1938 All. 358; *Ziaul Hasan* v. *Aziz Ahmad*, A.I.R. 1939 All. 896; *In re K.L. Gauba*, A.I.R. 1942 Lah. 105: *M.G. Kadir* v. *Kesri Narain Jaitly*, A.I.R. 1945 All. 67; cases which were not so clearly contempt include *In re Tushaf Kanti Ghosh Editor, Amrita Bazar Patrika*, A.I.R. 1935 Cal. 419; *In the Matter of Contempt of Court*, A.I.R. 1935 Lah. 212. Comments onpending matters which did not, and in some cases should not, perhaps, have attracted the contempt jurisdiction include *Re Kalidas Jhaveri*, A.I.R. 1920 Bom. 174; *In re Mohandas Karamchand Gandhi*, A.I.R. 1920 Bom. 175; *Government of Burma* v. *Saya Sein*, A.I.R. 1930 Rang. 124; *Sathappa Chettier* v. *C.R. Naidu*, A.I.R. 1932 Mad. 26 (no contempt); *Tujaram* v. *Governor Reserve Bank*, A.I.R. 1939 Mad. 257; *E.* v. *Tarpore*, A.I.R. 1940 Sindh 238; *In re Subramanyam* A.I.R. 1943 Lah. 329. Contrast *In the Matter of Ganesh Shankar Vidyarthi*, A.I.R. 1929 All. 81; *Demibai Genni* v. *Rowji* A.I.R. 1937 Bom. 305; *In re Vidya Sagar Kapur, Editor Daily Guru*, A.I.R. 1938 Lah. 815; *Anis Ahmed Abbasi* v. *Hakim Qari*, A.I.R. 1941 Oudh 399; *Hakim Quari* v. *Anis Ahmad Abbasi*, A.I.R. 1941 Oudh 67; *Hargovinadas B. Kotak* v. *Chimanlal Shah*, A.I.R. 1942 Bom. 86; *E.* v. *Tushar Kant Ghosh* A.I.R. 1946 All. 298; *E.* v. *Kaushal Chand*, A.I.R. 1945 Lah. 206.
36. *Mohd. Ibrahim* v. *Bhopal Singh*, A.I.R. 1948 Oudh 131; *Sukhdeo* v. *Brij Bhushan*, A.I.R. 1951 All. 667; *State* v. *Padma Kant Malviya*, A.I.R. 1955 All. 377; *Rao Harnarain* v. *Gumani Ram*, A.I.R. 1958 Punj. 273; *Press, Municipal Board, Fatehpur* v. *Raghubir Sahai*, A.I.R. 1958 All. 436; *Chunnilal Ken* v. *Shyamlal Sukhram*, A.I.R. 1959 M.P. 50; *E.T. Sen* v. *E data Narayan*, A.I.R. 1969 Delhi 201. *In the Matter of Mr. Hayles, Editor "The Mail"* A.I.R. 1955 Mad. 1; *R.K. Garg* v. *S.A. Azad* A.I.R. 1957 All. 37.
37. Constitution of India, 1950 Article 19(1)(a) and 19(2).
38. (1947) III C.A.D. 441 (29 April 1947); VII C.A.D. 711-87 (1 December 1949) while discussing the Draft Constitution circulated on 21 February, 1948.

39. B. Shiva Rao (ed.). *The Framing of the Constitution* (hereafter cited as Shiva Rao preceded by volume number) IV, 40.
40. X C.A.D. 394.
41. *Ibid.* 395-7.
42. *Ibid.* 398-400.
43. *Ibid.* 399.
44. *Ibid.* 401.
45. *e.g. E.M.S. Namboodripad* v. *T.N. Nambiar*, A.I.R. 1970 S,C. 1015 at pr. 11 p. 2019; *C.K. Daphtary* v. *O.P. Gupta*, A.I.R. 1971 S.C. 1132 at pr. 65 at p. 1145.
46. On the general validity of the law of contempt see *State* v. *Brahma Prakash*, A.I.R. 1950 All. 556 at pr. 10 pp. 559-60; *Legal Remembrancer* v. *Bibhuti Bhushan*, A.I.R. 1954 Pat. 203 at pr. 9 p. 206; *State* v. *Editors, Publishers and Printers of Eastern Times and Prajatantra*, A.I.R. 1952 Ori. 318 at 343; *State* v. *Editor, Publishers and Printers of Matrubhumi*, A.I.R. 1955 Ori 36 at 41.
47. *Lakhan Singh* v. *Balbir Singh* A.I.R. 1953 All. 342; *State* v. *Editor and Printers of Matrubhumi* A.I.R. 1955 Ori. 36; *In the Matter of Basanta Chandra Ghosh* A.I.R. 1960 Pat. 430; *Narayan* v. *Namboodripad* (1968) K.L.T. 299; *C.K. Daphtary* v. *O.P. Gupta* A.I.R. 1971 S.C. 1132 at 1142, 1143.
48. *Baradakanta Mishra* v. *Registrar of Orissa High Court*, A.I.R. 1974 S.C. 710 at 728.
49. The courts have assumed that freedom of speech does not include the right to commit contempt, that the law of contempt is a 'reasonable' restriction on the freedoms (including the freedom of speech and expression) enumerated in Article 19 even if—as was the case before the enactment of the Contempt of Courts Act, 1971—contempt was undefined and the courts drew on earlier decisions to elucidate the meaning and extent of the contempt jurisdiction: *State* v. *Brahma Prakash*, A.I.R. 1950 All. 556 at prs. 10-11 pp. 559-60; *State* v. *Editor and Publisher of Eastern Times and Prajapatra*, A.I.R. 1952 Ori. 318 at pr. 66 pp. 342-3; *Legal Remembrancer* v. *Bibhuti Bhushan*, A.I.R. 1954 Pat. 230 at pr. 9 p. 206; *Brahma Prakash* v. *State of U.P.* A.I.R. 1954 S.C. 10 at pr. 11 p. 13. (The issue of constitutionality is not specifically discussed); *State* v. *Editor, Printer and Publisher of Matrubhumi* A.I.R. I955 Or. 36 at pr. 7 p. 40; *R. K. Garg* v. *S. A. Azad*, A.I.R. 1957 All. 37 at pr. 19 p. 43; *Rao Harnarain Singh* v. *Gumani Ram*, A.I.R. 1958 Punj. 273 at pr. 30 p. 280; *State of Bombay* v. *Mr., 'P'*. A.I.R. 1959 Bom.182 at prs. 24-5 pp. 189-90 (on the validity of the procedure from the point of view of Article 21): *In the Matter of Basanta Chandra Ghosh*, A.I.R. 1960 Pat. 431 at pr. 9 p. 440; *Advocates General* v. *Ramana Rao*, A.I.R. 1967 A.P. 299 at pr. 19 pp. 310-11 and prs. 21-22 pp. 312-3 (where the summary procedure used in contempt cases also seems to have been approved);

Sher Singh v. *R. P. Kapur*, A.I.R. 1968 Punj. 217 at prs. 26-27 p. 230 (including a defence of the summary procedure on the basis of Article 14—the 'equality' article); *Narayan Nambiar* v. *E.M.S. Namboodripad*, (1968) 1 Kerala 384 at 418-20; 437 ff. 498-506; *K. P. Noordeen* v. *A. K. Gopalan* A.I.R. 1968 Ker. 301 at pr. 29 p. 309; *In the Matter of Hiren Bose*, A.I.R. 1969 Cal. 1 at pr. 8 p. 3; *E.P. Sen* v. *E. Narayan*, A.I.R 1969 Delhi 201 at pr. 10 p. 206-7; *C.K. Daphtary* v. *O. P. Gupta*, A.I.R. 1971 S. C. 1152 at pr. 65 p. 1145; *G. N. Verma* v. *Hargovind Dayal*, A.I.R. 1975 All. 53 at prs. 16-17 following *C.K. Daphtary's* case (*supra*).

50. *Ramakrishna Reddy* v. *State of Madras*, A.I.R. 1952 S.C. 149; *Aswini Kumar* v. *Arabinda Bose* A.I.R. 1953 S.C. 75; *Brahma Prakash* v. *State of U.P.*, A.I.R. 1954 S.C. 10; *Hira Lal Dixit* v. *State of U.P.*, A.I.R. 1954 S.C. 743; *R.C. Cooper* v. *Union of India*, A.I.R. 1970 S.C., 1318; *In re P. C. Sen*, A.I.R. 1970 S.C. 1821; *E.M.S. Namboodripad* v. *T.N. Nambiar*, A.I.R. 1970 S.C. 2015; *Perspective Publications* v. *State of Maharashtra*, A.I.R. 1971 S.C. 221; *C.K. Daphtary* v. *O.P. Gupta*, A.I.R. 1971 S.C. 1132; *Dinabandhu* v. *State of Orissa*, A.I.R. 1972 S.C. 180; *Govind Ram* v. *State of Maharashtra*, A.I.R. 1972 S.C. 989; *Baradakanta, Mishra* v. *Registrar of Orissa High Court*, A.I.R. 1974 S.C. 710; *Ram Pratap* v. *Daya Nand*, A.I.R. 1977 S.C. 809; *In re Sham Lal*, (1978) 2 S.C.C. 479; *In re S. Mulgaonkar*, A.I.R. 1978 S. C. 727.
51. *M.R. Parashar* v. *Farooq Abdullah* A.I.R. 1984 S.C. (617) at pr. 12 p. 618, pr. 9 p. 617 even though criticism was welcomed (pr. 10 pp. 617-8) along with, plea for moderation (pr. 11p. 618).
52. *E.M.S. Namboodripad* v. *T.N. Nambiar*, A.I.R. 1970 S.C. 2015.
53. *Ibid.* p. 2025.
54. This comment was made by *Blitz*—a leading left wing weekly.
55. *Surendra Mohanty* v. *State of Orissa*, C.A. of 1956 unreported, decided on 29 January, 1961.
56. Contempt of Courts Act, 1971 Section 3.
57. *In re P.C. Sen*, A.I.R. 1970 S.C. 1821; *A.K. Gopalan* v. *K.P. Noordeen*, (1969) 2 S.C.C. 734. Cf. M.R. Parashar *supra* note 51.
58. *Naraindas* v. *Government of M.P.*, 1974. Cri. L.J. 924.
59. See *Crown* v. *Aminduddin Sahrah*, A.I.R. 1949 Lah. 266; *Krishna Kant* v. *State*, A.I.R. 1953 M.B. 206; *State* v. *Vikar Ahmad*, A.I.R. 1954 Hyd. 175; *J.C. Medhi* v. *Frank Moraes*, A.I.R. 1954 Assam 201; *Legal Remembrancer* v. *Bibhuti Bhushan* A.I.R. 1954 Pat. 203; *In the Matter of Mr. Hayles, Editor "The Mail"* A.I.R. 1955 Mad. 1; *State of Bombay* v. *Mr. 'P'* A.I.R. 1959 Bom. 182; *In the Matter of Basanta Chandra Ghosh*, A.I.R. 1960 Pat. 430; *State* v. *Radha Krishna*, A.I.R. 1961 Punj. 113; *State* v. *Nityananda Mohapatra*, A.I.R. 1960 Ori. 133; *State of Bihar* v. *Gorakh Prasad Srivastava*, A.I.R. 1961 Pat. 360; *In the Matter of Basudeva Prashad* A.I.R. 1961

Pat. 436; *State of Bihar* v. *Shankarlal*, A.I.R. 1962 Pat. 2; *In the Matter of Hiren Bose* A.I.R. 1969 Cal. 1; *Sarat Chandra* v. *Surendra* A.I.R. 1969 Ori. 117; *T.N. Nambiar* v. *E.M.S. Namboodiripad*, (1968) K.L.T. 299; *State of Rajasthan* v. *Ram Narain*, (1973) Cr. L.J. 1340.

60. *Bankim Chandra* v. *Ananda Bazar Patrika*, A.I.R. 1950 Cal. 129.
61. *Government Pleader* v. *M. Manjooram*, A.I.R. 1959 Ker. 266.
62. *Crown* v. *Brish Bhan*, A.I.R. 1950 Pepsu 9.
63. *State* v. *Bishwanath Mohapatra*, A.I.R. 1955 Ori. 169; *R. Ali* v. *Beni Madho Baijpal*, A.I.R. 1957 All. 457; *Ramaswami* v. *J.L. Nehru*, A.I.R. 1958 Mad. 558; *K.P. Noordeen* v. *A.K. Gopalan*, A.I.R. 1968 Ker. 301.
64. *Ramaswami* v. *J.L Nehru*, A.I.R. 1958 Mad. 558.
65. *e.g. Leo Roy Frey* v. *R. Prasad*, A.I.R. 1958 Punj. 377.
66. *Harish Chandra* v. *Justice Ali Ahmad* A.I.R. 1986 Patna 65 at pr. 11 pp. 23-4 & cf. B.P. Sinha J. at prs. 21-24 pp. 76-7.
67. *Ramaswami* v. *J.L. Nehru* (*supra* note 64).
68. *R.* v. *Nayyar*, A.I.R. 1950 All. 549.
69. *Sukhdeo* v. *Brij Bhushan*, A.I.R. 1951 All. 667.
70. *State* v. *Editor and Publishers of Eastern Times and Prajatantra*, A.I.R. 1952 Ori. 318.
71. *Ramnik Lal* v. *Pranlal*, A.I.R. 1952 Kutch 74; see also an allegation of being vulgar with women, *State* v. *Bhawani Prashad*, A.I.R. 1954 Nag. 36.
72. *Lakhan Singh* v. *Balbir Singh*, A.I.R. 1953 All. 342.
73. *K.S. Vasan* v. *A.H.E. Taylor*, A.I.R. 1953 Mys. 103.
74. *State* v. *Editor and Publisher of Matrubhumi* A.I.R. 1955 Ori. 36.
75. On political incidents and matters see *Bankim Chandra* v. *Ananda Bazar Patrika*, A.I.R. 1950 Cal. 129; *R.* v. *Nayyar*, A.I.R. 1980 All. 549; *Ramniklal* v. *Pranlal*, A.I.R. 1952 Kutch 74; *State* v. *Ram Briksh Beni Puri*, A.I.R. 1953 Pat. 364; *State* v. *Bhawani Prashad*, A.I.R. 1954 Nag. 36; *State* v. *Radhagobind Das*, A.I.R. 1954 Ori. 1; *L.S. Shukla* v. *Ishwar Chand*, A.I.R. 1955 M.B. 183; *State* v. *Editor and Publisher of Matrubhumi*, A.I.R. 1955 Ori. 36; *Rahmat Ali* v. *Beni Madho Bali Pal*, A.I.R. 1957 All. 457; *Ramaswami* v. *J.L. Nehru*, A.I.R. 1958 Mad. 558; *Government Pleader* v. *Manjooran*, A.I.R. 1959 Ker. 266; *K.P. Noordeen* v. *A.K. Gopalan*, A.I.R. 1968 Ker. 301; *E.T. Sen* v. *Edata Narayan* A.I.R. 1969 Delhi 1. For direct attacks on politicians see *Bijoynanda* v. *Balkrishna*, A.I.R. 1953 Ori. 249; *State* v. *Editor and Printers of Matrubhumi Krushak* A.I.R 1954 Ori. 149; *Hare Krishna Mahtab* v. *Balkrishna*, A.I.R. 1954 Ori. 57. Clearly, the politicians of Orissa had learned the political uses of the law of contempt.
76. *Crown* v. *Brish Bhan*, A.I.R. 1950 Pepsu 9: *Sunnulal* v. *Yashwant Singh*, A.I.R. 1951 M.B. 98; *Bijoynanda* v. *Balkrishna*, A.I.R. 1953

Ori. 249; *Mankad* v. *Shah Pranlal Vakil*, A.I.R. 1954 Kutch 2; *State* v. *Bishwanatha Mohapatra*, A.I.R. 1955 Ori. 169; *State* v. *Faqir Chand*, A.I.R. 1957 H.P. 152; *District Magistrate* v. *Madhava Rao*, A.I.R. 1961 Mys. 12; *State of Bihar* v. *Shankar Lal*, A I.R. 1962 Pat. 2; *In re Vinod Maheshwari* A.I.R. 1967 M.P. 104; *K.P. Noordeen* v. *A.K. Gopalan*, A.I.R. 1968 Ker. 301.

77. *Ratnakar Jha* v. *Krishna Sewak*, A.I.R. 1954 Nag. 99; *Rao Harnarain* v. *Gumani Ram*. A.I.R. 1958 Punj. 273.

78. *Diwan Chand Chaudhry* v. *K. Narender*, A.I.R. 1950 E.P. 366; *Wasudeoraji* v *Gopal*, A.I.R. 1951 Nag. 26; *Wusudeorao* v. *Gopal Dattaraya Karkare*, A.I.R. 1951 Nag. 368; *T.B. Hawkins* v. *D.P. Mishra*, A.I.R. 1952 Nag. 256; *Dwarka Prashad* v. *Krishna Chandra*, A.I.R. 1953 All. 600; *Lakhan Singh* v. *Balbir Singh*, A.I.R. 1953 All. 342; *K.B. Vasan* v. *A.H.E. Taylor*, A.I.R. 1953 Mys. 103; *State of Himachal Pradesh* v. *Raghunandan Lal*, A.I.R. 1954 H.P. 70; *Ram Parikchan Pandey* v. *M.S.N. Sharma*, A.I.R. 1961 Pat. 217; *Rev. Fr. Sebastian* v. *Karunakaran*, A.I.R. 1967 Ker. 177.

79. *Mohd. Ibrahim* v. *Bhopal Singh*, A.I.R. 1948 Oudh 131; *Sukhdeo* v. *Brij Bhushal*, A.I.R. 1951 All. 667; *State* v. *Padma Kant Malviya*, A.I.R. 1955 All. 377; *Rao Harnarain* v. *Gumani Ram*, A.I.R. 1958 Punj. 273; *Pres., Municipal Board, Fatepur* v. *Raghubir Sahai*, A.I.R. 1958 All. 436; *Chunnilal Ken* v. *Shyamlal Sukhram*, A.I.R. 1959 M.P. 50; *E.T. Sen* v. *Edata Narayan*, A.I.R. 1969 Delhi 201; *In the Matter of Mr. Hayles, Editor "The Mail"* A.I.R. 1955 Mad. 1; *R.K. Garg* v. *S.A. Azad*, A.I.R. 1957 All. 37; *supra* notes 60-64, 71-74, 76-78.

80. A classification of the case law on the basis of punishment would be as follows: Imprisonment was given in *Crown* v. *Amin-ud-din Sahraf*, A.I.R. 1949 Lah. 266; *State* v. *Radhagobinda Das*, A.I.R. 1954 Ori. 1; *State* v. *Faqir Chand*, A.I.R. 1957 All. 657; *State* v. *Radhakrishna Khanna*, A.I.R. 1961 Punj. 113; *State of Bihar* v. *Gorakh Prasad Srivastava*, A.I.R. 1961 Pat. 360; *State of Rajasthan* v. *Shyam Narain Morivn*, (1973) Cr. L.J. 1340. Note the award of exemplary costs of Rs. 1,00,000 in *Sebastian's* case (*supra* note 8). Apologies were accepted and reprimands and warnings given (whether with or without a costs order) in *Mohd. Ibrahim* v. *Bhopal Singh*, A.I.R. 1948 Oudh 131; *Crown* v. *Brish Bhan*, A.I.R. 1950 Pepsu 9 (costs); *Sunnulal* v. *Yeshwant Singh*, A.I.R. 1951 M.B. 98 (costs); *Sikhea* v. *Brij Bhushal*, A.I.R. 1951 All 667 (costs); *Wasudeoraji* v. *A.D. Mani*, A.I.R. 1951 Nag. 26 (costs); *Ramnikal* v. *Premlal*, A.I.R. 1952 Kutch 74 (costs); *Bijoyananda* v. *Balakrishna*, A.I.R. 1953 Ori. 249; *J.C. Medhi* v. *Frank Moraes*, A.I.R. 1954 Assam 201; *State of H.P.* v. *Raghunadan Lal*, A.I.R. 1954 Nag. 36 (costs); *State* v. *Editor, Printer and Publishers of Matrubhumi, Krushak*, A.I.R. 1956 Ori. 149 (costs); *Harekrishna Mahtab* v. *Balkrishna Kar*, A.I.R. 1954 Ori. 67 (costs); *State v. Padma Kant Malviya*, A.I.R.

1955 All. 377; *R.K. Garg* v. *S.A. Azad*, A.I.R. 1957 All. 37 (costs); *Rahmat Ali* v. *Beni Madho Baijpal*, A.I.R. 1957 All. 457 (costs); *Le Roy Frey* v. *R. Prashad*, A.I.R. 1958 Punj. 377; *In the Matter of Basudeva Prashad* A.I.R. 1961 Pat. 436; *District Magistrate* v. *Madhava Rao*, A.I.R. 1961 Mys. 12; *State of Bihar* v. *Shankar Lal*, A.I.R. 1962 Pat. 2; *Rev. Fr. Sebastian* v. *Karunakaran*, A.I.R. 1967 Ker. 177. The Supreme Court has recently cautioned in *L.D. Jaikwal* v. *U.P.*, A.I.R. 1984 S.C. 1374 at pr. 6 pp. 1375-6 that the convenient expedient of an apology cannot discharge a contempt.

81. *Supra* note 65.
82. *Smt. Padmawati Devi Bhargava* v. *R.K. Karanjia*, A.I.R. 1963 M.P. 61.
83. *Digvijaya Narain Singh* v. *A.K. Sen*, (1971) 1 Delhi 14 (*Congress Party* case).
84. *Anil Kumar Gupta* v. *K. Subba Rao* (1974) 1 Delhi 1 (*Supersession* case).
85. B.B. Das Gupta introduced a Bill to amend and consolidate the law of contempt of court in the Lok Sabha on April 1, 1960.
86. Report of the Committee on Contempt of Courts (1963), the Bill was introduced in the Lok Sabha on April 1, 1968, 41 L.S.D. (Second Series) col. 9187. *Report of the Joint Committee on the Contempt of Courts Bill, 1968*: Government of India Gazette Extraordinary Pt. II Sec. 2 (23 February 1970).
87. *Ibid.*, p. 3: Chapter XII Conclusion (4) p. 58. This matter is discussed in Chapter III pp. 13-18.
88. *Ibid.*, 11, 19-20, 21, 36 f.n. 2 where the British Report is mentioned.
89. *Ibid.*, Chapter XI.
90. *Ibid.*, Conclusion 10 p. 59.
91. *Ibid.*, Conclusion 14(i) p. 59.
92. *Ibid.*, Conclusion 14(ii), the defence of the 'public good' was also recommended in such cases.
93. Report of the Joint Committee on the Contempt of Courts Bill, 1968 (*supra* note 86) pr. 16, comment on clause 3.
94. *Ibid.*, pr. 16—comment on Clause 3(2).
95. *Ibid.*, pr. 16—comments on Clause 6.
96. *Ibid.*, pr. 16—comment on Clause 12.
97. *Ibid.*, pr. 16—comment on Clause 13.
98. *Ibid.*, pr. 16—comment on Clause 16.
99. *Ibid.*, pr. 16—comment on Clause 20.
100. *Ibid.*, pr. 16—comment on Clause 21.
101. Minority Report of Bhupesh Gupta, V. Vishwanatha Menon, S.N. Banerjee, D. Sen Gupta prs. 2-4.
102. *Ibid.*, prs. 9-10.
103. *Ibid.*, pr. 18 (on the wilful contempt); pr. 23 (on the punishment clause).

104. (1971) 78 Rajya Sabha Debates (hereafter R.S.D.) No. 4 (18 November, 1971) cols. 203-56; No. 6 (22 November, 1971) cols. 104-63.
105. 78 R.S.D. (No. 4) col. 206 (18 November 1971).
106. *Ibid.*, col. 129, cols. 140-8.
107. Contempt of Courts Act, 1971 S. 2(c).
108. *Ibid.*, S. 3.
109. *Ibid.*, S. 3 Explanation.
110. *Ibid.*, S. 7.
111. *Ibid.*, S. 5.
112. *Ibid.*, S. 12 Explanation merely says that the qualified nature of an apology (*i.e.* "I apologize if I am guilty") should not be reason for its rejection. This does not mean that the hitherto unavailable defence of justification has been allowed. S. 8 of the 1971 Act presents any other defence which existed before the Act. 'Justification' was not available before 1971 and it is submitted cannot be read into the concept of a 'qualified' apology; see further *L.D. Jaikwal supra* note 80.
113. *Ibid.*, S. 13.
114. *Ibid.*, S. 12(1); on the possibility of exemplary costs see *Sebastion's* case *supra* notes 8 and 80.
115. *Ibid.*, S. 12(1) Proviso; on the limited use of apology see *L.D. Jaikwal supra* note 80.
116. *Ibid.*, S. 13.
117. *Ibid.*, Ss. 14-15; on the need for the consent of the Attorney or Advocate General see *Harish Chandra* v. *Justice S. Ali Ahmed* A.I.R. 1986 Patna 65 at pr. 6 pp. 70-1; *Haji Rasheed Muhammad* v. *D. Ramanujam*, A.I.R. 1986 Mad 119 at pr. 7 p. 121 that such consent is not necessary when court acts *suo motu*.
118. The Bombay High Court took the view that the the court cannot issue notices for contempt in respect of contempt of subordinate courts *suo motu*.. See *Vishwas Narayan Limaye* v. *Sharad Pawar*, 78 *Bombay Law Report* 616. Cf. *Vidya Chandra Mishra* v. *Sachindra Kumar* (1974) 2. I.L.R. All. 268.
119. Contempt of Courts Act, 1971 S. 20.
120. *Ibid.*, S. 18, cases on criminal contempt would be heard by a bench of not less than two judges except in respect of a judicial commissioner.
121. *Ibid.*, S. 19.
122. *Ibid.*, S. 16.
123. *Ibid.*, S. 22 (which claims to add to, rather than derogate from, other laws relating to contempt) and S. 8 (preserving existing defence not mentioned in this Act).
124. *Ibid.*, S. 9.
125. *Saloomuddin* v. *Sharfuddin*, A.I.R. 1980 Delhi 39 at pr. 26 p. 43; *Baradakant Mishra* v. *Bhimsen Dixit* (1973) Cr. L.J. 19 at prs. 15-6;

State v. *Bhim Singh* (1978) Cr. L.J. 1041 (H.P.); *Kalloo Mal* v. *Government of U.P.* (1974) Cr. L.J. 529 (All.); *Parkash Chand* v. *S.S. Grewal* (1975) Cr. L.J. 679 (Punjab); *B.N. Mulla* v. *Government of U.P.* (1975) Cr. L.J. 1283 (All.). This case is further complicated by the fact that the claim was time-barred. This does not wipe out the State's liability but it gives it a lever to evade the responsibility; *In re District Magistrate Rnjnadgaon* (1975) Cr. L.J. 1966; *Dr. P.L. Jauhar* v. *State*, A.I.R. 1975 Raj, 61; *State of Maharashtra* v. *J. Patra* (1976) Bom. L.R. 116; *Arun Kshetrpal* v. *Registrar, High Court, Jabalpur* (1976) Cr. L.J. 1539 (S.C.); *Dayanand* v. *Tahsildar, N.R. Pura* (1977) Cr. L.J. 971 (Kar); *A.J.K. Sehakari Sanstha* v. *State of Maharashtra* (1977) *Cr. L.J.* 1811 (Bom); *K.N. Sinha* v. *Sahadeo Jha* (1977) Cr. L.J. 1174 (Pat); *Jainarain Shr.ma* v. *Mahanth Pandey* (1979) BLJR 109; *Jitan Chaudhry* v. *State of Bihar* (1979) Cr. L.J. (N.O.C.) 85 (Pat.); *Hasmukhlal C. Shah* v. *State of Gujarat* (1978) 19 Guj. L.R. 378.

e.g. marriage (*Mira Bose* v. *Santosh Kumar* (1973) Cr. L.J. 7902); londlord-tenant matter (*Saleemuddin* v. *Sharfuddin* A.I.R. 1980 Delhi 39); contract (*Shamshul Hussain* v. *Kuber Nath* (1975) Cr. L.J. 898); property (*Chagaganbai* v. *S. Chandubhai* A.I.R. 1976 S.C. 1909); employment (*Purtabpur Co.* v. *C.P. Singh* (1976) Cr. L.R. 359); cinema licence (*Baburam Gupta* v. *Sudhir Bhashin* A.I.R. 1979 S.C. 1528); loan (*Smt. Pushpaben* v. *Narandas Badiani* (1979) 2 S.C.C. 399). This is just a random sample.

Clearly all of a person's rights under a contract, or in respect of property, are automatically suspended or taken away because the courts are seized of a dispute in relation to such a contract or property (see *K.T. Chandy* v. *H.R. Zade* (1974) Cr. L.J. 594; *Jose* v. *Alice Francis* (1979) K.L.T. 362). It is also not contempt not to obey vague or unclear orders (*Union of India* v. *Satish Chandra* (1980) S.L.J. 61). Litigants, therefore, find vagueness in orders or insist that certain things are not covered by orders (*e.g.* *R.N. Mulla* v. *State of U.P.* (1975) Cr. L.J, 1283—even though it was clear in this case that the government, being the litigant in question, did not want to honour a time-barred claim in a case where the payment of the past salary was not included in a reinstatement of a public servant case). Courts have also accepted pleas that certain thing may not be within a person's power (*Purtabpur Co.* v. *C.P. Singh* (1976) Cr. L.J. order from a superior to a subordinate officer (*Jitan Chowdhry* v. *State of Bihar* (1973) Cr. L.J. (N.O.C.) 85); 'the court stenography got the order wrong' (*S.P. Agarwal* v. *R.R. Upadhyaya* (1978) Cr. L.J. 789) or 'I got the wrong legal advice' (*A.T.K. Sahakari Sanstha* v. *State of Maharashtra* (1977) Cr. L.J. 1809) have been treated with more than suspicion. There has also been a tendency to wriggle out of obeying orders which are the product of a consent order (*Babu Ram* v. *Sudhir Bhashin* A.I.R.

1979 S.C. 1528). Cf. an undertaking given to a court in a similar situation (*Chagganbhai* v. *Chandubhai* A.I.R. 1976 S.C. 1909); *Hastings Mill* v. *Hira Singh* (1978) Cr. L.J. 560 (Cal).

126. *Punjab and Haryana High Court* v. *Ram Piara* (1973) Cr. L.J. 1106 (P. & H.); *State* v. *S.N. Dikshit* (1973) Cr. L.J. 1211; *State* v. *Rama Chandra Mahapatra* (1975) Cut. 604; *State of Karnataka* v. *Shivadeva* (1976) Cr. L.J. 1958 (Kar.); *Advocate General* v. *Abraham George* (1976) Cr. L.J. 158 (Ker.); *State* v. *R.N. Patra* (1976) Cr. L.J. 440 (Ori.); *Advocate-General, Andhra Pradesh* v. *R. Subba Rao* (1976) Cr. L.J. 746; *State of Rajasthan* v. *M.R. Mitrukha* (1978) Cr. L.J. 1440 (Raj.); *State* v. *Harihar Shukla* (1976) Cr. L.J. 507 (All.); *Ram Partap* v. *Dayanand* (1977) Cr. L.J. 579.

127. *Bhimsen Dixit* v. *Baradakant Mishra* (1971) Cut. 986; *Baradakant Mishra* v. *Bhimsen Dixit* (1973) Cr. L.J. 19 (S.C.); *Baradakant Mishra* v. *State of Orissa* (1976) Cut. 503; Special Leave Application (Civil No. 53 of 1967) (decided 6 February 1977); see further *State* v. *Baradakant Mishra* (1972) 2 Cut. N.R. 857; *State* v. *Baradakant Mishra* (1972) 2 Cut. W.R. 1872; *State* v. *Baradakant Mishra* (1972) 2 Cut. W.R. 1876; Criminal Appeal 174 of 1972; *Registrar, Orissa High Court* v. *Baradakant Mishra* A.I.R. 1973 Ori. 244; *Baradakant Mishra* v. *Registrar, High Court* A.I.R. 1974 S.C. 710; *Baradakant Mishra* v. *Chief Justice, Orissa High Court* A.I.R. 1974 Ori. 1. see also *Advocate General, Orissa* v. *Baradakant Mishra* (1974) Cr. L.J. 70; *Baradakant Mishra* v. *Chief Justic, Orissa High Court* (1975) Cr. L.J. 1 (S.C.); *Registrar, High Court, Orissa* v. *Baradakant Mishra* (1976) Cr. L.J. 405; *Baradakant Mishra* v. *Orissa High Court* (1976) Cr. L.J. 944 (S.C.)

128. *State of Karanataka* v. *Shivadeva* (1976) Cr. L.J. 1958 (Kar); *Advocate-General* v. *Abraham George* (1976) Cr. L.J. 158 (Ker.); *State* v. *Dhruba Charan* (1976) Cr. L.J. 246 (Ori.); *State* v. *R.N. Patra* (1976) Cr. L.J. 440 (Ori.); *Mohd. Osman Shaheed* v. *Mohd. Baqur Hussain* (1979) 2 A.P.L.J. 363.

129. *Rama Dayal* v. *State of U.P.* A.I.R. 1978 S.C. 921.

130. *Vishwas Narayan* v. *Sharad Pawar* 78 Bom. L.R. 616; *Anil Kumar Gupta* v. *K. Subba Rao* (1974). 1 Delhi 1; *G.N. Verma* v. *Hargovind Dayal* A.I.R. 1975 All. 52; *Manik Chandra Gupta* v. *Virendra Kumar* (1979) Cr. L.J. 412 (All.).

131. The courts have demanded a qualified apology at an early stage and have, therefore, eaten into the purpose for whieh the concept of a 'qualified apology' was introduced in Section 12 of the Contemp of Courts Act, 1971 (see *In re District Magistrate, Rajanandangaon* (1975) Cr. L.J. 1766; *High Court* v. *S.K. Mathur* C.I.T. (1975) 101 I.T.R. 180). The apology provisions were very harshly interpreted in *State* v. *S.N. Dikshit* (1973) Cr. L.J. 1211; *Manik Chandra Gupta* v. *Virendra Kumar* (1979) Cr. L.J. 412; see also *State* v. *Mohapatra* (1975) Cut. 604.

132. *S.C. Tyagi* v. *N. Gupta* (1974) Cr. L.J. 428 at pr. 429; *Manik Chandra Gupta* v. *Virendra Kumar* (1979) Cr. L.J. 412 (All.); *Rakesh Dwivedi* v. *Indra Gandhi* (1979) All. Cr. 217.
133. Contempt of Courts Act, 1971, S. 6.
134. *Punjab and Haryana High Court* v. *Ram Piara* (1973) Cr. L.J. 1106 (P. & H) at 1113 referring to Section 52 of the Indian Penal Code, 1860.
135. *State* v. *S.N. Dikshit* (1973) Cr. L.J. 1211 at pr. 11 p. 1216 citing Section 52 of the Indian Penal Code, 1860; *State* v. *Ramachandra Mahapatra* (1975) Cut. 604.
136. *State of Rajasthan* v. *M.R. Mitrakha* (1978) Cr. L.J. 1440 (Raj.); *State* v. *Harihar Shukla* (1976) Cr. L.J. 507 (All.).
137. *State* v. *D.K. Das Vidhi* (1973) Cr. L.J. 1271 (All.).
138. *State of Rajasthan* v. *Shyam Narain* (1973) Cr. L.J. 1340 (Raj.).
139. *Supra* note 132.
140. *In the Matter of D.B. Vohra* (1974) Cr. L.J. 899 (Delhi).
141. *G.N. Verma* v. *Hargovind Dayal* A.I.R. 1975 All. 52.
142. *Ragistrar, High Court* v. *Baradakanta Mishra* (1976) Cr. L.J. 405 (Ori.).
143. *Manik Chandra Gupta* v. *Virendra Kumar* (1979) Cr. L.J. 412 (All).
144. *Mohd. Osmam Shaheed* v. *Mohd. Baqur* (1979) 2 A.P.L.J. 763.
145. *Rakesh Dwivdi* v. *Indra Gandhi* (1979) All C.R. 217.
146. *In re Shamlal A.I.R.* 1978 S.C. 489. *In re Mulgaonkar* A.I.R. 1978 S.C. 727.
147. *Rama Dayal* v. *State of U.P. A.I.R.* 1978 S.C. 921; note also allegations against a Special Court Judge in *L.D. Jaikwal supra* note 80.
148. *State* v. *S.N. Dikishit* (1973) Cr. L.J. 1211.
149. *State* v. *D.K. Das Vidhi* (1973) Cr. L.J. 1271 (All.).
150. *Hargovind Dayal* v. *G.N. Verma* (1977) Cr. L.J. 1003.
151. *Supra* note 147.
152. *Ibid*. pr. 27-33 pp. 736-8.
153. *Supra* note 148.
154. *Ibid*. pr. 14 p. 928.
155. *Ibid*., pr. 10 p. 928.
156. *Ibid*., pr. 16 pp. 923-9.
157. *Ibid*., prs. 17-8 p. 929.
158. *Naraindas* v. *Government of M.P.* (1974) Cr. L.J. 924; *Anil Kumar Gupta* v. *K. Subha Rao* (1974) 1 Delhi 1 (*Supersession case*); *Y.B. Hanumantha* v. *K.R. Pattabhiram* A.I.R. 1075 A.P. 30.
159. *Vishwas Narayan* v. *Shard Pawar* (1973) 78 Bom. L.R. 616.
160. *Supra* note 58.
161. *Ibid*., pr. 6 p. 928.
162. *Supra* note 84.
163. *Y.V. Hanumantha* v. *K.R. Pattabhiram* A.I.R. 1975 A.P. 30.

164. *Ibid.*, pr. 32. *The Sunday Times* case (*Attorney-General* v. *Times Newspaper Ltd.* (1973 2 W.L.R. 452) is cited at pr. 7 p. 31 along with *In re. P.C. Sen* A.I.R. 1970 S.C. 1821 at pr. 8 pp. 31-2). It is submitted that the 'pre-judgment' test in the *Sunday Times* case is radically different from 'influence' test in the *Sen* case.
165. *Sunday Times Ltd.* v. *Government of the United Kingdom* 2(975), Mimeo.
166. *Haji Rasheed Mohammed* v. *Ramanujam* A.I.R. 1986 Mad. 119 at prs. 21 p. 125. However they accepted a *bona fide* apology (pr. 13 p. 126).
167. *Prabhakar* v. *Sadanand* (1975) Cr. L.J. 531.
168. Note the imbroglio created in 1978 when Justice Bhagwati and Chandrachud were accused of pusillanimity during the emergency for the cases see *supra* note 147; see also R. Dhavan and Balbir Singh, "Publish and be damned the press at the bar of the Supreme Court" (1979) 21 J.I.L.1.

5

PARLIAMENT AND ITS PRIVILEGES

I

Parliamentary privilege is an exciting jurisdiction. It recalls the history and growth of the English Constitution. Imported into other Constitutions of the world, the English experience is immediately deemed to be relevant in any discussion of the powers of legislative bodies to enforce their privileges. It is not surprising that until it was amended in 1976, the Indian Constitution decreed that the privileges of India's legislatures shall be those of the House of Commons.[1] All this makes a whole range of assumptions about the 'equivalence' (both 'equivalence-in-meaning' and 'equivalence-in-use') of legal concepts in differing legal and constitutional systems. It also makes assumptions about the importance of legal form and the in-built capacity of legal form to determine similar social and transactional meanings in differential contexts. In one sense, it was quite understandable for India's Constitution makers to make these assumptions. Since the Indian Constitution inelegantly borrowed, even if massively, from other Constitutions, such inelegance could only be sustained on the basis that 'form' and 'substance' were always similarly linked and that the constitutional practice of the country from whom the concept was borrowed was not only relevant but deserved to be emulated. In another sense, all these assumptions are difficult to sustain. Without getting into long drawn jurisprudential arguments about form and content, it is relevant to make a few observations. The view that legal concepts retain their form while permitting transformed use provides insufficient insights into both form and substance. It gives form a neutral character and diverts our attention to the volatile pathological use of legal concepts.

The form of a concept is not a neutral description. It has ideological dimensions. It projects an idea and persuades by definition. Its meaning lies not just in the legal context to which it belongs but in the political economy which requires the concept to be clothed in a particular way in order to give it ideological credibility and persuasive effect.[2] This is even more true of constitutional concepts which parade a whole range of legal meanings for political acceptability. From this point of view, to talk of the persistence of form over time or space seems either trivial or silly. The form is a socio-political idiom. It generates some practice without being able to settle it. Its initial or transformed meaning cannot be taken for granted. Nor is it meaningful to draw parallels or prescriptive solutions on the basis of an apparent similarity in form. When such parallels or prescriptive solutions are made, it is important to reserve the judgment that such an exercise may be trying to legitimate new demands under the cover of the acceptability of old ideologies.

It is difficult to say whether India's Constitution makers genuinely believed that institutions of English democracy could be transplanted into India. Despite the optimistic account of a foreign commentator on the constitution making process, it seems more realistic to believe that while using cosmopolitan concepts to legitimate a particular power structure, the makers of India's Constitution had analysed the *realpolitik* dimensions of what they were creating. That their predictive judgment was far from exact is another matter.

The English concept of parliamentary privilege was a radical intervention into English political history. Although parliamentary privilege is represented as providing institutional protection to a particular instrumentality of government, it did much more than that. As it happens that particular instrumentality of government (namely, parliament) constituted a mechanism which acculturated and advanced the power of certain emerging groups and classes of people. The history of the use of the privilege jurisdiction is littered with imperfect and unresolved outrages by parliament against its opponents. Such exercises of power continue to defy rational resolution. It represents a form of institutional bullying or hooliganism which gains acceptance because of the form it is clothed in. Since it is a power attributed to parliament, the defence of parliamentary privilege can—and is—represented as a defence of democracy. Used primarily by emerging elites against other institutions of government and political opponents, the limits of the jurisdiction were never too carefully defined. Operating in the name of democracy, a vast reservoir of power was claimed for the jurisdiction. This is why parliamentary privilege is much more than a courtyard jurisdiction and extends beyond the physical precincts of a legislature. Like contempt of court, it is designed to sustain a particular power connurbation in the political and constitutional system. Equally, like contempt of court, it has considerable difficulties in legitimating its absolutist claims. While American legislatures have allowed this jurisdiction to be jointly monitored by the intervention of courts, English (and Indian) constitutional law has struggled to answer jurisdictional questions concretely and clearly. In England, the problem has been assisted greatly by the jurisdiction becoming obsolete as part of intra-institutional conflict. As the competing elites who formed government became more cohesive, parliamentary privilege was used partly to discipline the practice of members as well as to contain the potential uses of a new non-governmental political arena: the press. There is now a high degree of consensus about the ground rules of government for the coercive aspects of parliamentary privilege to constitute a threat. However, the jurisdiction continues to remain a mild threat to non-conformist opponents in the press even though the press has succumbed into accepting the ground rules by which the distribution of power is made and critiqued. This represents the triumph of gradualism in the aftermath of the ideological and institutional assimilation of power by a consensus elite.

The Indian situation is wholly different. The Indian political system is a cauldron in which all kinds of class, group and factional disputes are brewing for recognition. Each of the formal and informal institutions of power are arenas of sharp, often unscrupulous, struggle. The new emerging corporate sector would like to see their power more artfully assimilated by democratically ordained institutional practice; but this is a luxury that has so far not been possible in an 'intermediate regime' that has bred a range of inexact alliances between 'power brokers' and their beneficiaries. The parliamentary privilege jurisdiction represents this chaos in a much more fertile way than any other process of government. Its untidiness makes it impossible to define the exact contours of the jurisdiction with any kind of exactness. Parliament is *tamasha* (spectacle) of which the privilege jurisdiction is a part. But it is a *tamasha* which is very heavily weighted in favour of those in control of parliament. However, since the jurisdiction belongs to parliament—and not to the ruling party—it has been used ruthlessly and effectively by the Opposition and free-lance members of parliament to embarrass leading politicians on all sides of the political divide. It has also been used as an arena to harass political newspaper opponents. However, the jurisdiction has a weak 'back up.' It cannot really use the power of imprisonment. The most effective weapon against newspapers is denial of access to the goings-on in parliament. Yet, to borrow a phrase, 'the process is the punishment';[3] and the process is quite intimidating. But, both the form and the content of the jurisdiction defy easy parallels with other constitutional systems even though the jurisdiction is notionally a transplant from the English constitutional law.

II

Since the emergence of Parliament entails some measure of representation of the people, it is not surprizing that Parliament was the last of the three divisions of government to emerge in British India. Although legislative councils had been introduced in 1861,[4] attempts at responsible government were first properly introduced in 1919.[5] Here, the legislators were given freedom of speech in the assemblies and immunity from legal proceedings for what they said and how they voted.[6] But the Act went no further than that. The assemblies had no punitive powers. Years later, members of India's Constituent Assembly complained that speeches made inside the assemblies were not always reported in the press. In particular, references were made in this connection to a significant speech by Shri Malviya.[7] At several conferences organised by the Presiding Officers of the Assemblies, there was a request that these officers should possess the power to rebuke for breach of privilege.[8] There were instances cited of both the Times of India and the Daily Telegraph (London) attacking the Presiding Officers of Indian assemblies with impunity.[9] There were suggestions that the privileges of the assemblies should be the same as those of the House of Commons in England.[10] However, the British government while anxious to protect their own executive and judiciary were reluctant to give Indian dominated legislatures punitive powers over others, which must, perforce, have included the government itself. Historically, the English Parliament's own use of its privileges was a good reminder that parliamentary privileges can be put to some very irksome uses.

The Government of India Act, 1935 which autonomized provincial power considerably gave members of both the Central and Provincial legislatures freedom of speech in the legislatures and immunity from legal proceedings for anything said or done in the legislature.[11] The legislatures were specifically denied a penal jurisdiction to enforce their privileges but an option was created to move the courts, where necessary.[12] These last two limitations were removed in 1947 as far as the Central legislature was concerned.[13] After 1935, there were some difficulties with the press. The *Statesman* had prematurely published a parliamentary report.[14] There was concern about the premature publication of other reports (though not Bills) and circulation of incorrect or false reports.[15]

The issue of parliamentary privilege was not seriously discussed by the Drafting Committees of the Constitution.[16] The first reference to this in the Draft Clauses of the Union Constitution gave the usual freedom of speech to members and the traditional immunity from legal proceedings.[17] However, the residuary privileges were deemed to be the same as those hitherto enjoyed by Indian legislatures until they were changed by a future Parliament.[18] A trade-off was suggested so that the discharge of judicial duties (except when considering the removal of a judge) could not be discussed by the legislatures and the irregularities in parliamentary proceedings could not be discussed in a court of law.[19] The latter discussion about residuary privileges is missing from N.G. Ayyangar's and A.K. Ayyar's memorandum on the Union Constitution.[20] The Provincial Constitution Committee thought that the residuary privileges should be the same as under the Government of India Act, 1935.[21] The Draft Constitution—for some reason that defies documentation—decreed that the residuary privileges shall be the same as those of the House of Commons.[22] Before the Draft Constitution was discussed on the floor of the Assembly, at least one person proposed the amendment that these residuary privileges should be those of the Indian dominion legislature and not the House of Commons.[23]

It was in the Constituent Assembly that some of the problems relating to parliamentary privilege were discussed for the first time.[24] There was no difficulty in persuading the Draftsmen that the privileges of the legislature should also extend to its committees.[25] The major thrust of the criticism was about the equation of parliament's privileges with those of the House of Commons. This was seen as something which was both vague and unnecessary,[26] an affront to the dignity of the Constitution and the concept of political independence,[27] a rejection of one's traditions[28] for a non-homogeneous, vague, unquantified and changing foreign code of privileges.[29] Some members did not see harm in such a reference to the House of Commons because India remained a member of the Commonwealth.[30] In the alternative, it was suggested that the privileges ought to be codified and collected in a Schedule of the Constitution.[31] The suggestion that the privileges should be the same as those of Indian dominion legislature[32] or the Constituent assembly was opposed on the ground that these assemblies enjoyed "no privileges" and that such a suggestion would tantamount to "a complete nullification of all our privileges".[33] A.K. Ayyar, the spokesman, rejected all these suggestions. He rejected the charge of imitation by asserting that ". . . to say that you are as good as Great Britain is not a badge of inferiority but an assertion of your own self-respect and also of the omnipotence of your parliament".[34] He reminded the House that this constitutional cross-reference to the House of Commons gave parliament the privilege to commit for contempt without affecting its power to change whatever it wanted.[35] Even so, an amendment specifically making each house the 'sole judge' of what it does was not specifically incorporated in the Constitution.[36]

The Constituent Assembly was also concerned that the immunity for the publication of parliament's proceedings extended only to official and not to newspaper and other publications.[37] It was argued that official proceedings are slow in appearing, that "there would be nothing known outside the House of the happenings inside the House for months to come".[38] It was feared that many speeches may not be reported. The example of Malviya's speech, which was not reported during the days of the Raj, was cited.[39] One member considered it hypocritical that those who criticised this limitation before Independence should support it now.[40] The crux of the issue was a fear that members would use parliament as a forum for giving wider publicity to all kinds of illegal and unsavoury matters.[41] This amendment was seen as

> enabling all kinds of defamatory statements, leaving alone for the time seditious statements.[42]

The critics replied that the Speakers of the various assemblies would have ample power to control what was said in the legislatures.[43] It was also submitted that

> freedom of the press is a very important right among the rights of the people. If anything could be published by or under the authority of this House, the press should have freedom to publish it.[44]

The front bench was not impressed.

The debate continued when similar provisions dealing with the State legislatures came before the Constituent Assembly.[45] Members pointed out that the press were very concerned about parliamentary privileges.[46] But, ironically, the press—as cited—seemed less concerned about their own rights and much more about the fact that the Constitution legislated by reference to an alien unwritten Constitution.[47] It was alleged that the Constitution makers had "more or less shirked, 'scamped' " their duties.[48] As alternatives India's own parliamentary experience and the fact that a future parliament could determine these matters was once again suggested.[49] The strongest alternative suggested was that of a Schedule listing all the privileges.[50] One member claimed that he had actually drawn up such a Schedule and would present it if required to do so.[51] But the debate was lost when B.R. Ambedkar, the chief front bench spokesman, made it clear that the privileges were needed not so much for the legislators but against the people and the legislators in order to safeguard the institutional viability of the House:

> But there is not the slightest doubt in my mind and I am also sure in the minds of the Drafting Committee that Parliament must have certain privileges, when that Parliament would be so much exposed to calumny, to unjustified criticism that the parliamentary institution in this country might be brought down to utter contempt and may lose all the respect which parliamentary institutions should have from the citizens for whose benefits it operates.[52]

The institutional protection of Parliament had become as important an issue with the Constituent Assembly as the institutional protection of the executive or the judiciary had become with the British in India.

The relevant provisions dealing with privilege of the Union Parliament in the Constitution were as follows:

105. *Powers, privileges, etc. of Houses of Parliament and of the members and committees thereof*

(1) Subject to the provisions of this Constitution and to the rules and standing orders regulating the procedure of Parliament, there shall be freedom of speech in Parliament.

(2) No member of Parliament shall be liable to any proceedings in any court in respect of anything said or any vote given by him in Parliament or any committee thereof, and no person shall be liable in respect of the publication by or under the authority of either House of Parliament of any report, paper, votes or proceedings.

(3) In other respects, the powers, privileges and immunities of each House of Parliament, and of the members and the committees of each House, shall be such as may from time to time be defined by Parliament by law, and, until so defined, shall be those of the House of Commons of the Parliament of the United Kingdom, and of its members and its Committees at the commencement of the Constitution.

(4) The provisions of clauses (1), (2) and (3) shall apply in relation to persons who by virtue of this Constitution have the right to speak in, and otherwise to take part in the proceedings of a House of Parliament or any committee thereof, as they apply in relation to members of Parliament.

Similar provisions were also made for the State legislatures.

Meanwhile, the Press Laws Enquiry Committee (1950) continued to take the stance taken by India's Constitution makers that "the privilege attached to speeches in the legislature cannot be passed on automatically to newspaper reports of such speeches".[53] The Press Commission (1952-4) recommended that a substantially true account of the proceedings of Central and State legislatures should not be liable for prosecution for criminal defamation.[54] It did not accept that a wider immunity from all legal proceedings should be given. It did, however, agree that an "unintentional and unavoidable transgression of the rulings of the chair (in respect of publication of proceedings) should. . . not be regarded as a breach of privilege".[55]

Quite apart from the constitutional implications, the press began to feel the raw edge of the laws relating to parliamentary privileges soon after the legislatures came to be established. This was made abundantly clear by the Press Commission which summed up the protests made by the representatives of the press as follows:

> Several representations have been made to us that the position of newspapers on the subject of the contempt of the legislatures requires to be clarified or elucidated. The Hyderabad State Government have stated that there are dark corners with regard to the law of contempt of legislatures. The Southern India Journalists' Federation have submitted that the laws should be strictly defined and rigorously enforced. The Indian Federation of Working Journalists have stated that the exercise of the powers by the legislatures with regard to contempt matters is causing them increasing concern. Both they and the All India Newspapers Editors' Conference have stressed the necessity of the newspapers not being penalized for publishing records of the proceedings which were subsequently ordered to be expunged. All India Newspapers Editors' Conference have further recommended that the powers of the legislature should be defined by statute and sparingly invoked. The Gujerati Patrakar Sangh have urged that where there is an alleging of the contempt of legislature, the matter should be referred by the Speaker to the High Court for decision. The Marathi Patrakar Parishad have adopted the Memorandum of the All India Newspapers Editors' Conference to the Press Laws Enquiry Committee in which a representation was made that newspapers should be fully protected when they published parliamentary proceedings.[56]

With the experience of a little over three years to go by the Press Commission was able to refer to cases like the Blitz case where the paper lost its credentials in the legislature because they talked of the Chief Minister's influence over the Speaker.[57] The Times of India lost its credentials for commenting on a

Speaker's vague understanding of the notions of the public interest.[58] Later it had to apologize for the premature publication of a Select Committee Report.[59] The Statesman was 'ticked off' for wrongly describing an account the 'official version' and finding it 'intriguing'.[60] The threat of withdrawal of credentials was made to some Mysore papers for criticising the legislature's attitude to gaming laws.[61] The Indian Express was threatened with admonishment for talking of the "confused atmosphere" in which a House decided a matter.[62] Three dailies, a weekly and a monthly were called to order for reporting on a press conference in which a Bill pending in the Madhya Bharat legislature was criticised.[63] There was some agitation when the Speaker of the Uttar Pradesh Assembly considered making rulings which would affect the rights of the press.[64] From all this the Press Commission reminded its readers that even the Supreme Court and High Courts were vulnerable to criticism and observed:

> Some of these cases, in our opinion, disclose oversensitiveness on the part of the legislatures to even honest criticism. . . It behoves our legislature not to resort lightly to contempt proceedings. The Press, as a whole, is anxious to maintain and enhance the dignity and prestige of our courts and legislatures and recognizes that within the precincts of the Assembly hall, the presiding officer's ruling is supreme and the freedom of the members absolute. . . [L]ike all prerogatives the privilege requires to be most jealously guarded and very cautiously exercised. Indiscriminate use is likely to defeat its own purpose. The fact that there is no legal remedy against at least some of the punishments imposed by the legislature should make them all the more careful in exercising their powers, privileges and immunities.[65]

Since the publication of parliamentary proceedings by newspapers and other private sources was immunized by clause (2), the Calcutta High Court held that such newspaper or private publication would be liable for criminal defamation and other legal proceedings.[66] The Parliamentary Proceedings

(Protection of Publication) Act, 1956 was passed to protect fair and accurate privately published accounts of proceedings in parliament. This applied only to the Central legislatures and not the states who were expected to pass their own laws on this matter.[67] This protection was removed during the Emergency (1975-77) by the Parliamentary Proceedings (Protection of Publication) Repeal Act, 1976. This repeal was bitterly opposed in Parliament as nailing the death of democracy and interfering with parliament's capability of communicating with the people.[68] The government's undoubted majority carried the day. Meanwhile the Constitution (Forty-second Amendment) Act, 1976 also amended the Constitution so that the House of Commons ceased to be the measuring device for discovering the privileges of Indian Parliaments from 1976 onwards.[69]

The Constituent Assembly had left an intractable problem for the Supreme Court and High Courts to solve. If Indian citizens and other persons had guaranteed fundamental rights, would the exercise of parliamentary privileges be allowed to react into these fundamental rights? Or, to put it differently, although the laws passed by both Houses of any Indian legislature were subject to the chapter on Fundamental Rights, would the privileges granted by the Constitution and assumed by one House have priority over and override fundamental rights?[70] This matter first came up in the *Blitz* case (1954)[71] where the paper had criticised the actions of the Speaker of the U.P. State Assembly over the withdrawal of accreditations of Blitz and alleged that he looked to the Chief Minister "for guidance . . . instead of trying to set up healthy parliamentary traditions". A refusal by the editor to disclose the name of his correspondent led to the editor's arrest and a consequent fundamental rights petition before the Supreme Court. The Supreme Court ignored the broad constitutional issues and concentrated on whether the warrant and arrest of the editor followed the procedure laid down in Article 22 of the chapter on Fundamental Rights. Article 22 had been violated because the editor was not taken before a magistrate within twenty-four hours. By implication, the exercise of the power of parliamentary privileges was made subject to fundamental rights. In specific terms, no such general constitutional doctrine was laid down by the Supreme Court in the *Blitz* case. Not surprisingly, the issue surfaced again in the *Searchlight* case [72] where an editor was issued a breach-of-privilege notice by the Bihar Legislative Assembly for he had published a portion of the proceedings which the Speaker had ordered to be expunged. This time, the editor also raised the question that the order of the Speaker violated his fundamental right to freedom of expression guaranteed in Article 19 (1) (a). As it happens, even though contempt of court had been included, parliamentary privilege was not one of the constitutionally permissible reasonable restrictions that could be made on the exercise of free speech.[73] The dissenting judge's solution to this case was to begin by denying the existence of a privilege whereby the Speaker could prohibit the publication of public debates.[74] But he went further and held that the privileges were subject to the free speech provisions.[75] The learned judge did not, however, clarify the matter much further. Was free speech absolute? Was contempt of parliament a reasonable restriction like contempt of court? If so, were the judges amending the Constitution by expanding the list of constitutional limitations on free speech? What was the dividing line between particular kinds of privileges which were absolute and those which were not? Were all privileges non-absolute? The majority of judges looked at the matter differently. They looked for a harmonious solution and came up with the prescription that general provisions in the Constitution must give way to specific provisions. In what was clearly a policy decision, they held that the general provision giving India's legislatures the same privileges as those of the House of Commons was more specific than the specific provision that freedom of speech and expression was subject to only some clearly specified restrictions found to be in the public interest.[76] The *Blitz* case was not seen as giving a general priority to the chapter on Fundamental Rights generally.[77] This approach was taken to even greater policy lengths when the Court also decided that the internal rules of the legislature were taken to meet the requirement of fundamental rights in Article 21 that a person should not be deprived of his liberty except by procedure established by law.[78] This quite clearly defeats the purposes of Article 21 which was designed precisely so that a person could be protected from informal and other rules and actions not specifically authorized by law. The majority in the *Searchlight* case did seem to make it clear that free speech was subject to the exercise of those privileges of the legislature which the Constituent Assembly had generously equated with those of the House of Commons.

Meanwhile, a much more important *non-press* case subsumed the entire controversy. A constitutional imbroglio was created when the Uttar Pradesh legislature issued warrants for the arrest of two Allahabad High Court judges who had released a petitioner imprisoned by the legislature for contumacious conduct.[79] Twenty-eight judges of the Allahabad High Court entertained a petition from the judges relieving them from the responsibility of complying with the order. The crisis continued. The President invoked the Supreme Court's advisory jurisdiction to resolve the constitutional entanglements that lay at the root of the problem. A compromise solution offered by the majority of the judges evaded the broad issue. They argued that a general warrant issued by the legislature for contempt of parliament was not really a privilege of the legislature and that, in the past, the courts had treated it as such on the basis of a general agreement and comity between them and the legislatures.[80] The dissenting judge—Justice Sarkar—rightly criticised this 'hovel argument' by refusing to accept that the courts created or administered law on the basis of agreement and concession.[81] Clearly, the majority's all too subtle argument had obscured the issue. But the majority did also make the basic point that the Supreme Court and the High Court's fundamental right (and other writ jurisdiction) was not really ousted by the existence of parliamentary privileges.[82] This really begs the whole issue. If the courts have jurisdiction, what is the basis on, and the extent to which, it exists? Several solutions are possible: (i) The court could inquire whether the privilege claimed actually exists and then back off. (ii) The courts could not only examine whether the privilege claimed exists but also consider whether the exercise of such a privilege in the instant case was a proper exercise of such privilege. (iii) The court could insist that an acknowledged privilege must meet the restraining impact of certain Fundamental Rights but not others. The list of rights to which the privilege provisions are subject would have to be justified on some rational or policy basis (*e.g.* it could just decide that the procedure used in cases of arrest for breach of privilege must follow the appropriate procedure used in the Fundamental Rights chapter). (iv) The courts could deem certain privileges to be absolute whilst treating others as not so absolute (*e.g.* a distinction could be made between breaches within the precincts of the legislatures and others or, between the privileges specifically mentioned in the Constitution (free speech in the legislature and immunity from legal proceedings for legislators) and residuary privileges which were simply equated with those of the House of Commons). (v) The courts could insist that the exercise of acknowledged privileges should feel the full impact of the Fundamental Rights chapter, including the free speech provisions. Indian courts seem to have followed all policies at all times.

The Court adopted solution (iii) in the *Blitz* case leaving open the case for solution (iv). The dissenting judge in the *Searchlight* case wanted solution (ii)—or a weaker variation of it—to be teamed up with solution (v). The majority in the *Searchlight* case adopted solution (i) with some modifications for solution (iii). The minority in the *High Court Judges* case adopted solution (i). The majority in this case gave an impression of adopting the minority judge's solution in the *Searchlight* case (who was also on the Bench that decided this case) but in fact left a large number of questions open. It seems to have rested its laurels simply on deciding that the privilege issue did not oust the fundamental rights and other jurisdiction of the courts. In *Tej Kiran* v. *Sanjiva Reddy*[83] (1970), the courts seem to have taken the view that their jurisdiction is totally ousted from considering a civil suit in respect of something said by a member in the House. The Court has used the language of total ouster but once again not resolved the issues with any clarity.

In recent years, some parliaments have avoided such a wrangle by taking no further action. In the *Chief Justice of*

India case (1981)[84] the Speaker disallowed a privilege motion on what the Chief Justice and his brother puisne judges had said about members of parliament during court proceedings. In *Govind Bhatt's* case (1982)[85] the Karnataka Speaker disallowed a motion about a former Chief Justice's criticism of a statute. These cases illustrate the reticence of the legislature in allowing any kind of discussion about judges. None of these cases really raised the jurisdictional conflicts where the institution in question would have no choice but to accept jurisdiction and then explain why it should intervene or refrain from intervening. In such cases, the legislature has sometimes sidestepped the issue.[86] Such a situation has arisen in the *Kerala Legislature* case[87] where the Kerala High Court gave relief to a petitioner who claimed that the exercise of parliamentary privileges by the Assembly violated his rights.

Irate pressmen and constitutional pundits have not teased the court for more exact solutions. It is clear that the courts will intervene if a pressman—or for that matter, any other person—is arrested and sent to jail by the legislature. It might offer him bail or require that the prescribed constitutional procedure should be observed. But on discovering that such a privilege is a legitimately acknowledged privilege, it would not go further. It is highly doubtful if the courts would themselves seek to resolve the fundamental reconciliation between parliamentary privileges and the freedom of the press. The *High Court Judges* case is a reminder that this is dangerous territory where judges should fear to tread. A solution that insists that the legislatures should be forced to accept to have their meetings publicised and commented upon in the public interest and under the scrutiny of the courts may not be within the political gift of the court.[88] It would also create an additional forum which would be ruthlessly exploited by those subject to the strictures of the legislature and content to sit by and watch a tense wrangle between two important divisions of government.

The legislatures of India have had a fairly free hand in exercising their privileges against the press. The list of instances is sufficiently large and wide-ranging to affirm the Press Commission's hesitant conclusion that the press were being unjustly treated. While the ultimate sanction has, in most cases, not been very severe, the procedure is sufficiently daunting to upset even the most vigorous editor. In the *Janagarajana* case (1965)[89] the paper carried an article: "Why does Bhansaheb Bandokar not attend the Assembly?" It criticised the *tamasha* going on in the Assembly, which was described as a fish market where several members spoke at once and which was a "waste of public money and time". Even though—in terms of the law of defamation—there might have been a good rolled up plea of justification and fair comment, the Committee of Privileges thought this brought the Speaker, the House and its legislators into ridicule and contempt. The editor's refusal to apologize led to committal to prison for contempt. Again, R.K. Karanjia, the editor of Blitz, was summoned and reprimanded for calling a member of parliament a liar.[90] Karanjia unsuccessfully tried to stall and by-pass the proceedings by petitioning the Supreme Court to reconsider the *Searchlight* case by giving priority to Fundamental Rights over parliamentary privileges. He was then subjected to the humiliating experience of a formal reprimand. Blitz was denied 'accreditation' privileges which were restored later. In the *Thaniram* case (1975),[91] a severe reprimand was given to a person who had questioned the partiality of the Speaker in not allowing a question about the Bangla leader, Mujibur Rehman. The error was trivial in nature and the punishment must be deemed to be related to the intransigence of the newspaper in not apologizing. A similar explanation for the punishment of reprimand can be made of the *Satyayug* case (1977)[92] where a legislator from West Bengal was maligned and where the feature writer did not apologize but the editor had. In the *Udayavani* case (1978)[93] the Karnataka legislature brought to the bar and reprimanded an unrepentant editor who had accused legislators of harassing educational institutions.

In the *Nagrik* case (1978)[94] an editor who criticised the alleged leak of a budget by the Chief Minister was subjected to simple imprisonment for a day. Here, the editor did not repent after the Chief Minister's explanation gave only what seemed like a qualified apology and disobeyed the summons to appear at the Bar of the house. In the *Times of India* case (1982)[95] the

Speaker artfully ducked the issue when he felt that it was beneath contempt for the House to take note of an allegation about the corruption of legislators in the house.

In the *Ravivarchi Loksattan* case (1983)[96] a state legislature faced with this situation did feel the need to express its strong displeasure.[97] In *Varsha Joshi and K.W. Deson* case,[98] the threat to institute legal proceedings against a speaker for allowing discussion on *sub judice* matters caused the Committee to recommend imprisonment as a punishment. The defence, probably realizing that much of this wrangle was wrapped up in local politics rather than genuinely raising substantive issues, decided to take no further action.

In all these cases, the power of reprimand relates less to the gravity of the offence or the *bona fides* of the journalist. It is linked to the attitude of the journalist. And a journalist making a *bona fide* defence in the public interest may discover that this is treated as recalcitrance justifying a use of the power of reprimand. The legislature uses this power against journalists to assert its status rather than deal with the issue. Generally most cases have been decided on the basis that the contemnor regretted a mistake and the matter has been dropped. Sometimes the paper has been told that it must make an unconditional apology and the matter has not been taken further. At others, a further condition has been stipulated. The paper has also been asked to publish (either on the front page or elsewhere) a correction and an apology. Sometimes the newspaper volunteers to do this or intimates to the legislature that it has already done so. In other cases, a reprimand is threatened unless the newspaper follows this course of action. The newspaper is usually given a chance to provide an explanation. This may be done before the Speaker rules on the matter. An opportunity for explanation, apology or representation is invariably provided by the Committee of Privileges. In *Thaniram* case (1975), the Kerala legislature did, however, rule that these proceedings were not judicial proceedings and there was no right to be represented by legal counsel.[99] In one interesting case, the Speaker actually consulted the Press Gallery Committee before making up his mind on what to do.[100] There is a sufficient flexibility in this procedure to manoeuvre a compromise and yet gain enough publicity to achieve any other political purpose that may be obtained from such proceedings.

Apart from the procedure and the mechanics of punishment, the 'law' evolved by the legislatures in dealing with the press has ostensibly tried to emulate the House of Commons. In particular, the latter's observations in the *Daily Mail* case on the importance of the press to parliament and the public have been relied upon by the Press Commission in various privilege cases like the *Dina Thant* case (1958)[101] in Madras and the *Nav Bharat* case (1957)[102] in Madhya Pradesh. In the former case, the Committee of Privileges observed:

> Just as members of the Vidhan Sabha (*i.e.*, legislature) have several rights to criticise and comment, the press too has constitutional rights to express its opinion and it is essential in the interests of the public that the rights of both of these institutions should not be encroached upon and their freedom should be safeguarded.[103]

The two notions which attend such a declaration of faith—and which were apparent in many cases—were the notion of *triviality* and the notion of *motive*. Thus, an inconsequential press report even if accompanied by some criticism is not proceeded with further. This is reinforced or accompanied by a finding that there was no motive (used interchangeably with lack of intent or lack of *mala fide*).

As to what is *trivial* is often a pragmatic political decision. In the *Hindustan Times* case (1981)[104] the U.P. Vidhan Sabha refused to proceed even though members of parliament had been compared to street gangs. The allegation was made by a well known communist who was himself a member of the Rajya Sabha and close to Mrs. Gandhi.

A large number of cases of simple or casual misreporting is dealt with thus, with or without preliminary investigation.

In the *Nav Bharat* case (1957),[105] a false and partial account of how the Speaker dealt with adjournment motions called for a *prima facie* investigation. But no contempt was found because the "gist of this contempt is *mala fide* publication" and no *mala fide* was found to exist in this case. No further action was recommended. In the *Times of India* case (1960)[106] a speech on the language issue in Assam did not correspond to what was said. Quite independently of the editor's regret and the expression of a hope that the reporter would be more careful, the Committee took the view that such matters should be settled between the complainant legislator and the paper. The *ratio decidendi* of the decision—if it can be called that—was that there was no contempt because "there was no malice but it was a case of careless reporting". The idea of the complainant and the newspaper sorting things between themselves is returned to in the *Statesman* case (1966)[107] where the House was satisfied with the explanation by the paper that they had printed the legislator's letter correcting the story. In the *Indian Express* case (1964)[108] a special correspondent was excused for falsely reporting that a legislator had apologized for what he had said because there was "no question of *mala fides* on his (*i.e.* the correspondent's) part". An expression of regret and a reminder to be "extremely careful in ensuring accuracy in reporting parliamentary proceedings" was deemed sufficient to dispose of the matter. In the *Times of India* case (1965),[109] a simple expression of regret in wrongly suggesting that the Finance Minister had criticised two legislators was deemed enough. The omission of the word 'too' in the *Statesman* case (1965)[110] while reporting on which language the Prime Minister would address the House was deemed not to have been "done in *mala fide* and we cannot conclude from this that it was done in malice to project something else". A *bona fide* error and the expression of regret for misreporting a speech in the Lok Sabha by the Rajya Sabha was considered adequate in the *Hindustan* case (1973).[111] This last case posed deeper problems about the restraint that legislators should themselves show in talking about other legislatures.

Many of these cases of careless reporting are best understood in their political context whereby the privilege jurisdiction is used to air grievances and harass political opponents. To take a more recent sample. In the *Hindustan Times* case (1979)[112] the real issue was about the takeover of the *National Herald.*

The editor expressed regret. In the *Hind Samachar* case (1980)[113] a minor misreporting was used to amplify aspects of the Baghpat rape case and the contribution of a particular member.[114] This is also true of the *All India Radio* case (1980)[115] regarding the misreporting of the party affiliation of a Janata(S) member as Lok Dal.

It is important to stop here for a moment to consider what the concept of *bona fide* or *mala fide* really means in the context of parliamentary jurisprudence. For the plea of *bona fides* (or lack of *mala fide*) is invoked freely and mechanically. Sometimes—as in the cases reviewed earlier—it is simply accepted. Consider the *Indian Express* case (1977)[116] where the opportunistic policies of a political party in respect of the passage of a legislation was in issue and the plea of *bona fide* was accepted even though the paper's hostility to the political party was well known. What exactly did *bona fide* mean? Perhaps, it signified simply an expression of regret. Not surprisingly many newspapers do not concentrate on the question of *bona fides* at all. They simply regret what has happened and that *sub silentio* serves the *bona fides* of the legislation.[117] Inevitably, the more important factors have become how trivial the occasion has been and the extent to which the newspaper shows regret and willingness to make amends if called upon to do so. An erroneous report accompanied by an expression of regret and the publication of a correction about a civil servant's alleged complicity in corruption was accepted in the *Alai Osai* case (1973).[118] The idea that the error was trivial and inadvertent is important in the *Alai Osai* and the *Hindustan* cases as well as the *Indian Express* cases (1963).[119] In the first *Indian Express* case it was wrongly reported that a bill had been passed when it was not.[120] In the second case, a leading politician was wrongly quoted as saying that the Prime Minister should not speak in Hindi.[121] In the first *Indian Express* case (1963) a correction had already been published. But some papers are asked to publish a correction with the threat that the matter would otherwise go to the Committee of Privileges. This is what happened in the *Hind Samachar* case (1962)[122] where the Speaker was wrongly described as castigating the *bewakufi* (foolishness) of some legislators. A milder threat was given in the *Indian Express* case (1967)[123] where the editor apologized for overcompressing a report to convey the impression that the legislator had supported the labour practice of *gherao* (temporary imprisonment by encirclement). It was suggested that "[i]f the House agreed, the editor may be asked to publish the correction and his regret in the next issue of his paper and the matter would be treated as closed". A similar attitude was taken in the *Indian Express* case (1970)[124] where a legislator was wrongly reported as opposing the government's action in giving travel documentation facilities to Nepal's former Prime Minister, B.P. Koirala.

The Committee of Privileges dealt with a case[125] where a misleading report was made about comments in the legislature about the Assembly and the newspaper. This error was further compounded by publishing information relating to the proceedings before the Committee of Privileges. A published unconditional apology and correction and a disarming plea of ignorance of the law of privileges were deemed to be enough to drop the matter. An allegation of misreporting was also considered by a Committee of Privileges in the *Semi-Sanj* case (1967).[126] Treating the official report of the proceedings as inconclusive, asserting the right to take oral evidence and accepting the apology, the Committee observed:

> It would appear that it would not be consistent with the dignity of the House to take too serious a view of every case of inaccurate reporting or misreporting. The Committee feels that the law of parliamentary privilege should not be administered in such a way which would fetter unnecessarily or discourage the reporting of proceedings of the House. In most of the cases where an apology is tendered the investigation into the controversial matter was not pursued and the matters were dropped by accepting the apology.

This reveals the policy of the legislature as opposed to the principles that underlie its decision-making. There is a considerable pragmatism in this approach which was explained by the Committee of Privileges of the Bihar Legislative Council in the *Bhrastachar Nirodh* (1977)[127] where allegations of corruption were made against certain legislators:

> [The] manager of this mushroom publication who may be prepared to descend to any depth to earn a name and fame for his paper. Any action will be a boon to him in disguise since it is bound to make an unwarranted publicity of his paper and give undue publicity to him.

Some of the cases about misreporting are trivial. In the *Patriot* case (1980)[128] the wrong party affiliation was attributed to a member of parliament. In the *Amrita Bazar Patrika* case (1979)[129] a name was 'suppressed' from the newspaper list of legislators who had asked a question. In some cases, the misreporting is important to the member. What was the truth about a minister's dealings with someone abroad?[130] Had a person agreed with the creation of a particular kind of commercial state?[131] Had a member called for the confirmation of President's Rule in Assam?[132] Had the opposition blocked proceeding?[133] Had a minister suggested that identity cards should be issued to even residents of Assam?[134] Had the Chairman of the Rajya Sabha criticized a minister over the handling of a fire tragedy?[135]

In many cases an apology is, therefore, accepted. Sometimes there is—as in the *Pratipaksha* (1976) and other cases[136]—an undertaking that such a breach will not be countenanced again. In certain cases like the *Satyajug* case (1977) and other cases[137] such an undertaking was a condition for the case being dropped.

While misleading reports cannot be made, it is now clear from a ruling of the Rajya Sabha that Parliamentary proceedings are public unless there is an order to the contrary.[138]

There have been several cases where the paper has tried to pass the blame on to the news agency which supplied the paper with the story. In the *Navashakti* case (1966)[139] the paper claimed that the reference to opposition legislators as "goondas" (ruffians) and "rowdies" was a translation error from the report of a news agency, PTI. It transpired that the PTI report could not possibly have lent itself to such a translation. The paper was let off because it expressed regret on the front page of three successive editions of its newspaper. In the *Indian Express* case (1967)[140] the news agency UNI's report was correct but the Indian Express had made an error in compressing a story about a legislator's support for the trade union tactic of *gherao* (encirclement). In the *Aryavarta* case (1968)[141] it was the news agency, Samachar which had made an error in reporting a speech on the Czech crisis. The plea of "no intention . . . to malign anybody" was accepted. Although the Committee of Privileges considered the case, no guidelines were laid down to prescribe the duty of care to be shown by news agencies. In the *Indian Nation* case (1970)[142] the Speaker of the Lok Sabha accepted the explanation that a respectable news agency, UNI was relied upon without in any way censuring the news agency. The issue reported on was a fairly important one relating to the travel facilities given to a former Nepalese Prime Minister. A similar forbearance was shown in the *Northern India Patrika* case (1970)[143] where it is not even clear whether the news agency reports of PTI and UNI had conveyed the impression whether a legislator was interrupting the speech of another. No proper investigation of the specific responsibility of the news agency took place. In the *Alai Osai* case (1973),[144] however, the news agency, PTI, apologized and published a correction about a false charge of corruption against a civil servant. In the *Hindustan Times, Indian Express, Times of India, UNI* cases (1974)[145] the news agency took the stand that its story on the 47th Report of the 'Committee on Public Undertakings' (CPU) on Modern Bakeries was essentially correct in highlighting that 'mouldy and stale bread' was being sold in the market. The Speaker took the somewhat unusual procedure of referring the matter to the CPU which reported that the headlines did not do justice to their findings. But having done all this, the Speaker dropped the issue. Excellent opportunities for working out guidelines for news agencies seem to have been missed. This opportunity continued to be missed in the *Hindustan Samachar and Loksatta* case (1981),[146] where the news agency made an important error about a statement made by a member of Parliament. An even better opportunity came in the *Hind*

Samachar case (1980)[147] where the news agency had reported correctly on the Baghpat rape case but not so the newspapers. In the *Swadesh* case (1981)[148] many satisfactory rulings were made about using the privilege jurisdiction for trivial cases but no comment was made on Swadesh's defence that the story came from a news agency. The relative liabilities of the paper and news agency should have been discussed.

This is all the more important because most newspapers—local and national—pick up their stories from news agencies. Most, if not all, newspapers cannot independently investigate news stories.

There are also some cases on the publication of material which should not have been published or was expunged. In the *Statesman* case (1957)[149] the proceedings had been published with the comment that the speech of one member was intriguing. The editor's regret—not a full apology—was considered enough to dispose of the matter. In the *Lok Satta* and *Indian Express* cases (1963)[150] regrets and apologies were accepted in the publication of two Bills as if they had been approved by the House. In the *Leaders Committee* case (1975)[151] an account of a confidential committee was leaked by legislators, who were requested not to do so again. Again, in the *Hind Publishing House* case (1973)[152] the deliberate and misleading publication of a Bill as virtually an Act was not discharged until a full and unconditional apology was made. The Committee of Privileges took this tough stand because the law publishers in question made the publication "with a view to make monetary gains by the sale of its copies". A categorical undertaking for the future was also requested in the *Pratipaksha* case (1974)[153] where unauthorized records were sold and there was a breach of the copyright of the legislature. The legislatures seem to have looked more at the motive of the contemnor rather than at the nature of the breach of privilege.

The cases involving the publication of material ordered to be expunged stand on a different footing. In the *Free Press Journal* case (1959)[154] an unconditional apology was given for this "oversight". In the *Hind Samachar* case (1960)[155] an unconditional apology and an assurance that a correction would be published was the course of action undertaken. Again, an apology was accepted in the *Hindustan Times* case (1966)[156] where such expunged remarks were made about a distinguished legislator. In the *Swadesh* case (1981)[157] the actual ruling on the question of expunged material is not clear. However, in the *Indian Express* case (1982)[158] the Chairman of the Rajya Sabha disallowed a privilege motion even though it related to expunged material although he did observe that disregarding the express wishes of the House was reprehensible.

While some consistency appears to have been achieved both in respect of the question of breach and the course of action to be followed the institutional rights of parliament to control the publication of its records do not appear to have been clearly and unequivocally enforced.

Now let us turn to the kind of allegations that are made by newspapers. There are certain cases where the newspapers are found to have made an inadvertent error. These cases are of various types. Some of these cases appear to be simple examples of what appears to be an *inadvertent error*. In the *National Herald* case (1981)[159] there was just the simple misreporting of a speech. But these matters are not always so simple. These cases are inevitably started by legislators who are not happy with a report or the manner in which they are projected or the political slant which may accompany such a report. Thus legislators often see many implications in what otherwise appears to be just an inadvertent error. In the *Indian Express* case (1966)[160] or the *Ananda Bazar Patrika* case (1980),[161] a legislator's name was missing from an exhaustive list of those who had taken a stand on a particular matter. In such cases the report is treated as being 'mixed up'.

Again—as in the *Jugantar* case (1977)[162]—the error may simply have been not to quote a member's speech in the newspaper. This may not amount to a breach of privilege and be treated indulgently but it may be sufficiently important for a legislator to raise it. Slightly more difficult are cases where the political implications are more overt and out in the open. In the *Patriot* case (1980)[163] a legislator was placed in the wrong party. In the *Hindustan Times* case (1979),[164] a legislator's political affiliations were wrongly described and other names were wrongly included. In the *Ananda Bazar Patrika* case (1980)[165] the dropping of certain legislators' names made the report somewhat meaningless. In the *Times of India* case (1965)[166] the newspaper mixed up the names of some colleagues about whom a legislator had made caustic comments. The *bona fides* of the newspaper were not doubted; and motive was taken as being crucial to the issue. This was also the issue in the *Samachar* case (1980)[167] where a person was wrongly described as a legislator. This case was further complicated because there was some distortion of parliament's discussion about the *Baghpat rape* case which had won a great deal of newspaper notoriety.

Again, legislators are concerned not to be seen as being rebuked or reprimanded by the Prime Minister—as in the *All India Radio* case (1978)[168]—or the Speaker—as in the *Times of India* case.[169] Still less—as in the *Mainstream* case[170]—do they take kindly to their contribution being described as "scurrilous". In this last case, which was riddled by the fact that the comment was made by a left wing paper on a right wing politician, the editor's apology made it unnecessary to consider whether this comment was justified as an opinion. Slightly more serious are cases like *All India Radio* (1980)[171] where a Speaker's ruling was seemingly suppressed; or, cases like the *Hindustan Times* (1979)[172] where important political information was distorted. In this latter case the newspaper falsely attributed to a Minister a statement concerning the takeover of another national newspaper. More serious are cases like *All India Radio* (1970)[173] and *Hindustan* (1977)[174] where aspersions were cast on legislators. In the *All India Radio* case (1975)[175] the allegations alleged to be made against a legislator were those of "cheating and forgery". The plea that there was a "genuine misunderstanding" because of the "terrible noise . . . din and uproar" was accepted and a strict attitude towards future transgressions promised. A reprimand was issued in the *Satyayug* case (1975)[176] where wrong reporting was used to make a legislator the "symbol of . . . torture" and associated with various illegalities. A less lenient attitude was taken in the *Hindustan* case (1977)[177] where a legislator in the Lok Sabha was alleged by the newspaper to have made allegations of political corruption against the Rajya Sabha. The issue was confused because it was not clear whether the report of the newspaper was accurate or not. In the *Assam Tribute* and *Natun Assamiya* cases (1959)[178] the official record did not bear out a report in the newspaper of an allegation that a legislator had given land to a Pakistani. Inadvertent reporting has more than a whisper of politics to it. And privilege motions are raised both to deal with this whisper and to take it further. In most cases—except in exceptional ones, as in the *Satyayug* case—no punishment is seriously considered. The object is to use the opportunity to make a clarification and further the political advantage of the legislator raising the privilege issue.

In the *Organiser* case (1969)[179] the newspaper added a sentence about the communal nature of the politics of a member. Although the error was treated as *bona fide*, a more vigorous examination might have shown that the paper used both the news item and the explanation as an opportunity to advance their partisan and communal views. Lip service was paid to the tests of triviality and *bona fides* to detract from the political issues which simmered beyond the formal complaint. In the *National Herald* case (1978)[180] the attributing of fictitious statements to the Ministry as regards the closure and expulsion of Coca Cola and IBM by the Janata Government was clearly political mischief. Fundamental to all these cases is the fact that the complainant legislator used the parliamentary forum to air the issues. This emerges much more clearly in the *Murasoli* case (1962)[181] where Bhupesh Gupta, a member of the Rajya Sabha, brought to the attention of the House a newspaper story and cartoon implying that he had spoken like a *goonda* (ruffian) in parliament. Gupta himself preferred the following solution:

> It is a gross breach of privilege. Even so, I would not bring a privilege motion but I would like that the opinion of the House be made known.

In the *Organizer* case (1962)[182] Gupta was accused of colluding with a newspaper and a foreign agent in the discharge of his parliamentary duties. The matter was referred to the

Committee of Privileges. Oddly enough, a qualified apology accompanied by a simple declaration of innocence and no further explanation seems to have satisfied the Committee. Gupta also brought the *Times of India* case (1966)[183] to parliament. The newspaper had given a misleading headline to a parliamentary report suggesting that a particular sabotage was caused by communists. The Speaker did not take the matter further. There is a strange mixture of grievance ventilation and political publicity underlying all these cases. Bhupesh Gupta (in the first case) and the Committee of Privileges and the Speaker (in the sccond and third cases respectively) did not really treat these cases as raising any issues other than those of creating political publicity and mischief. This is also true of the *Indian Express* (1963)[184] and the *Statesman* (1965)[185] cases where trivial errors were made in reporting on proceedings concerning the language in which the Prime Minister ought to address parliament. Here, the making of the complaint merely gave further publicity to political aspects of the language controversy.

India's various legislatures have permitted their members to use the privilege procedure to ventilate personal and political issues. In such cases, the legislatures record the complaint, sympathize, comment, punish and may, in certain cases, even help to evolve a compromise. In the *Assam Tribune* and *Natun Assamiya* cases[186] (1959)—a member felt that her involvement on the granting of land to a Pakistani was wrongly presented. Even though the story was concocted and did not correspond to the official record of the proceedings, after a series of meetings, the Committee of Privileges reported that the matter be dropped because "it was amicably settled between the parties". Indeed, the settlement could have come about by the legislator writing to the newspapers directly. The legislature did not seem to make too much of a meal about the point of incorrect reporting of its proceeding. It is clear that privilege procedure is used as a re-agitational device for the free-wheeling and re-airing of issues. Errors and allegations may be condoned and ignored because the legislator, Speaker, Committee of Privileges or the legislature may have felt that the finding of a breach of privilege was not the resolution of the real issue that lay at the root of the controversy in a particular case before them.

There are some cases which involve general attacks on parliament or its working. In the *Aina* case (1966)[187] legislators were accused of distorting history "committing an unpardonable crime of creating a gulf between India and Kashmir", being ignorant and, amongst other things, indulging in a "feverish outburst of narrow-minded and trouble-mongering nationalism". The Lok Sabha's Committee of Privileges took the indulgent view that

> the impugned article read as a whole does not constitute a breach of privilge and contempt of the House, though certain portions of it are couched in a rather strong and undesirable and irresponsible language which is unbecoming of a responsible newspaper. That matter does not deserve any further notice.

A similar attitude was taken in another case involving *Aina* (1966)[188] where the legislators were pungently described as ignorant. In the *Manorma* case (1966)[189] no breach of privilege was found where parliament was criticised for the administrative scheme it had set up in respect of the Kerala University. In the *Hindustan Times* case (1967)[190] the manner in which legislators handled a report was described as having "its root in the crookedness, timidity and perversity which perhaps has never been displayed on the floor of parliament before". Parliament was alleged to have shown a "display of absurdity, venom, character assassination and lack of wisdom . . . not in keeping with the dignity of parliament and its members". This case was slightly different in that allegations of corruption were also made. This time the Committee of Privileges recommended the accepting of an unqualified apology and made the finding that the editorial brought "parliament into disrespect and disrepute which amounts to a breach of privilege and contempt of the House". The case is not altogether different from the *Aina* case (1966)[191]—apart from the allegation of corruption which is not highlighted. The different attitude and result may be explained on the basis of the different political backgrounds of the cases.

Aina was about the Kashmir issue. This case was about one of the business houses of India. A good opportunity to clarify the law relating to scandalizing parliament—to adapt a phrase from the law of contempt of court—seems to have been lost.

The exact range of this privilege was not established by later cases. In the *Vikas* case (1976)[192] comments were made to the effect that future generations would be ashamed of the U.P. Vidhan Sabha in respect of an allegedly low level and absurd debate there. The issue appears to have been decided on the ground of lack of *mala fides* on behalf of the writer. Some guidance is given of the sweep of this privilege in that it was said that the *bona fides* of the legislature was not questioned by the writer. But this is not explained further. What appears to have clinched the issue is that such an incident "should not be taken as an important one involving any breach of privllege or contempt of the house". In the *Hindustan* case (1977)[193] the newspaper allegedly reported a general speech about corruption in the Rajya Sabha. Actually, there was a misreporting because many of these things were not said. Satisfied with a correction and apology, the Speaker did not go to the heart of the real question about the extent to which the reform of parliament could be discussed both within and without the houses of parliament. It was precisely this question which was raised in the *Udayavani* case (1978)[194] where a newspaper article talked of how legislators were indulging in rhetoric and corrupting educational institutions. Here a reprimand was made, but the extent to which newspapers could discuss the affairs of parliament were not discussed. The need for an adequate discussion is demonstrated by the *Illustrated Weekly of India* case (1978)[195] where an editorial—perhaps not without political implications—talked of the calibre of superannuated legislators. A partial apology with a plea that there was general respect of legislators appears to have settled the issue. Typically, these proceedings are conducted by negotiation with little or no reference to the substantive standards alleged to govern the subject.

There are also cases where a parliamentary committee, or its working has been criticized. In the *Bharat Jyoti* case (1966)[196] it was commented that the reports of the Public Accounts

Committee were becoming superfluous. No attempt was made to consider the case on merits, which the editor wanted. The apology clinched the issue without discussing the right to comment on the working of a powerful Public Committee of Parliament. In the *Dainik Deshbandhu* case (1976),[197] it was alleged that a Select Committee had undertaken an investigative trip by way of "entertainment and excursions". The defence that there was no intention to reflect badly on the committee coupled with an apology closed the issue. A similar pattern followed in the *New Age* case (1981)[198] where political influences were alleged to be at work in the Estimates Committee of the legislature of the State of Himachal. These are difficult areas in which to determine the range of permissible investigation, comment, opinion or speculation. The Committee of Privileges seems not to have attempted this task. The task of evaluating the work of committees has become ever more difficult in the light of two rulings on the famous *Kuo Oil Deals*.[199] The Rajya Sabha decided that it had no jurisdiction to deal with privilege motions over a joint committee of both Houses and the Lok Sabha took the view that a minister withheld information from such a Committee. The simple question of how much information is available to the Committees and the public for information, evaluation and critique needs to be pronounced upon. These rulings establish a supply of information in a parliamentary democracy.

Various legislatures have been very sensitive to criticism and sometimes reacted sharply to the newspaper putting forward a defence. In the *Hindustan Times* case (1956)[200] an editorial described the "wrong tactics" of the Congress Assembly Party in the Delhi Vidhan Sabha. The newspaper's plea of justification and fair comment was met with a 'mild warning' about its 'dilatory tactics'. In the *People's Guardian* case (1959)[201] a much more pungent protest was made about the "odious nature of Punjab politics" and how various legislators were running a campaign of vilification against the politician Kairon "prompted by the sordid interest of self-seekers, who are always looking for an opportunity or pretext to run down the party in power and take it a target of their fusillade of their abuses and cheap slander". A finding of breach of privilege was made and an apology was accepted because the editor was inexperienced. In the *Young India* case (1960)[202] a different attitude was taken. The newspaper commented on the Speaker's speech to describe the "shameless impertinence" of the whole Assam assembly in passing a resolution asking the centre to appoint a judicial inquiry into certain matters. The report was principally on what the Speaker said. The case was further complicated by the fact that the newspaper continued to report on the proceeding before the Committee of Privileges which it was not supposed to do. But its original article was found to contain an innuendo derogatory of the House and Speaker. Despite a disarming declaration that the House should not be oversensitive to criticism, the editor was deprived of all his privileges for a "flagrant violation" of the privileges of the House. This case contrasts with the *Bharat Jyoti* case (1966)[203] where a sharp attack was made on the reports of the Public Accounts Committee which were described as "becoming increasingly superfluous where they are not positively mischievous in their impact and incidence". The editor asserted his right to comment and apologised for any unintended disrespect, if any. With that the matter was closed. In the *New Age* case,[204] a similar approach was adopted except that the case is peculiar in that it suggests that journalist members of the Rajya Sabha (or, for that matter, any legislature) are outside the privilege jurisdiction of other legislatures even in respect of what they write as journalists in their respective papers. In the *Udayavani* case (1978)[205] the fact that the editor wanted legal counsel and was not very co-operative contributed largely to his reprimand. In all these cases, allegations of corruption appear to have been treated more severely. But otherwise, there is no consistency in the decision making of various legislatures in dealing with attacks on themselves.

A different kind of attack is on the conduct of members. In the *Navashakti* case (1966)[206] a report on rowdy scenes in the Rajya Sabha with the comment that the Opposition were "rowdy" or "*goondas*" (ruffians) was excused as a translation mistake from a news agency report and the incident was closed after an expression of apology and regret. In the *Aryavarta* case (1970)[207] an attack on the integrity and national loyalty of communist legislators was made while commenting on the loss of art and other national treasures in Kashmir. The explanation of lack of motive was accepted and a finding of fact made that this was an important issue on which no single legislator was criticised. The matter was not taken further.

In the *Jugantar* case (1977)[208] a communist legislator raised an issue of privilege over a comment about Russian influence over Parliament. The issue was closed after the newspaper provided an explanation that the sentence could only be explained in a political context and expressed regret for hurting anyone's feelings. Here was an allegation of political corruption—the permissible limits of which merited consideration. An attempt to weigh some of the factors taken into consideration was made in the *Indian Express* case (1979)[209] where a general allegation was made that a particular party (Congress-I) had been opportunistic in facilitating the passage of a Bill dealing with public safety. Attention was paid to whether there was *mala fide*, whether the aspersion cast was direct or indirect, whether the occasion was trivial or important and to the importance of the freedom of the press. On all these grounds the proceedings were dropped. Clearly there are differences between allegations of group corruption, the making of general epithets, attacks on the loyalty of certain groups and general comments on the policies of a party. It is unfortunate that well articulated standards have not been set. The fact that these cases were used by the complainant groups as a further exercise in politics suggests a greater interest in the politics generated by the complaint than in the evolution of clear guidelines for the future.

Specific comments on the conduct of individual legislators is differently treated. In the *Nav Prabhak* case (1958)[210] adverse comments on the speech of a member were deemed not to constitute a breach of privilege "as long as such comments and criticisms do not impute motives to members". In the *Jagran* case (1958),[211] in addition to stressing the point about the motive of the newspaper, the Committee of Privileges did not make a finding of breach where Labour legislators were merely criticised. At the same time, a strict liability concept was disjunctively set up as an independent head of privilege in addition to malicious statements and malicious falsehoods. In the *Patriot* case (1974)[212] a speech by Mr. Mavlankar, a legislator, on some political movement in Gujarat was described as 'moving' but it was stressed that the politics of Gujarat had outmanoeuvred him. The matter was dropped because there was no malicious intent on the part of the nswspaper and the comment related to a non-parliamentary matter. In the *Economic Times* case (1980)[213] a general comment was made that those legislators who had impugned the integrity of one of their colleagues and used the protection of Parliament to protect themselves, were themselves committing a breach of privilege. However the matter was not taken further because of an apology. The issue was a sensitive one involving India's technical collaboration with a foreign company.

Attacks on the integrity of legislators may fall into different categories depending on the gravity of the situation and the importance of the legislator. In the *Kalki* case (1958),[214] the paper alleged that the re-organisation of the electoral districts would increase the legislator's "monopoly of illegal power". This was not treated as a breach of privilege—even if in bad taste—because these matters were deemed to be about non-parliamentary matters. The rule as to what constitutes a parliamentary matter where the integrity of parliament or a member is in question was clearly defined. In the *New Age* case (1961),[215] a legislator's (Hem Barua) speech was described as "blinded by prejudice. . . (and) stooping to the lowest level of mendacity." The editor of of *New Age* claimed that this was *bona fide* opinion expressed without malice. The legislator did not press the motion even though he would have preferred an expression of regret. The Speaker criticised the paper but dropped the matter. In the *Blitz* case (1961)[216] the paper was formally reprimanded because it talked of a senior right wing legislator's "bad, bold and black lies" and "all uttered in a hysterical manner of a violent epileptic". There are difficulties in treating this case consistently with other rulings. The emphasis on the motive of the contemnor was not emphasised and a stronger test declared in its place:

> The crux of the question is whether the said comment can reasonably be construed to come within the bounds of a fair comment or justifiable comment or whether they are in the nature of contemptuous insults, gross calumny, foul epithets or libellous reflections on a member of the House on account of his speech or conduct in Parliament.

If this test were applied to other rulings which turned on the motive of the contemnor, many more breaches of privilege would have been recorded. In the *Kerala Janatha* case (1963)[217] a legislator was described as a *thug* and criminal for producing some confidential letters on the floor of the legislature. An expression of contrition was considered enough even though it was suggested that a libel on a legislator would constitute a breach of privilege. In the *Murasoli* case (1962)[218], a communist legislator, Bhupesh Gupta, who was called a *goonda* (ruffian) by a newspaper did not take the matter further. In the *Organizer* case (1964)[219] an allegation that Bhupesh Gupta and his party were destroying Indian unity was disposed of with an apology because there was no intent to cause disrespect. The same legislator was also involved in the *Times of India* case (1966).[220] He was unable to persuade the Speaker that there was a *prima facie* case of breach of privilege where a parliamentary debate was misrepresented to suggest that communists had caused a particular sabotage. In the *Nava Shakti* case (1966),[221] the Speaker took the same attitude to a description of the behaviour of the opposition parties in parliament being like the behaviour of rowdies and *goondas*. The explanation that this was the result of a mistake of translation seems to have been accepted. In the *Indian Express* case (1973)[222] a legislator was wrongly quoted as having said that the Prime Minister was surrounded by *goondas* who created a ring of protection around her. The matter was dropped on the basis that the reporter may have misheard the debate. This is a strange ensemble of cases. The communist legislators do not seem to have carried their brief too far. The left wing paper Blitz got an official reprimand for allegations not dissimilar in depth and intensity to those in other cases. On point of principle, inadvertent error seems to have been excused. Serious allegations are less lightly treated. But there is no clear principle and the rulings defy consistency.

The oversensitivity of the legislature is best demonstrated by the *Mail* case (1961)[223] where a legislator's speech against the police was presented as consisting of irresponsible generalizations and inspired by political motives. The Committee of Privileges refused to hear the representative of the All India Newspaper Editors Conference, found a breach of privilege, but excused the Mail because this was the first error in an otherwise clean record.

Serious aspersions against a legislator may inspire more stringent action. In the *Hindustan Times* case (1967)[224] the proceedings were misreported to make the serious allegation that the CIA supported some legislators. An apology and a correction on the front page was demanded and given. In the *Maharashtra Times* case (1969),[225] it was alleged that some legislators (not named) had accepted bribes and still had not done the things which they promised to do. The plea of inadvertent but *bona fide* was accepted and no further action was taken. In the *Indian Express* case (1960)[226] the paper successfully made a plea of unintended confusion where one legislator was wrongly accused of calling another a CIA agent. In the *Economic Times* case (1960)[227] a false statement was made about the motives of a member concerning his intervention in a debate over the government's foreign dealings. The Committee was in no doubt that this constituted a breach of privilege. It was only an apology by the Deputy Editor and the publication of an apology in the paper which prevented further action being taken. In the *Panchayanya* case (1980)[228] an apology was deemed to be enough to dispose of the matter even though it was an important disputed question of fact (as to whether a police officer had made allegations against a member) that had not been decided. In some instances—as in the *Nok-e-Kalan* case (1982)[229] the complainant himself, perhaps fearful of too much publicity, wanted to have the matter dropped even though the House was in no doubt that an allegation concerning a member being bribed was malicious beyond any reasonable doubt. In the *Probe* case (1982)[230] allegations by one member against another were not deemed to be a breach but the members were allowed to make an explanation. This pragmatic approach was taken in the *Times of India* case (1983)[231] where a 'cement pay off' to a member was alleged and the House did not deem it to be a breach of privilege. The case involved a political *cause celebre* concerning the Chief Minister. This was clearly an attempt to invite some more politics and sympathetic publicity for those involved in this famous imbroglio. However, the *ratio decidendi* of this decision appears to be that these allegations were not made in regard to the member's capacity as a member of the house. Contrast the mischievous complaint in the *Lok Sabha Who's Who* case (1981)[232] that a description of a member as a Barrister-at-Law and "unmarried" affected the election of that member. The complainant—a Communist Member, Mr. Basu—was not pacified by a Minister's explanation that there had been an oversight and he had to be formally denied consent to raise this as a question of privilege.

Even in these relatively serious cases newspapers are able to feign innocence and suggest inadvertent error. In the process of making these pleas and going through the ritual of contrition the more serious question of the kind of objective standards a newspaper should maintain seems to have gone by default.

There is also the question of the extent to which ministers can protect themselves from criticism by the use of this jurisdiction. In the *Bhrashtachar Nirodh* case (1977)[233] general attacks were made on both ministers and legislators. A *prima facie* breach was found and the matter dropped. In the *Hindustan Times* case (1977),[234] the Home Minister had made a statement in Parliament that former Prime Minister Indira Gandhi had intended to shoot the opposition. This provoked a spirited response from Mrs. Gandhi including allegations that this was part of a smear campaign. The Committee felt that this was a case where Mrs. Gandhi should have shown restraint even if she did not intend to disrespect the institutions. Although a caution was issued in this case, the important right of the public to reply to charges made in parliament was established. This case shows the extent to which such cases become part of a political repertoire. In this case the newspaper's role had been marginalized at the expense of a gigantic political quarrel. Important suggestions were made in two cases. In the *Assam Tribune* case (1980)[235] when allegations were made against a Finance Minister, it was suggested that Government should itself controvert such allegations straightway—suggesting, perhaps, that the use of the privilege jurisdiction was not appropriate in such cases. Here, the Committee felt that there was no *prima facie* case. In the *Pioneer* case (1968)[236] the issue concerned whether a minister had misbehaved with a woman in Singapore. The Uttar Pradash Vidhan Parishad applied a clearly articulated rule that this did not concern the Minister in his capacity as member or Minister. The political aspect of such cases cannot be ignored. In the *Nagrik* case (1981)[237] even after a Chief Minister had publicly denied that he had leaked the budget, the newspaper questioned his integrity and called upon him to resign. The newspaper was attributed constructive knowledge of the Chief Minister's statement and reprimanded for what was described as a slur on journalism. There is no doubt that the forum of parliamentary privilege has been used against newspapers also to further agitate political matters and to provide Ministers with a weapon to protect themselves from both responsible and irresponsible attacks.

Ministers usually do not wish to pursue such attacks through the privilege jurisdiction. Some journalists seek to invite privilege motions against them in the hope that the Minister will be drawn into further controversy. This was certainly true of the *Indira Gandhi Trust Scandal* case.[238] The legislature however dismissed these efforts as unfortunate but not worthy of consideration. The House proclaimed its generosity; and the ploy of the journalists to get further clarification and to indulge in further mischief was foiled.

Many cases involve comments about and allegations against the Speaker. In some of these cases, the Speaker is simply criticised. In the *Prabhat* case (1957)[239] the chair's impartiality was questioned on allowing a member to sit in the House. The

Speaker talked to the Press Gallery Committee which agreed that the conduct was reprehensible and a breach of privilege; and suggested that a warning should be administered after an apology was tendered. In the *Daily Karmudi* case (1957)[240] the paper offered a Nobel Prize to the Speaker for making a ruling which could not be respected. The Speaker chose to ignore this.

> What we are concerned with is whether partiality has been imputed to the Speaker. In one portion of the editorial it is made clear that they do not want to do so. . . . I would request the hon'ble House to be benevolent and to refrain from questioning the honesty of the sponsors of the editorial.

The argument of *bona fides* seems to have played a major part in the Speaker's ruling who appears to have decided the matter by subjective estimate. Having done so, the Speaker also made a different kind of tactical plea:

> It will be more prudent and more in keeping with the dignity of the House if we simply ignore such misuse of the inviolable rights of the freedom of the press and leave the rest to. . .decent democratic opinion without affording opportunity for sensation, the creation of which probably may be exactly what the authors of the editorial are in search of.

All this shows a shrewd understanding of the pathology of contempt cases and what they are about. In the *Hindustan Times* case (1969),[241] a legislator was wrongly quoted of accusing the Speaker of being used by the Prime Minister. The solution was to demand an apology and a printed correction before the matter was closed. In the *Janagarjana* case (1965)[242] the lack of control of the Speaker over the proceedings was lampooned ("Is the Speaker asleep in his chair?"). In this case, the editor was summoned and admonished even though there was no allegation of partiality, and no misrepresentation of the proceedings. The editor did, however, refuse to apologize taking the plea that he was describing a prevalent state of affairs and making a fair comment. In the *Zomin Ryot* case it was suggested that the speaker was emotional and lacking in adroitness and should be made a Minister. The House adopted the Committee's report that the matter was too trivial to take further. Where, however, aspersions were cast on the impartiality of the Speaker—as in the *Press Statement* case (1980)[244]—the matter was closed only after an unqualified apology. Here the real target was fellow members rather than the newspapers.

This case may be contrasted with the *Indian Times* case (1964)[245] where the allegation was that the Speaker had amassed a great deal of wealth. The House was more conscious of the effect of privilege proceedings rather than the merits of the issue or whether this was a matter of libel rather than privilege. The Prime Minister seemed to suggest that action should be taken only against a "regular" newspaper. Another legislator felt that privilege proceedings would only give greater publicity to an otherwise unknown news report. The course of action taken was to informally affirm faith in the Speaker and let the matter drop. These cases show how badly articulated rules merge with all kind of other considerations to emerge with pragmatic political solutions.

But there is a case for determining how well reasoned and dignified comments can be made about the Speaker's rulings and actions. In the *Thaniram* case (1975),[246] the Speaker's impartiality was questioned in not allowing an adjournment motion about the trial of Mujibur Rehman. It was true that a resolution had been passed by the Assembly but a plea had been made for what would, perhaps, have been another adjournment motion. The newspaperman who spoke of his "uncontrollable emotion due to the spirit of nationalism" demanded—and was denied—legal counsel—and pleaded that what he said was true and fair comment. The Committee of Privileges refused to examine the wider issue of free speech and argued that the contempt was aggravated by the editor rising to his defence and making submissions. Undoubtedly, the allegation of partiality was going a bit far. But it was made as a rhetorical rather than a serious allegation. A severe reprimand was given. Some consideration has to be given to the 'free speech' issue and the extent to which the Speaker's action can be discussed. In the *Hegde* case (1980)[247(a)] Lok Sabha Speaker was happy to provide an explanation before he closed the matter. Again, in the *Inderjit* case involving the *Tribune* (1982)[247(b)] the Speaker agreed to review a ruling in the light of comments that were made even though the ruling was not altered in the light of the review.

The newspapers are partly to blame for merging imputation with comment. But the legislatures have also made blanket use of this jurisdiction.

The press may also intrude into the legislature's right to be the primary forum through which public issues are discussed. Legislatures make a distinction between activities and proceedings within the House and proceedings outside the Legislature. Thus in the *Ganganatha Report* case (1950)[248] the release of a departmental committee's report before it was laid before the House was not deemed to be in breach of privilege. Again in the *Statesman-PTI* case (1967),[249] an account of the Minister's negotiation with the World Bank was not considered to constitute a breach of privilege. There is, however, an important parliamentary right which may have been obscured in these cases. The parliamentary system works on the assumption that it is parliament—and not some other body—which has the right to be kept informed about the working of government which is accountable to Parliament. The question is: to what extent should the law of parliamentary privilege be used to ensure that parliament and not the press is the forum where crucial and critical matters ought to be discussed first. In the *Statesman* case (1962)[250] an oil deal entered into by the government was mentioned in the paper. The newspaper had not got the information from the Minister. The Speaker let the matter be dropped because the life of the current parliament was at an end. But his reasons for so doing took the rather curious form of arguing that a Minister had a right to place an embargo on information which hethought was secret:

> The newspaper has somehow got this information which the Minister is not prepared to confirm or deny. I can only condemn the correspondent for having come out with this

> news item. Even if it be true, he is not helping the country by publishing it when the Minister thinks that it is in the public interest that it ought not to be placed before the House . . . I would urge upon all newspapers not to allow such things to be published. They will take note of whatever is happening here and if, in the interest of the public, it is considered either by the House or by me that an agreement which is made ought to be kept secret, they would also adopt that secrecy in the interest of the country and of proper journalism.

This ruling obscures the law relating to official secrecy (which it states too broadly) and confounds the issue about the right of parliament to information. The *Nehru* case (1967)[251] raises this latter point more clearly. Nehru had talked to journalists about the U.S. Seventh Fleet in the Indian Ocean when a call attention motion on that matter was due to be taken up by the House the next day. The Speaker, accepting that the comment had been made when some newspaper men surrounded the Prime Minister, seemed to severely cut down parliament's privilege to receive information:

> The position is very clear, and in fact, I had given my decision on that very day that there might be a question of courtesy, propriety and desirability but there was no question of breach of privilege at all. . . I have studied all the rulings up to this time not only in India but also in the United Kingdom. They are all uniform in the respect that statements by Ministers outside the House in regard to their policy matters or some such things do not constitute a breach of privilege of the House, though it is a matter of propriety, and courtesy also demands that they should be made in the House when the House is in session. . . I have the benefit of looking into decisions where really the matter had been on the agenda itself. Then too it has been held that it does not constitute in any case a breach of privilege at all. But courtesy demands that when there is such a thing then the statement should be made before the House. But there might be circumstances otherwise. . . .

Parliament's right to information seems to have made a question of conventional courtesy into a parliamentary privilege. A pragmatic attitude was taken in the *Statesman* case (1966)[252] where the newspaper alleged that the Minister was convinced that the left Communist party had plans for a countrywide sabotage. Was the Minister misleading the House? In an attempt to skirt the problem, the Committee of Privileges sought to say that there was a difference of opinion between the Minister and the newspaper about what happened and *bona fides* were not in question. The more important question about the general rights of parliament appear to have been ignored. Each case seems to have evolved its own strategy.

Many of these issues are raised as part of parliamentary political affray rather than seriously to explore the extent of parliamentary privilege. Thus, in the *Delhi Metropolitan Council* case (1980)[253] a prominent politician—Mr. Vajpayee—unsuccessfully questioned the propriety of the Home Secretary, Mr. Zail Singh, in not having informed the House of the dissolution of the Delhi Metropolitan Council. Similarly, L.K. Advani really raised a political point when he argued in the *Press Commission* case (1980)[254] that knowledge of the appointment of the Press Commission should first have been made to the House. This elicited the ruling that the House should be intimated about such matters as soon as possible. A political *cause celebre* was created in the *Railway Budget* case (1981)[255] where the Railway Minister took the view that the exact details were the product of an educated guess rather than a leak. A leak of the Budget was also alleged in another *Railway Budget* case (1982)[256] where prominent opposition leaders objected to details being disclosed by the Chairman of the Railway Board. While disallowing the question of privilege the House reiterated the view that while the 'property' in the budget document lay with the government, any information contained in the budget should be made by the Minister to the House.

A turnabout in these matters seems to have taken place in the *All India Radio* case (1978)[257] where the Minister had made a public statement about sabotage in certain vital sectors. The Privilege issue concerned the vital issue as to whether the statement should have been made to the house. It was decided that

> [E]arly information to the public in respect of the matters mentioned in the broadcast was necessary and the same was in the public interest.

Two issues are involved here. The first is the simple issue of timing. Here the statement was made to the press first. There was no intention not to make it to the house. But would this extend to important policy statements? The second question relates to the monopoly of the House to be informed and to debate matters. This is eventually linked to the whole issue of ministerial responsibility to Parliament which is a central feature of the Constitution. It would be impossible in this day and age not to give the government access to the public; or for that matter, the people access to the government. Equally, parliament has the right to consider policy statements. And it is this right to consider and influence policy statements that should fall within the purview of the rules.

This question has also been raised in respect of the right of the public to know what is going on in parliament. In the *Indian Express-UNI* case (1976)[258] and a case from Gujarat (1976)[259] legislators gave notice of their no-confidence motions against the government. Does the public have a right to know of these things? In one of the cases, the Speaker argued:

> any gentleman may come, give a motion, and then go out to the press. With all these campaigns against the Speaker it is very difficult for the chair to function.

This begs the issue. For, the point is whether these important public issues should be more widely discussed. And if so, when? The cut off point in the rules is when they are admitted. But cannot there be a campaign outside parliament to admit such a motion or a "call attention" motion? There may be a case for preserving the time of admission as the time for public debate. The general question of the extent to which a legislator or the press can inform the public about the former's activities remains. In the *Hindustan Times* case (1980)[260] the paper had published a legislator's advance publicity of his intention to oppose a bill. This was, it is submitted incorrectly, treated as falling within the rule of advanced publicity about notices to parliament. But it obscures the legislator's right to declare his attitude on various matters to the public. The idea that the legislator cannot state any views in advance wants rigorous examination even if we accept that such exercises may be designed to embarrass rather than enlighten. And, it could well be argued that such forms of political mobilisation are legitimate forms of political and newspaper activity.

The point was not clarified in the *Kerala Electricity Workers* case (1983)[261] where the Speaker simply disallowed a privilege without concerning advance publicity of a notice. In the *Hindustan Times and UNI* case (1978)[262] the Lok Sabha took the legalistic line that advance publicity of a notice violated Rule 334A and members should be more careful. This case may have been an opportunity to clarify the position because here a member was giving notice of his intention to oppose a Bill. But as soon as the issue is raised in parliament it can be publicised provided the information is not distorted or misrepresented.[263] Mr. Hidayatullah—Chairman of the Rajya Sabha—made the right of the public to know about the goings on *in Parliament* (after parliament has discussed them) quite clear in the *Director of Public Relations, Assam* case (1971),[264]

> The question, however, remains whether there can be a ban by legislation or executive fiat on any such (parliamentary) publication. Proceedings in the House are public property unless the House decides to the contrary. No executive fiat can issue to newspapers without authority of law. Proceedings which are open to the public must necessarily be open to the newspapers to report. The newspapers are the eyes and ears of the public not present in the House. Unless the House puts a ban, the newspapers must be held to have the right to reproduce fairly and faithfully and accurately the proceedings or any part thereof without

let or hindrance from any person not authorised by the House or by any law. The newspapers may not misrepresent by editing, adding or unfairly omitting to give a totally wrong impression.

However, the important question of pre-publicity to matters discussed in parliament has not been successfully resolved in favour of public participation. Parliament's right to be the first forum to which statements can be made was asserted again in the *Khandasari* case (1981)[265] where the Minister had made public a decision about the regulation of sugar without informing the House even though he was in the House on that day. This does create problems for lobbyists. By the time a decision or a policy is made before parliament, it is backed by an official commitment and has acquired a definite shape. It is less vulnerable to lobbying. Advance notice helps democracy. The 'parliament first' rule is more concerned with defending the privacy of the institution rather than the rights of the people.

The issue of lobbying does deserve more attention. What kind of pressures can be put on members of parliament? In the *Goanchen Rapon Karancho* case (1981)[266] fishermen sent a telegram to a member saying that they did not want the Marine Bill passed, that the masses could not be fooled forever and that they were "watching" the member. Although the matter was deemed undeserving of attention, it was clear that the limits of the kind of pressure that can be put were not clarified. The ruling takes the somewhat tough line that phrases like "we are watching you" might amount to undue pressure. But the press is always 'watching' legislators. It also causes them embarrassment, subjects them to adverse publicity and may even expose them. Let us examine some famous instances. In the *Prime Minister* case (1981)[267] it was alleged that the Prime Minister's comments about the results of an election campaign were contempt. It was decided that in such a case a denial by the Minister is enough to determine the issue. The situation was much more complex in the *Indira Grandhi Trust Scandal* case (1981)[268] where the Minister of Finance was held out by a leading journalist, to be a liar in misleading the House. The House decided not to take note of every technical error. But the central issue, concerning the extent of permissible comments, was not dealt with. *Arun Shourie's* (1981)[269] strictures on the Minister in an article entitled "Petty little lies in Parliament"[270] were similarly dealt with although the tone of the atricle was deprecated by the Chairman of the Rajya Sabha. Shourie had virtually invited the privilege jurisdiction to be inflicted upon him. Had the case gone further many questions about the range of permissible comment and lobbying of the House may have been settled. Was fair comment allowed? Could truth be pleaded as defence? Could proof of truth be offered to the House? Would the House simply take a formal view based on the kind of language used? Would a formal denial by the Minister be deemed to be enough? Could the truth content of such a denial be subjected to scrutiny by the press?

Individual members and Minister have also used this jurisdiction to protect themselves in respect of their activities outside Parliament. The *Organizer* case (1967)[271] has party political overtones. Here it was suggested that certain legislators had concocted an incident involving disruption within the precincts of the House. An apology was made to the Watch and Ward Staff who were also implicated and the matter dropped—over the complainant legislator's protest—on the tacit understanding that this was not an incident in the House. This tacit understanding of what is part of the 'House' appears to be wrong. Clearly the definition ought to be functional in nature rather than descriptive. The privilege was designed to protect legislators in the exercise of their functions. In the *UNI, Hindustan, Statesman, Times of India* case (1979)[272] even this approach was restrictively interpreted. Here a legislator alleged that the papers had made a misleading story about his arrest and the seizure of his jeep and two revolvers by the police. His attempts to make this a privilege issue on the basis that this interfered with his constituency work was not successful. These incidents were not regarded as relating to his work as a member of parliament.[273]

In the *Assam Tribune* case (1980) the Meghalaya Assembly went further and also insisted that comments on the failure by a Minister to consult colleagues in the cabinet or the Pay

Commission did not form part of the activities that fell within the privilege jurisdiction. The relative clarity of the law on the subject does not prevent people from using this jurisdiction for political purposes. The most glaring example of this was the *Pioneer* case (1981)[274] where allegations were made that a Minister should resign because a woman alleged that he had misbehaved with her in Singapore. Rather than institute a libel suit and contrary to settled practice, the privilege jurisdiction was used to fight this case further.

The question as to what constitutes the sweep of privilege is an important one. We have already seen that general allegations of corruption against members fall within this jurisdiction in respect of what they say in the house or their general activities as legislators. But where exactly does one draw the line? Consider the *Current* case (1978)[275] where allegations of financial dealings were made against a legislator of the Bihar Assembly but the name and photograph were of a member of the Lok Sabha. Here was a case for libel. Yet the Lok Sabha took the case up as a privilege issue and excused the editor after his explanation came through. The legislator then used this opportunity to insist that a regret and correction ought to be made. Such an allegation did not really concern the legislator's parliamentary work—however reprehensible the incident that occurred may have been.

The line continues to be blurred. In the *Pioneer* case (1976) it was held that a Minister's alleged misbehaviour with a woman in Singapore did not concern the House. This may be contrasted with the curious decision implied in the *Times of India* case (1983)[276] that 'cement pay offs' to a Minister were not in his capacity as member or Minister. These rulings may well be political responses to political mischief. As they stand they are not honoured by doctrinal consistency or clarity.

Perhaps, there is a case for greater clarity on what is regarded within the sweep of the legislature. In two cases[277] a rather neat point arose as to whether the Governor's address to the houses of the legislatures was part of the proceedings of the house. The answer that it was not merited greater deliberation. While there may be some difficulty in accepting the Press

Council's suggestion that these privileges should be codified, there is a case for a clearer description of what kind of press reports fall within the jurisdiction of the house. This may not prevent cases outside the privilege jurisdiction being brought to the legislature. These cases are not brought because there is a lack of clarity in the law but also to explore yet another forum to ventilate grievances and settle further personal and political differences.

Parliament has exercised some control in not getting too touchy about speeches made by government politicians outside parliament and by ignoring many unintended and inadvertent errors. It has even permitted criticism. But lack of consistency amongst various—and even the same—legislatures remains a problem. As with the courts of law, the use and abuse of the privilege jurisdiction has thrown up an interesting pathology. Characteristically, there is a large bulk of cases where the press is simply not careful enough. This applies equally to the cosmopolitan large newspaper 'quality' press as it does to the local and regional newspapers. But carelessness is not the only imputation made against the press. Undoubtedly, the law courts and the press engage in and proliferate political differences ranging from the incidental squabble and political in-fighting to genuine political differences between major political parties and politicians. 'Simple carelessness' acts as an intended and unintended addendum to such a use of newspapers. A newspaper that pleads carelessness may well be hiding an intriguing political background to its publication and the parliamentary response of the legislature's Committee of Privileges. The privilege jurisdiction is not used against the press purely as a corrective or warning device which both preserves an enforced code and establishes clear guidelines for the future. The jurisdiction has been used by newsmen, politicians and legislatures to promote further and better opportunities to exploit political and other differences. And it is not surprizing that this jurisdiction was rigorously put to political uses to attack a former Prime Minister, or a Minister, to throw more light on a social or political state of affairs. This insight into the pathology of the use of the privilege jurisdiction of the variou legislatures is crucial to an understanding of how the law relating to parliamentary privileges works and is interpreted and transformed.

III

Political and constitutional analysis has generally followed a two level approach. At the political level, there is an analysis of who assumes control of particular governmental institutions. From this there is a giant leap to an institutional level of analysis whereby the institution is depicted as autonomously working within its own ground rules. Such an analysis follows a standard form of philosophical practice of distinguishing between grosser and more reified forms of analysis. Thus, utilitarians distinguished between 'act' and 'rule' utilitarianism. The distinction between 'political' and 'constitutional' represents a similar pattern of justification proceeding from grosser forms of political action to entrenched and more reified forms of power consolidation in the form of constitutional practice. Such an analysis not only conceals power acculturations which lie concealed beneath constitutional practice, they also seek to stimulate a respect for a stable constitutional decision-making structure protected from the indiscriminate vagaries of crude politics. In such a state, constitutionalism is a preferred form of politics. Yet a closer look at constitutional practice might suggest different insights. Matured constitutionalism might be seen to represent the death of politics. It suggests a consolidation of power to the exclusion of those outside particular power groupings. It also implies a much more exacting control over the avenues and processes by which power can be obtained in any political and constitutional system. Constitutionalism both consolidates and legitimates. But in order that it may achieve all this it requires some consensus between the various elites who contend for power and recognition. The Indian Constitution has never really been able to build up the kind of consensus that is needed to maintain a constitutional structure.

In an earlier work, the present writer observed:

> The form of parliamentary government adopted by the Indian Constitution can only work if certain ground rules

> allow for certain predictable patterns of behaviour. The ground rules of the Indian political system, as they are constituted today, work on the theoretical assumption that every sectional interest in India can be politically effective if it uses the political and constitutional structure expediently, ruthlessly and without obeisance to the operational morality that the parliamentary system envisages. This theoretical assumption rests on the premise that various interests seek a quick translation of their ambitions and frustrations into political reality even if this means breaking conventional norms of political behaviour. This idea of a 'quick translation' of aspirations into reality introduces a certain speed into the system. The political system begins to reflect every twist and turn of political behaviour instead of stabilising itself. In time, the system itself, having compromised all its ground rules, begins to weaken unless some alternative rules are found to replace the previous ground rules.[279]

The Indian Constitution has not effected a respectable consolidation of power for its emerging elites and the intermediate regime of power brokers that have unscrupulously ediated this emergence. As it happens they have not been able to work out the ground rules between themselves. The two most volatile political arenas where fratricidal conflicts between various power brokers take place are the legislatures and the press. Where government by institution has consolidated itself, the press gives primacy and centrality to what is going on in such institutions. Where no consensus ground rules for government by institution are worked out, the press becomes a primary political arena competing with—and often surpassing—the institutions of government. Contemporary India displays this competition in abundance. Parliament uses its privilege jurisdiction to assert its supremacy. The press uses a combination of legal and publicity techniques to reduce the rigours of any consequences that might follow. All this is made infinitely more complex and exciting by the fact that the same people simultaneously use both political arenas to oppress each other. In formal terms, Parliament wins as the institutional forum beyond which there is no appeal. Informally, the press has the infinitely more damaging power of giving further and better publicity to its point of view. The real fight is not between the press and parliament, but between factions and groups who have in this contemporary interregnum made nonsense of both. We can only discover who has won after we have disabused ourselves of an analysis which seeks insights at the level of constitutional dialogue rather than at the level of political affray.

NOTES

1. See Articles 105(3) and 194(3) of the Constitution of India as amended by the Constitution (Forty-second Amendment) Act, 1976 and the Constitution (Forty-fourth Amendment) Act, 1978.
2. Cf. H.L.A. Hart: *The Concept of Law* (1961); and the more specific essay on Concepts: "Definition and theory in Jurisprudence" (1954) 70 *L.Q.*R. 37.
3. The title of Malcolm Feeley's book: *The Process is the Punishment* (1979).
4. Indian Councils Act, 1861 (24 and 25 Vict Chap. 67).
5. Government of India Act, 1919 (9 and 10 Geo. V Chap. 101.
6. *Ibid.* S. 24(7).
7. VIII Constituent Assembly Debates (hereafter C.A.D.) 146 (S.L. Saxena); 152-3 (L.L. Maitra)
8. Conferences of Presiding Officers were held in 1923, 1925, 1933 and 1938. A brief but invaluable account of these is contained in Hans Raj: *Privileges of Members of Parliament* (1978) 12-13.
9. Hans Raj, *ibid.*, 13.
10. *Ibid.* 14 and note the references to the discussions in the Indian Legislative Assembly.
11. Government of India Act, Ss. 21, 71.
12. *Ibid.*, Ss. 28 (3), 71(3).
13. *Ibid.*, Ss. 28 (4), 71 (4).
14. The Indian Independence Act, 1947 deleted Ss. 28 (5) and 28 (4) of the Government of India Act, 1935.
15. Hans Raj (*supra* note 8) 19.
16. It is not one of the issues earmarked for special discussion in the questionnaire issued by the constitutional Adviser; see the documents in B. Shiva Rao (ed.): *The Framing of India's Constitution* (1967) II, 441-447 (hereafter cited as *Shiva Rao* preceded by volume number).

17. Article 35 of a proposed Draft Clauses of Union Constitution—II Shiva Rao 511.
18. *Ibid.*, Article 35 (2) II Shiva Rao 511.
19. *Ibid.*, Articles 47-8—II Shiva Rao 517-8.
20. II Shiva Rao 544 pr. 10.
21. II shiva Rao 661.
22. Article 85(3), Article 169 (3)--Draft Constitution 1948, II Shiva Rao 546.
33. IV Shiva Rao 102, 124 (per A.C. Gupta).
24. VIII C.A.D. 145-56 (19 May; 1949); 578-84 (3 June 1949); C.A.D. 301-2 (16 October, 1949).
25. *Ibid.*, 144-5 (J.R. Kapoor) accepted at 156.
26. *Ibid.*, 147 (N. Ahmad) Cf. 149 (A.K. Ayyar).
27. *Ibid.*, 144 (H.V. Kamath), 152 (L.K. Maitra).
28. *Ibid.*, 144 (H.V. Kamath).
29. *Ibid.*, 147 (S.L. Saxena), 147 (N. Ahmad), 148 (P.S. Deshmkh), 151 (R.K. Chaudhri), 152 (L.K. Maitra).
30. *Ibid.*, 151 (R.K. Chaudhri), 135 (M.A. Ayyangar).
31. *Ibid.*, 146 (S.L. Saxena).
32. *Ibid.*, 144 (H.V. Kamath).
33. *Ibid.*, 145 (S.L. Saxena).
34. *Ibid.*, 148-9 (A.K. Ayyar).
35. *Ibid.*, 148.
36. *Ibid.*, 156 proposed 145 (K.T. Shah).
37. *Ibid.*, 146 (S.L. Saxena), 148 (P.S. Deshmukh).
38. *Ibid.*, 148 (P.S. Deshmukh).
39. *Ibid.*, 146 (S.L. Saxena) and especially 152-3 (L.K. Maitra).
40. *Ibid.*, 153 (L.K. Maitra).
41. *Ibid.*, 150 (J.N. Lal).
42. *Ibid.*, 153 (M.A. Ayyangar).
43. *Ibid.*, 151 (R.K. Chaudhri), 153 (L.K. Maitra).
44. *Ibid.*, 147 (N. Ahmad).
45. *Ibid.*, 578-84 (5 June 1949).
46. *Ibid.*, 579 (H.V. Kamath), 582 (B.B. Ambedkar).
47. *Ibid.*, 579. This seemed to be the substance of the reaction of the *Hindustan Times* quoted by H.V. Kamath.
48. *Ibid.*, 579 (H.V. Kamath).
49. *Ibid.*, 579 (H.V. Kamath on India's own experience), 581-2 (T.D. Bhargava on India's experience), 581 (P.S. Deshmukh that it should be left to each legislature).
50. *Ibid.*, 580 (N. Ahmad) and note B.R. Ambedkar's reaction at 583 that this is not really practical.
51. *Ibid.*, 580 (N. Ahmad).
52. *Ibid.*, 583 (B.R. Ambedkar).
53. *Report of the Press Laws Enquiry Committee* (1950) pr. 79—note

also the reference to this Report in the *Report of the Press Commission* (1952-54) pr. 1901 p. 418-19.

54. *Report of the Press Commission* (1952-54) pr. 1100 p. 424.
55. *Ibid.*, pr. 1101 p. 424.
56. *Ibid.*, pr. 1090 p. 418.
57. *Ibid.*, pr, 1106 pp. 425-6.
58. *Ibid.*, pr. 1107-1112 pp. 426-8 (re. a ruling from the Uttar Pradesh Assembly).
59. *Ibid.*, pr. 1114 pp. 428-29 (*Times of India* case) re. publication of confidential records of a Committee.
60. *Ibid.*, pp. 1115 pp. 429 (*Statesman* case about a slightly lively account of certain proceedings).
61. *Ibid.*, pr. 1116 pp. 429-430.
62. *Ibid.*, pr. 1117 p. 430.
63. *Ibid.*, pr. 1118 p. 430 (on criticism of the Madhya Bharat Municipal Bill).
64. *Ibid.*, pr. 1119 p. 430 (on certain rulings from Uttar Pradesh).
65. *Ibid.*, pr. 1120 p. 430.
66. *Suresh* v. *Pundit* A.I.R. 1951 Col. 176.
67. Parliamentary Proceedings (Production of Publication) Act, 1956.
68. Note that this Act was repealed during the Emergency by the Parliamentary Proceedings (Protection of Publication) Act, 1976 which was itself repealed and replaced by the Parliament Proceedings (Protection from Publication) Act, 1977.
69. Ss. 21, 34 of the Constitution (Forty-second) Amendment Act, 1976 amended the Constitution so that the privileges of the Indian Legislatures were determined by the past practice of Indian Legislatures rather than the House of Commons.
70. There is a considerable literature on the general subject of parliamentary privilege. Also see S.K. Nag: *Evolution of Parliamentary Privileges in India till 1947.* Ramachandran V.G.: *The Law of Parliamentary Privileges in India: A comparative study (1966)*; P. Govinda Menon: *Parliamentary Privileges and their Codification* (1968); D.N. Raju: *Privileges of Legislature and Freedom of Citizen*; P.S. Pachauri: *The Law of Parliamentary Privileges in U.K. and in India.* Arun Prokas Chatterjee: *Parliamentary Privileges in India* (1971); D.C. Jain: *Parliamentary Privileges under the Indian Constitution* (1975); Hans Raj: *Parliamentary Privileges in India* (1979); Kaul: *Parliamentary Procedures and Institutions* (1979). Also see further papers—"Privileges of Parliament and the Power of Court"—Chhail Bihari Lal Saxena, *A.I.R.* 1953 Jr. 62; "Parliamentary Privilege"—S. Swamikkannu (1963) 1 *M.L.J.* 31, "Privileges of members of Parliament against arrest"—S.K. Singh (1964) *I.J.P.A.* 662; "Legislative powers of Parliament vis-a-vis Parliamentary Privileges"—Satinder Mohan Mehta, 21 *L.R.* 48; "Privileges of M.P.'s". Editorial, 75 *CWN* 17-20, "Privileges of Parliament", Editorial 83 *CWN*

17-21; "Privileges of Parliamentarian", K.C. Joshi 24-25 *Pb. Univ. Law Rev*. 83-7; Privileges issues (generally refers to Jr. of Parl. Information and Privilege Digest) Codification of the Privileges of the legislature"—V.G. Ramchandran (1965) *I.A.* 16; "Power and Privileges of legislatures in India"—Sardar Hukam Singh (1965) *J.P.I.* 1; "Privileges of Indian Legislatures"—Om Prakash Motiwal (1966) *S.C.J.* 41; "Parliamentary Privileges of exemption from being summoned as a witness"—Bijai Narain Mani (1966) *L.R.* 105; "Parliamentary Privileges: An Approach"—G. Narayana Rao (1967) (July-Dec.) 7 *I.A.* 5; "Parliamentary Privileges and their codification"—P. Govinda Menon (1968) (April-June) II *J.C.P.S.* 1; "Parliamentary Privileges: The Press and the Judiciary"—M. Hidayatullah (1968) *J C.P.S.* 1; "Privileges and Immunities"—C.R. Pattabhi Raman (1969) *Lawyer* 7; "Parliamentary Privileges"—K.C. Joshi (1970) 2 *S.C.C.* 10-12; "Parliamentary Privileges" Editorial (1976-77) 81 *CWN* 47-8; "Parliamentary Privileges"—C.K. Daphtary (1977), 23 *J.P.L.* 385; "Parliamentary Privileges and Expulsion"—H.S. Sharma (1977) 11 *J.C.P.S.* 58-65; "Parliamentary Privileges. A Need for Codification"—Subhash Chander Gupta (1978) 10 *Lawyer* 1-10; "Parliamentary Privileges"—Shanti Bhushan (1978) 24 *J.P.I.* 203.

71. *Gunniput Keshwaram Reddy* v. *Nafisul Hasan* A.I.R. 1974 S.C. 636.
72. *M.S.M. Sharma* v. *Sri Krishna Sharma* A.I.R. 1959 S.C. 395.
73. See Article 19(2) Constitution of India,
74. *M.S.M. Sharma's* case (*supra* note 69) pr. 53-4 pp. 421-2; see now the ruling of ex-Vice President Hidayatullah in the Rajya Sabha.
75. *Ibid*., pr. 55 p. 422, pr. 44 p. 418 arguing that the freedom of speech remains preserved.
76. *Ibid*., pr. 26-28 pp. 408-410.
77. *Ibid*., pr. 28 p. 410 arguing that the *Blitz* case "proceeded entirely on a concesssion of counsel and cannot be regarded as a considered opinion on the subject."
78. *Ibid*. pr. 29 pp. 410-11 that a proceeding before the Committee of Privileges was in accordance with procedure established by law.
79. In *Re Article 143* A.I.R. 1965 S.C. 745.
80. *Ibid*. pr. 134-5 pp. 788-9 and note the view of H.M. Seervali: II *Constitutional Law of India* (1975) 1182. This does raise the whole question as to whether courts in England and elsewhere merely exercise judicial restraint in not interfering with the exercise of parliamentary privileges.
81. *Ibid*., pr. 170-72 p. 810.
82. *Ibid*., pr. 132 p. 788.
83. A.I.R. 1970 S.C. 1573.
84. (1981) XXV P.D. (No. 2)2 (Lok Sabha)
85. (1981) XXVII P.D. (No. 1) 18 (Karnataka).

86. *e.g. Shraddha Devi* v. *K.C. Pant* (1982) XXVII P.D. (No. 2) 17 (U.P. Vidhan Sabha) (on elections)); *Varsha Joshi and K.W. Desai* case (1982) XXVVI P.D. (No. 1) 14 on dismissing a matter that was *sub judice*.
87. *State of Kerala* v. *F. Sudarshan Babu* A.I.R. 1984 Kerala 1 (FB)—on the denial of credentials to Editor of *Deshabhimani*. Note also the *Eenadu* case (1984) where the newspaper, Peddam Golaba, March 9, 1983 caricatured the legislature which summoned the offending editor who was arrested on March 28, 1983, by a policeman despite a Supreme Court order of March 27. The Governor diffused the controversy by proroguing the House on March 30, 1984.
88. *In re Article 143*, A.I.R. 1965 S.C. 745.
89. (1966) XI Privileges Digest (hereafter P.D.) 9-11 Goa, Daman and Diu Legislative Assembly (1966).
90. (1961) V P.D. (No. 2) 28-36 (Lok Sabha) (1961).
91. (1975) XX P.D. (No. 2) 49 (Kerala Legislative Assembly).
92. (1977) XXII P.D. (No. 1) 18 (West Bengal Legislative Assembly) (1977).
93. (1977) XXII P.D. (No. 2) 47 (Karnataka Legislative Assembly (1976).
94. 1978 case reported (1981) XXVI P.D. (No. 1) 19 (Tripura Legislative Assembly).
95. 1981 case reported in (1982) XXVII P.D. (No. 1) 11 (Rajya Sabha).
96. (1983) XXVIII P.D. (No. 1) (Maharashtra).
97. *cf.* the English *Daily Mail* case reported (1983) XXVIII P.D. (No. 1) 26.
98. (1982) XXVII P.D. (No. 1) 14 (Gujarat).
99. (1975) XX P.D. (No. 2) 49 (Kerala Legislative Assembly) (1975).
100. *Pratap and Prabhat* case (1957) I.P.D. (No. 3) 17-20.
101. (1959) III P.D. (No. 4) 163-5. (Madras Legislative Assembly) (1958).
102. *Nav Bharat* case (1958) II P.D. (No. 2) 55-6 (M.P. Vidhan Sabha).
103. *Supra* note 101.
104. (1981) XXVI P.D. (No. 2) 26 (U.P. Vidhan Sabha).
105. (1958) II P.D. (No. 3) 99-100 (Madhya Pradesh Vidhan Sabha) (1957).
106. (1961) V P.D. (No. 2) 42-3 (Assam Legislative Assembly) (1961).
107. (1967) III P.D. (No. 1) 8-9 (Lok Sabha) (1966).
108. (1965) IX P.D. 7-8 (Rajya Sabha) (1964).
109. (1965) IX P.D. 6-7 (Lok Sabha) (1965).
110. (1965) IX P.D. 2-3 (Lok Sabha) (1965).
111. (1973) XVIII P.D. (No. 2) 24-26 (Lok Sabha) (1973).
112. 1979 case reported in (1980) XXV P.D. (No. 1) 4.
113. (1980) XXV P.D. (No. 2) 41 (Lok Sabha).
114. (1980) XXV P.D. (No. 2) 41 (Lok Sabha) regards another rape case in Sirson, Haryana.

115. (1980) XXV P.D. (No. 2) 42 (Lok Sab ha).
116. (1980) XXV P.D. (No. 2) 42 (Jammu and Kashmir Legislative Assembly) (1973), see also *Times of India* case (1979) XXIV P.D. (No. 2) 44 (Lok Sabha) (1978).
117. See further the *Dainik Deshbandhu* case (1976) XXI P.D. (No. 2) 42 (Madhya Bharat Vidhan Sabha) (1974); *Jugantar* case (1978) XXIII P.D. (No. 2) 1 (Lok Sabha) (1974); *Hindustan Times* case (1977) XXIII P.D. (No. 1) 3-7 (Lok Sabha) (1977); *Indian Express* case (1979) XXIV P.D. (No. 2) 48 (Jammu and Kashmir Legislative Assembly) (1978).
118. (1973) XVIII P.D. (No. 2) 26-7 (Lok Sabha) (1978).
119. (1968) XIII P.D. (No. 2) 74 (Maharashtra Legislative Assembly) (1963); (1964) VIII D.P. 3 (Lok Sabha) (1963).
120. (1968) XIII P.D. (No. 2) 74 (Maharashtra Legislative Assembly) (1963).
121. (1964) VIII P.D. 3 (Lok Sabha) (1963).
122. (1963) VI P.D. (No. 1) 11-12 (Punjab Vidhan Sabha) (1961).
123. (1967) XII P.D. (No. 2) 110-111 (Lok Sabha) (1967).
124. (1971) XVI P.D. (No. 1) 9 (Lok Sabha) (1970).
125. (1966) XI P.D. 27-8 (Punjab Vidhan Sabha) (1963).
126. (1970) XV P.D. (No. 2) 47-50 (Gujarat Legislative Assembly) (1967).
127. (1977) XXII P.D. (No. 1) 12 (Bihar Legislative Council) (1974).
128. (1984) XXV P.D. (No. 2) (Lok Sabha).
129. 1979 reported in (1980) XXV P.D. (No. 2) 52 (West Bengal Legislative Assembly).
130. *Blitz* case (1981) reported in (1982) XXVII P.D. (No. 1) 8 (Rajya Sabha).
131. *Hindustan Samachar and Lokgatton* case (1981) XXVI P.D. (No. 1) 13 (Rajya Sabha).
132. *Assam Tribune* case (1980) XXV P.D. (No. 2) 45 (Rajya Sabha).
133. *National Herald* case (1981) XXVI (No. 1) 13 (Rajya Sabha). Quaere: Was the delay of ten days in replying to the house really an excessive delay?
134. *Assam Tribune* case (1981) XXVI (No. 2) 16 (Rajya Sabha).
135. *Gujarat Samachar* case (1982) XXVII P.D. (No. 2) 12 (Rajya Sabha).
136. (1976) XXI P.D. (No. 2) 34 (Lok Sabha) (1974).
137. (1977) XXII P.D. (No. 1) 18 (West Bengal Legislative Assembly) (1975); see also 112A (1981) XXVI P.D. (No. 1) 12.
138. (1981) XXVI P.D. 12 at 13 (Rajya Sabha, 1980).
139. (1967) XII P.D. (No. 1) 20-21 (Lok Sabha) (1966).
140. (1967) XII P.D. (No. 2) 110-111 (Lok Sabha) (1967).
141. (1969) XIV P.D. (No. 1) 3-4 (Lok Sabha) (1968).
142. (1971) XVI P.D. (No. 1) 9 (Lok Sabha) (1970).
143. (1971) XVI P.D. (No. 1) 8-9 (Lok Sabha) (1970).
144. (1973) XVIII P.D. (No. 2) 26-27 (Lok Sabha) (1973).

145. (1974) XIX P.D. (No. 2) 40-42 (Lok Sabha) (1974).
146. (1981) XXI P.D. (No. 1) 13 (Rajya Sabha).
147. (1980) XXV P.D. (No. 2) 41 (Lok Sabha).
148. (1981) XXVI P.D. (No. 2) 24 (Madhya Pradesh Vidhan Sabha).
149. (1957) I P.D. (No. 3) 8 (Rajya Sabha) (1953).
150. (1968) XIII P.D. (No. 2) 74 (Maharashtra Legislative Assembly) (1963).
151. (1975) XX P.D. (No. 2) 44 (Lok Sabha) (1974).
152. (1975) XX P.D. (No. 2) 41-42 (Lok Sabha) (1973).
153. (1976) XXI P.D. (No. 2) 34 (Lok Sabha) (1974).
154. (1960) IV P.D. (No. 1) 3-4 (Lok Sabha) (1959).
155. (1961) V P.D. (No. 1) 4-5 (Punjab Vidhan Sabha) (1960).
156. (1967) XII P.D. (No. 1) 35.
157. (1981) XXVI P.D. (No. 2) 24 (Madhya Pradesh Legislative Assembly).
158. (1982) XXVII P.D. (No. 1) 6 (Rajya Sabha).
159. (1981) XXVI P.D. (No. 1) 13 (Rajya Sabha) (1981).
160. (1967) XII P.D. (No. 1) 13 (Lok Sabha) (1966).
161. (1980) XXV P.D. (No. 2) 51 (Rajya Sabha) (1979).
162. (1977) X .III P.D. (No. 1) 1 (Lok Sabha) (1977).
163. (1980) XXV P.D. (No. 2) 42 (Lok Sabha) (1980).
164. (1978) XXIII P.D. (No. 1) 10 (Lok Sabha) (1978).
165. (1980) XXV P.D. (No. 2) 51 (Rajya Sabha) (1979).
166. (1965) IX P.D. 6-7 (Lok Sabha) (1965).
167. (1980) XXV P.D. (No. 2) 41 (Lok Sabha) (1980).
168. (1978) XXIII P.D. (No. 1) 10 (Lok Sabha) (1978).
169 (1979) XXIV P.D. (No. 2) 44 (Lok Sabha) (1978).
170. (1979) XXIV P.D. (No. 1) 5 (Lok Sabha) (1978).
171. (1980) X .V P.D. (No. 2) 51 (West Bengal Legislative Assembly).
172. (1980) XXV P.D. (No. 1) 4 (Lok Sabha) (1979).
173. (1975) XX P.D. (No. 1) 12 (Lok Sabha) (1975).
174. (1977) XXII P.D. (No. 2) 48 (Lok Sabha) (1973).
175. (1975) XX P.D. (No. 1) 12 (Lok Sabha) (1975).
176. (1977) XXII P.D. (No. 1) 18 (West Bengal Legislative Assembly) (1975).
177. (1977) XXII P.D. (No. 2) 48 (Rajya Sabha) (1973).
178. (1961) V P.D. (No. 2) 40-42 (Assam Legislative Assembly) (1959).
179. (1969) XIV P.D. (No. 1) 6-7 (Lok Sabha) (1969).
180. (1978) XIII P.D. (No. 2) 44 (Rajya Sabha) (1978).
181. (196) XI P.D. (No. 2) 24 (Rajya Sabha) (1962).
182. (1964) XIII P.D. 7-8 (Rajya Sabha) (1963).
183. (1967) XII P.D. (No. 1) 37-8 (Rajya Sabha) (1966).
184. (1964) VIII P.D. 3 (Lok Sabha) (1963).
185. (1965) IX P.D. 2-3 (Lok Sabha) (1965).
186. (1961) V P.D. (No. 2) 40-42 (Assam Legislative Assembly) (1959).

187. (1967) XII P.D. (No. 1) 31-32 (Lok Sabha) (1966).
188. (1967) XII P.D. (No. 1) 38-39 (Rajya Sabha) (1966).
189. (1967) XII P.D. (No. 1) 9-10 (Lok Sabha) (1966).
190. (1967) XII P.D. (No. 2) 115-116 (Rajya Sabha) (1967).
191. (1967) XII P.D. (No. 1) 38-39 (Rajya Sabha) (1966).
192. (1976) XII P.D. (No. 1) 17 (Uttar Pradesh Vidhan Sabha) (1976).
193. (1977) XXII P.D. (No. 2) 43 (Rajya Sabha) (1973).
194. (1978) XXIII P.D. (No. 2) 47 (Karnataka Legislative Assembly) (1977).
195. (1978) P.D. (No. 2) 5 (Lok Sabha) (1973).
196. (1966) XI P.D. 1 (Lok Sabha) (1966).
197. (1976) XXI P.D. (No. 2) 42 (Madhya Pradesh Vidhan Sabha) (1974).
198. (1981) XXVI P.D. (No. 1) 16 (Himachal Vidhan Sabha) (1981).
199. *Oil Scandal* case (1982) XXVII P.D. (No. 2) 2 (Lok Sabha); *Oil Scandal* case (1982) XXVII P.D. (No. 2) 5 (Rajya Sabha).
200. (1957) II P.D. (No. 1) 9-12 (Delhi Vidhan Sabha) (1956).
201. (1960) IV P.D. (No. 2) 40-41 (Punjab Vidhan Sabha) (1959).
202. (1962) V P.D. (No. 1) 4-6 (Assam Legislative Assembly) (1960).
203. (1966) XI P.D. 1 (Lok Sabha) (1966).
204. 1976 reported in (1981) XXVI P.D. (No. 1) 6.
205. (1978) XXIII P.D. (No. 2) 47 (Karnataka Legislative Assembly) (1977).
206. (1967) XII P.D. (No. 1) 20-21 (Lok Sabha) (1966).
207. (1970) XV P.D. (No. 2) 43-44 (Lok Sabha) (1970).
208. (1975) XXII P.D. (No. 2) 34 (Lok Sabha) (1973).
209. (1979) XXIV P.D. (No. 2) 48 (Jammu and Kashmir Legislative Assembly) (1978).
210. (1958) II P.D. (No. 2) 55-56 (Madhya Pradesh Vidhan Sabha) (1957).
211. (1960) IV P.D. (No. 1) 10 (Madhya Pradesh Vidhan Sabha) (1958).
212. (1974) XIX P.D. (No. 2) 39-40 (Lok Sabha) (1972).
213. (1980) XXV P.D. (No. 2) 42 (Rajya Sabha) (1980).
214. (1963) VII P.D. 11 (Madras Legislative Assembly) (1958).
215. (1961) V P.D. (No. 2) 27-28 (Lok Sabha) (1961).
216. *Blitz* case (1961) V (2) P.D. 2 (Lok Sabha).
217. (1961) V P.D. (No. 2) 45-46 (Kerala Legislative Assembly) (1960).
218. (1962) VI P.D. (No. 2) 24 (Rajya Sabha) (1962).
219. (1964) VIII P.D. 7-8 (Rajya Sabha) (1963).
220. (1966) XII P.D. (No. 1) 37-38 (Rajya Sabha) (1966).
221. (1966) XII P.D. (No. 1) 20-21 (Lok Sabha) (1966).
222. (1973) XVIII P.D. (No. 2) 26-27 (Lok Sabha) (1973).
223. (1962) VI P.D. (No. 1) 10-11 (Madras Legislative Assembly) (1961).
224. (1967) XII P.D. (No. 2) 99 (Lok Sabha) (1967).
225. (1969) XIV P.D. (No. 1) 5-5 (Lok Sabha) (1968).
226. (1969) XIV P.D. (No. 2) 39-40 (Lok Sabha) (1969).
227. (1980) XXV P.D. (No. 2) 42 (Rajya Sabha).

228. 1980 reported in (1981) XXVI P.D. (No. 1) 12 (Rajya Sabha); see also *Srinagar Times* case (1983) XXVIII P.D. (No. 1) 12 J & K Assembly).
229. (1982) XXVII P.D. (No. 1) 12.
230. (1982) XXVII P.D. (No. 1) 3 (Lok Sabha).
231. (1983) XXVIII P.D. (No. 1) 16 (Maharashtra Legislative Assembly).
232. (1981) XXVI P.D. (No. 1) 3 (Lok Sabha).
233. (1977) XXII P.D. (No. 1) 12 (Bihar Legislative Council) (1974).
234. (1977) XXII P.D. (No. 2) 3-7 (Lok Sabha) (1977).
235. 1979 reported in (1980) XXV P.D. (No. 1) 11 (Meghalaya Legislative Assembly).
236. 1978 reported in (1981) XXVI P.D. (No. 1) 24.
237. (1981) XXVI P.D. (No. 2) 19 (Tripura Legislative Assembly) (1978).
238. *Indira Gandhi Trust* case (1981) XXVI P.D. (No. 2) 8 (Lok Sabha); *Arun Shourie* case (1981) XXVI P.D. (No. 2) 18 (Rajya Sabha).
239. (1957) I P.D. (No. 3) 17-20 (Punjab Vidhan Sabha) (1957).
240. (1957) I P.D. (No. 3) 10-11 (Kerala Legislative Assembly) (1957).
241. (1969) XIV P.D. (No. 2) 37-38 (Lok Sabha) (1969).
242. (1966) XI P.D. 9-11 (Goa, Daman and Diu Legislative Assembly).
243. 1979 reported in (1980) XXV P.D. (No. 1) 9 (Andhra Legislative Assembly).
244. (1980) XXV P.D. (No. 2) 37 involving the *Hindustan Times* and *Patriot*.
245. (1965) IX P.D. 1-2 (Lok Sabha) (1964).
246. (1975) XX P.D. (No. 2) (Kerala Legislative Assembly) (1971).
247a. (1980) XXV P.D. (No. 2) 37-8 (Lok Sabha).
247b. (1982) XXVII P.D. (No. 1) 1 (Lok Sabha).
248. (1959) III P.D. (No. 4) Parliament of India (1950).
249. (1967) XII P.D. (No. 1) 11-13 (Lok Sabha) (1966).
250. (1962) VI P.D. (No. 2) 23-4 (Lok Sabha) (1962).
251. (1964) VII P.D. 2-3 (Lok Sabha) (1963).
252. (1969) XII P.D. (No. 1) 27-30 (Lok Sabha) (1966).
253. (1980) XXV P.D. (No. 1) 7 (Lok Sabha).
254. (1980) XXV P.D. (No.2) 45 (Rajya Sabha).
255. (1981) XXVI P.D. (No. 1) (Lok Sabha) where the Speaker referred to the *Thomas* and *Dalton* cases of England, and article 105(3) of the Constitution of India to hold there was no breach of privilege, but that confidentiality should be maintained. (Quaere: Why?); see also *Daily Mail* case in England about pre-publication of a Committee Report reported (1981) XXVI P.D. (No. 1) 25.
256. (1982) XXVII P.D. (No. 1) 4 (Lok Sabha).
257. (1978) XXIII P.D. (No. 2) 34 (Lok Sabha) (1977).
258. (1976) XXI P.D. (No. 2) 36 (Lok Sabha) (1975).
259. (1977) XXII P.D. (No. 1) 18 (Gujarat Vidhan Sabha) (1976).
260. (1980) XXV P.D. (No. 1) 1 (Lok Sabha) (1978).
261. (1983) XXVIII P.D. (No. 1) 13 (Kerala Legislative Assembly).

262. 1978 reported (1980) XXV P.D. (No. 1) 11 (Lok Sabha).
263. *D.K. Ga g et. al.*, case 1980 reported in (1981) XXVI P.D. (No. 1) 5 (Rajya Sabha).
264. (1981) XXVI P.D. (No. 1) 12 (Rajya Sabha).
265. (1981) XXVI P.D. (No. 2) 25 (Uttar Pradesh).
266. (1981) XXVI P.D. (No. 2) 22 (Goa Legislative Assembly).
267. (1981) XXVI P.D. (No. 2) 8 (Lok Sabha).
268. (1981) XXVI P.D. (No. 2) 8 (Lok Sabha); see speech in Lok Sabha on 2 September 1981 *L.S.D.* column 333-4.
269. (1981) XXVI P.D. (No. 2) 18.
270. (Rajya Sabha) (1981) *Indian Express*, September 4.
271. (1978) XXIII P.D. (No. 2) 30-31 (Lok Sabha).
272. (1978) XXVI P.D. (No. 1) 3 (Lok Sabha).
273. It is difficult to draw a line. Consider the view that parliamentary privilege can be used for victimization in Hardwarilal: *Myth and Law of Parliamentary Privileges* (1979).
274. (1980) XXV P.D. (No. 2) 11 (Meghalaya Legislative Assembly) (1979).
275. (1981) XXVI P.D. (No. 2) 24 (Uttar Pradesh Vidhan Parishad) (1978).
276. (1978) XXIII P.D. (No. 2) 33 (Lok Sabha) (1976).
277. 1978 reported in (1981) XXVI P.D. (No. 1) 24 (Uttar Pradesh Legislative Council).
278. (1983) XXVIII P.D. (No. 1) 16 (Maharashtra Legislative Assembly).
279. *All India Radio* case (1975) XX P.D. (No. 2) 54 (Uttar Pradesh Vidhan Parishad) (1975); *Kare Koi Mare Koi* (1976) XXI P.D. (No. 1) 16 (Uttar Pradesh Vidhan Sabha).

6

ACCESS TO GOVERNMENT INFORMATION

I

Official secrecy has only recently been discovered by the law. Pre-capitalist societies operating within the framework of cohesive status relationships protected 'state' secrecy through these relationships. Information was a privilege within these relationships. A denial of the relationship could constitute an offence: as in the case of the offence of treason. Passing on information could be taken as constituting a denial of the relationship. An abuse of any privilege arising out of the relationship led to social and political ostracism. Those that were suspected of disloyalty were punished severely and stripped of both status and power. Undoubtedly all this was never enough; but it was efficacious.

The advent of capitalism and technology had two important effects on this apparatus of arrangements. Firstly the pre-capitalist structure of relationships had to be reconstituted into new legal concepts which represented the individual as a new kind of entity liberated from these relationships. He was, of course, ready for and immediately subjected to new relationships. The law refused to recognise new forms of group membership and projected the individual as a free market creature to be controlled individually and for whom others had no responsibility. Some rules were developed in order to establish the responsibility of superior principals. However, this new atomistic view of society precipitated an atomistic set of legal control mechanisms. This was one of the contradictions inherent in the new legal concepts. On the one hand the individual was thrown as a 'free agent' to fresh unscrupulous market forces; on the other hand, new theories of individual responsibility and liability meant the eclipse of forms of mass control. This was most clearly felt in the area of public order and labour law. It was also significant in the field of official secrecy. One of the major difficulties with the new law of official secrecy that was developed in the United Kingdom, in the nineteenth century, was that while it was notionally concerned with allocating individual responsibility for a person's actions, the heart of the legislation lay in trying to penalize a person for his contacts and relationships. The law that emerged was very wide, covering all kinds of activity, creating new concepts of preparatory offences and creating new widely phrased catch-all offences. Secondly, capitalism and technology necessitated legally conceptualising information as a category. New laws were created relating to copyright, trade mark and patents. These laws gave a new legal form to 'information' as a commodity. Yet this new legal form could not give protection to all forms of 'information' fetishism. A controlled information dispersal was the nexus between creative technological advance and the desired form of capitalist expansion. New kinds of information brokers mushroomed in society. While the press was a general broker, there were other more specific brokers who leaked and sold information. To some extent, information amongst certain categories of relationship was protected by the law relating to confidentiality. But the law knew no way to counteract the information explosion which accompanied the growth of journalism. Nor could it counteract the circulation of information at the expense of industry and the State. Too much slipped through the net of the law. Too much of the law acted after the event unable to prevent what it could only punish.

As it happened, much of the information was protected through unofficial means. Apart from personal, party, group and class loyalties, a fresh ideology was created in order to justify enfolding the processes of the modern State within the mantle of secrecy. The development of the concept of public interest provided the conceptive ideology for controlling information dissemination in society. While official secrecy was originally justified to meet the problem of foreign aggression and protect diplomacy, it did not take long for it to be stretched to protect all processes of government. The only way in which the preponderance of such laws could be justified in a liberal democracy was on the basis of an overriding appeal to the public interest. Each time the existence of these laws came to be questioned an exaggerated injury to the State was pointed to as an inevitable consequence if such laws were relaxed in their intensity. There was never a shortage of crises; so, there was never a shortage of appeals to the public interest. Willy nilly, the entire apparatus of government was potentially protected on this basis. In practical terms the continued use of official secrets legislation in non-espionage cases could only have delegitimating effects on the legal and political system as a whole. Official secrets legislation stood as a fall-back if rigorous informal methods of control failed. By and large, these informal methods were good. There was a considerable measure of agreement amongst governing elites about the kind of information that should be leaked. In time, capitalism produced a sophisticated working class who wanted to share both power and information. As these demands were assimilated into a structure of what has been described in the last chapter as 'government by institution', the concept of public interest was expanded to provide integrity and protection to institutional processes. Arguments for absolute protection were modified to provide a more partial but nevertheless effective protection to government by institution. Absolute laws relating to penal official secrets legislation continued after being subjected to gradual doses of liberalism. Capitalism having legally enshrined individualism to assist the development of the advantaged and facilitate the exploitation of the disadvantaged, had to appeal to new community concepts like the public interest and institutional viability in order to stabilise and preserve the distribution of power.

The Indian State did not develop it so systematically. The Imperial British State in India while slavishly imitating English legislation was in a far worse predicament in the late nineteenth century. Government by institution had not got firmly entrenched as part of the political structure. The informal methods of control did not operate outside the government and pro-government establishment press. The government itself had developed very complex diplomatic and class alliances with existing and emergent groups. Without the mantle of secrecy, the Imperial British government would not have been able to conceal the network of private deals within which the Imperial State functioned. Such a network while available in any modern State was even more marked in a rapidly transforming economy in which fresh alliances and compromises had to be struck between emerging and entrenched interests. The Imperial State passed on its legislation on official secrecy to its successor contemporary State. The extent and sweep of this legislation has not really been questioned despite the fact that it has to be adjusted within the framework of liberal constitutionalism.

II

The laws relating to protecting the executive can be traced back to the days of the British. One part of this legislation is about security of state, the incitement of disaffection, law and order and so on. The other part of the legislative efforts of the British to shroud the working of their administration is official secrets legislation.

The story about how official secrecy legislation was enacted in Britain in the late nineteenth century is well known. Following the Marvin (1878) and Anderson (1889) affairs, it became clear that there was no legal recourse against officials and others who 'borrowed' information and then returned it to their civil service safe.[1] Exactly the same position pertained in India. The initial strategy of the British in India was to deal with the matter internally. A series of administrative circulars dating from 1843 put an absolute embargo on official information being given to anyone else.[2] Later, it became clear that while senior officers would have to be given some discretion to explain the policy of the government, it was necessary—as in a famous resolution of 1878—

> to remind all officers of the government that information received by them in their official capacity, whether from official sources or otherwise, which is not from its nature obviously intended to be made public, cannot be treated as if it were at their personal disposal.[3]

But information was constantly leaked despite the fact that the government of India had assumed a tough policy on this question. Not surprisingly, when Britain enacted its first Official Secrets Act, 1889, it was quickly duplicated for India.[4] Both legislations were quite wide-ranging covering the leaking of information other than military secrets.[5] The Indian legislation, *inter alia*, made it an offence to "knowingly having control, possession or control over any such document, sketch, plan, model *or knowledge*" from any "fortress, arsenal, factory, dockyard, camp, ship, *office or like place*".[6] Officials were charged with a duty not to commit a criminal breach of trust.[7] In 1904, the Indian statute was amended making procedural changes, deleting 'offices' from the catchment of the Act,[8] including 'attempts' within the Act,[9] making the Act function for the wider 'public interest' rather than just the 'interest of the state',[10] and extending the Act to cover 'naval, military or civil' affairs of His Majesty.[11] In 1911, the English Parliament quickly enacted 'temporary' consolidating legislation in the form of the Official Secrets Act, 1911. This was extended to India.[12] In 1920, this statute was further amended to making communication with foreign agents a felony and making preparatory offences criminal. This was not extended to India. So, in 1920, India was governed by the two Indian enactments of 1889 and 1904 and the British statute of 1911 as unamended by the statute of 1920.

It was a typical tactic of the British to enact tough legislation under the guise of clearing up an existing confusion in the laws.[13] This applied to the move to enact a fresh official secrets legislation in India in 1922-23 in abundant measure. The Bill 'which later became the Official Secrets Act, 1923' was presented as a consolidating measure and the Select Committee dealing with the Bill was charged to "assimilate the law of British India relating to official secrets to the law in force in the United Kingdom."[14] When an Indian legislator—Mr. K.C. Neogy—protested that the English had much more sinister designs[15] he was promptly absorbed in the Select Committee itself and told:

> More than three-fourths of it is a purely consolidating measure . . . and the only effect will be, as the Honourable Member knew perfectly well, to leave the law in a confused state. Our main object in this Bill is to get the law into some real intelligible form at present and that is really the reason for the present measure.[16]

After the Bill returned from an allegedly "very representative Select Committee . . . (which) performed its labours most conscientiously",[17] it was heavily criticized in the Legislative Assembly[18] partly because it was seen as a "slavish imitation of the English statute"[19] and partly because it was much more wide-ranging in that "the language of the Bill is very wide and capable of much abuse in its interpretation".[20] After the attempt to re-commit the Bill to the Select Committee failed,[21] a series of amendments were tabled which tried to introduce a *mens rea* component in respect of many of the offences created by the Bill.

Indian legislators wanted to expand the Act to cover 'potential enemies' only to be told it was not necessary in the light of English interpretations of a similar statute.[22] Concern was expressed that people could be found guilty on the basis of their general "conduct and known character" and that mere communication with or possessing any information about or address of foreign agents—even if one did not know they were foreign agents—was an offence.[23] An attempt to delete this clause was defeated.[24] This led later to the inevitable following exchange:

> *Lala Girdharilal Agarwala*: . . . Is it proposed, Sir, to print the names of foreign agents in any publication for the guidance of the public?
>
> *The Honourable Malcolm Hailey*: . . . I am sorry the Honourable Member should think that we are so deficient in humour that we should even answer that question.[25]

Oddly enough, the 'catch all' clause 5, which covered official secrecy generally, did not come in for too heavy an attack.[26] The only real attack on it was that it should be used only where the offence 'prejudicially' affected the 'safety of the state' and not the general interests of the state.[27] This amendment was not accepted and a good opportunity to attack this wide-ranging clause was lost. The government was not prepared to give in to many wide-ranging concessions. It agreed to allow the courts to have a discretion not to accept the finality of evidence in the strict liability communication with foreign agents cases.[28] It also accepted amendments to the effect that the accused would have the right to determine whether or not he should be tried by a special Magistrate or a regular Court of Session.[29] But no major concessions were accepted. The British government had used the interesting manoeuvre of exploiting the consensus that spying must inevitably be decried as a bad thing. This had the effect of ensuring that the opposition confined themselves to legalistic questions and the manner in which the legislation would be enforced. Sir H.S. Gour summed up the strategy of the opposition:

> . . . I indignantly repudiate, both on my own behalf and on their (*i.e.*, the Opposition's) behalf, the charge that there was any intention to oppose the central principles of this measure. What we have opposed and what we should have continued to oppose are the details, which the occupants of the Treasury Benches have themselves confessed are of an exceptional and drastic character. We, as representatives of

> the people, had to see that these provisions were not unduly enlarged so as to let in through their wide meshes accused persons against whom justice and the evidence would not admit of conviction.[30]

Official secrecy—as an issue in itself—was not really mooted. Indian legislators had not really acclimatized themselves to looking at official secrecy as a whole.

The Official Secrets Act was amended again in 1967.[31] Once again the general stand taken by the government was that the "main point of the Bill is to make the offence punishable with greater sentences of imprisonment and make most of the offences under the Bill cognizable offences".[32] Security was made the major consideration.[33] One of the major critics of the Bill concentrated on the differential manner in which the government exercised its discretion to prosecute.[34] Another critic stressed that the government was not enforcing enough secrecy.[35] Parliament did not display enough concern about the problem of official secrecy as a whole. Only M.L. Sondhi—himself a former civil servant—added a note of caution:

> With regard to the question of official secrets, I speak with some experience, and it is my feeling that administrative reform is long overdue because if everything is marked "secret" then the very notions of secrecy are devalued.[36]

The whole Bill was reconstructed without giving too much attention to the issue of official secrecy as a whole.

Official secrecy has not figured as a major issue. The effect of the laws relating to official secrecy was analysed in part in a small book on press legislation in 1968.[37] A major international conference was held on the subject in India in 1978. It contributed to Indian journalists and others to look at the subject from a comparative perspective.[38] One editor hinted that the press ignored the secrecy classifications of the government and was convinced—clearly wrongly—that the 1923 statute did "not exhaust all the usual methods of administrative secrecy . . .(and dealt) only with the more serious aspects of the vital interests of the state".[39] But 'secrecy' has become a small political issue. The Janata government committed itself to examine it as an issue in its election manifesto in 1977. This was more by way of an adverse reaction to the Emergency of 1975-77 rather than because of a commitment to the issue. Indeed, when it came into power, a Working Group of officials from the Cabinet Secretariat and Ministries of Home Affairs, Finance and Defence reported that no change in the Official Secrets Act was necessary.[40] When an Opposition politician asked a Minister in Parliament whether India would follow the cosmopolitan contemporary trend in providing more access to information about government, he was told that the Official Secrets Act had been "amended from time to time to suit our requirement" and that—

> The provisions of the Official Secrets Act, 1923 are designed primarily to safeguard national security and not to prohibit legitimate access to official documents and, therefore, no legislation to guarantee access to official documents, other than those dealing with national security, is considered necessary.[41]

There is little or no climate in India for looking at the issue of 'openness' in government. The reason for this may be that information does pass hands informally anyway and, in any event, the press is not likely to put any such information to ambitious use.

The official secrets legislation in India is wide-ranging. Section 3 prohibits approaching, inspecting, or passing over or entering in the vicinity of a prohibited place; or making a sketch, plan or model or note which is intended to be, directly or indirectly, useful to an enemy.[42] But the section goes further, it is also an offence to obtain, collect, record, publish or communicate to any other person these items "or other document or information which is calculated to be or might be, directly or indirectly, useful to an enemy or which relates to a matter the disclosure of which is likely to affect the sovereignty and integrity of India, the security of the state or friendly relations with foreign states".[43] The section proceeds on the basis that even if the case is not proved against the accused, "his conduct or his known character as proved" could be used to presume that he acted out of a purpose "prejudicial to the safety or interests of the State".[44] Following the British courts, "enemy" has been interpreted to include "potential enemy".[45] Section 4 makes it unlawful to communicate with foreign agents or any person reasonably suspected of being a foreign agent. Again a wide ranging presumption states that a person will be presumed to have been in communication with a foreign agent if he had within or without India visited the address of such a foreign agent or had in his possession, or obtained, the address of such agent.[46] The terms "foreign agent"[47] and "address"[48] are widely defined so that a person would be guilty of an offence even if he himself did not know that a foreign agent was involved but there might have been reasonable objective grounds for suspicion. Section 5 is the 'catch all' section. It deals not just with information about 'prohibited places',[49] but relates to the wilful communication, uses, retention or failure to take care of all information—

> which has been entrusted in confidence to him (*i.e.* the accused) by any person holding office under Government, or which he has obtained or which he has had access owing to his position as a person who holds or has held office under Government or as a person who holds or has held a contract made on behalf of Government, or as a person who is or has been employed under a person who holds or has held such an office or contract.[50]

The voluntary reception, possession or control of any such information is also an offence if there is knowledge or reasonable cause to believe that such information is communicated in contravention of the Act.[51] Section 5 has been interpreted widely to cover, for example, budget leaks.[52] Section 6 not only prohibits admission or assisting others to gain admission to prohibited places, but also makes it an offence to retain, communicate and manufacture any secret code, password or *any official document* (whether in draft or otherwise), if it is kept for any purpose objectively determined to be prejudicial to the safety of the state.[53] There are penalties for obstructing the protection and policing of prohibited places[54] and harbouring spies[55] and a duty to give information about spying or attempts to spy.[56] The Act is extended to cover "attempts to commit or abet the commission of an offence under the Act".[57] Magistrates have the power to issue general search warrants where there is reasonable grounds of suspicion[58] and a general power of arrest is also given to the police.[59] Although the offence can be tried at the accused's option by high level Magistrates or the Court of Session[60] there is a power to exclude the public from the proceedings.[61]

Yet, after all this, it is ironic that there is very little reported case law on prosecutions under the official Secrets Act.[62] It is possible, but not really likely, that there were a lot of unreported prosecutions which were not appealed to, or reported by, the High Courts. It is really impossible to gauge the prosecutorial impact of the Act. The probable explanation for the lack of cases is not just that the statute was crystal clear and did not require interpretation by the higher judiciary. Even in other countries, such legislation serves as a symbolic statement and warning. And this has been its major impact in India—both during the days of Raj and since Independence.

Few of these cases concern themselves with the substantive interpretation of the Act. One of the leading cases is the *Karanjia* case.[63] Here, a leading paper had asked people to bring information about secrets of the government to the paper. The case was really concerned with whether the government could, under circumstances, impose a 'forfeitable deposit' on the paper. Answering this question in the affirmative, the Court also emphsized the wide range of official information covered by the Act. This interpretation was continued in the '*Budget Proposals*' case where pre-publication details about the budget were deemed to be covered by the statute.[64] These cases affirm and emphasize that the Official Secrets Act is not just concerned with spying and strategic and cognate secrets but all information which passes in and through the hands of the government. In a recent Calcutta case the Court extended this interpretation from the 'catch all' Section 5 to the spying section and decided that even in such cases the information, which formed the corpus of the offence, need not itself be 'secret' but only intended, calculated or otherwise useful to the 'enemy'.[65] We have already noted that 'enemy' here was interpreted, as in England, to cover a potential or future enemy or any unfriendly power which may later be involved in a war.[66]

Most of the cases have been concerned with procedural matters. Thus, the courts have decided that a Court of Session cannot quash a commitment for trial where an application had been made by the accused to have his case heard by the Sessions Court,[67] that a remand for bail should not be granted by a Magistrate not having the power to do so,[68] that bail could be refused under the Act where the accused was being tried for bailable and non-bailable offences under the Act,[69] that Magistrates have the power to deal with the investigative part of a case, and that the authority of the government was not needed in such matters,[70] that confessions recorded by a Magistrate could be used even where prior authorization for such recording of the proceedings was not taken under the Official Secrets Act,[71] that the Official Secrets Act was intended to be operated through a special procedure and that it was not necessary that all the documents of the case be made available to the accused,[72] that a lesser standard of proof was required in cases under the Act.[73] Some protection was given to the accused in respect of the extended presumption-of-guilt provisions and it was held that the fact that the accused knew where a particular office was located and the person who traced a document from that office does not create a presumption of guilt in a spying charge.[74]

All these procedural cases stress a very important point about the pathology of Indian litigation. A person accused of crime—or, for that matter, involved in a civil suit—leaves it to his lawyers to devise ingenious arguments to get him off the book or, where appropriate, prolong a case. While some of the procedural cases involve important points (*e.g.*, on the remanding to custody and presumption of guilt questions) the rest of the cases are really probing and strategic arguments which are designed to meander their way to success if the wind is blowing in the right direction.

Apart from the *Karanjia* case—which was not directly under this Act—none of the cases concerns the press. This suggests many things. To begin with, the Press itself does not conduct many investigations into the government. Gossip and conjecture are substituted for investigative reporting. There is a sufficient amount of rumour to whet the appetites of journalists and their reading public. At the same time, the government exercises a somewhat clumsy control over its official secrecy policy. Information is leaked, bought and available even if it is not used publicly. This does not apply to military secrets. But even here the spying case does not involve big spy rings but little 'alleged' spies connected with Pakistan and who are put on trial either because it is convenient to charge them under the Act or because it is useful to set an example.[75]

As if to lend credibility to the thesis about the pathology of litigation in India, there is a plethora of case law on the extent to which official documents can be used in litigation before the courts.[76] This issue, which is identified in English law, as concerning 'Crown privilege', is confusingly contained in two provisions of the Indian Evidence Act, 1972:

> *Section 123*: No one shall be permitted to give any evidence derived from any published official records relating to any affairs of State except with the permission of the Officer at the Head of the Department concerned, who shall give or withhold the information as he thinks fit".
>
> "*Section 162*: A witness summoned to produce a document shall, if it is in his position and power, bring it to the Court, notwithstanding any objection which there may be to its production or to its admissibility. The validity of any such objection shall be decided by the Court.
>
> The Court, if it sees fit, inspects the document, unless it refers to matters of state or to take evidence to enable it to determine on its admissibility".

Lawyers have fought many a hard battle on trying to get more information from the government. In the leading case,[77] the judges could not decide the extent of information which could be admitted in order to determine whether the document was secret or whether a blanket claim made by the government should be accepted. In time, the courts have gradually moved to accept a general cosmopolitan stance that the statement of the State should not by itself be sufficient.[78] But the issue has generally been treated as a lawyers' issue and it has been remarked: "[W]e find little discussion about the problem of official secrecy in Indian Democracy and the possible repercussions in India if the administration were called upon to be more frank in their disclosures".[79] Nor has the press used the 'Crown privilege' provisions in strategic litigation to get information out of the government.

Pressmen can also be called upon to disclose information which is needed by the State in connection with Commissions of Inquiry. The Indian law relating to Commissions of Inquiry contains provisions to force a person to make disclosures.[80] Any plea of confidentiality has to compete against other arguments which weigh with the public interest. However, an Ordinance[81] and later a statute amending the Official Secrets Act has been promulgated which prescribes a procedure for the exercise of discretion by the government in deciding whether a report of a Commission of Inquiry should be laid before the Lok Sabha or a Legislative Assembly. The government may decide to withhold such report if it finds that it would not be expedient in the interest of the sovereignty and integrity of the country.

How does the government of India operate its policy of official secrecy? Under the Constitution the President has the power to make "rules for the more convenient transaction of the business of the government of India."[82] Needless to say, these rules cannot transgress some other part of the Constitution; or presumably violate those provisions dealing with the freedom of speech and expression. The freedom of speech and expression can only be infringed upon by reasonable restrictions in respect of, amongst other things, the law relating to official secrecy.[83] A shroud of secrecy seems to surround the rules that have been made by the President. Published till ,973, these rules have now been declared confidential.[84] This was understandable during the period 1976-1978 when the Indian Constitution had been amended during the Emergency so as to prevent courts from having access to these already constitutional rules,[85] but no longer, now that amendment to the Constitution has itself been amended.[86]

The government of India runs an extensive system of official secrecy. Documents are divided into the well known categories of "classified" and "unclassified". The latter cannot be communicated to anyone outside government without a general or specific order. There are rules which suggest that government officials may not even without an official reason disclose information to their own colleagues. All communications to the press are communicated through the Press Bureau. "Classified" papers carry the designations—"top secret", "secret" "confidential" and "personal—not for publication". These terms are self-explanatory. The "top secret" category is reserved for military and cognate secrets, the "secret" and "confidential" categories intermix and represent a form of garding of what is available within the government itself.

All these documents locked in for thirty years. And even then only non-confidential information is available to a restricted range of people.[87]

There was no significant move to reform the law relating to official secrecy. When the matter was considered by the Press Laws Inquiry Committee in 1948, the Committee took the view that this legislation was necessary and that no move should be made to dislodge from the government its extensive and wide-ranging power to control the flow of official information.[88] It was assumed that a generous amount of official secrecy was necessary and that democratic government could be trusted to make sure that this power would not be abused by the government. The Press Committee of 1954 took a similar attitude. It shared the concern of newspaper lobbyists that the government could—and, indeed, did—designate information as 'secret' whenever it wanted to. But it was satisfied that the Official Secrets Act, 1923 was being administered in a "reasonable manner",[89] What the Commission should have done was not just to look at the paucity of prosecutions under the Act. Much rather it should have considered the whole system of official secrecy and how it influences the working of the press.

A government's Inter-Departmental Study was set up in 1977 to examine the working of the Official Secrets Act. But its secret report has not yet surfaced.[90]

All these questions were also not considered by the Law Commission when it considered the general area of Offences against National Security. After stressing that the operative Section 5 was badly drafted, the Law Commission was content with making a plea for a lenient policy of prosecutorial discretion. Equally, there was a recommendation that the punishment threshold should be increased where serious leaks of important secrets were involved.[91]

More recently, the Indian Law Institute has made various recommendations.[92] The Indian Law Institute has not only considered the matter thoroughly but has proceeded on a footing quite different from that of previous government commissions. It has refused to countenance the preliminary assumption that official secrecy is needed for all government activity. In fact, it has argued, there are certain distinct areas relating to defence, foreign relations, finance, law and order, confidentiality and privacy, trade secrets and the like which need specific protection. A defence has been proposed so that an accused can plead that a publication was in the public interest. It is not clear whether this defence should be made available to civil servants as well. Clearly, broad appeals to the public interest can always be made by any accused in any case. And the range is endless. Thus, to draw on an English example, a person accused of giving away nuclear secrets could easily argue that it is in the public interest that all nuclear war should stop. Faced with such a plea, it is more than likely that the courts may, in certain areas, repose the trusteeship of the public interest in the government. The Report recommends the shifting of prosecutorial responsibility in such cases away from the Attorney General to a proposed Committee including the Attorney General, the Chairman of the Press Council and one other person appointed by the latter. The Committee will not deal with espionage cases but only general prosecutions. But the report goes further and also suggests that it should be made obligatory on the government to disclose information and make it available to the general public in all except the specified categories which have been referred to above.

This Report has much to commend it and has been well received by the Press.[94] A lot really depends on the kind of role that the Press wishes to play. Given the relationships between the press and the government—and the power wielded by the latter—there are limits to the thresholds of investigation that the press will undertake. The relaxation of the rules of official secrecy will probably be more useful to those who wish to run private and public, and personal and political campaigns against politicians and bureaucrats. But it is only right that the whole question of official secrecy should be examined in the context of India's needs.

Lawyers and litigational concerns have loomed large in the interpretation of official secrets legislation in India. Otherwise, the public and the press have not really pressed the Indian government for more access to information.

Apart from weak protests, the request for reform in this area is as alien to the press and the public as it is to the traditional concept of government by and through which India is governed. Across all this, the Official Secrets Act, 1923 strides as a colossus declaring the symbolic aims of the government and successfully using a traditional and archaic social psychology to camouflage the activities of the government. Informal governmental controls and pressures and the temerity of the press does the rest. Except when spurred on by an imitative cosmopolitanism, the Indian press and its public is not really concerned with official secrecy or open government.

III

The Indian law of official secrecy, though similar to the law of the United Kingdom, grew up under very different circumstances. The Imperial Indian State sought to cloak its dealings with its headquarters State in England and its alliances with various classes and groups in India. The post-Independence Indian State possesses a Constitution which has invited a run on itself by holding out the promise of increased participation. Yet it offers real power to only a limited range of existing and emerging elites. The Indian State itself is an "intermediate regime" unable to assimilate power on a systematic institutional basis. India's contemporary rulers have smashed the institutional framework of government by a combination of an abuse of the ground rules and an equally indiscriminate use of patronge. At the hands of the 'intermediate regime' of Mrs. Gandhi, the Indian State was 'privatised' into a direct relationship with those who seek to control it. Official secrecy is useful not just to cloak the processes of government but also to reveal as little as possible about this process of privatization which is the hallmark of the development of the law and politics of the Indian State. The Indian State is riddled with scandals. To some extent, these scandals reflect on the dominance of group loyalties within the factions of the Indian State. At the same time, the emergent middle class and their power brokers have not been able to systematically consolidate their power. The laws of official secrecy notionally prevent a discovery of conspiracies amongst factions and the undisciplined takeover of the State by an unscrupulous intermediate regime of power brokers. The irony of all this lies in the fact that much of what is going on is known—if not as exact knowledge, at least through informed intuition. The crucial decision in India is not to know what is going on. The crucial decision is to decide when to offer what kinds of details for public exposure. The proper Indian method of indulging such exposure is to appoint Commissions of Inquiry. Hitherto, the task of Indian journalists was to bring about Commissions of Inquiry; and then to report on the findings of such inquiries. In time, such inquiries multiplied. Of late, Commissions of Inquiry serve two purposes. On the one hand, they divert attention from the even more real truths which lie at the root of Indian government. On the other hand, they are part and parcel of political witch hunts. Such witch hunts reached their high points in the aftermath of the Emergency (1975-77) when the

Shah Commission sat to investigate Mrs. Gandhi's emergency regime. Yet, it was the episode of the Shah Commission which made it abundantly clear that this whole Commission technique of investigating government was outmoded and ineffective. What was unleashed was a new journalism bent upon a more direct method of exposure. But the new journalism—of which Arun Shourie's *The Second Reign of Mrs. Gandhi*[94] is an example—suffers from a lack of overall direction. Often partisan, it struggles for a universal idiom. It represents class interests and is involved in factional disputes while claiming a wider interest in social justice. Its real target is to expose one part of the privatization of the Indian State reserving its investigative judgement on the rest. The government does not really wish to encourage new forms of investigative journalism or relax the laws relating to official secrecy. This view is shared by a bureaucracy which sees its own corruption less as a deviation from normative public standards and more as an inevitable concession to moral obligations generated by India's complicated socio-political structure. At the same time, the invitation to democracy and free speech also invites discovery of the privatization of the Indian State. At present, the demand for less official secrecy grows at the hands of factional and oppositional politics. As the corporate sector of India's political economy develops, it is possible that there might be a concomitant demand for more even-handed, rational and predictable treatment from the agencies of the State. When that happens, a much more genuine and complete attempt will be made to work out the extent to which the system can loosen its hold on official secrecy.

To sum up. The pre-independence Imperial State knew what it wished to protect, invited minimal participation in the affairs of the State and ruled through a network of institutions whose viability was protected in the public interest. The law of official secrecy was both an active threat as well as an ideological affirmation of the need to protect the methods of government. The post-independent State has really dissolved the significance of the law of official secrecy even though it cannot abandon its existence. The secrets are out in the open.

The institutions are undermined by their own masters; and the public interest is much too closely identified with private interests to justify its independent evaluation and protection. Official secrecy is significant in the area of espionage. Otherwise it remains a hardly used but active threat to the investigative journalism of the State. As things stand, it cannot be abandoned. It creates the circumstances under which the process of the privatization of the Indian State, although known, cannot be publicised. Newspapers print 'only the good news'. The rest is left to gossip rather than publicity.

NOTES

1. For the historical background see D.G.T. Williams: *Note in the Public Interest* (1968).
2. *e.g.* notifications of August 1843; (see Government of India, Home Department Public Proceedings (hereafter G.O.I.: H.O. August 1884 Nos. 213-220) July 1875 (*ibid.*); Treasury Minute of March 1884 and circular of August 1884 (*ibid.* 214), resolution of June 1865 (G.O.I.: H.O. June 1885 No. 162; All these have been researched and commented on by S. Maheshwari: "Secrecy in government in India" (1979) 25 *I.J.P.A.* 1101.
3. G.O.I.: H.O. January 1879 Nos. 95-6; see further S. Maheshwari (*op. cit. supra* note 2) 1103.
4. Indian Official Secrets Act (XV of) 1889 which applied (vide S. 2) *inter alia* to all these with British India, the Princely States and "all Native Indian subjects of Her Majesty without and beyond British India."
5. For the English Statute note the wider interpretation given to the statute in the unreported case of *R.* v. *John Doe* (1902).
6. (Emphasis added) Indian Official Secrets Act, 1889 S. 3.
7. *Ibid.* S. 4.
8. Indian Official Secrets Act (V of) 1904 S. 3. (a); but 'civil affairs' were included by S. 3 (b) (iii).
9. *Ibid.* S. 3 (e).
10. *Ibid.* S. 3 (b) (ii).
11. *Ibid.* S. 3 (c).
12. The background to these is to be found in D.G.T. Williams (*supra* note 1).
13. For another example of the use of this tactic see R. Dhavan: *Contempt of Court and the Press in Indta: A Preliminary Investigation* (Mimeo), 1980, Indian Law Institute—submitted to the Press Council of India—Chapter III.

14. See the Report of the Select Committee on the Bill to assimilate the laws in British India relating to official secrets to the law in force in the United Kingdom (1922).
15. The Bill was introduced on 25 March 1922 and was debated before going to the Select Committee on 6 September 1922 (III Legislative Assembly Debates) (hereafter L.A.D.) 130-4; and Neogy's speech at 130-2 pointing out that apart from statements in the House of Commons in England for a tougher law for India, "it has been our experience that the letter of the law is not so much at fault in India, as the spirit in which it is administered."
16. III L.A.D. 133 (per Sir William Vincent).
17. III L.A.D. 2244 (14 February 1923) (per Mr. L. Graham).
18. See generally the debate at III L.A.D. 2244-75.
19. III L.A.D. 2245 (per Dr. A.S. Gour).
20. III L.A.D. 2247 (per K.B.L. Agnihotri).
21. III L.A.D. 2247-2253. This motion proposed by K.B.L. Agnihotri, 2247-2251 was opposed by J. Chaudhri (2251-2) and L. Graham (2252) and provoked from Rao Bahadur T. Rangchariar the remark: "I am not ashamed of slavishly following the English of Englishmen".
22. III L.A.D. 2255-7; L. Graham referring impliedly to *R.* v. *Parrott* (1913).
23. III L.A.D. 2260-5 (on the known character amendment defeated by 38 votes to 26; on the 'foreign agents' issue see *ibid.* 2754-2761).
24. III L.A.D. 2265-2271.
25. III L.A.D. 2761.
26. III L.A.D. 27778.
27. III L.A.D. 2777. This was also sought to be introduced in earlier provisions—see III L.A.D. 2257-60.
28. III L.A.D. 2776-7.
29. III L.A.D. 2773-78.
30. III L.A.D. 2783.
31. Official Secrets Act (24 of) 1967.
32. (1967) 8 Lok Sabha Debates (IVth Series—hereafter L.S.D.) col. 19283—per V.C. Shukla.
33. *Ibid.* per R. Singh (cols. 19234-5); S. Goyal (19265-6); P. Shastri (19290-1); S. Nambiyar (19292-19293); K.N. Bajaj (19294-5). The tenor of the discussion may be summed up by K.K. Chatterjee's interjection (at 19292): "Should a traitor go scot-free?"
34. *Ibid.* 19286-89 (per S.M. Banerji).
35. *Ibid.* 19294-5.
36. *Ibid.* 19295.
37. Press Institute of India: *The Press in the Law* (1968)—note the contributions of C.P. Gupta, 49-51.
38. The papers are collected in a special issue of the *Indian Journal of Public Administration* (1979) Volume XXV: No. 4: 987-1360.

39. M. Chalapati Rau: "Official Secrets and Freedom of Information in India" (1979) XXV *I.J.A.P.* 1096.
40. See S. Maheshwari (*supra* note 2) 1112 who gives this a different interpretation and credits the protective attitude of the Committee to bureaucratic domination.
41. 17 L.S.D. (Sixth Series) No. 30 cols. 3294-5.
42. S. 3 (1) (a) (b) (c).
43. S. 3 (1) (c).
44. S. 3 (2).
45. See *Kutubuddin* v. *State of Rajasthan,* A.I.R. 1967 Raj. 257—see also the discussion *supra* note 22.
46. S. 2 (a).
47. S. 4 (2) (b).
48. S. 4 (2) (c).
49. S. 5 (1).
50. S. 5 (2).
51. *Nandlal* v. *State* (1965) 1 Cr. L.J. 393.
52. S. 6 (2).
53. S. 7.
54. S. 10.
55. S. 8.
56. S. 9.
57. S. 11.
58. S. 12.
59. S. 13.
60. S. 14. see further (1975) Cr. L.J. 832; and 304.
61. Shaken by the great spy scandal (see for example *State* v. *Jaspal Singh Gill* A.I.R. 1984 S.C. 1503) and apprehensive about spying, there is now an increasing alertness to the use of the Official Secrets Act see R. Jethmalani. "Espionage and fair trial" (1986) *The Law Magazine* (May) 10-17.
62. *R.K. Karanjia* v. *Emperor* A.I.R. 194′ Bombay 322.
63. *Nandlal* v. *State* (1965) 1 Cr.L.J. 393.
64. *Sunil Ranjan Das* v. *State* (1973) 77 C.W.N. 1061.
65. *Kutubuddin* v. *State of Rajasthan* A.I.R. 1967 Raj. 257 and Sunil Ranjan Das v. State (1973) 77 C.W.N. 1061.
66. *R.S. Diwakar Vakil* v. *State* A.I.R. 1958 All. 325.
67. *Safiulla* v. *State of Tripura* A.I.R. 1958 Tripura 34.
68. *State* v. *Coptain Jagjit Singh* A.I.R. 1962 S.C. 253.
69. *Kutubuddin* v. *State* A.I.R. 1967 Raj. 224.
70. *Rahmatulla* v. *State of Mysore* A.I.R. 1968 Mys. 95.
71. *Ramendra Singh* v. *Mohit Chowdhry* A.I.R. 1967 Cal. 533; of (1975) W.L.N. 137.
72. *Lal Chand* v. *The State* (1972) Raj. L.W. 675—a dismissed policeman who visited Pakistan and was seen in the company of spies was guilty of an offence.

73. *Mangi Lal* v. *State of Rajasthan* (1971) 21 Raj. 289.
74. *e.g.* cases in notes 65, 69, 72, 73.
75. See R. Dhavan: *The Supreme Court of India: A Socio-legal Analysis of its Juristic Techniques* (1977) 402-6.
76. *State of Punjab* v. *S.S. Singh* A.I.R. 1961 S.C. 493.
77. See *Amar Chand Butail* v. *Union of India* A.I.R. 1964 S.C. 1658; *State of Kerala* v. *Midland Rubber and Produce Co.* A.I.R. 1971 Ker. 228; *Muhummad Yusuf* v. *State of Madras* A.I.R. 1971 Mad. 468.
78. R. Dhavan (*supra* note 75) 456.
79 Commissions of Inquiry Act, 1952, Ss. 4, 6 offers some immunity that, in certain circumstances statements made by witnesses shall not be used in any civil and criminal proceeding (except prosecution for giving false evidence).
80. This is dealt with in part in the *Mrs. Gandhi* case decided by the Delhi High Court in 1979. For important English cases see *Att. Gen.* v. *Clough* (1963) 1 All. E.R. 420; *A.G.* v. *Mulholland* (1961) 1 All. E.R. 767.
81. Commission of Inquiry (Amendment) Ordinance, 1986 (reported in *Hindustan Times* 16 May 1986); see further *Hindu* 31 July 1986; 7 August 1986; also *Statesman* 13 July 1986; *Hindustan Times* 30 July 1986.
82. Article 77 (2) Constitution of India. I am indebted to Dr. S.N. Jain, formerly Director, Indian Law Institute for this point and for directing me to information about how the government operates its system of official secrecy; see further S.N. Jain: *Official Secrecy and Freedom of the Press* (1981); Mimeo study done by the Indian Law Institute for the Press Council of India); T.N. Chaturvedi (ed.) *Secrecy in Government* (1980).
83. Article 19 (1) (a) read with Article 19 (2) of the Constitution of India.
84. See Government of India (Allocation of Business) Rules, 1961; now not available.
85. Section 14, Constitution (Forty-second Amendment) Act, 1976 adding article 77 (4) to the Constitution.
86. Section 12, Constitution (Forty-fourth Amendment) Act, 1978 deleting Article 77 (4) of the Constitution.
87. On the classifications see S.N. Jain (supra) 21. The 'thirty year rule' is stated in the Archives Policy Resolution of 11 December 1972: also see "Permanent Secrets" reported in *Times of India*, 7 March 1986.
88. Report of the Press Laws Enquiry Committee (1951) prs. 44, 64.
89. Report of the Press Commission (1952-54) prs. 1044-1048, pp. 399-401.
90. Some information on this Group can be found in S. Maheshwari's contribution "Secrecy in Government" in T.N. Chaturvedi (ed.):

Secrecy in Government (1980) 126. I am indebted to Dr. S.N. Jain for directing me to this reference.

91. Law Commission of India: Forty-third Report—*Offences Against National Security* (1971 prs. 758-767, pp. 50-52.
92. S.N. Jain (*supra* note 82).
93. The press has responded to Dr. S.N. Jain's report favourably, see A.G. Noorant: "Secrets Act: an anachronism" *Indian Express* (10 June 1981) and S. Sahay: "A Close Look: Official Secrecy and the Press" *Statesman* (16 July, 1981). Note also the editorial: *Hindustan Times* (10 July, 1981).
94. The item was widely reported in the press, see *Financial Express* (8 July, 1981); *Patriot* (8 July, 1981); *National Herald* (9 July, 1981); *Times of India* (8 July, 1981); *The Times* (8 July, 1981); *Indian Express* (8 July, 1981); Hindu (8 July, 1981); *Hindustan Times* (8 July 1981); *Statesman* (8 July, 1981); *Financial Express* (24 July, 1981); *Times of India* (24 July, 1981).

PART THREE

Maintaining Law, Order and Morality

7

OBTAINING MORAL CONSENSUS IN A LAW AND ORDER SOCIETY

Public order has always been both an excuse and a reason for imposing restrictions on the press. It looms large as a justification for many of the restrictions that are imposed on the exercise of 'free' speech. By virtue of what has come to be recognized as a Hobbesian argument, a threat to public order is seen as threatening the very basis of society. And, at least this is how the argument runs, what could be worse than that?

On this basis, an apparatus of control is created which is only partly connected with the maintenance of public order and largely concerned with opposition to the government or a particular regime.

Newspapers and modern journalism presented an awkward challenge to the Common Law. During the seventeenth century in England, concepts like 'treason,' and 'sedition' were used to control the growth of political pamphleteering. It was naturally assumed that such mechanisms would be equally useful to deal with the aggressive and radical journalism which suddenly emerged on the political scene in the nineteenth century. However, there were problems. To begin with there was the ideological problem of reconciling such severe laws with the notion of 'liberty' and free speech which had acquired the political credibility of respectable doctrine. Fox's Libel Act of

1792, which made juries responsible for assessing whether a publication was libellous, and Lord Campbell's Libel Act of 1893 which allowed truth as a defence, represent the demands of this ideology on the system of socio-political control. There were, however, a great number of practical problems in permitting a too trigger-happy prosecution policy. As an Attorney General, in 1832, put it:

> A libeller thirsted for nothing more valuable than the advertisement of a public trial in a Court of Justice.[1]

The spate of prosecutions fell. Instead of testing and stretching the creativity of the Common Law, the prime strategy was to cripple the radical papers by taxes on paper, advertisements and publication. It was hoped that these taxes would make it impossible for the smaller newspapers to operate. In fact, these new controls had an adverse effect. The smaller radical newspapers simply invited continuing time and resource consuming prosecution by the State by not paying the taxes. The richer establishment papers found that these economic controls hurt them much more than they hurt the radical press. The removal of these restrictions in the mid-nineteenth century caused the establishment papers to expand, attract more advertising and fill their papers with attractive details which drove the serious—even if scandalous—radical papers out of the market.[2] Market conditions and 'free' enterprise did what the State control was unable to do. Constitutionally, the Common Law offences continued. But the newspapers were, henceforth, regulated by informal methods. The most formal of these informal methods is the 'D' notice which continues to this day.[3] Journalists seeking inside stories were forced to concede on the ground rules that form the basis on which they received—and would continue to receive—information. Some further controls were introduced during war time and, later, in the name of public order and race relations, the array of Common Law controls continued to exist as a backdrop. The jurisprudence of the law courts was used to give a more comprehensive meaning to the 'public interest' and indicate what could and could not be given publicity. New developments in the law of official secrecy, contempt of court and parliamentary privilege added further protection to the institutions of government. The new apparatus of formal and informal control was quite impressive and elicited some support from the 'establishment' press. The economies of journalism, agreed codes of operational morality and a fall-back reliance on legal controls had eliminated the possibility of the non-establishment radical press playing a significant oppositional role.

The Indian situation has evolved in a much lucid and less experimental manner. After the embarrassment of the early Calcutta papers, like *Hicky's Gazette*, and some vacillation amongst the authorities about the system to be imposed, a pincer strategy was worked out to deal with the press. Various pre-publication requirements were accompanied by an extremely strong penal law which was gradually strengthened over the decades of the late nineteenth and twentieth centuries. The Imperial government of the Raj was less troubled by the problems of democratic management than its parent regime in England. Parliamentary government in England based on an increasing adult suffrage forced the authorities in power to seek compromise to accommodate competing pressures before they could facilitate their needs. Every policy had to be explained in the language of democracy and liberalism. The regime in India was less troubled by such pressures, based its calculations on the new found philosophy of utilitarianism and sought to set a system of controls which would prevent 'constructive critique' from expanding into revolution. Yet we cannot make too much of the British having a free hand in India because of the absence of parliamentary government. Quite apart from adhering to a rock bottom 'minimum natural law' there were other constraints. The fact that John Stuart Mill worked in the India Office symbolises—and, perhaps, does no more than that—that liberal pressures of restraint were not wholly absent from British discourse about India. Both for themselves and the people they governed, the British had to try and obtain as much consent as they could for restrictive policies in a country strained by far more upheavals than 'establishment' histories of India would care to reveal. Using the broad argument of the public interest the British appealed to the 'rule of law' and argued that public order must be maintained at all costs. It was the secret success of Imperial jurisprudence to reduce all questions of freedom of speech and expression into questions of public order. By this token, any expression of free speech—ranging from street demonstrations and pamphlets protesting the effects of the Raj to armed revolts—were all interconnected as constituting an integrated threat to public order. A complex preventive and penal system was set up to control both peaceable and violent assemblies of people. From 1870, the Indian Penal Code was systematically extended to cover 'constructive' threats to public order through the press. It was not long before these powers were used to cover any kind of imaginary threat to the political administration system as a whole. Such a policy made a mild reformist seem like a criminal and a provocative pamphleteer like a dangerous revolutionary. This 'public-order-at-all-costs' argument gained acceptance as public policy and won considerable support from landed and commercial interests who saw its potential uses against those they oppressed. It helped to steer the emerging polity towards a 'government by institution' by insisting that the only acceptable form of influence on government had to come through the properly designated institutional and social channels. The success of this policy can be seen from the fact that even the Congress party of the early twentieth century gave the title of 'extremists' to its less compromising members.

The policy of public order was also projected as a neutral policy in that a lot of 'natural' strife was attributed to communal, caste and regional differences. Problems of public order were not deemed to arise from the policies of the Raj or forms of oppression arising out of the new economic order. They were alleged to be the product of endemic conditions pre-existing in the fabric of India's complex and excitable social polity. This method of classifying tensions, entrenched perceptions of public order had helped to justify the Raj's interventions as timely, necessary and just. Among other things, it also assisted the British in their quest to discover a conservative consensus morality which would be imposed on the political economy as a whole. The morality that was thus discovered would offend nobody. Since something always offend somebody, notions of public morality became more and more restrictive. The laws of public order and the laws of public morality formed the twin basis on which the morality of the Raj rested. It was argued that were it not for this part of the public law, India would collapse into its natural internal tensions. A sophisticated design was presented as practically necessary. The whole system was justified on pragmatic grounds in a way that the intrepid intrusions of liberal principles were easily shot down as academic and unworthy of consideration.

This important paradigm of British public policy has remained an important feature of Indian public law. Even as the constitution was being drafted the framers juxtaposed the threat of violence as the prime reason for restricting freedom of speech. The need for restraint was always regarded as more fundamental than the fundamental right to free speech. The Supreme Court of India had no difficulty in not questioning this paradigm either in relation to preventive detention or freedom of speech. Occasionaliy, the Court would remind the government to use their powers to prevent 'public order' and not just 'law and order'. Assuming they ever wanted to, the judges could not dislodge the firmly entrenched conventional wisdom about the primacy of public order. The American test of asking if there was a clear and present danger was sacrificed to a much more liberal test, and the existence of any potential threat was enough to justify the use of extended preventive and penal power.

The unquestionable supremacy of the strong public order paradigm proved a useful vehicle to deal with all forms of oppositional resistance. The first step in this process was to depict any threat to public order as a natural 'effluence' of India's complex structure. This enabled the State to claim that it entered into the fracas as a well meaning third party. The next step was to translate all civil liberties and socio-economic claims to some point on the public order scale which would form the sole basis for their evaluation. All forms of protest were deemed to be a threat which was susceptible to restraint. There were to be few—or no—'trade-offs' against competing values. In this way, the public order paradigm could be used against political opponents and social adversaries without pin-pointing their polarity to the regime. They were depicted as being caught up in a social affray which could disturb the peace rather than as opponents with a cause.

Contemporary India has not redressed its emphasis on public order by looking at the nature of social and political protest. They have reified public order so that it represents a self-contained and irrefutable logic. Such a process of reification has its roots in the nineteenth century when the public law of British India sought to create a system that would legitimate itself and camouflage political repression as publicly desirable legal action in the name of the rule of the law.

Looking back, it seems strange that the Indian Penal Code, as it was originally enacted in 1860, contained very few restraints on publication in the name of public order.[4] The original Code did not contain any laws relating to sedition or the incitement to disaffection. Nor were there any provisions relating to the promotion of enmity between classes or the outraging of religious feelings. All these were added much later. Macaulay's Draft Code of 1837 did contain a clause which punished "attempts to excite feelings of disaffection to the government" but not such "disapprobation of the measures of the government as was compatible with a disposition to render obedience to the lawful authority of the government and to support the lawful authority of the government against unlawful attempts to subvert or resist that authority".[5] This provision simply disappeared in the enactment of 1860. Why did this happen?

The explanation provided by Sir James Fitzjames Stephen, when introducing the 'sedition' provisions, appears to be that there was some kind of "unaccountable mistake".[6] This view was echoed by Sir Barnes Peacock in a letter to Sir Henry Maine in which he argued that the "omission of the . . . (sedition) section . . . must have occurred through mistake though I have no distinct recollection of it". He further observed:

> I am sorry that I cannot throw further light upon this matter, as I have no note as to the adoption or the rejection of this clause. I feel, however, that it was an oversight on the part of the Committee not to substitute some section for (this one).[7]

All this looks a little like feigned innocence. Sir Barnes Peacock had himself drafted an alternative section which the Select Committee had rejected because they had, amongst other things, found that "it was very much more severe".[8] The question of an extensive sedition law was discussed fairly thoroughly and then dropped.[9] The real question is why was this done?

The main reason for not creating specific offences against public order or the incitement to disaffection was the adoption of a more "wide ranging strategy" against the press. If the whole press could itself be stifled, there was no need to create, or defend the creation of specific offences. It is important to understand that what has earlier been called the "wide ranging strategy" remained an important part of the relationship between the British and the Press. The genesis of this strategy can be found in Sir Thomas Munro's famous minute on the subject:

> Those who speak of the press being free in this country have looked at only one part of the subject. They have not looked on further than to Englishmen and to the press as a monopoly in their hands for the amusement or benefit of their countrymen. They have not looked to its freedom among the natives to be by them employed nor whatever they may also consider to be for their own benefit and that of their countrymen. A free press and the dominion of strangers are things which are quite incompatible and which cannot long exist together. For what is the duty of a free press? It is to deliver the country from a foreign yoke, and to sacrifice to this one great object every meaner considera-tion; and if we make the press really free to the natives as well as the Europeans, it must inevitably lead to this result. . .[10]

This was accompanied by the sharp and perceptive realisation that the judicial and legal systems were so vulnerable and susceptible to manipulation and unpredictability that the creation of 'specific offences' was hardly likely to be effective:

> The law it may be supposed would be able to correct any violent abuse of the liberty of the press; but this would not be the case. The petty jury are shop-keepers and mechanics, a class not holding in this country the same station as in England—a class by themselves not mixing with the merchants or the civil and military servants, insignificant in number, and having no weight in the community. They will never, however differently the judge may think, find a libel in a newespaper against a public officer. Even if such a jury could act without bias, the agitation arising from such trials in a small society would far outweigh any advantage they could produce.[11]

This policy was embodied in the famous ordinance of 1823 and continued till 1835 when it lapsed—only to be revived for one year after the mutiny. The object of this policy was to put the press in "absolute control of the government".[12] This "wide ranging control" also lay at the root of later attempts to control the press through preventive measures and search and forfeiture powers rather than to wait until they actually committed an offence.[13]

The alternative system was to institute a system of registration—as was done in 1835 and refined in 1867[14]—which continues to this day. A concomitant of this alternative approach was to create 'specific offences' to preserve public order and the safety of the realm. Emergencies would be handled by emergency action:

> . . .(In) an extreme case of sudden and imminent danger, what government would hesitate to protect itself until the Legislature of India could provide for such a case.[15]

The alternative policy was not the expression of a

concessionary liberalism. Much rather, it was founded on a pragmatic prediction that the social and economic movements that were creating India's news press could not be repressed by the "wide ranging control" policy. This was readily recognised by Lord Canning when he introduced the "wide ranging control" system as a temporary device in 1857. He did so with "extreme reluctance"[16] and was supported by the Chief Justice, Sir James Colville, who said that the "gravity of the step which the Council was about to take could not be denied." There was a fear of distortion. No law existed to prevent it:

> It has been done sedulously, cleverly, artfully. Facts have been grossly misrepresented so grossly, that with educated and informed minds the very extravagance of the misrepresentations must compel discredit. But to native readers of all classes, scattered throughout the country, imperfectly acquainted with the proceedings of Government, and not well instructed as to what is passing even immediately around them these misrepresentations come uncontradicted, and are really credited. In addition to perversion of facts, there are constant vilifications of the Government, false assertions of its purposes, and unceasing attempts to sow discontent and hatred between it and its subjects.[17]

In 1860 the British government knew that it could use the "wide ranging control" system at any time it wanted. It, therefore, decided not to introduce a series of specific offences to exacerbate the feelings of an already excited and excitable press.

Then there was a change in strategy. Unwilling to introduce the "wide ranging control" and unable to resist the "specific offence" approach, a new approach was designed which over the years would incorporate both of these strategies. By 1870, the British Government took the view that specific offences would have to be created. "Sedition" was added to the list of offences in the Indian Penal Code.[18] In 1898, the further offence of promoting enmity between classes was also added.[19] And in 1927, an offence was also created which would deal with outraging religious feelings.[20] Meanwhile, the "wide ranging control" system was also gradually built into the system. In 1878, a statute was enacted to give wide-ranging powers of search in respect of the vernacular press.[21] Sir Alexander Arbuthnot made it clear that he preferred a system of extensive control of the kind that had been prophetically mooted by Sir Thomas Munro in 1823. Here was a policy of "prevention" to aid the "specific offence" approach:

> It would of course be possible to introduce into the Penal Code a provision rendering penal all writings calculated to inflame the minds of the people against their rulers, irrespective of the intention of the writers, but such a provision must be of general application and like the rest of the Penal Code, it must be essentially punitive. The principle of the Bill which I desire to lay before the Council is of a different principle. The provisions of the Bill will apply only to one class of writers, the writers of the vernacular press, and the measure is not so much a measure of penal, as it is a measure of preventive legislation. The machinery by which it will work is a machinery of checks rather than of penalties. Its object is to check mischievous writings . . . not by penal sentences but by requiring the offenders, or those in regards to whom it may be apprehended that they are likely to offend, to engage and deposit security for their good behaviour or by merely warning them and it is only in the event of the engagements being broken, or the warnings being disregarded, that the penalties which the Bill provides will be put in force. What is needed is a procedure more summary, and framed rather with a view to prevention than with a view to punishment.[22]

All this seems to present picture that the British having been faced with the choice of a "hard penal" approach and a cautious "preventive" approach, chose the latter. A similar picture was presented in 1898. By that time the Vernacular Press Act 1878 had been repealed in 1882. The British were anxious to move into a more comprehensive control. This is how the choice was presented:

> Recent events in India have called prominent attention to the law relating to seditious utterances and writings. We have had anxiously to consider the state of the law regarding these matters, and to decide whether, and in what respects, it required amendment. Two different lines of action were open to us. The first was to enact a Press Act similar to the Vernacular Press Act of 1878. The second was to amend the general law relating to sedition and cognate offences, so as to make it more efficient for this purpose. We have come to the conclusion that the second course is the right one for us to take.[23]

In actual fact, both systems were introduced. The penal law was made stronger. Sedition was more widely defined. Enmity between classes was added as an offence. And the Criminal Procedure Code was amended to include preventive control which was almost similar to the kind of control which existed under the Vernacular Press Act.[24] In the debates the Law Member made it clear that it was

> absurd to deal with them (i.e., a different press) by an elaborate State prosecution. We think that in most cases no prosecution at all will be required. It will be sufficient to give them an effective warning to discontinue their evil practices, and we think that the machinery we have devised will operate as an effective warning. The general power of revision possessed by the High Courts will secure that the machinery will not be used in any way oppressively; and we further propose that this new power should only be exercised by Presidency and District Magistrates or specially empowered Magistrates of the First Class.[25]

Clearly, the preventtive system had become a part of the ordinary law by the end of the nineteenth century. From this it was not a great distance to the Newspaper (Incitement of Offences) Act, 1908 and the Indian Press Act, 1910 which gave powers to impose deposits, forfeit securities and, in certain cases, even seize presses. The specific repeal of these measures, following the recommendations of the Sapru Committee, did not put an end to the preventive system[26] which was assimilated into the ordinary legislation further in 1926.[27] A tighter control system was introduced during the World War and in 1931.[28]

Ironically, even though a special Committee on the Press in 1948 had recommended the repeal of the tight deposit-forfeiture system of 1931 as being repugnant to the new Constitution,[29] fresh legislation was introduced in 1951 which continued a modified version of this system in the hands of the Sessions Judge with the right to appeal to the High Court.[30] This system continued till 1957.[31] By 1954 the Press Commission reported that these provisions were invoked in 134 cases with 88 demands of security and 48 orders of forfeiture. Such "action (was) . . . most successful in the State of Madras and least successful in the State of Delhi".[32] Even though the forfeiture-deposit system was revived again only during the internal Emergency (1975-77),[33] a pre-publication ban system has been incorporated in many statutes and has been specifically validated as not being unconstitutional.[34]

This excursus into history is important because it illustrates the importance that successive governments have attached to public order and the lengths to which they were prepared to go in order to control the press. Thus, we see the total control licensing system (1823-35, 1857-8), a registration system (1835, and then since 1867), the forfeiture-deposit system as a special system (1878-1882, 1908-1922, 1931-1951, 1951-1957, 1975-77), a less rigorous security system as part of the ordinary law (introduced in 1898 and strengthened in 1926), a specific offence approach (suggested by Macaulay in 1837 and introduced with ever increasing zest from 1870 and strengthened in 1898, 1927 and 1972) and a pre-publication ban system which has been declared to be constitutional since 1957. All this represents quite a formidable array of powers against the press. Although the special forfeiture-deposit system has been used only on special occasions, the rest of the techniques continue to be part of the control of the press. They are all presented in an absolutist form. The functional needs and requirements of the press as an institution are never really considered. All this has cast quite a gloom over the press. Journalists feel that they are being caught in a network of control in a spirit of total distrust. Some of these controls in respect of the forfeiture system apply specifically to the press. It is in this context that the Press Commission reported an unequivocal outburst from the submissions that were made to them:

> As one of the senior and respected journalists asked in the course of his evidence: Are we criminal tribes that there should be a special law for us?[35]

This puts the issue rather succinctly. The British tended to regard the press as a collection of criminal tribes. Much of their legislation was designed on this basis. Since the broad strategy of this legislation has been continued, the conclusion that the attitude of the Government of India remains the same is really quite irresistible.

II

The technique of introducing specific offences to prevent disorder and promote loyalty to the government began with the introduction of 'sedition' as Section 124A of the Indian Penal Code in 1870. The original section is somewhat curiously drafted. The substantive section made it an offence to "excite or attempt to excite feelings of disaffection against the government established by law in British India" by any "words . . . visible representation or otherwise". The punishment could be transportation for life (with or without fine) or imprisonment (including three years rigorous imprisonment whether with or without fine). But to all this was added an *Explanation* which seemed to cut down the import of the section:

> Such a disapprobation of the measures of the government as a compatible with a disposition to render obedience to the lawful authority of the government, and to support the lawful authority of the government against unlawful attempts

> to subvert or resist that authority, is not disaffection. Therefore, making of comments on the measures of the government, with the intention of exciting only this species of disapprobation is not an offence within the section.

What a provision! It is not surprizing that it was not used to prosecute for at least twenty years. Then came the *Bangobasi* case.[36] This case arose out of the controversy over increasing the age of consent in respect of child marriages. There was a great furore about this. The government was accused of being insensitive to Hindu opinion and was compared with arrogant and bigoted rulers of the Muslim era. That a jury was not prepared to convict in such a case has now become irrelevant. What is interesting is the manner in which the Chief Justice Petheram sought to extend the meaning of "disaffection" by stating that it meant—

> a feeling contrary to affection, in other words dislike or hatred. . . . It is sufficient for the purposes of the section that the words used or calculated to excite feelings of ill-will against the government, and to hold it up to the hatred and contempt of the people and that they were used with the intention to create much a feeling.

Further, the intention of the accused was to be gauged from the publications themselves. This interpretation of the section came to stay. It was relied upon by Justice Sirachey in the *Tilak* case (1897)[37] where an article was published in which the old Maharatta Chief Shivaji is made to visit British India and comment on the state of the nation and the manner in which his people were being treated. A conviction was found in this case which was not overturned in appeal by a Full Bench or the Privy Council.[38] It became clear that the section did not require the "disaffection" to be manifested in any way. Nor was it necessary that the accused "counsels or suggests rebellion or forcible resistance". "Disaffection" was just treated as the absence of "affection". The intention of the accused was to be gathered simply from "the natural and probable effect of reading such articles in the minds of the readers . . . to whom they were addressed". Much was left to intuition:

> It is not very difficult to distinguish between the language of hostility and the language of loyalty and goodwill, or of criticism and comment.

In the *Fratod* case (1897)[39] the article in question compared the Canadian situation with the Indian and argued that the Indian people were effeminate and not sufficiently spirited in making similar moves towards independence. Although the editor and the proprietor were sentenced to one year's rigorous and three months' simple imprisonment respectively, at least two judges—Justices Parsons and Ranade—seemed to take the view that the requirements of the section were that positive feelings of disloyalty should be engendered. Justice Ranade seemed to think what was said or written should be such as "makes men indisposed to obey or support the laws of the realm, and promotes discontent and disorder". This was a much more rigorous requirement than simply creating feeling of ill-will. In yet another case—*Amba Prashad's* case[40]—the inherent ambiguity of the *Explanation* to the section was highlighted. While the Explanation was not seen as varying the broad intent of the section, it was suggested that the section was about "disloyalty".

These three cases were enough to create a sufficient apprehension in the minds of the government about the desirability of clarifying the meaning of the section. Now where by "words . . . signs . . . visible representations or otherwise" the accused is guilty where he "brings or attempts to bring into hatred or contempt, or excites or attempts to excite disaffection towards the government of India". Important changes were made in the Explanation. The first Explanation made clear that "(t)he expression 'disaffection' *includes* disloyalty and all feelings of enmity". This seemed to resolve the inadequately declared discomfiture of the judiciary. Another Explanation kept alive the idea that there could be "disapprobation of the measures of the government" or its officers[41] provided the feelings mentioned in the main section were not aroused and provided that an attempt was made to achieve any alteration "by lawful means". Here was a blueprint for ensuring only mild criticisms through proper and designated channels. And that, too, in such a way that no feelings of ill-will were caused in respect of the government. This was the form in which the offence of sedition was left at the end of the century. This, to some extent, is also the form in which it continues to this day.

This section has been used for various situations. To begin with it has been used where it has been suggested that there should be a war or an armed insurrection against the government[42] or that the policy of non-violence should be given up for a policy of anarchy.[43] But sedition has also been found to exist where the government was accused of being reactionary,[44] or dishonest[45] or partial to landlords against peasants[46] or biased against the working classes[47] or insensitive in not attaching value to the lives of the subjects[48] or responsible for causing communal disharmony[49] amongst village folk.[50] A biased anti government account of history[51] or an account of freedom fighters found guilty of murder or dacoity[52] were all treated as seditious whereas a plea for a change of government[53] or an exhortation that people should fight for independence[54] was not seditious. Nor was it deemed to be sedition to ask people to boycott goods[55] or not to pay land revenue.[56] This last line of cases is not easy to explain. They are not really inconsistent with the Second Explanation that any criticism and proposals must be made in a lawful manner and not provoke an illegality. What then is the *ratio decidendi* of the exceptions. In effect, the emphasis seems to be on the severity of the criticisms and the extent to which the *bona fides* of the government are doubted.[57]

All this continues to have very serious implications for the press and for investigative journalism. In a democratic society which has guaranteed freedom of speech to its people, it is inevitable that there should be criticism of government.[58] It is a moot question as to who can claim the protection of this section and, therefore, has immunity from criticism? After all, this section seeks to protect the "government established by law" in India. Police officers[59] and subordinate officials[60] have all unsuccessfully sought to claim the protection of this section. The claim of Cabinet Ministers was dealt with rather more sympathetically by the Privy Council.[61] At least the Allahabad High Court took care to draw attention to the fact that section 124A could in fact be used for the purposes of stifling criticism of ministers.[62] The Allahabad High Court was quite prepared to declare this provision unconstitutional. Their view was not accepted by the Supreme Court,[63] which while declaring this section constitutionally valid, put an important gloss on the interpretation of this section.

The constitutional gloss on the sedition provisions has to be understood in the context of a difference of opinion between the Privy Council and the Federal Court. The Privy Council had constantly adhered to the view that the incitement to public disorder was not essential to maintain that an offence had been committed.[64] On the other hand, the Federal Court had taken the view that the section that the "acts or words complained must either incite to disorder or must be such as to satisfy reasonable men that is their intention or tendency.[65] The Supreme Court had to choose between these two interpretations in the light of a Constitution which guaranteed freedom of speech and expression and permitted reasonable restrictions, *inter alia,* in the interests of public order and security of state. The Supreme Court adopted the Federal Court's view and showed that since the section in question was limited to public order situations it was a permissible restriction on the freedom of speech. The view of the Supreme Court is really based on the view of the Press Laws Inquiry Committee (1950).[66] The Supreme Court made a distinction between a "government" and "the persons for the time being engaged in carrying on the administration" and further indicated that a person could with impunity make "a very strong speech or use very vigorous words in a writing directed to a very strong criticism of measures of government or acts of public officials."[67] But, after all this, the ambit of the section is still not clear. It seems that heavy criticism of this nature which produces, or may be deemed to have a tendency to affect public order would not only fall within the ambit of the sedition provisions but would also be constitutional. The Court seems to have lost its sense of history.

The sedition provisions were designed to prevent incitement to disaffection of a foreign power. Any sign of disaffection was seen as contributing to the fragility of that power. Any sign of criticism which made a telling point against the government was seen as striking another blow against that government. The transformation of this section in the context of Independent India strikes at the roots of the constitutional system which was created in 1950.

The Court seems to have ignored the fact that the essence of the sedition provisions is the criticism of the government in a form that would make the people or the general public hyper-critical of the government. The gloss relating to public order is one of the positive effects by which the nature of this criticism is to be adjudged. The reference to public order is not real. All that is needed is a tendency to affect public order. We are not talking of real effects. The section does not say that those who create public disorder are guilty of an offence. The section says that those who are guilty of deriding the government and causing disaffection towards the government will be guilty of sedition if implicit in their words or acts is a tendency to create public disorder. It is important to note that the Press Commission wanted this section repealed and replaced by a more direct section on the overthrow of existing method of government by violent means.[68] The sedition provisions have thus become a valuable instrument in the legal armoury of the government to prevent a full and vigorous discussion of the affairs of the state. The reference to public order does not represent the main thrust of the section. This is prime example of the manner in which the imperial powers of a foreign government are transformed into the normal powers of an independent regime.

Apart from the laws of sedition further provisions were also introduced to check the press. The first of these was section 153A designed to prevent the promotion of enmity between classes. At first it was suggested that this provision was introduced only to deal with problems between the Hindu and Muslim community.[69] Later a much more wide-ranging theatre of activity was envisaged for this provision when the Bill introducing it was finally considered in the Committee in 1898.

> . . .(I)n India the offence is a very dangerous one. When class or sectarian animosity is directed against any section of Her Majesty's subjects, the members of that section are in peril. Any accidental event may cause an explosion, and it is difficult to foresee the direction which the explosion will take. The persistent attacks made on the officers and helpers engaged in plague operations have already resulted in a loss of life. A squabble over an alleged mosque gave rise to a dangerous riot which at one time it was feared might turn into a general attack on the European community in Calcutta. We wish to trust to prevention rather than cure, and by taking power to punish people who foment class animosities to obviate the necessity of putting down the consequent disturbances with a high hand.[70]

Far from dealing with the problems of quarrelling natives, this provision was designed as an omnibus provision which would keep a tight control on the press as well as protect, amongst others, the European community and civil servants as a class as well. The section was very widely worded to cover "words. . . signs or. . . visible representations" which "promotes or attempts to promote feelings of enmity or hatred between different classes of Her Majesty's subjects." The position of the 'do-gooder' or the missionary was specifically protected by an *Explanation* which immunized those who lacked malicious intent and were honestly trying to remove enmity and hatred amongst classes.

Soon after the section was enacted it became clear that, far from being a measure which reduced tension amongst classes, this provision actually encouraged disputes between various classes of people. As soon as a group scented criticism, they rushed to the courts which they used as a forum to take the fight further. In one of the early cases,[71] one of the charges was that enmity was being created between clerks and poor Mohammedan rayats, and the activities of missionaries was being slighted. A significant distinction was evolved between the law relating to sedition and these provisions. It was made clear that in these provisions there must be a deliberate attempt to incite one class against another. In another case,[72] the Court had to consider an exhortation that Muslims should not make friends with Christians and Jews—and by Christians was meant the Christian race. The Court could not find an offence under this provision. Although the law relating to enmity between classes was designed as a wide-ranging law to protect various classes, it contained within itself the potential of giving rise to mischievous litigation. This is borne out by the subsequent cases in which this section was invoked.

At first the question of intent seems to have troubled at least the Allahabad High Court which took the view that there was no need to show a deliberate intent.[73] This could—as in the case of sedition—be inferred from the article itself. This view was not accepted by other courts[74] which appear to have settled for the stricter requirement that a deliberate intention, or at least some kind of positive intention, to cause enmity is needed. But for this, this provision would have been much more extensively used by various groups anxious to fight their group, and other, animosities in Court, and requiring no further proof other than to show that the words used could cause ill-will between classes.

It soon became apparent that this provision would be inevitably transformed into a battleground between communities rather than serve as a measure to prevent animosities. The section talked of "enmity or hatred between classes". What exactly did a class mean? Justice Nanavati of the Bombay High Court took it to mean

> a well defined and readily ascertainable group. . . (with) some element of permanence or stability. . . (and) sufficiently numerous and widespread to be designated as a class.

While refusing to accept that "class" was limited to religious and racial groups, he stressed that the expression could—but should not—be given too wide an interpretation.

> You may refer to people as diehards, or extremists or nationalists, as free traders or fair traders, as nationalists or communalists, as militarists or pacifists, as Imperialists or little Englanders; and it would be difficult to regard the people designated or meant to be designated by these and like expressions as forming classes sufficiently precise for the purposes of the criminal law.[75]

In the case before the court, the issue was whether capitalists were a class.[76] Any Marxist would provide an unequivocal answer to this; but not an answer which the Court could have agreed with.

It is at this point that the case law becomes a little confused. There was no doubt that religious and ethnic groups were "classes". This included Hindus and Muslims, Indians and Europeans.[77] But this did not include 'non-Bengalis'.[78] This latter decision must appear to be strange in retrospect if we remember that much of the agitation in Assam since 1980 has been on the influx of 'non-Assamese' people into their State. Again, an early decision seemed to take the view that "Babus" and "Meahs" in their treatment of Muslim rayats and Christian Missionaries in their treatment of converts were not a class.[79] A controversial decision of the Lahore High Court took the view that enmity must be caused between classes and this did not include criticism of a deceased religious leader or prophet.[80] Apart from religious groups, could other kinds of groups fall within the description of "class"? We have already seen that capitalists are not included in this term. It has also been held that this term does not also apply to shareholders in a joint stock company[81] or the workers who work in such a company.[82] Again, landlords are not a class;[83] but in certain circumstances they have been held to be a class where along with government servants they have been criticised for their treatment of tenants and of betraying the people.[84] A political party is not a class.[85] As is a group demanding a separate autonomous State or region where the government is accused of maladministration.[86] The simple criticism that a Ministry has been formed on a communal basis does not fall within these provisions.[87] But there is an instance of a case where a speech against the government has been considered to fall within the provisions of this section as well as the provision dealing with sedition.[88]

The point in all this is not the decision of the Court. In a sense the decision as to whether a particular group constitutes a class is not that important. What is significant is that there is sufficient play in the decisions so that a litigant can mobilize these provisions to use the Court to attack his critics. The fact that the sanction of the government or the authority of the magistrate may be needed has checked the random use of these provisions, but it has not wholly prevented the use of these provisions to further their quarrels.

In 1961, the scope of these provisions was widened.[89] Now, the "enmity or hatred" was between "different religious, racial or language groups or castes or communities" which was promoted (or an attempt was made to promote) on grounds of "religion, race, language, caste or community or any other ground whatsoever". This part of the section was not linked to public order. Equally, it seemed to affirm the view that no actual enmity or hatred need be caused. A new sub-section was added which sought to prevent

> any act which is prejudicial to the maintenance of harmony between different religious, racial or language groups or castes or communities and which disturbs or is likely to disturb the public tranquillity. . .

The Explanation which spoke of intent was deleted in 1961. This might mean that no 'deliberate intention' is needed in order to bring a prosecution within the gift of this section. The vulnerability of this section as a forum for fomenting political or social differences remains. In at least one case, an attempt was made to bring within the ambit of this section a plea in a newspaper that elections should be boycotted and revolutionary struggles organised.[90] The fact that this attempt was unsuccessful does not controvert the fact that this section was and may well continue to be so used. As always, what we do with the law has greater significance than what it is supposed to mean.

In 1971, a new provision—Section 1538—was added which dealt with "imputations" (and) assertions prejudicial to national integration. Here, no one could make an imputation questioning the truth and allegiance of any religious, racial, language or regional group or caste or community to the Constitution of India, or make a plea that such a group, caste or community be deprived of their rights or cause "feelings of enmity or hatred or ill-will between such members and other persons". This was undoubtedly by a political proposal and made at a time when there was a war with Pakistan over the future of East Bengal.[91] But we will notice that unlike the sedition provisions as finally interpreted by the Supreme Court, these provisions do not directly deal with disturbances to public order. This would normally have made them constitutionally suspect but for the Supreme Court's decision in *Ramji Lal Modi's* case that the Constitution permits restrictions 'in the interests of public order' and not just for the 'maintenance of public order'.[92] Be that as it may, the lack of an objective criteria about what constitutes 'ill-will' or enmity or hatred does pose serious problems. Inevitably, these sections can be mobilized for a wide range of purposes.

In 1927, the Lahore High Court took the view that a criticism of the Prophet did not fall within the provisions of Section 153-A.[93] While this decision was subsequently questioned by other High Courts,[94] it provoked the government to enact further legislation and include yet another provision—Section 295-A—in the Indian Penal Code. Accordingly, a "deliberate and malicious intention" to outrage the religious feelings of any class of citizens or insult or attempt to insult the religion or religious beliefs of that class. These provisions were declared constitutionally valid in *Ramji Lal's* case and were slightly strengthened in 1961.[95] Some of the controversies in this section have arisen because of the need to prove a 'deliberate and malicious intention'. Over time, the stronger view appears to be that such an intention cannot really be proved but must be inferred from the circumstances.[96] A very thin line exists between telling the true historical facts about a community (which is permissible) and commenting on matters in such a way that certain members may be annoyed, and be degraded in the eyes of the community.[97]

A lot may depend on the language that is used. A strong and abusive attack may fall within this section.[98] This may be inferred from the tone of the publication.[99] Problems are created where a person claims tohave at tacked the beliefs of others as well,[100] alleges that he is exercising the right to reply,[101] or asserts that his real aim was to shock people into reform.[102] Truth does not really constitute a defence. All this has imposed a certain amount of ambiguity into the interpretation of the section. While the overall thrust of the section is clear, it is not surprising that prosecutorial discretion has been involved each time a member of the community complains about something that has hurt his feelings. This section then becomes a vehicle for social revenge even if the ulimate decision goes against the complainant. An interesting example may be useful. A person who had bought a bull previously dedicated to Lord Shiva punctured the bull's nose and used it for ploughing. A case ensued on whether this hurt the feelings of the Hindu community.[103] The fact that complainant lost the case is beside the point. What is significant is that this section was used as a vehicle to bring the complaint forward.

There is at least one other provision of the Indian Penal Code which affects journalists, the press and the people who use them. This provision deals with a class of offences concerning the dissemination of false facts and rumours which are conducive to public mischief. The core of the controversy concerned the defence that the person in question believed the rumour to be true. Faced with great difficulties in proving criminal intent, the initial attitude of the British was that this should be an offence of strict liability:

> When, then, a man chooses to publish a statement, or circulate a rumour, which on the face of it is directly conducive to grave public mischief, he cannot complain if he is called upon to show that his intentions were not criminal.[104]

With the burden of proof shifted on the accused, a concession was made, ostensibly, to the demands of modern journalism:

> No doubt the statements, rumours and reports referred to are of a highly mischievous character, but having regard to the conditions under which modern journalism and the discussion of public questions are necessarily carried on, we think that when the statement, rumour report is published without any criminal intent, it is going too far to require the person who published it to prove its actual truth. To require such proof might be throwing an impossible burden on him and it should be sufficient for him to show that he had reasonable grounds for believing it, as for instance, by showing that he had made due inquiry before he had published it.[105]

The *Exception* apart, the substantive section is concerned with publications with intent to cause or which are likely to cause a mutiny or a failure to exercise one's duty in the Armed forces, fear or alarm to any section of the public so that he is induced to commit an offence against the State or public tranquillity or incite one class or community against another class or community. In 1969, further provisions were added on lines similar to the changes and amendments which were made in Section 153-A at the same time.[106]

These provisions are firmly linked with notions of public tranquillity and security of the state. That was the basis on which the constitutionality of this provision was saved.[107] An early decision[108] has established that if certain Nepalese coolies were alarmed by the rumour that a war was going to take place between India and Nepal and ran away from a plantation, no offence had been committed. These effects were not the likely or probable consequences of the publication. Praise of Mahatma Gandhi's assassin falls within this section[109] but pamphlets about the working of local authorities are not.[110] This provision can be used for stifling political discussion although the courts have emphasized the public order and security of state element.[111] But even there the exception has cut down the scope of the section even where public order has been involving communal riots, it was considered a defence under the Exception to plead that the publisher had reasonable cause to believe that the defence was true.[112]

This clause has not been actively mobilized by various groups against each other. Clearly, the provisions about mutiny seem to be appropriate. The courts seem to have checked some of the prosecutorial discretion which could have flowed out as a result of the incipient uses that this section can be put to. But the rest of the section has become an all-purpose section dealing with a very wide area. Apart from provisions concerning the armed forces, these provisions are not necessary, although the Exception is a salutary device which allows journalists and others to plead that they had verified their facts. This section is really part of an anachronistic overload.

In addition to all these provisions of the Indian Penal Code, there are a vast number of other statutes which deal with maintaining public order, and which restrain publications which interfere with public order, public tranquillity or security of state.[113] These have all been declared constitutional. The only restraints that have been imposed are that they must be connected with public order and not just law and order,[114] and that the executive should not have an untrammelled and arbitrary power.[115]

It will be recalled that the British had not just instituted a 'specific offence' techniques to control the press but also a 'wide ranging strategy in order to take preventive action'. This took the form of the deposit-forfeiture system and general powers of preventive action. These powers have been continued. Even under the Criminal Procedure Code, 1973[116] a Judicial Magistrate may require a person to execute a bond, whether with or without sureties, for his good behaviour for a maximum period of one year where the Magistrate is of the opinion that there are sufficient grounds for proceeding against such a person in respect of offences relating to certain public order offences we have discussed above, obscenity and the defamation of a judge.[117] These are very wide powers even if they have to be exercised under the authority of the State government or some other officer empowered on their behalf.[118] Equally wide-ranging powers exist in the State government itself[119] to issue search warrants for and forfeit where certain public order offences are committed or there is a transgression of the laws of obscenity.[120] There is some measure of judicial review and the government must explain why it has made a particular order and not simply recite a formal reason for its actions.[121] A special bench of the High Court may be moved within two months of the order for forfeiture.[122] These are all very drastic provisions, whose constitutionality is not really in question,[123] which exist independent of the normal powers of a court to issue a search warrant,[124] or a Magistrate's power to issue urgent and temporary orders of pre-censorship where he thinks that there is a danger to human life, health, safety or the possibility of public disturbances.[125]

In addition to all this there are powers in the post office and customs departments to intercept material which pertains to the public order and other offences we have considered.[126]

These are extensive normal peace time powers and co-exist with special power as we have seen, when an Emergency is declared.

III

This brief survey of the manner in which the laws relating to public order have applied to the press tells us many things. To begin with, it is clear that the British used the idea of public order as a legitimating device to devise extensive control over the press. These were two schools of thought about this in the British administration in the nineteenth century. One school led by Sir Thomas Munro took the view that the press was not to be trusted at all and must be controlled with great zest and in exacting detail. Another school led by Sir Charles Metcalfe seemed to be of the view that the press should be allowed to function freely, subject to some control in respect of registration and the restraining effect of some penal offences. Over the years, these controversies became stylized and unnecessary. In time the British administration saw that it would have to use a conglomerate of devices to control the press. The essence of such a policy was rooted in a total distrust of the press and what it was capable of doing. This conglomerate of devices included a wide-ranging system of fairly severe penal offences many of which were strict liability offences. In other words, they concerned themselves with what judges thought was the effect of an article rather than the intention of the writer. And this liability was made to stretch in most cases to the printer, the editor and the publisher as well. This was partly the result of the registration system and partly the consequence of judicial decisions.

Then there were powers of control and forfeiture and the right to demand securities from allegedly errant writers and publishers. So far, we are talking of an apparatus of 'ordinary' powers designed for everyday use. Superimposed on all these were the much more massive emergency powers of control and prevention. It is significant that Independent India has picked up this entire apparatus of power and virtually incorporated it as a part of its laws *in toto*. Very few modifications have been made. Very few concessions have beeen given. The essential paradigm that forms the basis of contemporary India's public order laws in respect of the press has not altered.

This wholescale acceptance of the British imperial model was done for various reasons. Neither the British nor its successor Indian government had given serious thought to a new relationship with the press. In the eyes of the government, the press has always consisted of a corps of people who were to be distrusted and who were always up to mischief. Undoubtedly, some of this is well founded. The Indian press has always operated at multiple levels of responsibility and irresponsibility. Its standards vary and it often reflects caste, communal, regional and other tensions with an unbridled ease. Successive governments have used the worst journalists as a model, and an excuse, in drafting laws. Laws have been evolved on the basis of a policy of distrust. And it is this distrust that continues to this day. No attempt to work out a new equation with the press has been made. Even the Press Commission, which reported in 1954, seems to have made recommedations on the basis that the old equations had to be revised but not reconsidered.[127]

Successive governments have pointed to difficult law and order situations to show that this elaborate apparatus of control is necessary. This mood was self-evident in the minds of the framers of India's Constitution. When the freedom of speech clauses came to be debated in the Assembly, the demands of public order occupied the minds of those in the Assembly greatly.[128] Undoubtedly, the first amendment to the Constitution reflects these demands. The amendment itself became necessary because the Supreme Court seemed to have argued that the original Constitution did not permit restrictions in the interests of public order but only in the interests of security of state.[129] The implications of all this alarmed at least a minority of members on the Press Commission (1952-54).[130]

The defence of public order has also been a favourite theme with the higher judiciary, and especially the Supreme Court. The judiciary has upheld the constitutionality of a large number of these extensive powers including the power of pre-censorship.[131] Some overall judicial control has been retained. In at least one non-press case—initiated by the famous politician Ram Manohar Lohia—the Supreme Court made it clear that such powers should be used to deal with problems of public order and not just ordinary law and order problems,[132] but these distinctions are often wasted on the government which uses its vast powers indiscriminately.

The picture that emerges is that the entire 'establishment' including the legislature, executive, bureaucracy and the judiciary, have given an overriding and virtually absolute priority to the notional demands of public order. It is important to use the word 'notional' here. There is very little information on how these laws are actually operated. The cases that come to the courts seem to confirm the feelings that there is a considerable amount of indiscriminate use. These powers used for ordinary situations and in emergency situations with the same alacrity. Often the use of these powers can only be fully explained after one has understood the political subterfuges that accompany the exercise of such powers. Often small party newspapers with small circulations are picked upon. This is either done for straightforward political reasons or in the context of local situations, or by way of political over-reaction.

All this has entrenched what has been well described as a 'hegemony' of ideas. In this 'hegemony' of ideas a certain set pattern has evolved between the government and the press on the issue of public order. No one seems to be looking at the real problems, asking how these powers have actually been exercised or considering the need for these extensive powers. The symbolic appeal to public order is so great that even the press have not seriously and systematically tried to re-evaluate and re-consider these ideas.

Quite apart from these larger questions about the public policy underlying these laws, the cases that we have looked at also provide other insights about the law and India's litigation system. Even where the laws are quite strict, India's litigation system operates in a way vulnerable to manipulative use. People who have learnt to use this litigation system know exactly how it works and how it can be used for a multitude of purposes in a multitude of ways. An editor running a campaign may, in certain cases, be quite willing to be drawn into a controversial prosecution, and then to get out of it as lightly as possible. This was certainly the strategy of Tilak and Gandhi, and it continues to be vigorously used in social and political situations. If we look at the cases on enmity between classes or incitement of religious tension, some very interesting patterns emerge. In many of the cases, public order questions are not really an issue. They are simply taken as read. The real issue is that the community which has been attacked in the press seeks to take public revenge in the law courts. The law courts become the public forum for further quarrels, not to enforce public order or to procure justice. Persons and groups have learnt to use these provisions to further their quarrels. "Government" officials and "ministers" have been described as a class and action has been taken under these provisions by their supporters against their detractors. The fact that these cases were not successful cannot obscure the fact that the opposite party were at least drawn into the litigative arena and subjected to all the problems of a law suit. The more adept a particular person or group is at using the law, the greater the chance of him using it adroitly against his opponents. The fact that many prosecutorial decisions are in the hands of the government or magistrates does not seem to have controlled the extent of manipulative use. In all this, the press both benefits and loses. Sometimes, it gets further and better publicity from these endeavours. Sometimes it is harassed by a combination of social, political and legal forces. The press is itself not a self-sustaining autonomous unit. It is a part of a network of relationships which is reflected in its activity. Depending on how it is placed in the social and political network, it both revels in and is a victim of litigation.

The law is a declaration by the government as well as intricate litigation system. As a declaration of the government, the public order laws are very severe on the government. They also represent a 'hegemony' of ideas which prioritize the need for governmental power at the expense of belittling the activities of the press. As a litigation system, these laws can be a source of both comfort and discomfort to the press. Also the litigation system itself becomes a public forum for giving vent to all kinds of social and political quarrels.

Notwithstanding all that, let us have one last look at the system of control as a whole. There can be no doubt that it is archaic and autocratic. It is possible that is the reason why the government has not seriously considered a rigorous re-examination of it.

IV

Quite apart from the demands of public order, the State also claims an interest in maintaining a public morality. In a sense, all law is concerned with the maintenance of a public morality. The law lays down norms which seek to regulate and determine what a person, institution or group may or may not do. But a plea has been made that the morality underlying law is a very special kind of decreed morality which must be kept quite distinct from other forms of individual ethics or social morality.[133] The nub of this controversy is concerned with the institutional mechanisms by which social morality is superimposed upon a society.[134] In our present context, we need to concern ourselves with certain special laws which are specifically designed to prohibit certain kinds of expression. This is done on the basis that these forms of expression are intrinsically bad and presumed to be not conducive to the public good. The particular laws in question deal with obscenity laws and prohibit what is called obscene speech. This relates virtually solely to expressions about sex.

The link between obscenity and sex goes back to the common law. In the United Kingdom, the courts have taken the concept of obscenity well beyond discussions about sex. The standard formula definition of obscenity in English law is that obscenity is that which "depraves or corrupts" the minds of those in whose hand it is likely to fall. This was a definition which was consecrated in a classic definition of the nineteenth century and which has now been given statutory recognition in 1959.[135] Of course, no one believed that reference of obscenity meant reference to anything other than sex. In two significant decisions English courts have extended the concept of obscenity greatly. In the first of these decisions it was held that a novel which advocated the taking of drugs was an obscene item.[136] Again, in the other decision, it was held that the depiction of bloody and violent scenes enclosed within a chewing wrapper was obscene.[137] These decisions take the definition of obscenity well beyond the accepted idea that obscenity is concerned with sex. If this trend of decisions is to be taken seriously, then obscenity will come to mean anything which the courts consider to be distasteful of depraving. This would be a very wide definition indeed. The law preventing obscenity could itself become the basis of a wide-ranging censorship on most social and moral issues.[138]

Till 1969, the Indian Penal Code did not define 'obscenity'. In time, the classic 'deprave and corrupt' formula was imported from English decisions into Indian Law. This view was also affirmed by the Supreme Court of India.[139] In 1969, an additional explanatory section was added which made it clear that "a book, pamphlet, paper writing, drawing, painting, representation, figure or any other object shall be deemed to be obscene if it is lascivious, or appeals to the prurient interest or if its effect. . ., if taken as a whole, is such as to deprave and corrupt persons who are likely, having regard to all the relevant circumstances, to read, see, hear, the matter contained or embodied in it".[140] This is wider than the English definition in that the words "lascivious" or "appeals to the prurient interest" are to be read disjunctively from the "deprave and corrupt" formula. A publication may be deemed to be obscene if it is "lascivious" or "appeals to the prurient interest", even where it may not "deprave or corrupt" those likely to read it.

The problem of definition is quite crucial in India. In India, there are many religious texts which deal with sex. Sex and sexual intercourse are depicted in many of the ancient religious and other sculptures and paintings. The phallus itself is an object of worship. It is for this reason that the original Code made a specific exception of such items which were "kept or used for any specific religious purpose".[141] When these provisions came to be revised in 1925, the Select Committee felt the need to preserve the religious exception but were sceptical about the *bona fides* of those who took advantage of this exception.[142] An amendment ensured that apart from references to allegedly obscene items found in temples and religious institutions themselves, any other use of the religious exception must be shown to *bona fide*.[143] Later, the religious exception was abolished altogether. The religious texts were either excused as forms of "primitive" expression[144] or as being generally acceptable in their own right.[145]

But in this, as in other cases, the pathology of litigation often creates definitions which belie the analytical expectations of the draftsmen of legislative statutes. Soon after the Code was enacted, the obscenity provisions came to be used in litigation for purposes which were more connected with community and individual disputes rather than the public interest in maintaining certain public standards. In two celebrated cases from Allahabad,[146] pamphlets were published as part of a propaganda war between Muslims and Hindus. These pamphlets sought to expose the alleged immoral tendencies in Islam in response to an allegation about the existence of sexual immoralities in the Hindu faith. The next stage of the quarrel was a successful obscenity indictment. In yet another case,[147] a newspaper published a description of sexual and other acts prohibited during the fast of Ramzan. This was considered to be obscene even though abstracted from religious sources. There are, however, also other cases where the general religious exception was applied in respect of items which might otherwise have been considered obscene.[148] All these cases are less easily explained on the basis of a discussion on the catchment area of obscenity legislation. It falls more easily into an explanation about the nature of litigation and the manner in which courts are used as a forum for the further social agitation of issues rather than their solution. The litigation is an end in itself. The success or failure of the litigation is subordinate. The use of the court as a forum for social agitation is much more significant. At least in respect of these religious cases, the litigative use of the obscenity provisions was more important than the enshrined definitions. After some time, the courts were able to check a use of these provisions by clearly laying down in a case from Bombay involving the Dawoodi Bohra community that no case in obscenity was made out where there was a denigration, abuse or ridicule of leaders.[149] It is not as if the courts ceased to be arenas for these religious disputes. Such disputes began to use other provisions of the criminal law as vehicles for their further perpetuation. This was considerably facilitated by the insertion, in 1927, in the Indian Penal Code of provisions which made it an offence to outrage the religious feelings of any class.[150] For some time, the religious exception became a cloak to commercially publish material which was regarded as obscene.[151] It was in order to block this kind of evasion that the amendment of 1925 stipulated that the religious exception was limited to *bona fide* cases. Publishers continue to publish photographs and materials taken from religious texts.[152] The Courts have permitted the publication of religious texts but have frowned upon attempts to publish selections from these religious texts,[153] or publishing of these texts with illustrations taken from modern photography.[154] It is still a moot question as to how an obscenity case reaches the courts in the first place. No study has yet been made on how obscenity litigation starts and who initiates it. Some cases are clearly extensions of individual and social quarrels. And, it would appear that the use of obscenity provisions for furthering social and political disputes is endless if a stray statement of *obiter dictum* of the Allahabad High Court is taken seriously. In this case, Justice Seth seemed to suggest that even the family planning programme of the government might fall within these provisions:

> In the present day society in India a book or a publication which deals with such matters cannot *per se* be said to be obscene. Great emphasis is being laid on family planning and in that connection it has become absolutely necessary to impart education about sex to the masses. Even so the books dealing with sex matters are to be so composed that they do not cross the bounds of decency and do not tend to become pornographic. Even a slight variation in the treatment of the subject in a book dealing with sex matters from the correct path may have effect of converting it into an obscene book.[155]

Such a statement is a gift to a politican looking for an opportunity to further his own political ends by attacking the family planning programme through the forum of law courts!

There are, of course, a lot of cases where the litigation has been initiated because of a genuine individual, group or social concern about a growing trend in the nature of obscene publications. This concern may be heightened by the fact that those who publish obscene items invariably find themselves making a lot of money. This takes us to the whole question of the putative purpose of obscenity laws.

There seems to be diverse explanations as to why obscenity laws exist. This diversity is as apparent in political circles as it is in judgments of Indian courts,[156] which echo, in part, the preoccupations of English courts.

The *first* way to look at obscenity legislation is with an emphasis on the importance of a consensus morality. Accordingly, obscenity is something that is not socially acceptable to the community. It is something that is "shocking", "crude", or "disgusting",[157] something that would offend the "ordinary" person.[158] This argument has posed considerable problems for courts. They have not always been able to determine whether they are supposed to maintain a notional standard of consensus morality or to answer the factual question as to whether a particular publication does, in fact, offend a particular community. In one early case, they refused to convict publications in a newspaper where the newspaper had a limited circulation.[159] Here the obscene items were not deemed to offend a significant section of the community.

By and large, courts have not concerned themselves whether the allegedly obscene item does cause offence to the community or a significant section of it. They seek to maintain what they consider to be an intuitive understanding of a consensus morality. This decision is made exclusively by judges who may rely on experts and other evidence.[160] Indian courts have been greatly troubled by the fact that this consensus morality differs from region to region and from age to age.[161] They have resorted to the technique of talking of the "ordinary person" as their yardstick.[162] This has not always led to satisfactory results. Some of the indicted publications claim to be religious in nature.[163] Others are defended on the basis that they constitute literature,[164] are part of educating people about sex,[165] or connected with the proliferation of medical or scientific knowledge.[166] Notionally, the court has been prepared to accommodate these claims. But it does so with a heightened sense of caution and skepticism. Indian judges seem to work on the assumption that any general exposure of, or discussion about, sex is really undignified and does not merit protection. Their attempt to maintain this position has not always led to logical results. Individual articles in periodicals have been declared not to be obscene even where an anthology of such articles is considered to be obscene.[167] There is a confusing collection of case law about whether discussion or depiction of sex is obscene *per se*. The conclusion that it is not was reached after a lot of agonizing.[168] Works of literature have not been considered in the light of their literary merit where the theme of sex has been dealt with *in extenso*.[169] The most celebrated case is the decision of the Supreme Court in which *Lady Chatterly's Lover* was considered obscene.[170]

A *second* approach to obscenity legislation may be called the "protectionist" approach. Here the emphasis is not on the maintenance of certain consistent standards but on protecting people from the insidious effect of such publications. To begin with thoughts about sex are in themselves considered to be impure and libidinous.[171] An individual is, therefore, deemed to need protection from the arousing of these thoughts. The strongest form of the 'protection' argument stresses the need to protect impressionable children.[172] This argument has been taken further by the Young Persons (Harmful Publications) Act, 1956. This statute is not limited to prohibiting obscene items but also extends to material which shows things of a repulsive, horrible, cruel or violent nature or which incites children to commit acts of violence or cruelty.[173] This legislation was obviously designed not just to protect children but also to control influences on adolescents and university students, because the intended beneficiaries of this statute are supposed to be persons below the age of twenty. The Indian Penal Code also contained provisions protecting young persons under twenty years of age.[174] It is important to note that the courts concern themselves with putative rather than actual effects. The courts neither ask nor answer the question: What is the actual effect of these publications on any particular individual or society? Courts assume that a harmful result must ensue if items which highlight the theme of sex are published. That being the case, the 'protection' argument is really another form of presenting the 'consensus' argument. Certain items shall be deemed to be 'harmful' because it is generally agreed that these kinds of items must, perforce, be deemed to be harmful. The 'protection' argument is less popular than it has been in previous years. Justice Hidayatullah's judgment in the *Lady Chatterly's Lover* case[175] seems to have shifted the emphasis away from the 'protection' argument to discussing the nature of obscenity in the context of public decency or morality. This shift in emphasis has been partly dictated by the fact that, as far as obscenity offences are concerned, the Constitution permits reasonable restrictions on freedom of speech only in the interest of "decency or morality".[176] If this constitutional limitation had been taken more seriously by the Court, the 'protection' argument may well have been laid to rest forever as being unconstitutional.

Justice Hidayatullah is also responsible for yet *another* approach to obscenity legislation. This approach may be called the "social advancement" approach. He seemed to put forward the view that free speech must have a "prepondering social purpose or profit" and that "obscenity is treating with sex in a manner appealing to the carnal side of human nature, or having that tendency".[177] He also saw free speech as being protected if its purpose was "to change political or social conditions or for the advancement of human knowledge".[178] Taking this approach further he saw obscenity legislation as improving national and regional literary standards.

> Today our national and regional languages are strengthening themselves by new literary standards after a deadening period under the impact of the English. Emulation by our writers of an obscene book under the aegis of the Court's determination is likely to pervert our entire literature because obscenity pays and true art finds little popular support.[179]

All this seems to set a totally different kind of test for the interpretation of the obscenity provisions. A person indicted for obscenity would not only have to show that an allegedly obscene item is consistent with an acceptable "consensus morality" or not "harmful." He would also have to show that it advances social or political conditions or the advancement of human knowledge.

Indian courts have discreetly followed yet another approach in obscenity cases. In many cases, the courts have concentrated on the motives of the accused and the advantages which have accrued to him as a result of a publication. Under the law, courts are not supposed to go into the motive of the publisher.[180] Equally, the intention of the publisher is supposed to be derived from what the court considers to be the effect of the publication.[181] In many cases, the court while looking at the effect of an obscene item seemed to have really been concerned with the motives of the publisher. Thus, the courts have concerned themselves with issues of the "low price" of a book or the fact that it was motivated with a view to get a large circulation.[182] Equally, judges have been prepared to ignore the extent of the circulation of a book where they have been satisfied about the motives of the publisher.[183] Indian judges have not, however, evolved a firm rule that they are primarily concerned with preventing the commercial exploitation of sex even if this has been at the back of their minds in some cases.

More recently in the *Samaresh Bose* case[184] Justice Sen seems to have ironed out some of the inconsistencies of the *Lady Chatterly's Lover* judgment and the law relating to obscenity in India generally. While approving the old Victorian test in *Hicklin's* case that obscene matter has a tendency to "deprave and corrupt"[185] and earlier rulings of the Supreme Court,[186] the court took greater note of the opinion of experts[187] as well as of the fact that the novel in question (*Prajapati*) sought to remove a social evil.[188] Clearly embarrassed by its earlier rulings[189] the Court, in effect, created a new variable test of obscenity which stressed upon literary opinion, the overall context and purpose of the book and the possible readership.[190]

Apart from making obscenity a penal offence, there are other provisions which deal with obscene items. The Criminal Procedure Codes, 1898 and 1974 empowers the Government to make forfeiture orders about obscene materials.[191] This is in addition to other powers under the Code whereby a person guilty of disseminating obscene items can be made to enter a bond—for up to one year, whether with or without sureties—to the effect that he would forfeit a certain sum of money if the offence was committed during that time.[192] These provisions were originally part of the law of sedition and designed to control the incidence of "sedition" against the British Empire in India. The extension of these provisions to the area of obscenity seems much too drastic a step. This is all the more important if we remember that statutes relating to the post office make it an offence to send "indecent, obscene, seditious, scurrilous, threatening or grossly offensive" items through the post.[193] This is a wide catalogue of offences and goes well beyond the standard definition of obscenity. Articles found to offend this list may be detained, returned or forwarded.[194] These are extremely wide powers to prevent and control the dissemination of a wide range of supposedly 'objectionable' material within the territory of India. Legislation dealing with customs gives a similarly wide power to make regulations to prevent the import and export of goods which might affect, amongst other things, decency and morality.[195] There is also the power to impose a fine. All this is subject to a system of quasi-judicial review.[196]

While these provisions control the circulation, import and export of obscene items, there are specific provisions prohibiting the advertisement of obscene material. Yet, at least one High Court has impliedly taken the view that the advertisement of obscene material is not *per se* an offence under the obscenity provisions of the Indian Penal Code.[197] The only direct restrictions on advertisements are to be found in the Drugs and Magic Remedies (Objectionable Advertisements) Act, 1954 which deal with cures for venereal and other diseases or offers sexual stimulants.[198] The Supieme Court seems, however, to have made clear that advertisements which are themselves obscene will not have the protection of the Constitution.[199]

Although we are not directly concerned here with films, it would be useful to note that a totally different kind of censorship system exists for films. Film censorship began in India in 1918. Under the Cinematograph Act, 1918 the government contained the power to license cinema houses and certify which films should be permitted for public exhibition. A new statute was passed in 1952[200] which gave a Censor Board set up by the government the power to lay down guidelines and recommend changes in a film. It could refuse to permit the exhibition of a film if its directions were not complied with. This has resulted in a massive and more or less complete pre-censorship of the film industry. This is particularly marked in the area of sex. Till recently, kissing was not permitted to be exhibited in Indian films. The government is empowered to lay down general principles for the Censor Board.[201] The general principles formulated by the government have been concerned with maintaining moral standards, preventing sympathy with "crime, wrongdoing, evil or sin", not ridiculing the country's laws or create sympathy for the violation of such laws and "having regard to the standards of the country and the people to which the story relates (and). . . not depraving the morality of the audience."[202] A Committee appointed by the government was not sufficiently critical of the censorship system.[203] Equally, the Supreme Court while providing relief to a petitioner who wanted to depict some of the realities underlying prostitution in Bombay, has accepted both the need for a broad pre-censorship system[204] as well as validated these extremely wide guidelines which have been laid down by the government.[205] Much of this censorship operates in the area of sexual morality and the Supreme Court itself seems to have taken the view that the same kind of guidelines as were used by the Supreme Court in dealing with publications under the Indian Penal Code should also apply in respect of films.[206] This leaves open the question as to whether films validated under the censorship system must also run the gauntlet of the obscenity provisions of the Indian Penal Code. Recently two prosecutions were begun against the famous Indian film actor, Raj Kapoor, concerning a film which had been cleared by the censorship board.[207] Although the Supreme Court took the view that he could avail of a defence in the Indian Penal Code to the effect that he acted, or thought he acted, lawfully, these cases show the wide scope of the obscenity provisions.[208] These cases also show how easy it is for an organised litigant to use the processes of the court and mobilize the provisions of the law against the media.

In sum, we can see that Indian law contains a multitude of restrictions on the press and media as far as obscenity and such matters are concerned. Initially, such controls were simply transplanted from the Common Law of England into the Indian Penal Code. They were also a part of the general policy of the British to keep publications in India in check with the use of diverse legal and other techniques. However, soon after these 'obscenity' offences were inducted into the Indian Penal Code, they were subjected to the vagaries of Indian litigation. Litigants used these provisions against their opponents rather than with a view to maintaining a public morality.

There is, however, a tradition in India for maintaining the appearance of a strong public morality. Such a tradition is an assimilative device. It has been used with considerable effect fulfilling social functions even if *dharmic* injunctions are ignored with impunity. The modern Indian judge and legislator faces the same problems that were faced by his ancient counterpart when he deals with matters of public morality. On the one hand, he cannot but take the view that standards of public morality have to be rigorously maintained. On the other hand, he has to devise ways and means not to deal with transgressions of morality in too hard and unrealistic a way. He resolves these problems by intuitively trying to understand what the general public wants and making decisions accordingly. It is this intuitive understanding that explains many of the decisions which have been made;[209] Justice Hidayatullah's decision declaring *Lady Chatterly's Lover* obscene is a good example of a decision where a judge feels that an undeclared public attitude would not suffer the validation of Lawrence's novel as literature.[210] By and large, judges in India seem to have been united in a commitment to preserve a public morality. As far as obscenity legislation is concerned, there have been no champions amongst the Indian judiciary of the libertarian attitude that people must be free to publish and read what they like. Much rather, the Indian judiciary inclines to the more conservative view that it is the business of the law and the judiciary to enforce public morals.

As it happens, no great public campaign has been raised against the nature of obscenity legislation or the manner in which it has been interpreted. The Press Commission of India (1952-4) virtually did not deal with this matter at all.[211] Meanwhile, the threshold of punishment was increased from time to time.[212]

In the sixties, a small campaign was fought to liberalize the laws relating to obscenity. This led to some interesting evidence being given to parliament.[213] This evidence demonstrates the dilemma the Indian legislator faces as do the Indian judges.

Indian legislators feel impelled to stress the need to maintain a public morality with the same zest with which they want to be seen to take a more liberal position in matters of free speech and expression.[214] The Indian solution to this dilemma lies in forcefully advocating both these positions. The amendment of the Penal Code in 1969 defined obscenity in unequivocal terms—using just the kind of language that is used in India to publicly condemn general discussions about sex. Thus, in addition to the general English formula that an obscene item must not deprave or corrupt those in whose hands it is likely to fall, the definition clause also made references to the fact that items would also be obscene if they were "lascivious" or "appealed to the prurient interest". The Law Commission's complaint that these new phrases have not made the concept of obscenity any clearer[215] seems to have missed the main social and political reason why these additions were made. At the same time, Parliament introduced a clause which stated that a publication would be deemed to be for the public good if it is in the "interest of science, literature, art or learning or other objects of general concern". The Law Commission wished to go further and make it clear that expert evidence should be permitted in such cases.[216] At present, expert evidence on these matters has been permitted but judges have made it clear that it is the judges and not the experts who must decide these matters.[217] The judges have not inquired into whether obscenity is, in fact, harmful. They do not wish to make such social inquiries about the nature of obscenity.[218] They prefer to rely on their own intuitive understanding of what they think constitutes a public consensus. Meanwhile, a lot of off-beat, imitative sexual material continues to silently circulate in India. As long as the image of a consensus morality is not publicly tarnished, no one cares unless they are forced to do so.[219]

V

The maintenance of public order and public morality is essential to every legal and political system. Public order and public morality represent a discipline and the State is the custodian of this discipline. The State has to strike a complex and difficult balance between competing and overlapping moral and legal orders. This is against a backdrop of forces which, short-sightedly but surely, seek to compel coherent patterns into a society. Much of that discipline in a modern society is achieved through routinization. But the re-ordering of modern society requires more than just a routine discipline. It needs the active acquiescence of various sectors of society to furthe agree to power allocations within society. This calls for all kinds of voluntary and enforced compromises. The future and the contours of existing disciplinary frameworks and moralitier have to be negotiated. Capitalist society faced with this labyrinth of disciplinary frameworks worked out an appealing political argument to de-recognise many of the group claims of what it designates as intermediate moralities. It treated the individual as the basic political monad; and juxtaposed the individual against the State. The basic equities that contended for recognition and solution were the demands of the individual and the State. It was in this mood that B.R. Ambedkar proclaimed to India's Constituent Assembly that the individual and not the group was to be the basic unit recognised by the Constitution.[220] In terms of political theory, the emphasis of the individual and the consequent de-recognition of the group wiped out at one stroke the inherent rights of existing and emerging groups. This was not because these groups ceased to exist or did not impose disciplinary frameworks on those that fell within their catchment. Much rather, it was because group rights had to be justified and tested against individual rights and any public interest articulated by the State. For example, trade unions were subjected to the dual attack that they restrict the rights of individual members *and* that they disrupt productive outputs in the economy as a whole.

Modern public law prefers to deal with individuals rather than negotiate the intervening strengths and moralities of individual groups. It has had to make certain concessions to group rights and traditional moralities by recognizing the freedom of religion and the right of minorities to their own culture. But even here, it has tried to stress the separation of

Church and State doctrine so that powerful, and otherwise strongly political, religious groups do not stray into politics. There is also the possibility that many groups would collapse if the Church/State doctrine were strictly adhered to and the groups in question were denied State protection and support. By juxtaposing both the public interest and individual claims against group demands, certain patterns of protest are denied legitimacy for both public and libertarian reasons. Yet whether we like it or not, all political activity and public and private protests are a product of group life. There is no gainsaying the fact that it is the group that must inevitably be the focus of socio-political activity in any society. Yet the legal and political systems of most societies will recognise the claims of institutional politics while scrutinizing the claims of groups through the individual rights and public interest lenses. It is not being suggested that groups are *sui generis*. Group demands are often manipulated to suit individual interests. At the same time, despite the alluring intervention of modern political theory, the group remains—as it must do—the basis for modern socio-political orders.

Beneath the facade of public order lies the real world of group conflicts seeking to entrench their gains in the legal and political system. There is never enough legal research done on who uses existing public order powers, against whom and for what? There is every reason to believe that the government in India has been using its public order powers to silence politicians from opposition groups. Yet, the debate has never really progressed beyond the public order situation and the equities of the case being discussed. India's Press Commission (1982) did collect a considerable amount of information to demonstrate that the press had become a public (and political) arena subjected to a huge range of pressures from various quarters. But it was not able to place all this evidence in a conceptual framework. The government itself was not absolved, but in the end, only accused of inactivity. The usual law and order prescription was suggested. But the government is a major participator in political and public affairs. By using public order as the reason for its interference it is able to cloak the use of its powers against opponents. Some of these opponents are regarded as opponents of the regime. But many opponents are not depicted as opponents to a regime but to the system as a whole; and, in certain cases, to 'civilized' life as portrayed in the notion of the 'rule of law'.

It was precisely this kind of use of public order powers that surfaced in the famous Bihar Bill controversy of 1982. Much of the controversy was devoted to, what must on analysis be regarded as, the wrong issue. The Bill created publishing an offence against "grossly indecent or scurrilous matter or matters intended for blackmail." This was punishable by imprisonment for up to two years (five years for second and subsequent convictions) or fine or both.

When the Indian Law Institute examined the provisions of the Bill on behalf of the Press Council of India, it was able to say no more than assert that the offences created were 'vague'. In a supplementary note, the Institute recanted its earlier view that persons would be tried under the Bill by an executive magistrate; but stressed, in the alternative, that the cognizability and non-bailability of the offences were unusual features except

> in such cases . . . which disturb the peace of the community or affect the law and order, or which constitute a serious threat to . . . life and property; and also offences in which there is a likelihood of the offender escaping the clutches of (the) law; and (cases where) if the suspect is not immediately arrested it may frustrate investigations of the case.[221]

The government argued that the Bill fell within some of these categories. However, that is—in a sense—besides the point. *The nature of the offence that was created was not the real nub of the controversy. An examination of cognate offences in the Indian Penal Code will show that the Bihar Bill was consistent rather than inconsistent with the basic strategy of the Penal Code to deal with newspaper offences.* Table 1 analyses the offences against newspapers in the Indian Penal Code.

TABLE 1

Offences by Publication in the Indian Penal Code

Year of Introduction: Section	*Offence*	*Punishment*	*Cognizable*	*Bailable*
(*1*)	(*2*)	(*3*)	(*4*)	(*5*)
1870. S. 124 A	Sedition	—Life and fine; or —3 years and fine; or —fine	C	NB
1898. S. 153 A	—promoting enmity between classes	3 years and/or fine or both	C	NB
	—promoting enmity between classes in place of public worship	5 years and fine	C	NB
1927. S. 153 B	—Imputations, assertions prejudical to national integration	3 years and/or fine or both	C	NB
	—If committed in a place of worship	5 years and fine	C	NB
1860. S. 292	—Sale of obscene books etc.	*1st Offence*: 2 years and Rs. 2000 *2nd and other Offences*: 5 years and Rs. 5000	C	B

(*Contd.*)

(1)	(2)	(3)	(4)	(5)
1860. S. 293	—Sale of obscene books to children	*1st Offence*: 3 years and Rs. 2000 *2nd and other Offences*: 7 years and Rs. 5000	C	B
1927. S. 295A	—Maliciously insulting the religion or religious belief of any class	2 years or fine or both	C	NB
1860. S. 499	—Defamation re. President, Governor, Administrator of a territory or district	Simple imprisonment for 2 years or fine or both	NC	B
	—defamation in other cases.	"		
S. 505	—False statement, rumour circulated with intent to:		NC	NB
1860.	(a) cause mutiny or offence against the public peace	3 years or fine or both	NC	NB
1898.	(b) create hatred, enmity, ill-will between different classes, religious groups etc.	3 years or fine or both		
1969.	(c) in a place of religious worship or performance of worships	5 years and fine	C	NB

It is clear from the Table that the Bihar Bill was, in fact, not different in various material particulars from the offences created in the Code. In fact, before 1973, the Indian Penal Code operated so that the executive magistrate tried—or committed for trial—many of these offences. *Far from deviating from the paradigm underlying the Indian Penal Code, the Bihar Bill is a classic affirmation of this paradigm.* If anything, the Bihar Bill is a comment on the basic strategy of Indian Law. To the extent to which the Bihar Bill controversy contrasted the Bill against provisions of the Indian Penal Code, it aired a non-controversy. The Bihar government argued that such provisions were necessary and could hardly be regarded as part of a strategy that was alien to the Indian legal system. The press, which had mobilised solid support, began a civil disobedience campaign, demonstrated in the streets, lobbied extensively, and picked on the arbitrary nature of the Bill. But, by Indian standards the Bill was not arbirtary. The real controversy was about whom the bill would be used against. It was suggested that like the Tamil Nadu and Orissa legislation, the Bill would be used against political opponents and those papers which criticised the unscrupulous Jagannath Mishra regime in Bihar. If the experiment worked in Bihar, it would be used as a Congress-I strategy in all the States they governed.[222]

At the root of the Bihar Bill lies a policy about political opposition. Public order and public morality offences sustain a framework within which political mobilization and discourse must take place. Successive Indian governments have been careful to organise this disciplinary framework so that it is justified and accepted by the people at large as the only sensible thing to do. This framework has been questioned twice in the last ten years. During the Emergency, no one seriously believed that the imposition of a new framework of censorship controls could be justified on any basis other than the personal and political needs of Mrs. Gandhi's regime. The Bihar Bill was the second occasion when the credulity of the public could not be strained into believing that the Bill was *pro bono publico.* Yet these two instances are treated as episodic examples rather than the visible tips of an existing iceberg.

India stands as a striking contrast to Western legal systems where pressure has been put to make real advances for individuals (and groups) against the public interest. This has been most successful in the area of public morality; and has had some impact on the area of public order. In India, the public order and morality argument has had an unassailable victory. This has acquired more and more insidious implications as the privatiza tion of the Indian State has increased. India's political economy has encouraged more and more parts of the Indian State to be directly controlled by private individuals, groups and classes. Indian politicians are enabling power brokers who either own and control parts of the State directly for themselves or for others who manipulate or corrupt them. The complexity by which this process works should not blind us to the gradual accretion of public power into private hands. It is difficult to say when this process will stop. A matured corporate sector may prefer a power structure which they manipulate better than others to a power structure which can easily be corrupted by anyone. At present, the distinction between private and public power is getting blurred in all respects other than the form in which the latter is expressed. That being the case, our real starting point of analysis must be to look at the private abuse of public power. The Indian debate on public order and the press is a false debate, which is trapped in a historically precipitated but ideologically impregnable paradigm. The real controversies concern the use of the press as a political arena and the extent to which the government poses as the biased umpire of the ground rules under which this political arena operates. As more and more government political institutions are subjected to direct manipulative control, the Indian press is becoming not just the prime but the only political arena for discussion and debate. It is not surprising that it is depicted as a kind of permanent threat to public order and the safety of the realm.

NOTES

1. Pelham (1832) 11 Hansard cols. 421-2 quoted J. Curran and J. Seaton: *Power without Responsibility* (1981) Chapter 2 note 2.
2. See generally J. Curran and J. Seaton (*supra* note 1) Chapters 3 and 4; see also P. Hollis: *The Pauper Press* (1970).
3. See generally D.G.T. Williams: *Note in the Public Interest* (1968) on the controversies on official secrecy. For the position in India see Chapter 6, *supra.*
4. The only real restraints on publication were the provisions dealing with obscenity (S. 292), defamation (Ss. 499-500) and causing mutiny and public alarm (S. 505).
5. Clause 113 of the Draft Indian Penal Code, 1837.
6. While introducing amendments to the Indian Penal Code on 2 August 1870. Extensive extracts from this and other speeches as have been reproduced in W.R. Donough: *The History of the Law of Sedition* (1914 Second Edition) 1.
7. Sir Barnes Peacock: Letter to Sir Henry Maine 7 June 1869—quoted in W.R. Donough *supra* note 6 2.
8. See James Fitzjames Stephen's speech of 2 August 1870 in Donough *supra* note 6 2-3.
9. Evidently, the draft was criticized by Norton and Huddleston in the *Second Report of the Law Commission on the Indian Penal Code.* Some other criticisms are mentioned in Sir Barnes Peacock's letter to Sir Henry Maine (*supra*)—see D. Gopalkrishna Sastri: *The Law of Sedition in India* (1962 Indian Law Institute) 13-14.
10. Sir Thomas Munro: *Danger of a Free Press in India*: Minute 12 April, 1822—quoted in W.R. Donough (*supra* note 6) 175.
11. *Ibid.* 176.
12. *Ibid.* 178.
13. See Regulation III of 1823 for the territories immediately subordinate to the Presidency of Fort William. A similar ordinance was passed in Bombay on 2 March 1825 and consolidated into a Regulation on 1 January 1827.
14. See the Regulation XI of 15 September 1835 and the Minute of Sir Charles Metcalfe of 17 April 1835.
15. Sir Charles Metcalfe quoted W.R. Donough *supra* note 6 181.
16. Lord Canning: Speech to the Legislative Council, 13 June 1857, quoted W.R. Donough *supra* note 6 184.
17. *Ibid.* 183.
18. S. 124 A, Indian Penal Code.
19. S. 153A Indian Penal Code.
20. S. 225A Indian Penal Code.
21. The Vernacular Press Act (IX of) 1878 passed on 14 March 1878. For a detailed account of the discussion in the Council see W.R. Donough *supra* note 6 189-202. On 16 October 1878 Sir Arthur

Arbuthnot reported that for the past seven months there had been no need to invoke the provisions: see W.R. Donough *supra* note 6 203. Even the Act was strengthened by Act XVI of 1878 after Lord Lytton has openly supported it: W.R. Donough *supra* note 6 205.

22. In the discussion before the Council 14 March 1878, quoted W.R. Donough *supra* note 6 192-3.
23. Speech of the Law Member before the Council, 1898 quoted W.R. Donough *supra* note 6 211.
24. Section 108, Criminal Procedure Code; see also the Report of the Select Committee (16 February 1898).
25. Speech of the Law Member, quoted W.R. Donough *supra* note 6 211-2.
26. Press Law (Repeal and Amendment) Act, 1931.
27. See Ss. 99A to G added to the Criminal Procedure Code of 1898.
28. Press (Emergency Powers) Act, 1931.
29. Press Laws Enquiry Committee (1948) pr. 3 of Summary of Recommendations.
30. Press (Objectionable Matter) Act, 1951.
31. The 1951 statute was repealed.
32. Report of the Press Commission (1952-54) pr. 1018 p. 387.
33. Prevention of Publication of Objectionable Matter Ordinance, 1975 converted into Prevention of the Publication of Objectionable Matter Act, 1976 (repealed on 9 April 1977).
34. See *Romesh Thapper* v. *State of Madras* A.I.R. 1951 S.C. 126; *Brij Bhushan* v. *State of Delhi* A.I.R. 1951 S.C. 129; *Virendra* v. *State of Punjab* A.I.R. 1957 S.C. 896; see also the Criminal Law (Amendment) Act, 1961 and the preventive measures in the Defence of India Act, 1962 and the Defence of India Act, 1971. The Central Censorship Order S.O. 275 of the Emergency (1975-77) was passed under the Defence of India Act.
35. *Report of the Press Commission* (1952-54) pr. 1007 p. 382.
36. *Q.E.* v. *Jogendra Chunder Bose* (1890) 19 Cal. 35.
37. *Q E.* v. *Bal Gangadhar Tilak* (1897) 22 Bom. 112.
38. *Bal Gangadhar Tilak* v. *Q.E.* (1898) 22 Bom 528.
39. *Q.E.* v. *Ramachandra Narayan* (1897) 22 Bom. 152.
40. *Q.E.* v. *Amba Prashad* (1897) 20 All. 55.
41. Explanation III to S. 124A.
42. *Parmanand* v. *Emperor* A.I.R. 1941 All. 156; *In re S.S. Batliwala* A.I.R. 1938 Mad. 758; *Emperor* v. *Phanendra Nath Mitter* (1908) 35 Cal. 945; see also simply threats that the government ought to be ousted, *Sodhi Pindi Das* v. *Emperor* A.I.R. 1938 Lah. 629; *Ram Saran Das* v. *Emperor* A.I R. 1930 Lah. 892; *Professor Indra* v. *Emperor* A.I.R. 1930 Lah. 870
43. *Anand Kishore* v. *Emperor* A.I.R. 1930 Lah. 306.
44. *M. Kanti Ghose, Keeper of the Amrita Bazar Patrika Press and Tarit*

Kanti Biswas, Publisher. . . In the matter of Amrit Bazar Patrika A.I.R. 1932 Cal. 738.

45. *Parmanand* v. *Emperor* A.I.R. 1941 All. 156.
46. *Narayan Vasudev Phadke* v. *Emperor* A.I.R. 1940 Bom. 379.
47. *Thakin Lay Maung* v. *The King* A.I.R. 1939 Rang. 169.
48. *Narinjan Das* v. *Emperor* A.I.R. 1931 Lah. 31.
49. *Gopal Lal Sanyal* v. *King-Emperor* A.I.R. 1927 Cal. 751; see also *Nageswar Prasad Sharma* v. *Emperor* A.I.R. 1925 Pat. 99; *Malik Amir Alam* v. *Emperor* A.I.R. 1930 Lah. 885: *Om Prakash* v. *The Crown* (1940) Punj. L.R. 382.
50. *V.S. Dandekar* v. *Emperor* A.I.R. 193 All. 324.
51. *Satyendra Nath Mazumdar* v. *Emperor* A.I.R. 1931 Cal. 337; see also *Lachhman Singh* v. *Emperor* A,I.R. 1930 Lah. 156.
52. *Kripal Singh* v. *Emperor* A.I.R. 1931 Lah. 106.
53. *Hanumanthiya* v. *Govt. of Mysore* (1948) 52 Mys. H.C.R. 265; also see *Manubhai Tribhovandas Patel* v. *State of Gujarat* (1972) Cr .L.J. 373 (Guj.).
54. *V. Bhusan Roy* v. *Emperor* (1907) 6 Cr. L.J. 297.
55. *V.O. Chidambaram Pillai and Subramanian Siva* v. *Emperor* (1909) 32 Mad. 3; *In re V.O. Chidambaram Pillai* (1909) 9 Cr. L.J. 140.
56. *Ibid.*; see also *Om Prakash* v. *The Crown* (1940) 42 Punj. L.R. 382.
57. No clear legal approach is discernible. In theory the courts continue to look at the natural and probable consequences of the words and not the intention of tne accused.
58. *Debi Soren* v. *The State* A.I.R. 1954 Pat. 254 at 261.
59. *Satya Ranjan Bakshi* v. *Emperor* A.I.R. 1929 Cal. 277; *Om Prakash Lalchand* v. *Emperor* A I.R. 1948 Nag. 71.
60. *Sagolsem Indramani Singh* v. *State of Manipur* A.I.R. 1955 Mani. 9.
61. Consider the implications of *Emperor* v. *Shiv Nath* A.I.R. 1945 P.C. 156.
62. *Ram Nandan* v. *State* A.I.R. 1959 All. 101.
63. *Kedar Nath* v. *State of Bihar* A.I.R. 1962 S.C. 955.
64. *K.E.* v. *S.N. Bhalerao* (1947) 74 I.A. 89.
65. *Niharendu* v. *K.E.* A.I.R. 1947 F.C. 22.
66. Report of the *Press Laws Enquiry Committee Report* (1948) 39.
67. *Kedar Nath* v. *State of Bihar* (*supra*) at pr. 24 p. 967; pr. 25 p. 962.
68. *Report of the Press Commission* (1952-54) p. 403. Note also the judgment in *Tara Singh* v. *State of Punjab* A.I.R. 1952 Punj. 27.
69. Mr. Chalmers when introducing the Bill on 25 December 1897 quoted W.R. Donough *supra* note 6 163.
70. Mr. Chalmers on 18 February 1893—see also the Report of the Select Committee on the Bill of 4 February 1898 quoted W.R. Donough *supra* note 6 164-5.
71. *Rungpur Bartabaha* case (No. 509 of 1910) before the Calcutta High Court—see W.R. Donough *supra* note 6 152-6, 167-8; *Joy Chandra Sarkar* v. *Emperor* (1911) 38 Cal. 214.

72. *Leakut Hossein Khan and Abdul Gaffur* v. *Emperor* App.No. 214 of 1908 reported W.R. Donough *supra* note 6 168-9, see further *Joy Chandra Sarkar* v. *Emperor* (1911) 38 Cal. 214. Note further W.R. Donough's comment (at 168): "In the case of *Emperor* v. *B.G. Tilak* (10 Bom. L.R. 848) a conviction was obtained under S. 153A, but it is not clear from the charge to the jury on what it is based."
73. *M.L.C. Gupta* v. *Emperor* A.I.R. 1936 All. 314. cf. *Harnam Dass* v. *State of U.P.* A.I.R. 1957 All. 538.
74. *Hirendra Prashad Ghose* v. *Emperor* A.I.R. 1927 Cal. 743, Cf. *Satya Ranjan Bakshi* v. *Emperor* A.I.R. 1929 Cal. 309; *Emperor* v. *Banomali Maharana* A.I.R. 1943 Pat. 382; *King Emperor* v. *Raj Pal* A.I.R. 1926 Lah. 195.
75. *Maniben Liladhar Kara* v. *Emperor* A.I.R. 1933 Bom. 65 at 67-69.
76. See also *Vishambar Daya Tripathi* v. *Emperor* A.I.R. 1941 Oudh 33.
77. See *Jaswant Rai* v. *Emperor* (1907) Cr. L.J. 439; *A M.A. Zaman* v. *Emperor* A.I.R. 1933 Cal. 139 (although no offence found); (*Swami*) *Chida Nand* v. *Emperor* A.I.R. 1930 Lah. 350.
78. *In re Paschim Bangal Patrika* (1951) 1 Cal. 235.
79. *Joy Chandra Sarkar* v. *Emperor* (1911) 38 Cal. 214.
80. *Raj Paul* v. *Emperor* A.I.R. 1927 Lah. 590. Cf. *Kali Charan Sharma* A.I.R. 1927 All. 654.
81. *Thakin Lay Maung* v. *The King* A.I.R. 1939 Rang. 169.
82. *Ibid.*
83. *Emperor* v. *Banomali Maharana* A.I.R. 1943 Pat. 382.
84. *Vishambhar Dayal Tripathi* v. *Emperor* A.I.R. 1941 Oudh 33.
85. *The State* v. *Sadat Jehan Begum* I.L.R. (1956) Hyd. 889. Cf. *Khan Gufran Zahidi* v. *State* (1964) All. L.J. 545.
86. *Debi Soren* v. *The State* A.I.R. 1954 Pat. 254.
87. *Ram P. Sadarangani* v. *Emperor* A.I.R. 1945 Sind 106; see further *State of Bihar* v, *Ghulam Sarwar* A.I.R. 1965 Pat. 393.
88. *Munshi Singh* v. *Emperor* A.I.R. 1935 Oudh 347.
89. By Act XLI of 1961. Further changes were also made and the punishment thresholds enhanced by the Criminal and Election Laws Amendment Act (35 of) 1969.
90. *Shiva Kumar Mishra* v. *State of U.P.*, (1978) Cr. L.J. 701.
91. Inserted by the Criminal Law (Amendment) Act (31 of) 1972; For the Statement of Objects and Reasons see Gazette of India Extra Pt. II S. 2 p. 582 (31 May, 1972).
92. *Ramji Lal Modi* v. *State of U.P.* A.I.R. 1957 S.C. 620.
93. *Devi Sharan Sharma* v. *Emperor* A.I.R. 1927 Lah. 594.
94. *Supra* note 80.
95. For *Ramji Lal Modi's* case *supra* note 88. The amending Act is the Indian Penal Code (Amending) Act (XLI of) 1961. The imprisonment is enhanced from "two" to "three" years.
96. See *Baba Khalil Ahmad* v. *State* A.I.R. 1960 All. 715; *In re P. Ramaswamy* (1962) 2 Cr. L.J. 146.

97. *Harnam Das* v. *State of U.P.* A.I.R. 1957 All. 538.
98. *Baba Khalil Ahamad* v. *State* A.I.R. 1960 All. 715; *State of Mysore* v. *Henry Rodrigues* (1962) 2 Cr. L.J. 564 (Mys.) Cf. *Lalai Singh Yadav* v. *State of U.P.* (on Sec. 153A) (1971) Cr. L.J. 1772.
99. *State of Mysore* v. *Henry Rodrigues* (1962) 2 Cr. L.J. 564; *The King* v. *Nga Shwe Hpi* A.I.R. 1930 Rang. 199.
100. *Shiv Ram Dass Udasin* v. *Punjab State* A.I.R. 1955 Punj. 28; or that the attack in question was universal; *N. Veerabrahman* v. *State of A.P.* A.I.R. 1959 A.P. 572.
101. *Shiv Ram Dass Udasin* v. *Punjab State* A.I.R. 1955 Punj. 28; *Baba Khalil Ahamad* v. *State* A.I.R. 1960 All. 715; *The King* v. *Nga Shwe Hpi* A.I.R. 1939 Rang. 199. In all these cases, the right to reply was not taken to be *bona fide*.
102. *The King* v. *Nga Shwe Hp* A.I.R. 1939 Rang. 199 where this was considered a defence but not where the accused simply had strong views about certain practices and beliefs; *State of Mysore* v. *Henry Rodrigues* (1962) 2 Cr. L.J. 564.
103. *Mukand Ram* v. *State* A.I.R. 1952 All. 26.
104. Law Member's speech to the Council, 1898 quoted W.R. Donough *supra* note 6 170.
105. *Report of the Select Committee* (1898) quoted W.R. Donough *supra* note 6 170-1.
106. S. 505 of the Indian Penal Code. The amendments inserted by the Criminal Election Law Amendment Act (35 of) 1969 concerned causing enmity between castes, groups and communities on grounds of caste, colour, religion, place of birth, residence or language, community; a 'good faith' requirement was also introduced in the Exception. The punishment threshold was increased from two to three years by the Indian Penal Code Amendment Act (41 of) 1961.
107. *Ramji Lal Modi* v. *State of U.P.* A.I R. 1957 S.C. 620.
108. *In the Matter of Mandir* ((1899) 3 Cal. W.N. 1.
109. *Gangadhar* v. *State of U.P.* I.L.R. (1962) M.P. 449.
110. *Kalicharan Mohapatra* v. *Srinivas Sahu*, I.L.R. (1959) Cut. 584.
111. *In the Matter of Mandir* (1899) 3 Cal. W.N. 1; see also *Kedar Nath* v. *State of Bihar* A.I.R. 1962 S.C. 955 at pr. 29 p. 970.
112. *K.R. Malkani* v. *State* (1972) 1 Delhi 393.
113. First and foremost note the Criminal Law Amendment Act, 1961 which empowers prosecution for threatening the safety, security or integrity of India by a magistrate without prior approval of the government (Section 2); prejudicial rumours or reports may not be circulated in a notified area (Section 3). There are also a large number of statutes dealing with public order even though all of them do not directly affect the Assam Maintenance of Order Act (11 of) 1947; Assam Maintenance of Public Order (Autonomous Districts) Act (16 of) 1953; Bengal Criminal Law Amendment Ordinance (2 of) 1947; Bengal State Prisoner's Regulation (Adaptation) Order 1947;

Bihar Maintenance of Public Order (Ordinance 4 of 1949 as amended by Ordinance 5 of) 1949; Bihar Maintenance of Public Order Act (1 of) 1950; Bihar Preventive Detention Ordinance (2 of) 1950; Bombay Public Security Measures Act (6 of) 1947; C.P. and Berar Goondas Act (10 of) 1946; C.P. and Berar Maintenance and Restoration of Public Order and Collection of Fines (Indemnity) Act (2 of) 1945; C.P. and Berar Public Safety Act (62 of) 1948; Cochin Criminal Law Amendment Act (27 of 1124 M.E.); Criminal Law Amendment Ordinance (29 of) 1948; East Punjab Public Safety Act (5 of) 1948; Hyderabad Public Safety and Public Interest Regulation (8 of 1358 F); and (12 of 1358 F); Hyderabad Public Security Act (12 of 1348 F); Hyderabad Special Tribunals Regulation (1 of 1358 F); Hyderabad Special Tribunals (Validation of Proceedings) Regulation (1 of 13.9 F); Indore Public Safety Act 1947; J & K Preventive Detention Act (4 of 2011 Samvat); J&K Public Security Act (14 of 2003 Samvat); Madhya Bharat Maintenance of Public Order Act (7 of) 1947; Madhya Bharat Maintenance of Public Order Ordinance (5 of) 1948: Madhya Bharat Public Security Act (12 of) 1953; Madhya Bharat Public Security Act (23 of) 1959; Madhya Bharat Public Security Measures Act (23 of) 1950; Madras Maintenance of Public Order Act (1 of) 1947; Madras Maintenance of Public Order Act (23 of) 1949; Madras Maintenance of Public Order Ordinance (23 of) 1949; Madras Maintenance of Public Order (Removal of Doubts and Amendment) Ordinance (1 of 1949); Mysore Public Safety Act (12 of) 1949; Orissa Maintenance of Public Order Act (4 of) 1948; Orissa Maintenance of Public Order Act (10 of) 1950; Patiala State Public Safety Ordinance (11 of 2003 Samvat); Pepsu Public Safety Ordinance (7 of 2006 Samvat); Punjab Disturbed Areas Act (1 of) 1947; Punjab Public Safety Act (2 of) 1947; Punjab Security of the State Act (12 of) 1953; Punjab Criminal Law Amendment Act (30 of) 1960; Rajasthan Public Safety Ordinance (9 of) 1948; Rajasthan Public Safety Ordinance (26 of) 1949; Saurashtra State Public Safety Measure Ordinance (9 of) 1949; Saurashtra State Public Safety Measures (Third Amendment) Ordinance (66 of) 1949; Travancore Cochin Public Safety Measures Act (5 of) 1950; Travancore Emergency Powers Act (1 of 1122 M.E). U.P. Maintenance of Public Order Act (11 of) 1949; U.P. Maintenance of Public Order Ordinance (2 of) 1949; U.P. Maintenance of Public Order (Temporary) Act (4 of) 1947; V.P. Prevention of Crime (Special Powers Temporary) Act (5 of) 1949; V.P. Criminal Law Amendment Act (Special Courts) Ordinance (5 of) 1949; W.B. Criminal Law Amendment (Special Courts Act (21 of) 1949; as amended by Act 12 of 1952; Act 24 of 1960; West Bengal Security Act (3 of 1943); West Bengal Security Act (19 of) 1950; West Bengal Security Ordinance (2 of 1949); West Bengal Security (Second Amendment) Ordinance

(2 of) 1949; West Bengal Special Courts Act (10 of) 1950; West Bengal Tribunal of Criminal Jurisdiction Act (14 of) 1952.

114. *Supdt. Central Prison* v. *Ram Manohar Lohia* A.I.R. 1960 S.C. 633; A.I.R. 1955 All. 193.
115. see *Virendra* v. *State of Punjab* A.I.R. 1957 S.C. 896.
116. S. 108, Criminal Procedure Code, 1973.
117. The offences in question are those contained in Ss. 124A, 153A, 153B, 295A, 292 of the Indian Penal Code, 1860 and the criminal defamation of a judge under that Code.
118. S. 108 (2), Criminal Procedure Code, 1973.
119. S. 95, Criminal Procedure Code, 1973.
120. The offences in question are those contained in Ss. 124 A, 133 A, 153B, 292, 293 and 295 A of the Indian Penal Code, 1860.
121. *Harnam Das* v. *State of U.P.* A.I.R. 1961 S.C. 1662; *State of U.P.* v. *Lalai Singh* A.I.R. 1977 S.C. 202, Justice Krishna Iyer quoting at pr. 20 pp. 207-08 a quotation from Chairman Mao along with American constitutional law.
122 S. 96 of the Criminal Procedure Code, 1973.
123. See *Harnam Das* v. *State of U.P.* A.I.R. 1961 S.C. 1662; see also *Veerabrahman* v. *State* A.I.R. 1959 A.P. 572; *Khalil Ahmad* v. *State* A.I.R. 1960 All. 715.
124. S. 93 of the Criminal Procedure Code, 1973.
125. An interpretation of S. 144 of the Criminal Procedure Code, 1973 for the general effect on free speech see *Babulal* v. *State of Maharashtra* A.I.R. 1961 S.C. 884; *Virendra* v. *State of Punjab* A.I.R. 1957 Punj. 1.
126. Section 27—(B), (C), (D), Post Office Act, 1898 envisages a procedure for seditious material analogous to the forfeiture provisions of the Criminal Procedure Code; see also S. 181-A Sea Customs Act, 1878.
127. *Report of the Press Commission* (1952-54) generally but specially Chapter XX.
128. The substantive debate took place on 1-2 December, 1948 and can be found in VIII C.A.D. 712-89 where the freedom of speech provisions were considered. For the preliminary discussions see G. Austin: *The Indian Constitution: Cornerstone of a Nation* (1966) 68-75.
129. Constitution (First Amendment) Act, 1951 following *Romesh Thappar* v. *State of Madras* A.I.R. 1950 S.C. 124 and *Brij Bhushan* v. *State of Delhi* A.I.R. 1950 S.C. 129.
130. *Report of the Press Commission* (1952-54) prs. 1142-1146 pp. 441-447.
131. See *Ramji Lal Modi* v. *State of U.P.* A.I.R. 1957 S.C. 620; *Virendra* v. *State of Punjab* A.I.R. 1957 S.C. 896; *Kedar Nath* v. *State of Bihar*, A.I.R. 1962 S.C. 955; *Babulal* v. *State of Maharashtra*, A.I.R. 1961 S.C. 884; *Santokh Singh* v. *Delhi Administration*, A.I.R. 1973 S.C. 1091. The Court refused to look at the actual necessity and rejected

in *Babulal's* case (*supra*) the plea that such powers are permissible only where there is a "clear and present danger".

132. *Supra* note 114.

133. This plea is to be found in J. Austin's classic: *The Province of Jurisprudence* (Hart edn. 1954) and H.L.A. Hart's celebrated essay "Positivism and the separation of law from morals" (1958) 71. Harvard *L.R.* 593.

134. Much of the controversy is about the autonomy of law as a separate system. The argument is really a political argument relating to the validity of law. Accordingly, the authority of an otherwise valid law cannot be shaken by appeals to morality.

135. The classic definition is to be found in Chief Justice Cockburn's judgment in *R.* v. *Hicklin* (1868) 3 Q.B. 360 at 371 and which is reproduced in Section 1(1) Obscene Publications Act, 1959 (United Kingdom).

136. *John Calder Publications Ltd.* v. *Powell* (1965) 1 Q.B. 509.

137. *D.P.P.* v. *A.B.C. Chewing Gum Ltd.* (1968) 1 Q. B. 159.

138. Cf. J.N. Mallick: *Law of Obscenity in India* (1966) 17 that there is no justification for limiting obscenity to sexual morality alone. In England the contrary view is expressed by D.G.T. Williams: "The Control of Obscenity" (1965) *Criminal L.R.* 522; G Zellick: "Violence as Pornography" (1970) *Cr. L.R.* 188.

139. *Emp.* v. *Indraman* (1881) 3 All. 837; *Emp.* v. *Hari Singh* (1906) 28 All. 100; *State* v. *Dina Nath* (1956) Cr. L.J. 415; *State* v. *Thakur Prashad* A.I.R. 1959 All. 49; *Zafar Ahmad* v. *State* A.I.R. 1963 All. 105; *Ranjit Udeshi* v. *State* (1962) 64 Bom. L.R. 356; *Public Prosecutor* v. *Markendeyulu* (1916) 18 Cr. L.J. 153; *Emp.* v. *Ghulam Hasan* A.I.R. 1917 Lah. 219. The Supreme Court affirmed the use of the deprave and corrupt formula in *Ranjit Udeshi* v. *State of Maharashtra* A.I.R. 1965 S.C. 881 at prs. 14-5 p. 887; *Chandra Kant* v. *State of Mysore* A.I.R. 1970 S.C. 1390 at pr. 5 p. 1392.

140. S. 292(1) Indian Penal Code, 1860 as amended by the Indian Penal Code (Amendment) Act (36 of) 1969.

141. The *Exception* to S. 292 in the original Indian Panel Code 1860 stated: "This section does not extend to any representation sculptured, engraved, painted or otherwise represented on or in any temple, or any car used for the conveyance of idols, or kept or used for any religious purpose."

142. See the *Report of the Select Committee* on the Bill to amend the Indian Penal Code, 10 February 1925.

143. The amendment by Act VIII of 1925 stated: This section does not extend to any book, pamphlet, writing, drawing, painting kept or used *bona fide* for religious purposes or any representation, sculptured, engraved, painted or otherwise represented on or in a temple, or in any car used for the conveyance of idols, or kept or used for

any religious purpose." It is important to note that while the scope of the publications protected was increased, the *bona fide* rule was attached to items in religious temples and processions.

144. *Emp.* v. *Vishnu Krishna Pusanik* (1913) 15 Bom. L.R. 307.

145. There is a suggestion in *Khirode Roy* v. *Emp.* (1911) 39 Cal. 377 that religious and classic works are not obscene. Here a poem had been taken from a sacred book from Orissa—the *Haribans*. Similarly in *Kishore Chander Roy Chowdhry* v. *Emp.* (1912) 13 Cr. L.J. 177 the book *Natu Churi* could not be deemed to suggest immorality to those who believed in the divinity of Lord Krishna. Cf. *Public Prosecutor* v. *Markondeyulu* (1916) Cr. L.J. 153 translations from the Telugu classics of *Srinadha* were sold at one anna a copy. Justice Sheshagiri Aiyar took the view that this fifteenth century classic was not written for the wide circulation of a printing press society! Now the emphasis is clearly on the manner in which a book is published and what is highlighted. See *State of U.P.* v. *Kunji Lal* A.I.R. 1970 All. 614 (involving the *Kamasutra, Rati Rahasya, Kamkala* and *Suhagraat, Anang Rang* and *Panch Sahayak* which were found to be obscene); *Ghulam Hussain* v. *Emperor*. A.I.R. 1917 Lah. 219—a newspaper article in Almunir, on sexual conduct prohibited during Ramzan was found to be obscene.)

146. *Emp.* v. *Indarman* (1881) 3 All. 837; *Emp.* v. *Hari Singh* (1905) 28 All. 100.

147. *Emp.* v. *Ghulam Husain* A.I.R. 1917 Lah. 219.

148. See the cases cited *supra* note 145.

149. *Rahimatalli* v. *Emp.* A.I.R. 1920 Bom. 402.

150. S. 295A, Indian Penal Code, 1860.

151. See *Public Prosecutor* v. *Markondeyulu* (1916) Cr. L.J. 153.

152. *e.g. Sukanta Haldar* v. *State* A.I R. 1952 Cal. 214 (photographs of temple architecture and other illustrations not connected with religion).

153. *Emp.* v. *Ghulam Hasan* A.I.R. 1917 Lah. 219 (passage from a religious book published in a journal).

154. *Sukanta Haldar* v. *State* A.I.R. 1952 Cal. 214 (see above); *State* v. *Kunji Lal*, A.I.R. 1970 All. 614 (classics and others reproduced in language and with pictures).

155. *Kunji Lal* v. *State* A.I.R. 1970 All. 614.

156. That there is a similarity between the attitudes of policy makers and judges is explored further later on.

157. *Emp.* v. *Harnam* A.I.R. 1947 Lah. 383; *Sreeram Saksena* v. *Emp.* A.I.R. 1940 Cal. 290.

158. *Sukanta Haldar* v. *State* A.I.R. 1952 Cal. 214 and used this test even with respect to a *quasi* scientific journal in *Ramamurthy* v. *State of Mysore* A.I.R. 1954 Mysore 164 at pr. 6 p. 166. However, the conviction was set aside in this case. The emphasis is not on the

effect on a person of wide culture *Kailash Chandra* v. *Emp.* A.I.R. 1932 Cal. 650 at 654 (in respect of the autobiography of a fictitious person). A different and more indulgent attitude seems to have been taken by the Supreme Court in a similar kind of case in *Chandrakant* v. *State of Mysore* A.I.R. 1970 S.C. 1390. The "ordinary man" is really a fictitious standard assembled together through the intuitive understanding of a judge. The emphasis on the effect on 'ordinary men' is clearly stated in Justice S. Aiyar's judgment in *Public Prosecutor* v. *Markondeyulu* A.I.R. 1918 Mad. 1195. "The opinion of men of the world and of persons who belong to the classes into whose hands this publication is likely to find its way is more entitled to weight than the judgment of scholars and of men of undisputed moral character". Note also the anthology of references compiled in *In re Chandrasekharan* (1957) 2 M.L.J. 539 at pp. 565-6.

159. *State* v. *Thakur Datt* (1917) P.R. 25:18 Cr.L.J. 126.

160. In *Ranjit Udeshi* v. *State of Maharashtra* A.I.R. 1965 S.C. 881 at pr. 3 p. 881 Justice Hidayatullah notes the evidence of an expert but clearly does not treat it as conclusive; see also *Chandrakant* v. *State of Maharashtra* A.I.R. 1970 S.C. at pr. 4 p. 1392.

161. *Sukanta Haldar* v. *State* A.I.R. 1952 Cal. 214 at pr. 4 p. 215; *Ranjit Udeshi* v. *State* A.I.R. 1962 Bom. 268 at pr. 9 p. 271; *State* v. *Dina Nath* A.I.R. 1956 Punj. 85 at pr. 14 p. 88; *Ramamurthy* v. *State of Mysore* A.I.R. 1954 Mys. 164 at pr. 3 p. 165.

162. *Supra* note 158.

163. See note 145 *supra*.

164. The defence of literature is very well stated in *Ranjit Udeshi* v. *State of Maharashtra* A.I.R. 1965 S.C. 881 at pr. 18 p. 888; prs. 27-28 pp. 890-1. But *Lady Chatterley's Lover* was declared obscene in this case; see also *Public Prosecutor* v. *Markondeyulu*, A.I.R. 1918 Mad. 1195 where a fifteenth century classic was to be judged according to the effect on ordinary people rather than scholars.

165. *Emperor* v. *Harnam Das* A.I.R. 1947 Lah. 383; see also *Ramamurthy* v. *State of Mysore* (1954) Cr. L.J. 1622 that education about sex on scientific lines was proper but that the journal *Kama Kala* was not connected with such education. See also *State* v. *Thakur Prashad* A.I R. 1959 All. 49 on whether a book called *Asli Kokshastra* was a scientific explanation of sex. A similar view was taken of a journal in *State* v. *Sukanta Haldar* (1952) Cr. L.J. 575.

166. This is made clear in *Ranjit Udeshi* v. *State of Maharashtra* A.I.R. 1965 S.C. 881 at pr. 9 p. 886 (while discussing medical treatises). But it obviously does not apply where the publication is not really a medical or scientific one: *State* v. *Thakur Prashad* A.I.R. 1959 All. 49 at pr. 17 p. 52; *Sukanta Haldar* v. *State*, A I.R. 1952 Cal. 214 at pr. 10 p. 215; Note the reliance on the experts in *Ramamurthy* v. *State of Mysore* A I.R. 1954 Mys. 164 at pr. 2 p. 165.

167. *Sukanta Haldar* v. *State* (1959) 1 Cal. 678; *supra* note 166.
168. See *Emp.* v. *Parashram* (1895) 20 Bom. 193; *Sree Ram Saksena* v. *Emp.* (1940) 1 Cal. 581; *Sukanta Haldar* v. *State* A.I.R. 1952 Cal. 214 and *State* v. *Thakur Prashad* A.I.R. 1959 All. 49 and the discussion on this in A. Sarkar: *The Law and Obscenity* (1967) 14-16.
169. Thus the literary eminence of an author may be irrelevant. *Public Prosecutor* v. *Markondeyulu* A.I.R. 1918 Mad. 1195. That being the case there is no difference in the approach of the court in respect of literary works and a nondescript account of sex in books like *Finding in Fire, The Dark Urge, The Shame of Mary Quinn* which were found to be obscene in *C.P. Prim* v. *State* A.I.R. 1961 Cal. 177. Superimposed in works of literature seems to be the condition that such works must be socially useful. In *Kailashandra Acharjya* v. *Emp.* (1932) 60 Cal. 201 where the sexual adventures of Rameshdar were not seen as serving any social purpose. The "social purpose" approach would have a far-reaching effect. At least the Supreme Court in *Chandrakant* v. *State of Maharashtra* A.I.R. 1970 S.C. 1390 was not prepared to declare a low-key story of this nature obscene where there was an allusion to sex but the book served no useful social purpose.
170. *Ranjit Udeshi* v. *State of Maharashtra supra* note 164.
171. Sometimes this is implicit. *In re Pandurangam* (1953) 1 M.L.J. 144 appears to work on the assumption that a book called *Kama Leelai* showing postures of intercourse must be bad. The definition of obscenity seems to have been copied from English sources and the reasoning of the court is not clear. For explicit statements see the cases cited in respect of the effect on children *infra* note 172.
172. *C.T. Prim* v. *State* A.I.R. 1961 Cal. 177 at pr. 8 p. 179; *Durlap Singh* v. *State* (1971) 73 P.L.R. 113; *Ramamurthy* v. *State of Mysore* A.I.R. 1954 Mys. 164 at pr. 6 pp. 165-6; *In re Chandrasekharan* (1957) 2 M.L.J. 559 at 567. Note also Justice Mitter's emphasis on the young in *Kailash Chandra* v. *Emp.* A.I.R. 1932 Cal. 651 at 654.
173. The Young Persons (Harmful Publications) Act, 1956.
174. S. 293, Indian Penal Code, 1860.
175. *Ranjit Udeshi* v. *State of Maharashtra supra* note 164 at pr. 7 p. 885.
176. See Article 19(2) of the Constitution of India.
177. *Ranjit Udeshi's* case (*supra* note 164) at pr. 22 p. 889.
178. *Ibid.*, at pr. 8 p. 885.
179. *Ibid.*, at pr. 21 p. 888-89.
180. *Kailash Chandra* v. *Emperor* A.I.R. 1932 Cal. 651 at pr. 651 (per Justice Sack) p. 654 (per Justice Mitter); *Ramamurti* v. *State of Mysore* A.I.R. 1954 Mys. 164.
181. *Ranjit Udeshi* v. *State of Maharashtra* A.I.R. 1965 S.C. 881 at pr. 10 p. 886; see also *E.* v. *Indramani* (1881) 3 All. 837; *Public Prosecutor* v. *Markondeyulu* A.I.R. 1918 Mad. 1195; *State* v. *Thakur Prashad*

A.I.R. 1959 All. 49; *C.T. Prim* v. *State* A.I.R. 1961 Cal. 177 (where pornographic stories were alleged to be sociological—see pr. 12 p. 180).

182. *Public Prosecutor* v. *Markondeyulu* A.I.R. 1918 Mad. 1195.

183. *Emp*. v. *Harnam* Das. A.I.R. 1947 Lah. 383 (involving a book to give advise about sex to married folk).

184. A.I.R. 1986 S.C. 967 (Justice Sen for Justice Pathak and himself).

185. *Ibid*. pr. 23 p. 977 quoting Cochburn C.J. in *R* v. *Hicklin* (1868) 3 QB 360.

186. *Ibid*. pr. 23-4 p. 976 (quoting *Ranjit Udeshi* v. *State of Maharashtra* A.I.R. 1965 S.C. 881); prs. 25-6 pp. 979-80 citing *Kakodar* v. *State of Maharashtra* A.I.R. 1970 S.C. 1390); also pr. 27 pp. 979-80, pr. 34 p. 984.

187. *Ibid*., prs. 8-14 pp. 969-72; and esp. pr. 34 p. 984.

188. *Ibid*. pr. 34 pp. 982-3.

189. *Ibid*. pr. 27 pp. 979-80; (and its difficulty in explaining the result in the *Lady Chatterly's Lover* case).

190. *Ibid*. pr. 34 pp. 982-4 even though the court disclaims (it is submitted wrongly) that it is deviating from earlier rulings (pr. 27 pp. 979-80). Perhaps, it followed this course of action because an open agreement would have required the constitution of a larger bench to reconsider the issue. Inroads into these earlier judgments were also made in *Miss Sadhna* v. *State* (*Delhi Administration*) (1981) XIX. Delhi Law Times 210 at 212 suggesting that *Udeshi's* case (*supra*) does not apply to cabarets or where the obscene exhibition (material) does not cause annoyance.

191. S. 99A Criminal Procedure Code, 1898. Under S. 99B the High Court may set aside the forfeiture—now see Ss. 95-96 Criminal Procedure Code, 1973.

192. S. 108 Criminal Procedure Code, 1898. The maximum time for which this surety can be entered is six months.

193. S. 20 Post Office Act, 1898.

194. S. 23 Post Office Act, 1898.

195. S. 11 Customs Act, 1962.

196. Ss. 111 and 113 of the Customs Act, 1962.

197. *Jag Narain Lal* v. *Emp*. A.I.R. 1928 Pat. 649. This involved an advertisement of a publication of the *Lok Shastra* and advertised as containing "coloured pictures (photos) of 84 postures (*avan*) of men and women with interesting descriptions of these".

198. The Drug and Magic Remedies (Objectionable Advertisements) Act, 1954. Note that the State of Punjab has a special statute about indecent advertisements; see Punjab Suppression of Indecent Advertisement Act (7 of) 1941.

199. *Hamdard Dawa Khana* v. *Union of India* A.I.R. 1960 S.C. 554.

200. Under S. 3(1) of the Cinematograph Act, 1952 a Board is created

with a chairman, five full-time and six part-time members—at least three of the latter being chosen from the film industry. There is an elaborate procedure for the films to be examined by the Board and—on application—by a Revision Committee (Ss. 4 and 5). There is a right of appeal to an appellate board (S. 5) and some limited powers of revision in the government (S. 6).

201. S. 5B of the Cinematograph Act merely echoes the same grounds of restrictions on films as those which are enumerated in Article 19(2) as permissible areas of restriction on the freedoms of speech and expression—namely, security of state, friendly relations with States, public order, decency or morality, defamation, contempt of court or the likelihood of the incitement to the commission of an offence.

202. This list of governmental directions has been paraphrased from the information cited by Chief Justice Hidayatullah in *K.A. Abbas* v. *Union of India* A.I.R. 1971 S.C. 481 at pr. 14 pp. 487-8.

203. *The Report of the Enquiry Committee on Film Censorship* (1969). For further literature on this see Bruce M. Boyd: "Film Censorship in India: A reasonable restriction of Freedom of Speech and Expression" (1972) 14 *J.I.L.I.* 501; V. Kesavan Kutty: "Film Censorship: Need for Radical Change" (1980) IV *Cochin Univ. L.R.* 377; see generally P. Shah: *The Indian Film* (1950); E. Barnouw and S. Krishnaswamy: *Indian Film* (1963).

204. *K.A. Abbas* v. *Union of India* A.I.R. 1971 S.C. at prs. 2-3 pp. 494-5.

205. *Ibid.*, at pr. 45 p. 495.

206. *Ibid.*, at pr. 54 p. 499 relying at pr. 50 pp. 497-8 on the fact that the government's committee on censorship (*supra* note 185) used the obscenity guidelines laid down by the Supreme Court.

207. *Raj Kapoor* v. *State* (*Delhi Administration*) (1980) 1 S.C.C. 528; *Raj Kapoor* v. *Laxmon* (1980) 2 S.C.C. 175.

208. S. 79 of the Indian Penal Code, 1860 provides a defence to anyone who commits an act justified by law or where he believes in good faith to be justified by law. The case with which this litigation started may suggest a need for procedural limitations being imposed restraining any individual from initiating such litigation.

209. See the cases cited *supra* note 169.

210. *Ranjit Udeshi's* case (*supra* note 164).

211. *Report of the Press Commission* (1952-54) Chapter XX which concentrates on the public order offences, defamation and contempt of court.

212. Thus the unspecified limit to the fines and three months maximum imprisonment in the 1860 Code were raised to limits of Rs. 2000 (fine) and two years (imprisonment) in 1969.

213. See Rajya Sabha: Joint Committee on the Indian Penal Code (Amendment Bill), 1963; Evidence (1967), which contains a wide

range of evidence from eminent lawyers, media men, actors and others.

214. For the debates on the Indian Penal Code Amendment Bills (1963 and 1967) see (1967) 62 Rajya Sabha Debates (hereafter R.S.D.) 2183-2228; 4263-87; 6289-90; (1968) 14 Lok Sabha Debates (hereafter L.S.D.) (IVth Series) 892; 16 L.S.D. (IVth Series) 274-87; see also Lok Sabha Report of the Select Committee on the Indian Penal Code (Amendment) Bill, 1967 presented 1 May, 1967.

215. Law Commission: *Forty Second Report on the Indian Penal Code* (1971) pr. 14. 13 p. 225.

216. Law Commission (*supra* note 215) pr. 14. 13 p. 225.

217. See *Ranjit Udeshi* (supra note 164) at pr. 3 p. 884.

218. English precedent would suggest that expert evidence cannot decide either what is obscene or be tendered in respect of the effect of obscenity on the public at large: see *R.* v. *Anderson* (1971) 3 W.L.R. 939; *R.* v. *Staniforth* and *R.* v. *Jordan* (1976) 2 All. E.R. 714; *Att. Gen. General Reference* (*No. 3 of*) *1977* (1978) 3 All. E.R. 1166.

219. There is a very limited literature on this subject. Apart from the literature on film censorship (*supra* note 20?) see J.N. Mallick; *The Law of Obscenity in India* (1966); A.K. Sarkar: *The Law and Obscenity* (1967); A Shah (ed.): *Roots of Obscenity* (1968); A.K. Sarkar: "Literature and Obscenity" (1965) 67 *Bom L.R. Jnl.* 121; C. Ranga Ratham: "Obscene posters, literature and publicities" (1965) 1 *M.L.J. Jnl.* 17; A.N. Grover: *The Law of Obscenity and Freedom of Expression* (1968); V.D. Sharma: "The Law relating to obscene publications in India" (1973) 22 *I.C L.Q.* 632; N. Raju Sekhar: "Law of Obscenity in India" (1969) *Lawyer* 117; P.S. Chaudhri: "Test of obscenity in *Ranjit Udeshi's* case" A.I.R. 1969 Jnl. 103; R.K. Raizada: "Khajuraho in the dollar market" (1971) *J.I.L.I.* 208; R.D. Garg: "Many facets of Obscenity" (1970-71) *A.L.R.* 72; K.C. Joshi: "The need for curbing obscenity" (1970-1) A.L.R. 97. Note also the editorial in (1969-70) 75 *C.W.N.* 139; (1975-76) 80 *C.W.N.* 29; (1976-77) 81 *C.W.N.* 35. The bulk of the material is to be found in works on criminal law: H.S. Gour: *Penal Law of India* (1972 edn.) II, 1994-2028; J. Nelson's: *Penal Law of India* (1970 edn.), 1329-42; see also Ratan Lal: *Law of Crimes* (1967 edn.) 221-222.

220. B.R. Ambedkar, Speech, (1948) VII *C.A.D.* 38-9.

221. Report of the Indian Law Institute to the Press Council of India on the Bihar Bill (August, 1982). I am grateful to the late Dr. S.N. Jain, the Director of the Institute for a copy.

222. The Bihar Bill created an opportunity to expose how the government in India can design the law to harass the Press. When the Bill was passed in Bihar's lower house, the latter was adjourned *sine die* (*Indian Express* 1 August, 1982) 'bedlam' broke loose (*Statesman*, 1 August 1982). Its passage through the upper house created

an 'uproar' (*Statesmen*, 4 August 1982). Much later it was said that Chief Minister Mishra had misled party legislators (see *Statesman*, 9 September 1982) and a special session was demanded (*Hindustan Times*, 19 September 1982). On his part Mishra thought the controversy unnecessary (*Amrit Bazar Patrika*, 6 August 1982) issued huge one page explanatory advertisements in several national papers (*e.g. Patriot*, 6 September 1982; *National Herald*, 4 September 1982; *Patriot*, 3 September 1982; *Times of India*, 6 September 1982). Mishra alleged that he would withdraw the Bill if the Press could come up with a code of ethics (*Patriot* and *National Herald*, 13 September 1982) and that the editors were wrong about the Bill (*Indian Express*, 15 August 1982). Justices Chowdhry and Sharma of Patna High Court refused to intervene on the constitutionality of the Bill (*Times of India*, 10 August 1982) while the editors wanted to move the Supreme Court (*Indian Express*, 11 August 1982). Meanwhile, an interim order was obtained from the Supreme Court on the comparable Tamil Nadu Act (*Statesman*, 22 August 1982) with an increasing interest by various people to intervene in the case (*Northern India Patrika*, 18 September 1982). Meanwhile, a Lok Sabha debate was initially not allowed (*Indian Express*, 6 August 1982). The Home Minister initially defended the Bill (*Indian Express*, 6 August 1982). There had been walk-outs of the Lok Sabha (*Indian Express*, 4 August 1982). Later on, assurance was given that the Bill would be scrutinized (*National Herald*, 10 August 1982). The Bill was likened to the Emergency (*Hindustan Times*, 10 August, 1982) and attacked bitterly (*Times of India*, 10 August 1982). The Press boycotted the houses of Parliament (*Indian Express*, 11 August 1982) and the opposition walked out (*Times of India*, 11 August 1982). Soon the Centre agreed to give proper consideration to the Bill (*Times of India*, 17 August 1982) and the Bill was remitted to the Centre (*Indian Express*, 18 August 1982) which was to review it (*Hindustan Times*, 20 August 1982). The relevant Minster agreed to meet representatives (*Indian Express*, 9 September 1982) and requested that all the alleged problems with the Bill be listed (*Indian Express*, 15 September 1982).

Responding to this agitation the Press Council initiated an inquiry *suo motu* (*Patriot*, 2 August 1982). After consultation with the Indian Law Institute, it published its own views (*Hindustan Times*, 20 August 1982) see also views of Kamath (*Sunday Express*, 7 November 1982) and asked the Bihar Government to appear before it (*Indian Express*, 29 August, 1982); *Amrit Bazar Patrika*, 12 September 1982). Nothing really came out of this initiative except that some anti-regime members in the Press Council were able to use the Press Council to momentarily embarrass the Government.

The Bihar Bill stimulated controversy about the Tamil Nadu Act which was agitated against (*Indian Express*, 18 September 1982).

There was a suggestion that Tamil Nadu would withdraw the Bill (*Statesman*, 14 September 1982). West Bengal (see *Patriot*, 3 September 1982) reacted strongly to the agitation. Rajasthan ruled out the possibility of such a Bill (*Hindustan Times*, 8 September 1982). It was alleged that the Orissa Bill was worse than the Bihar (*Times of India*, 30 August 1982) that its legality was doubtful (*Indian Express*, 2 September 1982) but that it had never been enforced in Orissa (*Indian Express*, 15 August 1982). As regards these Acts and the Bill, the nub of the attack was that the Bill made the executive the judge (*Indian Express*, 6 August 1982). As it happens that legal situation was perpetuated by a second Bill amending the Criminal Procedure Code (see *Statesman*, 20 August 1982). Note the Indian Law Institute's report to the Press Council had to be revised, when the true facts of the Bill came out. Some of the arbitrariness of the Bill was a matter of publicity rather than truth. I am indebted to the Dr. S.N. Jain, former Director of the Law Institute for information about the revised opinion.

The press had drawn up its own plans. The Editors Guild of India team including S. Sahay, K.R. Malkhan, Arun Shourie and K. Narendra met the Chief Minister of Bihar (*Indian Express*, 9 August 1982) only to be told by the Chief Minister a few days later that the editors were preaching mischief (*Indian Express*, 15 August 1982). Meanwhile, the press cautioned against the need to over-agitate (*Hindustan Times*, 16 September 1982). Perhaps, this was precisely what was in the mind of the Prime Minister (Mrs. Indira Gandhi) who denounced the stir (*Hindustan Times*, 2 September 1982), hinted at changes but took the view that the Bill did not destroy the press (*Indian Express* and *National Herald*, 2 September 1982). This obviously did not convince some in her party (*Indian Express*, 10 September 1982) and elicited a derogatory comment about the Prime Minister's relationship with the Press (*Financial Express*, 2 September 1982) and a rebuke from former Prime Minister Desai that Mrs. Gandhi was trying to shift the blame (*Statesman*, 12 September 1982). There was no doubt that she was trying to shift the focus from the Bill to the agitation generated by it.

The real attack on the Bill came in the form of what was really a popular uprising against the Bill. There was widespread agitation (*Statesman*, 11 August 1982). The Bhartiya Janata Party condemned the Bill in a memorandum to the President (*Indian Express*, 16 September 1982). They were joined by the lawyers (*Indian Express*, 9 September 1982), the remonstrations of ex-Chief Justice of India, J.C. Shah (*Times of India*, 12 September 1982), the vocal opposition of all the journalists and news agencies (*Statesman*, 11 August 1982), Bombay journalists (*Times of India*, 17 August 1982), other trade unions *e.g.* CITU (*Indian Express*, 13 August 1982). There were rallies in Bhopal (*Indian Express*, 30 August 1982) and Dhanbad

(*Times of India*, 24 August 1982). President Zail Singh's visit to Jaipur was boycotted by journalists (*Indian Express*, 1 September 1982) who also boycotted official functions (*Hindustan Times*, 29 August 1982). This was also true of Bhopal where Ministers' meetings were boycotted (*Hindustan Times*, 29 August 1982). Question hour in the Kerala Legislature was boycotted by journalists (*Times of India*, 21 August 1982). There was a *dharna* (sit in) by journalists in Bihar (*Times of India*, 13 August 1982). Resident doctors and young scientists opposed the Bill (*Indian Express*, 21 August 1982) and there were many seminars (*e.g. Hindustan Times*, 9 August 1982). International concern was expressed from London (*Indian Express*, 13 August 1984) Brussels and Kathmandu (*Indian Express*, 2 September 1982). It was successfully reported that there was widespread opposition (*Statesman*, 24 August 1982) even amidst news of violence (*Times of India*, 24 August 1982) and the blocade of streets by youth (*Times of India*, 25 August 1982) 2000 had filed letters before the President (*Times of India*, 2 September 1982). On one day it was reported that there were no newspapers (*Times of India*, 5 September 1982).

The opposition was determined to see that the stir continued (*Hindustan Times*, 19 September 1982).

The press had kept up the attack in a series of leaders *e.g. Statesman*: "Curbing the Prees" 2 August 1982; *Indian Express*: "Bihar's Black Bill" 3 August 1982; *Hindustan Times*: "The Last Resort" 3 August 1982; *Times of India*: "Curbing the Press" 4 August 1982; *Statesman* "Backdoor Methods" 11 August 1982; "Rights of the Press" 22 August 1982; *Economic Times*: "Obnoxious Bill" 12 August 1982; *National Herald* "Grain or Chaff" 26 August 1982. There were also several articles by various journalists including N. Eziekel and Rashid Talib.

The tail-end to the story is a comment on Mrs. Gandhi. She did nothing. The Bill quietly lapsed a year later. Chief Minister Mishra eventually resigned. But the occasion was not used for a thorough examination of the relationship between the press and the Government in the backdrop of tough law and order legislation. What was averted was the almost certain harassment of Bihar journalists at the hands of a Chief Minister whose scrupulousness could hardly be deemed to be above question.

8

PROTECTING PRIVACY

I

In one sense, there is no case to answer. Privacy can be made to include anything and everything. Invented as a legal concept to ponder over an intellectual concern rather than resolve a legal problem, there is some controversy as to whether privacy constitutes a concrete identifiable right or whether it is an otherwise 'meaningless' short-hand term to describe an aggregate of rights. For political and other reasons, English legislators and American judges have not been able to identify a concrete set of privacy rights. The problem is not just political. Conceptually, the notion of privacy represents all the negative and positive rights of the individual. To that extent, like the concept of liberty, it is an exercise in 'persuasive definition'.[1] It persuades more than it defines.

Although a retired Supreme Court judge has recently sought to espouse the cause of the "right to be left alone",[2] the right to privacy has not been an area of major concern in India. In 1964,[3] some attention was diverted to this area in a rather startling case where the police started paying domiciliary visits to a person at night. While all the judges were agreed that such domiciliary visits were unconstitutional, only a minority took the view that the privacy of an individual was part of th 'personal liberty' protected by the Constitution and could not be "deprived without procedure established by law".[4]

Ten years later, the Supreme Court was called upon to consider the surveillance power of the police.[5] This time the Supreme Court gave rather more serious attention to the concept of "privacy" and treated it as not just part of the limited right to "personal liberty" but took the view that "many of the fundamental rights of citizens can be described as contributing to the right of privacy". This judgment has been welcomed—as all good judgments should be.[6] But the Supreme Court has not really looked at the concept of "privacy" any further. Even in its constitutional context, it is not clear as to what "privacy" means and how far the right to privacy extends. So far, the concept of "privacy" has been used as a persuasive linguistic device. "Privacy" is a nice-sounding emotive phrase which persuades people that the Court is doing nice things. In any event, all this discussion on privacy has taken place in the somewhat limited area of restraining the government from interfering with the "privacy" of the individual.

In 1971, the Law Commission of India joined the privacy debate by suggesting the introduction of penal offences against unauthorised electronic and other eavesdropping devices and photography. However, it reserved the power of the State to violate these injunctions in the interests of catching criminals, administering justice and public order. These recommendations which offer a let-out to the only real potential offender (*viz.*, the State) were affirmed by the Press Commission of India in 1982. Anxious to legitimate the demands of the State, the Press Commission suggested that a government sponsored Council should act as an arbiter to privacy claims, whilst offering vague guidelines that private information may be revealed by the Press in the "public interest as distinct from news that may pander to prurient or morbid curiosity." Having said all this, the Commission confessed:

> Privacy is a very nebulous concept and criteria which may constitute its violation cannot be drawn up.[7]

Apart from determining the conditions under which government and others can cull information from an individual and publicise it, what exactly is privacy about? The law as it stands does not recognize the omnibus right to privacy. What the law does is simply to recognize separate rights which taken together may be said to constitute the right to privacy. These rights include—to follow a well known classification—the right to solitude and seclusion, disclosure of personal information about a person or representing him falsely in the eyes of the public and, finally, the appropriation of a person's name or likeness to the advantage of another.

Indian law—like English law—covers many aspects of this bundle of privacy rights. The right to solitude is protected, *inter alia*, through the torts of trespass and nuisance and the abuse of one's name, work and likeness is protected in part by the laws relating to passing off and copyright.[8]

Recently a bill was introduced to protect the right to privacy.[9] This Bill does not define privacy in a comprehensive way. The right against defamation and to confidentiality is not mentioned. Nor is the use or abuse of one's name. The privacy of a person is defined as the right to "preserve seclusion of himself, his family or his property from any other person".[10] A coach and horse can be run through the defences available against a suit for the invasion of one's privacy.[11] Consent and a legal justification are included—as, indeed, they must be. In addition, a person may plead that he did not invade another's privacy knowingly. There is not even a requirement that he should have acted in good faith. Mere lack of knowledge seems enough. The legitimate conduct of business serves as another defence. And, finally, a person may invade another's privacy to the extent to which it is reasonably necessary to comment in the public interest. This is a somewhat loosely drafted Bill. It does not protect many of the so-called privacy rights of a person. Nor does it deal with many of the things that affect the journalist.

II

Even though the concept of privacy may not have been treated as generally significant, the newspaper man in India has been affected by the laws relating to confidentiality and defamation.

Let us look first at the law relating to confidentiality. The law relating to confidentiality affects the journalist in two ways. On the one hand, the journalist can be called upon not to disclose confidential information. On the other hand, the journalist himself may have to plead the confidentiality of his sources if called upon to disclose them. The Indian law relating to confidentiality has not been adequately evolved. The only clear restraints are those which exist in respect of government documents. Some of these are found in official secrets legislation.[12] In addition to that the government can claim "Crown privilege" —as it has come to be called—for many of its documents if it is called upon to present them in Court.[13] All this is subject to the final decision of the Court which will decide if such a disclosure is in the public interest.[14] But the rest of the law on confidentiality is not really clear. Undoubtedly, a mixture of Common law and Equity can be used to restrain the publication of confidential information.[15] But the law restraining a journalist from disclosing confidential sources has not been completely evolved in India. Nor for that matter has Indian law seriously concerned itself with the converse situation where the journalist himself refuses to disclose his sources of information. There is no specific rule which gives professional exemption for journalists—of the kind that exists for lawyers[16] —in respect of informat on received in the course of their work. This may be a subject of further litigation if, and when, the law relating to confidentiality is further explored by Indian courts. It is possible that the law may be prepared to balance the claim of journalists against other claims in the public interest—including the claims of law courts. English law seems to be fairly clear that the general plea of confidentiality cannot be made in relation to investigations of a Commission of Inquiry investigating matters relating to espionage.[17] The Indian law relating to Commissions of Inquiry also contains provisions which can force a person to make disclosures.[18] In other matters, there is certainly a rule of evidence that a person —including a journalist—need not be made to disclose to a court more than what "a Court considers necessary in that particular case to the full understanding of the nature and effect of the statement, and of the circumstances under which it is made".[19] A more specific rule about disclosure seems to have been made by the Allahabad High Court in the area of criminal defamation. This case involved an allegation against the President of a local Anti-tuberculosis Society being accused of corruption and the misappropriation of funds. This case is also part of small newspaper rivalry. The defendant editor refused to disclose the name of his contributor. The Court did not force him to do so; but made the following observation:

> He (*i.e.* a journalist) also did not disclose the name of the writer and took shelter behind the spurious principle of journalistic ethics. Any principle which is devised by any group to defeat the ends of justice obviously cannot be accepted as ethical by any Court of law. If there is any such rule of etiquette, it is hardly better than the other maxim which prevails in the criminal world: "Honour amongst thieves". These rules also provide safety and success to groups engaged in particular law-breaking activities, but they are certainly against the interests of the community at large. The only conclusion that a Court can draw from such a conduct is that the publisher was in entire agreement with the writer and he was willing to take the full responsibility for the publication and face the consequences himself. . . . The courts in India have, in my view, taken too lenient a view of offences of this type.[20]

This judgment is highly unsatisfactory for various reasons even if the facts of the instant case before the Court were such that a stern rebuke of this nature was necessary. The Court did not seriously consider whether a disclosure could have been forced. Clearly, this was one of the factors the judge took into account while affirming the sentence of imprisonment. But many important issues were obscured by this grand denunciation of journalistic ethics. The Indian Penal Code itself expects men in public life to be the subject of comment.[21] Sometimes this has to be done after a considerable amount of investigative journalism and the obtaining of evidence in confidence. Many of these confidences have to be respected. On the other hand, there is a case for saying that where a journalist makes a serious charge against someone, he should normally not be allowed to shelter behind a plea of confidentiality. These are two points of views that need to be reconciled. The court made no attempt to do so. The problem is that Indian courts have not really looked very seriously at the problem of confidentiality as a whole. Confidentiality is both an intrusion into an individual's life as well as part of the investigative cloak of a journalist. Perhaps, Indian judges feel a little wary about exploring this area. They might feel—as the Allahabad High Court felt—that this would become yet another device that would be ruthlessly used by those who stand to gain from it.

The law relating to defamation represents both a playground and a pitfall for the newspaper. For those interested in publicity, a court case is a vehicle for further and greater publicity. Many issues which would otherwise have lain fallow get drawn into the excitement of publicity as a result of the very litigation which is intended to stop this publicity. At the same time, an involvement in litigation can itself be an enervating experience resulting, amongst other things, in the possibility of heavy damages, a fine or even imprisonment.

The Indian law of defamation comes from two sources. The civil law of defamation comes from the Common law and has been incorporated in India as part of justice, equity and good conscience.[22] The criminal law of defamation is part of the Indian Penal Code.[23] Its origins can be traced at least as far back as Macaulay. Macaulay took the view that a criminal law of defamation should not just be limited to where there was a breach of peace, and that truth should be a defence to a prosecution so that honest men could live in the security that it would be an offence for "one rogue to speak the truth about another rogue under the influence of passions excited in the course of a quarrel".[24] Aware that India was a country of considerable diversity, Macaulay also expressed the anxiety that defamation in India could mean many things to many people:

> We have thought it necessary, under the peculiar circumstances of this country, to lay down for the guidance of the courts a rule which if we legislate for a population among whom there was a uniform standard of morality, and honour, might appear superfluous. India is inhabited by races which differ widely from each other in manners, tastes and religious opinions. Practices which are regarded as innocent by one large portion of society, excite the horror of another large portion. A Hindoo would be driven to despair, if he knew that he was believed by persons of his own race to have done something, which a Christian or Mussalman would consider to be as indifferent or as laudable. Where such diversities of opinion exist that part of the law which is intended to prevent pain arising from opinion ought to be sufficiently flexible, to deal with othre diversities. We have, therefore, directed the judge not to decide the question whether an imputation be or be not defamatory by reference to any particular standard, however correct of honour, of morality, or of taste; but to extend an impartial protection to opinions which he regards as erroneous, and to feelings with which he has no sympathy.[25]

Feelings of imperial condescension apart, Macaulay seems to have both misjudged the nature of what might be called the morality of litigation as well as the long term pathology of litigation that would grow out of both the civil and criminal law of defamation. Litigation produces its own morality. People litigate for all kinds of reasons and to obtain all kinds of advantages. In particular, litigation in defamation cases is an exciting social game. It is a way in which people embarrass each other, square up with each other, intimidate one another and publicly ventilate their discomforts and irritation. This is not peculiar to India. Not surprisingly, the Indian litigants have taken to the defamation provisions with a ruthless alacrity.

We know that Hicky's Gazette was killed as a result of ruinous litigation. By the time the Indian Penal Code had been enacted in 1860 a lively civil and criminal litigation had already evolved. Many matters became the subject of civil litigation suits. The use of mere abusive language immediately brought the abused person to continue the quarrel in court.[26] A person asked for his railway ticket because it was apprehended that he might be travelling without one decided to take the matter into court.[27] A resolution by a trust that future transactions with a person would not be possible resulted in a successful defamation.[28] Letters to administrative officials pleading for the removal of a person became the subject of libel litigation.[29] Litigation ensued on the liability of judges,[30] parties[31] and witnesses[32] in respect of litigation in court. In other words, defamation suits were used to superimpose further litigation on existing litigation that was pending in court. The fact that a report was made to the police[33] became the subject of litigation as did pleadings in court.[34] Dismissed civil servants used the law of defamation to vindicate themselves.[35] All this is not peculiar to India. Litigants and their lawyers find as many avenues against their opponents as possible. At the turn of this century, that Indian litigants and lawyers should similarly go 'forum shopping' as well is not surprising. Much of this litigation dealt with some typically Indian problems as well. Imputations of a lack of chastity became the subject of litigation. That is unexceptional. But some of the litigation was devoted to considering the *locus standi* of the relatives on behalf of the maligned ladies.[36] Brothers felt that this is a cause that they must fight on their sisters' behalf.[37] The burning of an effigy gave rise to a defamation suit.[38] A large number of defamation suits have concerned themselves with questions of caste. A plaintiff was entitled to recover damages where he was declared an outcaste without being heard. The Court felt that the imputation had been made without due care and attention.[39] The case of a widow excommunicated by the head of her caste was treated differently. Excommunication was a prerogative of the caste and the head was merely doing his duty.[40] A false declaration that a person has been excommunicated is certainly defamatory,[41] as is the imputation of a wrong caste to a person or the person he has married.[42] Some of these disputes that have excited the defamation jurisdiction have arisen out of political differences,[43] the demands of the National movement for independence,[44] the desire of police officers to vindicate themselves.[45] Some have also been the product of electoral quarrels,[46] group fights[47] or personal differences. Some of these involve serious questions of defamation. Others simply use the law of defamation as a free wheeling device. A recent example illustrates this well. In one case,[48] an irate husband whose wife had left him and gone to stay with her brother, sent the brother a set of cheap bangles, and a tuft of hair. Later he threatened to beat him up. The brother responded with a defamation suit. The Court seems to have given this matter a very patient hearing both at the trial and appeal stage. The suit failed not just on the general basis that the sending of the tuft of hair was not necessarily insulting to the plaintiff but also on the technical ground that no such allegations were made in the plaint. May be, at the end of the day, even if the brother lost his case, he won his little counter-campaign.

It is important to note that these are not newspaper cases. They are all, by and large, civil cases. But the use of the criminal jurisdiction for all these matters is equally rich.[49] These cases merely illustrate that much of the law is what litigation makes it to be. Litigation determines the kind of use that is made of the law and virtually transforms its meaning and use in terms of its existence as social reality.

When the Press Commission came to consider the law of defamation in 1952-4, it asked itself a few routine questions, suggested that the law of criminal defamation should not be limited to where there was just a breach of peace,[50] and further took the view that unintentional defamation should not be a ground for liability.[51] It did not ask the important questions: who uses the law of defamation and why? Or, the further question: whom does the law of defamation affect adversely? Its major concern seemed to be to provide some kind of protection for civil servants. Here, the Commission, too, was concerned with the pathology of litigation and non-litigation. The crucial question became: how can this group of people (i.e, civil servants) use the defamation provisions more effectively to protect themselves in the public interest.' The Commission said:

> During the course of the evidence, many of the State governments have stressed the desirability of amending the law of defamation particularly in its application to public officers and Government servants. They have urged that many newspapers, particularly those which indulge in yellow journalism, make reckless allegations against public officials and Government servants, very often merely for the purpose of indulging in sensationalism and thus attracting more circulation. These officers find it extremely inconvenient and often very expensive to launch either a civil suit or a criminal prosecution particularly because of the delay involved in the conduct of these cases. When they do file such a suit or prosecution they are subjected to cross-examination which is aimed at throwing more mud on the reputation of these persons, and even if there is no truth in the allegations which are suggested in the cross-examination, some of the mud sticks. They are, therefore, extremely reluctant to take any legal steps for obtaining redress. Even if they are able to bring home the charge to the accused, he often tenders an apology when it begins to appear that there is no way of escaping conviction, and thus the matter is either compromized or the accused gets away with a nominal sentence or fine. The State governments have, therefore, stressed the desirability of amending the law in such a way as to enable the public servants to obtain relief without the handicaps involved in the present procedure.[52]

The Commission took the view that it was looking "at the problem not from the point of view of giving a favoured treatment to public servants but from the point of view of (the) public interest".[53] A minority in the Commission took the view that the fears of the majority were greatly exaggerated.[54] They also questioned the wisdom of the proposal that such cases should be subject to a special enabling procedure so that a magistrate can take cognizance of such alleged defamations "upon a complaint made in writing by some other public servant to whom he (*i.e.* the allegedly defamed public servant) is subordinate."[55] The Commission seems to have created a special law for civil servants which is, in some ways, analogous to the law of contempt. This law devises a special procedure initiated by bureaucrats to protect their colleagues from attack. Both the judiciary and the executive seem to have been given comparable protections—even if they vary in their extent and intensity.

The Commission also showed great awareness of the fact that a person who goes to the Court to complain about defamation often emerges more defamed even though he wins his suit.[56] The main reason for this lies in the availability of the right to an extended cross-examination of the complainant and plaintiff. This was particularly marked in criminal cases generally and in civil cases with respect to the quantum of damages. The Commission[57] took the view that the criminal law should be modified in a manner consistent with some rulings of courts of law[58] to the effect that such an extended cross-examination would not be permitted to show either that the person had no reputation or that it could not be lowered further.

The general strategy of the Commission appears to have been to check some of the abuses that flow from the litigation and non-litigation of defamation cases. But the view of the Press Commission can hardly be said to be balanced. It has not considered the public interest in ensuring that public officers are subjected to scrutiny and that public affairs are discussed at length. In fact, these matters from specific defences in the Penal Code itself.[59] American law seems to go further and suggests that those in public office should be quite used and prepared for a greater deal of criticism and scrutiny.[60] To provide lightning remedies for public servants and generally to limit the cross-examination of complainants seems to ignore the fact that many of the things that are said of these officials (or others) may well be said in good faith. Such restraints create an atmosphere in which a person accused of defamation may feel that some of the means by which he can fight back and expose the real reason for a defamation suit have been taken away. The general tone of the report suggests the assumption that most journalists are rightly accused of defamation and it is all really a question of how they can be booked, in as quick and undramatic a manner as possible. The major difficulty with the report is that it has not really concerned itself with how the law of defamation actually affects the press.

A litigant faced with the problem of pursuing a defamation claim in India is immediately faced with the problem of "forum shopping." Should he prosecute in criminal defamation? Or, should he file a suit in civil defamation? Although there is the technical right to pursue both remedies, some practical problems may arise in pursuing both remedies simultaneously.[61] But a person accused of adultery can certainly pursue these remedies one after the other.[62] A judgment from Calcutta suggests that a solicitor may negotiate damages in a defamation matter against a newspaper while a criminal suit is pending.[63] This would add greater strength to the allegedly defamed person and improve his bargaining position greatly. Newspapers would be placed under pressure to apologize, settle, give in or re-group. Where the civil action follows the criminal, the damages awarded in the civil case may be mitigated because of the conviction in the criminal case.[64] All this does create some room for manoeuvre as well. Thus it has been suggested that in at least one case the fact that the defamed person withdrew his criminal complaint after an apology was tendered may have reduced the quantum of damages.[65] Whatever the bargaining devices, there is no doubt that the criminal remedy is undoubtedly cheaper and the more effective one. No court fee is required.[66] And the matter can be moved at a magisterial level without too much difficulty. So much so, at least one High Court took the view that although the defamed person "has his rights and is entitled to pursue both his remedies. . . . when he does pursue both his remedies in this way, and only after he has tried out his evidence by the cheaper method of a criminal prosecution, he launches the action for damages, the circumstances can be properly taken into account in deciding what are the damages which should be awarded to him in a civil action."[67]

This view has been strongly contested by at least one other High Court[68] which has taken the view that a defamed person should be able to pursue both remedies with equal vigour without setting off his gains in a civil action against his victory in the criminal case. Judicial decisions should not deprive him of his legal entitlement given to him by the law.

The advantages of a criminal action over civil action have been partly exaggerated. *Prima facie*, there is some truth in the fact that criminal suit is cheap and quick. But what happens when an organised litigant is rich, has waiting power and wants to cripple his opponent through litigation. Such a litigant would go for a civil action as K.M.D. Thackersay did when he got an award of Rs. 1,50,000 against *Blitz*.[69] Blitz survived the shock. But this must have made a dent in its budget which could not have been recompensed by any increase in circulation which might have accrued as a result of that weekly's involvement in this controversy. Having said all this, it is important to note the conclusions of some research[70] which shows that the damages award in the *Blitz* case was certainly exceptional and that the usual damages in a representative sample of cases between 1914 and 1970 have been low. Politicians fighting elections got Rs. 2,000 in 1925[71] and Rs. 6,000 in 1956.[72] The next on the list were policemen accused of corruption [Rs. 2,500 (1929),[73] Rs. 2,250 (1936)[74]], jailors accused of brutality [Rs. 2,000 (1927)[75]] and widows whose chastity was called in question [Rs. 2,0:0 (1959)[76]]. The rest of the figures are really low.[77] A civil action does, however, take place in a more respectable way before a higher court. Forum shopping in defamation cases in India is a question of economic resources and institutional skill. Cases in civil defamation continue. The popular belief that civil litigation in defamation cases have stopped is simply not true. Poor people are constrained to prefer a criminal complaint and hope for the best. The richer and more organized a person or group is, the greater the chance of playing both the civil and criminal litigation game; or indeed, for that matter both games. Newspaper men must also be ambidexterous. And because these games can themselves be reported, while the allegedly defamed person asks for further and better particulars, the newspaper can indulge in greater and better publicity. It becomes a moot question as to who really wins and who loses.

First let us turn towards civil defamation. There are some important differences between English and Indian law. The first of these differences does not affect the press directly. In India, slander is actionable *per se.* No special damage has to be proved. The Penal Code makes no distinction between the written word (libel) and the spoken word (slander).[78] This is based, in part, on Macaulay's assumption that—

> In general . . . a man would rather see in a newspaper a story discreditable to him which he had the means of refuting than know that such a story though not published was current in society.[79]

Newspapers are newspapers and are not really to be ignored with such alacrity. Anyhow, Indian courts have virtually consistently taken the view that all kinds of slander are actionable *per se.*[80] This has been argued on the basis that the Indian law has been incorporated on the basis of "justice, equity and good conscience", and that the abolition of the distinction between kinds of slander that is actionable *per se* and slander where proof of special damage is required is consistent with justice, equity and good conscience.[81] In England itself the law was amended so that at least slanderous imputation of chastity became actionable *per se.*[82] It was precisely on this question that the Calcutta High Court took the view that special damage would have to be proved in such cases.[83] The English judge who decided this case took the view that English law would be deemed to be useful unless it was proven not to be so. He felt that the easy availability of criminal defamation would form a corrective in all cases where special damage could not be shown. This judgment is quite strange. And, more so, because it seeks to impose the requirement of special damage in India in the area of imputations of unchastity in India. That such an imputation would affect a lady's reputation adversely is axiomatic. Indeed, at least the British immigration service think so to this day because in 1979 they conducted a physical examination of a woman at Heathrow airport on the assumption that an unmarried fiancee must be *virgo intacta.* Later an undisclosed sum was paid as compensation. Indian law does not require proof of special damage before cases of slander can be allowed to proceed. This is not significant for newspapers. It may mean, however, that the catchment of cases in the docket of the Court will increase and extend greatly to trivial complaints.

Another distinction between Indian and English law was evolved which does affect the newspapers. This is in the area of unintentional defamation. The classic situation features a fictitious story about a person called Artemus Jones, which would certainly have been defamatory if Artemus Jones had existed. Well, as it happens, Artemus Jones did exist and was situated in circumstances analogous to the ones described in the newspaper. Under English law, the full rigour of the law of defamation visited the newspaper which printed this story—even though this has been modified by statute in such cases where the newspaper acted *bona fide.*[84] In India, the wisdom of this rule was doubted in a case where inadvertent statements were made about a lawyer. The Madras High Court was inclined to reject the English view in the *Jones* case on the ground that the latter was not consistent with justice, equity and good conscience—the classic formula which forms the basis on which the very foundation of the law of torts in India depends.[85] This case may have been complicated more by the fact that the lawyer wanted his damages increased to Rs. 2,000 (from Rs. 100). They were reduced to Rs. 10 because the court felt that he should have ignored the *peccadillo* against him. However, in a more recent case from Madras,[86] the *Dhinamalar* paper was held not to be liable where they published a story about opium being exported as incense sticks, which was attributed to the plaintiff. The Court was influenced by the fact that the newspaper had not only expressed its regret but also published a correction. These were both hard cases. What Indian courts have not clarified is the extent to which newspapers can plead unintentional defamation. All this borders on the question of good faith and the extent of a newspaper's responsibilities to avoid such unintentional defamation. There is a vast difference between publishing an innocent fictitious story and a fictitious story which consecrates an unverified rumour.

One more general point needs to be made before we go to examine civil and criminal cases on defamation. The press have no special privileges in India. In a famous case involving gross comments on the administration of criminal justice in India, the Privy Council made a classic statement in the *Burma Critic* case which has been quoted often.[87] Here it was made clear that there was a "... time worn fallacy that some kind of privilege attaches to the profession of the Press as distinguished from members of the public. The freedom of the journalist is an ordinary part of the freedom of the subject, and to whatever length the subject in general may go, so also may the journalist, his privilege is no higher. The responsibilities which attach to this power in the dissemination of printed matter may, and in the case of a conscientious journalist do, make him more careful; but the range of his criticisms or his comments, is as wide as, and no wider than that of the subject. No privilege attaches to his position."

All this obscures rather than clarifies the issues. There is no doubt that the press is not a public institution. Its ownership patterns, methods of accountability, channels of promoting equal access to all members of the public and its working pathology are such that it must be treated as a private group.[88] But it performs certain functions which are important to the public. There is, therefore, some kind of public interest in ensuring that the press performs these functions. Even if the press is treated on par with an individual—as it must inevitably be—it is a very different kind of individual. It does very different things. The effect of the statement of the Privy Council in the *Burma Critic* case[89] has been to perpetuate a general idea creating a hostility towards the press. The press is constantly reminded of its ordinary status[90] but also of its great power.[91] Editors are told that they should have a higher responsibility.[92] All this begins to represent a polar attitude which affects the interpretation of the law of defamation in a way that pays insufficient attention to the needs of the press to perform the functions which it seeks to perform in the public interest. For the press needs to investigate, inform, interest and comment; and also permit others to do so. That it does not always do so is another matter. The real question is whether the law should encourage it *when it does perform these functions.* The problem is not one of according the press special privileges. It is simply one of being prepared to balance the public interest in such a way that the press can deliver some of the goods that the public expects of them. Sometimes, the courts have been prepared to do this. One High Court stressed the role of an editor as an agent of the people in allowing people to ventilate their grievances, counteract complacency and promote the public interest. The Court felt that this should be borne in mind while determining the actual liability of the press.[93] Implicit in all this seems the view that the problems of the press need to be discussed as a matter of law and not just as an act of mercy in determining the sentence or fixing the quantum of damages. The crux of this issue pertains to the extent to which courts are willing to be sensitive to the demands of the press without compromising the working morality that is expected of a robust investigative journalism. It is also important to stress that this kind of attitude should be defended as part of the public interest.

Courts have often put a lot of moral pressure on the press by reminding it of the responsibility without assisting it to fulfi the expectations of the public interest. While doing this it is important to bear in mind that in a large country, the press is the major source of information. If it is in the public interes that such information should be made available, then some support for the press is also essential. It is possible to visualiz a political system in which the press does not play an importan role in the flow of investigation and information. In such a sys tem, the press plays a very different role. So does the law; anc indeed, the judiciary. But that is not the situation that we are face with in India today. In any event, some judges in India are ver conscious of the pressures on the press. In a case from Madhy

Pradesh,[94] the *Indore Samachar* had some evidence to make the assertion that communalism entered into the appointment of the Inspector General of Police (I.G.P.). The Court having investigated the case took the view that there was enough material for the newspaper to make this assertion and that the newspaper had acted in good faith. While not travelling too far away from the strictures of the Privy Council in the *Burma Critic* case, the Court sought to balance out an approach of the law so that the public interest in the press could be more adequately understood and appreciated. It observed:

> It is certainly in the public interest that anything shaky or unjust or improper in the conduct of a minister making appointments should be brought to the notice of the country at large. It is, in fact, criticism without which any democratic system is doomed to failure and ministers inevitably suffer absolute corruption by their unscrutinized exercise of power. Whether the conduct of any particular individual should be publicly criticised and would be in the public interest, would naturally vary with the circumstances of each case.
>
> If the person is any private individual and the incident does not in any real manner touch the public at large, then, of course, the criticism even, if otherwise, based on facts, and justified, would not be in a public interest. But the Minister in charge of a department getting appointments made to such a high office as that of an I.G.P., is doing something on which public attention should be limelighted. When the public does not show active interest in such appointments, it does not deserve to have a democratic Government and, will not, in fact be having it for any length of time.
>
> Every citizen (and the editor of a newspaper is a citizen and nothing more, nor less) is entitled to know at any rate, whether the appointment is being made really in the best interest of the public, or whether there is something ulterior. Certainly, he should not be hasty or unfair and should not mislead himself by false stories. But once the

> facts show that there is no ascertainable reason justifying the particular appointment except regionalism, he would be failing in his duty to himself and his fellow citizens if he does not come out with his criticism.

Even this balance is quite careful. Recently the Kerala High Court was faced with a case involving the *Manorama* newspaper which had inelegantly reported certain facts which were substantially true.[95] The Court took the view that that was enough to protect the journalist. It set its judgment in the context of changing times and the need to show a greater latitude to the press.

> It has also to be remembered that the standard of criticism indulged in by the newspapers is changing and in dealing with a newspaper report, considerable latitude is now allowed by the law as is seen from the trend of rulings on the subject. This does not mean that newspapers have any special rights or privilege to make unfair comments or can make imputations on character or motive. It means only that the tests of relevancy and honesty as well as defamatory language are interpreted liberally in the light of prevalent standards of public discussion and criticism. There cannot be any doubt that these standards are as strict now as they were formerly. . . . The important ingredient in the ninth exception is that the report must be substantially true and the comment made, basing itself on the facts, is supported by good faith. The latter element is the more important and if the accused fails to prove good faith, the whole defence is shattered. The mere fact that the report is based on facts will not by itself save the accused. The report should be true and faithful and the comment should be supported by good faith.[96]

These have been criminal cases. In a civil case where an allegation involving blackmarketing was made, the Court took the view that some support had to be given to the press where the factual information was substantially correct even if it was presented in such a way that it left a certain impression in people's minds. The Court explained its approach in this way:

> . . . (B)lackmarketing and corruption have become common and it is the duty of everybody to put a stop to the same; and it is the duty of the press to bring to the notice of the public the cases of such blackmarketing. It is true that the newspaper should know what it publishes is factual information. The defendant has not stated that the plaintiff is a black marketeer. He published that there is a report that when the plaintiff was President of the Stock-holders that account of shortage of Rs. 12043/9 shares of the Sethji were frozen. It is true that the shares were frozen. It is also true that the cases were handed over to the police. Therefore, there was justification as to what was published.[97]

However, any optimism that may be derived from these judgments has been immediately quelled by the Supreme Court in their latest judgment in the *Blitz* case.[98] Here the newspaper revealed that a detenu during the Emergency had illicit sexual contact with a married female lady. On being indicted, the newspaper requested that the Government's own report on the subject be made available to the Court. The report verified the newspaper's story. Should the newspaper have made further inquiries? If this was a matter that was inquired into, was it not in the public interest that the matter be revealed. Two judges (against one dissent) took the view that the newspaper could not take the stand that it had acted in good faith and that the revelation was for the public good. There is no doubt that this left wing newspaper had sought to highlight this story against a Jan Sangh and allegedly R.S.S. politician. But did this mean that the newspaper had not acted in good faith? The majority of judges presented a huge catalogue of factors which a journalist was supposed to take into account:

> Was the article published after due care and attention? Did the author of the article satisfy himself that there were reasonable grounds to believe that the imputations made by him were true? Did he act with reasonable care and a sense

> of responsibility and propriety? Was the article based entirely on the report of the Deputy Secretary or was there some other material before the author? What steps did the author take to satisfy himself about the authenticity of the report and its contents? Were the imputations made rashly without any attempt at verification? Was the imputation the result of any ill-will or malice which the author bore towards the political group to which the complainant belonged? Was the article intended to expose the rottenness of a jail administration which permitted free sexual approaches between male and female? Was the article intended to expose the despicable character of persons who were passing off as saintly leaders? Was the article merely intended to provide salacious reading material for readers who had a peculiar taste for scandal?[99]

Justice Chinnappa Reddy's catalogue stresses three factors: truth, the public good and good faith.[100] The difficulty with the catalogue is that it has no central emphasis, for the judgment does not indicate how the judge weighed up these various factors on the facts of the case. It is possible, and this is to some extent conjecture, that the learned judge may have given a considerable emphasis to the fact that the newspaper and the complainant were in opposite political camps. This is one of the factors that is mentioned in the catalogue. But, is it relevant? If a newspaper is satisfied of the truth of an item, has taken all reasonable care and attention to verify the facts and the information is for the public good, is the political—or for that matter even personal—animosity of the editor relevant? "Good faith" in this context cannot mean spite, malice or ill-will. It simply means acting with due care and attention. If the Court is satisfied that this was done, the question of ill-will is only relevant to the extent to which the Court might take the view that it is not in the public good that such quarrels be brought to the Court. And that inquiry pertains to the *bona fides* of the political complainant rather than the newspaper. In any event, it can be argued that a newspaper political rivalry is essential both to democracy and good journalism if the other two conditions of ascertaining the truth with due care and attention and the requirement of the public good are met. Justice Sen recognised that this was a matter of "great public importance".[101] He did not expand the meaning of good faith to mean good will and treated the question of public good as a fact. But apart from Justice Sen re-stating that the rights of the press were no greater than those of the ordinary citizen, he did not indicate either where the failure of good faith and public good lay. The dissenting judge—Justice Baharul Islam—took a different view. He felt that the public good can be assumed in certain cases and that the onus of discharging "good faith" should not be so high.

> The inquiry was made and the report prepared by a highly responsible officer and submitted to the Government. It was in pursuance of a complaint made by one of the citizens pointing out laxity in observance of jail rules and highly objectionable practices of some of the prisoners and seeking improvement in jail administration. The object was to see improved conditions, and maintenance of certain standards of moral conduct by prisoners, in jail. If the complainant and the consequent inquiry report be for the public good, and the respondents had reasons to believe its contents to be true they will be protected. . . . Even if the burden of proof of "good faith" be on the accused, "good faith" need not be proved beyond reasonable doubt. Once this is done, whether the publication was for the public good was a matter of inference.[102]

Justice Baharul Islam clearly took the view that here the newspaper had verified its facts from a credible inquiry and, *prima facie*, the public good requirement could be inferred,[103] no further questions were needed.

It is important to dwell on this case because this judgment is now the law of the land. It is clear that the Supreme Court seeks to continue the old approach which characterized the opinion of the Privy Council in the *Burma Critic* case. It merely shows that it might be a little while before the judiciary formulates a new approach in which the public interest in investigative and political journalism is more adequately represented.

To turn now to the major civil defamation cases, we have already explained the major differences between the law of civil defamation in India and in England. The rest of the law is the same. A pressman can plead "truth" as a "justification". Where the publication expresses an opinion, the defence pleaded is one of fair comment. This means that the opinion is an opinion and not an assertion of fact. It is fair. It is on a matter that is in the public interest. It ts not actuated by malice. In another case involving *Blitz* the Bombay High Court took the view that express and actual malice has to be proved.[104] Generally, an honest belief will suffice. The catalogue of inquiry in such civil cases is not as extensive as that suggested in Justice Chinnappa Reddy's judgment in the later *Blitz* case (1981 *supra*) in respect of criminal defamation. An absolute privilege attaches itself in respect of parliamentary proceedings and judicial proceedings, the official conduct of a judge, the statements of a witness in court, a lawyer's conduct in court and acts of state. A qualified privilege exists in respect of reports of Parliament, judicial proceedings and public meetings. A qualified privilege also exists where the maker of the defamatory statement can show that he had a moral, social or legal duty to make that statement. A qualified privilege can be rebutted if it is shown that there was malice which, in turn, is generally speaking taken to mean an absence of an honest belief. Not all these privileges affect the press although many intrude into its work.

A brief look at the major civil defamation cases involving the press unfolds an interesting classification of case law. Some of the cases arose out of group disputes about how a trust or estate should be administered.[105] Others involve the imputation of chastity in a woman,[106] the lack of professionalism with certain professionals,[107] attacks on the integrity or ethics of certain businessmen and traders,[108] cases which were part of the politics of the National Movement,[109] cases involving allegation of high-handedness or corruption in the police,[110] at least one case where it was suggested that an Englishman was able to manipulate British justice,[111] cases where politicians were maligned[112] and, finally, a miscellany of cases on various matters. We need to look at these cases.[113]

In the group disputes about the running of trusts or administration of property the courts were not anxious to take too interventionist a line. In the trust case involving the *Jam-e-Jamshed*,[114] there was a community dispute about the manner in which the plaintiff had gained prominence by sending threats. This was a small community newspaper. A plea of qualified privilege was made. Indeed, one could point out to a moral duty to make these facts available to the trustees before the trust meeting. But the Court took the view that the occasion was not privileged because this information had been publicly circulated in a newspaper. Thus, there was no duty to inform the general public. The other case involved the famous paper *Kesari*[115] and a dispute over the political and other legacies of the national leader Bal Gangadhar Tilak. One of the parties to the dispute was Tilak's son. The dispute had reached a fairly dramatic stage and a fast to death was already being staged as part of the drama. The Court did not want to get too deeply involved in an already matured attack and counter-attack. The Court stressed the fact that there was no malice in this case and that it was not just the actual sentences that mattered but the situation as a whole. The attitude of the Bombay High Court in this case[116] resembles the attitude of the Madras High Court in the *Madras Standard* case[116] involving the reputation of a lawyer where the Court gave extremely low damages because it took the view that the lawyer in question should really have not taken matters this far. The courts were much more vigorous in the defence of a Brahmin girl who was accused of not being chaste.[117] Again, in the *Gujerati* case where the public were told not to send their girls to a particular drama production because the future of the girl would be ruined, the Court did seek to protect the Parsees in charge of the production.[118] The courts have protected big businessmen accused of malpractices. Thus when the *Gujerati* accused a private company of being a set of adventurers, an award of Rs. 1000 was made even though the demand was for Rs. 50,000.[119] If we look at tariff of the award of damages, this is at the high end of the tariff.[120] But the *cause celebre* is the *Blitz* case where the newspaper had defamed the House of Thackersey. An award of Rs. 1,50,000 was made out of a claim of Rs. 3,00,000. This is the highest award made in a case in which the trial lasted 101 days.[121] Smaller businessmen accused of corruption have fared less favourably. We have already seen that in the *Indore Samachar* case,[122] the High Court sought to encourage inquiries into blackmarketing. Again, in the *Dhinamalar* case[123] a journalist was allowed to claim that a story about a smuggling operation was unintentional defamation which coincidentally implicated the plaintiff firm. Again, in the *Lok Jewan* case [124] imputations against estate agents yielded some damages but the plaintiffs had to bear their own costs. It is not being suggested that all the cases were not thoroughly investigated by the courts. But the bigger firms were obviously able to mobilize the law in their favour more effectively.

The real problems that have arisen in respect of the political cases were associated with the national movement and allegations of corruption made against police officers. The difficulty about the national movement cases was that the cases were a test for British justice. In the *Englishman* case[125] the newspaper had published a defamatory statement that Lala Lajpat Rai had been "tampering with loyalty of sepoys". This was not treated as an opinion but an assertion that Lajpat Rai was guilty of offences against the State under the Indian Penal Code. The Court rejected the newspapers' argument that similar comments had been made by the Nationalist leader in Parliament. This was taken to be an independent statement. Again, in the *Statesman* case,[126] involving Subhash Chandra Bose, the newspaper had made the allegation that Subhash Bose had been arrested not because he was a Swarajist but because he was a terrorist. This was taken to be an assertion of fact and not a comment in that Subhash Bose was being accused of an offence. The *Statesman*[127] was successfully sued by Baba Gurdit Singh when they accused all Sikhs on a ship of being in league with German agents and involved in a firing incident. These are all cases where the neutrality of the law is projected in cases involving a political movement. In fact, the Court seems to have leaned over to show that implicit in the National leaders' cases was an accusation of an offence and not just the assertion of an opinion.

The courts took particular care to protect the public administration. In an important case from the turn of this century, the Indian Daily News[128] published an article about the Sova Bazaar Tragedy and asserted the view that there was "a police conspiracy" and "a dastardly scheme to hang an innocent man". This was undoubtedly in the public interest. The Court awarded damages taking the view that this was not just the expression of an opinion. Considerable damages were awarded in the *Pardesi Khalsa*[129] case where there was an allegation that there was lawlessness in the Central Jail and that people were being beaten up. Instead of observing that the scrutiny of jails depends on proper investigative journalism, the Court thought it fit to remind journalists that they had no special privileges but, in fact, a greater responsibility. A slightly more difficult situation was created in the *Siyasat* case[130] where an allegation was made that a police officer was only just prevented from firing into some National Volunteers. The case was both political and trivial. The officer in question refused to give evidence and the Court granted minimal damages having already publicly set the story in order for the complaining police officer. These cases show clearly that the courts have been anxious to protect the administration from extended attacks even where the purpose of the newspaper may have been highlighting matters in the public interest. But having done this, the courts had no other choice but to legitimate the whole legal system by allowing claims of the Nationalist leaders on the grounds that it is difficult to legitimate a legal system unless it can be shown that what was sauce for the goose must be sauce for the gander. That the laws of defamation were used to protect the police administration is clear. The task became much easier because of the intellectual backdrop provided by the Privy Council in the *Burma Critic* case[131] where, as we have shown above, the Privy Council reminded journalists that they had no special privileges. However, all these legitimating devices seem to have failed in the *Rangoon Gazette* case[132] where the newspaper sought to show that an English Member of Parliament had been wrongly absolved from a charge of malicious prosecution and demanded an inquiry. The Court did not really deal with the core issue when a newspaper can demand a public inquiry.

The public inquiry question is both an important and a serious one. At what point in time is a newspaper justified in saying that there is a *prima facie* case for a public inquiry. By its very nature, the demand for a public inquiry implies that this is an area where the newspaper does not have sufficient information and it is hoped that the public inquiry will yield more information. In the *Hindustan Herald* case[133] a journalist, though not calling for an inquiry as such, asserted that the police had been very high-handed in respect of certain Kumbi women. The Court took the classical line that newspapers had no special privilege. Damages to the tune of Rs. 1,000 were awarded even though the newspaper indicated that the report was incorrect and the error regretted. But, there are instances where a newspaper genuinely believes that there is a case for an inquiry. Here the newspaper would place the facts available before it and then ask for an inquiry. The demand for an inquiry is not necessarily a fair comment but entails an imputation. Indian courts have not looked into this kind of question in any depth. Even though a nineteenth century case involving the *Times of India*[134] did stress the need for public men to be investigated and exposed as long as it was done in good faith.

There are several matters which have come up before the courts concerning politicians. A union leader was given a considerable amount of damages when she was falsely accused of trickery and of bringing hirelings to the Union. The Court took note of the fact that her career was ruined.[135] But in a case where a newspaper reported how a politician had been called a Godseite (Godse, being responsible for Gandhi's murder belonged to an extreme Hindu faction[136]) the damages awarded were low. Perhaps the Court felt that the real suit should have lain against the Speaker. Alternatively, there might have been an unexpressed feeling that unless special damage was shown, politicians were expected to take a great deal more in their stride. Or, they may not have had sympathy for the plaintiffs.

There are some miscellaneous cases involving the press. An accord and satisfaction between rival publications was obviously to be encouraged.[137] In an early case,[138] the Bombay High Court seems to have indulged in a wide inquiry about the previous malice of a defendant who had reprinted an article. We have already indicated that the proper inquiry in newspaper cases should usually be into lack of good faith and absence of honest belief. In another case involving the *Englishman*[139] the Calcutta High Court seemed to defend the right of a newspaper to defend its reporter after a person interviewed in the paper was allowed to have his protest printed. In a recent case from Punjab involving the *Sach* paper,[140] newspapers were reminded not to rely on unverified casual sources for their information and were reminded that they would have no course of action against such a source. The most remarkable of all these cases is a case which shows the extent to which the government interferes with the press.[141] Dissatisfied with a local journalist, an officer of the State government informed the employers of that journalist which included the leading news agency and some newspapers that he should be replaced, that he sided with politicians and was in the pay of a foreign embassy. The journalist was a good journalist and was virtually ruined. A considerable figure in damages—some Rs. 28,000—was awarded. This stern reminder may have gone unheeded. But all this does go to show that if journalists can find the resources and courage to litigate, they can use the law of civil defamation to ward off unscrupulous and unwarranted attacks and pressures on themselves.

Our survey of the important civil defamation cases indicates that the courts have not been anxious to get involved in defamation cases which are extensions of private disputes. Professionals and politicians are not expected to get over-sensitive unless they can show special harm and damage. Journalists who have been harassed and defamed by the government have been given protection. Imputations of chastity have elicited an unequivocal response from the courts. The interesting area has been the spirited defence of the police administration. A necessary *quid pro quo* has been to defend Nationalist leaders. But in all these cases, limitations have been put on the extent to which an inference has to be treated as the expression—even assertion—of an opinion—or a statement of a defamatory fact. Insufficient attention has been paid to the role of the press as a catalyst in asking for public inquiries. The small business owner has had less protection from the court rather than the big businessmen. Investigative journalism into the suspect affairs of small businessmen seems to have some sort of blessing from the Court. Bigger businessmen have been more successful in pursuing their claims. This is not because the courts are in awe of them. Much rather, it is because they have mastered the techniques and possess the resources to use this forum of activity effectively. The real problem in civil defamation cases is the extent to which the Court is willing to repose faith in the attempts of the press to keep the Government and powerful private bodies under scrutiny. Instead of holding that certain assertions are statements of fact requiring a complete justification as being true, certain assertions could be treated as statements of opinion or demands in the public interest requiring no more than good faith. This does not give the press any special privileges. It merely assists their honest endeavours—if and when such honest endeavours are made. Unfortunately, the courts in India have cause to believe that such endeavours are not always made by the Indian press. Further, Indian judges may also feel that when these endeavours are made, they are not always made honestly.

The criminal law of defamation is derived from the Indian Penal Code. English law makes defamation a criminal offence when the libel consists of the tendency to provoke a breach of peace. Macaulay explained why English law was wrong in principle and that a different kind of law should apply in India.

> Defamatory imputations of the worst kind may have no tendency to cause acts of violence. Words which convey no discreditable imputation whatever may have that tendency

> in the highest degree. Even in cases where defamation has a tendency to cause acts of violence, the heinousness of the defamation considered as defamation is by no means proportioned to its tendency to cause such acts; nay, circumstances which are greater aggravations of the offences, considered as defamation may be great mitigation of the same offence, considered as a provocation to a breach of peace. A scurrilous satire against a friendless woman published by a person who carefully conceals his name would be defamation in one of its most odious forms. But it would be only by a legal fiction that the satirist could be said to provoke a breach of peace. On the other hand, an imputation on the courage of an officer, contained in a private letter meant to be seen only by that officer and two or three other persons, might, considered as a defamation, be a very venial offence. But such an imputation would have an obvious tendency to cause a serious breach of peace.[142]

Macaulay seems to have overlooked the fact that the meaning of defamation as a social reality is determined by the pathology of litigation. And, as we have indicated, the pathology of litigation precipitated by these provisions was by no means limited to what was said about society ladies or imputations against the courage of army officers. Indian society took over the working of these provisions. Undoubtedly, they are a much more effective provision for the poorer sections of the community if they learn how to play the litigation game.

The defamation provisions in the Indian Penal Code are long and complicated. However, the Law Commission of India which examined these provisions took the view that it considered "the possibility of simplifying this lengthy statement . . . undesirable as it was likely to become less concrete and, perhaps, more difficult to understand".[143] The definition of defamation covers "words either spoken or intended to be read or . . . signs and visible representation". These will amount to defamation only when they constitute an imputation which is made or published "concerning any person intending to harm, or knowing or having reason to believe that such imputation will harm, the reputation of such person".[144] This is followed by four explanations and ten exceptions. The Explanations make it defamation to harm a dead person if the feelings of his family or near relatives would be hurt,[145] treat it as defamatory to make imputations against a company or association of persons,[146] make ironical innuendos defamatory,[47] and clarify that there is harm to a person's reputation when an imputation "directly or indirectly, in the estimation of others, lowers the moral and intellectual character of that person, or lowers the character of that person in respect of his caste or of his calling or lowers the credit of that person or causes it to be believed that the body of that person is in a loathsome state, or in a state generally believed to be disgraceful".[48] So much for definitions; these are very wide. But then come the Exceptions. For some time there was a lingering controversy as to whether some of the absolute privileges pertaining to judicial proceedings in respect of witnesses, counsel and judges in English law apply in India. After some hesitation,[149] it has been established that there is only a qualified privilege.[50] The Code itself protects substantially true reports of judicial proceedings or the result in any such proceedings, discussion on the merits of a decided case or the conduct of witnesses.[151] Any authority—including judges—having lawful authority over another and censuring that other in good faith has a defence.[152] Nor is it defamation to prefer in good faith an accusation against a person to any other person who has lawful authority over the former.[153] Apart from the Code, there is an absolute privilege in respect of what is said in Parliament and in respect to the reports of what was said and a qualified privilege in respect of fair and accurate accounts of such proceedings.[154]

But we have not exhausted all the Exceptions in the Penal Code itself—having left over the ones that affect the press more directly. The First Exception is similar but not wholly analogous to the defence of justification in civil cases. A truth may be published if it is for the public good. What is for the public good is a question of fact. It should be noted that apart from the requirement of the public good there is no requirement of good faith needed. A person publishing the truth for the public good cannot be deprived of this defence by showing that he did not act with due care or attention or that he behaved with ill-will. But let us turn to the Ninth Exception which states that "it is not defamation to make an imputation on the character of another provided that the imputation be made in good faith for the protection of interests of the person making it, or any other person, or for the public good". The relationship between the First and Ninth Exceptions has not been properly explored. It is imprecise to say that the First Exception is analogous to the defence of truth or justification in civil law and that the Ninth Exception deals with matters of fair comment. It is important to explore this point a little further because it is of fundamental importance to the press. It should be noted that the defence of justification in the First Exception has to be further supported by showing that the publication is for the public good. The fact that a thing is true does not mean that a person publishing such truths can escape the charge of criminal defamation unless it is shown that such publication is for the public good. But there is a more important point about the relationship between the First and Ninth Exceptions. The Ninth Exception is not limited to matters of opinion. A person can actually make a false defamatory statement and still claim a defence if he can show that it was made in good faith and in his own interests or in the interests of the public good. As far as the truth content of such a statement is concerned, all that he has to show is that he acted with due care and attention to find out the truth. The upshot of both these cxceptions is that all publications must be made in the interests of the public good. A statement should either be true; or, if false made after some kind of reasonable steps have been made to ascertain the truth. The defences available in the criminal law are, therefore, wider than those in civil law in that a false statement may also be published if it can be shown that the person making that statement believed it to be true. Much of the controversy in this area revolves around the meaning of "good faith". This is of great practical importance to journalists because it links it with the code of journalistic ethics. The whole question then becomes: at what point will the law say to a journalist: "You have done enough to ensure that you acted honestly and in good faith"? This is both a question of fact as well as law. If the courts impose a responsibility on the press to the extent that it must be totally and absolutely satisfied about the truth of an assertion, justification will become a part of the Ninth Exception. This links up to all kinds of policy questions as to how rigorous investigative journalism should be with itself.

While we ponder over that question, it is important to bear in mind that the Penal Code expected a good and effective response to any performance that was submitted to the judgment of the public. At the same time, there was also an expectation that the conduct or character of any public servant or any person[155] touching on any public question[156] was envisaged as falling within the scope of discussion and publication provided it was done in good faith.

The newspaper cases involving criminal defamation cover a diverse area. To begin with there are some cases where the libel was supposed to be such as threatened a breach of peace.[157] Other cases are involving the maligning of private individuals.[158] There are some cases where the newspaper maligned a group.[159] Undoubtedly, some of the cases are part of political infighting and involve allegations of incompetence or corruption against politicians.[160] Some of the cases concern some form of investigative journalism where allegations are made against municipal boards, the administration and politicians.[161] There are a miscellany of cases on various aspects of journalistic responsibility.[162]

The breach of peace cases belong to an area for which the English law of criminal defamation was designed. In the *Mulballigh*[163] case the paper was commenting on a social situation where Muslims and Hindus were present. The food had been blest by a Hindu priest. The assertion that it had been deliberately defiled by Muslims was seen as giving rise to communal tension which, in turn, would affect the peace. The Court gave a lecture to the press on the responsibilities of the editor. In the *Risalat* case[164] the Court awarded six months' punishment where the paper had suggested that a Hindu boy had been killed because he wanted to be converted to Islam.

Such cases belong not just to the area of defamation but also to the general area of seditious libel and causing religious tension. In fact, it is better that these kinds of cases—both of which were brought by the State in the name of the Emperor—should not be brought under the head of defamation cases. Criminal defamation trials can easily be stretched out with the defendant making either the plea of justification or that the publication was made with due care and attention in the public good. The fact that defamation will not ultimately be proved is really quite irrelevant. What is important is that the Court can be used as a forum to exacerbate greater tension.

There are some cases where personal imputations are made in the background of personal, social or political differences. In the *Rana Pratap* case,[165] the lady of a Health Centre was accused of having illicit love affairs and producing illegal abortions. In this situation, the High Court took a strict and severe attitude. A problem has arisen in cases of group libels. Where a whole group or party or caste is libelled, can an individual member sue? In certain cases, the Court assumes that a libel against the group affects the individual member. In other cases, the individual member has to specifically show that his reputation has been harmed. In the (*Aligarh*) *University Punch* case[166] girls of a particular hostel were deemed to be individually affected where comments were made on the licentious behaviour of all the girls in that hostel. In the *Statesman* case,[167] a person on behalf of the widows of his locality was allowed to prosecute the *Statesman* which talked of various social problems pertaining to childbirth of young mothers and of widows. A sentence highlighted that widows were regarded as God's curse.

In two cases involving films and film stars,[168] the courts took the view that a general attack on a group (like lawyers) will not attract criminal proceedings by way of defamation. Again, a film showing an orthodox Bengali Brahmin rebuking an Untouchable Bhangi was too general to be considered as applying to a particular person or group.[169] The real problems that arise have arisen in political cases. This can be illustrated by two cases involving *Blitz*. In the first of these cases,[170] Blitz made disparaging comments about an extreme Hindu political faction called the R.S.S. Although the Code makes it clear that imputation against an association or collection of persons can amount to defamation, the Court took the view that an individual member had to present more evidence to show how his reputation had been harmed or affected. In the second *Blitz* case[171] from Kerala the newspaper carried a report on an aspect of the agitation on the Kerala Education Bill. A photograph was taken of various people throwing stones at a building including the complainant. To this was added the caption: "Soldiers of the Goonda War in the compound of Bishop's Palace at Trivandrum for the Church bells to toll, the signal to attack". This case has more than a whisper of politics to it. The respondent ran a Communist weekly and supported the Communist government which was being agitated against. The complainant was the Chief Correspondent of the Malayalam Rajyam. Concentrating on the meaning of the word "goonda" (ruffian) the Court assumed that the complainant was defamed and that all that he had to show was that the "accused intended or knew or had reason to believe that the imputation made by him would harm the reputation of the complainant". But all that the *Blitz* reporter had done was print a photograph of a general incident. The caption was a comment and an opinion.

Would a non-participating Englishman or an unsympathetic Indian bystander have had a case in defamation if a newspaper report on Gandhi's famous Salt March included a photograph of a group in which this Englishman and Indian were included? Would it just have been considered as a group report? Would it have become defamation if it carried the caption: "Bloody revolutionaries on the move"? In such cases it cannot be so easily presumed either that there was intent to defame or that all members of that group were being criticised without further proof. All this is important both to the law on group libel as well as the reporting of general public incidents through the use of photographs. Much of modern politics involves group statements about the nature and politics of other groups. Those groups can—if they so desire—collectively prosecute for libel. Whether this facility should be available to the individual must depend on the extent to which that individual is harmed. Otherwise, newspapers with a nationwide circulation who comment on nationwide groups run the risk of being involved in a defamation suit in any part of the country at the whim of any individual member of the group.

It is important to give the politics of a country some lee-way to express itself. In the *Nagpur Times* case,[172] the Court took the view that a person complaining about what was said by a political journalist must not be general but must identity the actual words complained of. But apart from that the Supreme Court of India appears to have taken some note of the fact that it is the business of politicians to demand inquiries and make political comments. Thus, in a complicated case involving the affairs of the son of the erstwhile powerful Chief Minister of Punjab, Sardar Pratap Singh Kairon,[173] Chief Justice Gajendragadkar took note of the fact that the person accused of defamation was a respectable politician who was not acting out of political malice. This was not wholly borne in mind in the *Krishna Iyer* case[174] where it was ironically implied that the Ministry was being run incompetently and in a corrupt way. The Court was simply used as a forum for further political agitation. This is just one factor which helps the Court to determine whether the defendant acted in good faith by exercising all due care and attention. Rather than asking whether the politician-defendant had discovered the truth, the Court then seems to ask: given all the political circumstances, has the politician done all that he can to ascertain the truth, given his political status and his duty to the public? It must be made clear that it is no part of this argument that a politician is entitled to tell a total lie and indulge in conjectures. In the *Matrubhumi* case,[175] the newspaper quoted a statement of Ram Manohar Lohia that the Governor was a toy in the hands of the Congress and had secured an appointment for a relative in Assam Oil. It should be noted that here it was the newspaper which was prosecuted and the Court took the view that the newspaper had acted without due care and attention. But this sort of case does pose a problem for newspapers.

Much of a newspaper's information about political speeches is fed through news agencies. Should the newspaper simply refuse to report such allegations made by politicians? Should it report such allegations after an investigation of the facts? Should it report such a statement as representing not a state of facts but the opinion of a politician? Should the newspapers make it clear that it cannot say whether such a state of facts exists? To impose the duty of independent investigation on the newspaper in respect of each such statement will be too difficult and expensive. To say that a newspaper can simply say that the matter is "alleged" by the politician might be too light a control. Here politicians would themselves be liable for such a comment but might be prepared to take the risk of prosecution as a trade-off for publicly embarrassing their opponents. In a recent case involving the *Statesman*[176] a report indicated how a person was alleged to be a wagon breaker who had attacked the police. The Calcutta High Court took the view that "the publication was guarded enough, mentioning clearly and referring to the incident as 'alleged to be' and was published without express motive". In such situations, most newspapers act without an express motive. The real question is whether a newspaper should print certain kinds of allegations against a person at all or whether it can in all such cases hide behind the "alleged to be" formula? The newspaper itself is in a position of responsibility to gauge the nature of the defamation and determine the mischief with which it is made. The current situation whereby allegations against a Governor result in a successful prosecution but not allegations made against a political militant is far from satisfactory. The proper approach would appear to be that, given the circumstances of the case, a newspaper should publish opinions and general allegations but not specific allegations which are *per se* defamatory. The "magic formula" that an allegation was simply "alleged" should not be responsible for newspapers abandoning the control of the ethics of their profession to politicians and others. Undoubtedly, some mischief must abound. That is in the nature of politics, social life and journalism. The question is how much and to what extent? And, whether a newspaper should lose its control or abandon its responsibility as a monitor and transmitter of such mischief.

Many of the other cases involve both politics and investigative journalism. In one of the very early civil cases[177] the Court stressed the importance of the good faith requirement when allegations were made against a public person and an inquiry demanded while at the same time stressing the need for the investigation and exposure of public men. A more liberal stand was taken in the *Raja Bhakta Swadharma Nishta* case[178] concerning the exposure in good faith of police corruption where witnesses were turned hostile. In time, demands for an inquiry were less indulgently treated where it was alleged that innocent people had been fired upon in a shooting rather than others.[179] The Court frowned upon the newspaper tactic to publish the complainant's denial and leave it to the public to make up their minds. Similarly, in the *Nadar Nampan* case[180] an allegation that a Magistrate had been bribed with 'coconut, betel leaves, arecanuts, tobacco, bananas, lime fruits and sugar' was considered excessive. We have already referred to the *Kairon* case where the government itself invited the public to come out in the open to make allegations of corruption in respect of smuggling associated with Kairon's son. The Punjab High Court[181] took the view that a rival politician was rightly prosecuted for criminal defamation because he took up the challenge and made these allegations. The Supreme Court reversed the judgment of the Punjab High Court[182] permitted a politician to make public his investigations and took the view that, on the facts, he had acted in good faith and with due care and attention. There have been some important High Court decisions supporting the cause of investigative journalism. In the *Indore Samachar* case,[183] the newspaper was acquitted where it suggested that there had been a delay in making an important appointment and expressed the fear that communalism had entered into the making of the appointment. The inferences drawn by the newspaper were deemed to be fair comments. The Court was less helpful in the *Yogantra* case[184] where the source of information was not disclosed and accusations of corruption were made against a local public person. Unfortunately, the problem of disclosure was not properly canvassed. The problem of disclosure is linked to the issue of confidentiality which needed to be discussed more thoroughly before the Court made a comment about journalistic ethics. In any event, in criminal prosecutions the Court must be satisfied that a person acted in good faith—that is with due care and caution. The Court obviously felt that it could not be satisfied that such care and caution was exercised withon being apprised of all the evidence that was availabel before the newspaper. The cause of investigative journalism was fully represented in a judgment of the Madras High Court[185] where a reporter wrote a story about opperession in a village having made a proper inquiry into the facts and assured himself that there was an element of truth in what he said. Again, in a case from Allahabad involving the activities of a local official called a Lekhpal,[186] the Court—after making the new usual comment that a journalist's privilege is no higher than that of an ordinary citizen—stressed that:

> . . . the journalist owes certain duties to the public, the most important of which is the dissemination of news and views fully and truly expressed on matters affecting the public good. In so far as he does that he serves a social purpose, for by exposing the evils of the community or its servants to the public gaze he seeks to create a climate of opinion for their eradication. A newspaper editor, therefore, acts within his legitimate sphere when he offers criticism to what he considers and *bona fide* believes to be for the good of the community. But he is not protected if under the guard of criticism he employs language calculated to defame or degrade the character of a public servant or of a private citizen. In order to pass the last of fair comment the publication must be free from malice and made *bona fide* and in public interest. Mere exaggeration or inaccuracy in matters of detail does not make a comment unfair as long as what is expressed therein is materially true and for public benfit.

Here there was an emphasis on the functions of the journalist and his *bona fides*. There is a certain generosity in evolving some kind of rule that the article should be substantially true. This emphasis was also made in the *Manorama* case[187] (which has been discussed earlier). In actual fact, the Penal Code does not require truth as a component of the defence under the Ninth Exception. All that is needed is proof to the effect that the newspaper acted with due care and attention and made a reasonable effort to try and find the truth. Other decisions of the High Courts—like the *Mukti* case[188] where allegations of financial corruption were made about the Chairman of a Municipality—have also stressed the "right of the public to know the strength and foibles of its public men". The Supreme Court has—apart from the *Kairon* case—not been very supportive. In the *Kaliyug* case allegations were made about corruption in the police. The Supreme Court emphasized the power of the press more than it emphasized the need for investigation. At one stage it even suggested that truth may not be a defence even though it was not urged as a defence.[189] The Court took the view that the tenor of the article suggested that it was not for the public good or made with due care and attention. The judgment of the majority in the *Blitz* case (1981),[190] which has been discussed above, suggests that the Supreme Court has not yet matured a view on what constitutes due care and attention. Here *Blitz* had taken care to rely upon a government report which supported the story which was printed in the paper. This did not satisfy the majority of the judges.

In all these cases, editors are usually responsible for what is said in their paper unless they are away and have handed over responsibility to someone else.[191]

The sample of criminal cases shows that newspapers do abound in mischief. Some of it is part of group rivalries and some the product of individual or other animosities. The bulk of the cases do have a public face to them. Many of the allegations made against public men are tinctured with a touch of irresponsibility—and, sometimes, even more than that. Undoubtedly, politics plays a part in all this. Newspapers get drawn into defamation cases when they transmit political dialogue. Equally, politics and social conscience often gives rise to some investigative journalism and demands for public inquiries. British courts used the famous statement in the *Burma Critic* case to intimidate this kind of journalism, and this kind of demand, into silence in all but the most obvious cases. This attitude continues to this day even though some High Courts have taken the view that some concessions must be made to journalism. In the *Kairon* case, the Supreme Court also seemed to take the view that in law a *bona fide* political demand must be regarded as legitimate. But the courts have not taken the matter further. At times, implicit in the judgment of the courts is the view that newspapers should only publish what is true. Newspapers can only be expected to act with what appears, under the circumstances, to amount to due care and attention. This would not compromise journalistic standards. But courts may feel that Indian journalism is too varied and too irresponsible to merit a more indulgent attitude. Equally, they may feel that the State, and its administrative machinery, needs protection from attack much in the same way as the work of the judiciary is protected by the laws relating to contempt of court.

Having said all this, let us return to our initial assertion that the law relating to defamation in India is both a playground as well as a pitfall.

Some of the problems relating to the law of defamation arise from the lack of a good definition. The defamation in the Indian Penal Code is much too wide and extensive and provides no sort of guidance for the judges whatsoever. The words should normally be given their ordinary meaning. Most of the Indian cases go into too much background detail and into questions of express malice. The result is that the court case becomes a re-enactment of many of the idiosyncrasies which are part of the general dispute between the parties. Extended inquiries into malice should not in fact be permitted. The defence of justification in civil cases is, at present, different from the defence in criminal cases. The defence in the criminal cases is that the publication must be for the public good.[192] The criminal law rule can be jusitfied on the basis that they perform public functions. It is only right that they should be asked to justify the public interest which forms the basis of their rhetoric and—presumably—some of their activity. Truth should be taken to mean substantially true. It will be noted that in India a person can plead the Ninth Exception as an alternative to the truth-in-the-public-interest First Exception. This means that he can say that he does not know whether the statement was true but acted in good faith and took all the necessary precautions to ascertain the truth. This is a salutary rule and should be used as the basis for a new civil defence. In civil cases, a person can, at present, either claim justification or fair comment (or a 'rolled up' plea of both). He cannot plead due diligence. If any kind of investigative journalism is to survive, this new defence should be available in civil proceedings as well.

Confidentiality is a very important part of the armoury of a journalist. It is also an area that he intrudes upon. Some clear principles must be laid down so that a journalist may keep certain confidences in the public interest and also not violate confidences unless he can show that there is a clear public interest for doing so. Indian courts have not looked at the question of damages closely. Although the threshold of awards of damages is low, the picture is unclear. The law should clearly state the factors that should be taken into account and the circumstances under which an apology can be tendered. The remedy of asking for an injunction in certain cases should be made easier. Many of these defamation cases are a kind of *tamasha* or fancy fair. While an easy access to the court should be maintained, there might be a case for devising some kind of procedure to weed out vexatious and frivolous litigation. There is a danger in vesting the power in lower courts. Equally, there is a also a danger in creating yet another forum in the much more publicised higher courts where the issue of vexatiousness and frivolousness will be vexatiously and frivolously fought. These are merely some suggestions. They will become one more bargaining factor in litigation. Ultimately, all this must be subjected to the subterfuge of litigation.

Like all other laws, the law of defamation has been subjected to the vagaries of litigation. A closer examination of all the cases and the manner in which they have been fought suggests that the press have not been able to use this branch of the law effectively. In most of the major cases, they have been pitted against very powerful litigants who are either politicians, businessmen, or possess the backing of the state. Litigation is an expensive and skilful activity and few newspapers have the money and skill to play this game effectively in this complicated area of law in which many loopholes have to be found in order to advance the cause of the press. Nor has the press—apart from the exceptional *Blitz* case of 1961—learnt to draw out defamation trials under a blaze of publicity. The whole law of defamation operates under the shadow of certain paradigmatic assumptions that the press is not to be trusted, that the State necds to be protected and that the press should not be given any extended privileges. The *tour de force* of these paradigmatic assumptions is so great that all other aspects of the work, importance and functioning of the press are often overlooked. That the Indian press does not always inspire confidence is unexceptional. But, that may well be besides the point. The fact remains that when the press is drawn into the arena of litigation in defamation cases, it finds that it has too few skills, too few resources and too few allies to sustain a legal and jurisprudential campaign for more preferential treatment.

VI

No more than a very broad picture can be painted of the manner in which the law relating to public order, morality and privacy affects the press. The law that has been declared in statutes or imported from England as part of the Common Law has gone through many transformations before it has been translated into social reality. The threshold of social reality at which we have examined the law is both at the level of its declaration as well as in the manner of its litigative use. The fertility of litigation in India has transformed the social significance of many laws. Many laws have come to be used for purposes which have little or no connection with the purposes for which they were allegedly designed. And yet litigation itself is a skilful activity. In some cases, Indian newspaper men and publicists have used the litigation system casually. At times they have been drawn into it much more securely. In all these areas, the judges who have had to decide these press cases have followed a reliable intuition as much as they have followed the logic of the law. The intuition has, to some extent, been conditioned by a powerful jurisprudence developed during the days of the Raj that the press are a nuisance and must be treated as such. The judiciary has also been able to gauge the feeling of society when dealing at least with matters of public morality and defamation. Conscious of the existence and demands of a powerful State and administration, the judiciary has been sensitive to the demands of the administration in all these areas of activity. In doing all this, they have not jeopardized the fundamental assumption that the judicial system as a whole must carry social legitimation and conviction. This has led to the growth of a complicated jurisprudence which is, at times, wayward, confused and misleading. The press has not always benefited from this conglomeration of pressures. At times, it has fought some effective victories. At times, it has allowed itself to be, willy nilly, drawn into a losing litigation game.

The real difficulty lies in the fact that Indian society has always viewed the individual differently from the West. It places the individual within a network of relationships and rejoices in, rather than apologizes for, social intrusions into individual life. Indian perceptions visualise a wide measure of social participation in the life of the individual. Such participation does not have to be justified either on the basis of the incapabilities of a particular individual (as, for example, if the individual in question is a child or *non compos mentis*) or some overriding public interest. The individual is visualised as being voluntarily and involuntarily a part of various overlapping moral and social frameworks. It seems pointless to talk of a zone of privacy which provides autonomy to an individual and which must normally never be invaded. Such a perception of the individual is supposed to be both undesirable as well as an inaccurate description of social life. The individual is part of a mosaic of overlapping moralities and pressures which aid, support and oppress him. While it may be useful to isolate the individual in certain contexts, it seems a social heresy to create a wall of separation around the individual.

Indian society recognises that the individual is a part of several existing and emerging social and moral regimes. As to what should be made public is a complex social decision which cannot be over-simplified by asserting the right of the individual to voluntarily determine the moral regime to which he belongs or may wish to belong. The question is not to discuss the limits of individual autonomy but evaluate claims of competing and overlapping socio-moral regimes. In such situations, the notion of the autonomy of the individual is not helpful. A much bolder and more complex assessment has to be made about what is permissible. India has not agonized over the question of privacy. Individual rights are overtly and covertly treated as vehicles of social expression rather than assertions of an individual autonomy. Both Indian litigation and the Indian press are arenas where the contours of various social and moral regimes can be redrawn. A society that has been anxious to push the claims of social and moral regimes has been less concerned to create an individually based framework in which the claims of social and moral regimes are recognized.

The issue about privacy is a straw issue. Unattractive as a social doctrine and nebulous as an analytical concept, it has not assisted Indian law to concretize specific social claims as identifiable demands.

NOTES

1. The phrase is taken from C. L. Stevenson: "Persuasive definition" (1939) *Mind.* On privacy as a legal concept see generally Warren and Brandeis: "The right to privacy" (1890-1) 4 *Harvard L.R.* 193; Prosser: "Privacy" (1990) 48 *Columb. L.R.* 383: G. Dworkin: "The Common law protection to privacy" (1967) 2 . . .*Tasmania L.R.* 418; note also the Younger Committee *Report on privacy* (1974)
2. K.K. Mathew: "The right to be left alone" (1979) 4 *S.C.C.* (Jnl.); Cf. F. Nariman: "The right to be left alone—a fundamental right" (1977) 17 *Indian Advocate* 76; R. Dhavan and B. Kennedy; "Privacy —adventures of a concept" (1978) *Cochin U.L.R.* 18-48
3. *Kharak Singh v. State of U.P.* (1964) 1 *S.C.R.* 332.
4. Article 21, *Constitution of India.*
5. *Govind* v. *State of Madhya Pradesh* (1975) 3 *S.C.R.* 946.
6. F. Nariman *supra* n. 2.
7. *Report of the Second Press Commission* (1982) 77 pr. 43. For the views of the Law Commission see its *Forty Second Report*: *Indian Penal Code* (1971) Chapter 23.
8. For the copyright laws see the Copy Right Act, 1957.
9. Right to Privacy Bill (24 of) 1981, Gazette of India Extraordinary (Part 2: No. 16) 249, 20 March, 1981.
10. *Ibid.* clause 2.

11. *Ibid.* clause 3.
12. Official Secrets Act, 1923.
13. See S. 123 Evidence Act, 1872.
14. For India see *State of Punjab* v. *S.S. Singh* A.I.R. 1961 S.C. 493; *Amar Chand* v. *Union of India* A.I.R. 1964 S.C. 1658; *State of Uttar Pradesh* v. *Raj Narain* A.I.R. 1975 S.C. 865; and M.P. Jain and S.N. Jain: *Administrative Law* (1979) 622-9.
15. See *Frazer* v. *Evans* (1969) 1 All. E.R. 8; *Margaret, Duchess of Argyll* v. *Duke of Argyll* (1965) 1 All. E.R. 611: *Lord Ashburton* v. *Pope* (1913) 2 Ch. 469; *Prince Albert* v. *Strange* (1849) 1 Macdg. 25. Now see also *Attorney General* v. *Jonathan Cape Ltd.* (1976) B. 752.
16. S. 126 Indian Evidence Act, 1872.
17. *Attorney General* v. *Clough* (1963) 1 All. E.R. 420; *Attorney General* v. *Mulholand* (1961) 1 All. E.R. 767.
18. Commissions of Inquiry Act, 1952 Ss. 4 and 6 offering some immunity in that, in certain circumstances, the statements made by witnesses shall not be used in civil or criminal prosecutions or litigation.
19. S. 39 Indian Evidence Act, 1872.
20. *Ram Kumar* v. *State* (1962) Cr. L.J. 122 at pr. 16 p. 126.
21. See S. 499 Indian Penal Code, 1860 Exceptions II and III.
22. See *Hirabai* v. *Dinshaw* A.I.R. 1927 Bom. 322; *Naganatha* v. *Subramania* A.I.R. 1918 Mad. 700; see Derret: "Justice, Equity and Good Conscience" (1962) 64 *Bom. L. R. Jnl.* n 129, 145.
23. Ss. 499-501 Indian Penal Code, 1860.
24. Macaulay: *Report of the Indian Law Commission on the Indian Penal Code* 2 (14 October, 1837) reprinted in full *A.I.R. Commentary Indian Penal Code* (1974) IV, 655 at 709 col. 1.
25. *Ibid.* 706.
26. There is an impressive case law on this arising out of the legal controversy as to whether slander is actionable *per se* without proof of special damage. The answer to this was that no special damage was necessary see *Parvati* v. *Mannar* (1884) 8 Mad. 175; *Dewan Singh* v. *Mahip Singh* (1888) 10 All. 425; *Hirabai* v. *Dinshaw* A.I.R. 1927 Bom. 22; *Rahim Baksh* v. *Bachcha Lal* A.I.R. 1929 All. 214; *Narayana* v. *Kannamma Bai* A.I.R. 1932 Mad. 445; *Gayadin* v. *Mahabir Singh* A.I.R. 1926 Oudh 353; *H.C.D'Silva* v. *F.M. Potenger* (1946) 1 Cal. 157; *Murli Das* v. *Sricharan Mahapatra* (1949) Cut. 645; *Vasudevachar* v. *Gundachar* (1946) 50 Mys. H.C. 214. But this followed after a great moralistic stylistic debate on this question. The plethora of cases are collected in Alexander's *Indian Case Law on Torts* (1910, Fifth edn.) 288-290.
27. *South Indian Railway Company* v. *Rama Krishna* (1889) 13 Mad. 34.
28. *Shepherd* v. *Trustees of the Port of Bombay* 1 Bom. 477,

29. *e.g. Venkata Narasimha* v. *Kotaya* (1888) 12 Mad. 374; *Abdul Nakim* v. *Tej Chandra Mukharji* (1881) 3 All. 815; *Gurdutt Singh* v. *Gopal Das* (1866) All.H.C. Rep. 33: *Nathji* v. *Lalbhai* (1890) 14 Bom. 97.
30. *Raman Nayar* v. *Subramanya Aiyar* (1890) 14 Mad. 51.
31. *e.g. Hinde* v. *Bandry* (1878) 2 Mad. 13 and the cases cited in note 30.
32. *e.g. Ganesh Datta* v. *Mugniram* (1872) 17 Suth W.R. 283 (P.C.)
33. *Narasimha Shankar Derbhande* v. *Balmand Lakshman* (1903) 27 Bom. 585.
34. *Pachaepercemal Chettiar* v. *Dasi Thangham* (1908) 31 Mad. 401.
35. *J.M. Cursetjee* v. *Secy. of State for India* (1903) 27 Bom. 189.
36. *Girwar Singh* v. *Siraman Singh* (1905) 9 C.W.N. 847.
37. *Thakur Das Say* v. *Achar Chandra Missri* (1904) 32 Cal. 425—such a right was maintainable under the Criminal Procedure Code but not in tort as indicated in *Girwar Singh's* case (*supra* note 36).
38. *Pitambar Das* v. *Dwarka Prashad* (1870) All.H.L. Rep. 435.
39. *Vallabha* v. *Madusudanan* (1888) 12 Mad. 405; see also *Appaya* v. *Padappa* (1899) 23 Bom. 122.
40. *Keshavalal* v. *Baigirja* (1899) 24 Bom. 13.
41. For a criminal case see *Q.* v. *Sri Vidya Sankara* (1883) 6 Mad. 382; *Copposami Chetty* v. *Duraisami Chetty* (1910) 33 Mad. 67.
42. *Gaya Din Singh* v. *Mahabir Singh* A.I.R. 1926 Oudh 363; or even having committed adultery with a low-caste woman: *Daulat Singh* v. *Prem Singh* A.I.R. 1938 All. 447. On this kind of use of the defamation jurisdiction see Marc Galanter; "Untouchability and the Law" (1969) 134 *Economic and Political Weekly* and R. Ramamoorthy: *Law of Malicious Prosecution and Defamation* (1976) 146-152, 222-224.
43. See *infra* note 112.
44. See *infra* note 109.
45. See *infra* note 110.
46. See *infra* note 160.
47. See *infra* notes 105, 159.
48. *Subbrayudu* v. *Ramakrishna Rao* (1968) II Andh.L.T. 161.
49. For the caste cases see especially *Vengala Venkayya* v. *Thallam* (1915) 28 M.L.J. 58; *Makund Ram* v. *Emp.* (1909) 9 Cr. L.J. 535; *Bachcha* v. *Emp.* (1910) 11 Cr.L.J. 413; see further V. Mitter: *The Law of Defamation and Malicious Prosecution* (1978 Seventh edn.) 188.
50. *Report of the Press Commission* (1952-54) pr. 1130 p. 434.
51. *Ibid.* pr. 1140 pp. 440-1.
52. *Ibid.* pr. 1121 pp. 431-2.
53. *Ibid.* pr. 1131 p. 435.
54. *Ibid.* pr. 1159 p. 453.
55. *Ibid.* pr. 1134 p. 437. Proposals along these lines have been inserted as S. 198-B Criminal Procedure Code, 1898 (S. 199 Criminal

Procedure Code, 1973). Here a public prosecutor may initiate such litigation. Thus an administrative officer who feels defamed has the option either to sue himself or have the public prosecutor to sue on his behalf: *Muneshwar Nand* v. *State* A.I.R. 1961 All. 24. The Supreme Court refused to allow defendants to bog this procedure down by quibbling on procedural formalities: *Sabib Singh* v. *State of U.P.* A.I.R. 1965 S.C. 1451.

56. *Ibid.* prs. 1136-7 pp. 438-9.
57. *Ibid.* pr. 1138 pp. 439-40.
58. *Ibid.* pr. 1137 pp. 439-40 relying at pr. 1137 p. 439-40 on *D. Shastri* v. *K.B. Sahay* (1953) 32 Patna 276 and contrasting *Mannalal* v. *D.P. Singh* A.I.R. 1950 All. 455.
59. Exceptions II and III of S. 499 Indian Penal Code, 1860.
60. *N.Y. Times* v. *Sullivan* (1964) 376 U.S. 254; *Gertz* v. *Welsh* (1974) 418 U.S. 323.
61. *Asoke Kumar* v. *Radha Kanto* A.I.R. 1967 Cal. 178 and the comments on V. Mitter: *Law of Defamation and Malicious Prosecution* (see now Seventh edn. 1978, 27) at pr. 22 p. 183 of the judgment.
62. *Hirabai Jehangir* v. *Dinshaw Edulji* A.I.R. 1927 Bom. 22.
63. *Asoke Kumar* v. *Radha Kanto* A.I.R. 1967 Cal. 178.
64. *Hirabai Jehangir* v. *Dinshaw*, A.I.R. 1927 Bom. 22.
65. See *Govinda Charyulu* v. *Seshagiri Rao* A.I.R. 1941 Mad. 860. But as R. Ramamoorthy points out (*Law of Malicious Prosecution and Defamation* (1976) 259 f n. 116) "the Court did not express any opinion" on this question.
66. For the details of the court fee, see R. Ramamoorthy (*supra* note 65) 285-6.
67. *Ma Sein Tin* v. *Kyaw Muung*, A.I.R. 1936 Rang. 322.
68. *Edara Venkayya* v. *Pantulu Kalipattappa Chitti* A.I.R. 1940 Mad. 879.
69. *R.K. Karanjia* v. *K.M.D. Thackersey* A.I.R. 1970 Bom. 424. Note also the Rs.28,000 award in *State of Orissa* v. *Nyayapati* (1970) Cut. 1264.
70. R. Ramamoorthy (*supra* note 65) 268-72.
71. *Haraku Chand* v. *Ganga Prashad* A.I.R. 1925 All. 371.
72. *Ahsanali* v. *Hifazali* A.I.R. 1956 Nag. 264.
73. *Ogilvie* v. *Punjab Akhrat Co.* A.I.R. 1929 Lah. 561.
74. *Munshi Ram* v. *Mela Ram* A.I.R. 1936 Lah. 23.
75. *Khair-ud-din* v. *Tara Singh* A.I.R. 1927 Lah. 20.
76. *Maroti Sadashiv* v. *Godubhai N. Rao* A.I.R. 1959 Bom. 443.
77. See R. Ramamoorthy's (*supra* note 65) Table at 268-272 and the discussion at 257-65.
78. See S. 499 Indian Penal Code, 1860.
79. Macaulay: *Report of the Law Commission on the Indian Penal Code* (1837) *supra* note 24 p. 706.

80. See the cases cited in note 26 *supra.*
81. See *Hirabai* v. *Dinshaw* A.I.R. 1918 Bom. 22.
82. In England, it is now actionable *per se* under the Slander of Women Act, 1891.
83. *Bhooni Money Dossee* v. *Natobar Biswas* (1901) 28 Cal. 452 at 465.
84. *Hulton* v. *Jones* (1929) 2 K.B. 31.
85. *Naganatha* v. *Subramania* A.I.R. 1918 Mad. 700.
86. *T.V.R. Iyer* v. *M.A. Mohideen* A.I.R. 1972 Mad. 399.
87. *Arnold* v. *K.E.* (1914) 41 I.A. 149.
88. On the ownership pattern see *Report of the Press Commission* (1952-54), I, Chapters XV-XVI and of the Chapter 2 *supra.*
89. *Supra* note 87.
90. See *Vishan Sarup* v. *Nardeo Shastri* A.I.R. 1965 All. 439 pr. 16 p. 441; *M.B. Kanwar* v. *State* A.I.R. 1963 Punj. 201 at pr. 14 p. 205; *Gour Chandra* v. *Public Prosecutor* A.I.R. 1962 Ori. 197 at pr. 16 p. 202; *Dongar Singh* v. *Krishan Kant* A.I.R. 1958 M.P. 216 at pr. 11 pp. 217-8; *Dongar Singh* v. *Krishan* A.I.R. 1957 M.P. 162 at pr. 27 p. 164, pr. 31 p. 165; *T.C. Goswami* v. *State* A.I.R. 1952 Pepsu 165 at pr. 6 p. 168; *Balasubramania* v. *Rajgopalachariar* A.I.R. 1944 Mad. 484 at 491; *N.B. Khare* v. *M.R. Masani* A.I.R. 1942 Nag. 117 at 118; *Emperor v. J.M. Chatterjee* A.I.R. 1933 All. 434 at 435. This view is reiterated as we shall see in most press cases.
91. *Sahib Singh* v. *State of U.P.* A.I.R. 1965 S.C. 1451.
92. *Chellapan Pillai* v. *Karanjia* (1962) 2 Cr.L.J. 142.
93. *Durga Prashad* v. *State of Rajasthan* (1969) Raj.L.W. 202.
94. *Purshottam Vijay* v. *State* A.I.R. 1961 M.P. 205 pr. 32 p. 212.
95. *Chariyan* v. *Johnson* (1969) K.L.J. 507.
96. *Ibid* f.n 3 p. 600.
97. *Chhogalal* v. *Purshottam* (1969) Jab. L.J. 541.
98. *Sewakram Sobhani* v. *R.K. Karanjia* A.I.R. 1981 S.C. 1514.
99. *Ibid. per* Justice Chinnappa Reddy pr. 18. p. 1520.
100. Truth is necessary, however, for the Fourth and not the Ninth Exception to S. 499 of the Indian Penal Code, 1860.
101. *Ibid. per* Justice A.P. Sen pr. 12 p. 1519. The learned Judge does not (at pr. 11 p. 1519) distinguish the import of the First and Ninth Exceptions with any clarity.
102. *Per* Justice Baharul Islam pr. 31 p. 1523.
103. *Ibid.* pr. 21 p. 1521; pr. 24 p. 1522 pr. 27 p. 1522.
104. *R.K. Karanjia* v. *K.M.D. Thackersey* A I.R. 1970 Bom. 424.
105. *Nadirshaw Hormusji* v. *Pirojshaw Ratnaji Ratnagar* (1913) 15 Bom. L.R. 130; *Janardhan Karandekar* v. *Ramchandra Tilak.* A.I.R. 1947 Bom. 209.
106. *Venkayya* v. *Surya Prakasamma* A.I.R. 1940 Mad. 879.
107. *Naganatha* v. *Subramania* A.I.R. 1918 Mad. 700; *Mitha Rustomjee* v. *Nusserwanji Nowroji* A.I.R. 1941 Bom. 278.

108. *U.B. Guarantee Co.* v. *Thakore Lal* A.I.R. 1936 Bom. 114; *R.K. Karanjia* v. *K.M D. Thackersey* A.I.R. 1970 Bom. 424; *Chhogalal* v. *Purshottam* (1969) Jab.L.J. 744; *T.V.R. Iyer* v. *M A. Mohideen* A.I.R. 1972 Mad. 399; *Bal Ram* v. *Sukh Sampat Lal* A.I.R. 1975 Raj. 40.
109. *Lala Lajpat Rai* v. *Englishman* (1908-09) 13 C.W.N. 895; *Englishman* v. *Lajpat Rai* (1909) 14 C.W.N. 713; *Subhash Chandra Bose* v. *Knight and Sons* A.I.R. 1929 Cal. 69; *Baba Gurdit Singh* v. *Statesman Ltd.* (1934-5) 35 C.W.N. 845.
110. *A.J. Barrow* v. *Hem Chandra Lahiri* (1907-08) 12 C.W.N. 490; *Khairrudin* v. *Tara Singh* A.I.R. 1927 Lah. 20; *Dina Nath* v. *Sayad Habib* A.I.R. 1929 Lah. 129; *K.P. Narayan* v. *Mahendra Singh* A.I.R. 1957 Nag. 18.
111. *Hales* v. *Smiles* A.I.R. 1937 Rang. 105.
112. *Bina Bhowmick* v. *Tushar Kanti Ghosh* A.I.R. 1955 N.U.C. (Cal.) 487; *Narayana* v. *Narayan Iyer* (1961) 2 M.L J. 189.
113. *Makkhan Lal* v. *Panchamal* A.I.R. 1934 Nag. 226; *Kaikhenu Naoroji Kabraji* v. *Jehangir Byramji Murztan* (1890) 14. Bom. 532; *Englishman Ltd.* v. *Antonio* A.I.R. 1931 Cal. 81; *Gurbachan Singh* v. *Babu Ram* A.I.R. 1969 Punj. 201; *State of Orissa* v. *Nyayapati Ramanujaswamy* (1970) Cut. 1264.
114. *Nadirshaw Hormesji* v. *Pirojshaw Ratnaji Ratangar* (1913) 15 Bom. L.R. 130.
115. *Janardhan Karandekar* v. *Ramachandra Tilak* A.I.R. 1947 Bom. 209.
116. *Naganatha* v. *Subramania* A.I.R. 1918 Mad. 700.
117. *Venkayya* v. *Surya Prakasamma* A.I.R. 1940 Mad. 879.
118. *Mitha Rustomjee* v. *Nusserwanji Nowroji* A.I.R. 1941 Bom. 278.
119. *U B. Guarantee Co.* v. *Thakore Lal* A.I.R. 1936 Bom. 114.
120. See R. Ramamoorthy (*supra* note 65) 268-272.
121. *R.K. Karanjia* v. *K.M.D. Thackersey* A.I.R. 1970 Bom. 424.
122. *Chhogalal* v. *Purshottam* (1969) Jab.L.J. 544.
123. *T.V.R. Iyer* v. *M.A. Mohideen* A.I.R. 1972 Mad. 399.
124. *Bal Ram* v. *Sukh Sampat Lal* A.I.R. 1975 Raj 40.
125. *Lala Lajpat Rai* v. *Englishman Ltd.* (1908-09) 13 C.W.N. 895; *Englishman Ltd*. v. *Lala Lajpat Rai* (1909) 14 C.W.N. 713.
126. *Subhash Chandra* v. *Knight and Sons* A.I.R. 1929 Cal. 69.
127. *Baba Gurdit Siugh* v. *Statesman Ltd.* (1934-35) 35 C.W.N. 845.
128. *A.J. Barrow* v. *Hem Chandra Lahiri* (1907-08) 12 C.W.N. 490.
129. *Khairrudin* v. *Tara Singh* A.I.R. 1927 Lah. 20.
130. *Dina Nath* v. *Sayad Habib* A.I.R. 1929 Lah. 129.
131. *Supra* note 87.
132. *Hales* v. *Smiles* A.I.R. 1937 Rangoon 105.
133. *K.P. Narayan* v. *Mahendra Singh* A.I.R. 1957 Nag. 18.
134. *E J. Howard* v. *M. Mull* (1865-6) 1 Bom. H.C.R. (App) 85.

135. *Bina Bhowmick* v. *Tushar Kanti Ghosh* A.I.R. 1955 N.U.C. (Cal) 487.
136. *Narayana* v. *Narayana Iyer* (1961) II M.L.J. 189.
137. *Makkhan Lal* v. *Panchamal* A.I.R. 1934 Nag. 226.
138. *Kaikhuru Naoroji Kabraji* v. *Jehangir Byramji Murztan* (1890) 14 Bom. 532.
139. *Englishman Ltd.* v. *Antonio* A.I.R. 1931 Cal. 81.
140. *Gurbachan Singh* v. *Babu Ram* A.I.R. 1969 Punj. 201.
141. *State of Orissa* v. *Nyayayati Ramanujaswamy* (1970) Cut. 1264.
142. Macaulay: *Report of the Law Commission on the Indian Penal Code* ((1837) *supra* note 24) 705.
143. Law Commission of India: *Forty-second Report on the Indian Penal Code* (1971) 330-1.
144. S. 499 Indian Penal Code, 1860.
145. *Ibid.* Explanation I.
146. *Ibid.* Explanation II.
147. *Ibid.* Explanation III.
148. *Ibid.* Explanation IV.
149. Consider *Raman Nayar* v. *Subramanyu* (1894) 17 Mad. 87; *Jaganath Prashad* v. *Rafat Ali* A.I.R. 1934 All. 827.
150. Cf. *Lala Bhagirath* v. *Saiyed Ali* A.I.R. 1931 Oudh 392; *Kamla Patel* v. *Bhagwandas* A.I.R. 1934 Nag. 123; *Duraiswami* v. *Lakshman* A.I.R. 1933 Mad. 537.
151. S. 499 Indian Penal Code, 1860, Exceptions IV and V.
152. *Ibid.* Exception VII.
153. *Ibid.* Exception VIII.
154. Now see Parliamentary Proceedings (Protection of Publications) Act, 1977 and see also Article 361-A of the Indian Constitution as amended by the Constitution (Forty-fourth Amendment) Act, 1978.
155. S. 499 Indian Penal Code Exception II.
156. *Ibid.* Exception III.
157. *Aziz Ahmad* v. *Emp.* A.I.R. 1928 Lah. 865; *Mohd. Nazir* v. *Emp.* A.I.R. 1928 All. 321.
158. *M.B. Kanwar* v. *State* A.I.R. 1963 Punj. 201; *Dongar Singh* v. *Krishan* A.I.R. 1957 U.P. 162 and A.I.R. 1958 M.P. 216.
159. *Wahidullah Ansari* v. *Emp.* (1935) All. L.J. 676; *Mahin Chandra Roy* v. *A.H. Watson* (1928) 55 Cal. 1260; *T.C. Gupta* v. *R.K. Karanjia* (1962) All.L.J. 450; *Chellappan Pillai* v. *Karanjia* (1962) 2 Cr.L.J. 142; *Asha Parekh* v. *State of Bihar* (1977) Cr.L.J. 21; *Raj Kapoor* v. *Narendra* (1974) 15 G.L.R. 125.
160. *Balasubramaniam* v. *Rajgopalachariar* A.I.R. 1944 Mad. 484; *Harbhajan Singh* v. *State of Punjab* A.I.R. 1965 Punj. 215 reversed A.I.R. 1961 S.C. 97; *Gour Chandra* v. *Public Prosecutor* A.I.R. 1962 Ori. 197; *N.J. Nanporia* v. *Brojendra Bhowmick* (1974-5) 79 C.W.N. 531 (involving alleged political terrorists).

161. *Q.E.* v. *Girija Shankar Kashiram* (1890) 15 Bom. 286; *Emp.* v. *J.M. Chatterjee* A.I.R. 1933 All. 434; *State* v. *Packiraj* A.I.R. 1951 T.C. 105; *Harbhajan Singh* v. *State of Punjab* A.I.R. 1961 Punj. 215 rev. on appeal A.I.R. 1960 S.C. 97; *Purshottam Vijay* v. *State* A.I.R. 1961 M.P. 205; *Ram Kumar* v. *State* (1962) 1 Cr. L.J. 122; *Cheriyan* v. *Johnson* (1969) K.L.T. 597; *Bibhuti Bhushan* v. *Sudhir Kumar* A.I.R. 1966 Cal. 73; *Sahib Singh* v. *State of U.P.* A.I.R. 1965 S.C. 145; *K. Nair* v. *Thirumumnu* A.I.R. 1948 Mad. 266; *Vishan Sarup* v. *Nardeo Shastri* A.I.R. 1965 All. 439; *Sahib Singh* v. *State of U.P.* A.I.R. 1965 S.C. 1451; *Dongar Singh* v. *Krishan Kant* A.I.R. 1957 M.P. 162 and A.I.R. 1958 M.P. 216.
162. *e.g. Rumasami* v. *Lokanda* (1886) 9 Mad. 387.
163. *Aziz Ahmad* v. *Emp.* A.I.R. 1928 Lah. 865.
164. *Mohd. Nazir* v. *Emp.* A.I.R. 1928 All. 321.
165. *M.B. Kanwar* v. *State* A.I.R. 1963 Punj. 201.
166. *Wahidullah Ansari* v. *Emp.* (1935) All. L.J. 676.
167. *Mahin Chandra Roy* v. *A.H. Watson* (1928) 55 Cal. 1260.
168. *Asha Parekh* v. *State of Bihar* (1977) Cr.L.J. 21; *Raj Kapoor* v. *Narendra* (1974) 15 G.L.R. 125.
169. *Raj Kapoor* v. *Narendra* (1974) 15 G.L.R. 125.
170. *T.C. Gupta* v. *R.K. Karanjia* (1962) All L.J. 450.
171. *Chellapan Pillai* v. *Karanjia* (1962) Cr. L.J. 142.
172. *N.B. Khare* v. *M.R. Masani*, A.I.R. 1942 Nag 117; Cf. *Balasubramaniam* v. *Rajgopalachariar* A.I.R. 1944 Mad. 484.
173. *Harbhajan Singh* v. *State of Punjab* A.I.R. 1966 S.C. 97 at pr. 25 p. 104.
174. *R. Shankar* v. *State* A.I.R. 1959 Ker. 100.
175. *Gour Chandra* v. *Public Prosecutor* A.I.R. 1962 Ori. 197; see *Balasubramaniam* v. *Rajgopalachariar* A.I.R. 1944 Mad. 484 (attack on Rajaji).
176. *N.J. Nanporia* v. *Brojendra Bhowmick* (1974-75) 79 C.W.N. 531.
177. *E.J. Howard* v. *M. Mull* (1862-3) 1 Bom. H.C.R. (App.) 85.
178. *Q.E.* v. *Girija Shankar Kashiram* (1890) 15 Bom. 286. The facts are not clear. The Magistrate thought the article was for the public good. The High Court seems to have been concerned with only a technical point about the place of publication and jurisdiction.
179. *Emp.* v. *J.M. Chatterjee* A.I.R. 1933 All. 434.
180. *State* v. *Packiraj* A.I.R. 1951 T.C. 105.
181. *Harbhajan Singh* v. *State of Punjab* A.I.R. 1961 Punj. 215.
182. *Harbhajan Singh* v. *State of Punjab* A.I.R. 1966 S.C. 97.
183. *Purshottam Vijay* v. *State* A.I.R. 1961 M.P. 205.
184. *Ram Kumar* v. *State* (1962) 1 Cr. L.J. 122.
185. *Kelu Nair* v. *Thirumumnu* A.I.R. 1948 Mad. 266.
186. *Vishnu Sarup* v. *Nardeo Shastri* A.I.R. 1965 All. 439.
187. *Supra* note 95.
188. *Bibhuti Bhushan* v. *Sudhir Kumar* A.I.R. 1966 Cal. 473.

189. *Sahib Singh* v. *State of U.P.* A.I.R. 1965 S.C. 1451 at pr. 11 p. 1454. Truth was not being put forward as a defence in this case.
190. *Sewakram Sobhavi* v. *R.K. Karanjia* A.I.R. 1981 S.C. 1514.
191. *Ramasami* v. *Lokanda* (1886) 9 Mad. 387.
192. Cf. *Report of the Committee on Defamation* (1975) Cmnd. 5909 at pr. 137-140 pp. 36-7.

PART FOUR

Problems of Accountability

9

MAKING THE PRESS ACCOUNTABLE: THE EXPERIMENT OF THE PRESS COUNCIL

Is the press a public institution, or a private group performing functions which are important to the public? What is the basis on which the press can claim special powers and privileges? The press in India is, by and large, a private business, largely owned by private individuals. This can hardly be doubted even if the press does work in the shadow of the influence of the government. (The government, however, does *control* both radio and television.) The press performs many functions. It is a source of all kinds of private, commercial and public information. It is a forum for discussion. It is a means to expose and exercise the control of power. Superimposed upon all this are various other functions. As a source of information it is given an investigative function to determine the truth. As a forum for public discussion it performs the censorial function of evaluating what is said and provides a direction to what is said. Taken together all this makes the press quite a formidable quantity. As a business and an entertainer, the press must take its place along with other businesses and entertainers. But its information dissemination, investigative, truth verification, public discussion, censorial, public opinion stimulation and power management functions make the press responsible for matters of considerable public importance.[1]

Not all these functions are emphasised with equal effect in all countries. In some countries the press is publicly owned. Its information dissemination and public opinion stimulation functions are given greater importance than its investigative, truth verification, public discussion, censorial or power management functions.

In India, the press is theoretically supposed to perform all these functions. In actual fact, the performance of these functions meets all kinds of opposition. The press itself suffers from considerable ineptitude. It transmits information without independent investigation and truth verification. Owned by private business houses and manned by self-styled pundits, its censorial and power management functions are either transparently partisan or ineffective and pontificatory. It certainly moulds public opinion in a planned and unplanned way, and there is a growing concern to develop an independent journalism. This development has not wholly matured. The local and vernacular press are firmly established within their own setting and reflect marketplace gossip and local power.

Any discussion of the powers of the press is linked up to broader questions about our expectations from the press and our confidence in the press to perform the functions we expect it to perform. As long as we take the view that the press is merely a private group interested in furthering private interests and ambitions, there is an understandable reluctance to give the press increased powers and privileges. Accordingly, the press is treated as possessing no greater rights than those of other individuals[2] even though it is considered to be a group with a particular importance.

Normally, extensive powers and privileges are given to governmental institutions such as the legislatures, the army, police, civil services, and autonomous quasi-independent corporations. The focal point of the issue is, whether a collection of private bodies can be treated as constituting a public institution. Private institutions take out a lot of power for themselves and legitimate their possession of this power on the basis of the public importance of their work. If public notions of equality of opportunity, participation, access and influence are important, they are serious impediments in the path of the recognition of the press as a special public body. The press has constantly sought to play down its elite structure and emphasize its impartial dedication to all its functions. While not denying the importance of the press, people and governments have not been inclined to give the press the general status of being a public institution entitled to preferential treatment. At most, the importance of its tasks are recognised and preferential treatment accorded on an *ad hoc* basis. In America, the press is given a considerable amount of importance and many of its demands—in respect of the public functions it performs—have been met satisfactorily. A confrontation between the press and any other public institution (such as the bureaucracy, the judiciary, the executive or the legislature) is seen as a confrontation between two great public institutions and resolved on that basis.

In India, the demands of the press are not perceived as the demands of a public institution performing indispensable public functions. Indeed, the press is seen as a private group performing certain important functions which affect the public. A confrontation between the press and any other public institution is not a confrontation between two equals performing functions of co-equal public importance. The press is important, but subsidiary. Its demands have to be considered but can be rejected in favour of other public institutions whose importance is regarded as being unquestionably more than that of the press. And so, the demands of the press yield generously to the demands of official secrecy, protecting morality and decency, public order and contempt of court.

In 1950, the Constitution of India guaranteed freedom of speech and expression subject to reasonable restrictions in the interests of the "sovereignty and integrity of India, the security of the State, friendly relations with foreign states, public order, decency and morality or in relation to contempt of court, defamation or incitement of an offence".[3] Earlier suggestions that the freedom of the press should be specifically mentioned[4] were not reflected in the final text of the Constitution even though the importance of protecting the freedom of the press was emphasized on the floor of the Constituent Assembly.[5] In one sense, the fact that the freedom of the press is not specifically mentioned in the Constitution has not made much difference. The courts have assumed that the phrase 'freedom of speech and expression' includes, *inter alia*, the freedom of the press.[6] In another sense. the omission of a specific mention of the press has meant that the courts have been reluctant to give the press the preferred position it wants. By 1959, the Supreme Court echoed the view of Lord Shaw and argued that since freedom of the press was—

> only a right flowing from the freedom of speech and expression, the liberty of the press in India stands on no higher footing than the freedom of speech and expression of a citizen and that no privilege attaches to the press as such, that is to say, as distinct from the freedom of the citizen.[7]

The result is that the rights of the press as an institution (that is those rights which the press as a whole needs to enable it to effectively perform its functions) have never really been lobbied before, or considered by, the courts. Instead, the courts have refused to give special privileges to the press.[8]

The fact that the press performs an invaluable function in a democracy is not denied. But this has not led to a comprehensive examination of the institutional needs of the press. The Supreme Court has considered the importance of preserving certain kinds of working conditions for journalists.[9] It has also considered, in depth, the need for newspapers to retain some kind of control over the economics of production and distribution.[10] But no attention has been paid to the needs of the press to protect its right to investigate and report the truth, comment on what is going on or what has been discovered, and safeguard the methods by which these investigative, reporting and censorial functions are to be preserved. There is no doubt that in the performance of these functions the press often intrudes on the rights of others. If the press is an important institution in the working of a democracy, its institutional needs cannot be totally ignored. By not giving the press any greater rights than those given to an ordinary citizen, it has been put in the difficult position of having been given responsibilities with no special privileges to discharge these responsibilities.

All these have affected the interpretation of the constitutionally guaranteed right to freedom of speech and expression. There are very few occasions when the Supreme Court has not permitted the legislature and government to restrict or restrain the freedom of speech and expression. After an initial hesitation arising out of an alleged technical flaw in the drafting of the Constitution,[11] the Court has permitted the pre-censorship of newspapers,[12] validated a wide-ranging law of sedition,[13] approved of wide restraints of the freedom of speech and expression in the interests of public order and security of state,[14] approved a conservative law relating to obscenity,[15] upheld the laws relating to contempt of court[16] and even suggested that the parliamentary privileges can erode the constitutionally guaranteed freedom of speech and expression.[17] The provision that the restraints on the constitutionally guaranteed freedom of speech and expression must amount to a 'reasonable restriction' has been interpreted restrictively.[18] The approach has not been to give prominence to the protected freedom but to balance it against other factors so that it is one of many factors that have to be considered and not necessarily the most important one.

Granting additional powers and privileges to the press will undoubtedly affect both the life of an individual subject and other aspects of the public interest. A press claiming to investigate and publish matters in the public interest will intrude into an individual's privacy, violate his confidence and affect his reputation. The law works on the assumption that a private individual cannot make intrusions into the life of another individual except in two circumstances. Such intrusions are permitted either with the *consent* of the person affected, or in the pursuit of some legitimate freedom of the person making the intrusion. The press, as a private body, is expected to operate within these constraints. It can always get the consent of the person affected by its activities. Alternatively, the press must argue its case on the basis that as an individual body it is merely exercising its own undoubted rights. The law is constantly faced with the problem of adjusting conflicting claims.

The real problem is whether the press can constantly raise the plea that it serves the public interest. We allow the police and the tax inspector to intrude into the privacy of an individual. The government conducts and publicises damaging inquiries about private individuals. Courts and governmental institutions often demand a breach of confidentiality when they need information in the public interest. But even the government does not claim a blanket power to act in the public interest in respect of all issues and situations. Each grant of power is considered specifically. The press too cannot claim to make the broad plea of constantly acting in the public interest. They must exhaust all their private rights first and then claim additional privileges in certain situations. By and large, the law does not permit private individuals to make the plea of public interest. This is generally true of many aspects of law. People cannot enlarge their own rights or reduce others' rights simply by putting forward the claim that they are acting in the public interest (*i.e.* "I would have fulfilled this contract but it is not now in the public interest to do so"). Indeed if that were the case, everyone would claim to act in the public interest and we would be back where we started. The public interest is usually pleaded by a public body acting with, and considered deserving of, the authority to make that plea.

The claim of the press to be treated as a public institution is considerably weakened by the fact that it is privately owned and does not admit of any well developed system of accountability and representation other than whatever sense of self-restraint arises from its internal institutional morality. As a private group, the press must first establish that it deserves to be made the repository of certain aspects of the public interest. Then, it must show that the *public* interest it claims deserves to be recognised and have priority over other *public* interests (including the public interest in maintaining the rights of individuals). Therefore, three conditions should be satisfied before a private individual, group or institution is given the preferred powers and privileges of acting in the public interest:

(i) It must show that it deserves to be made the repository of this public interest. It must also show how it accommodates the public interest in fairness, equality of opportunity and the principles of public accountability.

(ii) The interest it claims to want to discharge must deserve to be recognised as part of the public interest.

(iii) It must claim to have priority over other aspects of the public interest (including the public interest in maintaining the rights of individuals). This will determine whether it deserves to be recognised and the extent to which it must be recognised.

Condition (i) cannot be ignored even if conditions (ii) and (iii) are met. Thus, the fact that the press theoretically performs functions fundamental to a democracy is not enough. The press in any country may, in fact, not perform these tasks but intrude upon other interests which deserve to be maintained. It is important to make this point because some people proceed on the assumption that just because certain things are in the public interest, it follows that the press must be given the task of dealing with these things.[19] The argument that the judiciary must not be corrupt is beyond challenge. It does not follow that the press is the best means of exposing this corruption. The institutional needs of the administration of justice, the track record of the press, and the efficacy and effect of all the alternative mechanisms have to be considered. The fact that the press is an otherwise unaccountable, non-homogenous and private group with differential levels of access, responsibility and efficiency cannot be ignored.

The law of defamation is designed to trust all people—even though the major beneficiaries of this are the press—to make honest, true, fair comments on other people in the public interest.[20] The public interest in free speech is reconciled with the private interest in maintaining other individuals' rights. In a law and order or national security situation, varying degrees of control are imposed on ordinary people and the press in various situations. The public interest in maintaining order has priority over the public interest in free speech. In the law relating to contempt of court, the press is given very limited powers because it is felt that the institutions which administer justice may need an extra layer of protection. While the need to preserve the public interest in the exposure of corruption and public discussion is not denied, the manner in which the press discharges this aspect of the public interest may create other complications. In India, additional complications are created because some sections of the press have not shown themselves to discharge this function properly while others, including some of the national press, have been docile.

It is important to pursue this point a little further. On the one hand, we have public institutions which demand that they cannot discharge their functions unless they are given certain powers and protected from certain kinds of criticisms and comments. This is not just a demand that is made by the courts alone but also by other institutions of government as well. Parliament claims certain privileges including the power to commit people for contempt of itself and its members. The executive protects its processes by the law of sedition and the laws relating to confidentiality and official secrecy. On the other hand, we have the press itself, claiming to be a public institution and discharging certain public interest functions. We have already explained that a private group—which has a limited, or no, system of public accountability, an unreliable and indifferent level of performance and promotes a differential access to it as far as all the members of a society are concerned—is not entitled to claim that it is a public institution which should also be given increased powers to protect its prestige and functioning viability.

The view that the press should be denied the status of a public institution does not mean that some of the functions that the press performs do not deserve to be protected. Apart from the duty or need to protect certain institutions it is in the public interest that the functions of investigation, truth verification, public discussion, public opinion formulation, power management and entertainment should be encouraged. It is in the public interest that people should have the right to have information about how public institutions work, the right to participate in issues and matters which concern or affect them. These matters are in the public interest not because there is a public institution—the press—which has the right to perform these functions or possess these rights. These matters are in the public interest because India has chosen a political system, the success of which depends on an effective distribution of these rights amongst a large section of the people. The right to informed participation is sufficiently important but may have to yield to the public interest in the viability of public institutions. But in a large democracy which has evolved a complicated pattern of communication, the bundle of rights connected with the right of informed participation have to be delivered through various highly organised methods. The question as to whether the press is a "public institution" and deserves additional "privileges" only confuses the issue. It conjures the image of giving special privileges to a private group of people because they claim to be important people doing important things. Both the phrases—"public institution" and "privilege"—are highly emotive. They dissuade rather than persuade. They also mislead.

The crucial question is: how are these tasks best performed? In various countries, the right to informed participation is theoretically catered to through a party machinery. The press plays a minimal role in all this. India has chosen to be a liberal democracy in which the transmission of information has been entrusted to a private group. Other alternative avenues for information and participation are inextricably enmeshed in the social system. We have to think of the development of the right to informed participation within the constraints of this framework. The problem is not of consecrating this group as a public institution with special privileges. The problem is of ensuring that the press does, in fact, do whatever it is supposed to do. This must entail protecting the rights of the press as a group. All this is not because the group is *sui generis*, but because something needs to be done and the press is an important mechanism through which it is done. In this formulation, the press is not a 'public institution' as such. It performs important functions. Any privileges that accrue out of this formulation do not go to the press but to the people. In its claim to protect its working and function, the press cannot be considered apart from the people it serves. Its claims for increased protection would be greatly assisted if it could show that it serves the public at large and not sectional social, political or economic interests.

This takes us to the question of accountability. We will distinguish between two forms of accountability—democratic accountability and functional accountability. Democratic accountability exists where there is a real informed participation by a large number of people. This leads to the creation of democratic structures which make such participation possible. Functional accountability does not concern itself with such concerns. Here, the press would argue that as long as it performs all its functions—in terms of information dissemination, investigation, truth verification, public discussion, censorial, public opinion stimulation and power management—it should not be asked to submit to forms of democratic accountability. And, of course, there are great difficulties in trying to design democratic structures for the press. Elections on a "winner-takes-all" basis are self-defeating exercises. This is equally true of either direct forms of governmental control or the interposition of trustees between the owners of a paper and its working journalists. Democratic structures can stretch to placing journalists in charge of the paper. This would, at least, solve one problem. The people who bring out the paper would be in a position of primary accountability. They cannot claim that they are not responsible for the paper. They cannot say that they are secondarily accountable to those whom they take orders from—whether this be the editor or the proprietor of the paper. But creating democratic structures within the newspaper does not mean that a system of democratic accountability involving the public has been created. Can the press make a plea of functional accountability? This is allowing a plea of the variety: "As long as I am doing my job well, how does it matter?" Indeed, this has been the plea of rulers who have ruled by Divine Right, dictators who believed in benign despotism and technocrats who have faith in their own efficiency. Democratic accountability was invented in order to offset the claims of functional accountability and to enable participation and not just the achievement of things.

Be that as it may, in a liberal democracy, the emphasis has been on evolving patterns of functional accountability for the press. The quest for forms of democratic accountability has been abandoned. The endeavour has been to ensure some kind of control whereby the press is able to perform all these functions. Sometimes, this control takes the form of direct governmental interference. Here, the government says that it is trying to create conditions to enable the press to perform its various functions. Thus, the formal reason for control of newsprint in India was to force an equitable distribution of this valuable material for the press. But governmental control creates its own problems. So, the strategy has been either to persuade the press to control itself or to create yet more institutions which will protect the press. Sometimes, both these strategies are combined in one. Some element of democratic accountability is sought to be introduced here. The press itself is persuaded to create institutions which will watch over it. All this seems a little strange. For we think of the press as a watch dog. Now, we seem to be talking of creating a watch dog to watch the watch dog.

II

The Press Commission of India was deeply concerned about the "standards and performance" of the press.[21] It wanted a certain amount of "accuracy and fairness".[22] This included the right to "propagate a point of view by marshalling facts and/or argument from facts or by the logical processes of inference or by deductions from any political, economic or other theory or set of ideas".[23] It required the press to supply "truthful, objective and comprehensive. . . news from all corners of the world. . . (because) . . .(t)he man behind the plough is eager to understand the world community of which he is a part".[24] At the same time, it seemed to be quite clear in its mind what the aims and objectives of the Indian Press ought to be:

> In our view, it is only a clear perception of the objective which can give meaning and significance to the vocation of journalism.
>
> The ultimate goal of Indian society has been very clearly defined in the directive principles embodied in the Indian Constitution. This is to secure and protect a social order in which justice, social, economic and political shall inform all the institutions of public life. Only the ever-present consciousness of such a definite purpose can give the journalist the ctiterion to judge what he writes. Without that background of some social philosophy, it would not be possible for him to correlate and interpret the multitudinous variety of events that take place every hour.[25]

Independent India seems to have found the need for an overwhelming emphasis of the concept of commitment. The concept of a committed press has its sequel in the concept of a committed judiciary which was floated in the early seventies and which was given as the theoretical reason for the supersession of certain judges in respect of their claims to be considered the Chief Justice of India.[26] One of the major difficulties with the concept of "commitment" is that this concept soon becomes a concept of "commitment" to the government rather than on independent criteria for evaluation and censorial comment. Equally, faced with a privately owned press which already seeks to try and project its own multiple versions of what social justice is, there are great difficulties in evaluating a sensible criteria. To keep such a press "professional" and within the bounds of accuracy, fairness and predictability is difficult enough. In many instances a loose concept of social justice serves as a legitimating device for the press and an instrument of control for those who wish to control it.

The Press Commission itself did a sample study of 5 national and 8 regional topics that where handled by the press.[27] Many of the mistakes of the press were unintentional,[28] even though there was yellow journalism,[29] sensationalism,[30] malicious attacks on public men,[31] indecency and vulgarity,[32] personal attacks on individuals[33] and several instances of objectionable writings which had been reported by the State government.[34] Its final verdict—which is not without relevance today—seemed to be:

> In the smaller States, where democratic government is being developed gradually, the papers are full of scurrilous attacks on politicians in office. In every part of the country, there have been examples of vulgarity, indecency and obscenity. . . . (T)he well established press have, on the whole, maintained a high standard of journalism. We are glad to state that they have avoided a cheap sensationalism and unwarranted intrusion into private lives. They represent a decisive majority of the total circulation in India. Objectionable features have been noticed in a small section of the press. Nevertheless, the large and well established newspapers suffer from certain weaknesses. Some of them are partisan in the presentation of news in respect of the financial interests with which they are allied; there is a certain timidity to expose courageously the shortcomings of those who are in a position of power and authority; there is an element of arbitrariness in the publicity given or denied to individuals; there is a tendency to suppress facts which are unfavourable to their own interests or the financial interests with which they are associated. These undesirable features are not singular to the Indian press. Despite these shortcomings we are of the opinion that the country possesses a number of newspapers of which any country may be proud.[35]

The Press Commission took the view that what was needed was a press council.[36] The purpose of this press council was not just to keep a watch on the press. It was also to enthuse a new perspective into journalists, do research and look at the ownership patterns of the press.[37] Someone who was a High Court judge would be nominated by the Chief Justice of India[38] to preside over the Council which would have 25 members out of which a majority of 13 members would come from the press. The Press Council would look at complaints and set up some uniform standards.[39] It would be financed through a levy of a cess of Rs. 10 per ton on the amount of newsprint consumed.[40]

In order to give effect to this recommendation, the government introduced a Bill in Parliament in July 1956. This Bill lapsed. The cause of a Press Council was again taken up by the National Integration Committee in 1962 until a Bill was introduced in July 1963 which was passed in 1965.[41] The Press Council itself was set up in 1966,[42] continued in 1970,[43] abolished during the Emergency in 1976,[44] and refloated in 1978.[45] The political discussions in Parliament on the Press Council are interesting because they indicate some of the profound confusions of the press and the Press Commission. There seem to have been many expectations of the Press Council—a kind of belief that the Press Council would clean the Augean stables on behalf of the government in the name of social justice.[46] Undoubtedly, parliamentarians kept a continuous watch over the Press Council in an effort to ensure that it did its job and controlled communalism, obscenity and the like.[47] The Press Council itself has tried to fashion out its role within the limitations of power, status and efficiency within which it is set.

The Statement of Objects and Reasons of the Press Council Act, 1965 stated the broad expectations from the Press Council which was to be "an autonomous body. . . and was to regulate its own procedure." It was "to safeguard the liberty of the press, evolve and maintain standards of journalistic ethics, keep under review developments tending towards monopoly and concentration of control and provide research and provide common services for the press." It was to consist of "people principally connected with the press. . . as well as a few members. . . represent(ing) the interests of education, literature, law and culture. . . and also public opinion through three members drawn from Parliament."[48] This was to be a judicious combination of a democracy and voluntariness. The papers were represented; and, it was alleged, so were the people. The Chairman was appointed by the Chief Justice of India.[49] The other members were to be six editors, seven other journalists, six proprietors, three persons appointed by the University Grants Commission, Bar Council of India and the Sahitya (Literary)

Academy and three Members of Parliament—two from the Lok Sabha and one from the Rajya Sabha, appointed by the respective Speakers of each of these Houses. The Members of Parliament could not be working journalists or newspaper managers or owners.[50] The Chairman and members were to hold office for three years.[51] The tasks of the Council were widely enumerated to include helping newspapers to maintain their standards, build a code of conduct, maintain high standards and "foster a due sense of both the rights and responsibilities of citizenship", to encourage a "sense of responsibility and public service among all those engaged in the profession of journalism", to review the concentration of power amongst newspapers and any other factors which may hinder the dissemination of news in the public interest and finally, to promote technical research.[52] But the powers that were given to the Press Council were not so extensive. It had the power to censure.[53] And that was all. It had the satisfaction of knowing that its decisions would not be questioned in any court of law.[54] In order to perform its functions the Press Council was given the power to summon and enforce the attendance of witnesses, require the discovery and production of documents, receive evidence on affadavits, issue commission for the examination of witnesses and documents, and require the publisher of any newspaper to furnish information on such points as the Council deems necessary.[55] It had the power to make rules and regulations,[56] was to be given a separate budget and was required to write Annual Reports[57] which were to be laid before Parliament.[58]

The Press Council Act, 1970 made some alterations. One of the principal changes was to include news agencies within the scope of the authority of the Press Council.[59] News agencies were also given membership on the Council.[60] Parliament was also concerned about the publications of the various foreign embassies in India. While the Press Council was not given a direct jurisdiction in respect of these foreign embassy publications, they were nevertheless supposed to undertake studies of such newspapers.[61] The Press Council was also asked to do an espionage operation and investigate the extent to which newspapers get subsidies from foreign governments.[62] The Press

Council was now required to "promote a better functional relationship among all classes of persons engaged in the production of or publication of newspapers or in news agencies."[63] This virtually made it some kind of chief negotiator in all press management and other disputes even though Parliament made it clear that the Council would not have any functions under the Industrial Disputes Act.[64] To its powers of censure were added the power to "warn and admonish" journalists and editors.[65] They were now also given the power to require the newspaper to publish the results of their inquiry.[66] The Council could requisition public records from offices and courts.[67] But it was made clear that a newspaper editor or journalist could not be compelled to disclose the sources of his information.[68] To all this was added the publicity power of making interim reports.[69] Its jurisdiction was extended to Jammu and Kashmir as well—probably to control the papers in that State.

The Press Council came to be abolished as part of the legislation against the press during the Emergency.[70] It was resuscitated with some ceremony in 1978.[71] The Joint Committee of both the Houses indicated some changes.[72] To begin with, it dispensed with the idea of the Chairman necessarily being a judge. Instead of being appointed by the Chief Justice of India, a part elective principle was introduced that he was appointed by a Committee consisting of the Speakers of the two Houses of Parliament and a person selected from the members of the Council.[73] The membership of the Council was expanded so that three members were to be appointed from the Lok Sabha and two from the Rajya Sabha instead of two and one respectively as enacted in the 1965 Act.[74] To avoid the domination of the English language papers, it was suggested that of the seven journalists, at least four had to be from Indian language papers.[75] The Committee took the view that the Council should not have the power to lay down a code of journalistic ethics which it was called upon to enforce.[76] The functions and powers of the Press Council were substantially the same as those contained in the 1965 and 1970 statutes.[77] But the Chairman was given the power to block a complaint if he did not think there was sufficient ground for holding an inquiry.[78] The Council was also given the power to levy a fee.[79] Certain members of Parliament had some misgivings about the Press Council developing a code of ethics. One dissenter protested that "no self-respecting person will relish the idea of a code of conduct." He felt that Indian society was going through "a transformation which it had never witnessed before." A code could only become obsolete.[80] Another dissenting member got to the nub of the matter when he feared "that a code of conduct in our Indian context, as manifested in more than one sphere of our public and national life. . . to mean a code of discipline." He suggested "caution and care"—hinting that such a code could itself become an instrument of repression and control.[81] This point was made even more clearly by a third dissenter who said:

> The big newspapers generally toe the line of the government and they may not mind entrusting the job of building a code of conduct to the Press Council. But the government can exercise indirect influence on the opposition parties by restricting the freedom of their newspapers through the Code of Conduct. . .[82]

These protests carry a significant undertone of diffidence about the whole enterprise of creating a Press Council. Implicit in the fears of these dissenting members is the feeling that while the Press Council can be a conciliation body in respect of complaints, it could also easily become an instrument of the Government of the day. This feeling is shared by many people and is characteristic of some of the work of the Press Council.

The Press Council Act, 1978 is really a copy of the earlier legislation[83] with a few additions pertaining to the election of of the Chairman,[84] the possibility of a Chairman who was not a judge[85] providing definite representation for journalists from Indian language papers[86] and providing the Press Council with the power to levy fees on registered newspapers and news agencies "after having due regard to their circulation and other matters".[87]

The Press Council which has been set up under these provisions is a strange body. It is an autonomous statutory body yet it is also built on the principle of the representation of news editors, journalists, and proprietors who will form a decisive majority if they stand together. The public is represented through litterateurs, lawyers, writers and Members of Parliament. The Council has been given a great number of assignments. In fact, these tasks are so massive that it is almost like a disciplinary committee, a Standing All-Purpose Press Commission and a Ministry of Information and Broadcasting all rolled into one. While its powers of requisitioning information are quite substantial, it can, eventually, only censure, warn, admonish or cause its findings to be published by a paper.

What has, and had, been created was a highly vulnerable body. The vulnerability of the Press Council stemmed from three factors. The first relates to finance, for, the Press Council could eventually take up only such questions as its financial and institutional capacity permitted. The second question relates to the free complainant procedure and the extent to which the Council's procedure would itself be abused or be effective. The third issue relates to the strategic confusion that is created in a body with multiple tasks and scarce resources trying to make up its mind about all of its seemingly equally important priorities.

Our study of the Press Council can be divided into two phases. The first phase began with its institution in 1966 and ended ten years later when it was abolished during the Emergency. The second phase saw the renewal of the Press Council experiment when the Janata government restored the Council and held out the expectation that the Council would be left with a measure of autonomy and not simply echo and facilitate government policy on the press. Both these phases need to be considered separately—as chronological and historical entities—even if the performance of the Press Council inspires a similar critique to the essentially similar perspectives cumulated in both phases of its life.

The First Phase

In this phase, the Press Council was very much a creature of the government. It was treated as a low financed government department and attracted the attention of the public and the press slowly. This is not to question the integrity of the judges who chaired the Council or of its members who found themselves the recipients of the patronage of their respective constituencies—a patronage that was not uninfluenced by intuitive estimates of government expectations. The Press Council soon got drawn into a framework of reference which the government had deemed to be appropriate to discussion about the press. The Council was not able to re-draw the boundaries of this framework. Nor was it able to act as the advisory conscience of the government. Within the contours of government initiated discussion, the Press Council reported on and prescribed the obvious. It allowed an indiscriminate use of its complaints jurisdiction with the same frightening results as those produced by the use and abuse of Indian litigation before courts. If it floundered for style it was because it paraded established hegemonic wisdom as newly inspired fresh insights.

Let us begin by looking at the budget of the Press Council. This is presented in Table I (*infra*).

For the great amount of work that the Press Council is supposed to do, the budget is pitiably low. The budget was increased slightly in 1970 when a new Press Council was considered. But even this, which was no more than an incomplete exercise in inflation proofing, was discontinued for the next year. The Press Council regime has done no more than inflation-proofed the budget of previous years. Salaries and establishment charges eat greatly into the budget. The contingency fund is really a massive addendum to the establishment budget. Very little money is earmarked for actual and separate investigations. The Press Council has come to operate as a complaint inquiry body with some of the trappings of the civil service and some of the style of a law court. Given its budget, it cannot really do much more than perform its complaint functions. These, too, have to be performed in the manner of a law court

TABLE I: Press Council Budget

Year	*Income or Expenditure*	*Pay of officers*	*Establishment*	*Allowances or Honoraria*	*Pension et al.*	*Contingency*
1968	Income Expenditure	3,01,316 2,38,815				
1969	2,67,390=59	53,215=42	38,177=25	76,885=93	22,562=48	47,720=21
1970	4,39,967=88	65,437=32	40,361=35	85,529=28	36,001=94	1,83,804=02
1971	3,61,787=52	69,374=28	33,124=40	1,06,125=21	19,301=55	1,17,959=33
1972	3,79,158=72	78,731=47	36,135=07	90,041=06	20,646=33	1,39,354=48
1973	3,97,769=80	75,481=00	39,502=00	1,02,219=00	15,274=00	1,32,901=00

Source: Annual Report of the Press Council: 1968,1969,1970,1971,1972,1973.

through the adverserial technique. The budgetary constraint is an important constraint on the working of the Council. The Council should seriously consider budgeting each item of its responsibility and prioritize them accordingly. So far, it has had to negotiate with the government on matters of finance. Now, it can raise money on its own if it wants to do so. But any such effort must, willy nilly, find the support of both the government and the press which is expected to contribute to it.

Let us turn now to the complaints jurisdiction of the Press Council which is the most important part of its work. The complaints jurisdiction—presided over as it has been—has acquired some of the dimensions of litigation. Just as litigation itself uses, abuses and transforms the nature of law as social reality, the complaints jurisdiction has also been used in such a way as to change and alter the nature of the jurisdiction. The complaints jurisdiction of the Press Council constitutes its most important function.[88] The Annual Reports of the Press Council devote a large amount of space to the work done on complaints.[89] Yet, none of the reports clearly set out detailed statistics which can give us a clear picture of who uses the jurisdiction and why. Table II sets out some of the information which is contained in these reports.

TABLE II: **Complaints before the Press Council**

Year	*Total No. of complaints*	*By the State*	*Against the State*
1967	29	(not known)	5
1968	32	14	3
1969	77	44	5
1970	58	26	11
1971	60		17
1972	125		22
1973	96		32
1974	95		39

Source: Extracted from Annual Reports of the Press Council of India.

Even these gross statistics tell a story. From the statistics available till 1970 it was clear that the Central and State Governments were a major complainant in almost a majority of the cases that were filed. The Press Council was being used principally by the government whenever the latter was dissatisfied with a report in a newspaper. This is hardly the kind of use that was envisaged. Even in 1967, there is evidence of the government being a major complainant. The Report of that year specifically identifies the Home Ministries of the Central and State Governments as being the principal Ministries that have been involved.[90] In an *Andhra Prabha* case the editor had to tender an apology to the Chief Minister of Orissa;[91] and in the *Mother India* case,[92] the editor gave an undertaking—which was accepted by the Ministry of Home Affairs—that he would not repeat these offences. The use of the Press Council machinery appears to have increased rather than decreased the control of the government. There have been several other instances where the government has brought cases about reporting on obscenity or communal clashes or even with a tinge of politics. The extended use of the Press Council in this way totally transforms the purposes for which the complaint jurisdiction was invented.

The Press Council has also tried to investigate cases where the government and others have been accused of putting pressure on the press. This has been entertained because a provision of the statute makes "help(ing) newspapers to maintain their independence" one of the specific functions of the Council.[93] This extension of the jurisdiction of the Council was opposed. The Advocate-General of Haryana gave the opinion that such inquiries were outside the scope of the Press Council. The Chairman used the Annual Report to state his reply and defend this extension.[94] By 1971, the Press Council felt sufficiently secure in this jurisdiction to express its displeasure at this jurisdiction being questioned.[95] The bulk of the cases against the Government have been summarized in the Report of 1972:

They are mostly directed against the State Government and

the bulk of them are based on the allegation that advertisements have been either refused or withdrawn because the news reportage in the papers is not to the liking of the government or that the editorial policy of the paper is directed against its lapses or shortcomings.[96]

The Press Council supported the Press Commission's attempt to solve this problem by laying down elaborate rules.[97] By and large, the government seems to use the Press Council more than the complaint procedure is used against it.

In cases other than those against the Central and State Governments, the success rate of the complaints is low. The powers of the Press Council are really limited to certain forms of censure. The Press Council's Annual Reports do not give a proper breakdown. But some statistics can be drawn from the text which are reproduced below:

TABLE III: **Details of Censures aud Admonitions**

Year	*Complaints against papers upheld*	*Censure*	*Admonition*	*Displeasure*	*Apology*	*Others*
1969	29	3	17	4	5	—
1970	10 (?)	2	2	4	?	—
1971	19	5	4	1	9	—
1972	11	3	2 (?)	1	2	—
1973	14	3	4	7	1	—

(?): Not clear
Source: Extracted from Annual Reports of the Press Council (1967-73).

It is clear from this information that the Press Council does not possess a considerable amount of power. It depends on the nature of its conciliatory machinery to try and procure a settlement of some kind between the complainant and the newspaper.

In this, it has achieved some measure of success although the turnover of cases which meander their way to its jurisdiction are too small and too random for a significant pattern to have emerged.

But the most significant aspect of the Press Council's complaint jurisdiction is the pathology of its use. It has been used by a large variety of people for diverse purposes. The government—as we have seen—has used it to keep the newspapers in check. Politicians have used its jurisdiction against their opponents. Communal politics has also been an important factor in the use of its jurisdiction. For example, in 1967, a politician complained that his name had been intentionally omitted from a list of candidates contesting an election.[98] This complaint was held to be justified. But the Press Council had no choice but to try and close a controversy around an article which gave a distorted picture of the culture and social conditions in Orissa. The matter got so out of hand that the Chief Minister of the State had to request that the matter be closed.[99] The Home Ministry moved against an English monthly called 'Mother India' where certain articles were deemed to be in extremely bad taste because they espoused a well-known research scholar's wildly different view of Mughal history. The Press Council's reasons for upholding this complaint are by no means convincing.[100] Then, there were also complaints against the Statesman about the manner in which it reported on news on the trade union movement. The Council took the view that the editor had the right to decide how a "continuing discussion on controversial subjects should be closed in its columns".[101] This case related to the very important subject of the right to reply. It is possible that the Press Council did not take too serious a view of this dispute because it might not have been convinced of the importance of the issue—seeing this as a social dispute into which it was being dragged. There is also evidence of complainants making complaints—presumably to intimidate newspapers—and then withdrawing them. Even the Government of Haryana has done this.[102]

In 1968, there were some cases on exaggerated reports,[103] one on plea for change of foreign policy,[104] some related to advertisements[105] or indecent and uncivilised language.[106] Some of the complaints were part of political and communal disputes.[107] In a case involving *Blitz*,[108] the Press Council took the view that the cartoon showing that India had been offered to the World Bank was in bad taste. Some of the complaints dealt with drawing unwarranted inferences or unverified news items,[109] editorial discretion[110] and inaccurate reports.[111] In one case,[112] teachers of Delhi University moved the Press Council as a threat against a newspaper which decided not to publish an advertisement containing their political views about the war in Vietnam. Having used the Press Council as a forum for further publicising their dispute, they did not take the matter any further. In 1969, cases involved allegations against a public servant,[113] a charge of inaccurate reporting,[114] a claim that to be anti-modern was against journalistic ethics,[115] a complaint that Mahatma Gandhi had been ridiculed,[116] examples of distorted reporting[117] and scandalous reporting,[118] the defamation of the community,[119] reporting on communal disturbances,[120] including a story about cow protection,[121] a complaint about the coarse narration of sex,[122] complaints about headlines and hyperbole.[123] Many of the items complained about relate to communal matters[124] and some are clearly against the administration or part of political disputes.[125] In at least one case the Press Council pointed out that exaggeration was not a part of press freedom.[126] The press seems to have taken a very straitjacketed view of the style of the press.

In 1970, the Press Council was very conscious of the fact that a dispute brought by the Delhi Mahila Samaj about the manner in which women in public life were discussed, had "political overtones".[127] The case is all the more interesting because it obliquely involved Mrs. Gandhi and one of the complainants was a member of the Home Ministry.[128] Many of the cases involved political differences about matters pertaining to religion and communalism.[129] In one case the Maharashtra Government lodged a complaint that a paper was inciting hatred against the Government.[130] In another case the Government of Tamil Nadu objected about the defamation of its Chief Secretary.[131] The complaint of the Government of Tamil Nadu had the effect of the newspaper's proprietor reporting to the Council that the editor responsible had been removed from his office.[132] Other complaints are clearly political and involve a use of the Press Council for the further agitation of a political dispute—using the Press Council as a free wheeling device for this purpose.[133] The report of the Press Council of 1971 deals with a variety of disputes including complaints about communalism,[134] the allegation that Roman Catholics are anti-national,[135] reporting about Naxalites,[136] the manner in which the police handled students,[137] the withdrawal of advertisement by the Government because of an editorial in a Punjab paper,[138] libellious attack,[139] improper use of photographs,[140] slander against the President,[141] undue exaggeration,[142] anti-India propaganda[143] and the publication of nude and semi-nude pictures.[144] The Press Council regarded some reports as frivolous.[145] It also issued censures in cases of false sensational reporting and reports of violations of modesty.[146]

In 1972, the Press Council dealt with complaints about indecency, obscenity [147] and news of molestations and reporting on communal matters,[148] attempts at blackmail,[149] journalistic impropriety,[150] and the balance in letters written to the editor.[151]

In 1973, some of the complaints that were made dealt with the rude manner in which the issue of a Sikh homeland was discussed.[152] Other complaints include allegations of slander,[153] prejudice regards Bangladeshis,[154] complaints about publishing letters against the policies of the Government,[155] the suppression of the views of opponents,[156] reporting on communal incidents,[157] offensive and abusive writings,[158] allegations about lasciviously stirring writings,[159] a dispute in a university[160] and a complaint about defamation in which the Press Council found that both the complainant and the respondent were to blame.[161] There were also complaints about journalistic impropriety.[162]

Many of these complaints are part and parcel of individual, group and political infighting into which the Press Council is, willy nilly, drawn as a participant, spectator, catalyst and agent for further and better publicity. This kind of pathological use of the complaint jurisdiction of the Press Council continues in respect of the Press Council established in 1978.[163]

In the same way as the law and the various jurisdictions of the Court acquire a meaning and dimension of their own through litigation, complaint jurisdiction of the Press Council has also acquired a social and political dimension of its own. It has been very effectively used by the States and by politicians to further their interests. It has been used to deal with the problems of communalism, of insults to various institutions of the State, and as a substitute to enforcing the laws relating to obscenity, decency and morality. It almost seems as if the Press Council has become another institution of the State using its power of moral censure to keep the press in check. And, there is no doubt that there is more than a whisper of personal political aggression and rivalry behind many of the complaints that have been presented on a *pro bono publico* basis. Very few cases actually deal with the problem of journalistic ethics in terms of the procedure followed by the newspaper. The issues that are presented in the Press Council's docket are precisely those issues for which penal offences exist. Nor has the Press Council taken the opportunity to try and deal with the cases that have come to it from the point of view of the ethics of journalism and with a view to evolving standards of fairness and perpetuate a synthesized attitude towards the procedure the press should adopt. It seems to have adjudicated on all these matters—much in the same way as a court of law might have done. But, the Press Council is not wholly to blame for this transformation of the complaint jurisdiction. The strategic use of this jurisdiction also greatly depends on the users of this jurisdiction. Where the users of the jurisdiction have trivialised the jurisdiction and seconded it to their use by violating all the ground rules through which the institution was going to work, the institution itself cannot be blamed for lacking a sense of strategic direction.

Earlier we have also suggested that some of the problems of the Press Council have arisen because it has been given a multiplicity of tasks but possesses scarce resources. Apart from its complaint jurisdiction, the Press Council has never really been able to state its priorities. When the Council was first established in 1966, it evolved an ambitious programme involving the evolution of a Code of Conduct,[164] a scheme for the training of journalists,[165] reviewing the concentration of ownership patterns[166] in the press and looking at the problems of parliamentary privilege and the press.[167] By 1967 some low-key work was done on all these areas.[168] It rightly concerned itself with some of the problems of free functioning of the press but only to deal with episodic issues in an episodic way.[169] It abandoned the attempt to create a code of ethics, hoping to create such a code through its case work.[170] As already suggested, it has dealt with its cases in such a way that no such pattern can be discerned. By 1968, the Press Council had become a bit of a lobby body—making its own suggestions on the Press Council Act itself[171] and the Criminal and Election Law Amendment Bill pending before Parliament.[172] It also began to look at the question of government loans to newspapers.[173] It seems to have resolved this problem by suggesting that no loans should be made until a Press Finance Corporation is set up.[174] This seems to be as impractical as it is oversimplistic. The Newspaper Corporation idea was worked on further in 1969[175] when the case for further changes in the Press Council Act were also canvassed.[176] Some guidelines were evolved on reporting on communal matters which in effect reiterate the provisions of the Indian Penal Code.[177] No real assistance is given on the procedure to be followed by a newspaper in such cases. The Press Council also lobbied for some change in the law relating to contempt of court.[178] By 1970, a new Press Council had been set up. It reverted back to the question of the economic pressures on the press.[179] It should not be forgotten that it was precisely at this time that the government was involved in a long and difficult battle with the larger newspapers, ostensibly on behalf of the smaller ones.[180] The Press Council seemed to be echoing some of the concerns of the Government. By 1971, the Press Council seemed to express annoyance of the Government because the latter did not take the Council into confidence over the government's moves in respect of monopolism in the press.[181] The Council also endorsed the Press Advisory system which had been set up during the Emergency rendered necessary by the Indo-Pakistan War of 1971.[182] By 1972, the war was over and the Press Council, along with the Government, returned to the question of monopolism and the structure of the press.[183] It did, however, make a plea with the government not to withdraw its advertisements from a paper, which the government was dissatisfied with.[184] By 1973—the last report available before its dissolution—the Council pursued the government's policy of looking at the concentration of ownership[185] and gave some thought to the question of foreign embassy advertisements.[186]

In this first phase, the Press Council did much to try and find its form. But, as it happens, the first phase coincided with the period when there was maximum tension between the government and the corporate press. This tension culminated in the famous newsprint supply case which the government lost in the Supreme Court.[187] In the long run, the government could hardly lose on the issue of newsprint. There was an endemic shortage in the supply of newsprint which invited both government intervention and arbitrariness. All that the Supreme Court had done was to spell out some of the limits beyond which this intervention could not go. But the government of those days was considerably short-sighted because of attacks by part of the corporate press on Congress leaders and Mrs. Gandhi's version of what Galbraith once called India's 'post-office socialism'. Despite the fact that the Press Council had got involved in those very issues about corporate power which the government wished to expose and project, the Council somehow came to be seen in government eyes as an enclave of opposition. This basic mistrust of the press led to the stringent censorship provisions which inaugurated the Emergency. The Press Council was one of the further casualties of the Emergency. In taking that step, Mrs. Gandhi's government lost an important mechanism to legitimate its rule. Authoritarianism is often accompanied by an unfortunate myopia.

The Second Phase

The Press Council was resurrected after the Emergency, more in anger than by design. As we have seen, the framework of the legislation was only marginally altered. Although a judge need not have been appointed as Chairman of the Council, Justice Grover found himself appointed to that post. This appointment was considered 'safe' enough to be affirmed by Mrs. Gandhi when she returned to power in 1980. Unlike Justice Mudholkar who was appointed Chairman to the first Press Council, Justice Grover had an undistinguished record of interest in matters concerning either the press or civil liberties.[188] The Janata regime may have tried to compensate him because his claims to become Chief Justice of India were superseded in 1973 and he felt obliged to resign from the Bench. Justice Grover's resignation may have been taken as representing a capacity for independence and integrity. That was hardly in question. The real considerations should have been his ability, perspicacity and pronouncements on press issues. While the Chairman held his job over many years, there has been a turnover of members in the Press Council between 1979-82. Over the first term of the Council (1978-81) the Annual Reports show that only nine of the original 1979 team have survived through to 1982.[189] In some cases, this was due to occupational changes. Editors ceased to be editors; and so on. But there is much in the patronage of appointments that suffers from further scrutiny. Undoubtedly the tune to which this patronage game is played has, in part, been orchestrated by political composers.

Let us begin by looking at the budget of the Council. This is presented in Table IV (*infra*).

The government has increased the initial budget to keep abreast of inflation. The Council's power to finance itself through a levy on the press has added to its budget.[190] This has caused the government's grant to settle at more or less a non-inflation proofed constant since 1979. The levy itself, though successful in theory, is already affected by problems of non-payment (Rs. 58,200 in 1980-1 and Rs. 2,30,804 in 1981-2)[191] which are increasing. To this extent, dependence on government has not weakened whilst newspaper ambivalence about the Council is tangibly expressed through the non-payment of the levy. Salaries continue to eat up most of its budget.[192] Apart from some research staff, the Council has had most of its research done cheaply through the Indian Law Institute even

TABLE IV

		Income		
Years	*Government Grant*	*Levy from Newspapers*	*Other*	*Total*
1978-79	5,00,000	2,05,900	18,307.80	5,00,896.41
1979-80	9,16,000	2,54,700	1,862.92	11,72,562.92
1980-81	9,09,087.20	*(3,61,312).00 3,03,112.00	39,470,13	12,25,411.30
1981-82	9,31,849.91	*2(5,53,446) 4,95,246	54,994.28	17,74,306.58
1982-83	8,11,253.10	6,99,598.00	*211,776.17	19.68,210.36
1983-84	10,87,889.81	7,72,702.00	*201,378.69	23,35,797.13
1984-85	12,93,056.08	7,38,450.00	*427,927.11	28,18,718.69

*Excludes existing balances etc.

*2Top figure includes amount over-due from previous years.

TABLE IV (*Contd.*)

Expenditure					
Salaries	*Contribution*	*Office*	*Travel*	*Other*	*Total*
1,62,355.90	19.50	2,81,841.9	56,679.10		*5,00,896.41
2,07,521.80	9,131.50	2,94,195.80	79,419.85	847.03	*11,72,562.92
5,57,238.50	19,379.00	3,96,909.57	86,906.70	2,183.76	*12,25,411.30
6,67,558.58	32,798.90	3,68,481.52	2,28,391.75	1,19,112.15	*17,74,306.58
8,29,793.75	64,624.10	4,17,037.77	2,06,194.60	1,76,733.51	1,96,840.36
9,10,474.24	65,163.83	6,18,130.78	1,95,103.50	642,904.08	*23,53,797.13
10,13,611.54	85,890.70	5,99,050.77	2,27,917.95	368,231.85	*28,18,718.69

*Includes excess of Income over expenditure.

Source: Based on the Press Council's Annual Reports 1979-84.

though its in-house staff have done some credible research on newspaper coverage.[193] The Chairman's extra allowance of over Rs. 1000 a month is matched by an ever increasing travel grant (for the Chairman and members) which is used more for 'public relations' than investigation and research.[194] Comfortable travel is expensive in India. Many quangos of government celebrate travel as a much to be sought after perk. This is invariably justified on the basis that a large country calls for extensive travel. That is unexceptional; but, by whom and for what? Operating through a network of up-market government and corporate contacts, the Council has not really spent money on trying to assert its role as an independent press body. It has joined protests by offering press releases which do not always reflect its independent assessment of the issues.[195] It has not really expended more resources on processing complaints although a claim to that effect has been made.[196] Its continued financial vulnerability is compounded by a lack of imagination in planning an enterprizing budget for the future. Some of the anxieties of the Press Council are expressed in the Annual Report of 1979 which states that the Council was not able to recruit competent staff because the Ministry of Housing treated the Council "as a non-participating office in the General Pool of Government residential accommodation".[197]

This hybrid position of the Press Council as a governmental and non-governmental body has important implications for its financial future. It is subject to government rules of expenditure and accountability. Yet at the same time it is deprived of the government perks which would enable it to work efficiently within the rules imposed by the governmental system of financial accountability. These rules would continue to persist even if the Council's revenue raising capability improves. It would still be treated as a government department permitted the kind of expansion which the government auditors think is appropriate and necessary.

The most crucial part of the work of the Council is the complaints jurisdiction. An overview of how this jurisdiction works is shown in Table V.

TABLE V: Press Council's Complaints Jurisdiction

Year	Total	Against Government									Against Press									
	Total New Cases	Filed	Suo Motu Action	Number dealt with	Outside Jurisdiction*[1]	Withdrawn	Adjudicated	Sustained or Intervened in*[2]	Rejected	Pending	Filed	Suo Motu Action	Number dealt with	Outside Jurisdiction*[1]	Withdrawn	Adjudicated	Sustained or Intervened in*[2]	Rejected	Pending	Total Pending
1979	91	40	—	10	9	1	—	—	—	30	47	—	27	15	6	3	—	3	23	53
1980	100	38 +	2 = 40	40	8	18	14	1	13	30	50 +	10 = 60	49	2	32	15	7	8	33	63
1981	226	97 +	6 =103	74	—	57	17	7	10	59	121 +	2 =123	83	64	—	10	7	12	34	93
1982	261	89 +	7 = 96	73	5 55	—	18	9	9	75	165	0	137	112	—	25	16	9	92	167
1983	383	79 +	4 = 83	91	63	—	28	9(8)*4	11	63	199 +	1 =200	137	118	—	19	16	3	134	197

1984	289	97	+ 2 = 99	97	46	51	22(11)*4	18	63	189	+ 1 =190	157	76	—	71	35(21)*4	15	125	188
1985	317	96	+ 7 =103	102*3	91	11	5(3)*4	3	64	214	—	198	155	—	19	11(4)*4	4	164	228

*1. This is a wide category including incomplete claims, *sub judice* cases and cases which are not within jurisdiction.

*2. Sustained cases include where the interaction of the Council produced a result even though no formal warning or reprimand was made.

*3. Discrepancy in (1985) A.R.9.

*4. Figures in brackets are compromized or settled cases.

Source: Press Council's Annual Reports 1979-1982.

Compared with its previous workload (1966-75) there is no doubt that the workload of the Council has increased. This is represented in the number of filings that are made before the Council. It is not wholly clear how many of these complaints are frivolous. We can see that many complaints are withdrawn or deemed to be outside jurisdiction.[198] Although the statistics on this are not clearly delineated, there is reason to suspect that many of the cases filed are filed in the knowledge that there is no substance in the complaint or that it would not attract the jurisdiction of the Council. The filing is itself constitutive of a litigational politics which has social and political implications. To some extent this is inevitable. But the incidence of such cases is extremely high and form a substantive part of the Council's docket. It is not clear how much of the Council's pending docket consists of 'loaded' cases which were initiated to provoke mischief rather than to invite resolution. Despite the Council's claim that the complaints wing has been strengthened,[199] this increase is not reflected in the dispositive efficiency of the Council to deal with its ever increasing docket.

It is quite crucial to try and discover who is using the Press Council's jurisdiction. We know that one part of its jurisdiction (concerning the government's curbs on the press) is being used by newspaper men in a strategic way—especially in respect of government advertising.[200] There is also some use of the Press Council's jurisdiction to examine complaints against the press.[201] However, if we look more closely at the representative sample of adjudicated cases which are reported in the Annual Reports of the Press Council, some disturbing trends continue to be visible. The least disturbing of these trends is the use of this jurisdiction by members of parliament to give further publicity to political in-fighting.[201] The most disturbing trend is the continued use of the Press Council's jurisdiction by the government to harass the newspapers. The sample of adjudicated cases in Annual Reports for four years suggest that the government is the largest and most effective complainant to have learnt to use the jurisdiction of the Press Council with enviable skill. The government is largely concerned with defending itself from attacks; and to discipline the press to keep in line with the government's notions of public order, communal disharmony and morality.[203] The Press Council itself does not appear to be particularly perturbed by this governmental claim on its jurisdiction. By a curious logic, it sees this as a 'healthy development'[204] because the government and public sector authorities do not use the courts instead. Since its jurisdiction allows complaints against the government, the Council seems to regard its use and abuse as a zero sum game. It has not, however, adequately done its sums on who wins and who loses. The Council's proximity to government cannot really be in question even though the government does permit the Council to act as a conscience brokering go-between within limits set by the former. This permissible and limited exposure of government helps to legitimate government in a more credible way. The tendency of the Press Council to act as some kind of agent of the government has two implications. At a simpler level, the Council's jurisdiction is coercive. Such proceedings are a nuisance. Resources and skill are required to counteract the allegations implicit in a government complaint before the Press Council. These complaints affect the reputation of a paper which is depicted as being communal, anti-patriotic or indulging in yellow journalism. At a deeper level, the Press Council becomes an important conceptive ideologist drawing out the government approved categories of permissible journalism. For the jurisdiction of the Press Council is triggered off by complainants; and the government is a powerful and astute complainant. In its deliberations, the Press Council encapsulates various kinds of ideological categories which have a deep impact on the general public's interpretation of political events and its assessment of particular forms of journalism. Many kinds of writing are classified as communal and seen as a threat to public order or the security of State without an adequate examination of the tensions that underlie such reporting. Along with the judiciary, the Council is a very important conceptive ideologist. The fact that it is a statutory body manned by pressmen adds weight to its pronouncements. Over the years, the Council has virtually declared certain kinds of reporting by certain kinds of newspapers as incontrovertibly false and mischievous. This has not been done by direct criticism but through a use of its discrete adjudicating processes. The government has used the Council's jurisdiction to obtain very important *fatwahs* (authoritative pronouncements). These *fatwahs* are more important than other menacingly toned declarations made by the government itself.

It is not surprising that the use of the Press Council's jurisdiction has come in for some criticism. In 1980, *Hitavada* called for the abolition of the Press Council.[205] It supported its plea strongly making the allegation that the Council had been politically motivated in entertaining irresponsible complaints about *Hitavada's* advertisement policy. Irritated by this allegation, the Council retaliated by taking *suo motu* action against the erring newspaper, reiterating the high principles on which it is supposed to work and thoroughly censuring the editor. The use of the Council's *suo motu* powers have increased. The principles on which such powers are exercised is not clear despite a formal clarification to the effect that action was taken—

> where it was felt that the complainants were not coming forward either because of lack of knowledge that they could not get their greivances redressed from the Press Council or they were fighting shy to come forward with specific complaints.[206]

As it happens, nothing could be further from the truth than this. Far from acting for some hypothetical uninformed or incapable complainant, the Council has acted on a much more policy orientated basis. It moved against the government when it thought the authorities in Punjab were harassing local journalists,[207] deprecated the prevention of the publication of newspapers in Bangalore[208] and protested against the arrest of journalists in Manipur.[209] These were important interventions against the government and carried a whisper of politics about them. It exposed allegedly marginal cases of government oppression and championed the cause of the Press Council as a negotiator between the government and others. The Council has acted *suo motu* on behalf of the press where newspaper offices have been attacked or blockaded.[210] But it has also acted *suo motu* against the press to protest about dummy advertising,[211] in support of government policy about reporting on communal tension in Moradabad[212] and to uphold its principles about reporting on women students.[213] These cases would probably have made it to the Press Council through the complaints jurisdiction. They are policy cases where the Council has mediated with the government and laid down prescriptive policy to give support to its own and the government's version of consensus morality and public order.

So far, the Council has arranged its docket to cover identifiable subject areas. In 1979, it concerned itself with editorial discretion.[214] However its adjudication seems to regard public participation as having therapeutic consequences for the public rather than being a meaningful part of public debate.[215] In 1980, it dealt with government advertising,[216] the government browbeating journalists,[217] the foreign infiltration of India's press,[218] the public's claim over editorial discretion,[219] norms about advertisements[220] and questions of public morality.[221] In 1981, it again took up cases on government advertising,[222] accreditation of journalists to government,[223] other forms of government pressure,[224] attacks on newspaper men and offices.[225] It also continued to explore problems concerning the discretion of editors,[226] the definition of public morality, the public interest and the national interest,[227] the right to reply[228] and the rules about scurrilous and defamatory attacks in the newspapers.[229] In 1982, the Council examined police, magisterial and government action against the press.[230] It also warned the press to verify its stories[231] and respect the privacy of the individual by refraining from defamation.[232] In 1983, the Press Council examined complaints by pressmen that it was attacked and harassed by political[233] and police authorities,[234] not given appropriate accreditation,[235] denied or pressurized by government advertisement[236] or fiscal[237] policy and the manner in which the Press and Registration of Books Act, 1867 worked.[238] There were also complaints about interference by party cadre[239] or by pressure by District authorities to disclose the source of information.[240] The press, on their part were accused of publishing stories without foundation,[241] casting aspersions on government,[242] not granting a right to reply,[243] publishing the wrong news,[244] indulging in communalism,[245] malicious stories and defamation[246] including a case of casting aspersions about working women.[247]

In 1984, there was the usual crop of complaints by the press about advertisements,[248] accreditation,[249] harassment and oppression by the police,[250] pressure (including assault) by the government[251] or other agencies (including the Shiromani Gurudwara Prabandhak Committee[252] and Post Office),[253] denial of access to information,[254] unfair treatment.[255] denial of travel facilities,[256] closure or threatened closure of newspapers,[257] unfair policy of newsprint,[258] bad legislation and its use against the press[259] and victimization.[260] In turn, the press was accused of communal writing,[261] misguiding advertisements,[262] or news,[263] unsubstantiated reports,[264] not giving the right to reply,[265] unfair covering of the Jammu and Kashmir elections,[266] defamatory and scurrilous reports,[267] obscenity,[268] causing alarm[269] and yellow journalism.[270]

In 1985, the press complained of harassment by police,[271] government officials[272] and security men,[273] denial of— or a discriminatory policy on—advertisements[274] and unfair treatment in respect of government accreditation of journalists and newspapers.[275] The press were accused by complaints of communalism,[276] malicious and defamatory writing,[277] yellow journalism,[278] and discrepancies in their stories,[279] violation of copyright[280] and unfair attacks on political parties.[281]

A pattern had developed in the case law which concentrates on the more obvious (and least defensible) forms of government oppression, the limits of editorial discretion and the imposition of consensus norms on the press in the public interest. Much of the deliberations of the Council concern the virile but vulnerable local and regional press. The corporate press is subjected to less scrutiny. The Press Council's work is more of a warning to the local press than its corporate counterpart. Many of these inquiries against the government are instigated by political promptings whilst many of the inquiries against the press are instigated by the government. Research conducted by the Indian Law Institute has shown that the deliberations of the Press Council can be quantified into a jurisprudence.[282] Settled principles are said to exist in the areas of defamation, intrusion of privacy, character assassination, obscenity and bad taste, non-verification of news, the right to reply and other forms of journalistic propriety. In part, these principles formally reiterate the law and government policy without examining the ground situation in which they operate. But, at the same time, the cumulation of this identifiable jurisprudence represents impressive ideological conceptualizations which reflect on how the Council visualises and seeks to control and contain the press.

Apart from the complaint jurisdiction, the Council has tried to pull together a coherent plan about what it wishes to do. In 1979, it projected itself as a body which would intervene in public controversies about the press and be better informed about its working.[283] It issued public statements against politicians who tried to oppress the press,[284] it tried to establish itself as a primary consultee on legislation concerning the press,[285] acted as a mediator with the government on the supply of newsprint[286] and set up a research wing to analyse newspaper reporting.[287] In 1980 the Council began to realise its helplessness and made the strange request that the government should withhold advertising from newspapers who were censured by the Press Council.[288] Such a plan would have forged yet another link with the government leaving the latter in charge. At the same time, the Council sought to establish its own financial autonomy by imposing a levy on newspapers.[289] This plan was implemented with partial success. It tried to establish codes of conduct for the press.[290] In doing so it made an important concession to government by accepting that

> safeguarding press freedom did not preclude those in authority from taking such action as may, in the totality of circumstances, be necessary to prevent the publication of material which encouraged anti-national movement like secession or disintegration or spread of communal

disharmony or violence but that this must be done without resorting to pre-censorship.[291]

This seems akin to blessing the techniques used by the Raj to reduce all protest to public order and security of State; and then taking tough consequent action to combat the nuisance. By 1981, the Chairman reported on the Council's willingness to "give all assistance to the authorities including the government"[292] and to break the alleged monopoly of the press by setting up a Newspaper Finance Corporation which would somehow not be subject to "political interference or patronage of any kind".[293] It negotiated with the government on newsprint supply[294] and lobbied the government on various cases of legislation to control 'scurrilous publications'.[295] The research reinforces many of the Congress government's views—before and during the Emergency—that India needs a 'committed' press which must be made to report 'responsibly' on social, political and public affairs.[296] Over the first three years, we can see that many of the Press Council's views were slowly travelling a way which could well have been designed by the government. In 1982, a renewed Press Council was established. The Chairman was happy to report on the cosmopolitan excellence that had been achieved.[297] The Council felt that it had created a basis for sustaining enduring traditions for both the government and the press. In particular, it offered advice on reforms in the field of official secrecy, parliamentary privilege, defamation and contempt of court.[298]

In 1983, the Press Council reacted sharply to the murder of the editor of *Madhya Yug* from Banda,[299] continued its opposition to the Bihar Bill,[300] sent in a response to the government reacting to the Second Press Commission,[301] considered the questionnaire of the Law Commission about the disclosure of sources of information,[302] inquired into the coverage of the Jammu and Kashmir elections,[303] sought to build a code of conduct,[304] studied accreditation rules and practice[305] and researched into the law of defamation.[306] The interest in the law of defamation[307] and the code of conduct[308] and press accreditation[309] continued in 1984. In that year it also recorded its opposition to the Andhra Pradesh Prevention of Dangerous Activities of

Communal Offenders Bill, 1984.[310] In 1985, it established a Press and Registration Appellate Board to hear appeals from Magistrates who refused to register or cancel declarations made by newspapers under the Press and Registration of Books Act, 1867.[311] It also gave its views on the Maharashtra Rape Bill[312] and continued its campaign to rationalise government rules of accreditation on a reasonable and equitable basis.[313] In the *Voice of Karnataka* case it sought legal opinion as to whethei the Council can continue to hear matters which are *sub judice* before the courts. If this question is answered in the affirmative, the "scope of (the work of the Press Council) would . . . widen perceptibly".[314]

Over the years, the Press Council has acquired broad hybrid functions as a mediator between the government and the press. Its total independence from the government cannot be assumed even we must accept that direct control of the Council has partly given way to a policy of systemic manipulation. More systematic than it was in its first phase, the Council has floundered for style in trying to steer between the pressures of government and the politics of the press. It has tried to establish standards acceptable to both the government and the corporate press without offering more than an eclectic critique of both. Given a wide ranging measure of responsibilities, it has made a cautious beginning constantly aware of its limitations. Its work has been episodic and its weak resources further accentuate its difficulties in becoming a more impressive presence on matters concerning the local and corporate press.

Over all, the Press Council was not able to establish a coherent strategy. It has echoed the views of the government on the problems of ownership. It has done a bit of lobbying on parliamentary privileges (1968-9) and contempt of court (1969). It has considered some specific problems and talked about many things. The Press Council established in 1978 has also tried to evolve a broad programme. But it has not yet gained either the momentum or the support which it needs to establish its institutional viability. Undoubtedly, politics plays more than a role in all this.[315]

III

We are still left with the problem of accountability. Earlier we asked whether the press could be made accountable either through the democratic processes or through the development of a code or process that ensures that it does what it is supposed to do. To impose a pattern of democratic accountability is almost impossible. *That journalists should control their own newspaper organisations is salutary but does not go far enough* for in that process the general public is left out of this operation. If the press is controlled by some democratic elected body, it is easy for such a system to drift into government control. If a quasi-autonomous body is interposed, there are enormous problems relating to the relationship of such an autonomous body to the government, to the press, to politicians and to the general public. Amongst all these, the general public are the least effective lobby. Nor is it really possible to achieve some kind of pattern of functional accountability whereby the press can at least be asked to become the transmitters of an information system which guarantees an equal distribution of the right of informed participation. The superimposition of a code will create problems as soon as an institutional agency begins to enforce it. Voluntary mechanisms are too greatly dependent on the good will of the press and the vagaries of the use of the complainant method. Recently, courts of law have entered into the arena as a possible institution which might further the development of a code of ethics. In a remarkable case,[316] a High Court took the view that it was part of the concept of the freedom of press that the government should give a right to reply and an equal right of access to those who wish to agitate matters of public concern through the publications of the government. The judgment itself has a very grand sweep to it. Taken to its logical conclusion it will completely wipe out the concept of editorial discretion and place on the government an extreme responsibility of accommodating all its critics. Perhaps, the answer lies in the much more gradual development of patterns of functional accountability through a use of various methods. Over time, a much more rigorous institutional morality may emerge. Undoubtedly such a development will constitute a consensus between the government and the corporate press. The Press Council may be an important third party in this process.

But to return to the Press Council. The Press Council is not really a watchdog which watches the watch dogs of the press. It has become an undernourished body, without a planned sense of direction and whose major complaint jurisdiction has been used by the government and others to deprive it of any strategic control. Notionally, an autonomous body, the Press Council, is neither a voluntary body nor wholly outside the ambit of the influence of the government. It depends greatly on the government for finance, ideas about its plan of action and the activation of its complaint jurisdiction. It is not a purely adjudicatory body but acts as if it is. It is supposed to be a democratic body but the democratic inputs into its work are not known and cannot be quantified. It has done many useful things but its work lacks consistency. In many matters, it seems to just potter along unwilling and unable to find its own feet. Its work can hardly be the justification for giving the press increased powers. The case of the press has to be considered without the window dressing of the Press Council.

NOTES

1. For a lively theoretical discussion see T.I. Emerson: *Towards a General Theory of the First Amendment* (1962) 1-15; C.E. Baker "The Scope of the First Amendment Freedom of Speech" (1978) 2 *U.C.L.: A.L.R.* 964; Lewis: "A preferred position for journalism" (1979) 7 *Hofstra L.R.* 595. Please note that a small part of this essay has been published as part of my report on *Contempt of Court and the Press* (1980).
2. The classic statement is to be found in *Arnold* v. *King* (1914) 41 I.A. 149 at 169.
3. Articles 19 (1) (a) and 19 (2) of the Constitution of India, 1950 (as amended).
4. B. Shiva Rao: *The Framing of India's Constitution* (1967) Volume II 75 (K.M. Munshi's Draft Proposals Article 5 (2)) and 87 (B.R. Ambedkar's Draft Proposals Article II (1) 12).
5. The debate on Article 19 took place on 1-2 December, 1948 (VII Constituent Assembly Debates (C.A.D.) 711-47 and 749-83). For

comments on the rights of the press see VII C.A.D. 716-7 (K.J. Shah), 763 (S.L. Saxena) and 780 (B.R. Ambedkar's reply); see also the discussion on sedition at 731-3 (K.M. Munshi) 780-1 (B.S. Mann) and 763 (S.L. Saxena and H.V. Kamath's views that these rights should be made absolute).

6. See *Romesh Thapar* v. *State of Madras* A.I.R. 1950 S.C. 124; *Express Newspapers Ltd.* v. *Union of India*, A.I.R. 1958 S.C. 578; *Sakal Newspapers Ltd.* v. *Union of India* A.I.R. 1962 S.C. 305; *Bennett Coleman* v. *Union of India* A.I.R. 1973 S.C. 106.
7. *M.S.N. Sharma* v. *Sri Krishna Sharma* A.I.R. 1959 S.C. 395 at pr. 13 p. 400; see also the discussion on defamation in Chapter VIII.
8. However, see *Prabha Dutt* v. *Union of India* (1982) 1.S.C.C.1.
9. *Express Newspapers Ltd.* v. *Union of India* A.I.R. 1958 S.C. 578.
10. *Sakal Newspapers Ltd.* v. *Union of India* A.I.R. 1962 S.C. 305.
11. Article 19 (2) as originally enacted permitted "reasonable restrictions" in the interests of "security of state" not "public order": *Romesh Thappar* v. *State of Madras* A.I.R. 1950 S.C. 124 and *Brij Bhushan* v. *State of Delhi* A.I.R. 1950 S.C. 124. The Constitution (First Amendment) Act, 1951 added "public order" to the list of permissible restrictions. Later the Supreme Court insisted that the amendment was not necessary: *State of Bihar* v. *Shaibala Devi* A.I.R. 1952 S.C. 329.
12. *Virendra* v. *State of Punjab* A.I.R. 1957 S.C. 896.
13. *Kedar Nath* v. *State of Bihar* A.I.R. 1962 S.C. 955.
14. *State of Bihar* v. *Shaibala Devi* A.I.R. 1952 S.C. 329; *Virendra* v. *State of Punjab* A.I.R. 1957 S.C. 896. *Ramji Lal* v. *State of U.P.* A.I.R. 1957 S.C. 620; *Santok Singh* v. *Delhi Administration* A.I.R. 1973 S.C. 1091; *Babulal* v. *State of Maharashtra* A.I.R. 1961 S.C. 884; *Madhu Limaye* v. *S.D.M. Monghyr* A.I.R. 1971 S.C. 2487; cf. *Supd. Central Prison* v. *R.M. Lohia* A.I.R. 1960 S.C. 533.
15. It is open to the courts to refuse to protect "objectionable" material as part of "free speech" (*Hamdard Dawakhana* v. *Union of India*, A.I.R. 1960 S.C. 533). The cases of obscenity were upheld in *Ranjit Udeshi* v. *State of Maharashtra* A.I.R. 1965 S.C. 881; *K.A. Abbas* v. *Union of India* A.I.R. 1971 S.C. 481.
16. *E.M.S. Namboodripad* v. *T.N. Nambiar* A.I.R. 1970 S.C. 2015 at pr. 11 p. 2019; *C.K. Daphtary* v. *O.P. Gupta* A.I.R. 1971 S.C. 1132.
17. *M.S.N. Sharma* v. *Sri Krishna Sharma* A.I.R. 1959 S.C. 395. *In Re Article 143* A.I.R. 1965 S.C. 745.
18. Apart from the general description of "reasonable restrictions" in *V.G. Row* v. *State of Madras* A.I.R. 1952 S.C. 196 at 280—note the wide interpretation to the words "in the interests of" in *Virendra* v. *State of Punjab* A.I.R. 1957 S.C. 896; *Santok Singh* v. *Delhi Administration* A.I.R. 1973 S.C. 1091 does not favour following more stringent American tests.

19. e.g. Soli J. Sorabjee: "Where Truth is no Defence" (1978) 15 *Vidura* 195.
20. See Chapter 7, *supra*.
21. *Report of the Press Commission* (1952-54) Chapter XIX pp. 339-56.
22. *Ibid.* pr. 914 p. 340.
23. *Ibid.* pr. 914 p. 340 last pr. sub-para (b).
24. *Ibid.* pr. 913 p. 340.
25. *Ibid.* pr. 911 p. 339.
26. For a classic statement of this position see Kumaramanglam: *Judicial Appointments* (1973).
27. *Report of the Press Commission* (1952-54) see prs. 915-6 pp. 341-2.
28. *Ibid.* pr. 916 p. 341.
29. *Ibid.* prs. 929-30 pp. 345-6.
30. *Ibid.* prs. 931-33 pp. 346-7, see also the comments on astrological predictions (pr. 934 pp. 347-8) and cartoons (prs. 935 p. 348).
31. *Ibid.* pr. 936 pp. 348-9.
32. *Ibid.* prs. 941-2 pp. 350-1.
33. *Ibid.* pr. 943 p. 351.
34. *Ibid.* pr. 944 p. 351. Note also attacks on castes and communities (pr. 940 p. 350).
35. *Ibid.* pr. 944 pp. 351-2.
36. *Ibid.* pr. 947 p. 352.
37. *Ibid.* prs. 951-2 pp. 353-4.
38. *Ibid.* pr. 952 p. 354.
39. *Ibid.* pr. 955 pp. 354-5.
40. *Ibid.* pr. 956 p. 355.
41. See *Press Council Annual Report* (1965) pp. 1-2.
42. Press Council Act (34 of) 1965.
43. Press Council (Amendment) Act (6 of) 1970.
44. Press Council Repeal Act, 1976.
45. Press Council Act (37 of) 1978.
46. For the debates on the Press Council Act, 1965 see (1964) 33 L.S.D. (Third Series) 2200-2 (17 September 1964; message from Rajya Sabha); (1964) 34 L.S.D. (Third Series) 4398-4432; 4558-62 (29-30 September 1964—Motion to refer to Joint Committee); (1964) 35 L.S.D. (Third Series) 28-29 (17 February 1965—motion to extend time of Joint Committee); (1965) 46 L.S.D. (Third Series) 7202-62; 6788-96 (23 September 1965—substantive debate); (1965) 47 L.S.D. 121-250, 13 November 1965—passed by Lok Sabha. For the Rajya Sabha see (1963) 45 R.S.D. 1042 (26 November 1963—introduced); 4 (1964) 49 R.S D. 386-422; 540-53; 563-98, 607-28 (8 September 1964), 754-773 (10 September 1964), 1405-1531 (15 September 1964). Motion to refer to Joint Committee from (8-15 September); 3975-6 (1 October 1964—Message to refer to Joint Committee); (1965) 51 R.S.D. 34 (17 February 1965—Presentation of Committee Report);

(1965) 53 R.S.D. 383-462 (17 August 1965); 530-600 (18 August 1965); 1118-1189 (24 August 1965); 1280-1302 (24 August 1965), 1303-80 (25 August 1965); 1481-1592 (20 August 1965). The substantive debate was from 17-26 August 1965.

For the debates on the Press Council Amendment Act, 1970 see Rajya Sabha: (1970) 71 R.S.D. 131 (26 February 1970—Introduced); 216-268 (3 March 1970); 146-258 (4 March 1970—Substantive debate on 3-4 March 1970). For Lok Sabha see (1970) 37 L.S.D. Fourth Series 237 (10 March 1970—message from Rajya Sabha); (1970) 38 L.S.D. 378-390 (30 March 1970—substantive debate; 226 (3 April 1970—passed).

On the Press Council Report Act, 1976 see Lok Sabha (1976) 56 L.S.D. (Fifth Series) 133-34 (23 January 1976—introduced) 140-179 (28 January, 1976—substantive discussion); 180-1 (23 January 1976—motion to pass); (4 February 1976—Message from Rajya Sabha arguing without amendment). For Rajya Sabha see (1976) 94 R.S.D. 256-8 (28 January 1976—message from Lok Sabha); 104-150 (passed).

On the Press Council Act, 1978 see Rajya Sabha (1978) 104 R.S.D. 154-245 (1 March 1978—introduced and recommended for Joint Committee procedure); 105 R.S.D. 29-33 (17 May 1978—message from Lok Sabha); 106 R.S.D. 161 (17 July 1978); 294-322 (3 August 1978); 186-289 (7 August 1978—substantive debate from 17 July—7 August 1978). For Lok Sabha see (1978) 10 L.S.D. (Sixth Series) 254-55 (3 March 1978—message from Rajya Sabha re Joint Committee); (1978) 15 L.S.D. (Sixth Series) 277-8 (15 May 1978 agreed with Rajya Sabha on Committee); (1978) 16 L.S.D. (Sixth Series) 385-87 (17 July 1978—Joint Committee Report tabled); (1978) 17 L.S.D. (Sixth Series) 220 10 August 1978—message from Rajya Sabha with Bill); (1978) 18 L.S.D. 361-72 (24 August 1978); 410-444 (28 August 1978); 227-283 (29 August 1978); 353-61 (30 August 1978—substantive debate from 24-31 August 1978); 109-13 (31 August 1978—motion to pass).

47. See (1965) 38 L.S.D. (Third Series) 28-29 (17 February 1965—request for Joint Committee of Bill); 682-3 (22 February 1965—giving adequate representation to periodicals and small newspapers in the Press Council); (1966) 54 L.S.D. (Third Series) 12748 (25 April 1966—on setting up the Press Council); (1966) 59 L.S.D. (Third Series) 7693 (29 August 1966—on the representation on the Press Council); 7632-33 (29 August 1966—on the composition and membership of the Press Council); (1967) 3 L.S.D. (Fourth Series) 2906 (5 June 1967—on the power of the Press Council to force a newspaper to stop indulging in yellow journalism. The government's reply that these powers are adequate is surprising); (1967) 3 L.S.D. (Fourth Series) 8941-4 (3 July 1967—on the differences between the

government and the Chief of the Indian Federation of Working Journalists); (1967) 7 L.S.D. (Fourth Series) 12304-5 (17 July 1967 on the working and setting up of the Press Council); (1967) 8 L.S.D. (Fourth Series) 17524-5 (7 August 1967 on the employment of retired people by the Press Council, the amount spent on the Chairman and Secretary and on the journalistic status of the Secretary); (1967) 10 L.S.D. 5958 (11 December 1967—on the Press Council's action against injudicious writing against India); (1968) 12 L.S.D. 2575-6 (14 February 1968—the Press Council's actions on indecent posters); 2316 (21 February 1968—on the boycott of the Press Council by the Federation of Working Journalists); (1968) 15 L.S.D. (Fourth Series) 1969 (3 April 1968—on the All India News Editors' Conference's concern about controversy over the working of the Press Council); (1968) 17 L.S.D. (Fourth Series) 2726 (8 May 1968—on the Chairman of the Press Council's visit abroad); 2750 (8 May 1978—on the Chairman of the Press Council's resignation); 2756 (8 May 1978—on the performance of the Press Council in respect of matters pertaining to obscenity and its attempts to evolve a code of ethics); 2756-7 on communal writings in *Mother India*—a paper); (1970) 42 L.S.D. (Fourth Series) 164-5 (30 July, 1970—on adequate representation in the Press Council); (1970) 44 L.S.D. 89 (27 August 1970—guidelines on communal writings); 92-3 (on the performance of the complaints jurisdiction of the Press Council): (1972) 18 L.S.D. (Fifth Series) 11-17 (23 August, 1972—on the Press Council's work on the concentration of ownership in the Indian Press); (1972) 19 L.S.D. (Fifth Series) 140-2 (on the Council's work on vulgar advertisements and the concentration of the ownership of newspapers in various business houses); (1974) 36 L.S.D. (Fifth Series) question No. 2863 (13 March 1974—on the working of the Press Council); (1974) 45 L.S.D. (Fifth Series) 31-32 (20 November 1974—on whether radio and television fall within the Press Council's jurisdiction); 107 (20 November 1974—on the suppression of press freedom by Central and State governments); (1976) 56 L.S.D. (Fifth Series) 121 (21 January 1976—on the Indian Federation of Working Journalists' views on a code of ethics); (1977) II L.S.D. (Sixth Series) 72 (22 July 1977—on the revival of the Press Council); (1977) 5 L.S.D. (Sixth Series) 188 (27 July 1977—on the reviving of the Press Council).

48. Gazette of India Extraordinary, S. 2 (26 November 1963) 768.
49. Press Council Act (34 of) 1965, S. 4 (1).
50. *Ibid.* S. 4 (2).
51. *Ibid.* S. 5 (1).
52. *Ibid.* S. 12.
53. *Ibid.* S. 13 (1).

54. *Ibid.* S. 13 (2). It was also protected from what it did in good faith (S. 20).
55. *Ibid.* S. 14.
56. *Ibid.* Ss. 22-23.
57. *Ibid.* Ss. 15-16, 19.
58. *Ibid.* S. 18.
59. Press Council Act, 1970 Ss. 9-10 (for changes in Ss. 12-13 of the Press Council Act, 1965. Consequently changes were made in other sections as well).
60. *Ibid.* S. 5 for changes in S. 4 of the Press Council Act, 1965.
61. *Ibid.* S. 9 for changes in S. 12 (2) (f) of the Press Council Act, 1965.
62. *Ibid.* S. 9 for changes in S. 12 (2) (g) in the Press Council Act, 1965.
63. *Ibid.* S. 9 for changes in S. 12 (2) (i) of the Press Council Act, 1965.
64. Proviso to S. 12 (2) (i) of the Press Council Act, 1965, as amended in 1970.
65. S. 10 of the Press Council Act, 1970 for changes in S. 13 (1) of the Press Council Act, 1965.
66. *Ibid.* S. 10 adding S. 13 (1A) to the Press Council Act, 1965.
67. *Ibid.* S. 11 for changes in S. 14 (1) (d) of the Press Council Act, 1965.
68. See S. 14 (2) of the Press Council Act, 1965 as amended in 1970.
69. S. 13 of the Press Council Act, 1970 adding S. 18 A to the Press Council Act 1965.
70. Press Council Repeal Act, 1976.
71. See debates on the Press Council Act, 1978 referred to in note 46.
72. *Report on the Joint Committee of the Press Council* (1978 Rajya Sabha 17 July).
73. *Ibid.* pp. vi-vii (on clause 5 (2)).
74. *Ibid.* p.vii (on clause 5 (3) (e)).
75. *Ibid.* p. vii (on clause 5 (3) (a): see also the comments on clause 5(3) (b) about two representatives each from the "big" "medium" and "small" papers.
76. *Ibid.* p. viii (on clause 14).
77. Press Council Act, 1978. The breakdown is as follows: Composition of Council (S. 5); Term of office and retirement (S. 6); Conditions of service of members (S. 7); Committees of Council (S. 8); Meetings (S. 9): Effect of vacancies not to invalidate Council's work (S. 10); Staff (S. 11); Authentication of work (S. 12); Objects and functions (S. 13); Power to censure (S. 14); General Process (S. 15); Levy of fees (S. 16); Payments to Council (S. 17); Fund of the Council (S. 18); Budget (S. 19); Annual Reports (S. 18); Interim Report (S. 19); Audit (S. 20); Protection for what is done in good faith (S. 23); Public servant status of members (S. 24); Power to make rules (S. 25); Power to make regulations (S. 26).
78. *Ibid.* Proviso to S. 14 (1).
79. *Ibid.* S. 16 (1).

80. *Ibid. Report of the Joint Committee* (*supra* note 72) (x)—per Srikant Verma.
81. *Ibid.* (x-xi)—per P.G. Mavlankar.
82. *Ibid.* (xi)— per Jagjit Singh.
83. Press Council Act, 1978 S. 5 (1).
84. *Ibid.* S. 5 (2).
85. *Ibid.* S. 5 (2).
86. *Ibid.* S. 5(3) (a).
87. *Ibid.* S. 16 (1).
88. S. 13, Press Council Act, 1978; S. 13 Press Council Act, 1965.
89. See Annual Reports of the Press Council (hereafter cited as A.R. and by reference to the years to which they refer)—(1967) A.R. 35-48; (1968) A.R. 10-40; (1969) A.R. 11-76; (1970) A.R. 15-96; (1971) A.R. 5-75; (1972) A.R. 7-146; (1973) A.R. 11-94; (1979) A.R. 14-25.
90. (1967) A.R. 40.
91. (1967) A.R. 39.
92. *Ibid.*
93. S. 12, Press Council Act, 1965. Now see S. 19, Press Council Act, 1978.
94. (1970) A.R. (v)–(vi). The question arose in respect of a complaint made by the *Tribune* about the Chief Minister of Haryana stopping government advertisements in that paper. Mr. Justice Ayyangar—former judge of the Supreme Court and the then Chairman of the Press Council, wrote a spirited and judicious defence of this jurisdiction.
95. (1971) A.R. 27-31 (once again on the *Tribune* case—*supra* note 94). On the reaction of the Press Council note the letter of the Chairman, 16 January 1971 (quoted at pp. 28-9).
96. (1972) A.R. (vi).
97. (1972) A.R. (vi)—(vii).
98. *Malai Murasu* (1967) A.R. 41.
99. *Ibid.* 42-3.
100. *Mother India, ibid.* 43-4.
101. *Statesman* 45-46.
102. *Ibid.* 47.
103. *Interview* 1 (1968) 21 (Result: Censure); *Nasheman* 27-8.
104. *Nasheman, ibid.* 29.
105. *Ibid.*, 32 (matter not pursued). One of the cases in the Delhi University teachers case (*infra* note 112) and the other re the advertisement of a house.
106. 33 (re local daily of Ajmer's comments on local Magistrate); *Lalkar* 13-14 (attack on lady school teacher); *Hardwar Darshan* 18-19, 20-21 (slander); 21.
107. *Daily Salar, ibid.*, 22-3 (on Kashmir); *Daily Salar*, 23-4 (Kannada agitation). On communal disputes see *Mother India* 12-3. *Interview*

21-2); *Desh Navajyoti* (on Sindhi community); *Karnatak Leader* 33-4.

108. *Blitz, ibid.*, 10-12.
109. *Daily Salar, ibid.*, 23—(unwarranted inferences).
110. *Andhra Patrika* and *Bharati* 14-15 (on non-publication of some articles).
111. *Hardwar Darshan* 19-20 (exaggerated claim about circulation); *Interview* 21-2.
112. *Ibid.*, 32.
113. *The Blade* (1969) A.R. 12.
114. *Ibid.*, *Hindu* 14-17.
115. *Ibid.*, *Daily Salar* 17-18.
116. *Ibid.*, *Mother India* 18-19.
117. *Ibid.*, *Nasheman* 19-20.
118. *Ibid.*, *Navasakti* 20-22.
119. *Ibid.*, *Mother India* 22-3; *Vivek* 40-1; *Organizer*, *Zam Zam* 56-7.
120. *Ibid.*, *Vikrama* 25-7; *Interview* 27-28; *Daily Aljamiat* 28-32.
121. *Ibid.*, re article "Ek Fazul Bahs" in *Daily Aljamiat* 28-29.
122. *Ibid.*, *Indian Observor* 33-4; *Confidential Advisor* 50-1.
123. *Ibid.*, *Hindustan* 34; *Urdu Reporter* 34-5; *Naqsh-e-Kokn* 35-6.
124. *Hayat-e-Millat* 36-37; *General Times* 37; *Mother India* 42-5; *Mother India* 49-50, 57-8.
125. *Ibid.*, *Vivek* 45-6; *Nama Nigar* 46-7; *Ranberi* 47-9.
126. *Ibid.*, *Nama Nigar* 58-9.
127. *Organizer* (1970) A.R. 15-18.
128. *Ibid.*, 16 and the Press Council's explanation at 18.
129. *Ibid.*, *Vivek* 23-5; *Vivek* 25-7; *Vivek* 28-29; *Sobat* 29-31; *Sobat* 32-33; *Masurashram Patrika* 33-35; *Masurashram Patrika* 36-8; *Marmik* 38-40; *Matru Bhoomi* 40-1.
130. *Ibid.*, *Vivek* 23-5; *Tanweer* 42-3; *Shoor Shipai* 41-2.
131. *Ibid.*, *Jeyaikodi* 43-4.
132. *Ibid.*, 44.
133. *Ibid.*, *Current* 44 (involving Mrs. Gandhi and Biju Patnaik). Note that in this year there were also some complaints about indecency—see *Confidential Advisor* 21-23.
134. *Vikrama* (1971) A.R. 6-10; *Nama Nigar* 10-12; *Dawat-e-Hug* 39-41; *Mujahid* 41-2; *Jayakranti* 42-3; *Mother India*; 44-5 *Kal* 45-6; *Loka Lok* on *Arya Samal* 61-2; cf. *Jamiat Times* 59-60.
135. *Ibid.*, *Masurashram Patrika* 12-15.
136. *Ibid.*, *Statesman-Tribune* 16-22 (purely as a law and order question).
137. *Ibid.*, *Kidi* 22-4.
138. *Ibid.*, *Tribune* 24-31.
139. *Ibid.*, *Haryana Mail* 31-36; *Bihan* 36-38.
140. *Ibid.*. *Haryana Mail* 31-36, see p. 36.
141. *Ibid.*, *Prabhat* 38-39; *Inquilab* 39.
142. *Ibid.*, *Dewat* 46-7.

143. *Ibid., Panch Janya* 52-55.
144. *Ibid., Jawani Diwani* 55-57; *Jawani Diwani* 57-58.
145. *Ibid., Lokasatta* 58.
146. *ibid., Marathawada Times* 60-61 (sensational reporting); and on molestation of women incidents see *Samata* 47-49; *Samata* 49-50; *Praja Sattak* 49-50.
147. (1972) A.R. on obscenity see *Blitz, Statesman, Amrita Bazar Patrika, Vishwamitra, Dharam Yuga, Cine Advance International* 69-90. The Council had some comments to make on *Blitz*. The Council gave a long determination on these matters almost in the style of a court judgment. On news of molestation see 90-102 (re *Northern India Patrika* and *Bharat*)—once again the ruling is long, discussive and judgment like.
148. *Ibid., Swadesh* 103-116; *Roshani-on Sindhis* 116-19; *Caravan* 119-21; *Veer Rashtray* 121-2; *Azad* 122-3; *Maharashtra Mihir* 123-4; *Mother India* 124-5.
149. *Ibid., Campus Reporter* 125-134; *Janasahayag* 134-8; *Daman Virodh* 138-140.
150. *Ibid., Homeo Prasanga* 140-2.
151. *Ibid., Indian Express* 142-46. See also *Prajapantru* 146—a case on confused reporting. That appears to be a dispute underlying this complaint.
152. (1973) A.R. 34-49 *Qaumi Ekta*.
153. *Ibid., Hindu* 49-51.
154. *Ibid., Parag* 51-2.
155. *Ibid., Insight, Times of India* 52.
156. *Ibid., Times of India* 55-60.
157. *Ibid., Vivtal* 60-65; *Imam-e-Inqalab* 69-71.
158. *Ibid., Rupangana* 65-9 (clearly a political dispute being fought out the through complaint jurisdiction of the Press Council).
159. *Ibid.. Blitz* and *Illustrated Weekly of India* 71-4.
160. *Ibid., Gandiva* 74-78.
161. *Ibid., Kewal Satya* 78-81.
162. *Ibid., Apne Log* 81-89; *Yug Mandal* 84-5; *Sigappu Nada* 85-88; *Navasakthi* 90-91; cf. *Nathigam, Dinamalar, Alai Osai* 91-94. Note in the *Dinamalar* case (88-90) politicians were also asked to be more careful with their press releases.
163. *Swatantra Bharati* (1979) A.R. 16-17 (re publication of letter), see also the Press Council Review (hereafter P.C.I. Rev.)—(1980)1 P.C.I. Rev. (Part I) (1-24) (re *Swatantra Bharat* case); (1980) I P.C.I. Rev. (Part 2) 18-20 (re *Campus Reporter* on advertisements being withdrawn by government corporation); 21-22 (re *Swatantra Doot Dainik* filed by newspaper against municipal authorities); 22-3 (re *Tribune* re article in *Tribune* about press censorship); (1980) I.P.C. Rev. (Part 3) 25-26 (re *Santaka Uvaach*—governments not giving advertisements);

26-8 (re *Urja*—about advertisements by a government corporation); (1980) 1 P.C.I. Rev. (Part 4) 12-16 (re *Hindu* about an academic's right to reply on a book review. This is a well considered ruling and to be welcomed); 16-18 (re *Charitra Vikas* on non-release of advertisements by government); on this also see 34-5 (re *Ala Osai* a case that was treated as withdrawn); 18-22 (re *Hitavada* on dummy advertisements;) 22-24 (re *Gava Kari*—on non-publication of rejoinder); 24-31 (re *Dainik Janabhumi*—on government pressure to toe the line); 28-31 (on the disaccreditation of a journalist); 31-32; 35-6 (re *Madhya Seemant Samachar*—on pressure from a municipality on a newspaper); 31-35 (re *Naveen Duniya*—a case re government advertisement that was not sustained).

164. (1966) A.R. 4.
165. *Ibid.*, 4-5.
166. *Ibid*,, 5.
167. *Ibid.*, 6-7.
168. (1967) A.R. 9-31; 92-117; (a compilation of some information on parliamentary privileges); 32-34 (training in journalism); 89-91 (questionnaire on monopolism in the press).
169. *Ibid.*, 48-58. Several cases are reported arising out of the reporting on West Bengal and the sacking by Governor Dharam Vir of his own Ministry (48-52). There is also a discussion on insufficient protection of an attack on a journalist from *Malayala Manorma* (52-3). The *Searchlight* of Patna asked for protection from mob violence.
170. *Ibid.*, 59-63.
171. (1968) A.R. 41-56.
172. *Ibid.*, 68-76.
173. *Ibid.*, 57-67.
174. *Ibid.*, 66-67 (see its decision in the *Loksatta* and *Jansatta* cases in respect of the government's loans).
175. (1969) A.R. 124-35.
176. *Ibid.*, 136-40.
177. *Ibid.*, 84-88. The guidelines are to be found at pp. 87-88.
178. *Ibid.*, 107-123.
179. (1970) A.R. 10; also the Newspapers Finance Corporation at pp. 7-8.
180. See *Bennett Coleman Ltd.* v. *Union of India*, A.I.R. 1973 S.C. 106.
181. (1971) A.R. 76 esp. the Resolution at pp. 79-80.
182. *Ibid.*, 82-84.
183. (1972) A.R. 3-5.
184. *Ibid.*, (vi)-(vii).
185. (1973) A.R. 9-10.
186. *Ibid.*, 5-6.
187. *Bennet Coleman and Co.* v. *Union of India* A.I.R. 1973 S.C. 106.
188. Justice Grover had written an article on censorship and obscenity: "Law of obscenity and freedom of expression" (1968) III *J.C.P.S.* 6;

In the famous *Fundamental Rights* case (*Kesavananda* v. *State of Kerala* (1973) 4 S.C.C. 225) he had delivered a joint judgment with Justice Shelat; it is not clear who had drafted it.

189. See (1979-82) A.R. It should be noted that the Press Council has been reconstituted since 1982. The members are a strange motley group. The influence of the corporate press and the government are discernible.

190. See (1979) A.R. 11 (where the government was lobbied to revise the rates prescribed in Rule 10 of the Press Council Rules, 1979 and which show the Government's influential say in these matters); (1980) A.R. 467 (where it was suggested that a levy on newsprint and paper would be a purchase tax outside the jurisdiction of the Central Government. Note: the detailed discussions between the Council, Ministry of Law and Ministry of Information and Broadcasting); (1981) A.R. 18-20 (on the enhancement of rates which would raise the potential revenue from Rs. three and half lakhs to Rs. six lakhs).

191. Certainly there was the expectation of a revenue of Rs. six lakhs ((1981) A.R. 20). There was some controversy about the exemption of Foreign Embassy journals ((1980) A.R. 7. The revenue raised fell short of the target being Rs. 2.54 lakhs in 1980 ((1980) A.R. 154) Rs. 3.03 lakhs in 1981 ((1981) A.R. 174) and Rs. 4.95 lakhs in 1982 ((1982) A.R. 128).

192. These full details are not available (see in the (1979) A.R. 30; (1980) A.R. 154-5; (1981) A.R. 174-176; (1982) A.R. 129)). Pay, allowances and travel dwarf the rest of the budget.

193. The Research wing is mentioned in (1980) A.R. 13-14; the research wing is heralded as representing just the kind of research needed by the Council to act *suo motu* (*ibid.* p. 13). However, the research planned is either farmed out to the Indian Law Institute (*ibid.* pp. 14-5) or to substantiate government rhetoric on social reporting by the press (*ibid.* p. 14). The research itself is summed up later ((1981) A.R. 220-28) but no conclusions have been drawn from it other than alleging the usual story about the irresponsibility and unevenness in reporting in social matters. Thus, the fact of research is its own fulfillment even if no conclusions were drawn (see (1982) A.R. 3). The Indian Law Institute continues to be the mainstay of research (see (1979) A.R. 8 outlining areas of research; and then, in later reports, see (1980) A.R. 14-15; (1981) A.R. 5; (1982) 26-27, showing what the Indian Law Institute has done.

194. On travel the rules are determined under Rule 4 of the Press Council Rules, 1979 (see (1981) A.R. 17-6). Meetings in other parts of the country were justified on the basis that this helped "to keep abreast of the problems of the press in the entire country as a whole and giving the entire press in the country a sense of participation in its affairs" ((1979) A.R. 5). It is not clear how this would happen if *in camera* meetings of the Council were held in Bangalore, Bombay,

Nainital, Trivandrum, Bhubaneshwar and Shillong? (see (1981) A.R. 2).

195. See (1979) A.R. 9-10 (pleading restraint to those politicians and those papers that did not toe the line); (1980) A.R. 9-10 (on the stoppage of papers in Bangalore and Assam); (1981) A.R. 3-4 (asking public and press men to display responsibility); (1982) A.R. 9-13 (following the advice of the Indian Law Institute on the Bihar Bill).

196. See (1980) A.R. 13 on the strengthening of the complaints wing. The British Press Council has taken the view that in certain classes of cases nothing short of immediate action is adequate (see *The Times* (London) 6 February, 1984, 2).

197. (1979) A.R. 4. Clearly the government has asserted its view of the levy ((1980) A.R. 4-7), on the allowances of Members of the Council ((1981) A.R. 17-18); on revising the levy (*ibid.* 18-20).

198. These categories are not distinguished in the Annual Reports after 1980. It is possible that the Press Council persuades some complainants to withdraw their case either on the basis of a settlement or otherwise. (see *Alai Osai* case (1980) A.R. 32 (case on government advertisements "dismissed as withdrawn"); *BHEL* case (1980) A.R. 36 (case on foreign contracts "allowed to rest"); *Hitavada* case (1980) A.R. 44 (case between Director of Information and Publicity and complainant compromised and case restored; and then dismissed as withdrawn); *Dainik Janmabhumi* case (1980) A.R. 56 (case dropped on an 'inconclusive basis'); *Central Press Accreditation* case (1980) A.R. 63 (referred to a government committee rather than decided); *Madhya Seemant Samachar* case (1980) A.R. 71 (complainant disinclined to pursue the matter); *Tribune* case (1980) A.R. 73 (case not taken further); *Dainik Sarvmath* (1980) A.R. 77 ("dismissed as withdrawn"); *India Today* (1980) A.R. 79 (matter treated as closed); *Khoon Naab* case (1981) A.R. 33 (complaint against government withdrawn); *Jayant* case ((1981) A.R. 41 (complaint closed after government assurance); *Ananda Bazar Patrika* (1981) A.R. 44 (case against West Bengal Government treated as closed); *Muzzaffarnagar Bulletin* case (1981) A.R. 57 (case closed after government assurance); *Shri Verma's* case (1981) A.R. 61 (case settled); *Campus Reporter* case (1981) A.R. 69 (withdrawn); *Antulay case* (1981) A.R. 73 (not proceeded after press release); *Mahajati* case (1981) A.R. 78 (withdrawn); *Samoiy* case (1981) A.R. 81 (Council report in the dark about settlement); *Indian Express* case (1981) A.R. 87 (case amicably settled); *Press Club* case (1981) A.R. 91 (dismissed for non-prosecution); *Blitz* case (1981) A.R. 141 (complaint withdrawn); *Hindustan* (1981) A.R. 145 (complaint dropped); *Daily Samaj* case (1982) A.R. 43 (dismissed for non-prosecution); *Shri Swamy* case (1982) A.R. 77 (referred to Accreditation Committee); *Hindustan Times* case (1982) A.R. 91

(case settled); *Maharashtra Times* case (1982) A.R. 95 (case withdrawn); *Weekly* case (1982) A.R. 96 (case settled); *Hindustan Times* case (1982) A.R. 109 (reconciliation effected); *Indian Express* case (1982) A.R. 110 (case settled): *Hindustan Times Assam Tribunal* case (1980) (withdrawn); *Hindustan Times* (1982) A.R. 113 (not proceeded against).

Two things should be noted about this list of cases. *First*, they represent the cases that came to the Council for adjudication even though the Council 'settled' them. *Secondly*, the sample suggests that complaints against the government and corporate press have a greater chance of being 'settled' or compromised.

199. *Supra* note 196.

200. These cases arise out of Section 13 of the Press Council Act, 1978 authorising to hear compla ints against the government. On advertising see the cases cited (1980) A.R. 18-53; (1981) A.R. 33-53; (1982) A.R. 23.

201. These cases arise under Section 14 of the Press Council Act, 1978.

202. For a political use of the Council see *Assam Tribunal* case (1980) A.R. 92; *Mahajati* case (1981) A.R. 78; *Indian Express* case (1981) A.R. 145; *Probe* case (1982) A.R. 88; *Gujarant Samachar* case (1982) A.R. 104; *Indian Express* case (1982) A.R. 110. Note: Such cases have only publicity value and tend to get settled. For other political use of the Council see *Chandi Kala Marg* case (1982) A.R. 101 (on Sikh politics).

203. For government intervention see *Malayalanadu* case (1980) A.R. 125 (obscenity; complainant: Ministry of Information and Broadcasting—hereafter Ministry); *Hindustan Times* case (1981) A.R. 98 (bad reporting; complainant: Ministry); *Sobat* case (1981) A.R. 151 (wrongly alleging Chief Minister communal; complainant: District Magistrate); *Saptahik Nilachal* case (1981) A.R. 154 (anti-national; complainant: Government of Assam); *Agradoot* case (1981) A.R. 157 (false reporting; complainant: Secretary to government); *Tribune* case (1981) A.R. 113 (false reporting; complainant: Ministry); *Indian Express* case (1981) A.R. 121 (false reporting; complainant: Ministry); *Blitz* case (1981) A.R. 141 (false reporting; complainant: statutory body); *Free Press Bulletin* (1981) A.R. 144 (false reporting; complainant: the police); *District Magistrate* case (1982) A.R. 46 (strange case of Ministry forwarding complaint about District Magistrate); *Dainik Asom* (1982) A.R. 82 (mischievous reporting; complainant: Government of Assam); *Readers Digest* case (1982) A.R. 85 (false reporting; complainant: Co-operative Bank); *Nai Duniya* case (1982) A.R. 94 (false reporting; complainant: Agricultural Marketing Committee); *Maharashtra Times* (1982) A.R. 95 (false reporting; complainant: police); *Free Press Bulletin* (1982) A.R. 97 (false reporting; complainant: police); *Gujarat Samachar* case (1982) A.R. 104 (false reporting and casteism; complainant; Ministry, and

politician;) *Blitz* case (1982) A.R. 105 (communal disharmony; complainant: Government of Bihar); *Hindustan Times* (1982) A.R. 108 and 109 (false reporting; complainant: Trade Fair Authority); *Hindustan Times* case (1982) A.R. 111 (casteism; complainant: government committee); *Indian Express* case (1982) A.R. 112 (false reporting; complainant: education department).

204. See (1981) A.R. 2. (1980) A.R. 1 casually mentions the government as complainant. In (1981) A.R. 2 the government's use of this jurisdiction is presented as healthy. Clearly (1982) A.R. 2 does not take this into account when passing the judgment that the government acted "without any interference".

205. For the original *Hitavada* case (1980) A.R. 115-120. For the *suo motu* action (1981) A.R. 95.

206. (1981) A.R. 2.

207. *Tribune* case (1979) A.R. 12.

208. See (1980) A.R. 9; and the adjudication at (1982) A.R. 51.

209. *Blitz* case (1982) A.R. 37.

210. See (1980) A.R. 9 (on journalists) and *Bangalore* case (1982) A.R. 51. There are several other cases against government harassment arising from complaints: see (1982) A.R. 22-72.

211. *Hitavada* case (1981) A.R. 97.

212. See (1980) A.R. 13. For these cases showing pigs with carcasses of men see *Dainik Jagran* case (1980) A.R. 132; *Asli Bharat* case (1980) A.R. 135; *Current* case (1980) A.R. 139. *Shree Warsha* (1980) A.R. 140; *Northern India Patrika* (1980) A.R. 142; *Malayala Manorama* (1980) A.R. 141.

213. *Hindustan Samachar* case (1981) A.R. 164.

214. *Swatantra Bharat* case (1979) A.R. 16.

215. *Ibid.*, p. 20 on the 'safety value' function of the correspondence columns.

216. On government advertising: *Campus Reporter* case (1980) A.R. 18 (complaint rejected); *Naveen Duniya* case (1980) A.R. 24 (complaint rejected); *Swantantra Doot Saptahik* (1980) A.R. 29 (complaint rejected); *Alai Osai* case (1980) A.R. 32 which was withdrawn; *Alai Osai* case (1980) A.R. 36 (where the government promised a review); *Charita Vikas* case (1980) A.R. 41 (allegation sustained); *Hitavada* case (1980) A.R. 44 (matter settled); *Sankata Uvaach* (1980) A.R. 53 (complaint rejected).

217. *Dainik Janmabhumi* case (1980) A.R. 56 (case closed even though ministerial conduct not above reproach); *J.P. Chaturvedi's* case (1980) A.R. 63 (complaint against the government's Accreditation Committee referred back to the latter); *Madhya Seemant Samachar* (1980) A.R. 71 (District Magistrate's harassment of press; matter not proceeded with); *Tribune* case (1980) A.R. 73 (police withholding press messages. Case not deemed to be proven, even though *suo*

motu inquiry); *Dainik Sarvmath* (1980) A.R. 77 (complaint against telegraph office dismissed as withdrawn).

218. *India Today* (1980) A.R. 79 (inconclusive evidence).
219. *Gavakari* case (1980) A.R. 86 (editor admonished for non-publication of rejoinder); *Assam Tribune* (1980) A.R. 92 (publication of material portion of rejoinder sufficient); *Romila Thapar* case (1980) A.R. 101 (non-publication of rejoinder deprecated).
220. *Hitavada* case (1980) A.R. 115, 120 (use of dummy advertisements denounced).
221. *Sunday* case (1980) A.R. 83 (editor warned for defamation); *Hindustan* case (1980) A.R. 110 (regrets for defamation published). *Malayalanadu* case (1980) A.R. 125 (charge of obscene writings not made out). In the following cases communalism was alleged and the papers informally admonished: *Dainik Jagran* case (1980) A.R. 132; *Asli Bharat* case (1980) A.R. 135; *Current* case (1980) A.R. 139; *Free Press Journal* case (1980) A.R. 140; *Shree Warsha* case (1980) A.R. 140; *Malayala Manorma* case (1980) A.R. 141; *Northern India Patrika* (1980) A.R. 142.
222. *Khoon Naab* case (1981) A.R. 33 (complaint of favouritism in advertising withdrawn); *Saptahik Chambal Varni* case (1981) A.R. 35 (complaint rejected); *Uttar Bangla Patrika* case (1981) A.R. 38 (complaint dismissed); *Jayant* case (1981) A.R. 41 (government promised to review case); *Ananda Bazar Patrika* case (1981) A.R. 44 (case against West Bengal Government treated as closed); *Manush Patrika* (1981) A.R. 49 (allegation upheld against government of Tripura). *Muzzaffarnagar Bulletin* (1981) A.R. 57 (government of U.P. assumes review); *Azimabad Express* case (1981) A.R. 64 (parties compromise).
223. *D.G. Kulkarni* case (1981) A.R. 53 (charge of wrongful disaccreditation not made out); *Muzzaffarnagar Bulletin* case (1981) A.R. 57 (disaccreditation to be reviewed).
224. *Campus Reporter* case (1981) A.R. 69 (charge of favouritism refuted); *Antulay* case (1981) A.R. 73 (Minister asked not to make derogatory remarks about the press); *Jugantar* case (1981) A.R. 73 (interference through union reprimanded); *Mahajati* (1981) A.R. 73 (pre-censorship complaint withdrawn).
225. *Samaj* case (1981) A.R. 81 (case settled); *Indian Express* case (1981) A.R. 81 (case settled); *Garhwal Press Club* case (1981) A.R. 91 (complaint dismissed for non-prosecution).
226. *Hitavada* case (1981) A.R. 95 (Press Council censured where newspaper seeks Council's abolition); *Hindustan Times* (1981) A.R. 98 (due care not exercised by correspondent); *Illustrated Weekly of India* case (1981) A.R. 130 (editorial discretion on an issue concerning Prime Minister's interview not properly exercised).
227. *Tribune* case (1981) A.R. 113 (haste in commenting on government not in the public interest); *Indian Expess* (1981) A.R. 121 (public

matters must be verified in the public interest); *Bombay* case (1980) A.R. 125 (ambivalent comments almost bordering on half-truths permissible); *Sobat* case (1981) A.R. 151 (charge of communalism dropped); *Saptahik Nilachal* (1981) A.R. 154 (story about secession of Assam censured); *Agradoot* case (1981) A.R. 157 (corruption allegation rejected); *Sunday Standard* case (1981) A.R. 160 (false story about death of woman admonished); *Hindustan Samachar* (1981) A.R. 164 (story about a woman slapping an 'eve-teaser': correspondent suspended).

228. *Image* case (1981) A.R. 127 (right to reply upheld); see also *Illustrated Weekly of India* case (1981) A.R. 130 at 134-5.

229. *Times of India* case (1981) A.R. 136 (charge of defamation not upheld); *Blitz* case (1981) A.R. 141 (withdrawn); *Free Press Bulletin* (1981) A.R. 144 (false report about police revolt admonished); *Hindustan* case (1981) A.R. 145 (false story: dropped); *National Herald* case (1981) A.R. 148 (distorted report; not upheld).

230. *Dainik Sambad* (1982) A.R. 23 (complaint against government of Tripura not substantiated); *Nav Bharat Times* case (1982) A.R. 34 (prosecution of correspondent not *bona fide*); *Himachal Times* case (1982) A.R. 36 (charge of police harassment not substantiated); *Blitz* (1982) A.R. 37 (arrest of journalists violative of press freedom); *Jai Ai Asom* case (1982) A.R. 39 (government criticized for maltreatment and humiliation of editor); *Daily Samaj* case (1982) A.R. 43 (complaints against Deputy Commissioner dismissed for non-prosecution); *U.P. Small and Medium Newspaper Council* case (1982) A.R. 46 (complaint against District Commissioner upheld. Note the government's public interest plea of communal harmony); *Yahan Wahaw* case (1982) A.R. 48 (complaint against police not warranted). The Council took *suo motu* action and condemned the blockade of newspaper offices in the *Indian Express et al* cases (1982) A.R. 51 (authorities reprimanded); *Indian Express* case (1982) A.R. 65 (cameraman's charge and allegation upheld); *Muzzaffarnagar Bulletin* (1982) A.R. 69 (cavalier attitude of government deplored); *Prachand* case (1982) A.R. 70 (complaint of maltreatment and harassment upheld); *Apni Duniya* case (1982) A.R. 74 (complaint of police harassment dismissed); *Malaya Manorama* case (1982) A.R. 75 (group raids on newspaper offices regretted). On advertisements see *Secular Indian Youth* case (1982) A.R. 79 (complaint rejected); on accreditation *Dainik Janta Express* case (1982) A.R. 77 (matter referred to Central Accreditation Committee).

231. *Dainik Asom* case (1982) A.R. 82 (fabricated stories about Assam; paper warned); *Reader's Digest* case (1982) A.R. 85 (non-publication of article: compromise and settlement reached); *Probe* case (1982) A.R. 88 (paper admonished for distorting interview and violating

confidentiality); *Hindustan Times* case (1982) A.R. 91 (case settled); *Nai Duniya* (1982) A.R. 94 (false report; allegation dismissed); *Maharashtra Times* case (1982) A.R. 95 (false report; case withdrawn); *Weekly* case (1982) A R. 96 (case settled); *Dainik Asom* (1982) A.R. 97 (paper willing to publish contradiction); *Free Press Bulletin* case (1982) A.R. 97 (paper warned); *Economic Times* case (1982) A.R. 96 (complaint rejected); *Indian Express* case (1982) A.R. 99 (action not substantiated). For cases on communal disharmony see *Chandi Kala Marg* case (1982) A.R. 101 (editor censured); *Gujarat Samachar* case (1982) A.R. 104 (editor admonished); *Blitz* case (1982) A.R. 105 (editor admonished).

232. *Hastinapur Samachar* case (1982) A.R. 107 (editor warned about defamation); *Hindustan Times* case (1982) A.R. 108 (complaint rejected); *Hindustan Times* case (1982) A.R. 109 (case reconciled by Council); *Indian Express* case (1982) A.R. 110 (case settled); *Hindustan Times* case (1982) A.R. 111 (case withdrawn); *Indian Express* case (1982) A R. 112 (allegation not substantiated); *Hindustan Times* case (1982) A.R. 113 (editor claimed good faith); *Bharati Leader* case (1982) A.R. 114 (editor censured); *Searchlight* case (1982) A.R. 116 (complaint not substantiated); *Hamara Nara* (1982) A.R. 117 (editor warned); *Quami Tanzeem* case (1982) A.R. 118 (editor warned: asked to publish contradiction).
233. *Deccan Chronicle* (1983) A.R. 16; *The Evidence Weekly* (1983) A.R. 19; *Huiyen Lampao* (1983) A.R. 21; *Blitz*—UNI (1983) A.R. 22; *Dainik Janambhumi* (1983) A.R. 26: *All India Small & Medium Newspapers Federation, Saharsa* (1983) A.R. 27; *Viplavi Mazdoor Weekly* (1983) A.R. 28.
234. *Patna University Student's* case (1983) A.R. 17; *The Pilot* (1983) A.R. 17; *Andhra Jyothi*, (1983) A.R. 18; *Aaina-E-Siasat* (1983) A.R. 18; *Khabaryaar*, (1983) A.R. 18; *The Tribune* (1983) A.R. 20; *Mahajati*, (1983) A.R. 24.
235. *Indian Express*, A.I.R. (1983) A.R. 29; *Blitz*, (1983) A.R. 35; *Sanchar Samachar Darpan*, (1983) A.R. 36; *The Pilot*, (1983) A.R. 36; *Sunday Standard*, (1983) A.R. 37; *Dainik Sambad* 1983 A.R. 38; *Eenadu*, (1983) A.R. 39.
236. *Saptahik Mujahid of Assam*, (1983) A.R. 31; *Saptahik Nilachal*, (1983) A.R. 32; *Ranchi Express*, (1983) A.R. 32; *Indian Nation and Aryavarta*, (1983) A.R. 33.
237. *Sanchar Samachar Darpan*, (1983) A.R. 36.
238. *Sunday Standard*, (1983) A.R. 37.
239. *Dainik Sambad*, (1983) A.R. 38.
240. *Arjun Baan Weekly*, (1983) A.R. 40.
241. See Section 14, *Probe's* case, (1983) A.R. 52.
242 *Dainit Kranti Krishna* (1983) A.R. 53.
243. *Indian Express*, (1983) A.R. 51.

244. *Hindustan Times*, (1983) A.R. 55.
245. *Havabaaz*, (1983) A.R. 56.
246. *The Indian Author*, (1983) A.R. 44; *Navhind Times*, (1983) A.R. 53; *Deccan Herald*, (1983) A.R. 57; *University Today*, (1983) A.R. 58; *Mumbai Sakal*, (1983) A.R. 59; *Yuva Pukar*, (1983) A.R. 60; *Bareilly Darshan*, (1983) A.R. 60; *Anchalik Kranti*, (1983) A.R. 61; *Prativedan*, (1983) A.R. 61; *Indian Express*, (1983) A.R. 63; *Randiant*, (1983) A.R. 63; *Free Press Journal's* case, (1983) A.R. 64.
247. *Radiant*, (1983) A.R. 63.
248. *Barendrabhumi*, (1984) A.R. 37; *Indian Personaliiy*, (1984) A.R. 39; *Eastern Express*, *Gangtok*, (1984) A.R. 41; *Coalfield Times*, (1984) A.R. 43; *Kungumam Publication*, (1984) A.R. 45; *Muzaffarnagar Bulletin*, (1984) A.R. 47; *News Week*, (1984) A.R. 50; *Yuva Prayas*, (1984) A.R. 51; *Daily Jangan*, (1984) A.R. 53; *Dinakaran*, (1984) A.R. 54.
249. *Yuwa Swapna*, (1984) A.R. 38; *Sona Sandesh* (*Weekly*), (1984) A.R. 46.
250. *Batari* and the *Assam Tribune*, (1984) A.R. 26; *Hirkhanda* (1984) A.R. 28; *Gana-Chabuk*, (1984) A.R. 29; *Republican* (*Harayana*), (1984) A.R. 30; *Adamya Weekly*, (1984) A.R. 31; *Bastar-ki-Awaz Weekly*, (1984) A.R. 32; *Malai Murasu*, *Evening Tamil Daily*, (1984) A.R. 34: *Blitz* (*Bombay*), (1984) A.R. 56; *Janata-ke-Vichar*, (1984) A.R. 61; *Tarsen Lal* (1984) A.R. 30-7.
251. *Blitz*, (1984) A.R. 13; *Prakatane*, (1984) A.R. 16; *The Telegraph*, (1984) A.R. 17; *Saptahik Adamya*, (1984) A.R. 18; *Daily Jagaran* (*Agartala*), (1984) A.R. 22; *Theme*, (1984) A.R. 23; *Bareilly Darshan*. (1984) A.R. 26; *Siwani Sandesh*, (1984) A.R. 29; *Dinakaran* (1984) A.R. 33.
252. *Daily Pratap* and *Daily Vir Pratap*, (1984) A.R. 25.
253. *Nav Bharat Times*, (1984) A.R. 64.
254. *West Bengal Newspapers' Rights Preservation Committee Burdwan*, (1984) A.R. 74.
255. *M.P. Chronicle's* (1984) A.R. 55.
256. *W. Bengal Newspapers' Rights Preservation Committee* (*Burdwan*) (1984) A.R. 57.
257. *Rehnuma-e-Deccan*, (1984) A.R. 63; *Munsif*, (1984) A.R. 65.
258. *S.T.C.*'s case, (1984) A.R. 58; *Rahnuma-e-Karnataka*, (1984) A.R. 72.
259. *Ethiroli*, (1984) A.R. 59; *Bihar Press Bill*, (1984) A.R. 63.
260. *The Light of Andamans*, (1984) A.R. 76.
261. Section 14—*Deshabhimani*, (1984) A.R. 102; *Daily Pratap*, (1984) A.R. 104; *Rajdhani* (*Bombay*), (1984) A.R. 104; *Aryavarta*, (1984) A.R. 105; *Times of India*, (1984) A.R. 106; *Rehnuma-e-Deccan*, (1984) A.R. 107; *Gujarat Samachar*, (1984) A.R. 107; *Mahasagar*. (1984) A.R. 108; *Kumkumam*, (1984) A.R. 109.

262. *Bhagirathi Sandesh*, (1984) A.R. 82.
263. *Sunday Observer*, (1984) A.R. 85.
264. *Kashmir Times*, (1984) A.R. 81.
265. *Hindustan Times*, (1984) A.R. 79; *Times of India*, (1984) A.R. 85; *Onlooker*, (1984) A.R. 98.
266. *India Today*, (1984) A.R. 87.
267. *Sunday Observer*, (1984) A.R. 86; *Ethiroli*, (1984) A.R. 97, 112, 113, 118, 119, 121; *Light of Andamans*, (1984) A.R. 98; *Murasoli*, (1984) A.R. 112; *Azimabad Express*, (1984) A.R. 116; *Hindustan Times*, (1984)A.R. 117; *Northern India Patrika*, (1984) A.R. 117; *Pooja Ke Den*, (1984) A.R. 123; *Trithabhumi*, (1984) A.R. 125; *Dainik Jagran*, (1984) A.R. 125; *Hindustan Times*, (1984) A.R. 126; *Economic Times*, (1984) A.R 127: *Nav Bharat Times*, (1984) A.R. 129; *Chikmaglur Patrika*, 1984 A.R. 130; *Punjab Kesari*, (1984) A.R 131; *Tej Pukar*, (1984) A.R. 131; *Hindustan Times*, (1984) A.R. 132; *Amrit Prabhat*, (1984) A.R. 134; *Aatmakatha*, (1984) A.R. 136; *Daily Pratap*, (1984) A.R. 137; *Vidrohi Swar*, (1984) A.R. 137; *Times of India*, (1984) A.R. 138; *Chingari*, (1984) A.R. 139; *Prajatantra*, (1984) A.R. 140; *Shatru Shaman*, (1984) A.R. 141; *Ravivar*, (1984) A.R. 141; *Hindustan Times*, (1984) A.R. 142; *Ek Baat Suni*, (1984) A.R. 144; *Free Press Journal*, (1984) A.R. 145; *Dinakaran*, (1984) A.R. 145; *Illustrated Weekly*, (1984) A.R. 146; *Jan-Varta* and *Gandiva*, (1984) A.R. 154; *Ravivar*, (1984) A.R. 155; *Yamuna Kinare*, (1984) A.R. 156; *Lokarth*, (1984) A.R. 156; *Naini Yatra*, (1984) A.R. 157; *Anokha Manav*, (1984) A.R. 157; *Amritha Weekly*, (1984) A.R. 158; *Uttari Herald*, (1984) A.R. 159; *Chhintey Aur Bacahharain*, (1984) A.R. 160.
268. *Illustrated Weekly*, (1984) A.. 161; *India 2000*, (1984) A.R. 169.
269. *Indian Express*, (1984) A.R. 80.
270. *Satya Sanaton*, (1984) A.R. 83; *Bareilly Darshan*, (1984) A.R. 84; *Jagpahiya*, (1984) A.R. 96.
271. *Dibakar Weekly*, (1985) A.R. 10; *Assault on Newsmen. . .* (1985) A.R. 12; *Prachand Weekly* (*New Delhi*), (1985) A.R. 12; *Newsmen's Harassment* (*Haryana*), (1985) A.R. 13; *Syandan Patrika*, (1985) A.R. 18.
272. *Mujhe Jeene Do*, (1985) A.R. 16.
273. *Hindustan Times*, (1985) A R. 11.
274. *Ibid. Pratush Sambad*, (1985) A.R. 17; *Marup* (*Tripura*) (1985) A.R. 19; *Gujarat Samachar*, (1985) A.R. 20; *Shailsuta*, (1985) A.R. 21.
275. *Hindustan Times*, (1985) A.R. 13.
276. Section 14—*Voice of Karnataka*, (1985) A.R. 33; *Organiser*, (1985) A.R. 34.
277. *Sainik Dhwani and Bundelvani*, (1985) A.R. 36; *Lalit Jyoti*, (1985) A.R. 37; *Sunehri Kiran*, (1985) A.R. 38; *Daily Pratap*, (1985) A.R. 39; *Murasoli*, (1985) A.R. 40; *Free Press Journal*, (1985) A.R.

41; *Chingari*, (1985) A.R. 42: *Krante Kathan*, (1985) A.R. 42; *Celebrity*, (1985) A.R. 45; *Hitavada*, (1985) A.R. 45; *Bareilly Darshan* (1985) A.R. 45.

278. *Amritha Weekly*, (1985) A.R. 24; *Free Press Bulletin*, (1985) A.R. 29; that some attacks on it as the one in this case were light-hearted.

279. *Gujarat Samachar*, (1985) A.R. 28.

280. *Ibid.*

281. *Illustrated Weekly of India*, (1985) A.R. 30 (attack on the *Communist Party* case).

282. This research consists of two books written by Usha Loghani: *Violation of Journalistic Ethics and Public Taste* (1984) and *Violation of the Freedom of the Press* (1986). They have (a) classified the cases as falling under distinct headings and (b) outlined what they believe to be the principles on which the Council is adjudicating matters. Their account tends to be generous. Lawyers would call much of what the Council has decreed *obiter dicta*. The Council tends to compromise many cases and not making their declarations a basis for an adjudicatory decision.

283. (1979) A.R. (ii) (Chairman's introduction), 6-7.

284. (1979) A.R. 9-10.

285. (1979) A.R. 11.

286. (1979) A.R. 10-11.

287. (1979) A.R. 7-8.

288. (1980) A.R. 3, The Council wanted the government to cut off advertisements to erring newspapers and deny accreditation to journalists found guilty of misconduct. This view was first aired by the Chairman in 1979 (see (1979) A.R. iii referring to the example of the Turkish Press Council).

289. (1980) A.R. 4-7. It was not able to convince the government to impose a cess on newsprint; or to extend the levy to foreign embassy journals in India.

290. (1980) A.R. 7-8. But the Council was heavily lobbied by various newspaper organisations and came to the conclusion that:

> "There was no need for it (*i.e.* the Council) to frame any guidelines or principles with regard to these matters for the present and that conventions could be allowed to develop and matters judged in a manner similar to the one applied for building up the code of conduct."

291. (1980) A.R. 10.

292. (1981) A.R. (ii).

293. (1981) A.R. (v).

294. (1981) A.R. 10-16.

295. (1981) A.R. 3 (on the Criminal Law Amendment Bill and on the Tamil Nadu Code of Criminal Procedure (Amendment) Ordinance 1981); 7-9 (on the Assam government notification No. PLA 1375/00/1 of 23 December 19ե0 on communal disharmony. The matter was *sub judice*).
296. See Chapter 2 (*supra*) generally.
297. (1982) A.R. (i)—(iii) (constantly comparing the work of the Council with other countries without looking for points of equivalence).
298. (1982) A.R. 17-21 based on the following reports S.N. Jain: *Official Secrecy and the Press* (1981); Rajeev Dhavan: *Contempt of Court and the Press* (1982); see also M.P. Jain: *Parliamentary Privileges and the Press* (1984) and also P.M. Bakshi: *Law of Defamation: Some Aspects* (1986). Note the general review of the previous Press Council's work (1979-82); the lobby report on the Bihar Bill (9-13) and submission to the Press Commission (13-16).
299. (1983) A.R. 1-2.
300. *Ibid.* 2.
301. *Ibid.* 5-7.
302. *Ibid.* 8-9.
303. *Ibid.* 9.
304. *Ibid.* 10-11.
305. *Ibid.* 11.
306. *Ibid.* 11.
307. (1984) A.R. 6.
308. *Ibid.* 7.
309. *Ibid.* 9.
310. *Ibid.* 10.
311. (1985) A.R. 6.
312. *Ibid.* 6.
313. *Ibid.* 7.
314. *Ibid.* 7.
315. This is certainly the verdict of the first chairman, J.R. Mudholkar: *Press Laws* (1975) 106; see also A.S. Abraham: "Powers for the Press Council: Playing into the Government's hands", *Times of India*, 4 September 1981.
316. *M. Shah* v. *L.I.C.*, *AIR 1981 Gujarat 15*; For the right to reply cases adjudicated by the Press Council see *supra* notes 219, 226, 228.

PART FIVE

The Press, Law and Politics

10

ONLY THE GOOD NEWS

I

Governments often decree that newspapers can publish 'only the good news'. A contrary tradition, which derives its strengths essentially from its contrariness, argues that printing what the government prohibits is, in fact, precisely what the 'good news' is. Dirigisme can hardly settle the question. Fulfilling or denying the expectations of a government, while pertinent, cannot be the whole story. The press has too multi-dimensional an existence in society to be judged on the sole consideration that it acts for or against regime interests. The 'good news' is defined by society in a lot of ways beyond the immediate interests and expectations of certain existing and identifiable groups and interests. Both 'fact' and 'value', the notion of 'good news' defines what constitutes 'news' as well as expresses a moral statement. In public and in journalists' minds, the 'good news' is offen inseparable from what is considered 'news'. The 'moral' is never too far from the 'fact'. Some papers are deemed not to publish 'news' because they do not write 'good news'. Papers are classified on the basis of the 'good news' they publish.

'Good news' is not just determined by political considerations. Apart from 'regime good news', there is a professional concept of 'good news' which itself draws texture and meaning from a variety of sources. For journalists this concept represents an internally and externally imposed disciplinary restraint. Such a discipline serves to present a picture that the 'good news' is the product of ardent neutrality.[1] It has the effect of acting as a restraint of trade and concerted practice for the profession and simultaneously builds up public notions of the 'good news'. Acting as a moral and political code, it marks out what is allowed and permissible. Not surprisingly, it is not determined just by the professional. What the professionals call 'good news' is constantly, socially and politically negotiated through a maze of articulated and inarticulated premises under pressure from the conflicting ideologies and interests that contend for acceptance.

In one sense, there is no concept of 'good news'. In that sense the 'good news' depends on what may appear to be 'good' to any person or group. But 'good news' has two other meanings. The more obvious of these meanings is associated with political censorship; the less obvious—but more insidious—is the professional concept of the 'good news'. Such a concept of 'good news' is not determined by government decrees. It is a moral virtue accepted by the press, mirrored in the law, reflective of politics and articulating a consensus on the methods and range of acceptable distortion. For 'good news' is 'bad news' in the shadow of an understanding of the permissible. Like 'law', the professional concept of the 'good news' pretends to be morally and politically neutral. It represents the way things are done as well as an end-product which is packaged so that it will influence without offence. Clumsily representing the interests of one group is 'bad news'.[2] The contours of 'good news' is not just marked out by professional agreement but delicately precipitated consensus values determined by various individual and institutional ideologues.

In all this, 'law' plays a crucial part. It represents an ideology as well as an institutional framework in which ideology, publicity, and decisions are negotiated.[3] Yet no study of law is complete without reference to a wider political context within which all political arenas—legal, media or otherwise—find substance and expression. This wider backdrop determines what the 'good news' is and also conditions the manner in which the laws of the press condition, repress or liberate the media. Here, we will first consider how we should view the 'law' and 'legal institutions' before we consider the wider political implications of the laws relating to the press in India.

II

The Press and the Law: Problems of Ideology and Pathology

One of the outstanding things about the law of the Indian press is the almost complete lack of material on the subject. In the sparse material that exists certain distinct approaches are discernible. The first kind of approach takes statute law to be the most important expression of social reality. A collection of the relevant statute law is taken to be central to the study of the law of the press. Typical of this kind of work is Justice Basu's *Law of the Press in India.*[4] This compends all the statutory cases, superimposes upon the words of the statute a commentary based on judicial cases and doctrine and ends up by telling us very little about the law of tbe press, how it actually operates and whom it affects. The second kind of approach concentrates on the legal doctrine generated by the courts and the institutions created by the government. Typical of this kind of approach is Justice Mudholkar's Tagore Law Lectures on *Press Law.*[5] While Justice Mudholkar—as a judge of the Supreme Court and the first Chairman of the Press Council—understood the problems of the press with an enviable clarity, he assumed that much of the debate about the press could be solved at the level of legal doctrine which, in turn, would manufacture consequential results. But the analysis does not stray beyond its legalistic framework or examine the social implications of legal doctrine. A third kind of approach has been to package law and legal doctrine with shrewd, even if intuitive, insights into policy perspectives. The picture is far from complete, accepts the law at face value and concentrates on questions of implementation.[6]

In this book, I have tried to explore the law and legal system against the backdrop of the Indian political economy in two distinct ways. The first is to look at the law as a complex ideology which defines, excludes, persuades and conditions. The second is to look at the legal system as a complex labyrinth which can, and within limits is, put to multiple differential uses. Disputes that become part of the litigation game are transformed as they are fed through the legal system. The winners often lose; and the losers lick their wounds but count their gains. Unable to look at actual negotiations and trials, I have tried to interpret court decisions, public pronouncements, legislation, parliamentary discourse and administrative decision-making as the basic data.

Ideological Components

The ideological components of the law are crucial to our understanding of the law.[7] Trapped in vulgar Austinian notions of the law as a set of rules—a view that was consecrated in the codification of Indian law in the late nineteenth century—we are apt to ignore the complex functions of law in defining reality, creating persuasive concepts, enabling argument and intellectual growth and settling the bases on which rights can be claimed as actual, moral, social and political. Law does not just address itself to lawyers and judges. It is a byzantine entity that addresses itself to society. It marks out enabling and disabling contours, adding and detracting moral, social and political force to what is, and should be deemed to be, acceptable to society. Modern law has reinforced its efficacy in this regard by pretending not to do all these things. The 'is' is separated from the 'ought' and there is a strict separation of the law from morals.[8] Conversely, there is much emphasis on the law as a rational development which has transformed earlier counterparts into a sophisticated modern rational entity.[9] The form of law cannot belie the sophisticated manner in which it grows and the social implications of its conceptual jurisprudence. In this sense, Hindu Law's *dharmasastris* were powerful conceptualists whose significance lay not in whether they were cited in courts or privy to dispute processing but in the invocations implicit in their conceptual reconstruction of society.[10] The *shastris* wrote not to control what was going on but to sharpen our awareness of what constitutes conventional wisdom. While modern law is more greatly concerned with the institutions of implementation, it is aware that many shadows stalk across its institutional framework. It is wrong to concentrate on just the institutional framework which in any event is, in practice, much more a property of society rather than of its creators. Law proposes a complex discipline which haunts every aspect of modern life. Much of what is proposed finds silent acceptance in the form of consensus ideology.

The advent of capitalism was a tremendous challenge to the law. A considerable amount of attention has been paid to the 'status/contract' metaphor and the extent to which contract formed the basis of the dispensation.[11] There is no doubt that contract recognised—perhaps enabled—a new transactional mould. Fitted into this mould were a new range of transactions. 'Labour' was presented as an 'exchanged' commodity rather than as a relationship. The information explosion called for new incremental development resting on the legality of new individual transactions. This obscured considerably the true nature of capitalism and the demands that it made on the political and legal system. Capitalism unleashed on society a series of new processes and group formations. It was the triumph of legal jurisprudence to have presented the legal reality of capitalism as a series of unconnected individual legal transactions. But the growth of capitalism is the growth of factories, of control on the movement of goods and grain, of the rise of the regulatory State, of the introduction of policing agencies, of the opening up and control of new public political arenas, of information explosions and the need to control the manner and extent of their proliferation, of the emergence of new groups and entities like companies and labour unions and of new bureaucracies both within the State and outside it. An honest jurisprudence would not have underplayed these developments and would have argued their merits and effects more rigorously and justly.[12] Instead, at least English law, played down the new groups, transferred much of the controversy from 'law' to politics,[13] allowed the growth of certain capitalist formations, and controlled, suppressed and refused to recognise the growth of certain emergent labour and other groups. Entire processes were encapsulated as 'property' rights and protected in the commodity transaction form.[14] It is highly doubtful if the commodity form was really essential to the development of capitalism as a *functional* device.[15] Little is known about the pathology of court litigation and out-of-court dispute settlement to suggest that contract suddenly became the crucial vehicle for enabling capitalist advancement.

The contract metaphor was an idea which helped to distort the ground conditions under which capitalism was being created. The contract metaphor helps to project the view that capitalism developed as a result of a series of individual transactions. To this is added the legitimating rhetoric that these transactions were entered into fairly, by equals. The contribution of the contract metaphor is not just that it formally camouflaged the substantive inequalities that lay behind the transactions of modern society. The real contribution is the effective way in which contract transactions depicted capitalism as an episodic development. American law mirrored and presented many of these developments much more accurately. The growth of anti-trust law is an example of the creation of new legal forms; constitutional law and jurisprudence developed in a much more outspoken way. Controversies in law replicated controversies in society. The group formations and institutional developments which accompanied capitalist development were given legal form in a more distinct way.

English law in India sought to accomplish three distinct objectives. The *first* was to accommodate and yet make invisible the economic changes that were taking place in Indian society. This was done by using both the 'status' and 'contract' form. Hindu law was notionally left intact as a traditional law. But, although notionally expressed in the form ordained by the *rishis*, it was made the forum in which the rights of old landowners, new claimants and money lenders were artfully reconciled.[16] Contract and property law individuated certain processes and represented the discrete retention or redistribution of power, wealth and status as isolated separate instances instead of being part of a wider process. The *second* objective was to ascribe, and yet play down, the primary position of the State as the regulator of the political economy. Public law was played down and private law was played up. However, the implications of codification were to accelerate a centripetal growth of law so that the law creation agencies of the State (*i.e.* the legislative council and law courts) alone became responsible for declaring 'law' in personal, private and public areas.[17] The State intervened in various ways. It had to deal with unrest, the growth of newspapers, the supply of goods and services, the control of investment patterns and of occupational mobility as a result of education and economic inducements. The State—although a mighty participant and ally to emerging groups—represented itself and its law as a 'neutral' intervention acting in the public interest. The *third* objective of British Indian law was to depoliticize 'law' (and the judiciary) so that it was presented as relatively autonomous and technical within a narrow framework rather than an independent entity.[18] Legal scholarship and court practice reinforced this image.[19] The law of contempt of court was specifically extended in 1926 by Sir Alexander Muddiman to ensure that political attacks on the judiciary did not reverse the depoliticized image British public policy had accorded to the judiciary.[20] A great deal went into the 'neutralisation' of law. The hold of this ideology continues to dominate legal minds in India today. The leading work on Indian Constitutional law continues to extoll the virtues of legal technique over matters of substance.[21]

Faced with the challenge of newspapers, the custodians of British Indian law displayed a strange but formidable combination of both an extreme personal neurosis as well as an amazing systemic complacency. The first batch of newspapers in the late eighteenth century were at the receiving end of this personal irritation and ruined by expensive litigation. It is around the time of India's Western renaissance (around the 1820's), that the press came to be regarded not just as an episodic irritation but as a new development that would have to be dealt with.[22] Throughout the nineteenth and twentieth centuries various kinds of regulatory controls were imposed on the press. Many of these controls—like the press registration system introduced in 1867 and which continues today—were depicted as routine necessity rather than heavy-handed State control. As soon as State control was recognised as overtly political—as was the case with the control of vernacular papers in 1880's—it excited a storm of protest.[23] This put limits to the extent on which the State regulatory system could be extended against the press. New legal methods, techniques and justifications had to be found.

The British Indian legal order responded to this challenge by basing the intervention of the law on need and necessity. From 1870 begin a series of amendments to the Indian Penal Code which underline the fact that the press was—and had the potential of being—not just a constructive critic but a massive threat to public order.[24] The importance of these provisions did not lie in their use against the press. Like the Official Secrets Act, these provisions were not used often by the State except to publicly reiterate the view that the press was a dangerous nuisance. The other emphasis in these provisions lay in the manner in which they identified the causes of public disorder. The sedition provisions emphasised that it was perfectly proper to critique the government. Thus, disorder was presented as arising from the actions of those who were not constructive critics but motivated mischief makers. In the 1898 and 1927 amendments to the code, disorder was projected as arising out of enmity between classes (not in the Marxist sense) and religious groups. Thus, disorder was publicly analysed not as arising from the policies of government or the results of emerging capitalism but as a 'natural' development arising out of traditional Indian society. British law allegedly intervened as a corrective to referee these unfortunate squabbles. 'Public order' was, therefore, represented as a State necessity required by circumstances that had nothing to do with the State, its policies, its allies or its systemic needs.[25]

All this helped to settle an important paradigm in Indian public law. All political expression and freedom of speech were directly translated into public order in a way that made any other consideration trivial or irrelevant. The debates in the Constituent Assembly were argued in a way that the importance of the freedom of speech and association provisions paled into insignificance. The Supreme Court of India refused to reconsider this value orientation. It continues to be reinforced from various quarters, including the pundits of the press.[26] Two successive Press Commissions have ensured that this paradigm has gone unchallenged.[27] Most significantly, the Press Council of India has allowed the government to use a large part of its jurisdiction to depict the press as irresponsible and to stress the primacy of public order over everything else.[28] Nurtured at the hands of the Law Commission and public and private conceptive ideologists, this essential ideology of Indian public law has triumphed. The infamous Bihar Bill was not an aberration of this policy but its expression.[29] By concentrating on particular personalities, the insurgent protest against the Bill cheated the possibility of re-assessment of this important legal stratagem.

The other major significance behind the new legal ideology lies in the fact that it constitutes a disciplinary framework which has a far greater impact outside legal institutions. Various legal concepts put together descriptively prescribe what constitutes the 'good news.' The rules of public morality,[30] the rules of public order,[31] the concepts that protect private reputations from public exposure, the notion of fair comment in the public interest,[32] the legal definition of what amounts to 'scandalising the judges',[33] the definition of 'good faith' as it applies to journalism,[34] the extent to which criticism of parliament, legislators[35] and courts[36] is in the public interest are all constituent elements of this disciplinary framework. The existence of this disciplinary framework does not mean that it is followed in practice. Nor does it mean that courts and other legal agencies are always successful in enforcing it. Its significance lies in the manner in which this framework creates images of what is 'good' as distinguished from 'bad' journalism. Such a view creates expectations about the news, about the style of journalism and the extent to which journalism can threaten or expose the *status quo*. Such a framework helps to answer questions of the variety: what kind of news constitutes the 'good news'? What kind of journalism is 'fair' journalism? On this basis many newspapers have been declared as producing 'bad news' through unfair journalism. In the fifties, *Blitz* invariably found itself accused of breaking the disciplinary framework. Its severe punishment at the hands of the Lok Sabha was less a comment on the immediate infraction and much more a comment on its style of journalism.[37] This is equally true of the recent Supreme Court case where the judges were unable to agree amongst themselves as to whether *Blitz* had acted in good faith.[38] The conceptual framework of law has been used by other bodies like the Press Council.[39] Recent research on the deliberations of the Press Council shows the extent to which good journalism has been influenced by government policy and the conceptual ideologies of the law.

Independent India—and especially Mrs. Gandhi's government—have added to these ideologies in significant ways. A major addition has been to define the purpose of journalism. Inaugurating a new approach which reached its high point during the Emergency, government has talked of a new kind of purposive developmental journalism. Even during the Emergency this won some support from journalists who were otherwise against the regime. This kind of argument won some support from the First Press Commission (1952-4), underlined the initial policies of the Institute of Mass Communications, and haunted the perspectives of the Kuldip Nayar Committee—in the Janata regime, as well as the Second Press Commission established after Mrs. Gandhi's return to power.[40] 'Developmental journalism' is wholly Statist in approach and concentrates on the nature, and success or failure of the government's socio-economic plans. It is not supposed to analyse the nature of the State, expose the kind of private deals that lie behind it, or look at the machinations which constitute the political economy behind the facade of the State. Being a constructive critic of State socialism is regarded as the true catchment area of developmental journalism. Such an approach is more overtly indicative of governmental and regime demands on journalism. This view is taking root in India and must, in the course of time, affect the law. Legal concepts such as the public interest, good faith, fair comment and the like are bound to find themselves re-interpreted in the light of this developmental ideology. Equally, the system of economic regulation through which resources are allocated to the press would reflect the priorities of developmental journalism. The great controversies over the pricing of papers and the supply of newsprint cannot be de-linked from the kind of newspapers and journalism that the government wished to encourage. Discussions about the policy of government advertising are linked to developmental journalism. The Second Press Commission seemed to endorse the view that government advertising can be taken away from certain kinds of unscrupulous non-development newspapers.[41]

The most important ideological innovation in recent years concerns the extent to which the press needs to be absorbed into the government system of economic and social regulation. The formal arguments are not controversial. Scarce resources need to be equitably distributed. Newsprint and patronage of government advertising, must, therefore, be equitably distributed. Newspaper finances must make allowances for an equitable wage structure. The newspaper industry must be free from monopolism and concerted practices. The upshot of all this is to insist upon the entire newspaper industry that it must submit itself to detailed governmental control.[42] The press has fought the government very hard on the extent to which such a control is necessary. The government's view that an enabling general control—of the kind it has secured in respect of public order—is necessary, was severely questioned by the Supreme Court in the *Bennet Coleman* case where the Court underlined the need for carefully and rigorously examining each governmental demand.[43] The government has reinforced its demands by attacking the monopolism of the establishment press, taking up the cause of the smaller newspapers and arguing for the need for government regulation on the basis of equity and freedom.

The Second Press Commission has advanced the arguments of the government further only to be told by an irate minority within the Commission that the government is waging an imaginary fight on behalf of an imaginary beneficiary.[44] Nobody can deny that there are vast differentials in the resources available to the various newspapers. But there is little evidence of monopolism or of concerted practices. Similar hegemonic viewpoints unite the establishment press. But the weakening of the establishment press does not necessarily mean the triumph of a critical journalism in India. The defeat of establishment journalism would weaken the credibility of the press as an important political arena. The left—who are suspicious of the establishment press—are right to continue to support the latter in keeping the institution of the press alive as a political arena. The establishment press has become dangerous not because it does not provide hegemonic support for the system of government. It is regarded as a potential threat because in-fighting and competition amongst the Indian bourgeoisie is being expressed by the emergence of new establishment journalism. A telling point has been made that the readership of this journalism is

> essentially the middle class, a class that needs an articulation of its role far in excess of its potentialities, a class extremely narcissistic but also predatory on the rest of society.[45]

Indian public law has been immersed in recent government demands to submit the whole of the press to the regulatory State. This has won sympathy with some judges.[46] But it has also arrested another field of exploration in constitutional law. In the *Price and Page* case[47] the Supreme Court was on the verge of not treating the press as a series of individuals but recognising the institutional needs of the press. This argument was weakly sustained in the *Newsprint* case and has collapsed thereafter.[48] The jurisprudence of the Court while anxious to monitor an abuse of government power has not really discussed the merits and demerits of the governmental system of regulation from the point of free speech, or the overall needs of the press in a democracy. This carries the implication that the Court will not challenge the overall principle of regulation but may monitor parts of the regulatory system.[49]

The ideas and ideologues of the law describe, persuade and threaten much more than the law itself does. They circumscribe both action and thought. The laws of British India did this by creating an administrative system of regulation, reducing all freedom of the press questions into questions of public order and creating an ideological disciplinary framework which conditioned public expectations about what constituted the good news. Independent India reinforced and refined the ideological canvass presented by its predecessor, stressed the need for a particular kind of journalism and is trying to force the press into a new regulatory framework. It is impossible to understand the law of the press in India without coming to terms with the powerful and sophisticated ideologues that inspired, and continue to inspire, it.

Pathological aspects

Without denying either their validity, their crucial importance or their effect, it is necessary to complete the picture by moving away from ideologies on which press laws are based. There is a lot that happens in the legal system which trades ideological clarity for pathological truth. For what happens within the legal system often misconstrues the best laid plans of legislators and conceptive ideologists. The ideologies survive as important measures of definition, discipline, argument and restraint. What happens within the legal system strains credulity and invites disbelief. This must not be taken to suggest that what happens is necessarily an unplanned and unintended effect. Many of the plusses and minuses of the regulatory framework of legal institutions—and the pathology they generate—are known. Winning—and not losing—every part of the game gives the game away and is, therefore, never an artful expectation.

Indian press laws are very exacting. If they were completely implemented, the Indian press would find itself constantly on the wrong side of the law. Indian press laws do not, however, just suffer from the problem of partial enforcement. Litigation completely transforms the nature of the legal system and renegotiates the nature and meaning of its normative framework. Litigation is a social exercise. Just as the fight over legal ideas is a social fight for the supremacy of certain ideologies, the fight for litigational advantages is the fight to obtain or avoid certain decisions and results. Litigation in the higher judiciary is also concerned with ideological spoils. Courts are very important ideological bargaining arenas. They formulate and re-formulate many issues by setting the contours within which discussion and debate should take place.

Litigation concerning the press reveals many interesting features about the pathology of the legal system. The sample that has been used in the book is a highly selected sample taken from reported cases. But even this sample tells an interesting story. An incisive American observer has noted how the defamation provisions of British Indian law were not really used to defend the reputation of individual persons. Litigation was a means to give publicity to caste disputes.[50] Many of the press cases do not concern important issues in the law of the press. They seem to have a life of their own. If we look at a sample of contempt cases, they are not really concerned with the contempt of court.[51] Consider the contempt case against Prime Minister Nehru accusing him of speaking on a matter that happened to be *sub judice*.[52] Not concerned with justice or the rights of the press, the litigation was frivolous and vexatious and designed to embarrass both Nehru and the judiciary. The judiciary twisted the then law of contempt and absolved the Prime Minister of an impertinence against Parliament, rather than throw out the case as an abuse of legal process. There are cases alleging that a magistrate was under the influence of a woman secretary of the Congress or "doing politics, misbehaving, creating groupism (and) discriminating".[53] These are, really, attempts to convert the court into a publicity carnival. A remarkable case finds a contemnor who is unable to establish his innocence unsuccessfully pleading that he is a poor brahmin whose daughter is ill, whose financial circumstances are poor and who is under such mental strain that he is going mad.[54] Many of the press cases concerning the law of contempt have been used by the press to their advantage. Far from protecting the judiciary, the law of contempt has been an embarrassment to the judiciary. The most celebrated instance of this is the case of the Oriyan Registrar who travelled up and down the law of contempt to give greater publicity to his views.[55]

The important question about the legal system is not what the law says but who uses the legal system and to what end. The rigours of the law of contempt find themselves broken down by the fact that alleged contemnors revel in attracting publicity through the cases framed against them. Such contempt cases are not just concerned with giving greater publicity to attacks on the judiciary. They are concerned with giving publicity to factional in-fights in Indian society. The game is played for social spoils in the knowledge that the price to be paid will be low. In contempt law, the ultimate punishment is a fine of Rs. 2000 or six months imprisonment. It is also known that incarceration is frowned upon and that abject apologies prostrated before the courts suffice to lighten the punishment. Even more startling is the threshold of punishment in defamation cases. Why should a newspaper be intimidated by the law of civil defamation if it is understood that the average defamation award against newspapers is about a thousand rupees. This may have something to do with the *ad valorem* fee that has to be deposited before the commencement of a case.[56] Alternatively, it may have something to do with judicial policy. Again, a British administrator complained bitterly, that the Indian press had made a nonsense of the laws of public order by putting up a series of dummy editors as defendants and compounding the error of their ways by continuing to disabuse the law by not complying with it.[57] The law relating to parliamentary privilege throws up an interesting pathology. It has been shown that many of the cases have nothing to do with the press and are really part of parliamentary in-fighting.[58] Parliament is acutely conscious of this transformation of the privilege jurisdiction and does not try and make too much sense of it. Its decisions are pragmatic rather than principled. The use of the jurisdiction continues to be as exciting as it is uncontrolled.

The transforming effect of litigation does much to change the meaning of specific laws. The pathology of litigation has softened the rigours of the normative demands of various press laws. This is not an accidental development. It reflects the abilities of various groups to use law better than others. It has been suggested that litigation requires certain skills. Those who have been able to acquire these skills are alleged to be better players of the game. Accordingly such players are better able to transform law to their advantage.[59] Implicit in this analysis is the suggestion that even the disadvantaged can become accomplished players of the game if they are able to make a concerted effort to acquire and consolidate certain skills. Indian litigation concerning the press suggests that such a view does not pay enough attention to the overall social advantages of such litigants. The press win the litigation game in India not because they are accomplished at playing the litigation game but because they are accomplished at playing their own press game and subordinating the litigation game to the press game. While it is true that the press has acquired some litigative skills, it has never allowed the legal controversy in any case to overshadow the publicity game which it regards as central. For them, the bargaining arena is the press and not the law. The situation is analogous to that of labour union leaders who want to avoid being trapped into making the litigation game the central focus of their dispute. It is not surprising that, apart from a few isolated instances, the press has not always tried to win any great legal battles. It has not tried to get a better deal from the law. Much rather, it has, in most cases, tried to leave the law exactly where it is, played a low key game within the litigation system and accorded centrality to the press game. It is possible that many of those who seek to control and humble the press would like to draw it deeper into the legal system as has been done in the case of trade unions. The press has, willy nilly, rather than by design, restrained itself from taking on a more serious commitment concerning the ideological and other legal gains that might result from a more vigorous use of the law. At present, they are drawn into the arena of the law; but they play their part casually without playing for high legal stakes. There is a cunning in this approach. In this way, loopholes in the law against the press are not highlighted. The press is able to criticise the law for being harsh as well manipulate it so that it does not affect them too harshly.

The transformation of law through litigation must undoubtedly affect prescriptive perspectives about particular laws. The law of contempt offers an example.[60] The law of contempt does not allow 'truth' to be a defence in cases where a judge is criticised. Analytically this sounds absurd and unfair. In actual fact, if truth were introduced as a defence judges would be accused of all kinds of corruption which would then be sought to be proved in long extended trials receiving extensive coverage in the press. The judge would, perhaps, win the case; but only after being subjected to a long legal trial by a newspaper which would scar his reputation for life. Reforming the laws of the press is surrounded with all kinds of complexities which do not always surface by examining the black letter law and the institutional framework through which it is enforced. Reformist perspectives have to take a multi-dimensional view of the socio-political system before an accurate picture of intended and unintended consequences materialises. This may, of course, be true of all laws which affect social and political behaviour. But it is more marked in the case of the law of the press because the press has the instant print capacity to force a reassessment of what happens on its own terms before a cultivated, if not captive, audience. It is not surprising that attempts to reform the law of the press have been few and far between. The press has trivialized many such efforts by transforming the aims of the reformers. It has fought many such attempts at the pre-legislative stage. On the other hand, it has much more readily agreed to surrender to informal control and enter into 'professional' agreements about its function and role.

The law of the press is wound up as much in the pathology of litigation as it is in the doctrinaire debates that surround discussion about free speech in a democracy. The press celebrates a multi-dimensional public presence. What it does, what it is allowed to do and what it agrees to do also needs to be considered in a wider political and constitutional framework. If anything, the press is an important public political arena which offers considerable competition to the constitutionally designated political institutions offered for public consumption and use.

III

The Press and Politics: An Emerging Political Arena in a Decaying Political System

The press is not *sui generis.* It cannot really be considered apart from the political system of which it is a part. Each political system has its own concept of the press. Each political system assigns a different status and function to the press. There are many political systems which use the press only for the purpose of conveying what has been decided by designated political institutions. This has both a theory and practice to it. The theory is contained in a not so well known correspondence between Lenin, when he was head of the newly formed Soviet State, and Comrade Myasnikov.[61] Comrade Myasnikov asked for more freedom of the press. Lenin felt that what was at stake was the right to informed participation which, in his view, was better catered to through the opportunities provided through the agencies of the party and other organisations. Under this theory, the press merely reinforced what the political system decided. And it was hoped—whether tongue in cheek or *bona fide*—that the political system would present many opportunities for informed participation. In such a set up, the press would still rise to some power and exercise both discretion and influence over what is done and not done. The press itself would operate within the framework of an ideological conglomerate of ideas which would circumscribe its work and determine the content of its publications. Political influence and control would play their part. But they are clearly meant to do so. Given a different political system, the press would play a totally different role. In a liberal democracy, the press would be assigned a much more major role in the determination of the right to informed participation. And yet, it is inherent in the nature of such a democracy that such an important instrument of influence be left free to devise its own use and abuse. This is what makes a liberal democracy acceptable, its vulnerability to manipulative influence being its strength. The 'haves' come out ahead because they know and understand the strategies of the system even though the system works on a principle of equal access. Other political systems seek to use the press in a combination of ways. The press can be part of a system of controlled propaganda. Again, it may not be that in a self-professed or conscious way. It may live in a political system in which the press is notionally free (in the liberal sense of the word) but at the same time intuitively conscious of the network of relationships and ideas of which it is a part. This intuitive understanding develops the press's notion of itself and the role that is imperceptibly assigned to it.

It is important to visualise the press in the context of the network of relationships of which it is a part and which must, perforce, determine its status, role and viability in that society. The network of relationships includes its relationship with the State, its relationship to those who own the press, the relationships of those working in the press amongst themselves, as well as the credibility of the press with the general public. These are all part of its perceived relationships. There are various institutions, mechanisms and *modus operandi* through which these relationships are cemented, broken and re-negotiated.

But the press also operates in the context of a network of ideas. These ideas determine what it is supposed to do, the extent to which it can or should allow itself to be manipulated, whether it should have a tight operational morality or a loose one. These areas also determine the kind of overall perspective of the press. Needless to say, not all these relationships operate as a consensus. They develop over time. They become part of a system of ideas and a system of thinking. They do not always emerge with an elegant clarity. But a whole system begins to operate on the basis of certain assumptions. Where these assumptions operate in largely an equivocal way, the major actors in the system know what they are doing. Where no assumptions operate, the system operates as a total free-for-all. Where many conflicting assumptions are superimposed on each other, there is some kind of confusion in the air. Sometimes, such a confusion is manipulated. Sometimes, it is just precipitated either as part of a historical residue or as a result of multiplicity of strains in society itself. Each strain seems to present a seemingly valid argument. A society seems to get locked into a kind of profound confusion from which it cannot escape. It is caught in a stalemate.

The Indian press is caught in a profound confusion. It cannot decide what it should do. Members of the press have called many conferences and written many books and articles which articulate this confusion with an ill-defined clarity. They cannot make up their minds whether they should be press men in the liberal mould operating principles of accuracy and fairness for those who have learnt to use them, whether they should throw in their lot with the powers of government acting as an aid and part time critic or whether they should cater to some new kind of ideology of social justice to inform and influence their work? Proprietors constantly seek to pressurise their badly paid newspaper employees into some kind of submission. The government puts both direct and indirect pressures on the press. The government also seeks to legitimate its influence by talking in terms of the press's commitment to the process of development and nation building. Just as the late sixties saw the reports of the Administrative Reforms Commission (1965-8) battling with the idea of a "committed" bureaucracy, the early seventies saw the floating of the idea of the committed judge.[62] The press was asked to be "committed" to certain developmental aims. No one was sure whether this meant "commitment" to certain principles of social justice or whether this meant a commitment to the government of the day. The "committed" judge, or bureaucrat or pressman was seen as an alternative to the "professional" judge, bureaucrat or pressman.

This really takes us to the heart of a discussion about our perceptions about the professions and their power. We can either think of various professions as being autonomous repositories of power or as being the transmitters of power on behalf of those who actually have it.[63] It would be impossible to think of the professions as having no power at all. Of course, they are powerful. But what kind of power have they been able to assemble for themselves? Indeed, what kind of power have they been permitted to have? It would be totally incongruous to think of the professions as possessing an autonomous repository of power so that they are seen as some kind of independent power filter. Clearly, those who possess real social, economic and political power will not allow the professions to accumulate this kind of power for any extended period in time. All this cannot happen in a world in which so many people have so much at stake. Since the profession possesses some measure of technical skill, it is in something of a bargaining position. It bargains either for higher economic stakes on an individual interstitial basis (another name for corruption) or for the benefit of the group as a whole. But its bargaining strength is not unlimited. If it is well treated and paid well, then it must give *quid pro quo* or some form of equivalence. What the professions offer in return is professionalism. *Professionalism is both a promise and a style.* It is a way of things. It represents predictability. It is a way of saying: "You can rely upon us. This is how we play the game and we promise you that we will do what we do in this way and in no other." The professional filter is not an autonomous power structure. It is a filter.[64] It is designed in such a way that only the most skilful and the most powerful can use it well. Occasionally, the professional will take to greed and violate the principles of professional ethics. He will try and strike an individual bargain. This is not done. It is frowned upon. The profession as a whole has struck some kind of bargain. It will stick to its bargain with those who have stuck to their bargain with it. The code of professionalism will be honoured. Lesser organised groups with a weaker bargaining position are not professionals. Their weakness stems from their availability and market conditions. But the whole concept of professionalism has not been developed on the basis of an explicit bargain. It is part of an understood gentleman's agreement. But it has to be presented on a liberal, available-for-all basis. Anything else would be too crude. Professionalism is a part of the working of a liberal market economy. If the professions were not organised in this way, those in power would not accept the 'transmitting' power that they have cumulated to themselves. The professions are left with this power because they promise to play the professional game according to predictable rules. The visible rules have to appear to be universalistic otherwise the entire enterprise would not carry credibility and weight. But the power that is lost in transmission through a group that uses a universaly applicable rhetoric is regained by the fact that the game is a game that requires skill and manipulation. And only the most fortunate are sufficiently well-grouped and well-equipped to have that kind of skill.

What kind of bargain we strike with our professionals really depends on what we want to do with them and what kind of bargaining strength they possess given the prevailing ideological and material conditions of the market economy within which they operate. In India today, the bargaining position of a skilful lawyer with a good social and economic background is really quite high.[65] He extracts great fees. He is able to talk in terms of his 'justice-for-all-if-they-can-afford-me' professionalism. The bargaining position of the less socially or otherwise qualified lawyer is much weaker. He may resort to more straight-forward corruption. The bargaining position of the judge is both weak and strong. He is the custodian of a power filter. But his profession has already made a bargain. He must abide by it. Usually, the bargain with him is adhered to in most liberal countries because of the importance of the institution of law and justice as a legitimating device. In India, the judge is under strain. And as his needs increase and his bargaining position gets weaker, manipulation and corruption have begun to creep in. The position of the bureaucrat is also weak. Recently, the very bottom of the bureacraucy were given an increase in allowances. The clerical and other staff have found it difficult to resist alternative bargains. And the higher echelons of the civil service are considering trading in their promise of professionalism for all kinds of new bargains, new rewards and new incentives.

The bargaining position of the Indian pressman is weak. Economically dependent on his proprietors, in a position to be harassed by the government, not wholly respected by society as a whole and suffering from a diffidence about the importance, status and efficacy of his own skills, *prima facie* the Indian journalist has little to offer by way of *quid pro quo.* He cannot offer professionalism to those who can intimidate, buy or manipulate him. The process by which he is manipulated is ideological, economic or social. For he is also part of a social network of relationships. He cannot offer to be a pliant lackey without losing his own self-respect as well as his utility to those who use him. Yet in many instances he has no choice but to do just that. So, he offers various things—both to others and to himself. To others, because they are the users. To himself, because his own self-respect is involved; and also because what he offers to himself improves his own bargaining position. The bargains which the Indian pressman has struck in India are quite fascinating. The term "bargain" is used throughout this essay to mean an implied social arrangement and not a specific agreement. It is a re-adjustment of relationships, both consciously and unconsciously worked out. It is sometimes explicitly stated and sometimes a part of the collective understanding of the groups involved. The term "bargain" will mislead if it is understood in any other sense. To the government, some pressmen have said: "We agree to support you; but we will have to do so in the name of social justice rather than direct support for government." Those who have struck bargains with their proprietors and others of that stock have said: "Right, you have our support but let us be seen to be independent and operate universal notions of right and access." Some have found more satisfying but less edifying bargains. And some are still trying to evolve fresh bargains with a new kind of investigative journalism. It is difficult to say where this bargain will come together and who will pay what for what. For the payment is a social payment. It is a long term bargain. We must wait to see who snaps up what kind of offer. The Indian pressman is in a state of profound confusion because he does not always know who to bargain with and to what end. Some sections of the press have already struck some bargains. Some of these bargains are crude and some are not. Confusion abounds. And, it will continue as long as the profession continues to contain such a heterogeneous collection of bargaining strengths.

Who is the press bargaining with? The first offer invariably comes from the proprietors. Proprietors are able to impose discrete bargains. But it is not to their advantage to impose indiscrete bargains when they deal with urbane metropolitan areas inhabited with people who know and understand the nature of these bargains and review the news accordingly. As the news industry gets better known, the bargain gets more and more sophisticated. It drifts towards the notion of professionalism. Here, the proprietor is willing to lose on an occasion or two as long as he can use the professional system better than anyone else. Professionalism is a good, presentable device. It seems to both give and take. But both the give and the take are determined by market conditions which are not apparent in the terms of the bargain itself.

The bargain with the government is slightly more difficult. The government of India has never really learnt to bargain with the press. The reason for this goes way back into the days of the Raj. The custodians of the British Administration always regarded the press as either a total nuisance or a nuisance which had to be tolerated. The first position was well represented in the regulations of Munro of 1823 while the second position was espoused by Metcalfe in his regulations of 1835. The habits of the Raj were grafted onto its successor governments. They have become, what has been called, a part of a hegemony of ideas.[66] The government has never really felt the need to strike a bargain with the press. It has tried to control it with a strict system of laws, pre-censorship control, manipulation through economic means, the use of its power of patronage and control through litigation and the use of the court system. The British operated near-emergency conditions throughout. The Indian government operated a weak Emergency model in normal times. It operated a full 'British' Emergency model during the famous Emergency of 1975-77. But the bargain that was struck on that occasion was weak. It was impossible to maintain it for an extended period of time. Nor was the press being offered anything other than shadowing the already nebulous Twenty Point programme. The press, thrown into temporary submission for a small period of time, hit back. Ironically, they took their wrath out on the Janata government. Any new bargain entered into by the press will really depend greatly on the honesty with which the government agrees to negotiate this bargain.

So far, the government's negotiating position has been weak and suspect. Nehru's government cultivated the press.[67] All the great editors were courtiers in Nehru's court. An interesting tradition of lobby correspondents was building up with Nehru and with various ministers in his government; even though many ministers were sensitive about both the press and publicity. The advent of Mrs. Gandhi represented a new round of bargains. The nascent lobby system was slowly dissolved. A war was waged on the press. This was done in the name of the smaller newspapers. This battle was fought over many rounds and through many methods. We have tried to show how even agencies like the Press Council got drawn into it. Since then, all kinds of moves have been floated. The press accuses the government of being insensitive, which it is. The government accuses the press of being incompetent and boring, which it often is as well. But once these home truths have been stated, there is no real movement. The government has tried to consolidate its powers by appealing to the general public and declaring that it needs to control the press in the name of public order, decency and morality, the institutions of state and in the name of the healthy development of the people as a whole. All this is part rhetoric and part truth. But the government and its allies are powerful. One part of the press seems to be attacking government on the basis that there are no more bargains to be struck with this government. Other pressmen have struck some kind of uncomfortable bargains. Some have acceded to the request that they should re-orient their thinking. Others still talk in terms of providing a predictable universalistic professionalism.[68] But the government needs the media. It cannot continue indefinitely to project itself through a not so respected 'chorus' press. But the bargaining has to be understood against the backdrop of a wider, complex political perspective. For the bargain is a social bargain to determine the limits of a particular kind of public activity.

Political arenas

The press is an important political arena. It competes with and often transplants existing political problems and its possibilities begin. The policy of any country is made up of diverse political arenas—some of which are part of the formal framework of government and some of which are not. In pre-capitalist economies the structure of government was designed to obtain consent through general ideology (*eg*. religion, notions of duty) and to reduce the public arenas for discussion, debate and influence.[69] The framework of government set out and rigorously maintained a pattern of obligations. Any attempt to desist the pattern of obligations was treated not just as an infraction but as being heretical. Peasant revolts were ruthlessly treated.[70] Private political arenas were set within obligatory relationships. Public political arenas were controlled and replicated much of the final discussions in private political arenas. The advent of capitalism introduced new patterns of economic and social mobility. New legal forms and ideologies were invented to express the demands of this mobility. The conceptual individuation of society depicted society as consisting of individuals who were trapped and fulfilled by their own self-chosen transactions. The reality was, of course, quite different. Old groups and relationships gave way to emerging groups and relationships. The law recognised and blessed some of these new patterns and intimidated and repressed others. At the same time, there was a considerable amount of pressure to open up new public political arenas for discussion and debate. The emergent bourgeoisie grudgingly made timely concessions on the formal sharing of power. The franchise was slowly extended. But they sought to pull back what they had conceded by prescribing and underlining the ground rules of institutional morality within which public institutions would operate. This is what has been called *government by institution* in this book. It became an important priority to ensure that the institutional capabilities of various organs of government were constrained, even if exaggerated claims continued to be made about their contribution to democracy and justice. Simultaneously, an effort was also made to de-politicise certain parts of government so that their work was not in the public eye and they were perceived as a public political arena. They were part of the rationalisation of the modern State. The work of the civil service and the judiciary was presented as self-contained and de-politicised. The army was also rationalised as separate special bureaucracy. This model of government with its restricted political arenas claimed much in the name of democracy and justice but conceded very little. However, this whole scheme was not easy to maintain. Internally, such a scheme was threatened by corruption and a failure to observe the institutional morality which carefully circumscribed the power and potential uses of these political arenas. Externally, there was a considerable amount of pressure to create new and fresh arenas as well as to 'corrupt' or transform existing arenas. These external pressures were greatly assisted by a continuous re-organisation of the social fabric into emerging groups as well as the proliferation of information on an ever-expanding scale that had—and has—no parallel. The attempt to create certain kinds of new political arenas were either ruthlessly crushed or rigorously controlled. When the working classes expressed their political tensions and demands in riots and demonstrations, this was immediately delegitimated as an acceptable form of politics. The law and politics of public order were devoted to creating an ideological and coercive framework to sustain this programme of counter-insurgency. The other major political arena that was created was the press. Here was an extremely powerful and alarming alternative. It is not surprising that English society in the first part of the nineteenth century did all it could to try and destroy the radical papers which had created a political market for themselves and which were second to none as a threat to the redesigned political system. What eventually killed the radical papers were the market conditions under which newspaper economics came to be set.[71] This was accompanied by a re-definition of the newspaper as a commodity. As a commodity, the newspaper became a vehicle for entertainment, advertising and comment. This new commodity description of newspapers complemented the economic strategy of making newspapers viable only for up-market investment. New rules had to be devised on how these newly designed newspapers would work. The primary consideration was to ensure that the newspaper (and, later, the emerging media) remained a secondary political arena which did not supplant the political arenas created by government by institution. This has been achieved in various ways. Direct formal and informal controls serve as a warning as well as a corrective. Attempts to keep the bargaining strength of the newspapers low have not always succeeded, especially where newspaper barons have been able to place newspapers on a sound financial footing. In such circumstances, the press has been accused of being monopolistic and acting against the public interest. But the most effective method of preventing the press from becoming a prime political arena has been to strait-jacket the press within the ideology of professionalisation. By depicting the press as 'professional' an attempt was made to de-politicise its potential as a political arena. Professionalisation imposed formal and informal ground rules so that the press is led to believe that they are careful 'transmitters' and commentators rather than activists and politicians. Neither newsmen nor those that manipulated them were able to get the press to wholly agree to adhere to these 'professional' guidelines. Papers overtly and covertly drift into politics. But professionalism has had a double effect. In addition to controlling journalists it also created an art form through which the public could be duped. By pretending to be 'professionally' put together, the 'news' reinforced attitudes by depicting them as objective:

> The . . . most important filter (by which news selects itself as 'objective' fact) is the cultural air we breathe, the whole ideological atmosphere of our society, which tells us that some things can be said and others had best not be said. It is the slow and almost unconscious pressure towards implicitly affirming the *status quo*, towards confirming 'the

> ordinary man' in his existing attitudes, towards discouraging refusals to conform. That atmosphere which comes (from the context in which news is set).[72]

The process by, and the limits within, which news is selected, presented and commented upon has the effect of both controlling the press as well as re-defining the package within which it is presented for public consumption. Despite all this a lot spills over. New kinds of journalism are born. *Watergate*, *Bofors*, investigative journalism, developmental journalism and the like all have their fair share of creative growth. They are absorbed and evaluated against value projections of what constitutes 'good news.' Investigative journalism can hardly be depicted as irrelevant; but may be treated as 'bad' news if it mixes investigation with speculative comment. A neat division of roles is suggested between the investigative journalist who discovers facts and the political commentator who interprets them. The role of the press is to feed the primary political agencies. None of this actually works except to heighten our intuition about the press and advance an ideology to contain and evaluate it.

The Indian press has struggled for political recognition. In the late eighteenth and early nineteenth century, the infant English and vernacular press opened up a new public arena which the British found disagreeable. The then British government first ruined it by litigation and then by a rigorous system of licensing and precensorship controls. This worked for a little while. By the last quarter of the nineteenth century it became clear that new political arenas were being devised by way of public demonstration, revolt and the vernacular press. This was infinitely more difficult to control. The licensing and pre-censorship systems—thought to be politically imprudent—were restored during certain times and were accompanied by a tough criminal law. An attempt was made to discredit native Indian journalism as disloyal, political, biased, and un-professional. What was at stake was not just the mischief created by specific news reports and articles. What was being created was a new political arena which could find more credibility than, and supplant, the existing political arenas which were designated for public use by the British government. Internally, British journalists tried to change the style of Indian journalism by arguing the case for 'professional' as opposed to 'political' journalism.[73] 'Professionalism' in this context was a moral ethic. It limited the press and created distorted expectations as to what could be regarded as 'good news'.

The post-British political period had to grapple with a different situation. The new constitutional set up had created new public political arenas. The press was given a subordinate 'professional' role to play in this new set up. In the Nehru regime, this ancillary was accepted by 'establishment' journalism and carelessly rejected by down market journalism. During—and since—Nehru's day, we have seen the privatisation of the Indian State. Designated political arenas have been made irrelevant as arenas within which serious public decisions takes place. Public power is manipulated by its direct corruption. The distinction between public and private power has been eroded by emerging groups and classes who have set up intermediate regimes. As the political arenas designated by the Indian Constitution have become more and more trivial, Indian politics has gone underground. Its public face is a facade. Nothing could be more dangerous to India's new system of government than public revelations about the privatisation of public power. Nor could this system of privatised politics survive the emergence of new political arenas which would constitute a radical alternative to the constitutional framework or threaten its behind-the-fence private dealings. The threat to the system came from corporate power which, while privy to the process of privatisation, were anxious to work through a more predictable 'rational' framework. The system was also threatened by intermediate groups unable to participate in private dealings. Most significantly, there was the threat posed by the disadvantaged who were being oppressed.

Fresh political arenas were being created. Activist grass root agencies sought to maintain political arenas where their power bases were located.[74] From Gandhian groups to Naxalites a new activism was taking shape in India. The government's strategy was either to crush these emerging political arenas or to try and absorb them within developmental programmes. A second arena which was acquiring a political dimension was the juidiciary. The first round of overt political use came in the fifties when the Zamindars used the courts to question the manner in which the government had passed on their property to an emerging class of acquisitive peasants in the name of socialism. In the years that followed the judiciary did much to stabilise and legitimate government programmes until it came to be used from the middle sixties to strongly, but publicly, agitate fresh issues before the higher judiciary. The government was forced to restrain the expansion of the courts into publicly acknowledged political arenas by a series of highly questionable, inelegant, but effective moves. The potential of courts as public political arenas has been re-discovered after the Emergency. The Supreme Court is at present encouraging this. But there is an uneasy tension in the air.[75] Lawyers and judges whose sympathies lie with the corporate and rich sectors of the Indian economy tend to feel that the rapid expansion of the higher judiciary into an overt public political arena might have the effect of throwing the baby out with the bath water by affecting the future of the judiciary as a whole. It is important to assert that the opening up of the higher judiciary as a political arena has much to do with elite in-fighting even though a much wider catchment of issues are finding their way to the courts.[76]

The third public arena that is emerging is the press. In many ways, it has the potential to supplant parliamentary government, the prime political arena. The government is concerned about this loss of primacy by the political institutions it has designated for public consumption and use. It has fought many battles against the press. The first and most prominent of these is to discredit the press as being mischievous, unethical, non-professional and dangerous. Using British ideologies to discredit the press, it is shown as a threat to public order. Ironically, the Press Council of India has been strongly used by the government to help to project the imperfections and lawlessness of the press. The second strategy of the government is to discredit the press as a fair potential public political arena. It has attacked the press as monopolistic and tried to undercut its financial base. In the early sixties, there was an effort to control price, page and volume of advertisement. In the late sixties, the control systems focussed on newsprint. In the seventies and eighties the government has tried to create a climate to control the financial viability and investment pattern of the larger newspapers. All this is done in the name of the smaller newspapers which are, in turn, being crushed by the denial of government advertisements and by physical coercion as well as by penal action.[77] Anxious not to lose out in this arena, the government has controlled radio and television[78] and tried to improve its own official and unofficial propaganda machines. A bitter struggle continues over the future of the Indian press and the extent to which it will be allowed to constitute an alternative framework of political activity. It is fair to point out that although this struggle is being waged in the name of freedom and civil liberties, it is being fought by the more advantaged interests in order that they can build up a power base in an alternative political interest. But any gains that are made must affect the wider cause of prizing up more—and alternative—political arenas for bargaining, discussion, intimidation and influence. It is, perhaps, for this reason that there is an unholy alliance between the right and left to try to fight for press freedom. Once stability is brought to this arena the right will indubitably use a combination of economic and ideological weapons to try and gain a more effective control over the political arena which is being campaigned for by both the left and right today.

IV

This study should not be taken to portray the press as a David fighting moral campaigns against the undesirable Goliaths who oppress modern society. The press is very much a part and parcel of the social forces which contend for supremacy. The Indian press is not all good. It is of uneven quality. Unscrupulous in style and not averse to yellow journalism, the press reflects local, regional and class formations. It has become a prime political arena through which dissent, opposition, discussions and comment have come to be formulated. We must recognise its transformed political use which is wider than the sterile party politics in which the other designated arenas of government have been caught. There is much that the press has to do to set its house in order. Its refusal to implement wage awards reflects the extent to which journalists are prevented from finding the economic security they need to come into their own. The press is being assessed—and is beginning to assess itself—in a political way. At the same time, the government of the Raj and its successors have arrested discussions about the press so that we cannot go beyond the paradigms of public order, developmental journalism and monopolism in which much, if not all, the debates about the press have been successfully trapped. Meanwhile, the press prints, and its readership reads, 'only the good news'.

NOTES

1. 'Discipline' is used here in a similar, but more extended, sense than the Sense in which it is used by Foucault: *Discipline and Punish* (1977) 215. "Discipline may be identified neither with an institution nor with an apparatus; it is a type of power, a modality for its exercising comprizing a whole set of instruments, techniques, procedures, levels of application, targets, it is a 'physics' or an anatomy of power, a technology." Here, discipline does not just indicate and legitimate a regime of social control but delineates a set of expectations which are reinforced by several conceptive ideologists (of the State, various professions and the market economy), recognised by the press in its internal organisation as well as its interactional relationship with the public and enforced by various individuals and institutions through a series of formal and informal methods. Not just a set of values it forms a constituting and self-constituting and self-perpetuating living tradition.
2. For an excellent study of how 'bad news' is manufactured under the guise of 'good news' see the Glasgow Media Group: *Bad News* (1978); *ibid*: *More Bad News* (1983).
3. This view of 'law' is to do away with the typically English institutional approach *viz.* law is what is accepted and enforced by institutions: (see H.L.A. Hart: *The Concept of Law* (1961)) and replace it with an approach which countenances 'two concepts of law' (see R. Dhavan: "Two Concepts of Law" (1981 mimeo)). The second concept emphasizes ideological aspects of the law; both in

support of, and in contradistinction to, the institutional approach.

4. D.D. Basu: *Law of the Press in India* (1980).
5. J.R. Mudholkar: *Press Law* (1975); see also E.S. Venkataramiah: *Freedom of Press: Some Recent Trends* (1984 Advocates Association Endowment Lecture, Bangalore); P.M. Bakshi: *Press Law: An Introduction* (1986).
6. C. Sarkar (ed.): *The Press and the Law* (1969).
7. There is an increasing interest in the ideology of law following the publication of E.P. Thompson: *Whigs and Hunters* (1975) which shows how the 'rule of law' was used to save many people from the gallows. Douglas Hay: "Property, Authority and the Criminal Law" in D. Hay, P. Linebaugh and E.P. Thompson (ed.): *Albion's Fatal Tree: Crime and Society in Nineteenth Century England* (1975) and for a case study D. Hay: "Poaching and the game laws in Cannock chase" in the same volume; also *ibid*: "Crime and justice in eighteenth and nineteenth century England" in N. Morris *et. al.* (ed.): *Crime and Justice: An Annual Review of Research* (1980), II, 45-84. For critical reviews from the left see R. Johnson: "Thomson, Genovese and Socialist-Humanist History" (1978) 6 *History Workshop* 79; cf. K.McClelland; "Some comments. . . " (1979) 7 *History Workshop* 101; see further A. Merritt: "The nature and function of law: A criticism of E.P. Thompson" (1980) 7 *Br. Jnl. of Law and Soc.* 192; D.P. Phillips: "A just measure of crime authority, hunters and blue locusts: The 'Revisionists' social history of crime and law in Britain in 1780-1850" in S. Cohen and A. Scull (ed.): *Social Control and the State* (1983) 50; D. Sugarman: "Theory and practice in law and history: A prologue to the study of the relationship between law and economy from a socio-historical perspective" in B. Fryer, A. Hunt, D. McBarnet and B. Monkhouse (ed.): *Law, State and Society* (1981) 70.

   For further studier on ideology see C. Sumner: *Reading Ideology* (1978) and D. Sugarman (ed.): *Legality Ideology and the State* (1983). In this book, the context will indicate that ideology is used in three distinct senses. In the first sense, ideology is *rhetorical*, designed to appeal emotionally. In the second sense, ideology is *constitutive*. It is a way in which social reality is described and re-cast. In the third sense, ideology is *conceptive*. In this last sense. it is a method of reasoning so as to create and reconcile values; and, as an aid to making and justifying decisions.
8. For the argument that analytical jurisprudence disguises a link between the rise of the sovereign power of kings and legislatures and the separation of law from morals see R. Dhavan: "The Basic Structure doctrine" in R. Dhavan and A. Jacob (ed.): *The Indian Constitution: Trends and Issues* (1978) 160 at 172-5. Thus, law creating authorities did not want an institutionally validated law delegitimated by an appeal to morals.

9. M. Galanter: "The modernization of law" in M. Wiener: *Modernization—The Dynamics of Growth* (1966); *ibid*: "The displacement of traditional law in Modern India" (1968) 24 *Jnl. of Soc. Issues* 65; *ibid.*: "The aborted restoration of indigenous law" (1972) 14 *Comp. Stud. in Soc. and History*, 53.

   The problem with the Galanter approach to 'modern law' is that he uses a Weberian approach to identify the cluster of features that belong to an ideal type description of modern law without placing this description within the context of the political economy which created modern law and which the latter services; see R. Dhavan's editorial introduction to M. Galanter: *Law and Society in Modern India*. (Delhi, O.U.P. forthcoming).

10. For a general analysis of its influence see P.V. Kane: *History of the Dharmasastra* (1968 edn. in 5 volumes) J.D.M. Derrett: *Dharmasastra and Juridical Literature* (1975): *ibid. History of Indian Law (Dharmasastra)* (1973); *ibid.*: *Essays in Classical and Modern Law* (1976) Volume I; Lingat: *Classical Law of India* (1974, Trans. with a critical introduction by J.D.M. Derrett). Derrett remains the most provocative and incisive of modern commentators.

11. The 'status/contract' metaphor derives from the writings of Sir Henry Maine: *Ancient Law* (1862); *ibid*: *Village Communities of the East* (1871); *ibid*: *Early History of Institutions* (1875); *ibid*: *Early Law and Customs* (1883); *ibid*: *Popular Government* (1885) who in his work on India displayed a much more exacting pragmatism in his administrative work on India (see Government of India: *Minutes of Sir Henry Maine 1862-9*). On Sir Henry Maine generally see M.E. Grant Duff: *Sir Henry Maine* (1884). For a use of Sir Henry Maine's metaphor see B.S. Cohn, "From Indian status to British Contract" (1961) XXI *Journal of Economic History* 613; D.A. Washbrook: "Law, State and Agrarian Society in India" (1981) 15 *Modern Asian Studies*, 649 esp. 653-4.

12. For an over-simplified approach to how such an 'honest' jurisprudence may be created see Z. Bankowski and G. Mungham: *Images of Law* (1976). Simpler and less consistent is U. Baxi: *Crisis in the Indian Legal System* (1982).

13. The 'black letter tradition' reinforces the institutional basis of law in courts and the legislature, separates law from morals, emphasizes the relative autonomy of legal systems and analyses the law in terms of its juristic conceptions. Its most famous and subtle contemporary exponent is H.L.A. Hart (supra note 3) even though Hart claims his work to be 'an essay in descriptive sociology'. The best traditions of such a scholarship are preserved in Seervai: *Constitutional Law of India* (1984). The most mechanical use of this tradition can be seen, for example, in Basu (*supra* note 4). The effect of the tradition is to isolate and autonomize the law and legal argument. For a brief but

incisive atternative, see P.M. Bakshi: *Press Law: An Introduction* (1986).

14. See Pashukanis, who seems to have been given scholarly revival, and stressed this point, see his *Law and Marxism* (1978 edn.).
15. Controversies abound on how English law in England and India (during the Raj) were able to use the 'commodity form' selectively so that vested interests could be served without a break with tradition; see (on England) D. Sugarman: "Law, Economy and the State in England, 1750-1914: Some major issues" in D. Sugarman (ed.) *Legality, Ideology and the State* (1983) 213, and on India D. Washbrook (*supra* note 11).
16. For the view that this was a good reconciliation see Derrett: *Religion, Law and the State in India* (1968) and also his *Essays in Classical and Modern Law* (1976-77) esp. Volumes II and IV. For a rigorous re-examination of this view see D.A. Washbrook (*supra* note 11). Interesting new historical research is being done by historians like Pam Price and Arjun Appadorai on law and society in the political economy.
17. To some extent one can be dismissive of the impact of utilitarians on India (see E. Stokes: *The English Utilitarians and India* (1965)) except in a very general sense. The 'real' discussion centred around much more pragmatic questions about the effects of the creation of particular legal and other processes on the mobilization of socio-economic interests (see R. Kumar: *Western India in the Nineteenth Century* (1968) 74-83; 153-160; 209-228). The law facilitated certain kinds of mobilization and disabled others. For the view that the British indulged a nice balance between new laws and traditional values see Derrett: *Religion, Law and the State in India* (1968); see also his "Tradition in India: Politics and Society" (Paper to a Seminar at London University, 1971).
18. Thus the judiciary's role as a political instrument or its particular pathological uses were rarely questioned. Judges themselves permitted those who attacked them (see R. Dhavan: *Contempt of Court and the Press* (1981) 41-58). Scholarship of Indian legal history continues to work on the colonial judiciary in a de-politicized context: C. Fawcett: *The First Century of British Justice in India* (1934); O.H. Mootham: *East India Company's Sadar Courts* (1983); and generally, M.P. Jain: *Outlines of Indian Legal History* (1966 edn.); J.K. Mittal: *Indian Legal History* (1982 edn.).
19. The various statutes enacted by the British produced their commentators foremost among them at the turn of the century was Sir D.F. Mulla whose works on various statutes are still updated standard texts *e.g.*, Mulla: *Civil Procedure Code* (1981 edn.); *ibid*: *Registration Act* (1973 edn.); *ibid*: *On the Law of Insolvency in India* (1977 edn.); *ibid*: *On the Sale of Goods and the Indian Partnership Act* (1979 edn.);

ibid: *Transfer of Property Act* (1973 edn.); Pollock and Mulla: *Indian Contract and Specific Relief Act* (1972 edn.). Mulla also produced codified texts of Hindu law (which ironically survives the codification of Hindu Law in 1956); see Mulla on *Principles of Hindu Law* (1982 edn.) and Muslim Law (which continues to enjoy pre-eminent authority); see Mulla on *Mohammedan Law* (1977 edn.). For an analysis of the techniques by which the black letter tradition is preserved see R. Dhavan: *The Supreme Court of India*: *A Socio-legal Analysis of its Juristic Techniques* (1977) Chapter II.

20. See R. Dhavan: (*supra* note 18) Chapter III.
21. H.M. Seervai: (*supra* note 17) I, ix.
22. See generally S. Natrajan: *History of the Press in India* (1962).
23. On the Vernacular Act see S. Gopal: *British Policy in India* (1965) 118-19; 144-5; 197, 199-200. Along with other discrimination, it formed the basis for an extended campaign by Indians; see also M. Edwards: *British India 1772-1942* (1967) 277-8.
24. *Supra* Chapter VII; see also W.R. Donough: *History of the Law of Sedition* (1914 edn.).
25. *Supra* Chapter III.
26. *Supra* Chapter III.
27. Note the emphasis on public order in the *Report of the Press Commission* (1952-4) pr. 1014 pp. 386-7 (on the necessity of a separate law to curb the press in the interests of public order); see also prs. 926-946 pp. 344-352; note dissent prs. 1142-1156 pp. 441-452; and, again in the *Report of the Second Press Commission* (1982) prs. 23-63 pp. 23-27 (on internal stability); prs. 27-32 pp. 30-34 (on public interest and the press); prs. 34-38 p. 38 (on pre-censorship). Cf. Minutes of Dissent on the excess of government control (prs. 15-33 pp. 352-4). Note also H.K. Paranjape's dissent on pre-censorship (pr. 38 p. 38); also p. 266 col. 1.
28. *Supra* Chapter 9.
29. On the Bihar Bill see *supra* Chapter 7.
30. *Supra* Chapter 7.
31. *Supra* Chapter 7.
32. *Supra* Chapter 8.
33. *Supra* Chapter 4.
34. Such a definition is used in relation to contempt of court (*supra* Chapter 4) parliamentary privilege (*supra* Chapter 5) and the law of defamation (*supra* Chapter 8).
35. *Supra* Chapter 5.
36. *Supra* Chapter 4.
37. *Blitz* case (1961) V P.D. (2) 2 (Lok Sabha).
38. *Sewakram* v. *R.K. Karanjia* A.I.R. 1981 S.C. 1514.
39. *Supra* Chapter 9.
40. *Report of the First Press Commission* (1952-4) prs. 910-911 p. 335

emphasizing that the ideals needed to be not just of the press were not just "accuracy, comprehensiveness and objectivity" but should fulfil the Directive Principles of State Policy in the Constitution. *The Report of the Second Press Commission* (1982) prs. 71-90 pp. 28-31 is much clearer in its view that the press has not, but should, pay attention to development. Mrs. Gandhi seems to have made her support clear in her speech in Gauhati before the Emergency (see U. Vasudev: *Indira Gandhi* (1974) 318-9). The Emergency remains the high point of 'developmental journalism' disguising regime interests (see *White Paper on Misuse of Media during the Internal Emergency* (1977)). The cause of developmental journalism was voiced by the media (e.g. S. Prasad: "Social Change and Newspapers (1966) 3 (1) *Vidura*; 'Vidura': "Development takes back seat" (1965) 2 (2) *Vidura*; D.K. Rangnekar: "Economic Journalists must show more dynamism" (1964) 1(3) *Vidura*; on the relationship between "The press and planners" see (1966) 3(4) *Vidura*. On concern that the media does not reach the villages see B.S. Thakur, A. Bradford, N.U. Tirtha: *Villages and the News*; also B. Sen Gupta "Newspapers don't reach villages" (1966) 3(3) *Vidura*. Apart from the work of the Indian Institute of Mass Communications (cited Chapter 1, *supra*) note esp. its *Development Journalism* (1976). Note there is a difference between 'development journalism' and the dissemination of information to make economic planning efficacious (see *Report of the (Amarnath Vidyalankar) Study Teams of the Five Year Plan's Publicity* (1965)). The Indian Institute of Mass Communications (see its *Evaluation: Sixth Anniversary*, 1980) seems to have conflated their two perspectives without much thought.

41. *Report of the Second Press Commission* (1982) Chapter XI Cf. Minority Report 224-262. The fact that the notion of direct financial patronage is rejected by the Commission seems to have made the Press Council ignore the import of this apparatus of control (Press Council's response to the Report of the Commission, *Indian Express* 22 August, 1984.
42. *Supra* Chapter 2.
43. *Bennett Coleman and Co.* v. *Union of India*, A.I.R. 1973 S.C. 136. Note the discussion on this and other constitutional cases in Chapter 3, *supra*.
44. *Report of the Second Press Commission* (198) 224-268 (Minority note of dissent). It is very surprising that the Minority (see pp. 224-264) did not file a separate Report. They seem to disagree with the majority on almost every major issue and, almost certainly, on the basic philosophy of the Commission.
45. C. Alvarez: "Marginal men" (1983) VII *Book Review* (No. 3) 143.6, reviewing Arun Shourie's *The Second Reign of Mrs. Gandhi* (1982).

46. The best and most cogent example of this is Justice Mathew's judgment in *Bennet Coleman* v. *Union of India* (*supra* note 43) and which was adopted by the *Report of the Second Press Commission* (1982) 33, 151, 156-160.
47. *Sakal Newspapers* v. *Union of India,* A.I.R. 1962 S.C. 305 and note the discussion in Chapter 3 *supra.*
48. Newsprint case: *Bennet Coleman* v. *Union of India* (*supra* note 43). For the collapse of this argument see *Maneka Gandhi* v. *Union of India,* A.I.R. 1978 S.C. 597. For an account of how this argument was whittled away see Chapter 3 *supra.*
49. *Supra* Chapter 3. cf. Justice Pendse's recent judgment in the *Bennett Coleman* case AIR 1986 Bombay 321.
50. M. Galanter: "Caste disabilities and Indian federalism" (1961) *J.I.L.I.* 205 at 208-211.
51. For a detailed analysis see R. Dhavan (*supra* note 18).
52. *Ramaswami* v. *J.L. Nehru,* A.I.R. 1958 Mad. 558. Note the views of the Minority (243-5) that the Press Commission adopted the philosophy and approach of Justice Mathew.
53. Shoorvir case, *State* v. *D.R. Das Vidhi* (1973) Cr. L.J. 1271 (All.).
54. *State* v. *Dhruba Charan* (1976) Cr. L.J. 246 at pr. 8. pp. 249-50.
55. See R. Dhavan: (*supra* note 18) 98-9.
56. There are only two reported cases where substantial damages have been awarded. The usual award of damages averages at about Rs. 800 (on the basis of the awards made in reported cases).
57. Sir William Vincent, speech reported at (1921) I L.A.D. 340 (22 February, 1921).
58. *Supra* Chapter 5.
59. M. Galanter: "Why the 'Haves' come out ahead; Speculation on the limits of legal change" (1974) 8 *Law and Society Review* 95.
60. See R. Dhavan (*supra* note 18) generally; and Chapter 4 *supra.*
61. Lenin: *32 Collected Works* 504 (Letter by Lenin to Comrade Myasnikov).
62. For the literature and discussion on a 'committed judiciary' see M. Kumaramanglam: *Judicial Appointments* (1973); N.A. Palkhivala (ed.): *A Judiciary made to Measure* (1973); K. Nayar (ed.) *Supersession of Judges* (1973); K.S. Hegde: *Crisis in the Judiciary* (1973); H. M. Seervai: *Constitutional Law of India* (1975) II, 1415-20; R. Dhavan (*supra* note 19) 27-29; for adjournment motions in the Lok Sabha see *L.S.D.* (V Series) Pt. 27 No. 46 col. 311-402 (2 May, 1973); No. 45 Col. 136-57 (26 April, 1973) No. 48 Col. 228-32 (27 April, 1973).
63. This argument is expressed in its most powerful form in Johnson: *Professions and Power* (1973). For a more dramatic attack on the professions see I. Illich (ed.): *Disabling Professions* (1977).
64. M. Cain: "The General practice of a lawyer and client: Towards a radical conception" (1979) *Int. Jnl. of Soc. of Law* 331, while

questioning the arguments put forward by Johnson is content to argue that lawyers (for example) translate expectations into 'law' and are conceptive ideologists. Here, we treat the professions as a kind of 'power filter' and seek to analyse the formation and sustenance of this power filter in the context of the structural and day to day demands of the market which uses the professions.

65. No work has been done on lawyers fees. There is, however, no doubt that 'good' lawyers command a daily case fee which is nothing short of fantastic when compared with the income of any other profession, other than corrupt politicians. There is very little work on how the legal profession works. For incisive and interesting accounts see R. Kidder: "Formal Litigation and professional insecurity: Legal entrepreneurship in South India" (1974) 9 *Law and Society Review* 11; C. Morrison: "Munshis and their masters: The organization of an occupational relationship in the Indian Legal System" (1972) 31 *Journal of Asian Studies*, 309; *ibid.* Clerks and Clients: Para-professional Roles and Cultural identities in Indian litigation (1974) 9 *Law and Society Review* 39; J. S. Gandhi: *Lawyers and Touts: A Study in the Sociology of Legal Professions* (1982); This is also true of the theoretical literature (*e.g.* T.G. Oomen: 'The Legal Profession in India: Some Sociological Perspectives' N.R. Madhava Menon (ed.): *The Legal Profession: A Preliminary Study of the Tamil Nadu Bar* (1984)) 1. What is needed is a study of the bar in the context of the State and political economy and not just in relation to their clients.

66. For an account of this hegemonic continuity see Chapter 2 *supra*; and especially Chapter 7 *supra.*

67. Cf. K.P. Sinha: "The attitude of the Prime Minister as regards freedom of the press in India" (1980) XIV *J.C.P.S.* 70.

68. For a review of the literature see Chapter 1 *supra.*

69. It is not proposed to defend this as a general statement other than to state that the pre-capitalist State is more of a direct intermediary on behalf of various interests. Such societies are kept together by an ideology that pattern status and transactions into a homogeneous whole. Capitalist societies use the State to mediate between transactions and status which high profiles the institutional features of the State and law. Hindu law (see *supra* note 10) represents a pre-capitalist ideological hegemony. Its transformation as a result of the advent of capitalism requires study (cf. Derrett: *Critique of Modern Hindu Law* (1970) as one account of this transformation); for the position before the advent of Muslim conquests see Derrett: "Law and Social Order in India before the Muhammadan Conquests" (1964) *7 Jnl. of Ec. and Soc. Hist. of the Orient 73.*

70. See Chapter 1 p. 19-20 note 45 *supra.*

71. See generally J. Curran: *Power Without Responsibility* (1982) Chapters III and IV and the literature referred to there; see further

J. Wiener: *The War of the Unstamped* (1970); P. Hollis: *The Pauper Press* (1978). Cf. G. Cranfield: *The Press and Society* (1978).

72. Glasgow Media Group: *Bad News* (1978); *ibid. More Bad News* (1980).
73. See V. Chirol: *Indian Unrest* (1910); P. Lovett: *Journalism in India* (1928).
74. On aspects of legal activism see R. Dhavan: *Public Interest Litigation in India* (1981, Report to the National Committee on Legal Aid). The Planning Commission seems to have recently affirmed its faith in a 'sponsored' activism from below (see B. Roy: "Voluntarism and the 7th Plan" *Indian Express* (17 August, 1984)) while the government harasses Marxists with detention and Gandhians with a vindictive inquiry under the auspices of an Inquiry Committee called the Kudal Commission (e.g. *Indian Express* 26 August, 1984).
75. Baxi in his *The Indian Supreme Court and Politics* (1980) seems to outstretch his argument from the descriptive to the prescriptive by urging the Supreme Court to pursue 'populist' causes.
76. See R. Dhavan: *Litigation Explosion in India* (1986).
77. *Report of the Second Press Commission* (1982) 96-100; on the manner in which newsprint is distributed see *Report of the Parliamentary Joint Committee on Offices of Profit* (13 August, 1984).
78. On the legality of the Government's radio monopoly see Justice Kapur evading the question by saying that alternative stations were not technologically possible: (*P.L. Lakhanpal* v. *Union of India* AIR 1982 Delhi 167.

    For the view that the monopoly may be unconstitutional see A.G. Noorani: "Autonomy for French Media" *Indian Express* 24 August, 1984. For discussion of these questions see (Chanda) *Report of the Committee on Broadcasting and Information in Radio and Television in India* (1965); G.C. Awasthy: *Broadcasting in India* (1965); R. Hardiwar: "All India Radio: A Case for corporate management" (1965) *Ind. Jnl. of Pol. Sc.* (July-September). A debate on the government monopoly radio and television is long overdue and may be initiated by Romesh Thapar's petition to the Supreme Court (*Indian Express* 29 April 1987) Indian cinema, heavily entrenched in the private market economy, stands as a strong contrast to television.

INDEX